MW01627440

The Wiley Handbook of Global Workplace Learning

## Wiley Handbooks in Education

The *Wiley Handbooks in Education* offer a capacious and comprehensive overview of higher education in a global context. These state-of-the-art volumes offer a magisterial overview of every sector, sub-field and facet of the discipline-from reform and foundations to K-12 learning and literacy. The Handbooks also engage with topics and themes dominating today's educational agenda-mentoring, technology, adult and continuing education, college access, race and educational attainment. Showcasing the very best scholarship that the discipline has to offer, The Wiley Handbooks in Education will set the intellectual agenda for scholars, students, researchers for years to come.

The Wiley Handbook of Global Workplace Learning
*by Vanessa Hammler Kenon (Editor) and Sunay Vasant Palsole (Editor)*

The Wiley Handbook of Action Research in Education
*by Craig A. Mertler (Editor)*

The Wiley Handbook of Mentoring
*by Beverly J. Irby (Editor), Fran Kochan (Editor), Linda Searby (Editor), Jennifer Boswell (Editor), and Ruben Garza (Editor)*

The Wiley Handbook of Problem-Based Learning
*by Mahnaz Moallem (Editor), Woei Hung (Editor) and Nada Dabbagh (Editor)*

The Wiley Handbook of Early Childhood Care and Education
*by Christopher Brown (Editor), Mary Benson McMullen (Editor) and Nancy File (Editor)*

The Wiley Handbook of Teaching and Learning
*by Gene E. Hall (Editor), Donna M. Gollnick (Editor) and Linda F. Quinn (Editor)*

The Wiley Handbook of Violence in Education: Forms, Factors, and Preventions
*by Harvey Shapiro (Editor)*

The Wiley Handbook of Global Educational Reform
*by Kenneth J. Saltman (Editor) and Alexander Means (Editor)*

The Wiley Handbook of Ethnography of Education
*by Dennis Beach (Editor), Carl Bagley(Editor) and Sofia Marques da Silva (Editor)*

The Wiley International Handbook of History Teaching and Learning
*by Scott Alan Metzger (Editor) and Lauren McArthur Harris (Editor)*

The Wiley Handbook of Christianity and Education
*by William Jeynes (Editor)*

The Wiley Handbook of Diversity in Special Education
*by Marie Tejero Hughes (Editor) and Elizabeth Talbott (Editor)*

The Wiley International Handbook of Educational Leadership
*by Duncan Waite (Editor) and Ira Bogotch (Editor)*

The Wiley Handbook of Social Studies Research
*by Meghan McGlinn Manfra (Editor) and Cheryl Mason Bolick (Editor)*

The Wiley Handbook of School Choice
*by Robert A. Fox (Editor) and Nina K. Buchanan (Editor)*

The Wiley Handbook of Home Education
*by Milton Gaither (Editor)*

The Wiley Handbook of Cognition and Assessment: Frameworks, Methodologies, and Applications
*by Andre A. Rupp (Editor) and Jacqueline P. Leighton (Editor)*

The Wiley Handbook of Learning Technology
*by Nick Rushby (Editor) and Dan Surry (Editor)*

# The Wiley Handbook of Global Workplace Learning

*Edited by*

*Vanessa Hammler Kenon and*
*Sunay Vasant Palsole*

WILEY Blackwell

This edition first published 2019


*Registered Office*
John Wiley & Sons, Inc., 111 River Street, Hoboken, NJ 07030, USA

*Editorial Office*
101 Station Landing, Medford, MA 02155, USA

For details of our global editorial offices, customer services, and more information about Wiley products visit us at www.wiley.com.

Wiley also publishes its books in a variety of electronic formats and by print-on-demand. Some content that appears in standard print versions of this book may not be available in other formats.



*Library of Congress Cataloging-in-Publication data applied for*
[Hardback] 9781119226994

Cover Design: Wiley
Cover Image: © istocksdaily/iStock/Getty Images Plus

Set in 10/12pt Warnock by SPi Global, Pondicherry, India

Printed in the United States of America

V10008834_031519

## Contents

About the Editors *ix*
Contributors' Biographies *xi*
Preface *xix*
Acknowledgements *xxi*

Part I Change Management *1*

1 Leadership as Shared Practice: A Means of Democratizing School for Its Goals Attainment *3*
*Joy-Telu Hamilton-Ekeke*

2 Effective Strategies for Workplace Learning *27*
*Annetjie Elizabeth Human and Victor Pitsoe*

3 Developing an Agile Global Workforce: Challenges and Critical Success Factors *45*
*Yoany Beldarrain*

4 The New Learning Economy and the Rise of the Working Learner *67*
*Hope Clark, Parminder K. Jassal, Sarah Blanchard Kyte, and Mary LeFebvre*

5 Inclusive Education and Work-Based Learning – Managing a Process of Change: The Arguments of Jennifer Todd, Thomas and Loxley *83*
*Elda Nikolou-Walker*

6 Using an Experiential Learning Model to Design an Assessment Framework for Workplace Learning *95*
*Yaw Owusu-Agyeman and Magda Fourie-Malherbe*

Part II Project Management, Partnerships, and Diverse Populations *119*

7 Measuring Innovative Thinking and Acting Skills as Workplace-Related Professional Competence *121*
*Susanne Weber and Frank Achtenhagen*

8 **Global Strategic Planning** *141*
*John D. Pessima and Bart Dietz*

9 **Global Talent Management** *155*
*John D. Pessima and Bart Dietz*

10 **The Confucius Institute Teachers' Workplace Training** *171*
*Xiaonan Wang and Wan Xiang Yao*

11 **Navigating Generational Differences in the Workplace** *181*
*Khamael Al Safi*

12 **Multicultural Curriculum and Cross-Cultural Workplace Learning** *201*
*Ana Ivenicki*

13 **Employee Learning Disabilities and Workforce Learning** *215*
*Damian Andreas Riviez*

14 **Digital Education in Career and Technical Education and the Support of Creative Professional Development** *241*
*Antje Barabasch and Alberto Cattaneo*

15 **Professional Development Meets Personal Development: Impact of a Master's Program on Alumni** *263*
*Yvonne Crotty, Margaret Farren, and Laura Kilboy*

**Part III Culture and Language** *277*

16 **Competency in Globalization and Intercultural Communication** *279*
*Qin Guo*

17 **Intercultural Communication in the Multilingual Urban Workplace** *301*
*Aditi Ghosh*

18 **Internationalization of Higher Education in the United Arab Emirates: Opportunities and Fears** *323*
*Sara AlAleeli*

19 **Are We Teaching and Assessing the English Skills Needed to Succeed in the Global Workplace?** *343*
*Maria Elena Oliveri and Richard J. Tannenbaum*

20 **Bridging the Cultural Gap in the Global Workplace: A Sociocultural Perspective** *355*
*Cynthia Carter Ching and George Sellu*

21 **Compensating for the Lack of Physical Non-verbal Cues in a Virtual Team Context, Based on Cultural Background and Preferred Communication Style** 369
*Yoany Beldarrain and Karen Diehl*

22 **Culture and Global Workplace Learning: Foundations of Cross-Cultural Design Theories and Models** 395
*Tutaleni Asino and Lisa Giacumo*

**Part IV Engagement and Motivation** 413

23 **Modern Meditation Training: An Innovative Technique to Increase Employee Learning and Achievement** 415
*Thomas F. Valone*

24 **Improving Leadership Communication Competencies and Skills through Training** 447
*Andreas Rupp*

25 **An Examination of Key Factors That Influence Employee Learning in the Workplace** 477
*G. J. Schwartz*

26 **The Effectiveness of Learning Communities in Increasing Employee Learning** 501
*George Sellu and Cynthia Carter Ching*

**Part V Workplace Technology Learning Trends** 521

27 **A Study of Attitude and Utilization of Interactive Whiteboards among Teacher Educators** 523
*Sunday Ayodele Taiwo and Emmanuel Olufemi Adeniyi*

28 **Gamification for Learning and Workforce Motivation** 539
*Kenneth R. Pierce*

29 **The Use of Gamification in Workplace Learning to Encourage Employee Motivation and Engagement** 557
*Hazel Grünewald, Petra Kneip, and Arjan Kozica*

30 **Impact of Gamification on Learning and Motivation of Workforce: A Student-Based Study** 577
*Ahmed Deif*

31 **Using Technology-Oriented, Problem-Based Learning to Support Global Workplace Learning** 591
*Emma O'Brien, Ileana Hamburg, and Mark Southern*

**Index** 611

## About the Editors

**Vanessa Hammler Kenon, EdD,** serves as the Associate Vice President for Information Management and Technology and is responsible to direct the management of the department's human resources, financial management, training, communications and marketing, and OIT's Faculty and Student Government committees.

As a key academic and technical liaison to UTSA students, faculty, and staff, Dr. Kenon serves on several UTSA committees and organizations supporting student success, community service, academic research, communications, and information technology. In addition, she is a lecturer in the African American Studies program of the College of Education and Human Development.

Dr. Kenon has worked in higher education positions of instruction, leadership, and management in both private and public higher education programs for more than 24 years with 22 of those years spent on managing educational departments and initiatives directly related to technology.

Some of her current UTSA projects include collaborating with UTSA Academic Affairs on continued enhancements to the Degree Works initiative, emerging student success initiatives, and the Labster, Google, and Lenovo launch as a part of the Bill and Melinda Gates Foundation's iPASS project.

A member of the UTSA Diversity and Inclusion Advisory Council (DIAC) and the Trinity University Alumni Education and Engagement Advisory Board, she also serves on the Board of Trustees for the Hallmark University System.

She has served as a facilitator and presenter at various conferences including the American Educational Research Association (AERA), Microsoft TechEd, Texas Association of State Systems for Computing and Communications (TASSCC), and The International Higher Education Reform Symposium. Additionally, she has served in these capacities for the Association for College and University Technology Advancement (ACUTA), The New Media Consortium (NMC), The International Society for Educational Planning (ISEP), DubLabs Unifying Mobility Conference, Achieving the Dream (ATD), and EDUCAUSE.

Dr. Kenon recently served on the 2017 EDUCAUSE IT Issues Panel and the 2018 Annual Program Committee. Currently, she serves on several EDUCAUSE committees including the CHIETA Global Benchmarking Committee, the Diversity Equity and Inclusion Task Force, the 2019 ETRAC Faculty and Student Study Content Creation Committee, and the Faculty for EDUCAUSE Leadership Institute.

**Sunay Vasant Palsole, PhD,** is the Assistant Vice Chancellor for Engineering Remote Education for Texas A&M. He is responsible for developing strategic innovative solutions for remote engineering education and advancing the mission and goals of the college for both academic and nonacademic courses for College Station and regional campuses. This includes developing online, blended, distance, and open programs and courses upholding high standards of quality and rigor.

He has taught at the undergraduate and graduate level in several institutions of higher education and has more than 20 years of experience in the academic technology field including distance and online learning. He has built and led multidisciplinary teams in various institutions and played a role in the creation of successful employee and student worker development programs. These programs involved a continuous evaluation schematic with upskilling and mentoring events designed to help colleagues elevate their achievements.

He is the co-developer of a Digital Academy, which was a finalist for the Innovation Award by the Professional and Organizational Development Network. He has been PI and co-PI on a number of grants related to education, educational technology, and online course development. His current research is focused on mapping techniques and technologies that support student success in alternative delivery environments, with focus on data modeling.

Over his career he has given numerous workshops nationally and internationally and served in various capacities in regional and national organizations.

Sunay is a strong proponent of active learning strategies in the classroom and is the creator of the space technology environment pedagogy (STEP) model for learning space design.

## Contributors' Biographies

**Frank Achtenhagen,** PhD, is a former Professor Emeritus at the University of Göttingen, where he taught for more than 30 years. He earned an MS in business education at the Free University of Berlin. In 1969, he obtained a PhD in the didactics of foreign language learning. A prolific author, he has written over 400 publications in vocational education and training. He is a member of the Finnish Academy of Science and Letters.

**Emmanuel Olufemi Adeniyi,** PhD, is currently a chief lecturer at the Federal College of Education, Abeokuta. He received his BEd in education/ special education in 1981, MEd in special education in 1985, and PhD in educational management in 2000 from the University of Ibadan. He has served as dean and deputy provost at the Federal College of Education, Abeokuta and as provost at the Federal College of Education (Special), Oyo.

**Sara AlAleeli,** PhD, a citizen of the United Arab Emirates, serves as Assistant Professor in the College of Education at the United Arab Emirates University. AlAleeli received her bachelor's degree at the American University in Cairo and her master's and PhD at Michigan State University. Her research interests focus mostly on the broad areas of second-language teaching and learning, the role of culture and innovation in developing nations' response to globalization, and education reform.

**Khamael Al Safi** lectures on organizational sociology at Middlesex University, Dubai. She also works for Exantium as a consultant in governance and organizational efficiency for governmental agencies in the Middle East. Her research interests include cross-cultural and intergenerational behaviors and their impact on the workplace and labor markets. She holds a Bachelor's (Honors) in Human Resources and Psychology from Middlesex University, Dubai and a Master's in Organizations and Governance from the London School of Economics.

**Tutaleni Asino,** PhD, is an Assistant Professor of educational technology in the School of Educational Studies at Oklahoma State University. His areas of research, writing, and presentations include: Open Access, diffusion of innovation, organizational development, adoption and use of emerging technologies and learning environments and mobile learning. Asino is an active member of the Comparative International Education Society (CIES), Association for Educational Communications and Technology (AECT) and Society for Information Technology and Teacher Education (SITE).

**Antje Barabasch,** PhD, works at the Swiss Federal Institute of Vocational Education and Training (SFIVET) as the head of the "Current Vocational Education and Training (VET)/Professional Education and Training (PET) context" research area. She holds master's degrees in adult education and applied geography and a PhD in educational policy studies and social foundations from Georgia State University. Her research focuses on creativity in Career and Technical Education (CTE), career transitions and guidance and CTE policy transfer.

**Yoany Beldarrain,** PhD, is Professor of business communication at ESB Business School, Reutlingen University. An international speaker, author, researcher and consultant, she has extensive experience in curriculum and instruction, e-learning, intercultural communication, and leadership. She has taught undergraduate and graduate courses at La Salle University, Duale Hochschule Baden-Würtemberg, and served as Instructional Leader at Florida Virtual School. Beldarrain earned an MS in educational leadership from Nova Southeastern University, and an EdD in education from Capella University.

**Alberto Cattaneo,** PhD, is head of the "Innovation in Vocational Education and Training" research field at the Swiss Federal Institute for Vocational Education and Training (SFIVET). His research concerns the integration of Information Communication Technology (ICT) and more specifically the use of visual aids and interactive videos for fostering the teaching-and-learning process. Cattaneo received his PhD in social, developmental and organizational psychology in 2005, presenting a thesis on blended learning and virtual learning environments.

**Cynthia Carter Ching,** PhD, is Professor of Learning and Mind Sciences and Associate Dean of Academic Programs in the School of Education at the University of California, Davis (UC Davis). Ching's research interests include child development, collaborative learning, gender and technology, learning in informal settings, qualitative methodology, and technology and identity. She is also a researcher in the UC Davis Foods for Health Institute's (FFHI) Children's Health and Education Program.

**Hope Clark,** PhD, is a Principal Research Psychologist at ACT Inc., an independent, nonprofit organization that provides assessment, research, analytics, and program management services in the broad areas of education and workforce development. She oversees validation and return on investment studies, impact research, program evaluation, and large-scale surveys to document the success of ACT's workforce solutions. She earned her master's degree in rehabilitation counseling, and her master's and PhD in industrial and organizational psychology, all from Northern Illinois University.

**Yvonne Crotty,** PhD, is an Associate Professor in the School of STEM Education, Innovation and Global Studies at the Institute of Education, at Dublin City University. Passionate about teaching and learning she was the winner of the Academic Category of the University President's Award for Teaching and Learning Excellence. She supervises Master's and PhD research students particularly in the area of educational multimedia and technology innovation in the workplace. Crotty has also developed an educational entrepreneurial approach to research.

**Ahmed Deif,** PhD, is an Assistant Professor of Industrial Technology at California Polytechnic State University. He received his master's and PhD in industrial and manufacturing systems at the University of Windsor, Canada. His current research interests are in supply chain management and lean and green manufacturing/service systems. He has more than 60 publications, some of which have won best-paper awards. Deif has a diverse portfolio in his industrial experience at various engineering and consultancy capacities.

**Karen Diehl,** PhD, a freelancer and an external collaborator in the European Research Council Project "Bodies across Borders: Oral and Visual Memory in Europe and Beyond," has lectured at the ESB Business School Reutlingen, Germany, since 2011. She studied general and comparative literature and eastern European studies at the Free University, Berlin and completed her MA in comparative literature at the University of East Anglia. She earned her PhD at the European University Institute.

**Bart Dietz,** PhD, is an Assistant Professor at Rotterdam School of Management, Erasmus University and Partner at Career Openers, an Amsterdam-based executive search firm. His research focuses on the management of salespeople, recruitment and selection. His articles appear in the *Journal of Marketing* and the *Journal of Applied Psychology,* and his research has been covered by several Dutch media and magazines for professionals. Dietz has consulted and presented for companies like Heineken, as well as Ernst and Young.

**Margaret Farren,** PhD, is an Associate Professor in the School of STEM Education, Innovation and Global Studies in the Institute of Education, Dublin City University and director of the International Centre for Innovation and Workplace Learning. She supervises Master's and PhD students who are using research approaches that contribute to personal and professional knowledge and knowledge in the field of practice. Her research areas include action research and transformative research approaches, pedagogy, and learning theories.

**Magda Fourie-Malherbe,** PhD, is an expert in higher education studies and has held several positions, including director of the Centre for Higher Education Studies and Development and vice rector of Academic Planning at the University of Free State and vice rector of Teaching and Learning at Stellenbosch University. A member of several professional associations including the European Higher Education Society, she is currently a Full Professor in the Centre for Higher and Adult Education at Stellenbosch University.

**Aditi Ghosh,** PhD, is an Associate Professor in the Department of Linguistics at the University of Calcutta. She obtained both her Master's and PhD in Linguistics from the University of Calcutta, where she was awarded a gold medal. She has also been a faculty member in the Department of Linguistics, Assam University, Silchar and a Research Fellow at the Asiatic Society, Kolkata. She is currently heading a major project on Intercultural Communication in Multilingual Urban Spaces.

**Lisa Giacumo,** PhD, is an Assistant Professor of organizational performance and workplace learning at Boise State University. Her research interests focus on developing competencies in instructional designers and the use of data, instructional design, and digital tools for global training initiatives and performance improvement. She has worked internationally as an instructional designer, trainer, and manager for businesses, universities, non-profits, and NGOs. She is a frequent presenter at AECT, ISPI, InsideNGO, and ISPI EMEA.

**Hazel Grünewald,** PhD, is a professor of organizational behavior and the Head of International Relations at ESB Business School, Reutlingen University. She has worked as a visiting professor at Zagreb School of Management and Economics and at Universiti Malaysia Pahang. Gruenewald was awarded a fellowship for innovation in teaching and has developed an innovative business simulation game, Quest 3C. Her research interests include gamification and motivation in the workplace.

**Qin Guo**, PhD, is currently a Senior Lecturer in international communication at Macquarie University, and an honorary professor of educational communication at South China Normal University. Her major research interest is in international communication and communication for social change. She has led a number of research projects in Australia and China, including Poverty Alleviation Strategy for Remote Areas in Guangdong, Enhancing Intercultural Understanding between Australia and China, and Media and Community Development in the Network Society.

**Ileana Hamburg**, PhD, is a research fellow and leader of the Lifelong Learning Study Group at the Institute of Work and Technology, Westphalian University of Applied Sciences, and lecturer for Informatics at the Open University of Hagen. She coordinates German and European projects particularly in the fields of eLearning, knowledge management, and innovation and new media. Hamburg is an EU evaluator for projects in different national and European initiatives and is active on the program committees of several international conferences.

**Joy-Telu Hamilton-Ekeke,** PhD, holds a PhD in health education from the University of Wales. Her research interests include teaching methodology to improve academic performance, as well as secondary school leadership. She has several publications in national and international journals. In addition, she is the author of *Social Constructivist Teaching and Dietary Knowledge,* published by Lambert Publishers, Germany. Currently, she is a Senior Lecturer and Head of the Department of Science Education at Niger Delta University.

**Annetjie Elizabeth Human**, DEd, is an expert on workplace learning strategies and human resource development. For 24 years, she worked within government to help managers and executives improve their effectiveness. As an experienced facilitator and study leader, she was responsible for organizational development and guided more than 200 executives to conduct research on various workplace problems in the South African Police Service. She received a DEd from the University of South Africa in 2017.

**Ana Ivenicki,** PhD, serves as a Full Professor at the Federal University of Rio de Janeiro, Brazil, developing activities in teaching, researching, and supervising in the Department of Educational Studies. She is also a researcher at the Brazilian National Council of Research. Ivenicki has authored books and articles in Brazil and abroad and served as an invited keynote speaker at international conferences and many institutions. She obtained her PhD in education from the University of Glasgow.

**Parminder K. Jassal**, PhD, leads the Learn + Work Futures Group at the Institute for the Future. Jassal investigates the future through three intersecting lenses: open economies, changing role of people, and dynamic environments. Par minder's current focus is on the transition from a world organized at the scale of large institutions to a world organized by distributed networks of social, political, and economic value.

**Laura Kilboy** was a research officer in the International Centre for Innovation and Workplace Learning. Her research interests include online learning, video, multimedia and critical pedagogy. She holds a BA in applied languages and international studies and an MSc and a diploma in management studies. She has experience in international adult education and training both in Ireland and abroad, where she is involved in volunteer projects such as an Irish-based charity in Eastern Romania.

**Petra Kneip**, PhD, is a Professor of HR management and organizational behavior at ESB Business School, Reutlingen University. A current member of the President's Office, she also serves as the head of the university's HR development department and is a member of the University Advisory Board. Her research interests center on digitalization in human resource management, employer branding, and motivation in work settings.

**Arjan Kozica**, PhD, is a Full Professor of Organization and Leadership at ESB Business School, Reutlingen University. Before joining ESB, he was an officer in the German Armed Forces where, among other things, he served as a unit leader for military logistics in the air force and as a research assistant in the German Armed Forces Command. His research topics are organizational change, change management and human resource management.

**Sarah Blanchard Kyte** PhD, is a researcher in the Office of Academic Affairs at the University of Arizona, where she focuses on leveraging academic advising for student success. A sociologist of education, Kyte's work examines structural and relational aspects of the transition to college and career with a focus on underserved students. Some of her recent peer-reviewed publications have appeared in *Social Science Research, Demography* and *The Journal of Pre-College Engineering Education.*

**Mary LeFebvre** is a principal research scientist—Workforce Policy at ACT Inc. Her primary focus is national workforce policy issues, competency supply/demand analysis, program evaluation, and K-Career longitudinal data matching. Prior to joining ACT in 2010, she was the workforce research manager at the Missouri Economic Research and Information Center within the Missouri Department of Economic Development. LeFebvre has an MS in industrial/organizational psychology from Christopher Newport University and a BS in psychology from Missouri State University.

**Elda Nikolou-Walker** is a Senior Lecturer in Work-Based Learning at Middlesex University, London. A prolific author in the field of work-based learning, Nikolou-Walker has made a new contribution to the growing body of literature in the field with her book titled *The Expanded University: Work-Based Learning and the Economy*. Its range of theoretical models and approaches assist in applying new insights and thinking to the vast array of prospective work-based situations.

**Emma O'Brien**, PhD, is a research fellow at the University of Limerick. In 2005, she obtained her PhD in digital workplace learning in small to medium enterprises (SMEs). She has coordinated several projects under the Erasmus Plus and lifelong learning programs in the areas of e-learning and work-based learning in SMEs. In addition, O'Brien teaches a number of distance and online modules to industry based learners within the University.

**Maria Elena Oliveri,** PhD, is a research scientist at Educational Testing Service and Associate Editor of *International Journal of Testing*. Her research focuses on fairness, validity, and innovative assessment design in support of learners from diverse cultural and linguistic backgrounds. Oliveri's master's and PhD are in measurement, evaluation and research methodology from the University of British Columbia. Previously, she was a literacy mentor to Vancouver schoolteachers, a teacher for disabled students, and a UBC lecturer.

**Yaw Owusu-Agyeman,** PhD, is a Fellow of the Higher Education Academy, UK, the Head of the Examinations Unit at Ghana Technology University College and an external researcher at the Centre for Higher and Adult Education at Stellenbosch University. He holds a PhD in curriculum studies from Stellenbosch University and has been involved in several international projects including one on the adoption of mobile money in Ghana, sponsored by the Bill and Melinda Gates Foundation.

**John D. Pessima** is a global talent management specialist, with more than 15 years of professional HR and talent management experience. Pessima has worked in various positions at the World Bank and Deloitte. He led the professional World Bank staff talent review process, a global talent management initiative. He has also led the design and development of key HR initiatives such as the institutional strategic staffing and talent review process and technology, as well as the implementation of position management governance.

**Kenneth R. Pierce** serves as vice president of Information Technology and CIO at Texas State University. He has previously served in roles such as vice provost for Information Technology, CIO and lecturer at the Universities of Texas at San Antonio and El Paso, as well as technical and executive management at The Boeing Co.. Pierce received his bachelor's in mechanical engineering from the University of Houston, and master's in information technology from Capella University.

**Victor Pitsoe** is a Professor in the Department of Educational Leadership and Management at the University of South Africa and deputy editor of Africa Education Review. A member of The World Institute for Nuclear Security, he has published more than 40 articles and ten book chapters, and edited two books. Pitsoe has published in an array of areas including management, citizenship and human rights education, philosophy of education, open distance learning, teacher education, and teacher professional development.

**Damian Andreas Riviez,** PhD, is an educator and writer living and working in Dubai. Focusing on leadership, education, management, and special needs, Riviez has more than 30 years' experience in academia and industry in teaching, research, management, operations, training, and consulting. His diverse cultural background and international experience encompasses working in 12 countries on four continents. Riviez has recently embarked on research projects that focus on working with individuals with learning differences pertaining to augmented learning strategies.

**Andreas Rupp**, PhD, is Director of the Institute of Medical Device at the Knowledge Foundation at Reutlingen University. Rupp earned his master's in educational theory and doctorate at the University of Tübingen. He is also the founder of the business consultancy r & k team, Mössingen, which offers consulting and training on organizational behavior, organizational learning and VET. He is also a part-time and guest lecturer at several universities in different countries.

**G. J. Schwartz,** PhD, is a Brigadier in the South African Police Service (SAPS) where he is the Section Head for Policing Research, responsible for inter alia research in crime detection, client satisfaction and management intervention case studies. He holds master's degrees in business administration and adult education, and a PhD in both leadership in performance and change, and in education. Schwartz is also involved in developing the organization's executive leadership.

**George Sellu,** PhD, is currently a Professor of agribusiness at Santa Rosa Junior College, where he teaches agribusiness courses and coordinates the agriculture business program. He has more than 20 years of experience providing technical advice and facilitating trainings for farmers and ranchers in sub-Saharan Africa and the United States. In addition to teaching, Sellu runs an agricultural diagnostic laboratory that provides a wide-range of services to farmers and ranchers in California.

**Mark Southern**, PhD, graduated from Nottingham Trent University in 1989 with a degree in engineering management and in 2004, obtained his doctorate. He is an experienced senior manager with an 11-year proven track record in multinationals and Subject Matter Experts (SMEs). He has led more than 20 national research projects with Irish manufacturing companies. In 2013, Southern was nationally recognized for his innovative efforts with Irish companies by winning the Enterprise Ireland Manufacturing, Engineering & Energy Commercialization Award.

**Sunday Ayodele Taiwo,** PhD, is chief lecturer and former Dean of the School of Education at the Federal College of Education (Special), Oyo. He has also served as the chair of the Committee of Deans. In 1988, he received his B.A. Ed. in education/ history at Obafemi Awolowo University. Taiwo also holds both a MA and an EdD in educational technology, which he obtained at the University of Ibadan and University of Ilorin, respectively.

**Richard J. Tannenbaum,** PhD, is a principal research director in the Research and Development Division of Educational Testing Service (ETS). He has strategic oversight for major Centers of Research that include more than 100 directors, scientists, and research associates. He holds a PhD in industrial/organizational psychology from Old Dominion University and has published numerous articles, book chapters, and technical papers. His areas of expertise include assessment development, licensure and certification, and standard setting.

**Thomas F. Valone,** PhD, PE, is a physicist and licensed professional engineer with 30 years of professional experience. In addition, he is a former patent examiner, research engineer, electronic device designer and an author, lecturer, and consultant. He has served as an expert witness and declaration writer for court cases and has appeared on CNN, A&E, History, and the Discovery Channels. A prolific writer, his works have been published in several languages including German, French, Romanian, and English.

**Xiaonan Wang** received her BA and MSc degrees at the Capital Normal University, China. Wang is currently a faculty member at The University of International Business and Economics, China and an instructor of Chinese classes at the University of Texas at San Antonio. Wang teaches Elementary and Intermediate Chinese classes at UTSA and teaches at Sunday School of the Confucius Institute at UTSA. Wang also offers workshops on Chinese culture, history, and society for American educators and other communities and is an experienced Chinese teacher and teacher trainer.

**Susanne Weber**, PhD, has served as a Professor and the director of the Institute of Human Resource Education and Management at the Munich School of Management since 2005. She obtained a master's degree in business education, political economy, business Administration and commercial law prior to earning her PhD. Her major research interests include vocational education and training, entre- and intrapreneurship, and intercultural learning. She has written more than 100 books and articles, and lectures worldwide.

**Wan Xiang Yao,** PhD, received his BS and MSc in Kinesiology from Beijing Sport University, China, and PhD in motor learning and control from Auburn University, USA. Yao has more than 20 years of research experience in the field of motor learning and control. He is currently a professor in the Department of Kinesiology, Health, and Nutrition, and director of the Confucius and East Asia Institutes at the University of Texas at San Antonio.

# Preface

Increasing globalization is the single most powerful driver of economic, social, and cultural change in the world today. Globalization of economies has had greater effects on political and personal life than any other force has had for generations. Companies are increasingly expanding their networks to take advantage of the global supply chain, resulting in greater interconnectivity between continents, countries, cities, towns, and villages. Integration of technology is facilitating rapid globalization and affecting the adoption, development, and dispersal of ideas, thoughts, and inventions faster than one can truly conceive.

Because of the rapid dispersal of global change and technologies, companies and governments need to adapt, adopt, and plan for this pace of transformation not only in terms of technology but also in terms of human capital development. The acquisition of updated knowledge, skills, and attributes (KSA's) by the existing workforce, and the developing workforce, is necessary to ensure longevity of the supports that are needed for these large-scale economic developments. These global movements affect all aspects of the economic chain, from K-12 through college, and in industry-based workforce training, reskilling, and skills updating. This breadth of development is needed to ensure that the modern global workforce keeps abreast of modern skills and work techniques along with the technologies that support them.

Cultural adoption and development plays an equally important role in workforce evolution, not only from the internal company culture perspective, but also from the international perspective as global supply chains mean a more diverse workforce in terms of ethnic origin. This complexity in ensuring proper development of KSA's has promoted the value of global workforce development to the front of the line. As businesses grow and expand globally, along with them comes the challenge of creating adequate cultural and technological development and training to ensure a thoughtful and proactive plan for skills development.

Addressing the complexity of global workforce development is in itself a complex task, and this handbook seeks to provide readers with some practical experiences in global workforce development. It is divided into five thematic sections: *Change Management, Project Management and Partnerships, Culture and Language, Engagement and Motivation,* and *Workplace Technology Learning Tools.*

Numerous people supported and contributed to the success of this publication. We would like to thank all the global editorial board members and authors who contributed time and material to the handbook. A special thank you is due to the Office of Information Technology at the University of Texas at San Antonio (UTSA) and former UTSA Provost, John Frederick; this handbook would not have been possible without their support. Nicole Duff in the Customer Relations, Communications, and Training group of the Office of Information Technology at The University of Texas at San Antonio has been an invaluable resource, coordinating, tracking, and managing the project along with the support of a dedicated team of student interns from the UTSA. We would be remiss if we did not convey our gratitude to the UTSA internship coordinators as well. Maia Adamina-Guzman in the Department of English, Richard Drum, Ph.D., in the Department of Educational Leadership and Policy Studies, and Red Madden in the Department of Communication, all provided a stellar group of interns to assist with this project over the years. Those student interns, who provided input and support on this project, reminded us daily of the reason why we hit the ground running at universities around the globe.

One of the most important benefits that students, scholars, industries, and even those who are just curious about the study of workplace learning will take from this work is learning the importance of work and family life balance. That said, we also thank our families and our spouses, Tia Palsole and Muhsin Kenon, without whose support we would not have been able to carry out our work on this project.

Vanessa Hammler Kenon
Sunay Vasant Palsole

## Acknowledgements

Nicole Duff—*Global Workplace Learning Handbook Project Manager*
Rosalind Ong—*Global Workplace Learning Handbook Project Coordinator*
Tirza Cardenas—*Senior Editorial Intern*
Samantha Fisher—*Senior Editorial Intern*
Danicia Steele—*Project Team*

Delia Swiger, EdD—*Project Team*
Nathaly Soto-Velez—*Editorial Intern*
Jessica Salinas—*Editorial Intern*
John Saldaña—*Editorial Intern*
Jacob Manear—*Editorial Intern*
Andrea Kraus Lozano—*Volunteer*
Texas A&M Engineering
The Office of Information Technology at the University of Texas at San Antonio (UTSA)

# Part I

# Change Management

# 1

# Leadership as Shared Practice

## A Means of Democratizing School for Its Goals Attainment

*Joy-Telu Hamilton-Ekeke*

*Niger Delta University*

A leader, according to Aghenta (2005) cited in Uwaifo (2012), is an individual who exercises positive acts upon others. He/she is an individual who exercises more important positive influences, and acts more than any other group in an organization he/she is in. A leader is one who is looked up to, whose personal judgment is trusted, and who can inspire and warm the heart of those he/she heads or leads, gaining their trust and confidence and explaining what is needed in a language which can be understood. According to Jennings (2003), "Leadership is the activity of influencing people to strive enthusiastically for group objectives." Leadership is the process of structuring, organizing and guiding a situation so that all members of the group can achieve common goals with minimum time and effort. In any organization, either formal or informal, productivity to a great extent depends upon the way and manner in which the leaders operate within the organization. Bennis and Nanus (1997) stated that leadership is a function of knowing oneself, having a vision that is well communicated, building trust among colleagues, and taking effective action to realize leadership potential. Also, Scouller (2011) sees leadership as a process that involves: setting a purpose and direction which inspires people to combine and work willingly, paying attention to the means, pace and quality of progress toward the aim, and upholding group unity and individual effectiveness throughout.

In order to run an organization successfully, a leader could among other things adopt a particular leadership style that could help him or her in achieving the goals of the organization. It is generally known that teachers learn to adopt positive or negative attitudes toward their work in accordance with whether they perceive the leadership behavior of the principal as supportive or harmful to their sense of personal worth and expectation. Oftentimes, principals seem too busy with all the day-to-day responsibilities of running schools that they do not have enough time to practice instructional leadership as expected.

*The Wiley Handbook of Global Workplace Learning*, First Edition.
Edited by Vanessa Hammler Kenon and Sunay Vasant Palsole.

## Leadership Concept

There is a rich history and body of research regarding leadership. Leadership is a very human activity, and is diverse and robust as any other human activity. There are a great many reasons for the strong popularity of the topic of leadership in this era, where everything is subject to change: people, groups and organizations, as in schools. Therefore, efficient effort is required to understand and navigate through these changes. The interpretation of various leadership models suggests that no single leadership style is adequate to run an organization effectively. Rather, a combination of styles is effective, if used appropriately as the situation demands. More importantly, achievement of goals should be the aim of any organization, especially of secondary schools as the intermediary of the educational system. The secondary school system has its own well-developed structure, ethics and well-established rules and regulations under which it operates.

The concept of leadership style has been universally accepted as a basic principle of effective and efficient management. This is essentially the human aspect of management. It can be seen as a process of formidable force to enhance teachers' job performance since followers' performance is dependent to a large extent upon how they perceive the leadership behavior of the leader. Campbell (2008) asserts that a thriving organization such as a school is one in which productivity, understanding and cooperation, job satisfaction and interpersonal relationships are involved. These attributes of profitability are functions of the extent to which the style of the school principal or management is able to influence the working environment to achieve the set goals of the organization.

Apart from other motivating factors, leadership styles could be mobilized with proper regard for interpersonal, emotional and environmental factors at working places (Ndubisi, 2004). In any organization such as a school, human factors should be recognized for the achievement of the organizational goals. The ultimate goal of schooling is learning on the part of students. What they learn, however, depends on teachers' performance, which is a product of many factors such as their commitment, professional growth, school environment, prevailing culture, innovativeness, and so forth. All of these factors, according to Mbiti (2007), have connections directly with the principal's actions or inaction. It is, therefore, important that school principals learn how best to relate to members of their organization (academic and non-academic staff, students and parents). Since the principal deals with humans, he/she must try to know the needs of all the stakeholders, as well as their backgrounds, emotions and interests. Principals must learn to relate with individuals in order to make the best out of them. A good principal is essentially a special friend to none, and this must be reflected in the administrative style in dealing with both teachers and students.

Principals are therefore expected to be sensitive to people's opinions and also expected to develop social skills in working with people and at the same time be competent in all aspects of their responsibilities. According to Shutters (2002), some principals feel however, that by the authority conferred on them and their status they are totally in complete control. While some individuals work effectively under autocracy, others with non-authoritarian values prefer a democratic leadership style. There are also other individuals who prefer working under conditions where there is no interference. To function effectively, they require complete freedom from their leaders. Nwankwo (2007) asserts that these groups of individuals perceived their leadership as a symbolic figure that has little or no authority over them.

The behavior of leaders has been identified as one of the major factors influencing the productivity of subordinates in any organization, schools included. The position of the principal is very important in the organization of the secondary school system. Nigeria's education goals have been set out in the National Policy on Education in terms of their relevance to the needs of both the individual and society (FGN, 2013). Toward this end, the National Policy on Education in Nigeria set up certain aims and objectives, which were to facilitate educational development in the country. In fostering these aims and objectives, the school principal has important roles to play. Among these roles include providing effective managerial behavior in secondary schools, thereby enhancing school goals attainment among students. How effective the principal is performing these roles has been a matter of concern to many educationists (Aghenta, 2001; Kadir & Manga, 2015; Ogungbemi, 2011).

The Federal Republic of Nigeria in its National Policy of Education (2004) (the White Paper document on education in Nigeria) set the broad goals of secondary education to be: preparation of individuals for useful living within the society and preparation of individuals for higher education. Specifically, secondary education shall:

- Provide all primary school leavers with the opportunity for education of a higher level, irrespective of sex, social status, religious or ethnic background;
- Offer diversified curriculum to cater for the differences;
- Provide trained manpower in the allied science, technology and commerce at sub-professional grades;
- Develop and promote Nigerian languages, art and culture in the context of the world's cultural heritage;
- Inspire students with a desire for self-improvement and achievement of excellence;
- Foster national unity with an emphasis on the common ties that unite us in our diversity;
- Raise a generation of people who can think for themselves, respect the views and feelings of others, respect the dignity of labor, appreciate those values specified under our broad national goals and live as good citizens;
- Provide the technical knowledge and vocational skills necessary for agricultural, industrial, commercial and economic development.

The achievement of these laudable goals of secondary school education in Nigeria will be possible through harnessing all sectors of a school administration and management. Principal managerial behavior implies the manner in which the principal of a school behaves toward teachers, non-academic staff and students in the school environment. Ibukun (1997) argued that the main task of the principal is to create an enabling atmosphere for teachers to be able to achieve desired changes in students. Supporting this argument, Ijaiya (2000) remarked that teachers in Nigeria express a desire for more participation in decision-making.

The way a principal relates with his or her staff could contribute immensely to his or her effectiveness or otherwise (Kadir & Manga, 2015). This chapter, therefore, examines principals' involvement of students in decision-making in the school and whether this translates to a school's goals attainment.

## Objectives/Purpose of Study

The primary function of a leader is the coordination of human and material resources toward the achievement of certain predetermined goals and objectives. The critical situational variables that moderate the relationship between leaders' effectiveness in terms of productivity in this case—students' realization of school goals—is the appropriate matching of the leader's behavior with maturity of the group and leadership shared practices. Ojo (2002) concluded that effective leadership is the key factor to the success or failure of an organization. There are several leadership styles in various literatures including democratic, laissez-faire, autocratic, pseudo-democratic and transactional. Ojombe (2003) stated that leadership style is concerned with ways or strategies one adopts in doing things toward the achievement of the goals and objectives of a group. In light of the above, the objectives of this study include:

i) Examining the effectiveness of the administrative style which a principal adopts for the attainment of school goals;
ii) Finding out the relationship that exists between principal and students to ensure effective administration;
iii) Ascertaining problems that students faced with their principal's leadership style.

## Perspective/Theoretical Framework

There are two perspectives of leadership, traditional and modern. Traditional perspectives perceive the concept of leadership as inducing compliance, respect and cooperation. In other words, the leader exercises power over the followers to obtain their cooperation (Anderson, Ford, & Hamilton, 1998). In addition, the old leadership perspectives are based on the leaders' role in formulating goals, and ensuring their efficient accomplishment. Maxwell (1999) is of a different opinion; he argues that the leader's attention is on what he/she can put into people rather than what he/she can get out of them, to build the kind of relationship that promotes and increases productivity in the organization. There are other views, which differ from the more traditional perspectives. Sergiovanni (2009), for example, perceives leadership as a personal thing comprising one's heart, head and hand. He says that the heart of leadership deals with one's beliefs, values, and vision. The "head" of leadership is the experiences one has accumulated over time and the ability to perceive present situations in the light of these experiences. The "hand" of leadership, according to him, is the actions and decisions that one takes. In essence, leadership is the act of leading, which reflects the leader's values, vision, experiences, personality, and ability to use past experiences to tackle the situation at hand. It may be argued that leadership is a display of a whole person with regard to intelligence, perceptions, ideas, values and knowledge coming into play, causing necessary changes in the organization.

Sashkin and Sashkin's (2003) and Hoy and Miskel's (2008) definitions of leadership appear to embody a more recent perspective. They define leadership as the art of transforming people and the organization with the aim of improving the organization. Leaders, in this perspective, define the task and explain why the job is being done; they oversee followers' activities and ensure that followers have what they need in terms of skills and resources to do the job. These kinds of leaders develop a relationship between themselves and their followers; they align, motivate and inspire the followers to foster productivity. This approach lays emphasis on transformation that brings positive change in the organization, groups, interpersonal, relationships and the environment.

Both the old and new concepts of leadership appear to agree on some characteristics of leadership. For example, both agree that leadership does not take place in isolation. Rather, it takes place in the process of two or more people interacting and the leader seeks to influence the behavior of other people. However, to a large extent, the old concept of leadership is based on exercising power over followers to maintain the status quo, while the new perspective is based on continuous improvement and power sharing with the followers. The new concept provides respect and concern for the followers and sees them as a powerful source of knowledge, creativity and energy for improving the organization. The issue of change and empowerment is the main focus of the new perspective on leadership.

Leadership is a complex concept. This is especially true because several philosophies have originated, several approaches or theories have been formed, and many models have been employed to provide meaning to the terms "leadership" and "effectiveness." Some of the theories include the Trait Theory, Situational Theory, Contingency Theory, Behavioral Theory and Path– Goal Theory (Adeyemi, 2010; House, 1996; Ogunsanwo, 2000; Walumba, Wang, Lawler, & Shi, 2004). The Trait Theory tends to emphasize the personality traits of the leader such as appearance, height, initiative, aggressiveness, enthusiasm, self-confidence, drive, persistence, interpersonal skills and administrative ability. The Situational Theory stipulates that leaders are the product of given situations. Thus, leadership is strongly affected by the situation from which the leader emerges and in which he/she operates (Adeyemi, 2010). The Contingency Theory is a combination of the Trait Theory and Situational Theory. The theory implies that leadership is a process in which the ability of a leader to exercise influence depends upon the group task situation and the degree to which the leader's personality fits the group (Sybil, 2000). The behavioral theory may be either job-centered or employee-centered. Job-centered leaders practiced close supervision, while employee-centered leaders practiced general supervision. The Path–Goal Theory is based on the theory of motivation (House, 1996). In this theory the behavior of the leader is acceptable to the subordinates only if they continue to see the leader as a source of satisfaction (Ajayi & Ayodele, 2001).

No man is independent of him/herself, as he/she cannot live in isolation. One belongs to a group that comprises different statuses of people ranging from superior to subordinate. Ojo (2002) noted that in such a grouping, each stratum performs different functions toward the realization of the goals of the group. Each group would have people (superiors) saddled with the responsibility of directing, controlling, guiding, monitoring and planning for the group, while the others (subordinates) obey and follow the laid down patterns of the first set of the people (superiors). Ojo (2002) said that those who agree to be bound by the dictated norm are the followers, while those that are fashioning their conduct are the leaders.

Ingiabuna (2004) opined that leadership has to do with the control or influence over a group. It is a group phenomenon. There cannot be a leader without a follower. This means that one cannot talk of leadership except with reference to a group. George, cited in Ingiabuna (2004), said that leadership is the activity of influencing people to strive willingly for the group objectives. Oyebamiji (2008) concurred by stating that for a leader to achieve his/her set goals and objectives, the leader must have demonstrated the capability for goals attainment. Osuji (2001) added that the basic prerequisite for the success of any school program is effective leadership. In secondary school administration, the success of any school in achieving its stated goals or objectives depends on the ability of the chief administrator, otherwise known as the principal, and which leadership style he/she adopts in administering the school. Ajibade (2000) noted that effective leadership roles provided by the principal will lead to the achievement of the school goals. The effectiveness of leadership style in goals attainment is encapsulated in the popular adage, "get the right man in the leadership job and all your problems will be solved." Ajibade (2000) noted that in cases where the leadership style of the principal is ineffective even the best school programs, most adequate resources and most motivated students will be rendered unproductive. Therefore, the importance of a good leadership style in an organization cannot be overemphasized. The teachers' and students' level of productivity in a school are indices of the principal's effectiveness.

## Leadership Styles

Leadership style means the nature of how someone acts when enacting a certain theory or model, e.g., to be autocratic, participative or laissez-faire in leadership style (Hersey & Blanchard, 1996). Osuji (2001) further opined that leadership style is a pattern or constellation of leadership behavior that characterizes a given leader. Osuji (2001) identified authoritarian, persuasive and participative styles of leadership as some leadership styles prevalent in the second tier of education (secondary schools) in Nigeria. Osuji (2001) further described the identified leadership styles as thus: the authoritarian leader is one who uses his/her power of office to impose his/her decision on his/her subordinate; the persuasive leader is one who uses logical reasoning to influence his/her subordinate; while the participative leadership is one who is willing to share decision-making and responsibilities equally with the subordinate. Osuji (2001) also identified and categorized leadership styles into autocratic, democratic and laissez-faire, transactional and pseudo democratic and Igwe (2000) added the coercive leadership style. As in any goal-oriented organization the concern for the effective leader is the attainment of the goals, which should be paramount.

Blake and Mouton (Gupta, 2009) proposed five leadership styles. They conceptualize leadership style in the form of a grid: "task" and "people." The grid categorizes leadership into five distinct styles: impoverished managers, country club managers, authority-compliant managers, middle-of-the road managers, and team managers. Impoverished managers are those leaders who are low on people and low on task:—such leaders exhibit lack of concern for the result of the assigned task or interpersonal relationship. Country club managers are those leaders who are high on people and low on task:—such leaders exhibit care and concern for the people, they create a comfortable and friendly environment while de-emphasizing the productivity of task. Authority-compliant managers are those leaders who are low on people and high on task:—these leaders have a strong focus on good planning and successful completion of tasks. They place little emphasis on relationships, motivation or communication with their subordinates. Middle-of-the-road managers are those leaders who are medium on people as well as on task:—these leaders are compromisers who have a weak balance between concern for people and task. They avoid any conflicting situations and try to get the work done by moderately focusing on both people and task. Team managers are those leaders who are high on people and high on task:—this style tries to maximize the concern of both task and people. Such leaders create strongly structured tasks, set clear priorities and track the progress on a timely basis. At the same time, they promote active participation and teamwork, create an open and comfortable environment, set guidelines for effective communication and empower the individuals enough to keep them motivated.

## Principalship in Secondary Schools in Nigeria

Principalship is a well-defined role in developed countries. The duties and responsibilities of the principal are documented and agreed upon in the literature of principalship in the United States, as described by Campbell and Cregg (1957). Berenji (1979 cited in Mbipom, 2000) presents the following as ten areas in which secondary school principals should function: administrator/ executive; community and public relations facilitator; curriculum and instruction supervisor; business services and budget facilitator; leader; change agent; evaluator; conflict reconciler; staff development planner; and student personnel organizer. In Nigeria, there tends to be a lack of consensus as to the sort of person who can be a school principal and what the role of the person should be.

## Functions of the School Principal

The functions of a school principal can be grouped into five broad responsibilities: staff development, finance and budget, public relations and the community, instructional program, and students' welfare. In terms of what this chapter is discussing – schools' goal attainment – the most crucial function of the principal, as will be discussed here, is an instructional program. Although, all five functions are interwoven and necessary for overall and effective school administration and management for school goals to be attained, this chapter will limit itself to the fourth and fifth broad functions of a principal, instructional program and student welfare.

## Instructional Program

The secondary school principal is the supervisor of curriculum and instruction of the school. He/she coordinates the instructional activities among staff. As a director of curriculum and instruction of the school, the principal devotes no less than 80% of his/her time to the improvement of instruction in the school. Students are sent to the school so that they may cultivate new skills that will change their lives in a positive way. Such changes are possible only where the principal monitors, directs and supervises the instruction that is given by the staff. Some principals try to excuse themselves from this huge task of supervision of curriculum and instruction in the school by hiding behind other managerial roles like record keeping, registration of students and payment vouchers which can be delegated to other senior staff to ensure that the principal has enough time to direct teaching and learning. The syllabus for secondary schools in Nigeria is centrally produced and supplied by the Ministry of Education. Principals are expected to spend time studying the syllabus and interpreting it into needed skills, competencies, activities, instructional materials, and so forth.

The principal should make it his/her priority to improve the quality of instruction in his/her school. The quality of instruction should be observed, evaluated, and discussed by the principal and staff. It is generally agreed that to any teacher, it is the little things that mean a lot. From the way a principal handles the small, seemingly insignificant items, teachers form their impressions of him/her as a human being, a colleague, and a supervisor of learning. The principal need not initiate outstanding changes in the curriculum to convince the staff that he/she is interested in learning. Only by working closely with them and exhibiting a candid interest in what they are doing in the classroom can the principal gain respect from his staff. If he/she is genuinely interested in better education for young people, the principal must go beyond the realm of preaching and pontificating. Instead, the principal must show by deeds rather than words, that his/her role as director of learning takes precedence over others.

When the principal takes the leadership role in improving instruction in the school he/she supervises the activities of all school functionaries, determines various services to aid the teaching and learning activities of the school, and ensures that the school is growing in a definite direction, which is the attainment of its goals.

## Student Welfare

The second core function of a principal as considered in this chapter is student welfare. The principal is the manager of students' personal matters. In this role, the principal directs, supervises, organizes, coordinates and evaluates all the activities that concern students (Mbipom, 2000). Apart from teaching and learning in the classroom, the staff and students are occupied with many extra-curricular activities that are geared toward developing the abilities, interest, and needs of individuals at various levels of maturity within the school. Many problems that affect the academic achievement of the students might be minimized if the guidance services of the school are properly organized and managed, students' difficulties are discovered in time and solutions for such problems found before it is too late.

Students should be disciplined in order to get the best out of the teaching–learning situation. Indiscipline in the family, society, class, and school is increasing. Indiscipline in school affects the work the child does and the way the teacher teaches. Any breakdown in the personal relationship or in the observance of rules that leads to disaster is indiscipline. It is the aim of the principal and staff that the students build up a level of self-control that will help them to learn as well as acquire and manifest good habits which encourage hard work. Some healthy habits in the school may include:

- Silence in the classroom, library and corridor;
- Respect for school authority—prefects, teachers, principals;
- Adhering to school rules;
- Wearing complete school uniform.

On the other hand, some common signs of indiscipline in secondary schools today include:

- Absenteeism and truancy;
- Untidiness in work dress and habits;
- Fighting and bullying;
- Deliberate vandalism of school property;
- Stealing of school property and other students' money or property;
- Laziness;
- Disturbances of those who want to work or read;
- Breaking of school rules (e.g., going out of bounds);
- Immorality (e.g., secret cult activities);
- Lateness at school.

## The School as a Formal Organization (Goal-Oriented)

Teachers teach and work in schools that are usually administered by managers, often known as principals or headmasters. School administration is itself often part of larger administration units. The conditions of teachers' working life are influenced by the administration and leadership provided by principals, and it is widely assumed that school leadership directly influences the effectiveness of teachers and the achievement outcomes of students (Organization for Economic Cooperation and Development [OECD], 2001; Pont, Nusche, & Moorman, 2008).

Formal organizations are established for the explicit purpose of achieving certain goals. A formal organization is bureaucratic. It is concerned with the division of labor, the allocation of power in the system and the job specifications for each position. It is interested in the efficiency of the system. Every formal organization has tasks to perform. There is a line of authority in the system. The formal organization is governed by rules in order to promote efficiency and discipline.

In the school, many people with different personal goals work together to try to achieve the goals for which the school was established. This type of formal organization usually needs a coordinator, a leader, a manager, or an administrator. The principal is responsible for using the financial or material resources and facilities and the human resources at his/her disposal for achieving the goals of the school. The principal ensures that each member of the formal organization is fully aware of his/her responsibilities. Where the formal organization is big or complex, other officers, who are usually hierarchically arranged below the manager, are chosen to assist the manager. Such officers include the vice principal, sectional head or head of department.

Denga (1990), cited in Mbipom (2000), submits that formal organizations are planned, rational, goal-oriented entities, which have the characteristics, or major features outlined below:

- Formal organizations set up common goals or purpose and work together to achieve them. The organizational interest is given priority over the individual's interest.
- Formal organizations are bureaucratic: this is to say that in a formal organization all members are given equal treatment. For example, rules and regulations are set up and enforced in the interest of the organization. There is a hierarchy of authority. A high degree of impersonality and standardized procedures are in operation.
- Resistance to change: although formal organizations are not static, it is difficult to channel massive changes through formal organizations. Hence, formal organizations may be said to be resistant to change.
- Authority: formal organizations have some form of authority for controlling, guiding, limiting, or managing the various units of the organization.
- Coordination: there is co-ordination of effort in the service of mutual help among the several units of the organization.
- Specialization: different members of the units of the organization perform different functions. There is division of labor. In education, some people specialize in teaching, others in service delivery like typing, the library service, meal service, and so forth.
- Order: human behavior and activities in a formal organization are regulated and constrained in order to ensure stability, continuity and decorum since formally defined objectives cannot be attained successfully if an organization is in a state of anarchy.
- Replaceability: the saying that "people come and go but the organization continues" is true. Members of the organization are replaced in order to curb the disruptions caused by individuals who for one reason or the other have to leave. When members resign, they are usually replaced.
- Compensation: in a formal organization, there is a system of rewards (mainly financial) which is designed to provide incentives for the staff to work harder. Some other rewards may be given to the workers in addition to their pay.

## How Leadership Styles Vary by Region/Country

In Sweden, the schools have been under strain for several decades and the school system is almost always on the political agenda. Economic resources allotted to schools have been decreasing since the 1990s, which has led to a reduction of the number of employees (Berg, 2003). The principal is responsible for both the educational program at his/her school and for keeping the budget of the school. Research on Swedish schools has indicated that the Swedish principal is under pressure from different directions (Svedberg, 2000; Wahlström, 2002). There are different interests and expectations between administration and education, state and local authorities (the municipality), curriculum and local traditions, between the responsible authorities and the profession (Scherp, 1998; Wingård, 1998).

A study was carried out by Hansson and Andersen (2009) on leadership style, decision-making style, and motivation profile in Sweden involving 200 Swedish principals (male and female) who responded to questionnaires concerning their leadership style, decision-making style and motivation profile. The results show that 49% of principals have a change-centered leadership style; 38% were primarily intuitive when making decisions; and 44% were achievement motivated. No significant gender differences were found. The results indicate that many principals have fair prospects of leading their schools successfully in times of change.

A similar trend was found in Saudi Arabia in a recent study carried out by Abdulghani (2016) which explores the relationship between principal's leadership styles and teachers' job satisfaction in girls' private elementary schools in Saudi Arabia. In that study, the researcher measured two main constructs: leadership styles and job satisfaction. Within leadership style, three sub-constructs were measured: transformational leadership, transactional leadership, and passive-avoidant leadership. Correlation analysis results from a sample of principals and teacher pairs from 55 schools revealed that the vast majority of principals who participated in the study practiced a transactional leadership style based on the use of rewards and punishments to motivate behavior. Additionally, evidence shows that the transactional leadership style is positively correlated with teachers' job satisfaction in the study context. The passive–avoidant leadership style has a marginally significant negative relationship with teachers' job satisfaction and the transformational leadership style is not significantly related to teachers' job satisfaction among participants.

Even in Organization for Economic Cooperation and Development (OECD) countries as elsewhere in the world, school leaders face challenges due to rising expectations for schools and schooling in a century characterized by technological innovation, migration and globalization. As countries aim to transform their educational systems to equip all young people with the knowledge and skills needed in this changing world, the roles of school leaders and related expectations have changed radically. They are no longer expected merely to be good managers; effective school leadership is increasingly viewed as key to large-scale education reform and to improved educational outcomes. Since at least 2001, with its series of reports, *What Works in Innovation in Education*, produced by the Centre for Educational Research and Innovation (CERI), the OECD has recognized the significant challenges faced by principals and school managers in member countries (OECD, 2001).

As countries increasingly turn to improving education to address an ever more complex world, many governments give school leadership more responsibility for implementing and managing significantly more demanding education programs. Globalization and widespread immigration mean that children, youth and their families represent an increasingly challenging clientele for schools in many countries. Also, the standards to which schools must perform and the accountability required of management raise expectations regarding school leadership to an unprecedented level. A recent OECD report, *Improving School Leadership*, summarizes the changing landscape of schools and their management over recent decades (Pont et al., 2008, p. 6): "in this new environment, schools and schooling are being given an even bigger job to do." Greater decentralization in many countries is being coupled with more school autonomy, more accountability for school and student results, and a better use of the knowledge base of education and pedagogical processes. It is also being coupled with broader responsibility for contributing to and supporting the schools' local communities, other schools and other public services.

The Organization for Economic Cooperation and Development [OECD] (2009) report argues that to meet the educational needs of the twenty-first century, the principals in primary and secondary schools must play a more dynamic role and become far more than an administrator of top-down rules and regulations, which tends to corroborate with the findings of the research which argues that school goals can be achieved through involvement of students in the everyday running of the schools, for instance in making their opinions count in the decision-making process. The OECD (2009) further stated that schools and their governing structures must let school leaders lead in a systematic fashion and focus on the instructional and learning processes and outcomes of their schools. The recommendations of OECD (2009) flowed from a field of education that has recently experienced a fundamental change in its philosophy of administration and even in its conception of schools as organizations. Research literature (Pont et al., 2008) indicated that what the public and other stakeholders of schools want as learning outcomes for students can only be achieved if school leadership is adapted to a new model. These changes are directly relevant to the working lives, professional development, instructional practices, pedagogical beliefs and attitudes and the appraisal and feedback of secondary school teachers and even students.

## Method

This chapter is centered on an empirical study carried out in a state in Nigeria-Bayelsa State, one of the 36 states of the Federal Republic of Nigeria. It is situated in the South-South Geo-Political zone of Nigeria. Bayelsa has about 26 public (government-owned) secondary schools in the capital metropolis, Yenagoa. Ten schools were randomly selected to be part of this study. Letters of consent were then sent to the schools eliciting their willingness to be involved in the study. Details of the objective and purpose of the research were outlined in the consent letter. All ten schools randomly selected for the study indicated their willingness to participate in the research. The students in the terminal class in Senior Secondary 3 (SS3) were involved in the study. The population of SS3 students in almost all of the participating schools ranges between 57 and 68 students. Forty-eight students from each of the ten schools were selected to make up the sample for the study. This selection was done by writing "Yes" on 48 pieces of paper and "No" on the rest. After shuffling the pieces of paper together, students were asked to pick one piece of paper and the 48 students who picked "Yes" were involved in the research.

The principals of each of the participating schools were also involved in the research, making a total of ten principals. The research was divided into two phases. Phase one helped to group participants into the different leadership style adopted by the head of the school, the principal, and phase two was to determine the academic performance of students under the various leadership styles.

**Phase One:** Two separate questionnaires (one for the principal and one for students, see Appendixes I and II, respectively) were developed by the researcher and validated by a team of experts in Measurement and Evaluation in the department of Educational Foundations at Niger Delta University in Bayelsa State, Nigeria. The reliability of the instruments was tested using the test–retest method of reliability where the same instrument was administered twice within an interval of 2 weeks to the same respondents not involved in the main sample for the study. The two data were collated and analyzed using the Pearson Product Moment Correlation Coefficient (PPMCC) and a coefficient of 0.84 was realized which is within the range for reliable coefficients.

The instruments for data collection in this study were a three-point Likert scale of "agreed," "disagreed," and "undecided" responses to the statement item around the three research questions posited for the study and Standardized General Knowledge Test (SGKT) questions adopted from past General Certificate of Education (GCE) and West African Examination Council (WAEC) examination question papers.

**Phase Two:** This phase included the administration of the Standardized General Knowledge Test. Both instruments (questionnaire and test questions) were administered by the researcher. Also, a cross-sectional interview session was held with some of the participants (students and principals) in order to triangulate the findings from the questionnaires. The responses were collated and analyzed to answer the research questions.

## Data Source

The data sources for this study were primary data generated from the student and principal questionnaires as well as the raw scores from the standardized test. These were analyzed using chi square and t-test statistics to answer the research questions and results presented in tables.

## Results

A large percentage of the respondents indicated that apart from the principal having regular meetings with the individual stakeholders of the schools (teachers, non-academic staff and students) principals also have a combination of meetings of all stakeholders totaling more than three meetings within a term (a term is 13 calendar weeks). Only a few of the respondents indicated that meetings were seldom held with all the three stakeholders in attendance. It was also found out from the study that decision-making and opinion sharing are not made only by the school head (principal) alone, but are collective responsibilities, with everybody's opinion/views counting, including the students', on which school goals are in their best interest. Including the students' opinions/views in the day-to-day running of the school gives them a sense of self-worth and inclusive administration. It also gives the students a sense of ownership and reason to work hard at their academics. In other words, all the participants –students and principals – agreed that school decisions are made by teachers, non-academic staff and the principal, while opinions or views are shared by all four (principal, teachers, non-academic staff and students) together.

These findings chime with the modern perspective of leadership put forward by Maxwell (1999). He argues that the leader's attention is on what he/she can put into people rather than what he/she can get out of them, so as to build the kind of relationship that promotes and increases goal attainment in the organization (this leadership style can be likened to a democratic leadership style), as opposed to the traditional perspective of leadership that perceives leadership as inducing compliance, respect and cooperation. In other words, the leader exercises power over the followers to obtain their cooperation (this can be likened to an autocratic leadership style). In addition, traditional leadership perspectives are based on leaders' role in formulating goals, and ensuring their efficient accomplishment (Anderson et al., 1998).

From the responses of this first phase of the research, the participating schools were divided into two leadership style groups: democratic leadership style group A and autocratic leadership style group B. Students from schools in both groups were then administered a standardized general knowledge test adopted from past GCE and WAEC test questions and the mean score of the two groups was compared using t-test statistics—the second phase of the research. It was found in phase two that students from schools where the principal's leadership style could be described as democratic outperformed students from schools where the principal's leadership style could be described as autocratic—not getting all the stakeholders involved in the decision-making and day-to-day running of the school. Also, during the cross-sectional interview with some of the participating students, the interviewees indicated that most of the time they are afraid of approaching their principals even if they have a problem or something meaningful to discuss with him/her. This probably might be a "culture phenomenon" where subordinates do not feel free to discuss with superiors (boss) for fear of being seen as rude or even seen as insubordinate.

The autocratic leader is the authoritarian dictator, who is proud and sometimes rude or harsh and uses threats to get work done. He/she is coercive, job-oriented, and feels that it is his/her responsibility to tell the staff what their duties are. An autocratic leader expects strict compliance without any excuses; his/her main concern is the achievement of the objectives to the letter. In most cases autocratic leaders believe that human beings are lazy by nature and so they should be made to work. The despotic leader tries to exact conformity from his/her staff through strict supervision. Autocratic leaders love power and authority and would not miss any opportunity of letting the world know they are in control. Autocratic leadership style is a traditional perspective of leadership. There is a paradigm shift from traditional perception to an all-inclusive modern perspective of leadership.

On the other hand, democratic leaders as the name implies, achieve high productivity through participation of their staff and students in decision-making. They discuss freely with their subordinates because they know that their staff as well as students have something to offer to the effective running of the school to achieve its goals. The democratic leader appreciates teamwork. The subordinates are given a high degree of freedom. The administrator sees his/her subordinates as partners in progress. This type of leader does not use harsh and abusive words while talking with his/her staff and students even when they are in the wrong. Intimidation and threats are not part of a democratic leader's corrective measures. The staff in this type of climate are more relaxed and committed to the achievement of the objectives of the school (which is increased performance by students) because they have been involved in building up the policy to be achieved. However, an effective administrator may not be expected to wait for staff's participation and consultation in case of an acute emergency.

This study investigated schools' goal attainment. The schools' goal is to turn out young adults who are worthy in character (behavior) and in learning (academic achievement), hence the second phase of this research. The findings from the second phase added to the debate are more or less narrative in the twist between leadership and management. There are so many differences of opinion among scholars and researchers about the concept of leadership and management. Some say that both are the same, but some others take management as a subset of leadership. Paul Birks says managers concern themselves with tasks, and leaders concern themselves with people. According to Hersey and Blanchard (1996), management merely consists in leadership applied to business situations or forms a subset of the broader process of leadership, or leadership occurs any time one attempts to influence the behavior of an individual or group regardless of the reason. Management is said to be a kind of leadership in which the achievement of the organizational goal is important (which fits into a school scenario). In light of this research, the principal's role is both a manager and a leader, as he/she ensures the school tasks are carried out to ensure high academic performance as well as concerns him/herself with the people to bring out the desired character/behavior in the students, which is in line with Birks' notion of a manager and a leader.

Among the five leadership styles proposed by Blakes and Mouton in Gupta (2009) discussed in the literature review, the findings from this study show that the fifth style, team manager, seems to be the one that can achieve the educational goals of a school, as the manager (the principal) needs to focus highly on both the students and teachers (people) as well as the task of teaching for the goals to be achieved. The principals who participated in this research fall into leadership styles three (authority-compliant manager – low on people – high on task) and style five (team manager who is high on people and high on task).

## Significance/Educational Implication of the Study

Education is viewed as the bedrock of any national development and it has been generally acclaimed that "no nation can rise above the quality of its educational system as the quality of its workforce will be determined by the system of education." The five main goals Nigeria endorsed as the necessary foundation for the National Policy on Education are the building of:

i) A free and democratic society;
ii) A just and egalitarian society;
iii) A united, strong and self-reliant nation;
iv) A great and dynamic economy and
v) A land full of bright opportunities for all citizens.

It is true that for these to happen, apart from enormous political will needed by the government to provide necessary human and material resources that will lead to the achievement of these goals, an understanding of leadership styles of the principal who is the accounting officer of the school is paramount. It could then be concluded that the principal's leadership style or behavior can improve schools' goals attainment, and that the principal's skills in conflict resolution and instructional leadership are important factors. There is a reciprocal relationship between leadership and management, which implies that an effective manager should possess leadership skills and an effective leader, should demonstrate management skills. In other words, management involves power by position and leadership involves power by influence. It is therefore recommended that principals as managers should be equipped with ample leadership skills and qualities to run schools successfully.

The study has limitations which include the findings cannot be generalized as there are other extraneous variables that can influence goal attainment that were not investigated in the study and also the generalization of findings is limited by the small sample size involved in the study.

## References

Abdulghani, N.K. (2016). *A correlational study of principals' leadership styles on teachers' job satisfaction in girls' private elementary schools in Saudi Arabia.* Unpublished PhD thesis, Pennsylvania State University, Graduate School College of Education, State College, Pennsylvania. Available at: https://etda.libraries.psu.edu/files/final_submissions/11734 Accessed October 11, 2018.

Adeyemi, T. O. (2010). Principals' leadership styles and teachers' job performance in senior secondary schools in Ondo State, Nigeria. *Journal of Education Administration and Policy Studies, 2*(6), 83–91.

Aghenta, J. A. (2001). *Educational planning: A turning point in education and development in Nigeria* Inaugural Lecture Series 58. Benin City, Nigeria: University of Benin.

Aghenta, J. A. (2005). *Fundamentals of educational management, department of educational administration and foundations.* Benin City, Nigeria: University of Benin.

Ajayi, I. A., & Ayodele, J. B. (2001). *Introduction to educational planning, administration and supervision.* Ado-Ekiti, Nigeria: Yemi Publishing Services.

Ajibade, E.S (2000). *The Relationship Between Principal Leadership Style and Staff Motivation in Selected Secondary Schools in Ibadan City.* An unpublished M.Ed. Project, University of Ibadan.

Anderson, T. D., Ford, R., & Hamilton, M. (1998). *Transforming leadership: Equipping yourself and coaching others to build leadership organization* (6th ed.). Boca Raton, FL: St Lucie Press.

Bennis, W., & Nanus, B. (1997). *Leaders: Strategies for taking charge.* New York, NY: Harper Business.

Berg, G. (2003). *Att förstå skolan. En teori om skolan som institution och skolor som organizationer (To Understand the School. A theory on the school as an institution and schools as organizations).* Lund, Sweden: Student litteratur.

Campbell, O. O. (2008). *Educational planning, management and school oganisation.* Yaba, Lagos: Ibrahim O. Campbell and Sons Publishers.

Campbell, R. E., & Cregg, R. T. (1957). *Administrative behavior in education.* New York, NY: Harper and Brothers.

Federal Republic of Nigeria. (2004). *National policy of education.* Lagos, Nigeria: NERDC.

Gupta, A. (2009). Leadership styles, *Practical Management: Designing a Better Workplace.* Available at http://www.practical-management.com/Leadership Development/Leadership-Style.html Accessed July 20, 2017.

Hansson, P.H. and Andersen, J. A. (2009). The Swedish Principal: Leadership Style, Decision-Making Style, and Motivation Profile. Available at: http://files.eric.ed.gov/fulltext/EJ987306.pdf Accessed March 10, 2017.

Hersey, P., & Blanchard, K. H. (1996). *Management of organization behavior* (6th ed.). New Delhi, India: Prentice- Hall of India.

House, R. J. (1996). Path–goal theory of leadership: Lessons, legacy and a reformulated theory. *Leadership Quarterly, 5*(3), 323–352.

Hoy, W. K., & Miskel, C. G. (2008). *Educational administration: Theory, research and practice* (8th ed.). Boston, MA: McGraw-Hill.

Ibukun, W. O. (1997). *Educational management: Theory and practice.* Lagos, Nigeria: Greenland Publishers.

Igwe, L. E. B. (2000). *Fundamental theories, concepts, principles and practice of educational administration.* Port Harcourt, Nigeria: Harvey Publication.

Ijaiya, N. Y. (2000). Failing schools' and national development: Time for reappraisal of school effectiveness in Nigeria. *Nigeria Journal of Educational Research and Evaluation, 2*(2), 42.

Ingiabuna, E. T. (2004). *Human social: An introduction to sociology*. Port Harcourt, Nigeria: Amethyst and Colleagues Publishers.

Jennings, A. (2003). *Management and hardship in the secondary school*. London, UK: Ward Book Educational.

Kadir, N. J., & Manga, S. D. (2015). Relationship between principal's managerial behavior and teachers' job performance in public senior secondary schools in Kwara State, Nigeria: Implication for counseling psychology. *Sokoto International Journal of Counseling Psychology, 3*, 227–239.

Maxwell, J. C. (1999). *The 21 indispensable qualities of a leader*. Nashville, TN: Tomas Nelson Publishers.

Mbipom, G. (2000). *Educational administration and planning*. Calabar, Nigeria: University of Calabar Press.

Mbiti, D. M. (2007). *Administration leadership foundation of school administration*. Nairobi, Kenya: Oxford University Press.

Ndubisi, B. E. (2004). Leadership theory. *The Nigerian Principal: Journal of ANCOPSS, 2*(3), 11–16.

Nwankwo, J. I. (2007). *Educational administration theory and method*. Ibadan, Nigeria: University Press.

Organization for Economic Cooperation and Development. (2001). Creating Effective Teaching and Learning Environments: First Results from TALIS – ISBN 978–92–64-05605-3.

Organization for Economic Cooperation and Development. (2009). Leading to Learn: School Leadership and Management Styles Chapter 6 available at: https://www.oecd.org/berlin/43541674.pdf. Accessed on March 12, 2017.

Ogungbemi, A.S. (2011). *Relationship among principals' managerial behavior, teachers' job performance and school effectiveness in Osun State secondary schools*. Unpublished PhD Dissertation, Department of Educational Management, University of Ilorin, Ilorin, Nigeria.

Ogunsanwo, O.A. (2000). Modern principles and techniques of management. External Studies Programme, Ibadan: Department of Educational Management University of Ibadan, pp. 24–90.

Ojo (2002). Effectiveness of teachers. *Journal of Teacher Education, 12*, 4–10.

Ojombe (2003). *Leadership effectiveness: A practical Guide for writers educational research projects*. Lagos: Educational Consultants and Publisher.

Osuji, E.E. (2001). Community Analysis Lecture Notes.

Oyebamiji, M.A (2008). The Challenges of Leadership in the promotion of Grassroots Development in Nigeria.

Pont, B., Nusche, D. and Moorman, H (2008). Improving School Leadership volume 1 Available at: https://www.oecd.org/edu/school/49847132.pdf. Accessed on March 16, 2017.

Sashkin, M., & Sashkin, M. G. (2003). *Leadership that matters*. San Francisco, CA: Berrett-Koehler Publishers, Inc.

Scherp, H.-Å. (1998). Utmanande eller utmanat ledarskap. Rektor, organization och förändrat undervisningsmönster I grundskolan (Challenging or challenged leadership. School management, the school organization and change of teaching patterns within the upper secondary school). Göteborg: Acta Universitatis Gothoburgensis.

Scouller, J. (2011). *The three levels of leadership: How to develop your leadership presence, knowhow and skills.* Milton Keynes, UK: Management Books 2000 Ltd.

Sergiovanni, T. J. (2009). *Rethinking leadership.* Arlington Heights, IL: Skylight Training and Publishing Inc.

Shutters, T. (2002). *School organization and management.* Lagos, Nigeria: Punmkar Nigeria Ltd.

Svedberg, L. (2000). *Rektorsrollen. Om skolledares gestaltning (The principal's role: A study of the formation of educational leadership).* Stockholm, Sweden: HLS förlag.

Sybil, J. (2000). *Introduction to communication for business and organization.* (pp. 31–42). Ibadan, Nigeria: Spectrum Books Ltd.

Uwaifo, V. O. (2012). The effects of family structure. Global Journal of Humanities and Social Sciences, 12(7). Available at: https://globaljournals.org/GJHSS_Volume12/7-The-Effects-of-Family-Structures.pdf Accessed November 6, 2018.

Wahlström, N. (2002). Om det förändrade ansvaret för skolan. Vägen till mål- och resultatstyrning och några av desskonsekvenser (On the shift of responsibility for compulsory schooling: the path to management by objectives and results and some of its consequences). Örebro: Örebro Studies in Education 3.

Walumba, F. O., Wang, P., Lawler, J. J., & Shi, K. (2004). The role of collective efficacy in the relations between transformational leadership and work outcomes. *Journal of Occupational and Organizational Psychology, 77*, 515–530.

Wingård, B. (1998). Att vara rektor och kvinna (To be a head and a woman). Uppsala: Acta Universitatis Upsaliensis.Uppsala Studies in Education 74.

## Appendix I
## Questionnaire on Effective Leadership Style on Secondary School Goals Attainment

(FOR PRINCIPALS)

**Section "A" Personal Data**
Name of School:...............................................................................................
Qualification:...................................................................................................
Teaching Experience:........................................................................................
Sex: Male:............................. Female:..................................................
Please indicate by ticking ( ) where applicable.

| | Questionnaire items | Agreed | Disagreed | Undecided | % | REMARK |
|---|---|---|---|---|---|---|
| **1.** | **How often do you organize meetings in a term to obtain school goals?** | | | | | |
| a. | Once | | | | | |
| b. | Twice | | | | | |
| c. | Thrice | | | | | |
| d. | More than thrice | | | | | |
| e. | Never | | | | | |
| **2.** | **Meetings with students** | | | | | |
| a. | Once | | | | | |
| b. | Twice | | | | | |
| c. | Thrice | | | | | |
| d. | More than thrice | | | | | |
| e. | Never | | | | | |
| **3.** | **Meetings with teachers** | | | | | |
| a. | Once | | | | | |
| b. | Twice | | | | | |
| c. | Thrice | | | | | |
| d. | More than thrice | | | | | |
| e. | Never | | | | | |

| **4.** | **Meetings with non-academic staff only** | | | | | |
|---|---|---|---|---|---|---|
| a. | Once | | | | | |
| b. | Twice | | | | | |
| c. | Thrice | | | | | |
| d. | More than thrice | | | | | |
| e. | Never | | | | | |
| **5.** | **Meetings with teachers/students** | | | | | |
| a. | Once | | | | | |
| b. | Twice | | | | | |
| c. | Thrice | | | | | |
| d. | More than thrice | | | | | |
| f. | Never | | | | | |
| **6.** | **Meetings with teachers and non-academic staff** | | | | | |
| | Once | | | | | |
| | Twice | | | | | |
| | Thrice | | | | | |
| | More than thrice | | | | | |
| | Never | | | | | |
| **7.** | **Meetings with students/non-academic staff** | | | | | |
| a. | Once | | | | | |
| b. | Twice | | | | | |
| c. | Thrice | | | | | |
| d. | More than thrice | | | | | |
| e. | Never | | | | | |
| **8.** | **Meetings with all three together** | | | | | |
| a. | Once | | | | | |
| b. | Twice | | | | | |
| c. | Thrice | | | | | |
| d. | More than thrice | | | | | |
| e. | Never | | | | | |

# Appendix II
# Questionnaire on Effective Leadership Style on Secondary School Goals Attainment

(FOR STUDENTS)

**Section "A" Personal Data**
Name of School:..........................................................................................
Class of Student:........................................................................................
Sex: Male:............................. Female:................................................
Please indicate by ticking ( ) where applicable.

| | Questionnaire items | Agreed | Disagreed | Undecided | % | REMARK |
|---|---|---|---|---|---|---|
| **1.** | **Is decision-making in your school made only by** | | | | | |
| a. | Principal | | | | | |
| b. | Principal / Teachers | | | | | |
| c. | Principal Teachers / Non- academic staff | | | | | |
| d. | Principal / Teachers / Non- academic staff/Student | | | | | |
| **2.** | **Are opinions in the meeting shared only by the:** | | | | | |
| a. | Principal | | | | | |
| b. | Principals / Teachers | | | | | |
| c. | Principal / Teacher/ Non-academic staff | | | | | |
| d. | Principal / teachers/ Non-academic staff/ Students | | | | | |
| e. | No respect for everyone | | | | | |
| f. | Delays of school activities | | | | | |

| **3.** | **Do principals influence students' academic achievement** | | | | | |
|---|---|---|---|---|---|---|
| a. | Positive | | | | | |
| b. | Average | | | | | |
| c. | Negative | | | | | |
| **4.** | **How effective is the Principal / Student interaction** | | | | | |
| a. | Very effective | | | | | |
| b. | Freedom to do what they want | | | | | |
| c. | Over bearing | | | | | |

# 2

# Effective Strategies for Workplace Learning

*Annetjie Elizabeth Human*[1] *and Victor Pitsoe*[2]

[1] *South African Police Service Academy*
[2] *University of South Africa*

**Note: Workplace learning**, for the purpose of this enquiry, refers to workplace learning that enhances workplace practices in the organization. It includes research in the physical workplace setting as well as other settings to involve the community.

Effective Strategies for Workplace Learning

## Background

The notion of "workplace learning" is not new in the South African Police Service (SAPS). It is increasingly being used more widely to develop leaders and improve their impact on the effectiveness and competitiveness of the organization. In an attempt to fulfill this need, the Human Resource Development (HRD) Division within the SAPS was mandated to the provision of an Executive Development Learning Programme (EDLP). The EDLP was, therefore, intended to develop the organization's leaders to address critical challenges in the organization. The program also contributes to equipping them with the ability and capability to perform tasks and fulfill leadership roles to the expected standard on a strategic level. The first author's involvement in executive development and workplace learning as well as a doctoral study on solving workplace problems on a strategic level formed the basis for this chapter.

This chapter explores Joseph Raelin's work-based learning model and leads into the application of the model to the SAPS context. The various learning modalities, which include the readiness level of the learners, the strengths and preferences of the facilitator, the support and attitudes at the workplace and the past practices of the sponsoring unit, are discussed (Raelin's Work-based learning model, Raelin, 1997). The chapter concludes by referring to the barriers to integrate newly gained information and knowledge in a shared mental modal, which informs decision-making and action. We argue that workplace learning is the critical link between strategy and operations. It is task-oriented which guides

*The Wiley Handbook of Global Workplace Learning*, First Edition.
Edited by Vanessa Hammler Kenon and Sunay Vasant Palsole.

thinking and actions. We also present global workplace learning as intertwined with general management principle in real life organizational strategies which challenges return on investment (ROI).

## Raelin's Work-Based Learning Model

Raelin (1998) reminds us that "the work-based learning model is premised on the simple idea that learning can be acquired in the midst of practice" and it is dedicated to the task at hand; it deliberately merges theory with practice and sees knowledge creation as the collective responsibility of every employee; to adopt a learning to learn culture; to eliminate underlying assumptions of practices and lastly to acknowledge the intersection of explicit and tacit forms of knowing (p. 280). For him, "the model has no set sequence since learning modalities are dependent on various conditions, such as the readiness level of the learners, the strengths and preferences of the facilitator(s), the support and attitudes at the workplace and the past practices of the sponsoring unit or organization" (p. 281). Learning is, therefore, not seen as a set of facts to be stored and recalled later, but rather a foundation to assist learners to deal with instant changes as well as new and unforeseen challenges in the workplace.

Raelin (1997) emphasizes, "At the individual level, work-based learning might start with conceptualization which provides practitioners with a means to challenge the assumptions underlying their practice. In experimentation, they engage their conceptual knowledge in such a way that it becomes contextualized or grounded in practice." Hence, the applications of the model can "spur conceptual and practical developments that might lead to a comprehensive theory of work-based learning" (Raelin, 1997, p. 563).

As Boud and Garrick (1999, p. 1) posit, "learning at work has become one of the most exciting areas of development in the dual fields of management and education as it attempts to solve innovative and interesting challenges" (p. 1). For them, "workplace learning is concerned not only with immediate work competencies, but considers also competencies to deal with future challenges. It is, thus, about the investment in general and specific capabilities of employees (p. 5).

Global workplace learning trends are, therefore, blended in terms of strategic direction, the identification of employees in need of development and subject matter experts to facilitate such learning. A practical, experiential, appropriate, transformative and collective approach to workplace learning equips learners to not only react to change, but also to anticipate change and be prepared for it.

## Raelin's Work-Based Learning Model in the South African Police Service Context

In the SAPS context, executive learners were also exposed to learning in the midst of practice. They were requested to identify a challenge in the workplace, conduct research on the problem and compile a report on the research with the intention to solve the problem and improve workplace practices. Research is, therefore, seen as another form of workplace learning which SAPS uses to involve employees from the workplace in the learning process. They were initially very ambitious to search for solutions to the identified problem. They worked very hard to manage their time as they concurrently performed their normal tasks. Workplace demands put them under enormous pressure to finalize these research studies in a given timeframe. They sacrifice valuable family time because of their own expectation to make a positive contribution toward current workplace practices and the body of knowledge.

Raelin (1997) further explains that the value which an organization attached to learning consequently influences whether research as part of a workplace learning strategy becomes a culture and is seen as a way of life in the organization. Although the EDLP learners received formal learning at the learning center, they had to conduct a workplace learning phase. The workplace firstly needs to be recognized as an environment for learning to take place, which requires that employees in the workplace understand the extent of the program as well as the value the organization attaches to it. Although Matthews (1999) opines that "the perception exists amongst most people that the workplace is simply a physical place to perform appointed tasks, the introduction of new technologies, policies, procedures, activities and changes in the workplace demands, imply and require continuous development and sharing of knowledge" (p. 18).

Through a scientific process the EDLP learners offer their opinions and contribute to the legitimacy of the scope of the problem in finding solutions for workplace problems (Raelin, 1997). This wider scope contributes to an increase in the acceptance of the findings and recommended solutions for possible implementation. This strategy provides meaning to inculcate a professional development culture. The effectiveness of the strategy is restricted to the inclusion in the strategic direction of the organization and the performance agreement in the workplace to ensure the necessary support, dignity and value of people's effort. Leadership development in the workplace involves face-to-face leadership that recognizes every person's contribution with diverse backgrounds, experiences, knowledge, skills, and interests by encouraging everyone to take responsibility and treat them as valuable partners in running the organization.

The workplace has concurrently become a platform where insights, knowledge and ideas are shared, and employees are influenced by the behavior, expertise and attitudes of others who contribute toward a culture of learning in the workplace. Learners have to handle the tension between learning outcome and performance agreement: they are distinctly assessed on their job performance in the workplace as well as the final research report at the learning center. The job performance, however, encourages development but does not include academic accomplishment. Although the organization expects employees to continuously improve their job performance and effectively deal with day-to-day challenges, little has been done to instill a culture of learning in the workplace.

A culture of learning in which knowledge is shared should therefore be a part of the workplace performance and organizational ethics and is vital to supporting everyone as they cope with challenges. The active engagement of practitioners, specialists and support systems becomes natural in encouraging and recognizing research as a workplace learning strategy (Lee & Lai, 2012, p. 2). It was, however, evident that the time spent on such learning was too limited and should be increased. Flexible learning time should also be considered for achieving the expected outcomes.

Development of leaders and employees becomes even more critical when an organization undertakes major changes and realizes new strategies. SAPS has gone through several organizational changes since 1994 and executive coaching becomes evident to facilitate such changes.

## Workplace Learning Strategies in Rethinking of Executive Coaching Through the Lens of Raelin

Workplace learning strategies in modern society demand a new approach of leadership (Raelin, 1997). Organizations employ highly educated employees as they have the potential to add more value to the profession. In a constantly changing society, the relationship between the organization and employee is continually changing. This makes it challenging for one person to lead the organization alone. An organization with the superfluity of leaders presents thus a leadership paradigm based on mutual leadership. Mutual leaders diplomatically allow employees to participate in a revolutionary new leadership approach that "transforms leadership from an individual property to a collective responsibility" (p.535). Raelin (1997) emphasizes that "leadership does not arrive from individual influences but emanates from practices of employees working together with a shared vision, especially in the discussion of important issues in preparation of new strategic interventions, or in the creation of meaning in the workplace or when proposing a change in direction."

A strategy where everyone in the workplace has an immediate opportunity to offer ideas that will occupy every person's imagination becomes fundamental. The team becomes fascinated in a comprehensive solution finding process while experiencing collective leadership. This collective nature of leadership incorporates the critical mechanisms of learning and constructs meaning in the workplace. The leaderful strategy is based on the following four approaches:

1) Leaders are concurrent, meaning that more than one leader can lead at the same time.
2) Leadership practice is collective and people might operate as leaders together. However, the same position leader does not give up on his or her leadership but many others offer their leadership at the same time.
3) Leadership practice is collaborative. All members of the organization have the opportunity to speak for the entire organization and may advocate a point of view that can contribute to the effectiveness of the organization. It is important in any organization to be equally sensitive to the opinions and feelings of every employee and to consider every person's viewpoints as equally valid and important.
4) Leadership practice is compassionate. The complete commitment demonstrates perseverance and dignity and considers people's views when making decisions if the situation allows.

Executive coaching is a strategy that is in line with Raelin's leaderful model by involving executives in discussions regarding performance breaches and the strategic direction of the organization. The focus in this strategy is on management and leadership development and encourages people to take responsibility to become partners with complete contributions to improve workplace practices. Executive coaching contributes to the creation of an enabling relationship to achieve high-level performance goals (Staman, 2007).

## Readiness Level of the Learner

Williams (2010) writes, "for an effective workplace learning culture to develop, the employee needs to practice self-directed learning by taking responsibility for their own development, obtain support to critically reflect on their own profession and be empowered to enhance the profession" (p. 628). The readiness level to learn increases as the person matures and fulfills different social roles, which require specific knowledge and skills, and it becomes inevitable to balance these different social roles. This, among others, implies that the focus is on competency and that an adult becomes ready to learn when his/her life situation necessitates a need to obtain knowledge with the intention to progress, to obtain a better understanding of how to fulfill these roles in society and to gain more confidence to compete on different levels in the organization (Cox, 2006, p. 398).

Executive development consequently depends on continuous professional education, which equips the facilitator to deliver focused learning which encompasses various aspects of life and practice (Day & Sachs, 2004). The need to develop on a strategic level arises when a learner has a strong desire to grow, experiences challenges to perform a specific role and when the past experiences are not sufficient to rely on in acting that role. The need therefore develops to search for new knowledge and ideas to be furnished to deal with these challenges more effectively. The search process becomes fundamental as positive reinforcement in the preparation for learning. Formulating goals, linking it the organization's strategic direction and redefining the tenacity of learning might confirm the commitment of the learners and ensure that they are in the same mind-set as their seniors by sharing the same goals of being shaped cognitively with new skills and knowledge for the benefit of the learner, the client as well as the organization (p. 4).

Illeris (2003) agrees, explaining that adults are skeptical about what others want them to learn but also realize the importance of discovering new knowledge, concepts, behaviors and action which might reinforce success (p. 173). The value of learning increases once the learner becomes so committed that he or she continues developing him or herself after completion of the program due to his/her intellectual curiosity. The organization and the workplace have the responsibility to stimulate this intellectual curiosity by creating opportunities for knowledge sharing and encouraging informal networks. It is therefore important that the development be appropriately acknowledged and rewarded as valuable and legitimate.

Various role players in the learning process might also reap substantial benefits when focusing on the generation of dynamic knowledge, which is subjected to critical reflection by subject matter experts and peers in various settings (Raelin, 1997). The organization expects employees to deal successfully with complex workplace challenges outside a learning center and hence needs to give them the opportunity to apply the knowledge accumulated during formal learning. This prospect can also underwrite in preparing the learner for future professions or equipping them to operate on a much higher level in the organization. It is thus important that the seniors of learners get directly involved in the process with the aim of finding work-related ways to capitalize on the learning experience. Clear expectations, necessary support and regular feedback therefore strengthen the learning culture (Hughes, Ginnett, & Curphy, 2015, p. 45).

## The Strengths and Preferences of the Faciliator(s)

The strengths and preferences of the facilitator(s) expose the learner to facts and theories of disciplinary knowledge during formal learning. Williams (2010) maintains that for an effective workplace learning culture to develop, the employee needs to continue practicing self-directed learning after accumulating theories and knowledge from the facilitator(s) at the learning center. By taking responsibility for one's own development and obtaining support to critically reflect on current practices, one becomes empowered to enhance the profession where required (p. 628).

Gosling and Moon (2001) identified the following interactive processes in workplace learning (p. 95):

- exposure to actual working experiences;
- reflection on experiences and highlighting particular elements of the workplace learning practice;
- conceptualization of learning through inductive reasoning to integrate content into logically sound workplace practices and theories; and
- practical experimentation to apply new knowledge in the workplace.

Workplace learning unfolds the discipline by encouraging and enabling the reading of authoritative textbooks, while the final proof of learning is confirmed in the workplace once the new knowledge is shared and applied (Kalantzis & Cope, 2008). The discourse of classroom talk, the sociocultural dynamics of sameness and the positive or negative experience during formal learning result in a certain kind of moral economy.

The moral economy represents a set of good norms and principles, which is characterized by good justice, respect and dignity. Didactic learning has a practical rationale behind its design. If learners experience formal learning as passive, boring and too challenging or achieve poor results, it might result in learners who lose interest in applying and sharing the knowledge back in the workplace (p. 25).

Good experiences during formal learning on the other hand stimulate information curiosity and inspire learners to search and produce new knowledge for themselves, the organization and the wider community. It excites sharing to bring positive transformation in the workplace (Kalantzis & Cope, 2008, p. 25).

Learners on the EDLP are actively involved in the learning experience and become active researchers in their own right by accumulating information, facts, policies, and practices. They have the opportunity to critically analyze and interpret the information to make positive recommendations regarding problems in the current practice with the goal of improving the profession. They are encouraged through the necessary guidance and support from study leaders throughout the program, which assist them with overcoming some theoretical challenges, and positive feedback secures the educational efforts in establishing a learning culture for the duration of the program.

The interdependent process of applying theory to solve real workplace matters, addresses the learners' desire to generate new knowledge and to make a positive contribution in the workplace. The organization instead has the opportunity to maintain growth and improvement. Successful learners share and apply the knowledge and become reflective knowledge-makers, which promotes the creation, and adoption of knowledge as constructed from multiple sources with different perspectives (Kalantzis & Cope, 2008, p. 46).

A good learning experience afforded by both the learning center and the workplace facilitates the opportunity to stay intact by shaping the richness of learning. For that reason, learners and facilitators become co-designers of knowledge that develops habits of stimulating the mind to produce new knowledge for sharing and applying. Mezirow (1997) regards transformative learning as the "essence of adult education which assists the learner to become high order, more autonomous thinkers that negotiate the meaning, value and purpose of learning" (p. 11). Tshelane (2014) thus argues that leadership is the ability to visualize the future, shape realistic and achievable goals in the organization and contribute to realization (p. 720). The ability to see reality that does not yet exist, combined with the will to identify current constraints and find solutions, minimalizes these constraints. Leadership development does not reside in one person, but in the relationship among all role players. It focuses also on social visualization and change (Alvesson & Spicer, 2012) in an attempt to prepare leadership for the extensive demands in the workplace, future challenges and possible job opportunities (p. 378).

The EDLP therefore develops leaders and prepares them to absorb what is going on in the safety and security environment and strategically plan to succeed in coping with the extensive demands globally. The program assists in generating knowledge to predict future challenges so that learners can feel equipped to contest prevailing values and practices with confidence. The ideal, however, is to inculcate a culture of leadership development in the workplace. It can be through spurring the prominence of leadership development.

Leadership development on a strategic level refers to the development of leaders in authoritative decision-making positions to take responsibility for and influence policies, structures, and practices. They make use of affordance for learning the integration of new theories and knowledge accumulated through research projects. A shared vision underpins a mental model, which guides decision-making and action. The background theories and context form a critical link between understanding strategy and the execution thereof influences attitudes and interactions with experts in the field and contributes to the enhancement of work performance. Even though the EDLP is compulsory for senior managers in the SAPS, the way in which it is presented inspires learners to grasp the value and importance of the program and appreciate the opportunity.

Although short-term goals, which include subject matter mastery and attainment of specific competencies to improve performance are important, the long-term goals for both the learner and the organization cannot be overestimated. These include developing learners to become socially responsible autonomous thinkers who effect change in the organization (Mezirow, 1997, p. 11). New information is only a source in the adult learning process that needs to be incorporated by the learner into a well-developed frame of reference. The adult educator can then help the learner to transform his or her frame of reference through a proper understanding of how the learning experience incorporates autonomous thinking regarding new trends in the global world of practice and living.

In order to remain relevant, new technologies, globalization, and diversity, the changing nature of work, various workplace demands, different identities and personalities of humans become important considerations in the creation of a learning culture. Facilitators, hence, have an important role toward observing change and constructively contribute in the direction the organization is urging. Their professional responsibility as change agents is not only to keep informed and updated in designing learning programs, which are current and relevant, but also to stimulate discussion. Successful transformative learning hereafter has a responsibility to equip learners with the necessary knowledge and skills to deal with current and future challenges in a knowledgeable fashion. This responsibility supports them to function effectively in a globalized society facing a range of extremely difficult choices. Facilitators consequently play a key role in assisting the leadership with understanding its responsibilities and accountabilities (Kalantzis & Cope, 2008). It is necessary, therefore, to grant learners opportunities to construct their own knowledge through experiential inquiry (p. 33).

Transformative learning reflects the changes that happen after learning has taken place in the workplace or at other learning communities outside the formal learning center. Facilitators assist learners to use their frame of reference in redefining workplace problems from different perspectives. These perspectives include scientific studies, historical practices and literary sources of knowledge. The amazing ability of the human brain to utilize multiple sources is nurtured by the technological intelligence surrounding human beings.

Theories, concepts and lecture material that were presented on the EDLP only serve as the foundation from which the learner illustrates the application to address current challenges in the workplace. The intention is to complete the learning experience and make a positive contribution toward the organization and broader society. The learners are encouraged by the facilitators and study leaders to become knowledge searchers and avail opportunities to collect information, analyze the information and argue critically with authoritative subject matter experts to arrive at implementable recommendations. General leadership principles are consequently illustrated by exposing learners to real life challenges in the workplace and to gain personal growth while simultaneously searching for creative solutions for these workplace challenges. The frame of references shapes a person's expectations, perceptions, feelings and knowledge, which influence actions to accept or reject challenges.

In a case study among EDLP learners who successfully completed the program, it was evident that a positive frame of reference inspires the participants to accept the challenge, to overcome their own insecurity, enter the unknown world of research and co-create knowledge with other people inside and outside the organization. This real life challenge formed part of workplace learning to look beyond the short-term growth cycle in which learners fall back on what is known and tested and to manage their day-to-day tasks in such a way that they also succeed in their academic responsibilities and practice to complete the learning experience. This learning experience contributes toward a lifelong learning approach in the sense that it refreshed continuous learning as some learners were inspired to take up their personal studies. It is manifest that the majority of students quit personal studies because of the academic scars caused by research methodology. The facilitators manage to get the learner to understand his or her engagement in such a multifaceted learning experience. Learners were fortified to utilize every opportunity to gain experience in a specific professional domain.

The HRD division, which affords the learning opportunity, realizes that in the current global economic state, growth on an executive level is imperative to assure meaningful performance in becoming knowledgeable leaders. However, in the broader organization, especially in the workplace, leadership is not so much concerned regarding positive changes as a result of the learning and wants the learners to finish their studies and concentrate on the job. Leadership involvement and support throughout the learning could be significant in understanding and acknowledging the value of the program in solving workplace challenges.

## Organizational Support

A powerful mechanism in the success of any workplace learning approach is the buy-in, rendered to the learner by the learning center's management and personnel as well as management and personnel in the workplace (SA, 2011). A meaningful workplace learning experience exposes learners to global technologies, which equip them with new and current knowledge to the benefit of the organization. Thus, it is necessary that the anticipated benefit for the organization and for the individual correlates with the money that the organization is prepared to invest in development. The workplace accordingly produces concrete outcomes, which is important for stability and growth in a competitive society.

Support includes inspiring the learner to be committed and backing the learner throughout the entire development process. It is consequently important that all role players understand the value and importance of the learning and the contribution it has to the world of professional practice (SA, 2011).

In this case study the HRD division fortified senior staff in the workplace to get involved in the learning process by supporting learners in an endeavor to find implementable solutions for burning workplace issues. Senior staff were involved in discussions regarding workplace problems for which the organization was in desperate need of solutions. Even after the research project was done, the organization provided an opportunity for the learner to explain the process followed for collecting data, analyze the data and recommend possible solutions to solve the problem. A PowerPoint presentation was given to a panel of subject matter experts, including senior management in the different provinces, to validate the reliability of these studies and to support implementation of the recommendations. This process provides leadership, including line managers, with a comprehensive knowledge of the project for critical revision.

The attitude of leadership, peer employees, the learner's knowledge of the learning program, previous experiences, knowledge levels and the expectations of the organization, the workplace and the learner assist in the value attached to such a learning journey. The employee internalizes specific values, norms, attitudes and professional standards, which enables him/her to identify the need to develop. Kirpal (2004) reiterates that organizational identity is grounded in the learning culture that exists which is informed by an employee's attitude, organizational values, processes and work procedures (p. 201). A structured environment considers research as an advantage to the generation of knowledge. A crisis, however, occurs when a conflict of interest arises among these elements concerning the value and expected outcome of the learning. Conflicts of interest among the organization, the management at the workplace and the learner have a direct influence on the sustainability and value of the learning program.

In a global knowledge economy education and training is of great importance for learners with knowledge on trends in a specific discipline. Hence, Berglund and Andersson (2012) maintain that formal learning is as valuable as informal learning and just as important to the organization as to the individual. Equally important is a strategy to facilitate the recognition of earlier achievements and experiences as well as knowledge and skills developed to improve workplace practices (p. 75).

There are different approaches to enhance the integration of formal learning and workplace challenges. As a result, is it important to consider an approach, which aligns learning, organizational strategies and workplace practices for the mutual benefit of the learner, the workplace and the organization (p. 13). A holistic educational strategy that considers future workplace demands and promotes the integration of real life experience and new market trends is needed. Mbango (2009) regards the integration of workplace learning in the learning program as the starting point to apply the theory in an authentic workplace context. It is, therefore, important to re-evaluate the value of any learning in order to nominate the most talented person, which can affect the required transformation for specific growth.

## Workplace Learning as Tool for SAPS Leadership Development

Gulcan (as cited by Tshelane, 2014) argues that leadership is the "ability to see the future, shaping a realistic vision and set achievable goals for the organization" (p. 720). A leader should share the vision and target with all people in the organization in realizing it. Julie (as cited by Tshelane, 2014, p. 720) postulates the ability of leadership to see the reality that does not yet exist. Leadership is, therefore, seen as the individual's will to identify current constraints and stretch him or herself mentally in collaboration with others to set achievable meaningful goals (Alvesson & Spicer, 2013). Leadership thus does not reside in a person, but in the association between people, and emphasizes social involvement and change (p. 67).

Workplace learning as a tool for SAPS leadership development exposes learners to education, training, the transfer of knowledge and the ultimate application of these skills in the workplace. Furthermore, workplace learning improves the value of a learning program as the leader gains the opportunity to demonstrate his/her knowledge and skills. Most importantly, workplace research might have more individual and personal value for the learner as for the organization as it develops the skill to consult different sources before making informed decisions, acknowledging people's uniqueness and treating them accordingly. It empowers leaders to be experts in their practice by gaining experts' knowledge and experience while building networks and enhancing personal relationships. Workplace learning contributes to personal growth, organizational development and enhancing return on investment. The learner is involved in utilizing newly gained knowledge in leading people in the workplace (Wills, 2011, p. 19).

Personnel development, socialization, qualifications, and competency development require immediate action and application of knowledge. The leader becomes a learner in the organization in which knowledge and skills are obtained, theory and practice are integrated to effect modification. Gosling and Moon (2001) look at a different viewpoint to WPL and are of the opinion that a curriculum is based on Kolb's (1984) learning cycle that occurs in four stages:

1) The first stage is concrete experience, which provides the learner the opportunity to get actively involved in the learning process.
2) The second stage involves reflective observation. The learner's attention is therefore focused on the reflection of specific elements in the learning experience.
3) The third stage is called abstract conceptualization. The learner analyzes observations and explains them using logical sound theories through inductive reasoning.
4) The last stage is active experimentation. This is where the learner considers how to implement what was learned.

To sum up this section, the adult learner on a strategic level has distinctive learning experiences and appearances with unique job accountabilities and demands. This requires different types and levels of knowledge and expertise. Learning in the workplace deviates in a sense from formal learning at learning centers because it requires more action than just writing an assessment. The action demonstrates the ability and knowledge to address the strategic goals and needs of the organization. Organizational structures, instructions, policies, regulations, and institutional practices need to be considered and analyzed in the learning process. The learning content is more contextual and dynamic in the workplace than in a learning center. The environment and the emotional climate need to create circumstances that affect learning and performance. It develops conditions in which leaders can flourish in preparation to manage the extensive demands in the workplace and stay well-informed regarding global trends and predict future challenges.

## Workplace Learning as Task-Oriented

Workplace learning as task-oriented enables leaders to focus on supporting the strategic direction of the organization, defining different roles and responsibilities, giving direction, setting timelines, and indicating how to achieve the goals. The necessary motivation, equipment, and technical backing are needed to finish tasks within a specific timeframe (Northhouse, 2010, p. 25). Consequently, expectations are clarified in assigning responsibilities to people. Progress is monitored and while the leaders are concerned about employees' needs, they decide how to utilize their personnel effectively to achieve their set goals and objectives (Yukl, O'Donnell and Taber, as cited in Holloway, 2012, p. 24). Atkinson (in Hughes et al., 2015) claims that powerful achievement orientation makes every effort to accomplish socially acceptable endeavors (p. 12).

People with a strong aspiration to achieve goals, feel rewarded when they solve problems prolifically and master tasks. Hughes et al. (2015) maintain that leaders who understand the different motivational theories are more likely to negotiate strong expectations, provide the required support and resources, create a conducive working environment of social interests and disperse interesting and challenging tasks (p. 339). Maslow (as cited by Hughes et al., 2015) advocates that higher-order needs become prominent once the basic lower-order needs are satisfied (p. 341). Different approaches in achievement orientation leadership underwrite the energy people are prepared to expend in accomplishing the task and tend to set and achieve higher personal goals. Task-oriented leaders are thus more likely to expend the time and effort needed in completing high quality tasks.

The National Commissioner in the SAPS conducts planning sessions and sets organizational goals, which need to be achieved within a specific timeframe, and focuses much of his attention on achieving these operational goals (South African Police Service [SAPS], 2015, Operational Plan). Thus, it was understandable that learners who were responsible for these operational goals found it challenging to accomplish learning goals concurrently. The performance agreements of employees in senior positions need therefore to accommodate operational goals as well as developmental expectations in order to ensure maximum commitment and achievement. Global workplace learning is thus a tool for transformational leadership.

## Global Workplace Learning as a Tool for Transformational Leadership

The workplace affords learners the perfect opportunity to participate in transformative ways of workplace practice (Billett, 2004) and to enhance the understanding of formal learning (p. 314). Nevertheless, training and development activities place heavy demands on HRD functions, which have to interact with stakeholders regarding changing information and conditions (p. 314). An interdependent process compromises negotiations between the aspiration of the learner to be successful, the operational accountabilities, and the opportunities afforded by the organization in the workplace to transform. The quality of the learning experience afforded by both academic institutions and the workplace shape the richness of the learning outcomes.

Work-integrated learning therefore emphasizes the importance of enabling the learner to integrate the theory learned through formal learning with the practical knowledge gained in the workplace or professional context to enhance the return on investment and the return on expectations. Formal and informal learning depends on the circumstances in which the learning takes place and influences the transformation it has on the learner and the organization. A balance between the compliance with stakeholder requests, global market trends in the profession, and legal regulations contribute to effective and efficient workplace learning in support of transformational leadership.

The South African Police Service is characterized by many uncertainties, and rapid, continuous changes in global crime trends and community demands. This has placed a renewed prominence on equipping managers on a strategic level with current, relevant skills and competencies not only to solve current workplace problems, but also to shape the workplace for future challenges in the profession. People in modern society therefore constantly define themselves and are publicly defined by their occupation and the work they are doing. Innovative technologies and artificial intelligence (AI) profoundly affect the profession and the community. Therefore, workplace learning strategies deserve some rethinking to make the workplace a better place to work and learn.

Although the implementation of newly gained knowledge is the ideal, there are always risks and barriers that hinder the implementation thereof.

## Barriers that Hinder the Implementation of Newly Gained Knowledge in the SAPS

Even though the SAPS HRD Division executes the mandate to develop leadership in the organization, the following barriers limit the effectiveness of research as workplace learning strategy:

### Lack of understanding

Following an interpretivist methodological approach in the case study, which involved face-to-face interviews, it portrays that a lack of understanding of the value of research on a strategic level resulted in restraining transformation in the workplace. However, Personal Educational Theory contributes toward continuous personal and social growth, which influences the development of and change in educational and workplace practices (Atkins & Wallace, 2012). Perceptions of disbelief in the value of the learning method as well as the doubt regarding the worth of the program for the organization did not discourage learners from completing the program successfully to their own advantage (p. 130). They understand the expectations of the organization concerning taking responsibility for one's own progress to deal with challenging workplace demands.

It was, however, understandable that some learners became disillusioned and frustrated taking into consideration the time spent on research, utilizing personal and office time, as well as sacrificing family time, and took responsibility for their own development through self-directed learning to the benefit of the workplace and the organization. A lack of understanding of the extent of the learning process and poor workplace involvement result in a skeptical view concerning the acceptance of the outcome of workplace research. Another aspect reflects that senior managers who did not utilize their own opportunity on the EDLP effectively to gain the necessary perspective and insights on research as a knowledge generating tool, usually lack the cognizance of securing a conducive environment to acknowledge intellectual contributions to the advantage of the organization.

#### High management turnover

High management turnover while the development process is in progress influences the continuity of sustainable support until the learning program is finalized. Research, as a workplace learning strategy, can be most informative once management who approved the topic and research proposal in the workplace maintain the same. It assists in being consistent in ensuring continuous support, understanding and accepting the research process as scientific, reliable and relevant. Although, in this case study, some learners are positive toward the support during workplace research, a general feeling exists that workplace learning is not valued as much as learning at the tertiary level. Brindley (2004) emphasizes a sustainable, responsive learner-support system to be imitated in the learning philosophy and values of the organization. Therefore, the expectations of the organization, the HRD Division, the workplace, and the learner need to be housed in such a learning philosophy (p. 112).

High turnover influences the reason why development is offered and challenges the learner, whether it is the learner who got promoted to another post or the manager who got transferred to another section. It definitely has an influence on the enthusiasm, commitment and passion to complete the learning program successfully. It is also evident that although the original workplace problem still exists, the learner who is affected by the turnover is not in the favorite position to bring about change. This emphasizes the importance of including the development of executives in the strategic direction of the organization.

#### Competing interests

The workplace calls for operational outputs on which the learner's performance is measured; it also demands a research output from the HRD Division on which the learner is academically assessed. Therefore, it is a challenge for top management to acknowledge the impact and benefits of research in the workplace. Their primary interest is in rapidly addressing the current demands in the workplace and operational difficulties and not conducting research to improve workplace practices in the long run.

Although research projects require intellectual stimulation, it is important to create a platform for sharing newly gained knowledge. The emotional climate and workplace conditions have a significant impact, which invite and encourage intellectual stimulation regarding workplace practices as part of the performance agreement of the learner. Apart from the development is the implicit learning that influences attitudes and self-confidence by having a broader scope of knowledge regarding the expectations of clients. It is, therefore, important to have a strategy to facilitate the recognition of experiences and previous knowledge, generating new knowledge and skills development in the workplace. Such a strategy will allow eligibility for employee progression (Berglund & Andersson, 2012) and create a platform to share these experiences, knowledge and skills to establish a knowledgeable workforce (p. 75). Management needs to inform the people in the workplace of the challenges regarding research studies as part of workplace learning, the value research might have on current workplace practices and difficulties surrounding research in order to ensure a better understanding of what the learner goes through in conducting workplace research projects and to avoid competing interests.

Leadership must play an active role in shaping the performance of executives to meet the expectations of the organization. Adult learners who are nominated for development usually have expectations and a predetermined goal for their own development, which they need to share with their management prior to attending the program. It is thus important to have a high degree of ownership from both the learner and the management to drive the learning process. This is a purpose of being more motivated to participate in the learning and headed for exceptional results of making an impact. The return on investment will be evident in the generation of knowledge, change in insights and outlooks as well as addressing the expectations of management, the organization and the learner through changes in thinking patterns (Erasmus, Loedolff, Mda, & Nel, 2011, p. 87).

### Involvement of management

Managers do not always have time to be development partners who request regular feedback on progress and to be actively involved in the development process. However, they can support and encourage learners by availing time in the workplace, provide advice or referring learners to experts in the field and allowing them to interview people in the workplace as well as outside the workplace during working hours (Richard, Robert, & Gordy, 2015, p. 473). The success of any learning can be influenced by the involvement of management regarding intrinsic motivators, support, guidance, sharing of knowledge, providing resources and administration.

### Acknowledgement of learning in the workplace

Organizations in our modern society go through extensive restructuring processes. Owing to quick succession and changes in top management structures, the mere size of organizations and its diverse processes might take a considerable amount of time to finalize these new organizational structures. Moreover, the implementation of fresh research results are most often delayed for long periods of time coupled with uncertainty on the strategic direction of the organization. Research completed during these periods often loses its value or impact owing to the shelf life of knowledge (Thomson, 2011, p. 33). The logic of mind is to analyze all research done in an organization and recognize newly gained knowledge in steering restructuring processes in well-thought through strategic directions. If top management is committed to the development of employees in senior positions, and have agreed upon a shared vision concerning the purpose and outcome of development, the value in informing the strategic direction will be considered.

The reasons why organizations train and develop senior managers need to be adopted in the learning culture of the organization. The culture needs to make provision for acknowledging new knowledge arrived from learning. This might also encourage further research on the specific practice to keep knowledge generation current and relevant. Research as a workplace learning strategy can provide a platform for the creation of a conducive environment for working and learning (Massyn & Wilkinson, 2014) where employees can grow with the organization (p. 95). The predetermined desire of the learner to make a positive contribution in finding solutions for problems strengthens the will to learn, the aspiration to make a positive input and to engage in community scholarship (Peterson, 2009, p. 541).

### Key performance area (KPA)

If workplace research is not one of the key performance areas on which a manager's performance is measured, it creates a huge challenge in encouraging the learner to finalize the learning program successfully. From the 27 interviews that were conducted in this case study, 20 participants cited misalignment of research as one of their key performance areas. The study, therefore, suggests that the organization needs to understand that research is a portion of a person's development and should be included in the performance agreement. This will contribute to work-directed learning where learners are encouraged by senior manager's acknowledgment of the importance of workplace research projects to the advancement of the workplace and the organization (Brockbank and McGill, 1998 as cited in SA, 2011, p. 32). Return on investment can be effectively evaluated through the regular generation of new research and the reflection on it before taking the responsibility for implementation (Brewster et al., 2005). This contributes toward a good strategy to identify the strengths of leaders (Reiss, 2009) in order to continue to assist people to produce the required output in their personal and professional lives (p. 201).

## Conclusion

Research is a recommended workplace learning strategy only if the learner is conditionally released from normal day-to-day responsibilities. The development of executives is monitored and measured until the workplace learning phase is completed. The return on investment will be measured once back in the workplace.

In this chapter, we have explored Joseph Raelin's work-based learning model in the South African Police Service context. Our central argument is that workplace learning as a task- oriented approach is both a tool for SAPS leadership development and transformational leadership. Lastly, we proposed rethinking of research and executive coaching as workplace learning strategies through the lens of Raelin (1997, 1998).

## References

Alvesson, M., & Spicer, A. (2012). Critical leadership studies: The case for critical performativity. *Human Relations, 65*(3), 367–390.

Alvesson, M., & Spicer, A. (2013). *Critical Perspectives on Leadership*. Oxford: Oxford University Press.

Atkins, L., & Wallace, S. (2012). *Qualitative research in education*. London, UK: Sage.

Berglund, L., & Andersson, P. (2012). Recognition of knowledge and skills at work: In whose interests. *Journal of Workplace Learning, 24*(2), 73–84.

Billett, S. (2004). Workplace participatory practices. *Journal of Workplace Learning, 16*(6), 312–324.

Boud, D., & Garrick, J. (Eds.) (1999). *Understandings of workplace learning. In understanding learning at work*. London, UK and New York, NY: Routledge.

Brewster, C., Sparrow, P., & Harris, H. (2005). Towards a new model of globalizing HRM. *The International Journal of Human Resource Management, 16*(6), 949–970.

Brindley, J. (2004). Practitioner research and evaluation skills training in open and distance learning. In *PREST handbook 6: Researching tutoring and learner support*, The Commonwealth of Learning. Harlow, UK: Longman Group.

Cox, E. (2006). An adult learning approach to coaching. In D. Stober, & A. Grant (Eds.), *The handbook of evidence-based coaching* (pp. 193–218). Chichester, UK: Wiley.

Day, C., & Sachs, J. (Eds.) (2004). Professionalism, performativity and empowerment: Discourses in the politics, policies and purpose of continuing professional development. In *Day, C. and Sachs, J. (eds.), International handbook on the continuing professional development of teachers* (pp. 3–33). Berkshire, UK: McGraw-Hill Education.

Erasmus, B. J., Loedolff, P. Z., Mda, T., & Nel, P. S. (2011). *Managing training and development in South Africa* (5th ed.). Goodwood, South Africa: Oxford University Press.

Gosling, D., & Moon, J. (2001). *How to write learning outcomes and assessment criteria*. London, UK: SEEC Office. University of East London.

Holloway, B. J. (2012). Leadership behaviour and organizational climate: An empirical study in a non-profit organization. *Emerging Leadership Journal, 5*(1), 9–35.

Hughes, R. L., Ginnett, R. C., & Curphy, G. J. (2015). *Leadership enhancing the lessons of experience* (8th ed.). Singapore: McGraw-Hill Education.

Illeris, K. (2003). Workplace learning and learning theory. *Journal for Workplace Learning, 15*(4), 147–178.

Kalantzis, M., & Cope, B. (2008). *New learning elements of a science of education.* Cambridge, UK: Cambridge University Press.

Kirpal, S. (2004). Researching work identities in a European context. *Career Development International, 9*(3), 199–221.

Kolb, D. A. (1984). *Experiential learning; Experience as the source of learning and development* (Vol. *1*). Englewood Cliffs, NJ: Prentice Hall.

Lee, L.S. and Lai, C.C. (2012), Global trends in workplace l earning. Paper presented at the 6th International Conference on Complex, Intelligent and Software Intensive Systems (CISIS-2012) and the 6th International Conference on Innovative Mobile and Internet Services in Ubiquitous Computing (IMIS-2012). July 4–6, 2012, Palermo, Italy.

Massyn, L., & Wilkinson, A. (2014). Adapting to the contemporary learning environment: From instructional design to learning design. *Progressio, 36*(1), 93–107.

Matthews, P. (1999). Workplace learning: Developing an holistic model. *The Learning Organization, 6*(1), 18–29.

Mbango, P. (2009). Work-integrated learning (WIL). Retrieved from http://www.uj.ac/marketing/workintegratedlearning/tabird 26 October 2014.

Mezirow, J. (1997). Transformative learning: Theory to practice. *New Directions for Adult and Continuing Education,* (74), 5–12.

Northhouse, P. G. (2010). *Leadership: Theory and practice* (5th ed.). Thousand Oaks, CA: Sage.

Peterson, T. H. (2009). Engaged scholarship: Reflections and research on the pedagogy of social change. *Teaching in Higher Education, 14*(5), 541–552.

Raelin, J. A. (1997). A model of work-based learning. *Organization Science, 8*(6), 563–578.

Raelin, J. A. (1998). Work-based learning in practice. *Journal of Workplace Learning, 10*(6/7), 280–283.

Reiss, K. (2009). Leadership coaching. In J. Knight (Ed.), *Coaching: Approaches and Perspectives* (pp. 166–191). San Francisco: Corwin Press.

Richard, L. H., Robert, C. G., & Gordy, J. C. (2015). *Leadership enhancing the lessons of experience* (8th ed.). Singapore: McGraw-Hill.

South Africa. (2011). South Africa Council on Higher Education. Work-Integrated Learning: Good Practice Guide. HE Monitor No. 12 August, 2011. Retrieved from www.che.ac.za/documents/d000087on 25 August 2011.

Staman, J. (2007). The impact of executive coaching on job performance from the perspective of executive women. Unpublished Doctoral dissertation, Capella University, Capella, MN.

Thomson, R. (2011). *Managing people.* New York, NY: Routledge.

Tshelane, M. (2014). Democratic postgraduate student leadership for a sustainable learning environment. *Journal of Higher Education, 28*(3), 717–732.

Williams, C. (2010). Understanding the essential elements of work-based learning and its relevance to everyday clinical practice. *Journal of Nursing Management, 18*(6), 624–632.

Wills, J. (2011). Understanding the executive development challenge. Retrieved from https://www.clomedia.com/2011/11/28/understanding-the-executive-development-challenge October 12, 2018.

# 3

# Developing an Agile Global Workforce

## Challenges and Critical Success Factors

*Yoany Beldarrain*

*Reutlingen University*

There is no denying that organizations, whether domestic or global, whether educational, governmental, or business, are undergoing rapid transformation. However, what is causing it? Prompted by the need to remain relevant and competitive, organizations constantly try to reinvent themselves. Those that do not, according to the laws of economics, will simply serve no purpose and will eventually cease to exist. Regardless of sector or industry, an organization's success pivots around its human talent. Hence, it is crucial to manage it and cultivate certain traits, knowledge, and skills. In today's global economy, organizations are more interconnected than ever before and thus the challenges they face require that employees possess not only expert knowledge, problem-solving, cross-cultural, and cross-functional teaming skills, but also good communication skills and agile thinking.

Organizations must therefore unlock the potential of their workforce but also understand the challenges and critical success factors behind the implementation of agile concepts. In an effort to gain insight into these issues, this chapter explores the perspectives of employees and upper managers of medium to large global companies. Two case studies capture additional clues as to how global companies are dealing with this challenge. The goal of this chapter is to identify relevant themes that may be a springboard for future studies and potentially help organizations become more agile.

At first glance, it may appear that agile thinking simply involves quick thought, but upon closer look it involves more than that. Although the concept of agility was first introduced by Winston Royce in the 1970s as the waterfall model (Royce, 1987) in the context of software development, it has, over the decades, been adapted to all kinds of organizational needs and strategic planning. Agility is described in today's business world as encompassing more than just tools, methodologies, and frameworks; it includes organizational values. These values are reflected in the internal culture as well as the branding strategy of a company. In its most basic definition today, the concept of agility involves the ability to adapt quickly to seen or unforeseen changes by following a process of iterations (Abbas,

*The Wiley Handbook of Global Workplace Learning*, First Edition.
Edited by Vanessa Hammler Kenon and Sunay Vasant Palsole.

Gravell, & Wills, 2008). For product developers, it may mean being able to iteratively make changes to the product as they collect feedback from users throughout the design and/or product lifecycle. For project managers, it may mean that team members work on distinct yet connected parts of the project, and therefore the final product is a better product because team members will continuously communicate, test the smaller sections, and make changes as needed.

It is important to point out that the term agile or agility is an umbrella term for a compilation of different elements. Methodologies such as Scrum, Extreme Programming, Dynamic Systems Development Method, Crystal (Dingsøyr, Nerur, Balijepally, & Moe, 2012; Silva et al., 2015) and frameworks such as the Stacey Matrix (Stacey, 2002) or the Cynefin framework (Snowden & Boone, 2007) are all tools available to organizations wishing to be more business-agile. These methodologies and frameworks, also known as agile flavors, can be mixed and matched to fit the specific requirements of a project (Tal, 2015) and decrease complexity.

Agile organizations are able to respond quickly to market trends, imminent competition, and social or technological changes. They are also better positioned to leverage networks, create synergies, strategize, and seize opportunities. There is a dilemma, however, an agile organization needs an agile workforce. On one hand, it may be simple to train employees on Scrum development methods (Schwaber, 1997) for example, but on the other, it may prove quite difficult to permeate agile thinking throughout the organization.

## Agile Thinking, Agile Mindset

Researchers and practitioners alike have defined agile thinking in different ways. A comprehensive definition was proposed by Wendler and Gräning (2011). In their definition, they integrated organizational values and principles such as responsiveness, competency, flexibility, speed (Zhang & Sharifi, 2000), creation, proaction, reaction, learning of change (Conboy, 2009), and the Agile Manifesto (2001) with different factors that are believed to influence agile thinking at both the individual and the organizational levels.

Based on an extensive review of the literature, Wendler and Gräning (2011) identified three categories of influencing factors: the individual, the team, and environmental factors surrounding the team. Accordingly, the individual factors describe the individual's own competencies and sense of responsibility, while the team factors include power distribution, team size, communication, and decision-making processes, all of which influence the team dynamics. The environmental factors, nevertheless, center around the processes that might be external to the team, such as the satisfaction level of customers, their level of collaboration during iterations and feedback loops, project documentation as a quality indicator, as well as the flexibility of pricing models for agile approaches. When looking at all the possible influencing factors however, Wendler and Gräning found that communication indicated a true agile attitude regardless of whether the individual was a regular employee or an important decision-maker in the company. Open and flexible communication therefore facilitates agile thinking. More and more organizations are realizing the benefits of agile thinking. From lean supply chain management or manufacturing (Harris, 2004) to design thinking (Wölbling et al., 2012), *agile thinking can further enhance a company's ability to simplify complex processes.*

## Rethinking Groupthink

True agile thinking increases the effectiveness and the quality of the outcome because team members with an agile mindset can openly interact and communicate. This minimizes the potential for groupthink, which naturally hinders creativity (Esser, 1998). The groupthink phenomena is counteractive to the goals of agility, even though it may cause a team to agree on a potential solution faster. The more cohesive the group, the higher the risk for members to become victims of groupthink (Janis, 1971). One method of controlling groupthink is to limit the group size; Wendler and Gräning (2011) found a positive relationship between group size and the ability of the team to think more agilely. Incorporating customer feedback in the decision-making process could also potentially help minimize groupthink. Although this remains to be explored, it can be hypothesized that by bringing in fresh perspectives in the way of pilot testing, focus groups, and other forms of direct feedback, the individual team members are forced to consider multiple options.

Agility is also about having the right mindset to be able to self-organize. An agile mindset means that each team member is involved in the different aspects of the project and therefore all information is shared; they effectively use the agile concepts, methods, and frameworks to make decisions as a team (Stellman & Greene, 2015). One of these methods is known as *kanban*, a term born out of manufacturing and repurposed for software development by Anderson (2010). Kanban methods require that the team work within its own limitations. Expanding on Anderson's work, Stellman and Greene propose that agile teams adopt kanban in order to eliminate wasteful processes and become leaner thinkers.

## An Agile Workforce

Much has been predicted about the future workforce and the talent war, where companies are fighting to attract the most talented workers (Michaels, Handfield-Jones, & Axelrod, 2001). Some of these predictions depict work environments that are more personalized, more socially connected and engaging, with social learning and professional development that bring together employees regardless of generation or location (Meister & Willyerd, 2010). As it is well known, Google strives to create this type of work environment to attract young, promising talent. Google is therefore explicitly "...looking for people who can bring new perspectives ... who are big thinkers eager to take on fresh challenges as a team..." (Google, 2016). In other words, Google seeks agile thinkers. Even if someone is employed at Google for a short period of time, his/her employability in another company is automatically higher because s/he has acquired and/or demonstrated certain skills, knowledge and agile mentality. This is a phenomenon that cannot be ignored.

A key concern in human resource development (HRD) pertains to talent management. Old recruitment practices might no longer be conducive to attracting candidates with a more agile mindset. Gravett and Caldwell (2016) adamantly recommend hiring a learning-agile workforce, not only to increase their agile acumen and professional potential but also to strategically plan for sustainable talent management and succession. The Korn Ferry Institute (Hallenbeck, Swisher, & Orr, 2011) conducted a study of 1245 managers and executives who were considered to be "high learning-agile," meaning that they had the ability to learn fast and adapt in different situations. Within the sample, seven categories of learning-agile leaders emerged: problem-solvers, thought-leaders, trailblazers, champions, pillars, diplomats and energizers. Among the commonalities across all categories, five dimensions were identified as being indispensable for learning-agile leaders: mental agility, people agility, change agility, results agility and self-awareness. It is therefore imperative that recruitment practices and talent management strategies attract and keep individuals who are high learning-agile. Rothwell, Graber, and McCormick (2012) caution against poor workforce planning, pointing out that both quality and quantity are equally important. Another report by the Korn Ferry Institute (Lamarca & Eaton, 2016) reveals a strategy for recruiting high caliber global talent: honing in on not only learning agility but also cross-cultural, mental, and change agility. This strategy is based on the Institute's extensive work with global companies.

As a consequence, previously designed professional development activities might be obsolete. The entire HRD strategy might have to be reconsidered. This will certainly take time, effort and plenty of resources. Implementation of an organization-wide agile strategy is therefore not feasible until it is in alignment with the HRD strategy, which should be aligned with the overall strategic orientation of the organization.

Change-management literature points out the importance of communication and trust. Because organizational change itself is a slow process that may span a period of up to 10 years, Kotter (1996) specifically recommends closely monitoring employees as they experience the change process. This requires transparency and an open feedback loop. Clear and open communication may be more difficult to achieve for very large organizations whose workforce is geographically dispersed. In an empirical study involving 515 organizations in the United Kindgom, Breu, Hemingway, Strathern, and Bridger (2002) found that workforce agility increased when organizations used communications technology for collaboration. Therefore, an appropriate infrastructure must be in place.

There are other potential constraints in the implementation of agility. Differing cultural contexts may present barriers in terms of language, time, values, roles, expectations and perceptions, among others. Even if the organization successfully communicates the need to be agile and provides extensive training for employees, it does not mean that a global team will actually behave in an agile way and find solutions together. Concerns about interpersonal competence and intercultural competence all come to mind. Hosein and Yousefi (2012) found that emotional intelligence also plays a role in workforce agility. They found that factors about interpersonal competence such as self-awareness, self-control and self-motivation have a more significant effect on workforce agility changes than factors associated with social competence. The role of interpersonal competence in this study is concurrent with the findings of the Korn Ferry Institute (Hallenbeck et al., 2011). Unfortunately, the literature is void of information about the relationship between intercultural competence and agile thinking.

On one hand, implementing agility brings obvious benefits and yet on the other, it presents multiple challenges. Like any organizational change, there are a myriad of variables that may influence successful implementation. First and foremost, leadership must keep in mind that change management is a holistic approach, and therefore, implementation of agility cannot be isolated to one department or function. In order for agile thinking to truly permeate the organization, the interdependencies of departments, functions, and individuals must be clearly understood. The organizational structure is a direct reflection of the organization's strategic orientation. The flatter the organization and the more decentralized the decision-making process, the more likely the organization is to increase its workforce agility (Alavi, Wahab, Muhamad, & Arbab Shirani, 2014).

If the strategic orientation changes, the organizational structure might have to be redefined. This is often the case when a company re-brands, follows an expansion strategy, or even downsizes. The same holds true for implementing agility; implementation of agility as an organization-wide strategy will not be successful unless the organizational structure is appropriate and the connection between stakeholders is clearly understood. Only then can leadership effectively manage the change that is about to take place.

The process of implementation of agility to actually attaining measurable results takes considerable time. As organizations strive to remain relevant and highly competitive, they will have to rely on an agile workforce. The Greek philosopher Heraclitus wrote that the only thing that is constant is change. The ability to adapt to this constant change begins with the individual employee, who then influences the dynamics of the team, which subsequently impacts the success of the organization. This chapter explores employee perceptions and expectations concerning agility and presents insight into challenges as well as success factors for implementing business agility and developing an agile global workforce.

## Challenges and Success Factors

In order to gain an understanding about the challenges as well as potential success factors behind the implementation of agile concepts, it is necessary to talk directly to those trying to put these concepts into practice. This section presents a mixed-method, exploratory study (Stebbins, 2001) that aimed to identify these factors from the employees as well as management's perspectives. This research is further extended by focusing on two case studies that showcase how global companies are dealing with the implementation of agile concepts.

The target population of the study included employees of medium to large organizations accessible to the researcher. Two sample units were identified based on company role as either: (a) low to mid-tier employee or manager, or (b) upper management position.

## Data-Collection Methods

Convenience sampling (Borg & Gall, 1989; Lavrakas, 2008) was deemed the most suitable sampling method for this study because the researcher wanted to include only companies with a well-established brand name in the global market, and that were easily accessible. The rationale for this pre-selection criteria was based on the assumptions that well-established global brands are more likely to be aware of the benefits of business agility, have more experience with the topic, and are under global pressure to remain competitive. By excluding companies outside the researcher's professional networks, the sample units were easy to identify but were less likely to be representative of the population. Because of the inherent limitations, the results cannot be generalized. Nonetheless, the results of this study provide insight into the experiences and perspectives of the two specific units of study and can serve as a stepping-stone for future investigations.

An anonymous online survey (Denscombe, 2004; Jackson, 2011), targeted sample unit 1. Structured expert interviews targeted sample unit 2. It was necessary to collect data separately for each group because the questions in the survey were different from those in the structured interviews. The open-ended interview questions addressed agility issues associated with the role of upper management, versus the survey questions that addressed agility issues from the perspective of low- to mid-tier employees. Variable data collection allowed for the exploration of both perspectives independently, thus giving deeper insight into the salient themes of each perspective. The exploration of the potential relationship between salient themes was not within the scope of this study but may be of relevance in future studies.

The sample unit of *low- to mid-tier employees/ managers* was a heterogeneous group of professionals across the globe, working in ten medium to large companies that were accessible to the researcher and met the pre-selection criteria. A unique survey link (SurveyMonkey) was sent to a sample size of 100 individuals via the researchers′ professional networks. The response rate for this group was 38%. The second sample unit, *upper level managers*, consisted of a heterogeneous group of upper-level managers in Europe and North America. These individuals also worked in medium to large companies that were accessible to the researcher and met the pre-selection criteria.

Qualitative, structured interviews originally aimed at gathering information to create mini-case studies about different companies. Due to the sensitivity of some of the feedback however, interviewees requested to remain anonymous as individuals but also requested that the name of the company be withheld. Only two case studies emerged from this effort, The Bosch Group and Hugo Boss AG. These two case studies augmented the data-collection methods by providing crucial insight into the success factors as well as the challenges global brands face when implementing business agility.

The sample size for the structured interviews included 20 upper level managers in ten different global companies. The global companies represented different industries such as banking, automotive, food, apparel, and commercial services and supplies. Content validity for the survey, as well as the structured interview questions, was enhanced by conducting two feedback sessions with five members of each sample unit, also chosen based on convenience and proximity. After piloting the self-developed questions and conducting member-checking (Creswell & Miller, 2000), the survey and interview questions were revised.

The survey questions addressed three main areas:

1) The participant's own perceptions; for example: "My organization currently has problems adapting to the changing needs of the market."
2) Their expectations; for example: "I expect my teammates to have a flexible mindset and adapt to rapidly changing circumstances."
3) The factors they believe have an impact on a company's ability to be agile; for example: "understanding the company's strategic goals." Participants rated the factors in order of importance.

For areas 1 and 2, participants rated the statements using a 4-point ordinal Likert scale ranging from strongly disagree, disagree, agree, to strongly agree. The extreme, insignificant answers received a value of zero. The online survey results were analyzed using univariate descriptive analysis, while the qualitative data from the expert interviews was coded (Miles & Huberman, 1994) to identify emerging themes. Questions for the interviewees aimed to get a more specific, richer description of the situation as perceived by the participants. It also addressed company and function specific issues, for example: "How does the Human Resources department contribute to the agility of your company?" In order to ensure anonymity of the interviewees, the findings are reported in a summary format and are not correlated to any particular company or individual.

### Data Analysis for Sample Unit 1: Low- to Mid-Tier Employees and/or Managers

Respondents from ten medium to large global brands participated in the survey. The average age of the 38 respondents was 31 years old, which indicates a generational as well as an experience difference with the expert group. Only four individuals were between the ages of 44 and 49, one was aged 50–55, and three were 56 or older. There was also a noticeable difference in gender, with 59.5% being female compared with 30% females in the upper-level managers sample unit. The overwhelming majority (31) were located in Western Europe, with only seven located in the United States. The functional areas represented were more diverse than in the expert group. As shown in Figure 3.1, nine areas were identified, with the largest percentage (36.4%) of participants working in finance and accounting, and 18.2% in marketing, followed by 15.2% in sales.

On average, participants had worked in the company for three years, with only six indicating they had worked at the company longer than 7 years, and only eight indicating they had been trained to use agile methods. This presents a conundrum because 15 of them said they were familiar with the concept of agility. It is possible that respondents had learned about business agility on their own and not through any particular company strategy, or only very few had actually been trained at the time even if the company was pursuing agility.

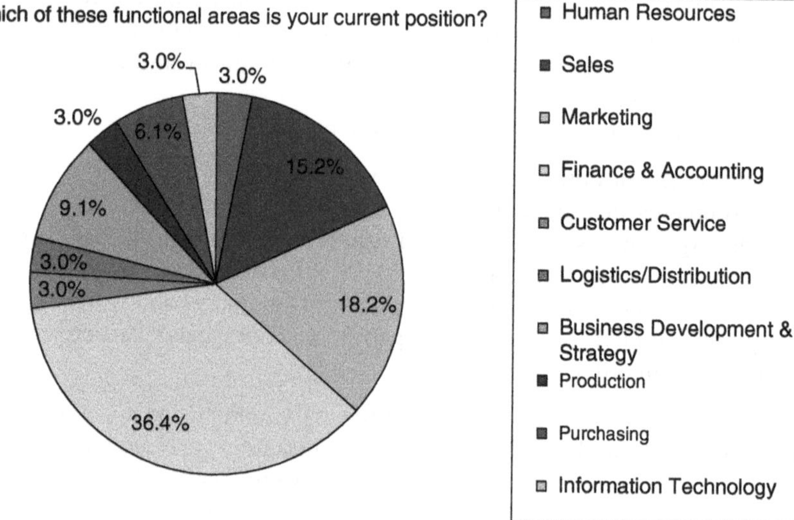


**Figure 3.1** Functional areas represented in the low- to mid-tier employees and/or managers sample unit

The perceptions among respondents of this sample unit indicate that younger employees, especially new business graduates, have a high level of awareness about business agility. They are also more likely to see the potential consequences if their organization does not become more adaptable. The majority (18 agree, 10 strongly agree) believe that their company will suffer adverse consequences, although 19 agree that the organization currently has problems adapting to the changing needs of the market. This could mean that as employees, they perceive the company is indeed adapting successfully, yet are cautious about the ability to sustain success. Overall, participants almost evenly were divided when asked if they considered their company to be agile. A total of 18 had a negative perception, whereas 20 had a positive perception.

Despite the ambivalence in perception of whether or not their company is currently agile, only ten respondents said they were not aware of any specific activities leading to agility, and only one said the company is not doing anything at all to become agile. As shown in Figure 3.2, respondents identified a variety of activities currently taking place in their companies, from general knowledge workshops all the way to recruitment.

Twenty-eight of the 38 respondents in this sample unit did not think their colleagues understood what agility is all about, and expect them to be trained (30 agree, four strongly agree). The overwhelming majority (34) agreed or strongly agreed that using agile methods would improve their team's results. All but two respondents agreed or strongly agreed that they expected their teammates to have a flexible mindset. Their expectations about colleagues mirror their opinion about the expectations of supervisors; 17 participants agreed that their supervisors expect them to have a flexible mindset, and 20 strongly agreed.

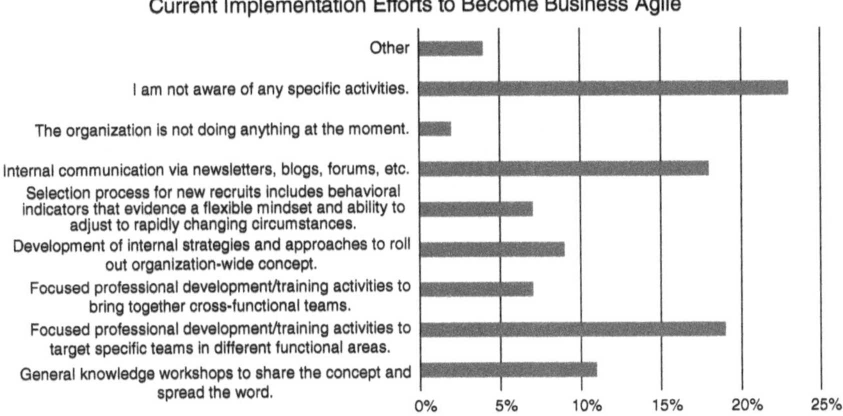


**Figure 3.2** Current implementation efforts to become business-agile

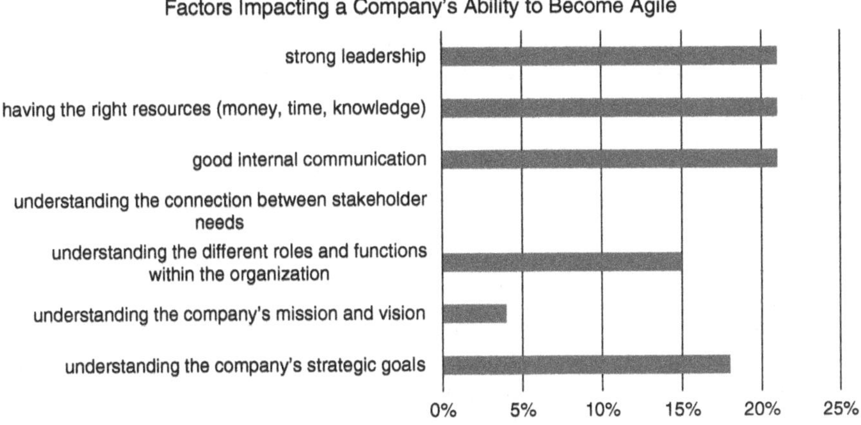


**Figure 3.3** Factors impacting a company's ability to become agile

When asked to rank in order of importance the factors that might impact a company's ability to become business-agile (see Figure 3.3), no single factor emerged as the clear priority. Instead, strong leadership, resources, and internal communication were identified as equally important (eight responses for each factor). Understanding the connection between stakeholder needs was the only topic not considered an influential factor by any of the respondents.

Additional factors mentioned were the ability of suppliers to meet the same agility requirements, strong understanding of the industry environment, and workforce diversity.

Data Analysis for Sample Unit 2: Upper-Level Managers

The 20 upper-level managers from ten companies were distributed across five different industries and four functional areas, as illustrated in Table 3.1. The average length of time working in the company was 9.5 years, and the

**Table 3.1** Distribution of upper-level managers

| Industry and number of companies | Functional area of expert interviewees | | | |
|---|---|---|---|---|
| | Business development and strategy | HRD | Marketing | Production |
| Apparel (3) | 2 | 3 | 1 | 0 |
| Automotive (2) | 2 | 1 | 1 | 2 |
| Banking/Finance (1) | 0 | 1 | 1 | 0 |
| Food (2) | 1 | 2 | 0 | 0 |
| Commercial Services (2) and Supplies | 1 | 1 | 0 | 1 |
| Total Participants | 6 | 8 | 3 | 3 |

participants'average age was 44. There was again, an imbalance in terms of gender, with 14 of the participants being male.

Twelve of the participants worked in global companies based in Western Europe, ten in Germany and two in France. The remaining eight worked for global companies in North America; seven in the United States and one in Canada. Out of the ten companies represented, seven have made their agility endeavors public via the company website, and the remaining three have yet to do so—however, they indicate the reason is because they are still in the very early stages of implementation.

Emerging Themes and Discussion

The emerging themes were coded in three different stages: transcription, reducing data inductively as patterns were identified, and revising the thematic clusters (Miles & Huberman, 1994). As shown in Table 3.2, internal communication was the most frequently occurring theme across the functional areas represented in the sample unit, followed by leadership, whereas branding, core values, and Industry 4.0 emerged only once. It can be said that some emerging themes reflect the typical activities under each functional area, and that seasoned upper-level managers in global companies see internal communication as a highly relevant theme to the topic of business agility. It is not clear, however, why some themes seem to be more important in certain functional areas than in others.

Although internal communication was the most frequent theme, it was not the top priority in any of the functional areas. Instead, leadership was the first concern for three out of the five functional areas. One inteviewee referred to visionary leadership as "having the guts to be exposed and vulnerable because you think you know where you should go, but recognize that it may be the wrong direction." The preoccupation with internal communication, combined with the concern for leadership, indicates that even global players are struggling to translate vision and mission into strategy, and strategy into business tactics. All 20 expert interviewees expressed a general dissatisfaction with the way corporate leadership communicated strategic goals and how those goals were supposed to be achieved. As one participant explained, in an attempt to respond quickly to

**Table 3.2** Emerging themes based on functional area and order of importance

| Functional area | Emerging themes |
|---|---|
| Business Development and Strategy | Leadership<br>Strategic positioning<br>Internal communication<br>Recruiting |
| HRD | Leadership<br>Internal communication<br>Recruiting<br>Professional development and training |
| Marketing | Leadership<br>Branding<br>Core values<br>Internal communication |
| Production | Industry 4.0<br>Strategic positioning<br>Internal communication<br>Professional development and training |

the changing needs of the market, corporate leadership "shoots and then points" at the seemingly moving targets. This perception stems from the fact that many of the companies represented are undergoing transformation in order to remain competitive. Furthermore, if such companies fail to manage change properly, stakeholders, especially employees, will not fully understand in which direction the company is now moving. This underscores the importance of communication (Kotter, 1996; Wendler & Gräning, 2011) in change management. The same holds true in the early stages of agility implementation because it implies a massive organizational change.

Fifteen participants indicated that although the company currently strives to implement business agility, the efforts are not commensurate with the needs. For example, a common mistake companies in the earlier stages of implementation make is to focus all their efforts on training a core group on Scrum methods first, without necessarily thinking of an organization-wide strategy. All 20 individuals agreed that without a sound implementation strategy, the specific needs of the company cannot be met. The majority of the participants also agreed that specific training such as Scrum is necessary, but it would have minimal impact if there was no bigger idea behind it. One respondent was "exhausted from all the different professional development activities" that were never really put into practice. For those in HRD, the main concern with Scrum was that early training tends to lose momentum unless there are other activities built around it. Overall, employees should not just hear about agility occasionally or be presented with abstract definitions. Instead, it should first be presented as a new way of working and collaborating and a new way of thinking.

Moreover, the three interviewees from marketing saw business agility as a more holistic concept. For them, the core values of the company played a large role in agility implementation. In their opinion, "CEOs can come and go," but the guiding principles or values that are the essence of the company should not be altered. Some of those values may include "trust," "innovation" and "integrity," among many others. They are part of branding, and they must be communicated and evidenced in day-to-day business life. Other interviewees shared the view that core values are "intertwined" with agile business practices, as in the case of innovation, and one cannot be achieved without the other.

Participants working in business development and HRD functional areas both highlighted the topic of recruiting. Overall, 14 interviewees considered this a key success element. They were concerned with attracting the best candidates, but not just in terms of knowledge. When asked to describe the candidate best suited to work for a company that is implementing business agility, the answers of the 20 experts were somewhat paradoxical and challenging to code. Below is a description of the ideal candidate, along with preliminary interpretations based on the emerging themes.

> ***Mindset***: The ideal candidate is highly flexible. S/he must pursue his/her own ideas yet integrate the ideas of other team members to produce a better outcome.
> ***Skills***: The ideal candidate is not afraid to learn new skills, or apply old skills using a new method. S/he is visionary but old school. S/he is an expert, but also a jack-of-all-trades.
> ***Knowledge***: The ideal candidate is well versed in current methodologies, frameworks, and models applicable to the specific business area, but questions everything.
> ***Personal attributes***: The ideal candidate has thick skin to withstand criticism, but is sensitive enough to reflect on self-improvement and the improvement of the team.

Conceptual flexibility is crucial for successfully adapting to a new situation. One must quickly assess the options and reconsider the stance, approach, or solution. If individual team members do not see themselves as experts who can speak up, then the danger of groupthink is higher, thus the quality of the final product is compromised. Every team member's contribution is valued, and the sum of those contributions should achieve the best possible outcome. In terms of skill set, potential team members must have the appropriate level of experience for the job. On one hand, they have to immediately integrate themselves in a fast-paced company environment and perform, yet on the other, they must be open-minded and willing to learn new things quickly.

Hunger for knowledge, curiosity, and an explorer-like attitude will enable a fresh recruit to find new perspectives, test the known boundaries, and remove barriers. Through constant reflection, this person strives to grow personally and professionally, thus his/her contributions to the team are of higher quality and stronger impact. Overall, the team dynamics are positively affected.

Recruiting individuals with the right agile mentality is not the only challenge, however. Interviewees, especially those from HRD and production, also indicated that training current employees to think in more agile ways often presented a bigger obstacle to successfully implementing agility concepts.

When asked to define business agility, experts from business development and production placed more emphasis on strategic positioning than the others. Coincidentally, this theme emerged as the second most important for both groups in terms of success factors. One hypothesis might be that in these functional areas, the direct consequences of strategic positioning are felt more so than the other areas, however, it is not clear how. One interviewee from business development revealed that his biggest challenge is "how to translate agile activities into increased brand awareness and market share." More research is needed in order to understand the reasons why certain themes might be more important in certain functional areas.

Other definitions of business agility hinted at leveraging change agents to catapult the organization into competitive advantage. These change agents, most certainly, are supposed to be the individual team members guided by the core values of the organization, the mission and vision, and, of course, visionary leadership.

The functional areas represented in this particular sample unit seem to contribute to the company's agility in function-specific ways. One reason might be that all ten companies are organized into divisional structures where waterfall strategies abound, hence the challenges to becoming agile. Because of the more traditional organizational structure, the different functional areas seem to be perpetuating functional stereotypes. For example, recruiting is something that only HRD should care about, while strategic positioning should be left up to those in business development and strategy. All interviewees agreed that these structural barriers must be removed for agile thinking to take hold.

It is clear that there are many potential variables that influence an organization's business agility. The findings from both sample units and the emerging themes provide useful insight for organizations wishing to become more agile.

## Organizational Impact

This section presents two case studies that illustrate the challenges associated with the implementation of strategic and tactical business decisions to increase agility. The case studies further augment the findings of the mixed method, exploratory study discussed previously, especially because these two global brands were included in the second sample unit, *upper level managers*. The case studies are based on direct data gathered via the qualitative interviews previously described, as well as from secondary data sources publicly available.

### The Bosch Group

Founded in 1886, as the Workshop for Precision Mechanics and Electrical Engineering in Stuttgart, Germany, the Robert Bosch GmbH company exemplifies the transformational power of an agile mindset. According to historical accounts, Mr. Robert Bosch himself was driven by curiosity, hunger for knowledge, and a passion for innovation; he showed some of the attributes that researchers today associate with agile thinking. Today, the Bosch Group, which consists of Robert Bosch GmbH and approximately 450 subsidiaries, maintains a strong global presence in four different sectors: mobility solutions, industrial technology, consumer goods, and energy and building technology, each with multiple divisions and extensive product lines. Despite the long history of successful expansion strategies, the Bosch Group, like other global players, has to rethink its strategic positioning.

As a result, the Group has recognized the need to add more flexibility to the traditional waterfall organizational structure and is actively pursuing business agility across the different sectors. Because the Bosch Group has a well-articulated mission – *We are Bosch* – and vision to become one of the world's leading internet of things (IoT) companies – the journey to agility can be more easily communicated to stakeholders (Bosch, 2016).

Business agility also allows the Bosch Group to be proactive instead of reactive, as in the case of mobile technology and connectivity. To Bosch, user-centricity has proven to be a highly important enabler of business agility and it is therefore core to IoT strategic positioning. According to the *Bosch Today* 2016 (Bosch, 2016) report, three out of four smartphones worldwide use Bosch sensors. This is a major strategic feat, and it is testament to the collaborative efforts of different cross-functional teams.

The right operational agility is also likely to help improve other sectors that have accounted for less sales revenue in recent years, such as the industrial technology sector and energy and building technology sector (Bosch, 2016, p. 11). Changes in the market place therefore might cause the company to be more reactive in those sectors, which is not ideal. The only way to counterbalance the effects of a weak or fluctuating market is to increase adaptability and reduce reaction times.

Communication is key to Bosch's implementation of agile methods, concepts, and frameworks. Internal and external branding strategies are in sync; from HR branding to the Bosch Group image branding, agility is embedded in company blogs, newsletters, and social media. One clear example is the *Bosch ConnectedWorld Blog* (2017), which has a dedicated page explaining specific agile projects to all stakeholders as well as the public at large. Current examples noted on the blog include an agile business incubator, agile engineering for cars, and even agile engineering for asparagus growers (Denner, 2015). Sharing details about such projects, especially less-known applications as in the case of developing heat sensors to help farmers grow asparagus more successfully, portrays the company's innovative spirit and adds to its image as an agile company. Internally, the digital platform *Bosch Connect* facilitates internal collaboration across functional areas. Collaboration is further rewarded via incentives linked to worldwide as well as division-specific target goals, thus increasing feedback as well as the focus on the Group's long-term goals.

An additional yet key benefit to becoming business-agile is that it opens up new opportunities to collaborate and leverage synergies with other agile companies. Through its agile processes and strategies, Bosch currently collaborates with Tesla to provide chassis and safety systems (Denner, 2015) as well as with IBM to provide connectivity to millions of IoT devices in an effort to accomplish Industry 4.0 objectives (Bosch, 2017).

Professional development and training is also fundamental to Bosch's successful implementation of agility. Bosch associates can become an agile master to guide agile teams, which in turn enhances the overall team's performance. There are numerous efforts to train teams on methods such as Scrum and Kanban across different divisions and functions, and more specifically, to adapt known frameworks to company needs. In doing so, Bosch developed its own interpretations of agile flavors that are congruent with the company's strategic orientation. The flavors are applied in functional strategies such as HR's focus on recruiting team oriented, social, digital, and mobile individuals (Beleiu & Jockel, 2016).

The Bosch Group has bolstered its agility strategy by investing in state-of-the-art IT infrastructure to connect all of its employees (Bosch, 2015). This should further support communication and collaboration, and hence facilitate agile processes. With a total sales of more than 70 billion euros in 2016 (Bosch, 2016) and plans to continue growing, the Bosch Group is well on its way to becoming fully business-agile.

## Hugo Boss AG

Hugo Boss is one of the market leaders in the upper premium segment of the global apparel market. It focuses on development and marketing of premium fashion and accessories for men and women.

Founded by Hugo F. Boss in the small town of Metzingen, Germany, in 1924, the company has been in constant motion throughout its history. Not only has it expanded its brands and portfolios over the decades, but it has changed ownership several times, each time with a different focus. Despite the growing pains, the company has managed to expand into new markets, open new sales channels, and position itself in the premium segment of fashion and accessories. Boasting net sales of 2.8 billion euros in 2015, Hugo Boss AG recognizes how current macroeconomic as well as microeconomic constraints affect its ability to sustain growth across all markets and all of its brands (Hugo Boss, 2015). As a consequence of these constraints, the company recently experienced yet another change in ownership, leadership and, once again—strategic orientation (Hugo Boss, 2015;Langer, 2016; Weber, 2016). Faced with declining profits, especially due to the overall weakened premium and luxury apparel markets globally, and the change in customer behaviors and expectations (Langer, 2016; Weber, 2016), the company swiftly re-prioritized its goals in 2016.

The strategic framework for the group strategy is formed of five attributes. First and foremost, Hugo Boss wants to ensure that all its activities are consistently aligned in a customer-oriented manner. Taking this as a basis, the group must act in a digital, agile, sustainable, and global manner in all areas. In many ways however, "it will force the company to cease operating in functional silos and embrace cross-functional teams instead," says Frederic Klumpp, Senior Vice President of Global Human Resources (F. Klumpp, personal communication, Personal interview with Yoany Beldarrain. Metzingen, Germany, January 4, 2017). Mr. Klumpp also points out that the traditional waterfall strategy must be flipped, thus empowering employees and increasing the agility of the company.

The timely reaction to the changing needs of the market required an agile, strategic mindset on the part of leadership. In a bold move to save its brand image, the company identified clear, measurable goals that revolve around the customer. A candid assessment of strengths and weaknesses led to the repositioning of the brand with two specific target groups and unique brand identities: BOSS, Hugo Boss offering premium business and casual wear, and HUGO, offering a more affordable yet fashionable 24-hour look (Langer, 2016; Weber, 2016). In doing so, the company wants to reinforce its core brand BOSS and leverage its experience in menswear, and successfully expand womenswear by 2020 (Hugo Boss, 2017). How can the company operationalize these strategic goals so quickly, especially if the rebranding efforts mean changing the previous growth strategy?

Through a more sound, leaner operational framework, leadership seeks to not just optimize but to reinvent the way Hugo Boss AG does business. Digitization of the business model is expected to lead to more customer centric practices, innovative operations such as Industry 4.0, development of omnichannels, and global interconnectedness (Hugo Boss, 2016; Langer, 2016; Thomasson, 2016). Simultaneously, the company pursues a more balanced, transparent pricing strategy across different regions of the world. Relying on agile methodologies and concepts, leadership intends on rapidly revitalizing its bottom line, becoming profitable again well into 2018 (Langer, 2016; Langer, 2017; Weber, 2016).

Driven by the mission *HUGO BOSS inspires people toward success*, the company seeks to inspire from within. Its recruiting endeavors focus on attracting highly qualified, motivated, and committed individuals who aspire for continuous personal and professional growth (Hugo Boss, 2017). The company strives to live its core corporate values of respect, quality, innovation, cooperation, passion and engages employees in a myriad of training and professional development opportunities via its own Hugo Boss University (Hugo Boss, 2017). This level of corporate commitment is crucial for permeating an agile thinking culture.

The radical transformation that Hugo Boss wants to achieve will most certainly be challenging. A major challenge will be developing the agile mindset of new recruits versus developing seasoned employees because they have different needs, expectations and organizational knowledge (F. Klumpp, personal communication). Younger, newer recruits might be more likely to have certain attributes and the propensity to think and behave agile due to the selection process, their educational background, and training at university. Agile methods provide greater flexibility and decentralize the decision making process, thus some seasoned employees who are used to more structure might not know what to do with their new freedom. Another challenge pertains to communication. According to Mr. Klumpp, true cultural change can only come about if the approach toward agility is in alignment with the leadership approach. A strong communication strategy is therefore core to organizational and cultural change.

Because of self-reflection and strategic agility, Hugo Boss AG is more likely to navigate the seas of market change and position BOSS in the upper premium segment. Competitors such as Prada, Burberry, Ralph Lauren, among others, are trying to do the same. Such a huge transformation entails embarking on the arduous journey of organizational and cultural change, but the company cannot afford not to do so. Leadership is key. As Mr. Klumpp puts it, leadership at Hugo Boss needs to "play like a jazz band, adapting to the rhythm as each person brings his/her own expertise."

## Flexible Structures, Boundless Possibilities

The findings of the exploratory study, combined with the case studies, confirm the critical role of business agility in an organization's competitiveness. The impending market changes bring challenges but also opportunities. Business agility, however, cannot happen without an agile workforce.

Recruiting individuals with an agile mindset is only the beginning, as companies must also ensure that current employees understand that agility is more than just methodologies and frameworks for organizing and doing work. Professional development endeavors should nurture agile thinking in highly collaborative, dynamic, diverse teams. Although the literature is void of information about the relationship between intercultural competence and agile thinking, it is known that higher intercultural competence positively impacts the dynamics of culturally diverse teams. Team members should be trained in the different concepts and methodologies that facilitate agile processes but also in related strategies such as lean thinking. The goal is for individual team members to have the conceptual flexibility and knowledge to apply the approaches most suitable for the given situation. The approach to leadership must in turn create an organizational culture of empowerment and trust.

Leadership and communication were the top two themes across the study, regardless of position or functional area. Leadership and communication also emerged as key organizational challenges for the Bosch Group and Hugo Boss Group. These findings indicate that leadership must, first and foremost, elaborate an agile strategy that includes clear, measurable goals, and also a robust communication network through which these goals and agile thinking are promoted. As a result, the strategic orientation is better understood, hence better operationalized. Communication strategies should also aim at sharpening the company's brand image both, internally and externally. Business agility is nowadays associated with innovation; therefore, different stakeholders should be aware of how the different agile strategies and processes add value to the service or product. Most importantly, business agility should be communicated not just as *what* the company does or *how*, but mainly as *who* the company is, and *why* it exists—thus clearly reconnecting agile strategic orientation with the organization's mission and vision. Stakeholders must clearly understand what the company's agility means for them as customers, suppliers, employees, and so forth.

The findings indicate that upper level managers tend to focus on themes that are traditionally associated with their functional area. Although the sample size for both sample units was rather small and the convenience sampling methods make it rather difficult to make generalizations, the case study of Hugo Boss AG supports the assumption that waterfall-type of strategies and structures create organizational silos. Agile organizations therefore need flexible structures that encourage cross-functional dialog. The literature also indicates that agility flourishes more easily in flatter organizations, hence it can be said that organizations wishing to implement agile strategies, concepts, methodologies, and frameworks must reflect on their organizational structure.

A company's success pivots around the people behind it, from the front desk secretary to the CEO. An agile workforce is more likely to think and behave proactively, flexibly, and strategically. An agile workforce has the right skills, knowledge, and personal attributes required for their position but also the right mindset to move the organization forward.

## References

Abbas, N., Gravell, A. M., & Wills, G. B. (2008). Historical roots of agile methods: Where did "agile thinking" come from? In J. Garbajosa, X. Wang, & A. Aguiar (Eds.), *Lecture notes in business information processing: Vol 9. Agile processes in software engineering and extreme programming,* (pp. 94–103). Berlin, Heidelberg, Germany: Springer. https://doi.org/10.1007/978-3-540-68255-4_10

Agile Manifesto. (2001). Manifesto for agile software development. Retrieved February 27, 2017, from http://www.agilemanifesto.org

Alavi, S., Wahab, D. A., Muhamad, N., & Arbab Shirani, B. (2014). Organic structure and organizational learning as the main antecedents of workforce agility. *International Journal of Production Research, 52*(21), 6273–6295. https://doi.org/10.1080/00207543.2014.919420

Anderson, D. J. (2010). *Kanban: Successful evolutionary change for your technology business.* Sequin, WA: Blue Hole Press.

Beleiu, R. & Jockel, J. (2016). *Agile flavors at Bosch and how they taste for HR.* Presentation at Agile HR Conference 2016, Köln, Germany. Retrieved February 27, 2017, from https://hr-pioneers.com/wp-content/uploads/2016/04/Bosch.pdf

Borg, W. R., & Gall, M. D. (1989). *Educational research: An introduction* (5th ed.). New York, NY: Longman.

Bosch. (2015). Boosting agility on the job. [Press release]. Retrieved February 27, 2017, from http://www.bosch-presse.de/pressportal/de/en/bosch-invests-in-the-workplace-of-the-future-42993.html

Bosch. (2016). *Bosch today 2016.* Retrieved February 27, 2017, from http://www.bosch.com/content2/publication_forms/en/downloads/Bosch_Today_2016.pdf

Bosch. (2017). Bosch and IBM start collaboration for industrial IoT [Press release]. Retrieved February 27, 2017, from http://www.bosch-presse.de/pressportal/de/en/bosch-and-ibm-start-collaboration-for-industrial-iot-89409.html

Bosch ConnectedWorld. (2017). Blog. Retrieved from http://blog.bosch-si.com

Breu, K., Hemingway, C. J., Strathern, M., & Bridger, D. (2002). Worforce agility: The new employee strategy for the knowledge economy. *Journal of Information Technology, 17*(1), 21–31.

Conboy, K. (2009). Agility from first principles: Reconstructing the concept of agility in information systems development. *Information Systems Research, 20*(3), 329–354. https://doi.org/10.1287/isre.1090.0236

Creswell, J. W., & Miller, D. L. (2000). Determining validity in qualitative inquiry. *Theory Into Practice, 39*, 124–130. https://doi.org/10.1207/s15430421tip3903_2

Denner, V. (2015). *Agility at Bosch: Mission impossible?* [Bosch ConnectedWorld Blog]. Retrieved February 27, 2017, from http://blog.bosch-si.com/categories/internetofthings/2015/06/agility-at-bosch-mission-impossible

Denscombe, M. (2004). *The good research guide for small-scale social research* (2nd ed.). Berkshire, UK: Open University Press.

Dingsøyr, T., Nerur, S., Balijepally, V., & Moe, N. B. (2012). A decade of agile methodologies: Towards explaining agile software development. *Journal of Systems and Software, 85*(6), 1213–1221. https://doi.org/10.1016/j.jss.2012.02.033

Esser, J. K. (1998). Alive and well after 25 years: A review of groupthink research. *Organizational Behavior and Human Decision Processes, 73*(2), 116–141. https://doi.org/10.1006/obhd.1998.2756

Google. (2016). Recruitment page. Retrieved May 15, 2016 from http://www.google.de/about/careers/how-we-hire

Gravett, L. S., & Caldwell, S. A. (2016). How to sustain a culture of learning agility. In L. S. Gravett, & S. A. Caldwell (Eds.), *Learning Agility* (pp. 95–107). Basingstoke, UK: Palgrave Macmillan. https://doi.org/10.1057/978-1-137-59965-0_7

Hallenbeck, G., Swisher, V., & Orr, J.E. (2011). *Seven faces of learning agility. Smarter ways to define, deploy, and develop high-potential talent* (Research report). Retrieved from Korn Ferry Institute website: http://www.kornferry.com/media/lominger_pdf/Seven_faces_of_learning_agility.pdf

Harris, A. (2004). Reaping the rewards of agile thinking. *Manufacturing Engineer, 83*(6), 24–27. https://doi.org/10.1049/me:20040603

Hosein, Z. Z., & Yousefi, A. (2012). The role of emotional intelligence on workforce agility in the workplace. *International Journal of Psychological Studies, 4*(3), 48. https://doi.org/10.5539/ijps.v4n3p48

Hugo Boss. (2015). *Sustainability report 2015.* Retrieved February 28, 2017, from http://group.hugoboss.com/en/sustainability

Hugo Boss. (2016). *Hugo Boss presents its strategic development plan* [Press release]. Retrieved February 28, 2017, from http://group.hugoboss.com/en/news/16112016-hugo-boss-presents-its-strategic-development-plan-13000910

Hugo Boss. (2017). Growth strategy 2020. [Corporate website]. Retrieved February 28, 2017, from http://group.hugoboss.com/en/investor-relations/investment-case/strategy

Jackson, S. L. (2011). *Research methods and statistics: A critical approach* (4th ed.). Boston, MA: Cengage Learning.

Janis, I. L. (1971). Groupthink. Psychology Today, 5, 43– 46. https://web.archive.org/web/20100401033524/http://apps.olin.wustl.edu/faculty/macdonald/GroupThink.pdf

Kotter, J. P. (1996). *Leading change.* Boston, MA: Harvard Business School Press.

Lamarca, G. & Eaton, D. (2016). *What color is your passport?* (Research report). Retrieved from Korn Ferry Institute website: https://www.kornferry.com/institute/what-color-is-your-passport Accessed October 13, 2018.

Langer, M. (2016). Group strategy. Investor Day 2016 (Presentation). Retrieved February 28, 2017, from https://group.hugoboss.com/files/user_upload/Investor_Relations/Events/2016/ID2016_Group_Strategy_Mark_Langer_final.pdf

Langer, M. (2017). Kepler Cheuvreux German Corporate Conference 2017. (Presentation). Retrieved February 28, 2017, from http://group.hugoboss.com/files/user_upload/Investor_Relations/Events/2017/2017-01-18_Kepler_Cheuvreux_GCC_FFM_HUGO_BOSS_short.pdf

Lavrakas, P. J. (2008). *Encyclopedia of survey research methods*. Thousand Oaks, CA: Sage. https://doi.org/10.4135/9781412963947

Meister, J. C., & Willyerd, K. (2010). *The 2020 workplace: How innovative companies attract, develop, and keep tomorrow's employees today*. New York, NY: Harper-Collins.

Michaels, E., Handfield-Jones, H., & Axelrod, B. (2001). *The war for talent*. Boston, MA: McKinsey and Company.

Miles, M. B., & Huberman, A. M. (1994). *Qualitative data analysis* (2nd ed.). Thousand Oaks, CA: Sage.

Rothwell, W. J., Graber, J., & McCormick, N. (2012). *Lean but agile: Rethink workforce planning and gain a true competitive edge*. Nashville, TN: AMACOM Division American Management Association. e-Book ISBN: 9780814417782.

Royce, W.W. (1987). Managing the development of large software systems: Concepts and techniques. *Proceedings of the 9th International Conference on Software Engineering*, Los Alamitos, CA, USA, 328–338. Full text retrieved from https://dl.acm.org/citation.cfm?id=41765&picked=prox

Schwaber, K. (1997). Scrum development process. In J. V. Sutherland, D. Patel, C. Casanave, J. Miller, & G. Hollowell (Eds.), *Business object design and implementation*, (pp. 117–134). London, UK: Springer. https://doi.org/10.1007/978-1-4471-0947-1

Silva, F. S., Soares, F. S. F., Peres, A. L., de Azevedo, I. M., Vasconcelos, A. P. L., Kamei, F. K., & de Lemos Meira, S. R. (2015). Using CMMI together with agile software development: A systematic review. *Information and Software Technology, 58*, 20–43. https://doi.org/10.1016/j.infsof.2014.09.012

Snowden, D.J. & Boone, M.E. (2007). A leader's framework for decision making. Harvard Business Review, Retrieved from https://hbr.org/2007/11/a-leaders-framework-for-decision-making

Stacey, R. D. (2002). *Strategic management and organizational dynamics: The challenge of complexity* (3rd ed.). Harlow, UK: Prentice Hall.

Stebbins, R. A. (2001). *Exploratory research in the social sciences*. Thousand Oaks, CA: Sage.

Stellman, A., & Greene, J. (2015). *Learning agile. Understanding scrum, XP, and Kanban*. Sebastopol, CA: O'Reilly Media, Inc.

Tal, L. (2015). *Agile software development with HP Agile Manager*. Berlin, Germany: Apress. https://doi.org/10.1007/978-1-4842-1034-5

Thomasson, E. (2016). Hugo Boss sees revival plan bearing fruit in 2018. Reuters. Retrieved February 8, 2017, from http://www.reuters.com/article/us-hugo-boss-strategy-idUSKBN13B0JG

Weber, D. (2016). Investor meeting presentation. German Senior Investor Day Munich. (Presentation). Retrieved February 28, 2017, from http://group.hugoboss.com/files/user_upload/Investor_Relations/Events/2016/2016-11-30_UBS_German_Senior_Investor_Day_Munich.pdf

Wendler, R. & Gräning, A. (2011). How agile are you thinking? An exploratory case study. In A. Bernstein, and G. Schwabe (eds.), *Proceedings of the 10th International Conference on Wirtschaftsinformatik [Business Informatics] WI 2.011: Vol. 2*, (pp. 818–827). Zurich, Switzerland: Lulu. doi:https://doi.org/10.5167/uzh-60516.

Wölbling, A., Krämer, K., Buss, C. N., Dribbisch, K., LoBue, P., & Taherivand, A. (2012). Design thinking: An innovative concept for developing user-centered software. In A. Maedche, A. Botzenhardt, & L. Neer (Eds.), (Series eds.) *Management for professional series. Software for people*, (pp. 121–136). Berlin, Heidelberg, Germany: Springer. https://doi.org/10.1007/978-3-642-31371-4_7

Zhang, Z., & Sharifi, H. (2000). A methodology for achieving agility in manufacturing organizations. *International Journal of Operations and Production Management, 20*(4), 496–513. https://doi.org/10.1108/01443570010314818

# 4

# The New Learning Economy and the Rise of the Working Learner

*Hope Clark*[1]*, Parminder K. Jassal*[1]*, Sarah Blanchard Kyte*[2]*, and Mary LeFebvre*[1]

[1] *Institute for the Future*
[2] *The University of Arizona*

Until recently, we thought of learning, working, and living as separate parts of our lives. In our younger years, we went to school. Then, we spent our adult years working. In between, we wove in personal events into the time that remained when we were not working or learning. Now, and in the future, working, learning, and our personal lives will become increasingly inseparable, not by choice, but in order to thrive in a rapidly evolving learning economy.

In this chapter, we highlight the features and trends of the new learning economy fueled by the rise of the working learner. We identify the barriers associated with integrating living, learning, and working and suggest strategies for reducing the struggles of working learners through increased collaboration, and coalition-building across global economic development, workforce development and education systems. Finally, we summarize actionable research that provides additional insights and key understandings of the rise of the working learner and present a new framework for organizing and understanding various work-and-learn options.

The rise of the working learner in the new learning economy signifies a dramatic shift in how we think about working and learning and the relationship with overall life satisfaction. Just like any other economy, the new learning economy operates at many different levels: global, regional, state and local, creating an ecosystem whereby working, learning and living are integrated functions (Institute for the Future, 2015, see also Jassal & Clark, 2016) (see Figure 4.1).

Innovation in work-and-learn options can occur at all levels, with interactions occurring between the various levels to produce a fluid ecosystem that supports working, learning and life satisfaction. For example, global economic and labor market trends driven by technological innovation influence national policies on education and workforce-development strategies. These strategies support bringing new work-and-learn innovations to scale. Policies are then developed

*The Wiley Handbook of Global Workplace Learning*, First Edition.
Edited by Vanessa Hammler Kenon and Sunay Vasant Palsole.

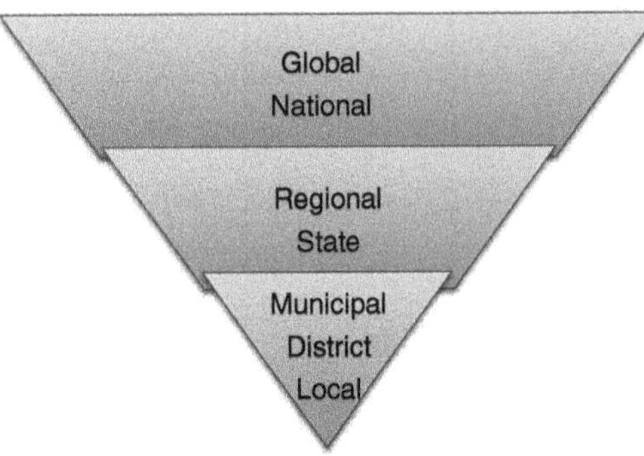


**Figure 4.1** Fluidity of learning economies

that influence funding decisions and funds are passed down to the state and local levels to implement these innovative solutions for working learners at the ground level. Many of these innovative solutions require curators to think about the interplay of working, learning and living to achieve an ideal balance that is personalized for the individual.

Historically, research on working and on learning have been analyzed and reported as parallel and separate paradigms with little or no intersection (Lundvall, 2004). These studies typically examine factors related to negative or positive working or learning outcomes but not how these factors coincide and interact to impact workplace or educational success. Research on working and learning is a new and emerging field, and only recently have attempts been made to pull the two fields together (Jassal & Clark, 2016). For example, The Higher Education Quality Council of Ontario (2016) provides an outstanding guide on work-integrated learning and offers information on how colleges and universities can implement effective structured work experiences into their educational programming.

On the other hand, alternative solutions are led by the working learner themselves. A report by Randstad (2016) predicts the future workplace in 2025 underscored by the rise of the agile workforce. This report, based on a survey of 1500 business executives and 3160 workers, found that nearly 11% of the workforce is made up of full-time agile workers or workers who perform temporary, freelance or contractual work. Furthermore, 39% of permanent workers (i.e., non-agile) surveyed said they are likely to take a position in the future that falls in the category of agile. Usually in this case it is because there is a need or desire to balance work, life and learning and there is tremendous motivation to seek opportunities that integrate and support their living, learning and working worlds. Examples of work-and-learn options that are sought that support this balance include the rising popularity of the Freelancer's Union and learners using applications like Duolingo, UpWork, Guru and Outsourcely (Jassal & Clark, 2016). Figure 4.2 represents the new work-and-learn ecosystem where the activities of working, learning and

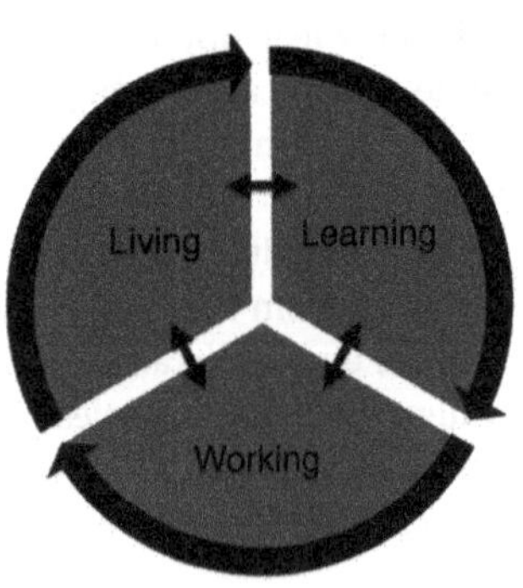


**Figure 4.2** Working, learning and living ecosystem

living become more integrated. This work has only just begun and will continue to evolve as new technology and innovative solutions are created to support successful learn-and-earn outcomes that lead to workplace success and life satisfaction.

## The Evolution of the New Learning Economy: Moving From Knowledge to Performance-Driven Learning

In 1996, the Organization for Economic Cooperation and Development (OECD) published a report that defined the knowledge-based economy as one that is "directly based on the production, distribution and use of knowledge and information" (Organization for Economic Cooperation and Development [OECD], 1996). The knowledge economy reflected economic trends driven by growth in high-technology investments in high technology industries requiring highly skilled labor leading to higher productivity gains. During the late 1990s and early 2000s knowledge distribution occurred through formal and informal networks where codified information was transmitted through computer and communications networks in the emerging "information society."

The knowledge economy also required tacit knowledge, which is associated with skills such as leadership, emotional intelligence, and communication. Tacit knowledge is much harder to transfer from one individual to another than is formal knowledge, because it is not easily captured by knowledge-management systems. These skills are needed to adapt codified knowledge, to drive innovation and performance. In a knowledge-based economy, innovation is driven by the interaction of producers and users in the exchange of both codified and tacit knowledge. This requires dynamic interactions between industry, government, and academia in the development of real-time learning opportunities in order to drive economic growth.

During the early 2000s, Lundvall (2004) published a paper on a new economy driven by learning and competence building. He argues that it is useful to rethink the concept of this new economy as a "techno-economic" paradigm shift with a focus on the ability for individuals to "cope with and use the full potential of the new technologies." This paradigm shift marks the beginning of what we now call "the new learning economy," with an emphasis on demonstrating "what we can do with what we know," not just simply recalling what we have learned. Fast forward 20 years from the time that the knowledge economy was first defined to the present day, and we are witnessing a revolution of new work and learn options supported by innovative technologies. The new learning economy is being fueled by the rise of the working learner, with a new focus on a performance-based outcome such as applying what is learned to achieve workplace goals.

The American Council on Education (ACE) published a report on the "readiness for a new learning economy," based on insights from OECD's *Survey of Adult Skills on Workforce Readiness and Preparation* (Soares & Perna, 2014). In their report, they define the new learning economy as "the intersection of the knowledge economy and human capital development." During the twentieth century, technological improvements in agriculture and industry enabled people with minimal skills to be economically successful via mass production. In the twenty-first century, technology is having the opposite effect. Technological innovation is having a profound impact on the information-processing, academic, and technical skills required not only for newly created jobs but also for existing jobs. A learning economy has emerged in which success requires continuous knowledge and adaptation to changing workplace processes and is measured using organizational performance metrics.

Historically, working and learning were thought of as separate paradigms following parallel paths with little or no intersection (Jassal & Clark, 2016). The rise of the working learner in the new learning economy signifies a dramatic shift in the way we think about working and learning in life. In the new learning economy, working, learning, and living are integrated and harmonious, resulting in new economic opportunities and overall life satisfaction. Billet (2009) offers a common definition for work-integrated learning that has been adapted by work-and-learn stakeholders:

> work integrated learning refers to the process whereby students come to learn from experiences in educational practice settings and integrate contributions of those experiences in developing the understandings, procedures and dispositions required for effective professional practice, including criticality. Work integrated learning arrangements include the kinds of curriculum and pedagogic practices that can assist, provide and effectively integrate learning experiences in both educational and practice settings.

The new learning economy is driven by a new vision of labor that is student-centered, focusing on competency-based models of learning. For example, federally recognized "Work Colleges" were established under federal legislation which defines a Work College as a special type of degree-granting institution where a "comprehensive work-learning-service program" is an "integral and stated part of the institution's educational program and part of a financial aid plan that decreases reliance on grants and loans and encourages students to participate in community service activities" (U.S. Government Publishing Office, 2017). It is a competency-based (rather than credit hour-based) model of learning. Unlike federal work-study programs, which are solely need-based, all students work, regardless of their academic program or their financial need. Currently there are only eight Work Colleges in the United States that meet the federal definition and guidelines as overseen by the U.S. Department of Education. For example, at Berea College in Lexington, Kentucky, the vision of their Labor Program is to provide opportunities for the Berea College community to develop goals for both the learning and workplace performance of students and to reflect on local and global issues in the world of work. According to research by the Work College Consortium (2011), Work College graduates report that their experiences at the college better prepared them for their current job as compared to their peers. They also report that their college costs are significantly lower than their peers' (Work College Consortium, 2011).

In a newly proposed "work-to-study" model, working environments influence students' health, well-being, and academic outcomes via two mediating constructs: work–study conflict and work–study facilitation (Owen, Kavanagh and Dollard, 2017). Decreasing work–study conflict and increasing work–study facilitation, can improve course grades, increase academic engagement and increase program completion. Similar models are being applied in Colorado via a program called CareerWise which is a type of apprenticeship program that is designed to let students earn a competitive wage while earning an advanced technology degree offered through eight state colleges and universities (Cordell, 2017). Students typically spend 16 hours a week in the workplace and the rest of the week in the classroom. As they progress, they spend less time studying and more time working – up to around 32 hours per week during the final years of study.

The envisioned new learning economy provides working learners with improved access to relevant learn and earn opportunities, better connections to work pathways, clearer and more attainable learning outcomes, and increased life satisfaction. The highly integrated new environment of living, learning, and working demands high levels of performance and the ability to successfully navigate a blended digital–physical world. These new "work-and-learn" environments remove barriers for non-traditional learners, which translates into significant economic opportunity for individuals who embrace this change.

## Who Are Working Learners?

Having described the current context as one in which individuals' performance and capacity to learn play an increasing role in economic competitiveness, we now turn our attention to the individuals at the center of these changes – working learners. Working learners have been identified as those working for pay while simultaneously enrolled in some form of formal post-secondary education or training (Carnevale, Smith, Melton, & Price, 2015). In the U.S., this definition fits 14 million adults (8% of the labor force) roughly and three in four college students (ibid.). By including workers who engage in informal learning in this category, such as those involved in self-directed and more passive forms of learning, this number swells to include virtually all workers (Van Noy, 2016).

These insights help fuel a growing recognition of learning as a lifelong process as well as engagement with learning as a defining characteristic of many of today's workers (Beaudry, Green, & Sand, 2016; Jassal & Clark, 2016; Pew Research Center, 2016). Across cohorts, advantages in opportunities to learn new skills at the workplace and to receive training from employers have declined for incumbents with bachelors' degrees, pressing both degree holders and those without bachelor's degrees to seek educational opportunities outside of work (Blanchard Kyte, 2017a). Indeed, among all workers, 37% enrolled in courses related to their jobs, 22% enrolled in courses related to personal interests, and 73% pursued informal learning outside of work (Blanchard Kyte, 2017a). This engagement with education varied by industries with some of the greatest engagement among those working in growing sectors of the economy – namely, health, education, and public administration. Moreover, Blanchard Kyte's (2017a) analysis of data from the Survey of Income and Program Participation (SIPP) estimated that over a five-year period, working learners saw greater earnings increases, even if they did not complete a formal credential, than peers not learning while working. Taken together, this intensive engagement with education while in the labor force challenges prior conceptualizations of education and work as separate and sequential (Phelan & Peters, 2016).

Consequently, working learners were previously an invisible population, those who divide their time and effort between working and learning are now the norm rather than the exception (Jassal & Clark, 2016). A recent report from the Georgetown University Center on Education and the Workforce makes the case that the prevalence of the working learner in formal, post-secondary education masks heterogeneity across industries, work experiences and key demographic characteristics, including age, income, race/ ethnicity, and gender (Carnevale et al., 2015). In addition, the authors provide evidence that although it is no longer possible in most cases for college students to pay their tuition exclusively through full-time work, college students who work while enrolled may benefit from this balancing act.[1] This is especially true for students who are able to gain work experience relevant to their fields of study during their postsecondary education (ibid.). Yet, these benefits are the exception rather than the norm; in an analysis of national data, fewer than one in five working college students reported that their jobs were related to their major and less than one-third saw their jobs as helping their career preparation (Blanchard Kyte, 2017b). Though largely descriptive, the Georgetown study is arguably the first to bring working learners as a distinct group into focus.

Engagement with paid work often precedes post-secondary enrollment, and recent scholarship has documented the experiences and prospects of high school-aged working learners. Half of high school students report working for pay, with roughly one in four working more than 15 hours each week (Blanchard, 2016; LeFebvre, 2016). Among the national pool of high school students taking the ACT achievement test, those who reported working 15 hours or more each week tended to have greater certainty of their career plans compared to their peers (LeFebvre, 2016). To the extent that students' career success will hinge on their ability to align their educational and work trajectories around defined ambitions (Schneider & Stevenson, 1999), quality working and learning experiences may offer these students a powerful advantage.

The decision to work as a high schooler is not made in a vacuum. After examining the linkages between family income, academic readiness for college, and the decision to work, Blanchard (2016) finds a distinct pattern among low-income high school students relating to work and academic preparation for college. Consistent with LeFebvre (2016), students in the general population who work more than 15 hours each week tend to be less academically prepared for college compared to those who work fewer hours or not at all. However, among students whose family incomes are below or close to the poverty line, those who are the most academically prepared for college also engage the most intensively with paid work while still in high school (Blanchard, 2016). Thus, family resources shape the balance working learners attempt to strike between working and learning even as they prepare for the transition to college.

From another perspective, working and learning presents an opportunity to meet the needs not only of working learners themselves but also of local employers and communities. Promising examples of innovative partnerships between post-secondary institutions and employers have been shown to advance the interests and well-being of each. In one outstanding example of such a partnership, the United Parcel Service (UPS) established a public/ private partnership between state actors and post-secondary institutions in Louisville, Kentucky (Riggert et al., 2004). Rather than relocate a hub from Louisville to another location due to high employee turnover, UPS invested a fraction of the potential cost of relocation into 50% tuition coverage, book reimbursements, and academic bonuses for student workers. In turn, turnover among employees was cut by 70%, and the partnership resulted in over 2500 post-secondary credentials, largely among underserved students. By facilitating the partnership and offsetting the remaining 50% of tuition and infrastructure costs, the public partners were able to retain the second-largest state employer and cultivate a stronger local pool of talent (Corporate Voices for Working Families, 2012). Indeed, such shining examples of synchronicity are the exception rather than the norm; however, they illustrate how leveraging the potential of working learners offers access to an untapped and often ignored resource. Thus, a working learner perspective offers significant opportunities not only to the working learners themselves but also to employers and communities as a whole.

## The Work vs Learning Conflict: Barriers to Integrating Living, Learning and Working

Despite these promising findings, a theme across the emerging scholarship on working learners is that they face significant barriers to the successful integration of working and learning that dampens their ability to thrive. As articulated by Perna (2010), the balance between school and work – and often family – that working learners attempt to strike is often a precarious one, especially for individuals from historically underserved groups. Moreover, students with more resources accessible through their families, social networks, employers, and educational institutions are better able to manage this balancing act (see also Carnevale et al., 2015). By contrast, among college students, first-generation and low-income students are more likely to work, and in turn, are more likely to pay a penalty in terms of degree persistence. For example, Blanchard Kyte (2017b) documented how students enrolling in four-year universities who work more than 15 hours each week are less likely to graduate within six years, and that this disadvantage is magnified for students from low-income households. This double-bind suggests that, at present, working and learning often poses a barrier to getting ahead (Blanchard Kyte, 2017b; Carnevale et al., 2015; Perna, 2010). Within post-secondary institutions, scheduling flexibility and a culture that affirms work as a part of an increasing share of students' lives are integral elements to the success of working learners (ibid.). Simply put, the old paradigm of education and work as distinct phases persists, and its institutional and structural remnants present barriers to the emerging working learner reality.

For example, this paradigm of learning and work as separate and sequential also looms large in the mindsets of most employers.[2] Rather than a competitive advantage, recent evidence suggests that individuals attempting to balance education and work face considerable barriers through contemporary hiring practices that undervalue working learners (Phelan & Peters, 2016). In particular, those with post-secondary credentials in progress are typically screened out of the pool of job candidates even though human resource professionals often lack an empirical basis for the advanced credentials identified as hiring criteria (ibid.). This tendency is not without cost to employers; the authors argue that the pervasive undervaluing of working learners undermines the cultivation of diverse internal talent pipelines of high-potential individuals (ibid., see also Lumina Foundation, 2016). Paradoxically, recent studies suggest that a majority (83%) of employers offer tuition reimbursement or education assistance to incumbents while simultaneously undervaluing ongoing education in prospective hires (International Foundation of Employee Benefit Plans [IFEBP], 2015, see also Society for Human Resource Management [SHRM], 2013). This example illustrates how the barriers faced by working learners may negatively impact employers and firms as well.

Taken together, the rise of working learners reflects social forces, including the arrival of the new learning economy as well as the decisions that individuals make in the face of the opportunities and constraints presented by this context. In the coming decades, workforce and labor market scholars have predicted that working learners will increase in numbers (Carnevale et al. 2015, see also Jassal & Clark, 2016). Therefore, alleviating institutional and structural barriers is necessary to accommodate working learners and, in doing so, maximize outcomes for educational institutions, employers, and the communities that stand to benefit from their efforts. Moreover, integrating working and learning from an institutional perspective requires not only increased flexibility to accommodate the extensive demands on working learners' time but also new multi-level and cross-institutional frameworks. This vision is the focus of the concluding section of this chapter.

## The Future of Work and Learn Options: A New Framework

The evolution of the knowledge economy to a new learning economy, driven largely by new technological forces and digital signals, presents a shift in how we design and develop "work and learn" options and assessments that incorporate both informal and formal learning approaches with a new focus on performance-based outcomes. The new era of growth in work and learn options is part evolution and part revolution where working learners drive their own work and learn trajectory, increasing the need to broaden conceptions of learning to include a range of informal learning opportunities (Van Noy, 2016). Demand has led to unparalleled growth in offerings by third parties and new options driven by working learners that combine working and learning through a variety of formal and informal combinations. This has implications for how we think about assessment of learning, especially as it relates to a new emphasis on performance-based outcomes.

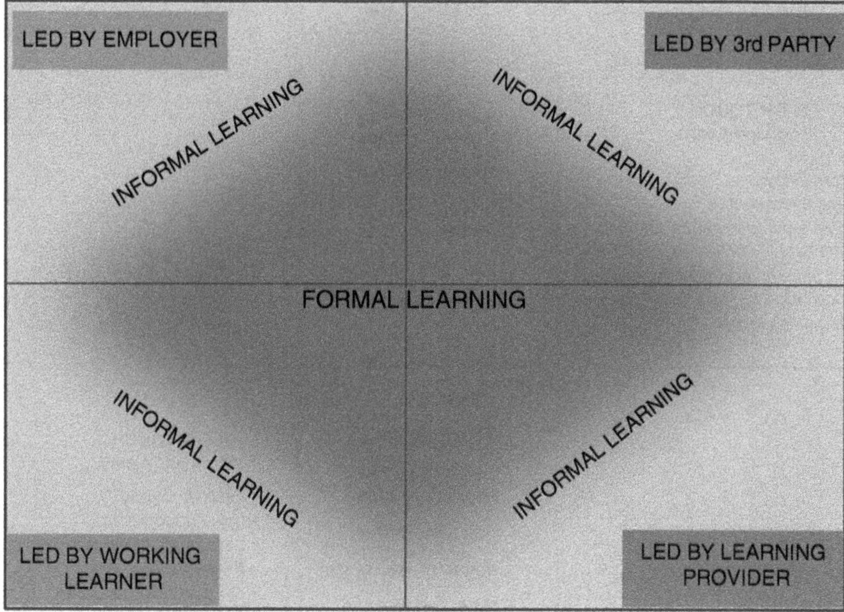


**Figure 4.3** A new framework for work and learn options

Emerging from this evolution/revolution or "evo-revolution" is a new framework for work-and-learn options that incorporates a new dimension of learning that is driven by working learners and their use of new technologies. This new framework represents a spectrum anchored by the level of coordination needed for the work-and-learn option and who offers the work-and-learn option (see Figure 4.3). The framework is categorized by whether the work-and-learn option is driven by (a) the employer, (b) the learning provider, (c) a third party or (d) the working learner.

Work and learn options range from being highly structured (high touch), such as registered apprenticeships, to loosely defined (low touch), such as employers hosting study zones in the workplace (See Figure 4.4).

These options can be further categorized along the formal versus informal learning continuum that has a direct relationship with the type of infrastructure needed (e.g., online versus bricks-and-mortar classrooms) and supports (e.g., childcare, flexible course schedules, etc.) in order to be successful. These variables will also determine how we measure success and the type of assessment that is most appropriate to measure learning outcomes and demonstrated performance. Options led by working learners, which tend to be low-touch, informal and supported by mobile technologies, are experiencing explosive growth, as evidenced by new social networks and start-up companies offering opportunities for working learners through non-traditional channels. These new work-and-learn options offer working learners the opportunity to create real-time, customized and personalized career pathways. An enhanced framework for

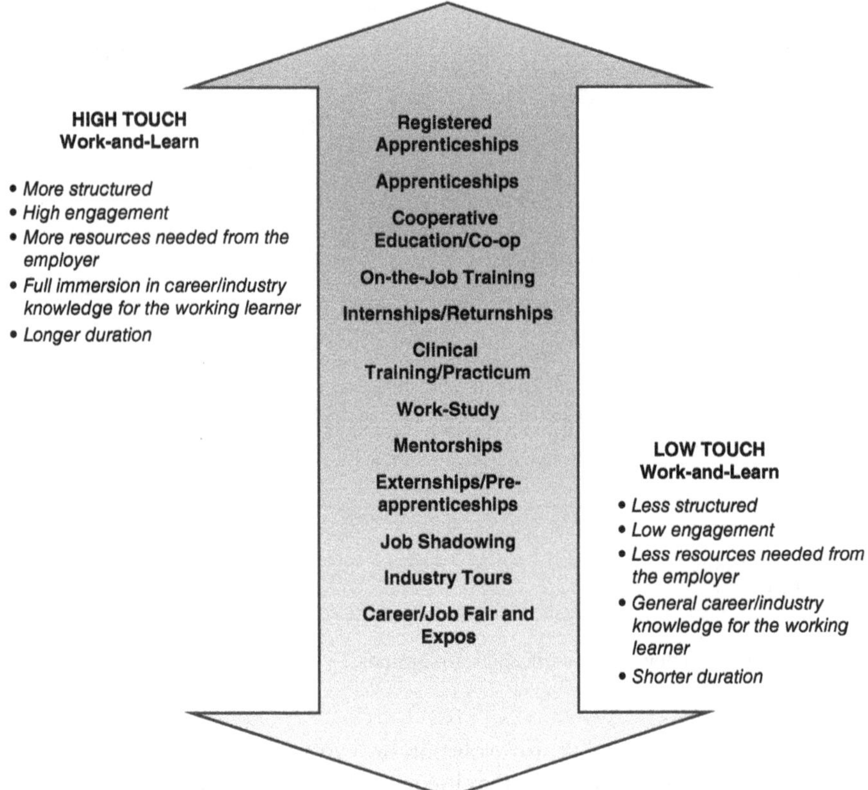


**Figure 4.4** Work and learn options: low-touch vs high-touch. For more information on the definitions of the various work-and-learn programs see: *Work and Learn in Action: Successful Strategies for Employers. Source:* National Network of Business and Industry Associations (2015)

these various work-and-learn options that incorporates the various dimensions of learning along a continuum is presented in Figure 4.5.

According to a research report commissioned by the Higher Education Quality Council of Ontario, the benefits of work-integrated learning on the social and human capital of post-secondary education graduates (with specific reference to the quality of student learning and labor market outcomes associated with work-and-learn programs), outweigh the challenges (Sattler, 2011). Work-integrated learning was strongly endorsed as an important element of the overall student experience, with a range of student benefits including career exploration, career clarity, improved prospects for employment, opportunity to apply theory to practice in real workplace and community settings, and the development of marketable workplace skills. Benefits to employers included improved productivity and service-delivery enhancements, streamlined recruitment and screening processes, reduced training costs for new hires, better connections and understanding between employers and post-secondary institutions, and demonstrated commitment by employers to the community and profession. Post-secondary

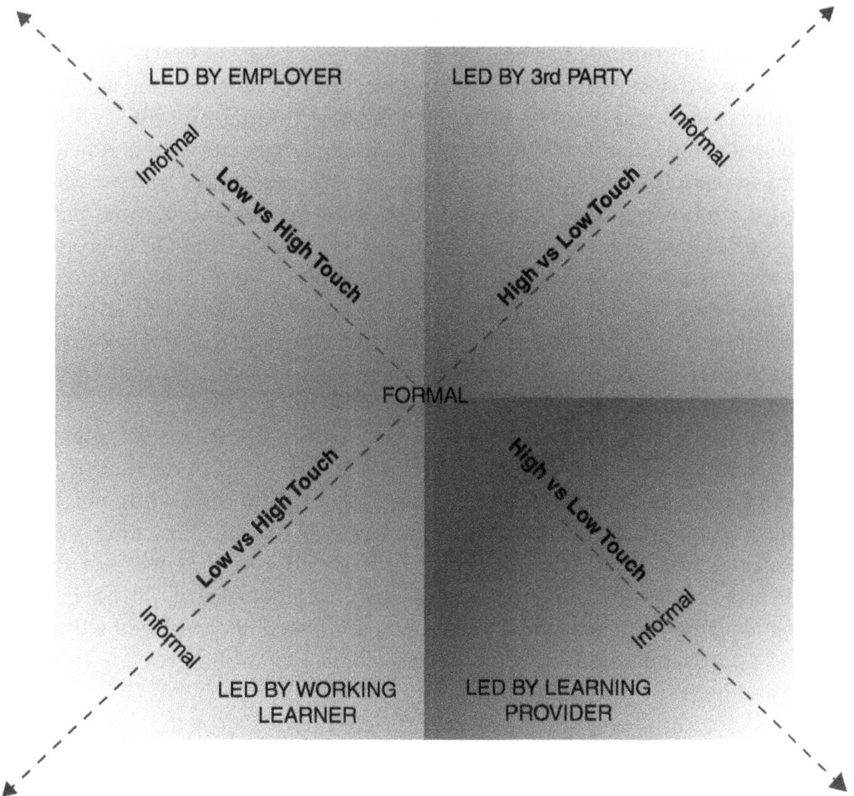


**Figure 4.5** An enhanced framework for work-and-learn options

institutions cited strengthening community partnerships and enhancing institutional and program reputation – and the associated positive impacts on student recruitment, alumni relations, and program development, through employer feedback – as the most significant benefits to work-integrated programs.

The movement toward work and learn integration presents its own set of challenges as education providers work to scale these new innovative approaches that tend to be more personalized and customized in order to effectively balance working, learning, and living. Challenges for work and learn program providers identified by the HEQCO include the following: volume of administration and paperwork; securing sufficient student placements and meeting employer demands for students; economic situation and financial pressures on employers; managing expectations among faculty; students and employer partners; institutional bias and lack of institutional supports; developing and implementing work and learn curriculum and the need for faculty buy-in; and the changing nature of the workplace (Sattler, 2011). Employer and community partners identified similar challenges, with some additional barriers related to managing workload and staffing to enable student supervision; working through educational institution processes and procedures; matching organizational planning cycles with student availability; concerns about student quality; physical workplace limitations; and managing expectations of students, education institutions, employees, and customers/ clients (Sattler, 2011).

While there are significant challenges in successfully implementing work-and-learn options for all stakeholders involved, the opportunities presented allow for high levels of partner satisfaction in spite of the challenges presented. Key work-and-learn stakeholders, such as working learners, educators and employers indicated the following opportunities: better coordination and communication between education and employers; expansion of higher education programs incorporating work-integrated learning components; greater engagement of higher education in applied research; tax credits and financial incentives; increased university commitment to community service learning; revitalization of apprenticeship programs; and the emergence of innovative interdisciplinary work-and-learn models (Jassal & Clark, 2016).

Historically, degrees, grades, and résumés have been the traditional tokens of value or currencies in the workplace, but that is changing. The value of these traditional educational currencies is shifting as the pace of innovation quickens, laying the groundwork for the emergence of new assessments of learning, including micro-credentials, certifications, badges and stealth assessments that capture informal and formal learning blends (Institute for the Future, 2015). In this emerging learning economy, old assumptions are tested and replaced with new ideas and approaches that allow for better synchronization between working, learning and living.

Unbound learning resources are driving continuous growth, opening the future to new possibilities and aspirations for working learners. Blending digital and physical experiences is creating new platforms that make it easier to integrate learning into workflows and is blurring the lines between work, life, and learning. These new platforms allow for continuous actionable feedback that helps us adapt and shape our environments to our personal needs, passions, and life circumstances. The integration of these new technological resources, platforms and programs is fueling a continuous cycle of future learning and earning realities that will require new measurement approaches and unconventional thinking about how we evaluate educational outcomes, measure workplace success, and ensure life satisfaction.

## Notes

1 For a summary of the literature on working college students from a higher education perspective, see Perna (2010).
2 For exceptions see Carnevale et al. (2015) pp. 49–59.

## References

Beaudry, P., Green, D. A., & Sand, B. M. (2016). The great reversal in the demand for skill and cognitive tasks. *Journal of Labor Economics*, *34*(S1), S199–S247.

Billet, S. (2009). Realising the educational worth of integrating work experience in higher education. *Studies of Higher Education*, *34*(7), 827–843.

Blanchard Kyte, S. (2017a). *Equity in Working and Learning Among U.S. Adults: Are There Differences in the Opportunities, Supports, and Returns?* ACT Center for Equity in Learning. Iowa City, IA: ACT Inc. Retrieved from http://equityinlearning.act.org/wp-content/uploads/2017/08/EquityInWorkingAndLearning.pdf. Accessed October 12, 2018.

Blanchard Kyte, S. (2017b). *Who Does Work Work for? Understanding Equity in Working Learner College and Career Success. ACT Center for Equity in Learning. Iowa City, IA: ACT Inc.* Retrieved from: https://equityinlearning.act.org/wp-content/themes/voltron/img/WhoDoesWorkWorkFor.pdf. Accessed October 12, 2018.

Blanchard, S. (2016). *Getting Ahead, Getting Through, or Getting By? An Examination of the Experiences and Prospects of High School Working Learners.* ACT Foundation. Retrieved from: https://equityinlearning.act.org/wp-content/uploads/2017/07/Getting-Ahead-Through-By-pdf-Sarah-Blanchard.pdf. Accessed October 12, 2018.

Carnevale, A. P., Smith, N., Melton, M., & Price, E. W. (2015). Learning while earning: The new normal. The Georgetown University Center on Education and the Workforce. Retrieved from https://cew.georgetown.edu/wp-content/uploads/Working-Learners-Report.pdf. Accessed October 12, 2018.

Cordell, K. (2017). *The new school.* 5280 Denver's High Mile Magazine. Retrieved from: http://www.5280.com/2017/08/new-school. Accessed October 12, 2018.

Corporate Voices for Working Families. (2012). *A Talent Development Solution: Exploring Business Drivers and Returns in Learn and Earn Partnerships.* http://www.americaspromise.org/resource/talent-development-solution-exploring-business-drivers-and-returns-learn-and-earn. Accessed October 12, 2018.

Higher Education Quality Council of Ontario. (2016). A practical guide for work-integrated learning: Effective practices to enhance the educational quality of structured work experiences offered through colleges and universities. Retrieved from: http://www.heqco.ca/en-ca/Research/ResPub/Pages/A-Practical-Guide-for-Work-integrated-Learning.aspx. Accessed October 12, 2018.

Institute for the Future. (2015). *Learning is Earning in the National Learning Economy.* http://www.iftf.org/fileadmin/user_upload/downloads/learning/IFTF_ACT_LearningIsEarning_ResearchMap.pdf. Accessed October 12, 2018.

International Foundation of Employee Benefit Plans. (2015). *Educational Assistance Benefits: 2015 Survey Results.* https://www.ifebp.org/pdf/educational-assistance-survey-results.pdf. Accessed October 12, 2018.

Jassal, K. P. & Clark, H. (2016). *The New Learning Economy and the Rise of the Working Learner: An Anthology of Recent Evidence.* ACT Center for Equity and Learning and ACT Foundation.: https://pages2.act.org/riseofworkinglearners.html. Accessed October 12, 2018.

LeFebvre, M. (2016). *Work/Learning Balance: Is it Possible for Students?* Paper presented at the annual meeting of the American Educational Research Association, Washington, DC.

Lumina Foundation. (2016). *Talent Investments Pay Off: Cigna Realizes Return on Investment from Tuition Benefits.* Retrieved from https://www.luminafoundation.org/files/resources/talent-investments-pay-off-cigna-full.pdf. Accessed October 12, 2018.

Lundvall, B. (2004). *Why the New Economy is a Learning Economy*. DRUID Working Paper No. 04–01 See: https://ideas.repec.org/p/aal/abbswp/04-01.html. Accessed October 12, 2018.

National Network of Business and Industry Associations. (2015). *Work-and-learn in Action: Successful Strategies for Employers*. http://www.nationalnetwork.org/wp-content/uploads/2016/10/WALGuidebook_10.25.2016.pdf. Accessed October 12, 2018.

Organization for Economic Cooperation and Development. (1996). *The Knowledge-Based Economy*. https://www.oecd.org/sti/sci-tech/1913021.pdf. Accessed October 12, 2018.

Owen, M. S., Kavanagh, P. S., & Dollard, M. F. (2017). An integrated model of work-study conflict and work-study facilitation. *Journal of Career Development*. https://doi.org/10.1177/0894845317720071

Perna, W. L. (Ed.) (2010). *Understanding the working college student: New research and its implications for policy and practice*. Sterling, VA: Stylus Publishing.

Pew Research Center. The state of American jobs. Washington, DC: Pew Research Center. 2016. Retrieved from http://assets.pewresearch.org/wp-content/uploads/sites/3/2016/10/ST_2016.10.06_Future-of-Work_FINAL4.pdf. Accessed October 12, 2018.

Phelan, F., & Peters, R. (2016). *Hiring practices and working learner success in the learning economy*. Herndon, VA: ACT Foundation. Retrieved from http://actfdn.org/actionable-research/hiring-practices-working-learner-success-learning-economy. Accessed October 12, 2018.

Randstad. (2016). *Workplace 2025: Embracing disruption in a post-digital world*. Retrieved from: http://experts.randstadusa.com/future-of-work-workplace-2025. Accessed October 12, 2018.

Riggert, C. S., Ash, D., Boyle, M. A., Kinney, J., Howarth, D. A., & Rudy-Parkins, C. (2004). Metropolitan college: Building community value through education–business partnerships. *Innovative Higher Education*, *29*(1), 7–19.

Sattler, P. (2011). *Work-integrated learning in Ontario's postsecondary sector*. Toronto, Canada: Higher Education Quality Council of Ontario.

Schneider, B., & Stevenson, D. (1999). *The ambitious generation: America's teenagers, motivated but directionless*. New Haven, CT: Yale University Press.

Soares, L. & L. W. Perna. (2014). Readiness for the learning economy: Insights from OECD's survey of adult skills on workforce readiness and preparation. http://www.acenet.edu/news-room/Documents/Readiness-for-the-Learning-Economy.pdf. Accessed October 12, 2018.

Society for Human Resource Management. (2013). *2013 Employee Benefits: An Overview of Employee Benefits Offerings in the U.S.* https://www.shrm.org/hr-today/news/hr-magazine/Documents/13-0245%202013_empbenefits_fnl.pdf. Accessed October 12, 2018.

U.S. Government Publishing Office. (2017). Title 34: Education, Part 675 – Federal Work-Study Programs, Subpart C – Work-Colleges Program. Retrieved from: https://www.ecfr.gov/cgi-bin/retrieveECFR?gp=andSID=19510d2314b346907b450a1ad4c7244fandmc=trueandn=sp34.3.675.candr=SUBPARTandty=HTML. Accessed October 12, 2018.

Van Noy, M. (2016). *Reconceptualizing learning: A brief on informal learning.* Herndon, VA: ACT Foundation. Retrieved from https://smlr.rutgers.edu/sites/default/files/images/Research_Documents/informal-learning_final.pdf. Accessed October 12, 2018.

Work College Consortium. (2011). *Understanding and measuring success of work college graduates.* Retrieved from: http://www.workcolleges.org/professionals/research. Accessed October 12, 2018.

# 5

# Inclusive Education and Work-Based Learning – Managing a Process of Change

## The Arguments of Jennifer Todd, Thomas and Loxley

*Elda Nikolou-Walker*

*Middlesex University*

This chapter discusses the concept of inclusive education. In order to do this, two main authors in this area of work are examined: Jennifer Todd ("post-structuralist" theory), and Thomas and Loxley. All three scholars are proposing that inclusive education needs to progress, arguing that a radical assessment of both *theory* and *practice* is now feasible. This process is illustrated through a Work-Based Learning (WBL) approach – the paper argues that WBL can become a successful tool of delivery for the intimated progress.

This article also compares and contrasts Todd's views with those of Thomas and Loxley and draws relative conclusions as to how these might best fit with special educational needs. Though the research methods adopted by all researchers involved differ, these scholars are fundamentally in agreement regarding a common approach toward inclusive education. Todd places herself, for example, in the center of the research, basing her new theory of *post-structuralism*, as well as other narratives, on her own experience, usually validated by her fellow educational psychologists (using, among other means, "face–face" interviews).

Thomas and Loxley, on the other hand, judging from their, otherwise similar in nature research, seem more remote. Thomas and Loxley's use of "passive" language, "third party" terms, and generic terminology makes this research, some could argue, harder to validate.

Attempts are made to indicate that for inclusive education to be successful it is imperative for the *traditional* roles, usually carried out by individuals representing the various professions (i.e., teachers, psychologists, etc.), as well as parents and children, to *change*. This is not, however, a seamless change, but, instead, one which involves a significant "culture shift," in order to accommodate the revised demands being placed upon the *developing* new roles.

Finally, the paper considers the direction inclusive education is taking and suggests that WBL may be the catalyst to assisting and/or providing a pragmatic method for its implementation, drawing on the possible benefits of WBL, in order to further inclusive education.

*The Wiley Handbook of Global Workplace Learning*, First Edition.
Edited by Vanessa Hammler Kenon and Sunay Vasant Palsole.

## Critical Analysis of J. Todd's "*Post-Structuralist*" Argument

Before examining the developments within inclusive education, it is necessary to commence with an explanation of what special educational needs actually means. This terminology, it is argued, chiefly denotes those children with learning difficulties or disabilities, who present greater challenges to learning when compared with children of their same age. These children, therefore, require additional support, which can come from *within*, or *outside* the school. Like the actual *need* itself, this support may be permanent or temporary, which is the subject of assessment by professionals. This assessment usually determines whether or not the child can be educated in a mainstream school (or requires specialist support from a specialist institution). The debate around inclusive education, it has to be stressed, addresses both approaches with the child at the *center* of the discussion.

Inclusive education, therefore, attracts many interpretations and definitions, one being provided by Allen (1999) as being "about responding to diversity about listening to unfamiliar voices, [about] being open, [about] empowering all members and celebrating 'difference' in dignified ways."

From this perspective, the goal is not to leave anyone *out* of school. Thomas and Loxley also define inclusion as being about "comprehensive education, equality and collective belonging." These scholars, therefore, consider inclusive education as being *more* than integrating children with special educational needs into mainstream schools, or about these needs necessarily emerging from learning difficulties, or disability. It is argued that children who are, for any reason, disadvantaged should not be excluded from mainstream education.

In relation to inclusive education, Todd places the concept of *partnership* at the center of her research. Todd's views on working alongside parents and children are pivotal to successfully moving toward *real* inclusive education. She calls this process, an enabling practice, "an involving one, working alongside parents and children in ways that engage with an agenda for inclusion" (Todd, 2007).

Thomas and Loxley (2007) also believe that inclusion is part of a more complex process (than the one currently in existence), a process which is *more* than how teachers and academics conceptualize the differences.

Today's need for inclusion attempts to involve those children and young people who society has possibly excluded, as they are considered different because they do not conform to societal norms in terms, for example, of "behaviors," "language," "learning," and "beliefs." However, Tawney (1964), through his "social model" for inclusion, suggests that a (truly) civilized society strives to reduce the inequalities that arise from "given" and from its relative organization. The organization of society's institutions, such as schools, should "lighten," in order to reduce those inequalities (that frequently arise from birth or circumstances), rather than exaggerate them.

It is generally accepted that current approaches to teaching are incorporated into a world where *hypothesis testing* is widely used, for example, to solve difficult mathematical or scientific problems. This (scientific) approach, indisputably, justifies an accepted level of objectivity, as solutions to problems usually derive from a formula being developed, in order to prove a corresponding theory; thus, it is *believed* to be achieving an informed outcome.

The latter attaches to this historical scientific rationale a high *authority* and one which, it could be argued, would be difficult to challenge. An earlier approach by Mezirow (1991), though, also considered the need to challenge people's perceptions regarding inclusive education, in order to *change* them and (ultimately) move forward. "...conceptualized transformative learning [can only occur] as development through challenging old assumptions and creating new meanings that are more inclusive, integrating, discriminating and open to alternative points of view" (Mezirow, 1991).

Todd, also, soon became aware that any *new* theory attempting to further inclusive education would have to be "brave." Todd, therefore, developed her "post-structuralist" theory, in order to encounter individual perspectives and acquire the capacity to critically analyze the themes and discourses which underlie the concept in question.

According to Todd, special needs is a fluid concept which grows with people and it is, therefore, desirable for people to govern their own actions in accordance with their circumstances.

Todd considers a partnership approach (professionals, parents, child) to be the key to resolving problems regarding inclusive education. Todd argues that it is through effective discussions between *all* the partners that the children will receive meaningful help to separate themselves from their problems. She identified that such an approach would be crucial to inclusive education and has argued that the process has either been entirely absent, paid "lip service" to, or has been badly managed (Todd, 2000).

Increasing the levels of communication between the parent, child and professionals, Todd believes, will lead to establishing a revised set of accepted norms. Both the individual, and family, as well as the community, it is then hoped, will equally share these.

Thomas and Loxley (2007) are, some would argue, even more radical in their thinking, as they believe that inclusive education is based upon the fact that similar difficulties (as described by Todd) are constructed out of an *assumption* regarding concepts of for example, "deficit," "weakness," "disturbance" and "vulnerability."

If inclusive education is to be seriously considered it will mean a *change* in the *traditional* roles of those involved, namely the professionals, parents and children. It is accepted that within schools, senior staff are, frequently, trained to undertake, among others, the role of "Inclusion Managers." Duncan observes that "[p]arents, unfortunately, are afforded no such opportunity [of training/retraining] and such roles would cause them undue stress" (Duncan, 2003).

The training of senior staff can in itself be viewed in two contrasting ways:

Firstly, it can be seen as holding onto traditional pedagogy. For example, senior staff who carry with them their teaching experience would, perhaps, be capable of molding this new ideology (inclusive education) into the *existing* teaching fabric and possibly justify the current "status quo." Secondly, though, (and perhaps more akin to "Change Management"), would be the attempt to convert individuals who are negatively pre-disposed. Once these senior staff, it could be argued, have been convinced of the merits and benefits that inclusive education brings, they can expound such advantages, in order to significantly increase the pace for introducing, and/or furthering inclusion, within their individual schools.

The use of senior staff may also help with what Armstrong, Galloway, and Tomlinson (1993) term as the "deferment of responsibility." Senior staff, inevitably, create their own reputation over their working years. Thus, any disability exhibited by a child can be attributed to *other* causes, as opposed to a teacher's (possible) failings. For instance, "the deferring of responsibility from the teacher to other causes accommodates the teachers' own integrity and reputation, as they [teachers] can redefine their roles in terms of skills associated with teaching 'normal' children." Newly appointed teachers, however, could have a much harder job with such deferments. Securing the teachers' "buy-in," could contribute to the "shift from treating it [special education] as [a] marginal and problematic aspect of the state-maintained schooling, to a more central component in the wider 'inclusion' project" (DfES, 2001).

It has been argued that starting to give the parent and the child a "voice," resulted in the breakdown of the traditional model of "teacher–psychologist" partnership which, however, produced a "teacher-led" solution. Indeed, Morgan (2000) also argued that "for inclusive education to take place professionals should adopt practices that help people develop their own preferred identities."

Todd acknowledges that her research showed that some professionals view themselves as actual representatives of the parent and/or child. This, it is claimed can result in the professional views being considered, but not necessarily being assimilated to the opinions or choices that the parent or child *may* consider important. Thomas and Loxley (2007) also agree with seeking the views of children, as their "freshness and common sense in these suggestions derive in large measures from the fact that they are uncluttered by the constructs, dreams and jargon of the professional educators."

Psychologists also appear to be aware of the need to increase the involvement of the child and have developed many tools and methods to do this (Hobbs, Taylor, & Todd, 2000). It has been argued that any lack of involvement for the child can disengage him/her from the process of finding a solution for his/her inclusion. In that case, therefore, the solution will be the one which the teacher, or psychologist(s) considers the best fit. However, it can also be argued, that the latter perspective has helped, until now, to shift the element of blame, (problem), from the "child," to, possibly, other causes (i.e., the "school," "family," "community," "culture," etc.).

Thomas and Loxley (2007) considered inclusion to be much more problematic as they argue that "it cannot be effected simply on the basis of the way that teachers and academics conceptualize difference: it is part of a complex picture."

Todd's "post-structuralist" theory removes the need for professionals to give a "child" or "young person," a label, which best identifies them because of the nature of their disability. Todd suggests that facilitating scrutiny of both "language" and "processes" (which have been constructed around the disabled child), would help the consideration of whether these actually *help* or *hinder* that child. These can then be deconstructed, as Parker (1999) also stated, in a process of critical reading and unraveling of "loaded" terms, that construct *how* we "read" our place in culture, "relationships" and *how* we think about who we are and what it might be *possible* for us to be. This deconstruction of terms and language used, supported by Todd's collaborative approach, has resulted in a change of emphasis from the "need" for a child to get an education, to a "right" for a child to receive an education.

The latter point was also supported by Article 2 of the "European Convention for Human Rights," which concerned the "Right to an Education." This has subsequently, been incorporated into the UK (within the "Bill of Rights"). All of these legislative requirements, although not yet primary legislation within the UK, further the inclusion education approach by highlighting the need to embrace *diversity*. However, this intention has, some could argue, "fallen short" of protecting the "vulnerable" (i.e., those with special education needs), as it has failed to find its way into current education law.

It has also been argued that a successful method of aiding inclusive education is the use of "multiagency" working. This involves the partnering of various organizations working together, in the interest of the child. With regards to special educational needs, a typical composition of a "multiagency" team would be, for example, an "educational psychologist," an "occupational therapist" and a "speech and language therapist." This composition of the team is, usually, convened when the teacher identifies that a "child" or "young person" is underperforming.

Some scholars have argued (Thomas & Loxley, 2007; Todd, 2007) that a possible danger of this process is the inherent understanding that the child has already been labeled; therefore, the team sets about introducing both the *objectivity* and *rationale* needed, in order to decide if a problem actually exists and the "label" is an *appropriate* one. Todd (2007), argues that these "multi-professional assessments can be seen as combining rationality, objectivity, bureaucracy, and control into 'totalising identities.'" Watson also illustrated this (as early as in 1999), by arguing that "the label may become the child's identity whereby everything related to the child being explained by their impairment" (Watson et al., 1999).

"Multiagency" teams, therefore, can also lead to actual exclusion for the child who is being assessed. The parents are usually invited to the school to discuss (or be informed about) what intervention the school believes will serve the child's best interest. The exclusion, it has been argued, emanates from removing the child from its normal classroom activity for assessments, away from its peers and inviting the parents to the school, outside the normal "parent–teacher" meeting schedules. Questions are frequently encouraged from those who are not afforded the same attention.

Corker and Davis (2002) have claimed that "disabled children and their parents become the objects of scrutiny and separation from the moment the impairment is identified, and identification leads to separation in terms of policy and practice, irrespective of grand claims of inclusion." Thomas and Loxley (2007), also agree that the aforementioned approach could be counterproductive to the problems it was trying to remedy. As these authors reveal, "These kinds of feature [sic], with assumptions of deficit and all attendance paraphernalia of special pedagogy and its 'remedial' and segregative methods, exaggerate existing difference."

Developments around inclusive education are indeed continuing. It is important, as Todd claims, to move away from the "problems." Instead, people have to be viewed as part of a "*system*." The consultation document "Every School is a Good School: The Way Forward for Special Education Needs (SEN) and Inclusion," has in itself been criticized, as there is a strong belief that its structure lends itself more to the re-packaging of the historical approach, rather than a fundamental re-visioning of special needs education and inclusion, for example, within Northern Ireland (Smith, 2010). Allen and Slee (2009) are also in agreement, claiming that "attempts are made to get behind the meaning of the word, [though] little real substance, and/or confusion is found."

The document also interchanges the words "integration" and "inclusion": "integration" seems to be concerned with ensuring that children with "special needs" are placed in mainstream schools alongside other children without these needs, whereas "inclusion" is presented as the process of the assimilation of children with "learning difficulties," "sensory impairments," or "physical disabilities" to mainstream schools. This definition also has its critics as the terminology of "special needs" can also have its limitations- in this case, it frequently continues to involve a concept which excludes *any* child, for *any* reason, from mainstream schooling. This, in the past, resulted in Warnock (DES, 1978) redefining "special needs," as a move away from "labelling," or "categorizing" the children, into a more accepted approach to define "child's needs, as and when they arose" (DES, 1978).

The document itself, it can be argued, still revolves around the language of "barriers to learning," or "child's difficulties." This, when compared with Armstrong's "deferment theory," still puts the onus of *blame* on the child rather than considering the education system as an entity (i.e., "school," "education professionals," "environment," etc.)

The document, though, considers a school improvement policy and a wider education reform for those who "support, govern, inspect and work in schools," but there is still no mention of those who *use* the schools (i.e., the children).

The entire premise for these improvements seems to center around resources and the suitability for the planned improvements. However, very early in the document the DE sets out that, "the Department is also reviewing its funding allocation policy for schools." Is this, possibly, demonstrating that the DE is merely committed to providing a framework for these improvements, but will (inevitably?) leave it up to individual schools to "action" this framework? Would, perhaps, a more committed approach from the DE, be to have indicated a suitable budget which schools can "tap into," as they develop their inclusive projects?

Inclusion is argued to be placing the child's *needs* at the center. With that in mind, as a key principle, it could possibly be argued that this document contradicts itself regarding this central role: though it refers to the "absolute centrality of the role of the classroom or subject teacher," it also refers to "the interests of the pupils rather than the institutions" as having to be at "the centre of efforts." Is the latter conforming to the ideology of inclusion, whereas the former isolates this single entity from the systematic improvement required?

The document, however, has harnessed Todd's (2007) "activity" approach, as it intends to involve all stakeholders, "the improvement process is a collaborative one, requiring communication and co-operation within the school and between the school and its parents and wider community that it serves"(Todd, 2007). However, there is little mention of how this will be catered for and/or specifically what finances will be available to implement this, due to the *changing roles* of all involved.

The document recognized that educational law does not bestow legal responsibilities on the strategic decision-makers. Is it, therefore failing to grasp this opportunity to rectify this and assign such roles and responsibilities in its improvement policy which the legislation fails to provide?

A reader might also argue that the document uses statistical information (i.e., "one half," or, "one third"), more as a defensive mechanism of the educational system, as opposed to deriving real learning from its mistakes. Is the presentation of current performances somewhat "masked" by passive terminology (i.e., "generally good," or "not good enough," etc.)? Perhaps these terms would be more meaningful if actual numbers were used and the reader could ascertain what the current levels or standards of inclusion are, and what, if any, improvements are achieved through this approach?

## Discussion of the Implications of Inclusive Education for Work-Based Learning in Higher Education Institutions

It is argued that inclusive education can be effectively implemented through a WBL approach, as opposed to *mainstream* studying. The structure of WBL programs, arguably, places the student at the center of learning, while the teacher provides the guidance and direction required to achieve the desired outcomes. This is one of the ways then, that the teaching becomes both "learner-centred and experience-led." (Boud & Solomon, 2001).

Also, a WBL program usually includes (from the beginning of the learning), the crucial partnering and/or collaboration, which is an absolute requirement for all-inclusive education programs. Both the pace of this learning and the pressures surrounding the learner can, usually, be facilitated, in order to ensure that learning continues.

Costley (2006) stated that the issues around quality assurance regarding inclusion and management of the barriers to learning can, indeed, be delivered through three main elements: Costley talks of "descriptors" as general statements defining what each module, or subject, entails. It is reckoned that the language, or conveyance of these details can be in a format best suited for the learner to understand; while "learning outcomes" should be agreed with the individual in advance, in order to clarify what are the expectations regarding what it is to be achieved. This process is viewed as particularly important, since it aspires to provide the learner with a "picture" for the learning journey; in other words, what the learner will be capable of achieving after the subject has been covered. Finally, Costley talks about the "assessment criteria" as being elements through which the individual declares commitment and discovers, long in advance of the critical "testing" time, the ways in which he/she will be assessed, in order to ensure that the actual learning has taken place.

In general, within main school pedagogy, children only have certain landmarks in their minds with regards to their testing (i.e., how much they have learned). Typically, these are Key Stage tests (i.e.,: "11+"and/or "P7 Transfer tests," etc.) where a child's *only* choice in the latter, is to possibly "opt out." With WBL, the involvement of the learner from the onset can help deal with these stages more effectively, as the lead-in period would, arguably, be more guarded.

A WBL approach would support inclusive education programs, as it could be argued that it can effectively cater for stakeholder partnerships, such as those made-up from a selection from, or all of, the "teacher–child–parent–professional" network. This collaboration is also hoped to be effective in reducing any resistance to change; thus, increasing the *ownership* of important decisions made to solve difficult problems. This *ownership* is intended to be "spread across" each distinct party involved; thus avoiding the element of "blame" being afforded to just one person- the language is transferred to "situations," as opposed to "people."

Arguably, the aforementioned process can be demonstrated throughout a WBL program, where the "content," "teaching methods," "attendance patterns" and the actual "assessment processes," are previously *discussed* and *agreed.* It is then hoped that all can have a "voice" which can lead to steer the learning process to ensure that everybody's objectives are fulfilled. The issue of removing a child from the peers for the purposes of assessment can also be subtly managed through WBL. WBL requires interaction on a one-on-one basis, whereby the tutor guides the student individually, to achieve the relevant "learning outcomes."

This is, generally, accepted as the usual norm for studying. This approach can ensure that any barriers to learning are accommodated and confidentiality is usually retained between the individual concerned and the teacher; though it has also been argued that it is *exactly* because of these inherent elements of "secrecy," that there is the possible danger that this approach can, indeed, "mask" difficulties to learning for the individual!

Work-Based Learning and the close relationship between the teacher and the learner can also be used to optimize the opportunity for the individual to share any problems external to the learning which may have an impact on the actual learning process. These can derive from a "cultural," "family," "environmental" context. WBL, however, also facilitates an opportunity for the student to discuss other issues which impact upon their learning that can be, generally, "missed" by a teacher, due to, for example, other classroom activities and inherent distractions, (such as other pupils).

However, WBL methodology, it is argued, has the virtue of avoiding segregation from other students, thus successfully addressing most issues underlying the rationale for inclusion.

If government ministers and policy-makers are resolute in their plight for inclusive education, they should, perhaps, adopt a stance that removes such barriers. A WBL approach would be particularly helpful to mature students who are in full-time employment, but return to study for career and/or personal development purposes.

An analysis of the current education law identifies that the aforementioned group of people can find no protection, or recourse of mistreatment, therein.

Their barriers to learning, however, usually derive from having a "family and children," as well as other commitments linked to adulthood (i.e., full-time employment). The mature students' time should, therefore, be equally divided among all of these priorities.

Also, the need to pay university fees can provide an additional burden for the mature student. These fees, which are usually required as soon as a learning program starts, can significantly limit the training budgets' capacity to accommodate all interested participants, frequently leading to disappointed candidates, purely on a financial (not intellectual) basis.

It is hoped that WBL has eased many of the barriers disadvantaging the mature student. If educational policy-makers, however, want to realize their vision of an all-inclusive education society, then it seems that they will have to make, as a priority, the relevant funds available, in order to support the mature student and ease the additional pressures that education, usually, places on an already strained "family budget"!

## Discussion of the Implications of Inclusive Education for the General Practice of Work-Based Learning

It is argued that WBL makes a major contribution to resolving learning barriers through creating an inclusive educational approach (i.e.,: flexibility/time/structure of classes, one–one tutorials, a close relationship and support from the course leader, etc.). All these elements culminate in a more "student-friendly" product which facilitates the individual's domestic, working and studying life.

Hence, it can be argued that the increased implementation of WBL can, indeed, influence the pace at which inclusive education is developed, (especially for the mature student in full-time employment). WBL accommodates the current changes within the working environment from one that was entirely based in an industrial economy to one that now recognizes the contribution and value that *knowledge* can make to the individual, family, schools, universities, employers, and communities in general. It represents a new paradigm in education but one which continues to evolve as *knowledge* becomes increasingly more valuable.

> Work-Based Learning is situated within the context of a paradigm shift from industrial to knowledge society. The rhetoric of knowledge and work is persuasive and dominant in a developed world. *(Nikolou-Walker, 2008)*

It is believed by some scholars that the concept of inclusive education can be realized through WBL. Its programs are structured upon the premise of learning partnerships. The make-up of these partnerships can be tailored to the individual and consists of various stakeholders (i.e.,: "student," "teacher," "parents," "employers," "universities," "communities," "other agencies," etc.)

In reference to tackling the issues of "integration" and "segregation," a WBL approach has a greater tendency to *mask* the underlying reasons behind the original need to integrate or segregate the learner.

This need for integration, possibly, becomes an issue when *others* are aware of the "difference" (i.e.,: when attention is unnecessarily drawn to the "special need" differentiating the learner from their peers). WBL, it can be argued, also removes the need to segregate the learner from their peers, as all learners follow the same learning pattern and one–one contact with the course tutor becomes the norm. (In these cases, does anyone else need to know or be informed of the "special need," outside of the stakeholders involved in the aforementioned partnerships?)

The structure of WBL programs also facilitates learning as they are usually more flexible than traditional modes of study. (The mature student in employment can then liaise with their employer to secure time off, etc.) The relationship built up between the learner and the tutor can help, with the tutor identifying any other "barriers to learning," which the teacher in a traditional classroom situation may "miss." This is a direct result of the student feeling more comfortable and potentially releasing more information for the tutor to manage, as the WBL program rolls out.

It has also been argued that WBL as a vehicle for implementing inclusive education can cater for both the needs of the education system, as well as those of the learner. The one–one WBL structure, allows the learner to ask and seek additional support without being "labeled" by their peers. This may form one of the barriers of learning for the individual, without however, being readily apparent (i.e., inability to write quickly and take notes during lectures, difficulty in copying from a board, etc.).

The progress of the WBL learner is measured through assessments as opposed to examinations. This removes the pressures from traditional examinations which have a tendency to test what the individual can remember under pressure instead of what the individual is capable of.

It is hoped that the use of WBL can harness and embrace the issue of diversity and deliver the aims and objectives of an inclusive education system. The contribution and effectiveness of WBL remains, however, at the mercy of the firm hold of *traditional* education approaches.

## Conclusion

Inclusive education is less about integrating children with special needs into mainstream schools and more about ensuring that any encounters with barriers to learning experienced by any child are sensitively managed to prevent the child being overtly treated differently from their peers.

The ways that this practice is maintained may call for those in authority to explore *new* arrangements for schooling and learn the lessons of alternative approaches to education which have, already, been demonstrated to have a positive contribution to make in progressing inclusive education initiatives.

These new ways must safeguard the child's integrity and gain their involvement on what affects them. Their parents, too, must be supported and involved to ensure the decisions being made, regarding the child's education, are ones which the child has contributed to, and not ones which only teachers, and professionals think would be best fitted to them.

Todd (2003) has also considered the use of "Parent Partnership Schemes" (PPS). These were set up in local authorities to train independent parents whose children had been identified as having special needs. However, there is little evidence of widespread take-up for these (Duncan, 2003). Todd (2003), had, indeed, her reservations regarding PPS, as she felt that they were further removing parents from the *real* center of decision-making.

Work-based learning has become a helpful way of learning, supported generally by both government and employers/employees. It can therefore, assist those students who have *other* barriers to learning (i.e.,: "family commitments," "challenges with personal finances," etc.), as WBL claims to be addressing the aforementioned "disruptions" to learning.

Is there an inherent danger in what Robbins famously referred to as "if you always do what you have always done, you will always get what you have always got!"? This was reinforced within the inclusive education debate by Sketic (1995) who stated that "rather than resolving the special education problems of the late twentieth century, the inclusion debate will reproduce them in the twenty-first century."

Thus, any change to the current schooling system and the challenges of inclusion will most definitely have to be "brave"; but nonetheless, perhaps if based upon the foundations of the learning and experiences afforded by WBL, (already adopted by some Higher Education Institutions), these will be, ultimately, justified and proved effective.

WBL should not be about a controlled acquisition of predetermined skills, knowledge and working practices. It is rather, hoped that WBL helps to formulate what type of learning should be covered, how the success of such learning can be measured and most importantly, how this process will be developed. Such approaches, it is argued, can help the development of inclusive education and the special needs concept can have the assumption of predictability reduced especially, in relation to the usefulness and impact of the various pedagogical interventions.

## References

Allen, J. (1999). *Actively seeking inclusion: Pupils with special needs in mainstream schools.* Brighton, UK: Falmer Press.

Allen, J., & Slee, R. (2009). *Doing inclusive education research.* Rotterdam, Netherlands: Sense Publishers.

Armstrong, D., Galloway, D., & Tomlinson, S. (1993). The assessment of special education needs and the proletarianisation of professionals. *British Journal of Sociology, 14*(4), 399–408.

Boud, D. J., & Solomon, N. V. (2001). *Work-based learning; a new and higher education.* Buckingham, UK: Society for research into Higher Education and Open University Press.

Costley, C. (2006). Work-based learning: Assessment and evaluation in higher education. *Assessment and Evaluation in Higher Education, 32*(1), 1–9.

Corker, M., & Davis, J. (2002). Portrait of Collum. The disabling of a childhood? In R. Edwards (Ed.), *Children, home and school: Regulation, autonomy or regulation?* (pp. 75–91). London and New York: Routledge/Falmer.

DES (1978). *Department of Education for Northern Ireland. Code of Practice on the Identification and Assessment of Special Educational Needs.* Bangor: DENI.

DfES. (2001). *Inclusive schooling.* London, UK: DfES.

Duncan, N. (2003). Awkward customers? Parents and provision for special educational needs. *Disability and Society, 18*(3), 341–356.

Hobbs, C., Taylor, J., & Todd, L. (2000). Consulting with children and young people. Enabling educational psychologists to work collaboratively with children and young people. *Educational and Child Psychology, 17*(4), 107–115.

Mezirow, J. (1991). *Transformative dimensions of adult learning.* San Francisco, CA: Jossy-Bass.

Morgan, A. (2000). *What is a narrative therapy? An easy-to-read introduction.* Adelaide, Australia: Dulwich Centre Publications.

Nikolou-Walker, E. (2008). *The expanded university: Work-based learning and the economy.* Boston, MA: Pearson Custom Publication.

Parker, I. (1999). Deconstructing psychotherapy. In I. Parker (Ed.), *Deconstructing psychotherapy* (pp. 169–170). London, UK: Sage.

Sketic, T. (1995). *Disability and democracy: Restructuring special education for post-modernity.* New York, NY: Teacher's College Press.

Smith, A. (2010). *The influence of education on conflict and peace building: Background paper prepared for the Education For all Global Monitoring Report 2011, 'The Hidden Crisis: Armed Conflict and Education' Education For All, Global Monitoring Report'.* Paris: UNESCO.

Tawney, R. H. (1964). *Equality.* London, UK: George Allen and Unwin.

Thomas, G., & Loxley, A. (2007). *Deconstructing special education and constructing inclusion* (2nd ed.). Maidenhead, UK: Open University Press.

Todd, E.S, (2000). *The Problematic of Partnership in the Assessment of Education Needs.* Unpublished Ph.D. Thesis, Newcastle University.

Todd, L. (2003). Disability and the restructuring of welfare: *The problem with partnerships with parents. International Journal of Inclusive Education, 7*(3), 281–296.

Todd, L. (2007). *Partnerships for inclusive education: A critical approach to collaborative working.* Abingdon, UK: Routledge Falmer.

Watson, N. Shakespeare, T., Cunningham-Burley, S., Barnes, C., Corker, M., Davis, J., and Priestly, M. (1999). *Life as a Disabled Child. A Qualitative Study of Young People's Experiences and Perspectives.* ESRC Research Programme. Children 5–16: Growing into the Twenty-First Century, Grant. Swindon. ESRC Report.

# 6

# Using an Experiential Learning Model to Design an Assessment Framework for Workplace Learning

*Yaw Owusu-Agyeman*[1] *and Magda Fourie-Malherbe*[2]

[1] *Ghana Technology University College*
[2] *Stellenbosch University*

## Rationale for Assessing Workplace Learning

This chapter focuses on the development of a framework for assessing workplace learning, using experiential learning theory as the basis for the design. Workplace learning has become an important component of the development of the knowledge, skills and attitudes of workers and students in the modern era (Avis, 2010; Evans, Hodkinson, Rainbird, & Unwin, 2006; Jacobs & Park, 2009; Noe, 2008; Tynjälä, 2013), because it serves as the foundation for developing and applying new knowledge in a work environment. Inquiry into workplace learning within a global context can be categorized into micro and macro perspectives (Bauer & Gruber, 2007; Billet, 2004; Gherardi, 2006). Macro perspectives describe how industry and external factors such as a changing market situation, the effect of globalization (Bauer & Gruber, 2007) and technological advancements impact workplace activities and learning. Micro perspectives, on the other hand, explain how employees work and how they are assessed, based on their output and competencies within the work environment, often referred to as communities of practice (Fuller, Hodkinson, Hodkinson, & Unwin, 2005). This study adopts a micro perspective that identifies the relationship between workers and their immediate environment in a workplace setting.

While workers and secondary school graduates obtain advanced qualifications by enrolling in higher education and non-tertiary programs, knowledge and skills are also acquired in the workplace, hence the need for structured assessment criteria of workplace learning. Billet (2004) suggests that the structure of workplace learning should be distinguished from that of formal learning that takes place in an educational setting. As an example, legitimate peripheral participation (Fuller et al., 2005; Lave & Wenger, 1991) can be regarded as a form of situated workplace learning, as it denotes learning opportunities in the workplace by being inducted into communities of practice in order to enable newcomers to become competent individuals and to contribute to the development of the organization.

*The Wiley Handbook of Global Workplace Learning*, First Edition.
Edited by Vanessa Hammler Kenon and Sunay Vasant Palsole.

As the competencies of employees are defined in terms of knowledge, skills and behavior (Bauer & Gruber, 2007; Jacobs & Park, 2009; Tynjälä, 2013), it is important for an assessment system to incorporate all three elements. Furthermore, workplace learning has been conceptualized as consisting of informal learning (Barnett, 1999; Colley, Hodkinson, & Malcolm, 2003; Evans & Rainbird, 2002; Sambrook, 2005), formal learning (Barnett, 1999; Colley et al., 2003; Evans, Hodkinson, and Unwin, 2002; Sambrook, 2005) and non-formal learning (Colley et al., 2003). This study focuses on developing a generic assessment framework that could be used for all types of learning and in all workplace learning settings.

In developing a framework for assessing workplace learning, we argue that the competencies of workers could be assessed by first identifying the knowledge required of them to perform specific tasks, and here we identify the self-concept (Elliott, 2014) as key to enhancing individual and group output. In order to provide a coherent argument in support of a generic assessment framework, we adopt a basic system model which assesses the activities of workers in a learning environment according to input, process, output and impact. We then integrate the model with Kolb's theory of experiential learning (Kolb & Kolb, 2005). Using a social realist approach that defines knowledge as a historical and social entity, we propose a generic assessment framework embedded in experiential learning that incorporates the input, process, output and impact domains of work competencies. In order to optimize the effect of the global assessment framework, we were guided by the following design objectives:

- To develop a comprehensive generic assessment framework that supports workers to blend theoretical knowledge with practical application in the field of work.
- To enhance the application of theoretical knowledge and practical skills of workers, who are also students, by means of structured assessment criteria in the workplace.
- To develop a feedback loop that allows information from assessment procedures to serve as the basis for policy decisions and improvement actions by the management of organizations and educational institutions.

## Theoretical Overview

### Emerging Trends in Global Workplace Learning

In modern organizations globally, workplace learning has evolved to include a conscious process of developing the knowledge and skills of workers through a series of activities aimed at promoting work output, while measuring the progress of employees through a feedback loop. Jacobs and Park (2009, p. 134) define workplace learning as a "process used by individuals when engaged in training programs, education and development courses, or some type of experiential learning activity for the purpose of acquiring the competence necessary to meet current and future work requirements." Although Jacobs and Park (2009) provide a succinct description of what workplace learning is, and integrate the concept of experiential learning in their definition, they do not provide information on how the competencies of these individuals are assessed.

Lave and Wenger (1991) describe two key processes, namely communities of practice and situated learning, as essential in social activities that support group participation and contribution. In conceptualizing the assessment processes in a work environment, we distinguish between the development of the knowledge and skills of existing staff rather than the introduction of new entrants into a working environment and work processes.

Although workplace learning has been in existence for several years, its prominence in the current training and development landscape could be attributed to four main factors: (i) increasing expectations of employers for employees to produce quality output; (ii) exigencies of learning teams as an integral part of organizational learning (Crossan & Berdrow, 2003; Kayes, Kayes, & Kolb, 2005); (iii) the importance of technology as an evolving tool for perfecting output; and (iv) the impact of the work process on organizational goals (Gherardi, 2006). The authors posit that beyond the development of competency frameworks (Garavan & McGuire, 2001) lies the need to assess the performance of workers in organizations through a structured process that is underpinned by theoretical assumptions.

Firstly, the expectations of employers regarding work processes and responsibilities from a global perspective are often based on contractual considerations that call for employees to perform their obligations, while employers also seek to satisfy employees' expectations. Although the role of employees in meeting organizational goals continues to attract attention globally, the evaluation of individual jobs has become even more important because it also comes along with a learning process that needs to be measured.

Several authors (Fuller et al., 2005; Gherardi, 2006; Reedy, King, & Coupland, 2016) have espoused the benefits of developing individual skills and knowledge to promote both group and individual goals within the work environment. We posit that organizational learning (Argote & Miron-Spektor, 2011; Egan, Yang, & Bartlett, 2004; Jiménez-Jiménez & Sanz-Valle, 2011) is an important driver of knowledge acquisition through team effort in the workplace. On the global front, technology continues to alter the workplace environment, primarily because it challenges workers to adapt to evolving techniques used in getting work done at a faster pace and with greater precision. The need for workers to learn the application of new technology and also to have their work activities evaluated, places an even greater responsibility on them to acquire advanced skills in technology application. The authors consider the assessment of work processes that involve technology adaptation as particularly useful in ensuring that workers gain the most from any assessment regime and also use technology effectively.

## Knowledge and Skills Enablers in the Workplace

This chapter considers knowledge and skills acquisition in the workplace as important to the production of quality goods and services. The process domain of learning provides information on empirical, epistemological and conceptual considerations that also define how individuals obtain relevant knowledge and skills in specific fields (Hager, 2004). From a human resource development (HRD) perspective, Mohrman (2003) espouses the term *knowledge work* and suggests that it often involves obtaining information from different sources, applying different methods of using the information to meet specific goals, and developing new ideas and work processes from the information obtained. While the advantages of learning at the workplace have evolved to include the promotion of knowledge and skills acquisition among workers (Eraut, 2004; Gherardi, 2006; Lam, 2000; Webster-Wright, 2009), this study considers the assessment of knowledge and skills acquisition as complementary. The development of knowledge in a global workplace learning environment could be categorized in two processes: first, as a standardized production process where work is seen as different units with no relation to one another nor to the bigger domain, and second, as a relationship between several parts with little or no relationship with the whole (Gamble, 2006). Workplace learning could be described as a potential source of knowledge (Lam, 2000) and practical skills that transform workers. Beyond the acquisition of skills and knowledge, workplace learning also allows workers to construct their identity (Filliettaz, 2013) through a sustained process that incorporates the organizational structure and culture.

The technical knowledge that is required of employees is defined by Bernstein (1999) as vertical discourse. In the context of workplace learning, vertical discourse explains the structured form of knowledge acquisition that is coherent and clear to the learners. What is very important is that the relationship between the learner and the object of study is defined by the knowledge and skills expectations of employers that are also coded as technical languages. Therefore, vertical discourse – as distinguished from horizontal discourse – suggests that while vertical discourse of knowledge acquisition identifies the depth of knowledge acquisition in the specific technical area, horizontal discourse explains the segments of knowledge that are not only related to the technical aspects of the work processes, but also to other relevant aspects that are necessary in the promotion of work.

### Experiential Learning in the Global Workplace Learning Environment

The rationale for choosing experiential learning as the theoretical underpinning for the development of an assessment framework in a global workplace learning environment emerges from two main factors: first the need to develop new ideas and work processes in daily activities (Ackerman, 1998; Evans et al., 2002; Jacobs & Park, 2009); and, second, the need to reflect on these activities (Bauer & Gruber, 2007; Eyler, 2002) to enable workers to develop relevant knowledge and skills. We discuss experiential learning in the context of our study from two main perspectives, namely the micro environment of workplace learning and the integrated assessment framework.

Jacobs and Park (2009, p. 134) suggest that the structure of workplace learning consists of three key domains: "(a) the location of the learning, (b) the extent of planning that is invested in developing and delivering the learning experiences, and (c) the role of the trainer, facilitator, or others during the learning process." Although these key domains are all aspects of the micro environment of workplace learning, we argue that the assessment of workplace learning rather requires, as a starting point, the critical analysis of these three domains. The purpose of the assessment of workplace learning is to ensure the effectiveness of learning, which will provide workers with the professional development they need to perform their jobs optimally. Noe (2008) suggests that employee development (the various processes and opportunities that ensure that employees achieve their career goals) could be enhanced through an assessment of workplace learning that is supported by a feedback loop.

Experiential learning as the theoretical underpinning focuses attention on two main domains as espoused by Kolb and Kolb (2005): *modes of grasping experience* and *modes of transforming experience* (see Figure 6.1). The modes of grasping experience in the context of global workplace learning and our model involve two key domains: input (abstract conceptualization) and process (active experimentation). On the other hand, we consider the modes of transforming experiences as consisting of the output (concrete experience) and impact (reflective observation) domains. Using the basic system model, we identify the input domain as the first level in the assessment design. Here, workers' qualifications and work experience in the global context are important elements in the assessment design; hence we consider them as contextual factors. We argue that the input factors are necessary for the assessment of workplace learning because they consist of new information that is received by workers and later transformed into work processes.

The input domain therefore provides an explanation of the learner identity (Lave & Wenger, 1991), which is important in assessing the knowledge and skills gathered by the worker over the years through co-participation. The process domain is the second assessment domain, and here we consider active experimentation as key to the application of knowledge and skills by workers in the workplace.

The modes of transforming experience relate to the output and impact domains. While the output domain shows how concrete experiences are necessary

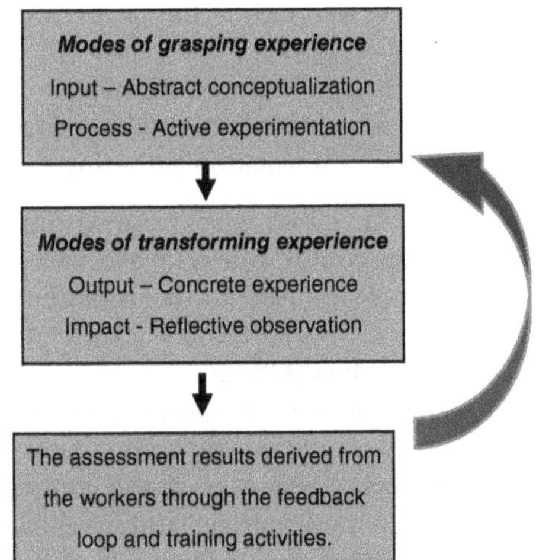


**Figure 6.1** The Generic Assessment Feedback Loop. *Source:* Adapted From Kolb and Kolb (2005) and Jacobs and Park (2009)

in producing goods and providing services, the impact domain explains how reflective observation enables individuals and teams to assess the extent to which their products or services meet the needs of consumers. Again, the modes of grasping experience consist of concrete experience and abstract conceptualization where workers attempt to develop their conceptions of the work processes and the job requirements in order to meet their goals. Another factor worth considering is concrete experience, and this describes the skills of workers that serve as input factors in the learning process.

### Assessment framework

This study adopts the Context–Input–Process–Output–Outcome system model (Carvalho & White, 1996; Scheerens, Glass, & Thomas, 2003) in the development of an assessment framework and integrating the framework with experiential learning theory. Additionally, we argue that the assessment design is relevant to all organizations across different geographical locations, primarily because it influences the information required from both assessors and workers in the trajectory.

The design framework exhibits the system model that can be used to collect detailed information on workers' performance and information that is relevant for general improvement, since an assessment system focuses on giving feedback and direction to the trainee (Fleischer, 2005). It provides information on the input, process, output and outcome measures that are required when assessing the performance of workers in a workplace environment. Based on the design framework and the key components in the framework, the input–process–output–outcome system model was considered in optimizing the knowledge and skills enablers by showing that:

- The assessment framework provides a measure of the most important concepts in the assessment of workers in the workplace setting.
- The assessment framework is validated to incorporate workers' progression toward the desired outcomes and set benchmarks by employers.
- The assessment framework is tested to ensure continuous application over time while also having the propensity to incorporate new approaches in the design.
- The assessment framework allows comparisons to be made over a period between actual appraisal results and feedback on assessments that are informed by coherent information gathering.

Figure 6.2 shows the Context–Input–Process–Output–Outcome system model in the context of workplace learning. Additionally, it provides an overview of the framework used for the assessment design.

### Context indicators of the assessment

The context domain, as shown in Figure 6.2 above, provides information on the working environment that stimulates individual performance through the input–process–output–outcome continuum. The authors refer to the context indicators in the empirical study as the knowledge and skills enablers, depicting the institutional structure and arrangement that support workplace learning.

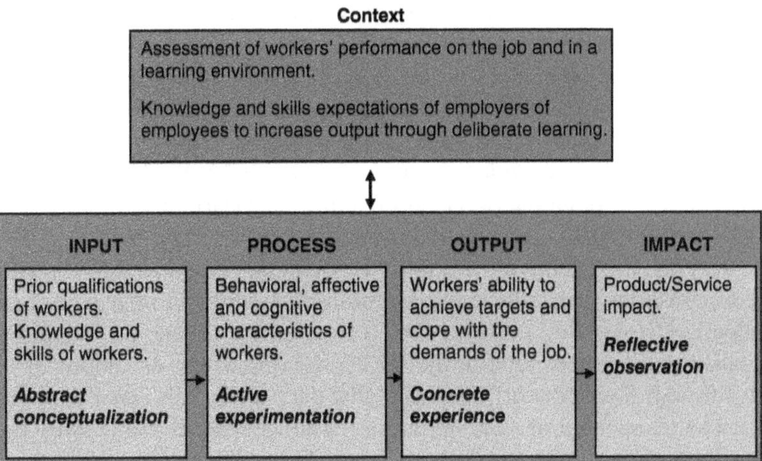


**Figure 6.2** Workplace assessment indicators. *Source:* Adapted From Owusu-Agyeman (2011) and Scheerens et al. (2003)

The workplace assessment context, as shown in Figure 6.2, refers to the characteristics of the institution that are responsible for developing assessment indicators for evaluation by supervisors and managers in job settings. The elements of the context domain consist of the following: assessment of workers' performance on the job, and knowledge and skills expectations of employers to increase output. The performance of workers in workplace learning is often driven by the expectations of management and the organizational culture that supports learning on the job (or not).

### The input indicator

The input indicator provides demographic information of respondents as well as their level of experience and qualifications. Additionally, the input indicator as shown in Figure 6.2 explains the background information that could influence the performance of workers on the job. We posit that the input indicator provides the needed information on workers that is essential for developing their knowledge and skills in order to meet the expectations of employers, while also aiming at increasing their output.

### The process indicator

The process indicator for assessing the performance of workers in the job setting consists of three main variables: the affective, cognitive and behavioral. The **affective variable** is the first element in the domain. It consists of attitudes, feelings and emotions of workers. The key drivers or determinants of the affective variable include: activities that motivate workers to learn and develop their skills on the job; encouraging workers to improve on their output and providing them with regular feedback on their performance; providing workers with opportunities to improve their performance; encouraging workers to be responsible for their decisions and activities; and informing workers of their work expectations and responsibilities.

The second variable in the domain is the **behavioral variable** that is made up of the explicit actions of workers that affect their work output in the organization. The behavioral variable in the context of workplace learning also explains the conduct of workers in the workplace environment that directly affects productivity. Here we identify change in individual response to work processes and requirements as important to the concept of workplace learning and also to the development of the organization as a whole, often referred to as organizational learning (Argote, 2011).

The third variable that is used in the assessment of workers in the process domain of workplace learning is the **cognitive variable.** This variable explains the detailed knowledge and skills that are required of workers to perform their work excellently. Crossan and Berdrow (2003) encapsulate the cognitive abilities of individuals in a workplace environment as consisting of the development of knowledge through a process of "intuiting" that recognizes the experiences of individuals. The assessment of workers in the cognitive domain will identify the knowledge, application, understanding and problem-solving skills of workers that are aimed at improving work processes and output.

### Output Indicators

The output indicators describe how products and services are developed or rendered by workers in the workplace setting. Additionally, output indicators are often seen as the visible results of the application of knowledge and skills by the worker. Importantly, output indicators provide information on how workers' products and services are measured within a defined period.

### Impact Indicators

The outcome or impact indicators refer to the satisfaction derived from using the product or services. In other words, the outcome or impact indicators describe the advantages that users of products or services obtain from the product or services. It is important to note that the impact or outcome indicators are the results of the application of knowledge and skills that are achieved through the production of goods and the provision of services in the job setting. In the context of workplace learning, measurement of the impact or outcome achievement could occur by way of feedback obtained from users of products or services. While specific feedback on the use of a final product can only be provided in terms of feedback from the use of products, measurement of the impact or outcome indicators of individuals who provide services can be done through feedback provided by the beneficiaries of services. The importance of assessment in a workplace environment would be to identify the strengths and weaknesses of workers and to be able to implement processes that allow such workers to develop their knowledge and skills through reward systems and further training.

## Method

In order to establish the relationship between the assessment of workplace learning and the integration of experiential learning, an interpretive paradigm was adopted. The authors relied on an exploratory research design that sought to develop the assessment structure based on the views of workers and management officials from 13 different organizations in Ghana. While the workers were provided with questionnaires to be completed, five management staff members from the 13 organizations who voluntarily obliged to respond to the interview questions provided their perspectives through responding to an unstructured interview schedule.

To establish the relationship between workplace learning and experiential learning by way of an assessment design system, the authors used the Partial Least Square approach to structural equation modeling (PLS-SEM) on SPSS Amos V.21 software. Additionally, the authors reduced the datasets into a smaller number of factors in order to avoid information loss from the large number of data gathered initially.

#### Population and sampling technique

The study population was 1380 staff members from 13 different organizations in Accra, the capital of Ghana. The respondents were drawn from financial institutions, engineering firms, pharmaceutical companies, educational institutions, construction firms and service personnel trading organizations. The researchers adopted a simple random sampling method to select respondents from the 13 organizations. The advantages of the simple random sampling method include: its appropriateness when gathering data from a large population, its representativeness and its acceptability across different fields (Cohen, Manion, & Morrison, 2011; Creswell, 2008; Lindlof, 1995). A sample of 520 workers who had completed either a first degree or a higher national diploma was included in the survey. From the total number of questionnaires distributed, the authors received 379 survey responses. Seven responses were invalid, resulting in 372 valid responses, representing 74.4% of the sample. We performed an analysis of the responses of the 372 valid responses by way of a structural equation model, explained in more detail in the results section of the chapter. We also conducted interviews with five management staff members from five organizations from the same sample, using purposive sampling. Responses of the interviewees are discussed in the Results section.

#### Data Collection

The survey required workers to provide their opinion on the constructs that we developed. All the measures of constructs used by the authors in this chapter were culled from relevant literature on experiential learning (Kolb & Kolb, 2005; Roberts, 2012), workplace learning (Evans et al., 2002; Jacobs & Park, 2009) and the development of individual knowledge and skills (Fuller et al., 2005; Reedy et al., 2016). The survey was categorized into five main sections: biographical information; knowledge and skills enablers; input factors; process factors; output factors, and impact factors. Using a five-point Likert scale that ranged from 1 (strongly agree) to 5 (strongly disagree), the respondents provided their responses on each of the constructs.

The interview schedule, on the other hand, sought to glean from the respondents their perspectives on institutional policies that were designed to support the assessment of workplace learning in their various organizations. Additionally, information regarding the methods of assessing employees through both formal and informal means at the workplace was also gathered. Details of the responses are discussed in the Results section.

### Validity, Reliability, Ethical Consideration and Unidimensionality

Prior to the administration of the questionnaires, a pilot questionnaire was distributed to workers in the education and construction industries, and following the responses we gathered, the questionnaire was re-developed to ensure that workers understood the underlying reason for the study and that the data we sought to gather indeed measured the constructs that we intended them to measure. We undertook the initial survey piloting by gathering the initial data, primarily because we sought to strengthen the construct validity of the datasets which could affect the findings of our study (Chmiliar, 2010; Cohen et al., 2011; Creswell, 2008). Additionally, we avoided biases by providing instructions to respondents during the administration of questionnaires, and by ensuring that we presented reliable data in the compilation of datasets as well as in the analysis of datasets (Chmiliar, 2010; Lindlof, 1995). The importance of reliability of scales and unidimensionality has been espoused by Anderson and Gerbing (1982) as necessary to develop convergent and discriminant validity. In order to measure the validity and reliability of the constructs in the workplace learning assessment framework, an analysis of the latent variable was computed. The unidimensionality, on the other hand, was developed to show the degree to which the items in the various scales on the workplace assessment framework provide meaning to the constructs by way of values.

#### Research hypothesis

In order to espouse the underlying features of workplace learning, using an experiential learning based assessment design, the following research hypotheses were developed to guide the study:

$H_1$: Knowledge and skills enablers for the assessment of workplace learning are positively influenced by abstract conceptualization (input factors).
$H_2$: Knowledge and skills enablers for the assessment of workplace learning are positively influenced by active experimentation (process factors).
$H_3$: Knowledge and skills enablers for the assessment of workplace learning are positively influenced by concrete experience (output factors).
$H_4$: Knowledge and skills enablers for the assessment of workplace learning are positively influenced by reflective observation (impact factors).

## Results

We analyzed the data we gathered through the Partial Least Square approach to structural equation modeling (PLS-SEM) by way of SPSS Amos V.21 software. Kock (2013) argues that PLS-SEM accommodates the operationalization of a hierarchical model by way of incessant application of manifest variables. What this means is that, in computing the PLS-SEM, one does not necessarily have to compute for multivariate normality, since the approach makes room for modeling with small sample sizes (Henseler, Ringle, & Sinkovics, 2009).

**Measurement of Hierarchical Structure Using PLS**

The authors performed a series of principal component analyses (PCA) to assess the uniqueness and relationship between the variables, whereas the measurement model for the theoretical structure was computed to demonstrate the validity and reliability of the factors (Chin, 1998; Hair, Hult, Ringle, & Sarstedt, 2013). The variables used for the study were: KSE (Knowledge and Skills Enablers), INPU (Input factors/ abstract conceptualization); PROC (Process factors/ active experimentation); OUTP (Output factors/ concrete experience) and IMPA (Impact factors/ reflective observation). We thereafter tested the hypothesized causal relationships among theoretical constructs to reveal the key factors that were considered necessary in developing an assessment model using experiential learning as the theoretical underpinning.

Table 6.1 shows the correlation between the constructs with the AVE, CR and Cronbach's alpha. The mean scores and the standard deviation revealed high mean value for IMPA (M = 4.29, SD = 0.46), as compared to INPU (M = 4.07, SD = 0.47), which demonstrated the least mean values. Table 6.1 also provides information on the strength of association between the five variables. We observed a statistically significant relationship between all five constructs. Conspicuously, INPU and PROC ($r = 0.72$, $p < 0.01$) revealed the highest correlation, while KSE and OUTP ($r = 0.49$, $p < 0.01$) demonstrated the least correlation, albeit at an acceptable value. The correlation between INPU and PROC, however, suggested that respondents who identified the knowledge and skills enablers in the assessment of workplace learning as important, also considered active experimentation as essential in assessing the knowledge and skills of workers. In expounding this phenomenon, we noted that only 52% ($R^2 = 0.52$) of the variance is explained by the relationship between the two constructs. The study also

**Table 6.1** Correlation among the constructs showing the mean, STDEV, AVE, CR and α

| | Mean | STDEV | CR | α | KSE | INPU | PROC | OUTP | IMPA |
|---|---|---|---|---|---|---|---|---|---|
| KSE | 4.23 | 0.57 | 0.85 | 0.84 | **0.66** | | | | |
| INPU | 4.07 | 0.47 | 0.78 | 0.73 | 0.52 | **0.58** | | | |
| PROC | 4.16 | 0.47 | 0.82 | 0.82 | 0.51 | 0.72 | **0.68** | | |
| OUTP | 4.16 | 0.48 | 0.79 | 0.81 | 0.49 | 0.52 | 0.6 | **0.61** | |
| IMPA | 4.29 | 0.46 | 0.78 | 0.77 | 0.51 | 0.56 | 0.64 | 0.59 | **0.58** |

All correlations are significant at the $p < 0.01$ level.
STDEV – Standard deviation.
CR – Cronbach's alpha.
α – Composite reliability.
AVE – Average Variance Extracted.
*Note:* Diagonal elements in bold are the square roots of AVE.

revealed a significant relationship between PROC and IMPA ($r = 0.64$, $p < 0.01$), therefore demonstrating that 41% ($R^2 = 0.41$) of the variance in active experimentation could be explained by salient factors in reflective observation within the assessment framework.

The authors proceeded to compute the reliability test for each construct, the convergent validity and the discriminant validity of the workplace learning assessment indicators (Gefen, Straub, & Boudreau, 2000). Additionally, the reliability of each individual item was measured by evaluating the assessment hierarchical structure to support the measurement model. The reliability and validity of the lower-order constructs were first evaluated by analyzing the factorial loading, composite reliability (CR) and Average Variance Extracted (AVE) (Chin, 1998; Hair et al., 2013). The rule regarding the confirmation of convergent validity suggests that the variance of the average variables extracted (AVE) should not be above 0 > .50 (Fornell & Larcker, 1981). Additionally, all the composite reliability indicators as well as $\alpha$ present strong framing with values above the required threshold of 0.7 (CR= > 0.782, $\alpha$= > 0.728). In order to determine the convergent validity, the AVE was computed and this revealed the least value as 0.782. The variance explained in the model was more than those that could not be explained among the variables associated with the constructs (Fornell & Larcker, 1981).

Next, the Cronbach's alpha ($\alpha$) and composite reliability were derived, with each of the constructs scaled against the recommended threshold values of the reliability. The reliability coefficient often termed as Cronbach's alpha (Cronbach, 1951) was used to test the reliability of the scale with values that were 0.70 or greater than 0.70, and these were deemed to be showing good-scale reliability (Cohen et al., 2011; O'Leary-Kelly & Vokurka, 1998). We show that all the variables that support the development of workplace learning revealed a high reliability value that was close to 1, based on the alpha coefficient value range between 0 and 1.

The rule of thumb regarding composite reliability was observed, primarily by ensuring that the individual constructs showed composite reliability that was equal to or greater than the acceptable minimum level of 0.70 (Hair et al., 2013; Nunnally & Bernstein, 1994) which shows satisfactory reliability. We proceeded to compare the square root of the AVEs to confirm whether the discriminant validity actually exceeded the correlations between the various constructs in the workplace assessment structure.

### Kaiser–Mayer–Olkin (KMO) and Bartlett's test

The strength of association among the workplace learning assessment variables was derived through the computation of Principal Component Analysis (PCA), while the process also ensured that the principal factors associated with the 34 items within the construct were computed. We measured the construct validity of our datasets using Bartlett's Test of Sphericity as well as the Kaiser–Mayer–Olkin (KMO) method. In order to obtain relevant data to carry out further assessment, the KMO was also used to detect multi-collinearity issues that were observed in the model, and this process ensured that all insignificant variables found in the model were obliterated. We again computed the KMO from a range of 0 to 1 with values between 0.6 and 1, representing strong figures that were

**Table 6.2** KMO and Bartlett's Test

| | | |
|---|---|---|
| Keiser-Meyer-Okin measure of sampling adequacy | | .547 |
| | Approx. chi-square | 13012.85 |
| Bartlett's Test of Sphericity | Df | 561 |
| | Sig. | .000 |

relevant for performing factor analysis. We did not use values that fell below the required KMO threshold of 0.6. Table 6.2 shows that the values obtained support the model's aptness for factor analysis, with results for the Bartlett's test of Sphericity and KMO revealing highly significant values. Additionally, the analysis was carried out on eigenvalues that showed all 34 factors. Hair et al. (2013) posit that variables with loadings that are higher than .30 are significant; loadings of value greater than .40 are more important; loadings that are greater than .50 are very significant.

The correlation matrix as shown in Table 6.1 suggests that each of the variables (knowledge and skills enablers, input indicators, process indicators, output indicators and impact factors) has a significant relationship with the workplace learning assessment framework. Seeing that the values shown in Table 6.1 demonstrated a sturdy association among the various constructs, we proceeded to conduct further tests on the model fit by way of a rotated component matrix.

The values shown in Table 6.3 indicate a strong affiliation of items to a factor, while factors with higher loadings were expounded as abstaining a higher affiliation between an item and a specific factor. We posit that each factor in the analysis shows strong relationships with the items in the workplace assessment construct. The model in this study thus proposes general criteria of acceptance for items with loadings of 0.60 and greater (see Table 6.3). Values that were less than 0.60 were not included in the table.

### The model fit

To provide credence to the model by way of unidimensionality in the five workplace assessment factors developed, we used Confirmatory Factor Analysis (CFA) to further explain the consistency of the measures of construct and the workplace learning assessment model proposition. The computation of the CFA was, however, preceded by the piloting of each workplace learning assessment construct in the model. In approximating the CFA models, we adopted the maximum likelihood estimation while using other gauges such as the Adjusted Goodness-of-Fit Index (AGFI), the Root Mean square Residual (RMR), Comparative Fit Index (CFI), and Goodness-of-Fit Index (GFI). A summary of the CFI, RMR, GFI and AGFI tests has been provided in Table 6.4. The CFI values are all close to 1 and therefore display Goodness-of-Fit Model (Bentler, 1992; Raykov & Marcoulides, 2000). The results of the Model Fit, as shown in Table 6.4, represent a good model with high values of CFI attained, ranging from .91 to .98.

We explicate our earlier argument that the Goodness-of-Fit Index displays the proportion of the variance in the sample covariance matrix that is accounted for by the model (see Table 6.4). Therefore, when the value exceeds 0.9, it specifies a

**Table 6.3** Rotated component matrix[a]

| Descriptors | Items | F1 | F2 | F3 | F4 | F5 |
|---|---|---|---|---|---|---|
| *Knowledge and skills enablers* | | | | | | |
| Motivation to acquire practical knowledge and skills | KSE1 | | | | | 0.60 |
| The exigencies of self-discipline in knowledge acquisition | KSE2 | | | | | 0.61 |
| The exigencies of punctuality in knowledge acquisition | KSE3 | | | | | 0.68 |
| The importance of team work in knowledge acquisition | KSE4 | | | | | 0.67 |
| Openness to suggestions and correction in learning | KSE5 | | | | | 0.66 |
| Ability to control emotion in the learning process | KSE6 | | | | | |
| Impact of good relationship with superiors and peers | KSE7 | | | | | 0.61 |
| *Input indicators* | | | | | | |
| Prior knowledge of work processes | INPU1 | | 0.66 | | | |
| Importance of critical thinking in the learning process | INPU2 | | 0.64 | | | |
| Importance of problem solving skills in workplace learning | INPU3 | | 0.60 | | | |
| Experience in work processes as essential tool in workplace learning | INPU4 | | 0.72 | | | |
| Familiarity with the organization's core operations | INPU5 | | | | | |
| Age as an important factor in workplace learning | INPU6 | | 0.63 | | | |
| Academic qualification as an important factor in workplace learning | INPU7 | | 0.72 | | | |
| Adherence to rules and regulations as essential to workplace learning | INPU8 | | 0.61 | | | |
| The importance of leadership qualities in workplace learning | INPU9 | | 0.61 | | | |
| *Process indicators* | | | | | | |
| Ability to work both independently and in a team | PROC1 | | | | 0.65 | |
| The importance of continuous practice | PROC2 | | | | 0.61 | |
| The exigencies of effective supervision on workplace learning | PROC3 | | | | | |
| Initiative, motivation and desire to obtain knowledge and skills | PROC4 | | | | | |
| Conducive workplace environment as essential to learning | PROC5 | | | | 0.64 | |

**Table 6.3** (Continued)

| Descriptors | Items | F1 | F2 | F3 | F4 | F5 |
|---|---|---|---|---|---|---|
| Feedback systems and its importance to workplace learning | PROC6 | | | | 0.66 | |
| *Output indicators* | | | | | | |
| Individual ability to assess work at the workplace periodically | OUTP1 | | | 0.62 | | |
| Assessment feedback on workers output by supervisors | OUTP2 | | | 0.73 | | |
| Comparing actual worker output against standards set | OUTP3 | | | 0.77 | | |
| The effect of knowledge and skills acquisition on output | OUTP4 | | | | | |
| The impact of workplace learning on workers' personal development | OUTP5 | | | 0.79 | | |
| Relationship between workplace learning and output | OUTP6 | | | 0.82 | | |
| *Impact indicator* | | | | | | |
| Ability to demonstrate initiative and resourcefulness in job roles | IMPA1 | 0.61 | | | | |
| Adequate willingness to learn other tasks to meet group goals | IMPA2 | 0.72 | | | | |
| Exercising sound judgment in decision-making | IMPA3 | 0.80 | | | | |
| Responding positively to constructive criticism that arises | IMPA4 | 0.60 | | | | |
| The relevance of continuous learning cycle at the workplace | IMPA5 | 0.76 | | | | |
| The importance of peer monitoring and advising | IMPA6 | 0.63 | | | | |

Extraction method: Principal Component Analysis.
Rotation method: Varimax with Kaiser Normalization. Loadings that are 0.60 or less are not shown.
[a] Rotation converged in 14 iterations.

**Table 6.4** The results of model fit

| Factor Indicator | P value | GFI | AGFI | CFI | RMR |
|---|---|---|---|---|---|
| Knowledge and skills enablers | 0.001 | 0.907 | 0.902 | 0.906 | 0.01 |
| Input indicators | 0.001 | 0.932 | 0.928 | 0.926 | 0.04 |
| Process indicators | 0.001 | 0.987 | 0.921 | 0.978 | 0.02 |
| Output indicators | 0.001 | 0.968 | 0.962 | 0.95 | 0.04 |
| Impact indicator | 0.005 | 0.954 | 0.95 | 0.95 | 0.03 |

good model. The Adjusted Goodness-of-Fit Index (AGFI) is an alternate index to the GFI which has the value of its index adjusted for the given number of parameters within the model (all are above 0.9), as shown in Table 6.4.

## Hypotheses Testing

The structural equation model as shown in Figure 6.3 specifies a good fit, as the workplace learning assessment model's probability, the p value, in this study was supposed to be less than 0.05 for a good fit sign (Hair et al., 2010).

We show in Figure 6.3 that the model has an $R^2$ of 0.63 for knowledge and skills enablers, and this signified that 63% of the variance connected with KSE was accounted for by the four remaining predictor variables: input factors, process factors, output factors and impact indicators.

Table 6.5 shows the results of the hypothesis testing with the values for Critical Ratio (CR), path coefficients, p value and the empirical conclusion. Importantly, all four paths hypothesized in the model were significant at $p < .01$. $H_1$: Knowledge and Skills Enablers (KSE) for the assessment of workplace learning by way of Abstract Conceptualization (input indicators) showed a positive and significant relationship between the two variables ($\beta = 0.41$, $p < 0.001$). $H_2$: the relationship between Knowledge and Skills Enablers and Active Experimentation (process indicators) also revealed a positive and significant relationship among the variables ($\beta = -0.42$ $p < 0.001$) while, $H_3$ revealed a positively significant relationship between the Knowledge and Skills Enablers (KSE) and concrete experience ($\beta = 0.18$, $p = 0.001$). $H_4$: the relationship between Knowledge and Skills Enablers (KSE) and Reflective observation (Impact indicators) revealed a positive and significant relationship among the variables ($\beta = 1.27$ $p < 0.001$).

### Interviews

The interviews with the top-management officials from five industries revealed that, although workplace learning was a continuous cycle in the workplace, assessment of workers' performance was not carried out because most employers depend on appraisal reports for making decisions on promotions and salary adjustments. In the words of one of the managers, "We have not considered assessing the efforts of workers on the job for the purposes of simply measuring their performance for learning. We advise our supervisors to ensure that employees are constantly given feedback while working." The responses from most of the management staff we interviewed revealed that the assessment of workplace learning was not considered in the scheme of affairs at the workplace.

In response to a question on how the organization considered the development of the knowledge and skills of workers through a generic assessment system that integrates the context–input–process–output–outcome/impact domains, the management member stated that, while the concept sounded plausible, its implementation could be time-consuming, especially when the feedback was only meant for improvement purposes and not as a reward mechanism. The response from a second interviewee showed that integrating a reward scheme could be ideal for maximizing the benefits of the generic assessment framework,

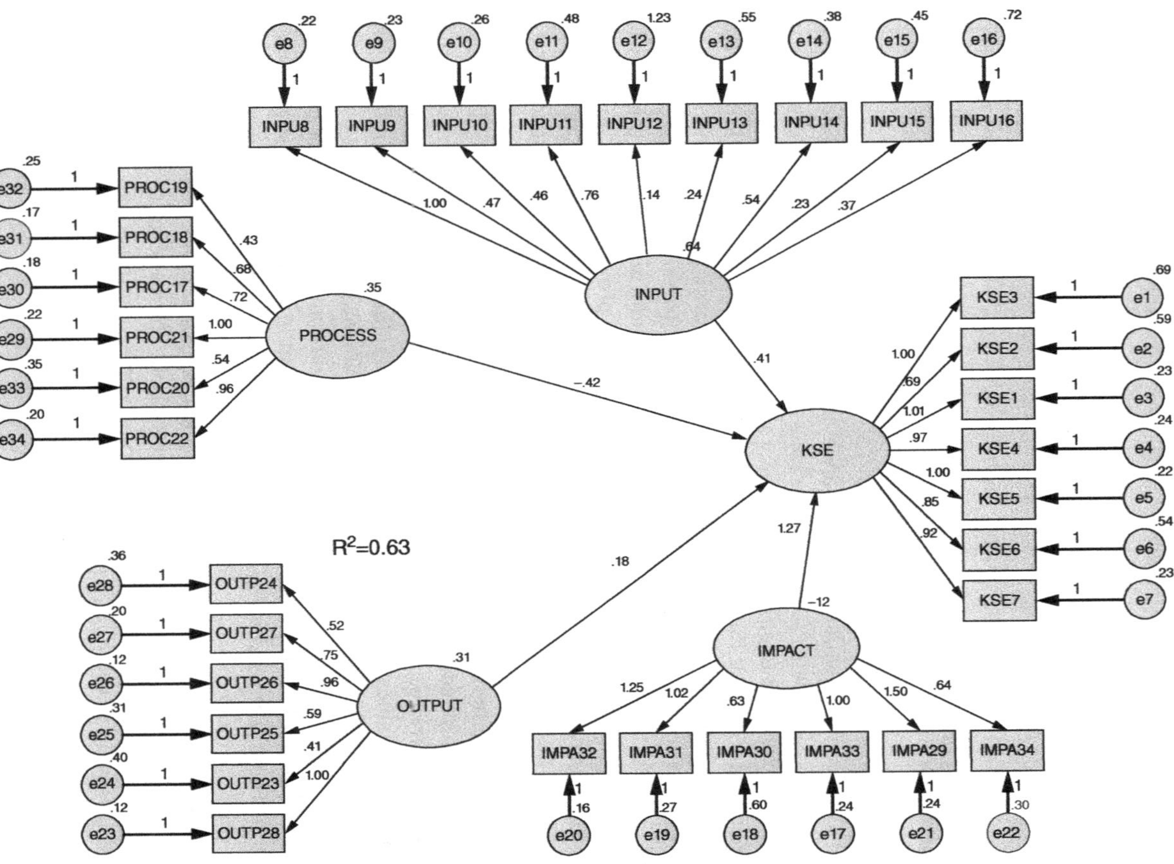


**Figure 6.3** The Workplace Learning Assessment Model

**Table 6.5** Results of Hypothesis Testing

| Relationship | Hypothesis | CR | Path coefficients | p value | Empirical conclusions |
|---|---|---|---|---|---|
| INPU → KSE | $H_1$ | 5.38 | 0.41 | 0.001 | Supported |
| PROC → KSE | $H_2$ | 6.49 | −0.42 | 0.001 | Supported |
| OUTP → KSE | $H_3$ | 9.62 | 0.18 | 0.001 | Supported |
| IMPA → KSE | $H_4$ | 8.44 | 1.27 | 0.001 | Supported |

although it could come along with several challenges, such as design of a reward package and the change in assessment focus from formative to summative considerations.

**Discussion**

The assessment of workers' performance in the job setting is global, because it provides workers with feedback on essential areas in the work processes that could be developed to enhance efficiency and productivity. Also, the assessment system and feedback mechanisms allow workers to obtain relevant knowledge and skills in their workplace based on standardized work processes and employers' expectations. In the context of this study, the purpose of assessing workers' learning was to develop their knowledge and skills and also to align the knowledge and skills expectations of employers with those provided by the workers.

Additionally, the generic assessment framework was designed to serve as a knowledge and skills development tool that relies on a feedback loop incorporating a process of judging and valuing the output of workers based on systematic information gathering.

The study revealed that the knowledge and skills enablers, which serve as the dependent variable, showed a positive and significant relationship with the predictor variables such that the input factors (*abstract conceptualization*; $\beta = 0.41$, $p < 0.001$), process factors (*active experimentation*; $\beta = -0.42$ $p < 0.001$), output factors (*concrete experience*; $\beta = 0.18$, $p = 0.001$) and impact factors (*reflective observation*; $\beta = 1.27$, $p = 0.001$) served as important indicators for assessing workplace learning. The results also showed that, although workplace learning continues to evolve in modern work settings (Bauer & Gruber, 2007; Evans, Hodkinson, Rainbird, & Unwin, 2006; Gomez-Mejia, Balkin, & Cardy, 2007), very little has been done to inform managers of organizations about the benefits of incorporating assessment systems in the process. Additionally, the generic assessment model also revealed a close link between the basic system model and experiential learning theory as a cogent framework for the design of an assessment system for workplace learning globally.

In conceptualizing the generic framework in the context of global workplace learning, we argue that the process of assessing workers' performance in a learning environment could be differentiated into two main categories: formative and summative assessment (Taras, 2005).

Formative assessment (Nicol & Macfarlane-Dick, 2006; Taras, 2005) of workplace learning is carried out to improve the performance of workers, which could also lead to improvement in the quality of products and services provided. Importantly, formative assessment, if properly structured, produces relevant information required of workers to develop their knowledge and skills. In developing a case for a generic workplace learning assessment framework that could be used globally, this study posits that consistent information and feedback (refer to Figure 6.1) provide opportunities for workers to improve their performance. Again, in workplace learning, formative assessment could ensure the early detection and fixing of weaknesses and deficiencies, thereby preventing avoidable cost, losses and operational setbacks that could be found in the working environment. This study did not adopt a summative assessment design, because the intent of the workplace assessment framework is to develop the knowledge and skills of workers without making the assessment forms the object of the workplace learning process.

The authors posit that the concept of assessment could be described as a process of putting in place measures to develop set parameters for the achievement of individual and group goals in an organizational setting. Similarly, the goal of assessment in organizations includes the following: to obtain information on the strengths and weaknesses of employees and to develop interventions for promoting the knowledge and skills of workers in order to meet the expectations of employers (Gomez-Mejia et al., 2007).

## Conclusion and Implications of the Study

This study revealed that the generic assessment framework for workplace learning could be enhanced by integrating experiential learning and the basic system model that aggregates workers' performance through a four-stage approach: input, process, output and outcome domains. Importantly, the authors showed that, although learning takes place at the workplace in both formal and informal structures (Diefenbach & Sillince, 2011), its assessment is necessary to provide workers with information on their performance, which is also required for their career development.

It is important to note that while workers learn on the job, they also attempt to apply theories they have learnt either in the classroom setting or on their own. The application of theories in a practical environment is essential to the development of knowledge and skills of workers in the workplace, because it allows for the introduction of new ideas and innovative work processes. While workers are required to solve problems and to be creative while they critically examine the work processes and attempt to develop solutions to fix the problems that arise, an assessment framework can best serve as a feedback tool for enhancing work processes.

Theoretically, this study showed that the adoption of experiential learning theory (Kolb & Kolb, 2005; Roberts, 2012) in the design of a generic assessment framework could be explained in three ways: (i) understanding the makeup of workers and the context of the workplace which is global; (ii) identifying the two elements that are relevant in understanding experiences in the workplace – abstract conceptualization and active experimentation, and (iii) understanding the modes of transforming experience through concrete experience and reflective observation that are universal and applicable in all organizations. We further argue that the development of the knowledge and skills of workers requires a detailed process of constructing and reconstructing knowledge through active engagement and constant feedback systems (see Owusu-Agyeman, Larbi-Siaw, Brenya, and Anyidoho (2017). Veering from the conventional experiential learning model (Kolb & Kolb, 2005), we argue that abstract conceptualization and active experimentation are relevant in understanding experiences and their assessment in the workplace globally.

Concrete experience and reflective observation serve as the basis for transforming experiences in the workplace, while also providing managers with new implications for decisions to be made regarding employee knowledge and skills. Additionally, the implications of employee reflections could be actively tested to serve as leads for new experiences.

Practically, organizations in different industries could adopt the generic assessment framework as a means of developing the knowledge and skills of workers through a detailed structure that is informed by the context–input–process–output–outcome/ impact domains. This ensures that the various domains in the system model are assessed in order to generate appropriate feedback for further training. Importantly, as organizations continue to develop the knowledge and skills of their workers, assessing the various learning processes for the purpose of formative feedback rather than for summative purposes that are inherent to appraisal systems, has become important. At the micro level, the benefits of such assessment systems could include preparing workers for more challenging leadership roles, and breaking the barriers of formal structures that inhibit a camaraderie-type of workplace environment that supports learning and makes feedback systems more flexible for employees.

## References

Ackerman, F. (1998). *The changing nature of work*. Washington, DC: Island.

Anderson, J. C., & Gerbing, D. W. (1982). Some methods for respecifying measurement models to obtain unidimensional construct measurement. *Journal of Marketing Research, 19*(4), 453–460.

Argote, L. (2011). Organizational learning research: Past, present and future. *Management Learning, 42*(4), 439–446.

Argote, L., & Miron-Spektor, E. (2011). Organizational learning: From experience to knowledge. *Organization Science, 22*(5), 1123–1137.

Avis, J. (2010). Workplace learning, knowledge, practice and transformation. *Journal for Critical Education Policy Studies (JCEPS), 8*(2).

Barnett, R. (1999). Learning to work and working to learn. In D. Boud, & J. Garrick (Eds.), *Understanding learning at work*, (pp. 29–44). London: Routledge.

Bauer, J., & Gruber, H. (2007). Workplace changes and workplace learning: Advantages of an educational micro perspective. *International Journal of Lifelong Education, 26*(6), 675–688.

Bentler, P. M. (1992). On the fit of models to covariance and methodology to the bulletin. *Psychological Bulletin, 112*(3), 400–404.

Bernstein, B. (1999). Vertical and horizontal discourse: An essay. *British Journal of Sociology of Education, 20*(2), 157–173.

Billet, S. (2004). Workplace participatory practices. Conceptualizing workplaces as learning environments. *Journal of Workplace Learning, 16*, 312–324.

Carvalho, S., & White, H. (1996). *Implementing projects for the poor: What has been learnt?*. Washington, DC: The World Bank.

Chin, W. W. (1998). The partial least squares approach to structural equation modeling. In G. A. Marcoulides (Ed.), *Modern methods for business research*, pp. 295–336. Mahwah, NJ: Lawrence Erlbaum Associates.

Chmiliar, L. (2010). Case study surveys. In A. J. Mills, G. Durepos, & E. Wiebe (Eds.), *Encyclopedia of case study research*, (pp. 761–765). Thousand Oaks, CA: Sage.

Colley, H., Hodkinson, P., & Malcolm, J. (2003). Understanding informality and formality in learning. *Adults Learning, 15*(3), 7–9.

Cohen, L., Manion, L., & Morrison, K. (2011). *Research methods in education*. New York: Routledge.

Creswell, J. (2008). *Educational research: Planning, conducting and evaluating quantitative and qualitative research* (3rd ed.). Upper Saddle River, NJ: Pearson Prentice Hall.

Cronbach, L. (1951). Coefficient alpha and the internal structure of tests. *Psychometrika, 16*(3), 297–334.

Crossan, M. M., & Berdrow, I. (2003). Organizational learning and strategic renewal. *Strategic Management Journal, 24*(11), 1087–1105.

Diefenbach, T., & Sillince, J. A. A. (2011). Formal and informal hierarchy in different types of organization. *Organization Studies, 32*, 1515–1537.

Egan, T. M., Yang, B., & Bartlett, K. R. (2004). The effects of organizational learning culture and job satisfaction on motivation to transfer learning and turnover intention. *Human Resource Development Quarterly, 15*(3), 279–301.

Elliott, A. (2014). *Concepts of the self* (3rd ed.). Cambridge, UK: Polity.

Eraut, M. (2004). Informal learning in the workplace. *Studies in Continuing Education, 26*(2), 247–273.

Evans, K., Hodkinson, P., Rainbird, H., & Unwin, L. (2006). *Improving workplace learning*. Abingdon, UK: Routledge.

Evans, K., Hodkinson, P., & Unwin, L. (Eds.) (2006). *Working to learn*. London, UK: Kogan Page.

Evans, K., & Rainbird, H. (2002). The significance of workplace learning for a "learning society." In K. Evans, P. Hodkinson, & L. Unwin (Eds.), *Working to learn*, (pp. 7–28). London, UK: Kogan Page.

Eyler, J. (2002). Reflection: Linking service and learning – Linking students and communities. *Journal of Social Issues, 58*(3), 517–534.

Filliettaz, L. (2013). Affording learning environments in workplace contexts: An interactional and multimodal perspective. *International Journal of Lifelong Education, 32*(1), 107–122.

Fleischer, J. (2005). Lessons for Leaders. *Call Centre Magazine*, 18, 8–10.

Fornell, C., & Larcker, D. (1981). Structural equation models with unobservable variables and measurement error. *Journal of Marketing Research, 18*(3), 39–50.

Fuller, A., Hodkinson, H., Hodkinson, P., & Unwin, L. (2005). Learning as peripheral participation in communities of practice: A reassessment of key concepts in workplace learning. *British Educational Research Journal, 31*(1), 49–68.

Gamble, J. (2006). Theory and practice in the vocational curriculum. In M. Young, & J. Gamble (Eds.), *Knowledge, curriculum and qualifications for south African further education*, pp. 87–103. Cape Town, South Africa: Human Sciences Research Council Press.

Garavan, T. N., & McGuire, D. (2001). Competencies and workplace learning: Some reflections on the rhetoric and the reality. *Journal of Workplace Learning, 13*(4), 144–164.

Gefen, D., Straub, D., & Boudreau, M. C. (2000). Structural equation modelling and regression: Guidelines for research practice. *Communication of the Association for Information Systems, 4*(7), 1–79.

Gherardi, S. (2006). *Organizational knowledge: The texture of workplace learning*. Melbourne, Australia: Blackwell Publishing.

Gomez-Mejia, L. R., Balkin, D. B., & Cardy, R. L. (2007). *Managing Human Resources*. Upper Saddle River, NJ: Pearson Education Incorporated.

Hager, P. (2004). Lifelong learning in the workplace? Challenges and issues. *Journal of Workplace Learning, 16*, 22–32.

Hair, J. F., Anderson, R. E., Tatham, R. L., & Black, W. C. (2010). *Multivariate Data Analysis: A Global Perspective* (7th ed.). Upper Saddle River, NJ: Pearson Prentice-Hall.

Hair, J. F., Hult, G. T. M., Ringle, C. M., & Sarstedt, M. (2013). *A primer on partial least squares structural equation modeling* (PLS-SEM) (1st ed.). London: Sage.

Henseler, J., Ringle, C. M., & Sinkovics, R. (2009). The use of partial least squares path modeling in international marketing. *Advances in International Marketing, 20*, 277–319.

Jacobs, R. J., & Park, Y. (2009). A proposed conceptual framework of workplace learning: Implications for theory development and research in human resource development. *Human Resource Development Review, 8*(2), 133–150. https://doi.org/10.1177/1534484309334269

Jiménez-Jiménez, D., & Sanz-Valle, R. (2011). Innovation, organizational learning, and performance. *Journal of Business Research, 64*(4), 408–417.

Kayes, A. B., Kayes, D. C., & Kolb, D. A. (2005). Experiential learning in teams. *Simulation and Gaming, 36*(X), 1–25. https://doi.org/10.1177/1046878105279012

Kock, N. (2013). *WarpPLS 4.0 User Manual*. Texas: ScriptWarp Systems.

Kolb, A. Y., & Kolb, D. A. (2005). Learning styles and learning spaces: Enhancing experiential learning in higher education. *Academy of Management Learning and Education, 4*(2), 193–212.

Lam, A. (2000). Tacit knowledge, organizational learning and societal institutions: An integrated framework. *Organization Studies, 21*(3), 487–513.

Lave, J., & Wenger, E. (1991). *Situated learning*. Cambridge, UK: Cambridge University Press.

Lindlof, T. R. (1995). *Qualitative communication research methods*. Thousand Oaks, CA: Sage.

Mohrman, S. A. (2003). Designing work for knowledge-based competition. In S. E. Jackson, M. A. Hitt, & A. S. DeNisi (Eds.), *Managing knowledge for sustained competitive advantage: Designing strategies for effective human resource management*, (pp. 94–123). San Francisco, CA: Jossey-Bass.

Nicol, D. J., & Macfarlane-Dick, D. (2006). Formative assessment and self-regulated learning: A model and seven principles of good feedback practice. *Studies in Higher Education, 31*(2), 199–218.

Noe, R. A. (2008). *Employee training and development.* New York: McGraw-Hill.

Nunnally, J., & Bernstein, I. H. (1994). *Psychometric theory.* London: McGraw Hill.

O'Leary-Kelly, S. W., & Vokurka, R. J. (1998). The empirical assessment of construct validity. *Journal of Operations Management, 16*(4), 387–405.

Owusu-Agyeman, Y. (2011). Workplace Learning and Collaborative Learning in Higher Educational Institutions: Design of assessment indicators for students on industrial attachment programmes in Ghana. International Conference of Education, Research and Innovation, November 14 to 16, 2011, Madrid, Spain. (http://library.iated.org/view/OWUSUAGYEMAN2011WOR)

Owusu-Agyeman, Y., Larbi-Siaw, O., Brenya, B., & Anyidoho, A. (2017). An embedded fuzzy analytic hierarchy process for evaluating lecturers' conceptions of teaching and learning. *Studies in Educational Evaluation, 55*, 46–57. https://doi.org/10.1016/j.stueduc.2017.07.001

Raykov, T., & Marcoulides, G. A. (2000). *A first course in structural equation modeling.* Mahwah, NJ: Lawrence Erlbaum Associates.

Reedy, P., King, D., & Coupland, C. (2016). Organizing for individuation: Alternative organizing, politics and new identities. *Organization Studies, 37*(11), 1553–1573.

Roberts, J. W. (2012). *Beyond learning by doing: Theoretical currents in experiential education.* New York: Routledge.

Sambrook, S. (2005). Factors influencing the context and process of work-related learning: Synthesizing findings from two research projects. *Human Resource Development International, 8*, 101–119.

Scheerens, J., Glass, C., & Thomas, S. M. (2003). *Educational evaluation, assessment, and monitoring: A systematic approach.* London, and New York: Taylor and Francis Publishers.

Taras, M. (2005). Assessment – summative and formative – some theoretical reflections. *British Journal of Educational Studies, 53*(4), 466–478.

Tynjälä, P. (2013). Toward a 3-P model of workplace learning: A literature review. *Vocations and Learning, 6*(1), 11–36.

Webster-Wright, A. (2009). Reframing professional development through understanding authentic professional learning. *Review of Educational Research, 79*(2), 702–739.

# Part II

# Project Management, Partnerships, and Diverse Populations

# 7

# Measuring Innovative Thinking and Acting Skills as Workplace-Related Professional Competence

*Susanne Weber*[1] *and Frank Achtenhagen*[2]

[1] *Ludwig-Maximilians-University Munich*
[2] *University of Göttingen*

## Problems of Fitting the Needs of the Current Labor Market

So-called "megatrends," for example globalization and internationalization of economies and businesses, demographic challenges, migration and an increasing use of communication technologies, have consequences for economic growth, but also for generating a skillful and professional workforce. A special challenge in this context is to prepare youth for the effects of workplace changes (Achtenhagen & Grubb, 2001; Achtenhagen, Nijhof, & Raffe, 1995; Buttler, 2009; Furlong & Cartmel, 2007; Goller & Paloniemi, 2017; Griffin, McGaw, & Care, 2012; Malloch, Cairns, Evans, & O'Connor, 2011; Mulder, 2017; Parker & Bindl, 2017; Roberts, 2011; The Partnership for 21st Century Learning, 2017).

Routinized manual work in the production area is being superseded by highly technology-based work in the production area. The same is true for the immense increase of communication- and service-oriented workplaces, not only in the service sector. These developments call for new and unfamiliar thinking and acting skills, often at a high level. Employers expect employees at all hierarchical levels to work in teams, solve problems proactively and independently, execute decisions autonomously and contribute to companies' goals with a high level of initiative (Goller & Paloniemi, 2017; Mayer & Solga, 2008). These dynamic changes and instabilities co-occur with limited work-contracts, lack of apprenticeship training positions and (temporal) unemployment, which leads to irritation especially among youth at all levels of education and training. These challenges evoke uncertainty, pressure for achievement and (often unguided) self-regulation in the early life stages. They produce drop-outs from vocational education and training (VET) programs including apprenticeships. Other effects are an increase in waiting-time for a job, multiple education trails, and a prolongation of time spent in education together with later take-up of full-time work. Simultaneously, these challenges extend the transition process between school and work, the transition

*The Wiley Handbook of Global Workplace Learning*, First Edition.
Edited by Vanessa Hammler Kenon and Sunay Vasant Palsole.

process to adulthood (du Bois-Reymond & Lopez Blasco, 2003; European Group for Integrated Social Research [EGRIS], 2001; Furlong & Cartmel, 2007; Hamilton & Hamilton, 2014; Mayer & Diewald, 2007; Roberts, 2011). All this demands a higher degree of attention to self-regulation, autonomy, responsibility, work agency or employability.

One can observe today that many industrialized countries are challenged to reorganize their skill-formation regimes, especially in VET (Busemeyer & Trampusch, 2012) and tertiary education. The central goal is mastering the transition from school to work, crafting a strong workforce which contributes to the companies' success as well as avoiding unemployment. Young people's transition from compulsory education to work has been becoming more difficult and challenging over the past few decades. According to the United Nations' World Youth Report (United Nations, 2012), difficulty in accessing secure workplaces has increased among young people globally. Youth unemployment, and youth drifting out of the labor market, has also become a serious problem in industrialized countries (ILO, 2012). In various economies there is growing evidence of young adults not being able to find a job that pays a middle-class wage (for the US see Hamilton & Hamilton, 2014; Symonds, Schwartz, & Ferguson, 2011). There are significant variations between countries: while the unemployment rate for 15/16–24-year-old youth in Germany was 6.4% and in the US 9.1%, it was even higher in Spain. at 37.2%, and in Greece at 42.8%. The average rate for the OECD was 13% and for the EU 16.6% (OECD, 2012). The reasons seem to be manifold, going beyond temporary economic levels of prosperity (Weber & Lehtinen, 2014): the lack of basic skills and work ethic needed for many jobs; new and challenging jobs that require so-called 21st-century skills (Binkley et al., 2012; Carnevale, Smith, & Strohl, 2010; Goller & Paloniemi, 2017; Mayer & Solga, 2008; National Research Council, 2012; Symonds et al., 2011); high drop-out rates from post-secondary programs (high school, community college, Bachelor's degree courses, apprenticeships) as young people do not see a clear, transparent relationship between educational programs and opportunities in the labor market (Symonds et al., 2011). It seems to be a governance issue to master such overarching VET and societal problems. There is a necessity to develop a highly equipped workforce that meets the requirements of the labor market, but also to enable social cohesion for a productive adulthood, especially at the level of middle-skilled professionals (Massey & Johnston, 2015; Mayntz, 2010).

Experiences with different skill-formation regimes with their various historically minted components (Busemeyer & Trampusch, 2012) suggest that neither a one-sided boosting of VET systems nor a one-sided fostering of modes of tertiary education will produce the desired political and economic effects (for the various components and effects, see, e.g., Weber & Lehtinen, 2014). We have evidence that a unidirectional emphasis on tertiary education may lead simultaneously to an unemployment of academics (e.g., Scandinavia or Korea) and a loss of medium-skilled employees for production, services and administration. Additionally, many ad-hoc measures for workplace learning/ training ignore the importance of formal certification which encourage employees to continue learning and to be mobile and flexible in the labor market.

We are convinced that the success of such transition processes does not only depend on human capital, historically developed VET systems, investment or structures, but also on what comes out of the manifold processes at the end of the programs and endeavors (Rauch & Frese, 2007). That means the competences (knowledge, skills, and attitudes) that the individuals have acquired and can offer to the labor market. This central problem of the mismatch of school and work is heavily featured in the scientific literature (cf. Weber & Lehtinen, 2014). On the other hand, employers try to overcome their opaque, poorly structured local and regional labor supply situations by seeking to recruit employees with advanced competences across the globe. Correspondingly, we find various strategies in International Human Resource Management (IHRM) or Global Talent Management (GTM) (McCracken, Currie, & Harrison, 2016; Scullion & Collings, 2011; Stahl et al., 2012; Tarique & Schuler, 2010). In our estimation, such strategies are time- and cost-intensive and underestimate the potential locked in the employees and apprentices of their own companies (Rupietta & Backes-Gellner, 2015).

To cope with such circumstances, we need new broad monitoring strategies. The level of formal education and traditional career paths are not as decisiveas achieved competences. Research questions (RQ) in this context are:

(RQ1) How is it possible to visualize and measure such innovative thinking and acting skills in the sense of intrapreneurship (IP) competences?
(RQ2) Which contextual success factors for developing IP competence have to be considered?

Regarding the global importance of an adequate preparation for the workplace experience and the difficult current situation for employees and employers, it seems necessary to develop a monitoring strategy which also allows an international comparison of skill-formation regimes to identify strengths and weaknesses, but also to get hints for supporting and hindering structures for fostering such new competences. Such comparison can be run close to existing international large-scale assessments (e.g., Program for International Student Assessment (PISA) and Trends in International Mathematics Study (TIMS) studies in the area of compulsory education, or thee Adult Literacy and Lifeskills Survey (ALL) and Program for the International Assessment of Adult Competencies (PIAAC) studies in the fields of adult education). In the following, therefore, we present with regard to RQ1 (1) a framework for a large-scale assessment of VET; (2) an attempt to identify common tasks at workplaces in the area of business and administration across European countries; (3) a prototype for the assessment of workplace competences; and (4) a proposal to visualize and measure IP competence. We, then, discuss RQ2 in terms of contextual success, and factors promoting such IP competences.

## Modeling and Measuring Workplace Competence

### A Framework for a Large-Scale Assessment of VET

As a first approach to visualizing and measuring workplace competence, the German Federal Ministry for Education and Research set up an initiative to develop a proposal for a large-scale assessment in VET. Baethge et al. (2006) prepared such a proposal in cooperation with a group of experts from 18 industrialized countries (including the US and Australia). At two international "curriculum conferences" (Frey, 1981; Hansen, 2008) the following three overarching goals of VET were formulated (Baethge et al., 2006, p. 11):

1) The development of individual occupational adjustment from an individual user's point of view, taking self-regulation and autonomy into consideration. This goal is in contrast to a too-narrow interpretation of workplace learning focusing primarily on performance.
2) The safeguarding of human resources in a society. This focuses on the necessity to develop and use the potential of all employees and workers.
3) The warranty of social share and equal opportunities. This goal strengthens the educational and political dimensions of learning in the workplace: to be responsible as a member of a workforce within society.

These goals function as reference points for the identification of workplace-related competences. The whole proposal discusses how these goals can serve as a basis for a large-scale assessment together with the corresponding educational, organizational and political variables.

### Identifying Common Workplace Needs and Experiences Across Eight European Countries

As a first consequence of this frame for a large-scale assessment of VET, a European cross-national comparative study was run to identify commonalities of workplace experience (Baethge & Arends, 2009). The overarching question is: *How can occupational fields and work activities be identified and internationally related to each other with regard to the differences in job-classification schemata?* The study investigated four major occupational fields: car mechatronics, electricians, business and administration and social and health care, addressing 359 experts from eight European countries. A basic difficulty of such international comparison stems from the fact that the tasks and items cannot be directly taken from the corresponding national curricula. Each country defines school curricula, qualification requirements and occupational goals and tasks according to its tradition, its work structure and labor market structure under different historical and political assumptions. This includes different perspectives on school and apprenticeship careers for individual learners who intend to acquire the necessary qualifications for task fulfillment at the worksite. The same difficulty applies to tertiary education and training.

Thus, the research groups of this comparative study developed a questionnaire relying heavily on three instruments: ISCED (International Standard Classification of Education; UNESCO, 2006), ISCO (International Standard Classification of Occupations; ILO, 2008) and O*NET (US Occupational Information Network; Peterson, Mumford, Borman, Jeanneret, & Fleishman, 1999) to identify necessary work activities and to enable the setting up of comparable categories.

With regard to the occupational area of business and administration, national expert groups from six countries: Austria, Denmark, Finland, Germany, Slovenia and Switzerland ($n$ = 70 experts), conducted questionnaire-based comparative analyses. For the first instrument the interviewers set entrance level ISCED 3 B, a prior compulsory schooling of nine years and an entrance age of 15 or 16; this gave gives access to the labor market. For the second instrument the experts had to choose occupations according to ISCO 08 category 33. This is related to all forms of vocational education and training: school-only, practical training-only or mixed forms, which take three or four years in all countries. With regard to the use of O*NET, all occupational tasks are assigned to job zones 3 or 4 (medium or considerable preparation) and to a SVP range (duration of specific vocational preparation) of 6.0 to <8.0 (which includes one to four years of specific vocational preparation) (cf. Breuer, Hillen, & Winther, 2009).

As a result of their analyses all expert groups agreed on nine occupational tasks as *representative* for the fields of business and administration. After rating these tasks according to their *relevance* three tasks showed the highest congruent judgments over all six countries: "Prepare invoices, reports, memos, letters, financial statements, other documents"; "Respond to customers'/ suppliers' inquiries about order status, changes, cancellations"; and "Review files, records, and other documents to obtain information to respond to requests." These tasks are also those with the highest *frequency* found at the worksite, which means according to the judgment of the experts they refer to the common day-to-day work processes of industrial clerks (Breuer et al., 2009, pp. 74/75).

The results of these analyses give fruitful hints for defining curricula and instruction, but also for assessment as well as modes of competence measurement in VET.

## Prototype for Assessing Workplace Competences

To visualize and to measure these workplace competences necessary to master the identified workplace tasks, the German Federal Government launched an initiative to create corresponding assessment tools (Achtenhagen & Winther, 2009), aiming to show that it is possible to model and measure workplace competences in a way which could serve principally as a basis for a large-scale assessment. In this context Achtenhagen and Winther (2009), cf. also Achtenhagen & Winther, 2014; Winther, 2010) developed a virtual technology-based company, ALUSIM Ltd., in which workplace tasks, as they had been identified by comparative cross-national studies, were simulated and created as authentic test items. Furthermore, the authors drew on research results to construct complex teaching–learning environments for the fields of business and administration to model this virtual company and its workplaces authentically (Achtenhagen, 2001; Achtenhagen et al., 1992; Achtenhagen & Weber, 2003; Cognition and Technology Group at Vanderbilt, 1997; Doyle, 2000; Janesick, 2006; Mayer, 1999). They constructed a comprehensive data package for the virtual company with all means and data necessary to generate realistic business processes. Data included, for example, balances, cost accounting and prices for different products, descriptions of workplaces of different departments and customer demands. On this authentic basis, realistic tasks were created as test items. Experts from real companies appraised all the tasks (test items) to be fulfilled in the virtual company for representativeness. Agreement was unanimous. The tasks were converted into a web-based format. The virtual company, ALUSIM, fabricates aluminum packages (the modeled real company is part of a worldwide operating trust with about 100,000 employees). The company's products are beverage cans (Coca-Cola), cosmetics (Nivea), and food packaging. Authentic parameters of modeling were used, including company history and reporting (e.g., balance sheet, profit and loss statements, cash-flow analyses). Authentic large volume production and its corresponding costs were included, together with real-world customers and suppliers. An important criterion for authenticity was to embed the tasks sequentially in processes to avoid an unrealistic static handling of isolated tasks. The virtual company was constructed to offer workplace tasks in three departments, reflecting those identified by the international feasibility study: sales department (three sequences of tasks); purchasing department (four sequences); and production planning department (two sequences). This also included the development of different technology-based tools such as storyboards of authentic business processes, applications of integrated Enterprise Resource Planning (ERP) units, including customer and supplier lists, in-depth analyses of the designed company and so on.

All these products and modeling steps were necessary to stimulate performance in authentic vocational situations and work processes as key elements of competence measurement. In other words, a simulation of real-world conditions ensures measurement of authentic abilities without bringing those being tested into such real-world situations. Therefore, the business simulation contains complete business processes. This focus guarantees interpretability of test results. The simulation ensures a content-related and cognition-based characterization of the test environment. It also provides a valid description of personal abilities and item difficulties with regard to concrete test challenges. This permitted a psychometric modeling approach.

All domain specific challenges are video-based and refer to a complete sequence of tasks (e.g., work processes). The test subjects navigate through the tasks using an interactive desktop which encompasses all documents, ERP units, filings and helping tools to test the ability to cope efficiently and effectively with the tasks. The solutions serve as a basis for the measurement of competence. Starting a video opens the domain-specific challenge. The test subjects watch a dialog between a trainee and an employee, which contains useful information and a reference to solving the problem. However, different work processes structure each challenge. The sales challenge, for example, starts with two steps. First, the test subjects must enter the customer demand data into the ERP system. Therefore, they must review all relevant customer information, the ERP requirements, the production, and also the delivery process.

In a second step, another test situation, the testee receives information from the production department that the sale cannot be closed on usual terms. The trainee must manage that situation by contacting the customer. The outlined work process demands a deep understanding of sale records, business conditions, customer buying patterns, and sensitivities. The test subject must anticipate the entire production process to find the new delivery date, make the right decision and inform the customer correctly and politely (to prompt a long-term relationship with the customer). This behavior component is also measured as part of the corresponding test item. Such work processes refer to different complexity levels and stay as examples for the whole bunch of tasks to be fulfilled within business workplaces.

This prototype of test was run with 264 participants (third-year apprenticeship of industrial clerks) in 15 classrooms in 7 commercial schools in 3 German States. The subjects were between 20 and 23 years old. The test consists of 34 items related to business actions and 26 items related to the comprehension of business processes.

The analyses were conducted by applying a multi-dimensional random coefficients multinomial logit model out of the family of item response theory (IRT) for competence measurement (Adams, Wilson, & Wang, 1997) using the software ConQuest (Wu, Adams, Wilson, & Haldane, 2007). The results show that the model fits the empirical data. All values for validity and reliability of the test results are very good (Achtenhagen & Winther, 2014; Winther, 2010).

## Visualizing and Measuring Intrapreneurship Competence

Inspired by this first prototype, the German Federal Ministry for Education and Research started the ASCOT initiative (Technology-based Competence Development in Vocational Education and Training; http://ascot-vet.net) on this basis for the VET areas business and administration, technology, health and care (Beck, Landenberger, & Oser, 2016). Two special projects were run within the business and administration sector: one following and enlarging the ALUSIM approach for industrial clerks (Winther, University of Paderborn); the other (Weber et al., 2016; Weber, Trost, Wiethe-Körprich, Weiß, & Achtenhagen, 2014) also followed the ALUSIM approach, but brought in a new dimension by modeling and measuring explicitly IP competence as a decisive twenty-first century skill (Di Fabio, 2014).

Intrapreneurship (IP)-competence is meanwhile an explicit part of the official curriculum of apprenticeships in the area of business and administration (Wiethe-Körprich, Weber, Bley, & Kreuzer, 2017). An intrapreneur is understood to be an entrepreneur within an organization (Antoncic & Hisrich, 2001). Actions of intrapreneurs are focused on organizing and structuring resources with regard to the generation of innovative ideas and their realization within a complex bureaucracy (Perlman, Gueths, & Weber, 1988). IP is related to innovative actions as "idea generation" and "planning and implementing" these innovative ideas. Typical IP-projects are (a) the foundation of business units within existing organizational structures (new venture business), (b) organizational change by renewal of key ideas and concepts (self-renewal), (c) technologically related development of products or services (redesign of the product line) (cf. Antoncic & Hisrich, 2001; Perlman et al., 1988). Such projects are also part of BA and MBA programs. The construction of the IP competence model follows the proposals of Blömeke, Gustafsson, and Shavelson (2015), Weinert (2001), Shavelson (2010a, 2010b), and Pellegrino, DiBello, and Goldman (2016).

On the basis of extensive domain analyses as well as intense pre-studies, Weber et al. (2014, 2016) developed 49 items to measure this latent competence construct IP and tested it by a pre-test ($n = 357$) and by a German-wide main-test ($n = 906$). The modeling of IP-competence followed the international discussion of competence measurement (cf. Mislevy, Almond, & Lukas, 2003; Pellegrino et al., 2016; Shavelson, 2012; Wilson, 2005; Wilson, DeBoeck, & Carstensen, 2008), using the following central concepts:

1) *Construct map:* Extensive domain analyses: reviewing scientific literature, curricula, training regulations, textbooks, job advertisements as well as running observations of school instruction and training behavior in firms, show the "big picture" of IP within the apprenticeship of industrial clerks (Trost & Weber, 2012; Weber et al., 2014; Weber, Wiethe-Körprich, et al., 2016): 1) innovative hints for IP are given within the curricula, the instructional and training processes and assessments; 2) most frequent are processes in the sales departments (e.g., introduction of new products or identification of new sales lanes) and in the personnel departments (how to get new personnel, especially apprentices); 3) for mastering these domain-specific situational challenges, innovative behavior becomes relevant. Many authors, e.g., Pinchot (1987) focus on the fact that IP competence mainly consists of two latent dimensions: idea generation, with the two situation-specific skills of problem perception and generation of innovative new intrapreneurship ideas; and planning and implementing, with the specific skills fourfold structure of information and project planning, implementation of the intrapreneurship project, distribution of the intrapreneurship idea and reflection and evaluation.

   According to the evidence-centered design approach (Mislevy & Haertel, 2006; Mislevy & Riconscente, 2006; Pellegrino et al., 2016), the latent competence facets were operationalized by situation-specific skills and, then, related to observable actions. The mechanism is shown by Figure 7.1. The operationalization was done for all facets and skills in this way (Wiethe-Körprich et al., 2017). We, here, demonstrate the process for the fourth competence facet within the latent dimension "Implementation of the IP project." We determine situation-specific skills for reaching this facet and show, then, which observations secure evidence for inferring it to the latent IP competence construct.

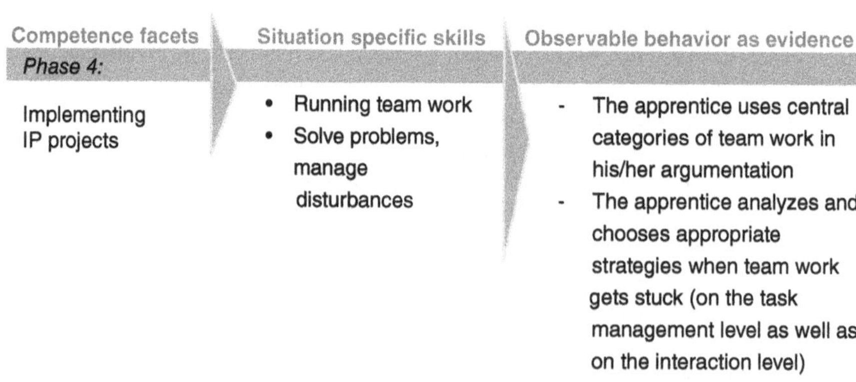


**Figure 7.1** Mechanism of operationalization – one example

2) *Item design:* On the basis of these operationalization processes, 19 authentic tasks with 49 test items were constructed. The tasks are introduced by video clips. As they are presented via the virtual company ALUSIM Ltd. (Achtenhagen & Winther, 2009, 2014), the testees can use all given firm information. The tasks are assigned to two scenarios according to the results of the domain analyses: lack of qualified personnel; or implementation of a sales structure for new products (aluminum back covers and bumpers for smartphones). Different formats of the tasks and items are chosen which can be answered locally independently.

   All tasks and items were validated by thinking-aloud studies ($n$ = 26 apprentices) and expert ratings ($n$ = 9 teachers and trainers) and also rated with regard to their difficulty. The dimension of "idea generation" is judged to be more difficult than "planning and implementing."
3) *Outcome space:* The coding schema was constructed in accordance with the expected solution space. The data were dichotomously and polytomously coded. The prescriptions are fixed by a coding guide. Intensive coder training was run. The intercoder reliability was 0.9 (Cohen's kappa), together with a consensual validation.
4) *Statistical model:* The validation of the competence model was done by using IRT (de Ayala, 2009). The analyses are also run by using the multi-dimensional random coefficients multinomial logit model (Adams et al., 1997; Wu et al., 2007) for scaling up and visualizing the person's abilities and test item difficulties on the same logit scale. Pinchot's assumption of a two-dimensional structure of IP competence was confirmed by the pre-test ($n$ = 357) as well as the nation-wide main-test ($n$ = 906) (Weber, Draxler, et al., 2016). Figure 7.2 presents one central result.

Figure 7.2 shows the distribution of the apprentices according to IP-competence levels. Remarkable is that about three-quarters of the apprentices have reached the medium and higher levels of IP competence and that about 30% reached the highest level of IP behavior. This means that this group might function as candidates for leading positions. Simultaneously, this opens new possibilities to recruit company-own "high potentials."

## Monitoring Contextual Success Factors for Intrapreneurship Competence

After having found a promising way of visualizing respectively modeling and measuring the indispensable competence of IP, it was also necessary to identify success factors that support the development of this workplace competence, our RQ2 (Achtenhagen & Weber, 2008, 2009; Baethge et al., 2006; Deutsche Forschungsgemeinschaft, 1990; Weber, 2013).

The ASCOT initiative approached this endeavor by linking diagonally a sub-project on investigating context factors (Baethge-Kinsky, Baethge, & Lischewski, 2016) as well as a sub-project on basic skills like mathematics and German language (Ziegler, Balkenhol, Keimes, & Rexing, 2012). Important factors include:

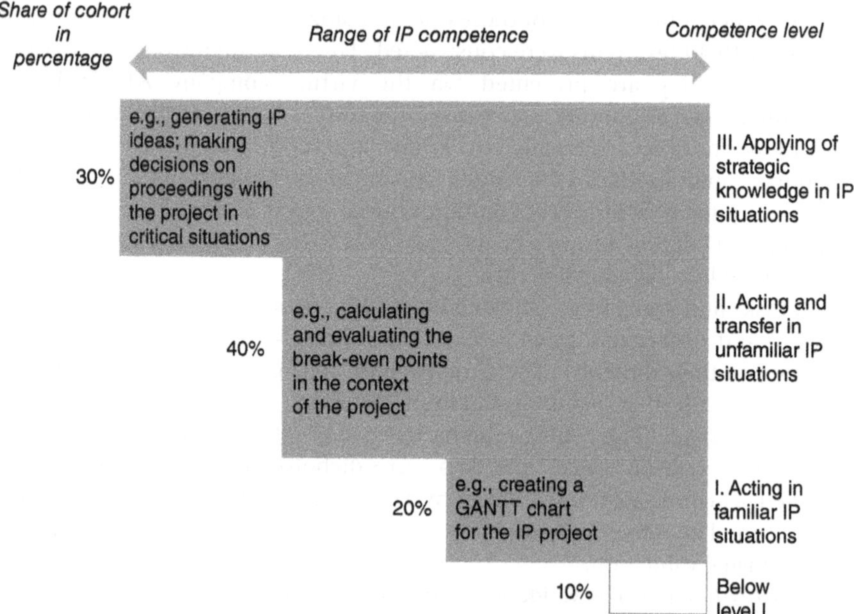


**Figure 7.2** Levels of intrapreneurship competence for apprentices

1) *Local context factors*: Besides the overarching regimes, local conditions (labor market structure, demand on labor), social environments and culture also seem to influence people's behavior (cf. Reich, 1997; Tynjälä, 2013; Weber & Rippen, 1999; Welter, 2010). Thus, it is important how supportive local factors are to the fostering of intrapreneurial behavior and which supportive means are offered. Support may be provided by chambers of industry and commerce, job centers, science parks, etc. There is also the matter of the influence of actors who collaborate with students, offer awards for the best elaborated projects and work, offer sponsorships, hire expert speakers from various local organizations and industry for educational courses, or serve on jury boards (see Achtenhagen & Johannisson, 2014; Weber & Funke, 2014).
2) *Social context factors of the apprentices*: Vocational and professional competences (like IP) are learnable and teachable (Boon, Van der Klink, & Janssen, 2013; Gibb, 2002; Kreuzer, Weber, Bley, & Wiethe-Körprich, 2017; Littunen, 2000; von Graevenitz, Harhoff, & Weber, 2010). But such learning and teaching processes might differ. They depend on various inputs such as socioeconomic background, education, individual needs, prior knowledge, career aspiration, migration background and the social climate in which certain occupations are more highly regarded than others. Previous work experiences, domain-specific prior knowledge or relevant basic and cross-functional skills also play a decisive role (Ziegler et al., 2012).
3) *Institutional context factors as the organization of apprenticeship in companies and vocational schools*: From various studies on school quality and school improvement we know that the mode of the processes of teaching and learning, as well as the corresponding learning environments are decisive for

learning success (Cortina, 2006; Tynjälä, 2013; Weber, 2013; Welter, 2010). This is also the case in vocational education and IP (Kreuzer et al., 2017). Thus, it is important to observe the learning climate and the allocated tasks to be mastered, but also the quality of instructional support and feedback at the workplace as well as at vocational schools.

4) *Individual educational interaction processes in vocational schools and at the workplace*: The teaching–learning interaction is a core element of the educational process. Following a competence-oriented approach, a mixture of different kinds of "knowledge" and corresponding "instruction" seems to be necessary to develop vocational and professional competences successfully. For example, there is clear evidence of the utility of systematic academic knowledge for giving orientation, skills for enabling practical problem-solving, as well as attitudes toward personal growth (including professional identity, motivation and taking responsibility) (Schiro, 2013; Weber & Funke, 2014).
5) *Acquired individual competences and certificates*: We suggest, in line with the international discussion on modeling and measuring work-related competences, using a multi-dimensional, holistic and integrative model of competence (cf. Baethge et al., 2006; Blömeke et al., 2015; Rychen & Salganik, 2003; Weber & Achtenhagen, 2014, 2017; Weinert, 2001; Winterton, 2009; Winther, 2010). This integrative model of competence includes both input and output variables (focusing on attributes a person must possess in order to perform competently, plus their demonstration by performance). Such an integrative model is also successfully used within the labor market database "O*NET" (Occupational Information Network) initiated by the US Ministry of Labor (Peterson et al., 1999). Within O*NET particular job/ situational requirements and corresponding worker/ individual-related traits/attitudes, knowledge, skills and experiences are matched (Peterson et al., 2001).

Although these contextual analyses are still going on, first results highlight that "having learning opportunities" and a stimulating "innovative climate" are the most boosting context factors (Weber, Draxler, et al., 2016).

## Conclusion and Educational Impact

Based on this review, a promising monitoring strategy can be crafted: a strategy by which competences in VET can be visualized, high potentials can be discovered and success factors can be identified. The major point to be stressed, here, is the fact that many companies underestimate the possibility of detecting and identifying high potentials among their employees, especially, their apprentices.

The revisited studies demonstrate that an apprenticeship system is not just able to generate skills for dealing adequately with isolated, specific workplace requirements. Apprenticeship systems are also able to foster highly estimated innovative behavior in the sense of IP competences.

Primary trials to develop an international comparison in the field of VET (16 European countries, the US and Australia) show that it is possible to come to a commonly shared understanding of work areas and occupational tasks, as well as qualification requirements.

First developments of assessment tools demonstrate that it is possible to measure vocational and occupational competences authentically regarding the dimensions of knowledge, skills and attitudes. This is visualized, here, for the field of business and administration, but also valid for other areas of VET.

This contribution presents examples for competence modeling and measurement won in the fields of business and administration. Departing from the cornerstones of the skill formation regime in Germany (Busemeyer & Trampusch, 2012), we highlight two major problems of VET in Germany, but which are also given for other industrialized countries: to prepare youth for the increased complexity of tasks at the workplaces and to sensitize employers for their employees' hidden potentials. The discussion above should have made clear that it is not enough merely to formulate desired competences, respectively competence domains. It is necessary not only to link the competence construct to theoretical approaches (Blömeke et al., 2015) as well as to an overarching theoretical frame (Baethge et al., 2006); but, also, one must relate competences to the current labor market and its antecedents and corresponding needs. Domain analyses (e. g. O*NET) as well as international comparisons may clarify which kind of knowledge, skills and attitudes are relevant and which content is necessary in this changing world (accounting, IP, etc.) (Baethge & Arends, 2009; Breuer et al., 2009).

The two studies on the prototype (Achtenhagen & Winther, 2014) as well as on IP competence (Weber, Draxler, et al., 2016) show how it is possible to visualize and to measure workplace competences. Thereby, a necessary precondition is the applied procedure of aligning clearly formulated goals, authentically simulated workplace assessment tasks and corresponding model-based psychometric measurement (Embretson, 2010). This procedure enables a highly valid interpretation of the latent competences by evidentiary reasoning (Pellegrino et al., 2016). By additionally embedding these measurements into the context (Weber, Draxler, et al., 2016), success factors for fostering workplace competences can be identified.

We are convinced that our suggestion – referring to international approaches of large-scale assessments – is a solid base for establishing a monitoring system in VET and is also a good point of departure for international comparative studies in VET. This perspective opens potential for guiding youth through their transition from school to work as well as for employers to identify the high potentials within their workforce.

Our study demonstrates that a successful adaptation of VET to the needs of a changing work-site requires a lot of time for stringent long-term research, as well as continuous political support.

## References

Achtenhagen, F. (2001). Criteria for the development of complex teaching-learning environments. *Instructional Science*, *29*, 361–380.

Achtenhagen, F., & Grubb, W. N. (2001). Vocational and occupational education: Pedagogical complexity, institutional diversity. In V. Richardson (Ed.), *Handbook of research on teaching* (4th ed., ed.) (pp. 604–639). Washington, DC: American Educational Research Association.

Achtenhagen, L., & Johannisson, B. (2014). Context ideology of entrepreneurship education in practice. In S. Weber, F. K. Oser, F. Achtenhagen, M. Fretschner, & S. Trost (Eds.), *Becoming an entrepreneur* (pp. 91–107). Rotterdam, The Netherlands: Sense Publishers.

Achtenhagen, F., Nijhof, J. W., & Raffe, D. (1995). *Feasibility study: Research scope for vocational education in the framework of COST social sciences. European commission: Directorate-general science, Research and development, COST technical committee social sciences* (Vol. 3). Brussels, Luxembourg: ECSC-EC-EAEC.

Achtenhagen, F., Tramm, T., Preiß, P., Seemann-Weymar, H., John, E. G., & Schunck, A. (1992). *Lernhandeln in komplexen Situationen* [learning and acting in complex situations]. Wiesbaden, Germany: Gabler.

Achtenhagen, F., & Weber, S. (2003). "Authentizität" in der Gestaltung beruflicher Lernumgebungen ["Authenticity" in designing vocational learning environments]. In A. Bredow, R. Dobischat, & J. Rottmann (Eds.), *Berufs- und Wirtschaftspädagogik von A-Z* [vocational education from A to Z] (pp. 185–199). Baltmannsweiler, Germany: Schneider.

Achtenhagen, F., & Weber, S. (2008). Transferability, flexibility, mobility as targets of vocational education and training – The COST action A 11. In F. Rauner, & R. Maclean (Eds.), *Handbook of technical and vocational education and training research,* (pp. 683–695). Dordrecht, The Netherlands: Springer.

Achtenhagen, F., & Weber, S. (2009). Zur Bedeutung der beruflichen Aus- und Weiterbildung [On the importance of VET]. In J. M. Fegert, A. Streeck-Fischer, & H. J. Freyberger (Eds.), *Adoleszenzpsychiatrie – Psychiatrie und Psychotherapie der Adoleszenz und des jungen Erwachsenenalters,* (pp. 48–65). Stuttgart, NY: Schattauer.

Achtenhagen, F., & Winther, E. (2009). *Konstruktvalidität von Simulationsaufgaben: Computergestützte Messung berufsfachlicher Kompetenz – am Beispiel der Ausbildung von Industriekaufleuten* [Construct validity of simulated tasks: computer-based measurement of VET competences]. Bericht für das BMBF. Göttingen, Germany: Seminar für Wirtschaftspädagogik.

Achtenhagen, F., & Winther, E. (2014). Workplace-based competence measurement: Developing innovative assessment systems for tomorrow's VET programmes. *Journal of Vocational Education and Training, 66*(3), 281–295.

Adams, R. J., Wilson, M., & Wang, W. C. (1997). The multidimensional random coefficients multinomial logit model. *Applied Psychological Measurement, 21*(1), 1–23.

Antoncic, B., & Hisrich, R. D. (2001). Intrapreneurship: Construct refinement and cross-cultural validation. *Journal of Business Venturing, 16*(5), 495–527.

Baethge, M., Achtenhagen, F., Arends, L., Babic, E., Baethge-Kinsky, V., & Weber, S. (2006). *PISA-VET – A feasibility study.* Stuttgart, Germany: Steiner.

Baethge, M., & Arends, L. (Eds.) (2009). *Feasibility study VET-LSA. A comparative analysis of occupational profiles and VET programmes in eight European countries. International report.* Bonn, Germany: BMBF.

Baethge-Kinsky, V., Baethge, M., & Lischewski, J. (2016). Bedingungen beruflicher Kompetenzentwicklung: Institutionelle und individuelle Kontextfaktoren (SiKoFak) [conditions of developing VET competences: Institutional and individual context factors]. In K. Beck, M. Landenberger, & F. Oser (Eds.), *Technologiebasierte Kompetenzmessung in der beruflichen Bildung [technology-based measurement of competences in VET]*, (pp. 265–299). Bielefeld, Germany: Bertelsmann.

Beck, K., Landenberger, M., & Oser, F. (Eds.) (2016). *Technologiebasierte Kompetenzmessung in der beruflichen Bildung. [Technology-based measurement of competences in VET]*. Bielefeld, Germany: Bertelsmann.

Binkley, M., Erstad, O., Herman, J., Raizen, S., Ripley, M., Miller-Ricci, M., & Rumble, M. (2012). Defining twenty-first century skills. In B. McGaw, E. Care, & P. E. Griffin (Eds.), *Assessment and teaching of 21st century skills*, (pp. 17–66). Dordrecht, Netherlands: Springer.

Blömeke, S., Gustafsson, J.-E., & Shavelson, R. J. (2015). Beyond dichotomies. Competence viewed as a continuum. *Zeitschrift für Psychologie, 223*(1), 3–13.

Boon, J., Van der Klink, M., & Janssen, J. (2013). Fostering intrapreneurial competencies of employees in the education sector. *International Journal of Training and Development, 17*(3), 210–220.

Breuer, K., Hillen, S., & Winther, E. (2009). Comparative international analysis of occupational tasks and qualification requirements for the labor market and assessment tasks at the end of VET in participating countries – Business and administration. In M. Baethge, & L. Arends (Eds.), *Feasibility study VET-LSA. A comparative analysis of occupational profiles and VET programmes in eight European countries. International report*, (pp. 71–84). Bonn, Germany: BMBF.

Busemeyer, M. R., & Trampusch, C. (2012). The comparative political economy of collective skill formation. In M. R. Busemeyer, & C. Trampusch (Eds.), *The political economy of collective skill formation*, (pp. 3–38). New York, NY: Oxford University Press.

Buttler, F. (2009). To learn makes people large and strong – Developing trends in gainful occupation, learning competence and social inclusion in an international perspective. In F. Oser, U. Renold, E. G. John, E. Winther, & S. Weber (Eds.), *VET boost. Towards a theory of professional competencies. Essays in honor of frank Achtenhagen*, (pp. 361–370). Rotterdam, Netherlands: Sense Publishers.

Carnevale, A. P., Smith, N., & Strohl, J. (2010). *Help wanted: Projections of jobs and education requirements through 2018*. Washington, DC: CEW Georgetown.

Cognition and Technology Group at Vanderbilt. (1997). *The Jasper project: Lessons in curriculum, instruction, assessment, and professional development*. Mahwah, NJ/London, UK: Erlbaum.

Cortina, K. S. (2006). Psychologie der Lernumwelt [psychology of learning environment]. In A. Krapp, & B. Weidenmann (Eds.), *Pädagogische Psychologie*, (pp. 478–524). Weinheim, Germany: Beltz.

de Ayala, R. J. (2009). *The theory and practice of item response theory. Methodology in the social sciences*. New York, NY: Guilford Press.

Deutsche Forschungsgemeinschaft. (1990). *Berufsbildungsforschung an den Hochschulen der Bundesrepublik Deutschland*. Denkschrift [Research on VET at German Universities]. Weinheim, Germany: VCH.

Di Fabio, A. (2014). Intrapreneurial self-capital: A new construct for the 21st century. *Journal of Employment Counseling, 51*, 98–111.

Doyle, W. (2000). *Authenticity*. Paper presented at the AERA Annual Meeting, New Orleans.

du Bois-Reymond, M., & Lopez Blasco, A. L. (2003). Yo-yo transitions and misleading trajectories: Towards integrated transition policies for young adults in Europe. In A. L. Lopez Blasco, & A. Walther (Eds.), *Young people and contradictions of inclusion: Towards integrated transition policies in Europe*, (pp. 19–42). Bristol, UK: The Policy Press.

European Group for Integrated Social Research. (2001). Misleading trajectories: Transition dilemmas of young people in Europe. *Journal of Youth Studies, 4*(1), 101–118.

Embretson, S. E. (2010). Measuring psychological constructs with model-based approaches: An instruction. In S. E. Embretson (Ed.), *Measuring psychological constructs. Advances in model-based approaches*, (pp. 1–7). Washington, DC: American Psychological Association.

Eteläpelto, A., Vähäsantanen, K., Hökkä, P., & Paloniemi, S. (2013). What is agency? Conceptualizing professional agency at work. *Educational Research Review, 10*, 45–65.

Frey, K. (1981). *Curriculum-Konferenz: Gebiet Mikroprozessor* [Curriculum conference]. *Report 45*. Kiel: IPN – Leibniz Institute for Science Education.

Furlong, A., & Cartmel, F. (2007). *Young people and social change: New perspectives*. Maidenhead, UK: McGraw-Hill/ Open University Press.

Gibb, A. A. (2002). Creating conducive environments for learning and entrepreneurship: Living with, dealing with, creating and enjoying uncertainty and complexity. *Industry and Higher Education, 16*(3), 135–148.

Goller, M., & Paloniemi, S. (Eds.) (2017). *Agency at work*. Cham (CH), Switzerland: Springer.

Griffin, P., McGaw, B., & Care, E. (Eds.) (2012). *Assessment and teaching of 21st century skills*. Dordrecht, The Netherlands: Springer.

Hamilton, S. F., & Hamilton, M. A. (2014). Mentoring, social capital, and human capital. *Unterrichtswissenschaft, 42*(3), 206–223.

Hansen, K. H. (2008). The curriculum workshop: A place for deliberative inquiry and teacher professional learning. *European Educational Research Journal, 7*(4), 487–500.

ILO. (2008). *ISCO. International standard classification of occupations*. Geneva, Switzerland: Author.

ILO. (2012). *Global employment trends 2012. Preventing a deeper jobs crisis*. Geneva, Switzerland: Author.

Janesick, V. J. (2006). *Authentic assessment*. New York, NY: Lang.

Kreuzer, C., Weber, S., Bley, S., & Wiethe-Körprich, M. (2017). Measuring Intrapreneurship competence as a manifestation of work agency in different educational settings. In M. Goller, & S. Paloniemi (Eds.), *Agency at work*, (pp. 373–399). Cham (CH), Switzerland: Springer.

Littunen, H. (2000). Entrepreneurship and the characteristics of the entrepreneurial personality. *International Journal of Entrepreneurial Behaviour and Research*, 6(6), 295–309.

Malloch, M., Cairns, L., Evans, K., & O'Connor, B. N. (Eds.) (2011). *The SAGE handbook of workplace learning*. Los Angeles, CA: Sage.

Massey, A., & Johnston, K. (Eds.) (2015). *The international handbook of public administration and governance*. Cheltenham, UK: Edward Elgar.

Mayer, R. E. (1999). *The promise of educational psychology: Learning in the content areas*. Upper Saddle River, NJ: Pearson.

Mayer, K. U., & Diewald, M. (2007). Entwicklung als soziale und kulturelle Konstruktion [development as social and cultural construction]. In J. Brandstädter, & U. Lindenberger (Eds.), *Entwicklungspsychologie der Lebensspanne*, (pp. 510–539). Stuttgart, Germany: Kohlhammer.

Mayer, K. U., & Solga, H. (2008). Skill formation. Interdisciplinary and cross-national perspectives. In K. U. Mayer, & H. Solga (Eds.), *Skill formation. Interdisciplinary and cross-national perspectives*, (pp. 1–18). Cambridge, UK: Cambridge University Press.

Mayntz, R. (2010). *Governance im modernen Staat* [governance in modern states]. In A. Benz (Ed.), *Governance – Regieren in komplexen Regelsystemen* (2. Aufl (pp. 37–48). Wiesbaden, Germany: VS Verlag für Sozialwissenschaften.

McCracken, M., Currie, D., & Harrison, J. (2016). Understanding graduate recruitment, development and retention for the enhancement of talent management: Sharpening "the edge" of graduate talent. *The International Journal of Human Resource Management, 27*(Issue 22), 2727–2752.

Mislevy, R. J., Almond, R. G., & Lukas, J. F. (2003). *A brief introduction to evidence-centered design*. Princeton, NJ: Educational Testing Service.

Mislevy, R. J., & Haertel, G. D. (2006). Implications of evidence-centered design for dducational testing. *Educational Measurement: Issues and Practice, 25*(4), 6–20.

Mislevy, R. J. and Riconscente, M. M. (eds.) (2006). *Evidence-Centered Assessment Design: Layers, Structures, and Terminology. PADI Technical Report 9*. Menlo Park, CA: SRI International.

Mulder, M. (Ed.) (2017). *Competence-based vocational and professional education*. Cham (CH), Switzerland: Springer.

National Research Council. (2012). *Education for life and work: Developing transferable knowledge and skills in the 21st century*. Washington, DC: The National Academies Press.

OECD. (2012). *Youth unemployment rate*. DOI: https://doi.org/10.1787/20752342

Parker, S. K., & Bindl, U. K. (2017). *Proactivity at work*. London, UK: Routledge.

Pellegrino, J. W., DiBello, L. V., & Goldman, S. R. (2016). A framework for conceptualizing and evaluating the validity of instructionally relevant assessments. *Educational Psychologist, 51*(1), 59–81.

Perlman, B., Gueths, J., & Weber, D. A. (1988). *The academic intrapreneur*. Strategy, innovation, and management in higher education. New York, NY: Praeger.

Peterson, N., Mumford, M. D., Borman, W. C., Jeanneret, P. R., & Fleishman, E. A. (Eds.) (1999). *An occupational information system for the 21st century: The development of O*NET*. Washington, DC: American Psychological Association/ Cambridge University Press.

Peterson, N. G., Mumford, M. D., Borman, W. C., Jeanneret, P. R., Fleishman, E. A., Levin, K. Y., ... Dye, D. M. (2001). Understanding work using the occupational information network (O*NET): Implications for practice and research. *Personnel Psychology, 54*(2), 451–492.

Pinchot, G. (1987). Innovation through intrapreneuring. *Research Management, 30*(2), 14–19.

Rauch, A., & Frese, M. (2007). Let's put the person back into entrepreneurship research: A meta-analysis on the relationship between business Owners' personality traits, business creation, and success. *European Journal of Work and Organizational Psychology, 16*(4), 353–385.

Reich, R. B. (1997). *Die neue Weltwirtschaft – Das Ende der nationalen Ökonomie* [The work of Nations]. Frankfurt, Germany: Fischer.

Roberts, S. (2011). Beyond "NEET" and "tidy" pathways: Considering the "missing middle" of youth transition studies. *Journal of Youth Studies, 14*(1), 21–39.

Rupietta, C. and Backes-Gellner, U. (2015). High quality workplace training and innovation in highly developed countries. *Swiss Leading House Working Paper No. 74.* Zürich, Bern.

Rychen, D. S., & Salganik, L. H. (2003). A holistic model of competence. In D. S. Rychen, & L. H. Salganik (Eds.), *Key competencies for a successful life and a well-functioning-society,* (pp. 41–62). Ashland, OH: Hogrefe and Huber.

Schiro, M. S. (2013). *Curriculum theory: Conflicting visions and enduring concerns* (2nd ed.). Thousand Oaks, CA: Sage.

Scullion, H., & Collings, D. G. (Eds.) (2011). *Global talent management.* London, UK: Routledge.

Shavelson, R. J. (2010a). *Measuring college learning responsibly. Accountability in a new era.* Stanford, CA: Stanford University Press.

Shavelson, R. J. (2010b). On the measurement of competency. *Empirical Research in Vocational Education and Training, 2*(1), 41–63.

Shavelson, R. J. (2012). Assessing business-planning competence using the collegiate learning assessment as a prototype. *Empirical Research in Vocational Education and Training, 4*(1), 77–90.

Stahl, G., Björkman, I., Farndale, E., Morris, S. S., Paauwe, J., Stiles, P., ... Wright, P. (2012). Global talent management: How leading multinationals build and sustain their talent pipeline. *Sloan Management Review, 53*(2), 25–42.

Symonds, W. C., Schwartz, R. B., & Ferguson, R. (2011). *Pathways to prosperity: Meeting the challenges of preparing young Americans for the 21st century.* Boston, MA: *Harvard* Graduate School of Education.

Tarique, I., & Schuler, R. S. (2010). Global talent management: Literature review, integrative framework, and suggestions for further research. *Journal of World Business, 45,* 122–133.

The Partnership for 21st Century Learning. (2017). *Framework for 21st century learning.* Retrieved from: http://www.nea.org/home/34888.htm

Trost, S., & Weber, S. (2012). Fähigkeitsanforderungen an kaufmännische Fachkräfte – Eine kompetenzbasierte Analyse von Stellenanzeigen mittels O*NET [abilities of commercial employees – A competence-based analyses of job advertisings using O*NET]. *Zeitschrift für Berufs- und Wirtschaftspädagogik, 108*(2), 217–242.

Tynjälä, P. (2013). Toward a 3-P model of workplace learning: A literature review. *Vocations and Learning, 6*(1), 11–36.

UNESCO. (2006). ISCED 1997 *International Standard Classification of Education.* Re-edition. Online: http://www.uis.unesco.org/TEMPLATE/pdf isced/ISCED_A.pdf

United Nations. (2012). *World youth report*. Youth employment: youth perspectives on the pursuit of decent work in changing times. United Nations: Department of Economic and Social Affairs.

von Graevenitz, G., Harhoff, D., & Weber, R. (2010). The effects of entrepreneurship education. *Journal of Economic Behavior and Organization*, *76*(1), 90–112.

Weber, S. (2013). Sense of workplace learning. *Vocations and Learning*, *6*(1), 1–9.

Weber, S., & Achtenhagen, F. (2014). Fachdidaktisch gesteuerte Modellierung und Messung von Kompetenzen im Bereich der beruflichen Bildung [modeling and measuring competences in VET]. In E. Winther, & M. Prenzel (Eds.), (Hrsg.)*Perspektiven der empirischen Berufsbildungsforschung. Zeitschrift für Erziehungswissenschaft, Sonderheft 22* (pp. 33–58). Wiesbaden, Germany: Springer VS.

Weber, S., & Achtenhagen, F. (2017). Competence domains and vocational-professional education in Germany. In M. Mulder (Ed.), *Competence-based vocational and professional education*, (pp. 337–359). Cham (CH), Switzerland: Springer.

Weber, S., Draxler, C., Bley, S., Wiethe-Körprich, M., Weiß, C., & Gürer, C. (2016). Der Projektverbund COBALIT: Large scale assessments in der kaufmännischen Berufsbildung – Intrapreneurship [Large-scale assessments in VET – Intrapreneurship]. In K. Beck, M. Landenberger, & F. Oser (Eds.), (Hrsg.)*Technologiebasierte Kompetenzmessung in der beruflichen Bildung* (pp. 75–92). Bielefeld, Germany: Bertelsmann.

Weber, S., & Funke, S. (2014). A research- and evidence-based entrepreneurship education program at Ludwig-Maximilians University (LMU), Munich. In S. Weber, F. K. Oser, F. Achtenhagen, M. Fretschner, & S. Trost (Eds.), *Becoming an entrepreneur*, (pp. 177–195). Rotterdam, The Netherlands: Sense.

Weber, S., & Lehtinen, E. (2014). Transition from school-to-work and its challenges. *Unterrichtswissenschaft*, *42*(3), 194–205.

Weber, S., & Rippen, J. (1999). Das duale Ausbildungsprogramm C.A.T.S. (commercial advancement training scheme) als element der südafrikanischen Berufsausbildung [the commercial advancement training scheme as element of south-African VET]. *Zeitschrift für Berufs- und Wirtschaftspädagogik*, *95*(1), 34–62.

Weber, S., Trost, S., Wiethe-Körprich, M., Weiß, C., & Achtenhagen, F. (2014). Intrapreneur: An entrepreneur within a company – An approach on modeling and measuring intrapreneurship competence. In S. Weber, F. K. Oser, F. Achtenhagen, M. Fretschner, & S. Trost (Eds.), *Becoming an entrepreneur*, (pp. 279–302). Rotterdam, The Netherlands/Boston, MA/Taipei, Taiwan: Sense.

Weber, S., Wiethe-Körprich, M., Bley, S., Weiß, C., Draxler, C., & Gürer, C. (2016). Modellierung und Validierung eines Intrapreneurship-Kompetenz-Modells bei Industriekaufleuten [modeling and validating an intrapreneurship competence model]. *Unterrichtswissenschaft*, *44*(2), 149–168.

Weinert, F. E. (2001). Concept of competence: A conceptual clarification. In D. S. Rychen, & L. H. Salganik (Eds.), *Defining and selecting key competencies*, (pp. 45–65). Seattle, WA: Hogrefe and Huber.

Welter, F. (2010). Contextualising entrepreneurship: Conceptual challenges and ways forward. *Entrepreneurship Theory & Practice*, *35*(1), 165–184.

Wiethe-Körprich, M., Weber, S., Bley, S., & Kreuzer, C. (2017). Intrapreneurship competence as a manifestation of work agency: A systematic literature review. In M. Goller, & S. Paloniemi (Eds.), *Agency at work* (pp. 37–65). Cham (CH): Springer.

Wilson, M. (2005). *Constructing measures*. Mahwah, NJ: Lawrence Erlbaum.

Wilson, M., DeBoeck, P., & Carstensen, C. H. (2008). Explanatory Item response models: A brief introduction. In J. Hartig, E. Klieme, & D. Leutner (Eds.), *Assessment of competencies in educational contexts* (pp. 91–120). Göttingen: Hogrefe.

Winterton, J. (2009). Competence across Europe: Highest common factor or lowest common denominator? *Journal of European Industrial Training, 33*, 681–700.

Winther, E. (2010). *Kompetenzmessung in der beruflichen Bildung* [Competence measurement in VET]. Bielefeld: Bertelsmann.

Wu, M. L., Adams, R. J., Wilson, M., and Haldane, S. A. (2007). *ACER CONQUEST. Version 2.0.* Camberwell: ACER Press.

Ziegler, B., Balkenhol, A., Keimes, C., & Rexing, V. (2012). Diagnostik "funktionaler Lesekompetenz" [Diagnosis of "functional reading competence"]. *bwp@ Ausgabe Nr. 22 | Juni* 2012. http://www.bwpat.de/ausgabe22/ziegler_etal_bwpat22.pdf

Ziegler, B., Frey, A., Seeber, S., Balkenhol, A., & Bernhardt, R. (2016). Adaptive Messung allgemeiner Kompetenzen [Adaptive measurement of general competences]. In K. Beck, M. Landenberger, & F. Oser (Eds.), *Technologiebasierte Kompetenzmessung in der beruflichen Bildung* [Technology-based competence measurement in VET] (pp. 33–53). Bielefeld: Bertelsmann.

# 8

# Global Strategic Planning

*John D. Pessima*[1] *and Bart Dietz*[2]

[1] *The World Bank Group*
[2] *Erasmus University*

The business environment has increasingly become global, forcing organizations to have a robust strategy in place as their customers come to expect to be served wherever they are in the world. This, together with the accelerating rate of change, requires interactive and agile planning designs and a culture of continuous learning and adaptation (Roy & Singh, 2015). Leading organizations are developing HR operating models that are flexible enough to allow for local implementation and agile enough to adapt to local markets and business trends (Deloitte Human Capital, 2014).

To be successful in today's global business environment, national as well as multinational corporations (MNCs) must deploy their resources against competitors in a highly integrated and agile approach. Organizations undertake strategic planning to align markets and competition through effective deployment of their in-house capabilities and resources. This requires aligning their human capital, market positioning, financial capital and environmental analysis in novel ways, that offer them hard-to-copy strategic options. The development of an organizational strategy provides a long-term road map for growth, profitability and sustainability and is critically important in light of the constantly changing and uncertain economic circumstances in which businesses operate.

Strategic planning is a critical process used by organizations to compete in the marketplace. The strategic statement provides the bedrock for the entire organization to create and execute tactics for future business through prioritization of goals. It helps align organizational priorities, resources and customer demands/expectations with the competitive landscape. Strategic decisions taken as part of the strategic planning process are far more difficult to reverse and often involve critical organizational stakeholders' alignment. Such decisions dictate a long-term vision of the organization. Despite the perceived benefits of strategic planning, it appears to be grossly underutilized by many stakeholders involved in the process.

*The Wiley Handbook of Global Workplace Learning*, First Edition.
Edited by Vanessa Hammler Kenon and Sunay Vasant Palsole.

Strategic planning is defined by Varkey and Bennet (2010), as a set of organizational processes for identifying the desired future of the organization and developing decisions, guidelines and frameworks for how an organization will achieve its objectives and goals. Strategic planning is a process to provide organizational resources and unifying attempts to achieve goals and long-term vision regarding internal and external limitations. It can be seen as both an "art" and a "science" or an inspired combination of the two (Broderick, 2011). Rajasekar and Raee (2014), defined strategic planning broadly as the execution of plans produced through comprehensive analysis and systematic procedures. The term has varying understanding and interpretations to various stakeholders.

While some stakeholders see the process as the vision that shapes the future of the organization toward growth and competitiveness, it is also experienced by many as a tactical endeavor involving intense exercises with a plan designed to capture advantage in the market place with human capital, market analysis and positioning, financial and technological capabilities and environmental analyses as input variables. Although there are different understandings and interpretations of the process of strategic planning, focusing on internal and external limitations and opportunities, engaging in the process and making strategic choices as an organization are critical to achieve alignment around the vision and mission of a business. These also provide guidance for issues like product/ market improvement, enhancement of operational processes, community engagement, and bottom-line productivity. Strategic planning is seen by many organizations as the coping mechanism for the constant growth and rapid changes in their environment (Rajasekar & Raee, 2014).

There are many interpretations of the terms strategy, strategic management, and planning. Central to the different definitions is the long-term horizon and the desire to achieve an impactful organizational goal. While this chapter will not focus on definitions, it will elaborate on the process of strategic planning in the global context. Strategy is a portfolio of initiatives with the intention of moving the organization from its present state to a future and desired state. A robust strategy focuses resources, clarifies decisions and intent, energizes execution, manages risk and unleashes potential (Broderick, 2011). The choice for a global strategy for organizations is precipitated by various factors: it could be a response to a local market need while avoiding competitiveness on a global scale and/or a defensive move to protect market share. Successful multinational corporations (MNCs) promote a unified vision and work toward aligning everyone behind it (Broderick, 2011).

Crafting a business strategy in a rapidly changing market is more than just visioning, forecasting and planning. It involves redefining all substantive issues of strategy such as issues of implementation and actual positioning in the competitive marketplace as well as a comprehensive review of the company's capabilities.

Given the fast pace and unpredictable context of the business environment, many organizations are realizing that strategies that worked well in the past no longer deliver the anticipated results (McGrath, 2013). Dramatic changes in the global business environment described by volatility, uncertainty, complexity and ambiguity (Johansen, 2007), have unearthed major gaps between traditional models to strategic planning.

According to Roth (2015), most organizations are bogged down in the traditional approaches to strategic planning that take too long to develop, and lack the agility required and produced results often become obsolete even before they are implemented. The traditional strategic planning approach driven by the notion of competitive advantage, as proposed by Michael Porter, is less suitable for understanding the current markets, competition and the operating context to deliver sustainable competitive advantage. The markets around the world have become faster-paced than they were a decade or more ago, such that old models of understanding and responding to the market competitive forces are becoming inefficient and ineffective to responding to such market threats and customer demands. Such models don't seem to make sense of the huge wave of data pouring in on organizations. The length of time a company might expect its competitive advantage to last had steadily declined since the 1960s (Kiechel, 2010). Competitive advantage, the ability of a firm to outperform rivals on profitability and other stakeholder values, depends on how a firm can create value for its customers that exceeds the firm's cost of creating a product. It is the key to long-term value creation that is considered as the main objective behind the management of strategic decisions (Roy & Singh, 2015).

We like to build on the ideas of McGrath (2013), a leading strategy consultant, who has proposed a shift from the sustainable competitive advantage school associated with Michael Porter, which has become hard to realize and defend for most of today's organizations, toward more adaptive forms of strategy. Also, others like Kiechel (2010) have noted the concept of adaptive strategy, which requires that instead of top-down dictated strategy based on analysts' predictions and deductions, the goal would be to develop and sustain optimal conditions for the continuous emergence of superior strategies through an adaptive and evolutionary process. This would require giving more regulatory responsibility to those in proximity to the market, like customers and suppliers.

Globalization is dissolving the difference between local and international businesses. Almost all organizations are affected by trends toward global marketing, trade barriers and tariffs. Even those who do not trade outside their national borders are increasingly affected by competitors and trends from other countries. Fast-paced technological changes disrupting existing business models have made the process even more complex. This requires most existing strategy tools be used with caution. Hypercompetition has added another layer to the challenges facing organizations. Indeed, we agree with Blythe and Zimmerman's (2004) notion that global strategic planning is a process of identifying market positions across national boundaries, seizing on the opportunity to develop global competitive strengths and capabilities which would not be otherwise developed if they decide to stay local. Organizations implementing global strategic planning perceive key opportunities and threats beyond their domestic markets. Globalization generates economies of scale and allows firms to spread risks. However, global strategies can also lead to problems of adaptation to meet local conditions in the target markets.

This chapter presents an outline of global strategic planning, its challenges, the tools currently in use and the approaches to adapt the strategic thinking and tools to the markets in which they operate. It also covers a series of contextual factors.

## Strategic Planning in a Global Context

Having looked at why organizations do strategic planning, the current political, environmental, social, technological, ethical and legal (PESTEL) factors, and how they have helped to shape the process, this section will look at the global context and some of the thinking around strategic planning. Many organizations viewed long-term strategic planning as a leadership responsibility (Varkey & Bennet, 2010). The Chief Executive Officer (CEO), Chief Strategy Officer (CSO), or Chief Operations Officer (COO) drives the process together with the leadership team. Other organizations have a strategic planning unit staffed with professionals from various input units of the organization such as Human Resources, Finance, Marketing, Product Development/ Operations, Information Technology and Legal, all tasked with the responsibility of spearheading the strategy development exercise, as well as monitoring progress against target. Still other organizations hire consulting firms or independent strategy consultants to help with the process. Whether the process is led by senior management using a team of staff or a team of strategy consultants, it remains an art as well as a science. An art in the sense of which inputs or combination of inputs to take into the planning process and how much detail would be needed to provide sufficient insight. It involves the science of evidence-based decision-making, balancing the array of risk factors spanning the range from planning risk, search risk, business model risk, organizational risk to management risks (Kim & Mauborgne, 2005).

Strategic planning efforts traditionally have four important phases. The process starts with an understanding of a firm's situation relative to the competition (environmental scanning) which is a key driver for strategic planning. The second phase is the definition of long-term objectives and short-term goals. Such understanding of the organization's strategic context will help transform a company to compete more effectively on local and global markets. Various tools and frameworks are used to assess the internal and external context of organizations to discover what is happening and how it might be affecting the organization's competitive position and to plan appropriate strategies to address them. The seminal strategy thinker Peter Drucker (1973), long ago proposed fivekey questions in helping to understand a firm's strategic direction:

- What is the business that the organization operates?
- What customers does it intend to serve?
- What is the value it provides for its customers?
- What would be the business it intends to run 3–5 years from now?
- What should be the business 3–5 years from now?

While Drucker's ideas originate from over four decades ago, they are still relevant to the strategic planning process of many organizations today. Kiechel (2010), also proposed the following boundary strategy questions: (a) what would be the right way to define the market or segment; (b) how should the competition be understood and approached? And, (c) how broad of a scope must the organization consider for its value chain. To answer these questions requires a deep dive into an understanding and analysis of the organizational strengths, weaknesses, opportunities and threats (SWOT) and other market forces. The internal audit approach can also be used to study the flow of the organizations including inputs, throughputs, and outputs in combination with the SWOT analysis. Trend analysis and the reference projection tools are also valuable approaches in helping to best scan the environment. The reference projection helps to identify past and present trends and to project them into the future (Roth, 2015).

The question of what is the business the organization is involved in will help to articulate the vision/ mission of the organization. This depends on the customers it is servicing, the value it delivers for those customers and the competitive landscape within which it operates. The question of what will be the business the organization will be delivering is a projection of the current trend with everything else being equal which is hardly the case in today's unpredictable market environment. The strategic visioning model by Peter Drucker hardly works for many organizations today given the transient nature of markets and the plethora of data points to inform decisions. Organizations make strategic decisions in an evolving or adaptive manner driven by their customer demands and competitive pressures. The critical question of what should be the future business of the organization is what drives the strategic planning process.

Van den Heijden (2005), referred to three main schools of thought on strategic management and planning. These are the rationalist, evolutionalist and processual schools of thought.

> The rationalist school of thought believes in the concept of the best solution. The strategic planning team or strategist is tasked with the mandate to craft the best strategy for the organization or to develop the best solution or find the best answer. This school of thought bestowed the strategy planning process to a few elites within the organization to convene and formulate the strategic plan to which all relevant units will need to align.
>
> The evolutionary school of thought on the other hand focuses on the past and retrospect. This approach to strategic planning believes that an organization has a memory of previous successful strategies that can inform future success. Unsuccessful strategies are filtered and successful strategies used to drive business success and extrapolated to form the future direction of the organization.
>
> The processual school of thought asserts that although it is not possible to craft optimal strategy through rational thinking alone, organizational strategic planning teams can design a process within the organization that is flexible and adaptive and that is capable to learn from failures. This school of thought is based on the theory that alternative futures are possible through the utilization of change management processes and concepts. Authors like Labib (2014) reason that individuals and organizations learn from failures. Incremental learning which tends to be control-oriented, therefore, seeks to maintain predictable operations, and minimize variations, while radical learning seeks to increase variations to explore opportunities and challenge the status quo. This school of thought lends from the traditional school of thought which emphasizes learning from success (Labib, 2014).

Multinational corporations put in place global strategy teams to lead their global strategic planning process. Varkey et al. suggest that the strategy-formulation process is best carried out by the executive team with assistance from the management team. This provides them with a worldview of the markets they serve, the opportunities they pursue and challenges they face in these markets. A global strategic planning team would need to be regionally balanced. When dominated by one country it will not have a true global view of the challenges and opportunities that need to be factored in the strategy-planning process. Other organizations contract global strategy consulting firms such as BCG, Bain, Deloitte, McKinsey, PWC or renowned individual strategy consultants to help with their global strategic planning process, including markets competitive analysis and assessments.

In addition to the national strategies of member firms, MNC's also have a global strategy in place. The latter is not the sum of national strategies but a deliberate vision and mission of the global organization to achieve a sustainable or transient competitive advantage depending on the markets it serves or the opportunities it pursues. A company which is a cost leader in its domestic market, could be a differentiator in a foreign market either because its products are unknown outside of its domestic market or it has incorporated capabilities into the product or its functionality that are unique in the foreign market. The global positioning of a firm's product and services is a very challenging exercise, involving a range of analytical tools to understand and adapt to the pace of change of the business environment.

Blythe and Zimmerman (2004) argue that firms seeking to formulate effective global strategies will be affected by the following factors:

- An intense and gruesome competition. In many global markets, competition has moved from joking for positions, as presented by Michael Porter in his work on competitive advantage, to hypercompetition in which disruption and surprises have become the new normal;
- Rapid shifts in the business environment induced by frequent entry of new and unknown competitors from other countries and markets;
- The difficulty in predicting future trends in an information-swamped planning environment that is precipitated by volatility, complexity, uncertainty and ambiguity.

## The Strategy-Planning Process

The strategyplanning process forces leadership of organizations to look diligently into the future direction of the organization. It forces organizations to develop the capabilities to get to market early, to understand what is going on in their markets, develop scenarios, and make tough choices to succeed in a perpetually fast-changing world of unpredictability and dilemmas without resorting to a false sense of certainty (Johansen, 2007). Furthermore, it forces leadership to ask tough questions about the future of the organization, its competitiveness and future challenges. It encourages leadership to re-evaluate past assumptions and

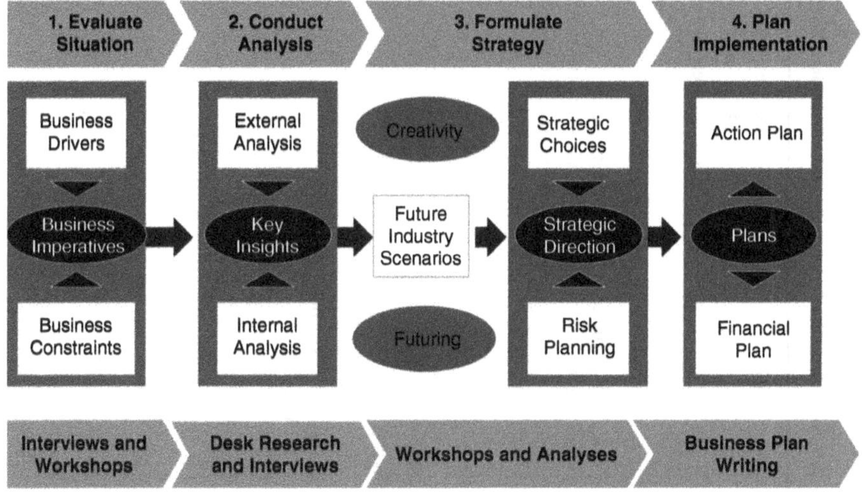


**Figure 8.1** The Strategy-Planning Process

scenarios constantly considering new circumstances and facts. The exercise when conducted on a global or national scale demands an in-depth understanding of the internal capabilities of the organization and its external context. It helps focus on what matters for the future survival of the organization. According to Broderick (2011)), strategic planning also has psychological benefits. As a tool, it promotes collaboration, creates a sense of renewal and mission around the organizational goals and provides the opportunity to generate excitement and buy-in by re-energizing all stakeholders about the potential outcome of strategic plans, the challenges the organization has to face and the opportunities to pursue. The process also helps to specify the roles and responsibilities to make this happen. The model in Figure 8.1 is a strategy-planning model developed by the authors. It illustrates four phases of strategic planning, the processes that support each phase and the output that is generated.

## Strategy Development

The process of strategic planning uses a plethora of analytical tools and models (Jowkar, Nia, & Far, 2015; Rajasekar & Raee, 2014; Siddique, 2015) to make sense of the organization's capabilities, constraints, customer demands, competition and PESTEL factors. These tools can be applied in different contexts whether the organization is developing a blue or red ocean strategy (Kim & Mauborgne, 2005), deliberate or emergent strategy (Petkovic & Jasinskas, 2016) or developing capabilities for a transient competitive advantage (McGrath, 2013). A novel combination of some of these tools helps to generate unique insights that support strategy development. Table 8.1 is an analysis of the strategy-development process, the tools that companies can use and their sources of reference.

**Table 8.1** The Tools that Companies Can Use in Their Strategy-Development Process

| Strategy-development process | Strategic process | Tools | Referencing authors | Stakeholder engagement |
|---|---|---|---|---|
| Evaluation of company situation | Business drivers | Strategy map | Evans, 2013 | Expert interviews and workshops |
| | Business constraints | Strengths, Weaknesses, Opportunities, Threats (SWOT) analysis | Evans, 2013; Van den Heijden, 2005 | Staff engagement surveys |
| Conduct internal and external analysis | Internal analysis | SWOT analysis | Evans, 2013; Van den Heijden, 2005 | Desk research, interviews, outsource to strategy consulting firms |
| | | The capability gap | Evans, 2013 | |
| | | Engagement survey | | |
| | | Assessing demand for people | Turner, 2002 | |
| | | The People Process Map | Turner, 2002 | |
| | External analysis | Political, Environmental, Social, Technological, Ethical, Legal (PESTEL) analysis | Evans, 2013 | |
| | | Porter five forces model | Evans, 2013; Kiechel, 2010; Van den Heijden, 2005 | |
| | | The pyramid principle | Evans, 2013 | |
| | | McKinsey's 9-box matrix | Kiechel, 2010 | |
| | | Boston Consulting Group (BCG) growth-share matrix | Evans, 2013; Kiechel, 2010 | |
| | | BCG competitive environment matrix | Kiechel, 2010 | |
| | | GE/McKinsey attractiveness/advantage matrix | Evans, 2013 | |
| | | Market intelligence reports, Hoof demand forecasting | Evans, 2013 | |
| | | Factors contributing to the need for strategic human capital management | | |

| | | | | |
|---|---|---|---|---|
| Formulate strategy | Strategic choices | Grant resource and capability strength/ importance matrix | Evans, 2013 | Workshops and analysis |
| | | Ansoff product/market matrix | Evans, 2013 | |
| | | Scenario planning | Evans, 2013; Van den Heijden, 2005 | |
| | | Scenario/option matrix | Van den Heijden, 2005 | |
| | | Porter generic strategies | Evans, 2013 | |
| | | Value innovation | Kim & Mauborgne, 2005 | |
| | | The four actions framework | Kim & Mauborgne, 2005 | |
| | | Strategy canvas | Kim & Mauborgne, 2005 | |
| | | The eliminate–reduce–raise–create grid | Kim & Mauborgne, 2005 | |
| | | The four steps of visualizing strategy | Kim & Mauborgne, 2005 | |
| | Risk planning | The Suns and Clouds chart | Evans, 2013 | |
| | | Six principles of blue ocean strategy | Kim & Mauborgne, 2005 | |
| Implementation planning | Human capital plan | The manpower plan | Turner, 2002 | Developing robust implementation plan |
| | | The human resource plan | Turner, 2002 | |
| | Product/ marketing plan | McCarthy 4Ps marketing mix | Evans, 2013 | |
| | Financial plan/ target | Market contextual revenue review | | |
| | Operational plan | Creating a culture of success – Seven key levers | Turner, 2002 | |
| | Technological plan | Christensen disruptive technological change | Evans, 2013 | |
| | Manage project and change management communications | Options to communicating in a networked organization | Johansen, 2007 | |
| Monitoring and evaluation | | | | Various monitoring and evaluation tools (Strategy Monitor, Performance Dashboards) |

Firms charting global strategies face challenges orchestrating an inclusive planning and reviewing process. Major stakeholders at the country and regional levels need to be actively involved in the planning process. It is also important that the newly crafted strategy is tested not only in its current markets but also in emerging markets to determine its adaptability to varying market demands.

The strategy-planning process often starts with an assessment or evaluation of the internal capabilities. This involves assessment of current business activities, staffing, service/ product portfolio, pricing strategies, input from employee engagement surveys, market surveys, speed-to-market and financial capabilities to support the desired strategy. Given the fact that the external environment in which organizations operate is changing so rapidly, the strategic planning process needs to be very swift and adaptive in order to remain relevant and useful (Broderick, 2011; McGrath, 2013). It needs to be able to flex and bend to changing customer demands and competitive pressures.

The following analysis and analytical tools help to put the external market analysis into perspective: market assessment, industry trends and competitive landscape analysis, growth rate of core products and services, and competitive positioning. The external analyses such as the Porter's Five Forces analysis, PESTEL analysis, the pyramid principle, McKinsey's 9-box matrix or attractiveness/advantage matrix, Growth-Share matrix analysis, BCG's competitive environment matrix all help to identify high-impact trends, products and service needs and gaps with existing offerings and for testing competitive positioning within global markets. Input from key clients, customer feedback, secondary research on the state of the market and competitive landscape also serve as secondary sources of data into the strategy-planning process. Foresight of disruptive technologies that might threaten planning over a 3–5-year horizon allows for incremental steps in achieving significant changes in strategic intent such as expanding into new markets, growth strategies for such capabilities in-house, remaining flexible enough to respond opportunistically to market shifts, resource changes and external events.

Most organizations have developed templates to consistently capture strategic drivers for summarizing the external analysis and capturing the internal capabilities. Various other models exist to support the strategy-development process. The choice of which tools to deploy is discretional to the strategy-planning team. According to the stages of planning as proposed by (Kiechel, 2010), organizations can be mapped into the four phases of strategic planning based on the effectiveness of strategic decision-making and the value they want to create:

- **Phase 1**: financial planning looks at the annual budget and functional focus of the organization as the starting point. Organizations at this level are focusing on meeting budgetary demands.
- **Phase 2**: forecast-based planning which involves multi-year budgets, gaps analysis based on actuals against planned forecasts and the static allocation of resources in the realization of strategic objectives. Such organizations are labeled as predicting the future.
- **Phase 3**: externally oriented planning with robust situational and competitive analysis, evaluation of strategic alternatives and dynamic allocation of resources. These organizations are termed as thinking strategically.

- **Phase 4**: strategic management organizations have well defined strategic framework with widespread strategic thinking capabilities, coherent reinforcing management processes for negotiating objectives, reviewing progress and incentivizing with a support value system and climate. Organizations on this path are termed: "creating the future."

William Roth (2015), proposed another four phases of strategic planning: (i) environmental scanning, (ii) definition and articulation of long-term objectives and short-term goals, (iii) definition of an implementation strategy or a vehicle for realizing the proposed goals and objectives, and (iv) evaluation, monitoring and control of the resultant changes. While both Roth and Kiechel cover the same phases of the strategic planning process, each phase is prescribed differently. During environmental scanning which is the first phase according to Roth, participants examine both the internal and external environments to discover what is happening and how it might be affecting the organization. In Kiechel's sequencing of the process, this is addressed in phases, 1, 2, and 3. This reiterates the fact that there is no fixed approach to conducting strategic planning. However, all strategic planning process undertakes these four critical phases to fully understand their competitive position and to craft a strategy for realizing their short-term goals and long-term objectives. The formulation of the strategic objective is critical to its realization.

## Strategy Implementation

A strategy without a strong execution plan creates confusion rather than clarity and is hardly successful. Organizations are not only made of top or middle management but everyone from top management to the front lines. Lack of inclusiveness of employees is among the range of barriers Petkovic and Jasinskas (2016), mentioned affecting strategy formulation. Strategy implementation is done at the unit level with a continuous, rigorous monitoring process, measuring progress against plan. It is when all levels of the organization support the strategy for whatever it is, that will help to set the organization apart as a consistent executor of strategy.

Strategy implementation is taking various shapes and forms in organizations depending on the size and complexity of the organization, the industry segment in which the organization operates and the complexity of the strategy. Irrespective of these implementation-defining factors, its pace of implementation; people's minds and hearts must align with the new strategy to get their buy-in and commitment to its execution. This requires a culture of trust and commitment that would motivate people to execute the agreed strategy as planned. According to Kim and Mauborgne (2005), to build people's trust and commitment deep in the ranks and inspire their voluntary cooperation, organizations need to build execution into strategy planning right from the start. Kim and Mauborgne (2005) reason that this would minimize the management risk of distrust, non-cooperation and sabotage, which are relevant to the execution of both blue and red ocean strategies.

Oversight for the strategy implementation is either allocated to a strategic planning and monitoring unit or confined to the COO, CFO, CEO, or a partner on the executive committee assigned to oversee implementation and monitoring. The head of strategy monitoring and evaluation meets with the heads of the products and services teams or heads of the implementation teams on a regular basis for progress on implementation. They assess performance against plan, propose directional changes and provide feedback to the respective leads. The process can utilize the support of a knowledgeable facilitator to guide the brainstorming process for an efficient process and to also serve as an external validator of the strategic statement (Varkey & Bennet, 2010). The strategy implementation and review meetings help senior management of the organizations to keep informed on the direction of the business and implementation progress, surface potential problems early and re-assess strategic choices. Necessary adjustments can be made to the implementation plans to reflect the market dynamics of the business and to keep an eye on the expected results.

## Monitoring and Evaluation

What gets measured, gets managed (Weatherly, 2003, p. 4). Roth (2015), refers to evaluation as keeping track of the obstacles that arise during each step of the implementation process. However, strategy evaluation is not an easy process. It demands an attitude toward the goals, activities and results of an organization that is connected to the development of each activity and individual staff members (Petkovic & Jasinskas, 2016). Given the integrated nature of service offerings within organizations today, obstacles arising in one part of the organization can invariably create a cascading effect in other parts. Identifying the right monitoring and reporting tools and reports is critical to the success of strategy implementation. Employees should be capable of adapting when something unexpected happens. If the measurement or metric is inappropriate or measures the wrong outcomes, it is useless. Peter Drucker made a very fundamental distinction between doing things right and doing the right things. It is one thing to measure the right metrics wrongly, quite another to measure the wrong metrics correctly.

Many organizations have monthly and/or quarterly progress reports. Those operating in hypercompetitive markets have real-time monitoring and reporting capabilities to allow the product divisions, service leaders or head of the talent division to monitor progress 24/7. Some organizations co-opt periodically or have real-time customer feedback and employee engagement surveys to assess progress against strategic intent. Keeping a constant eye on the markets and competitive trends that would potentially impact the strategic plans is a critical part of the implementation agenda. Progress with strategy implementation and performance can be reported at different levels using the concept of a strategy monitor – a strategy-implementation reporting and monitoring tool that can cascade information on strategy implementation to the various management levels. For the strategic activities to be successful, the quality of the available data and its interpretation is critically important. It also depends on cooperation with employees, attention to their opinion through surveys and other feedback mechanisms.

## Integrating Risk Management Into Global Strategic Planning

There is no strategy without risks, as the process of strategy development involves risk-taking in the pursuit of investment opportunities (Kim & Mauborgne, 2005). The strategy-planning process is fraught with risks of various types ranging from planning risks with the narrow focus of the strategy on incremental improvements to the creation of innovations that change the competitive landscape. The process can also involve selecting a wrong business model or not having the focus on existing customer demand, which can lead to scale risk. Furthermore, if proper execution is not built in the strategy-planning process with adequate people resources and expertise to support implementation, it would suffer from change management risk. Risk and the strategy-planning process are inseparable but can be managed through the awareness of the strategy team in terms of the risks they are faced with.

## Conclusion

Global Strategic Planning is not a static, but a dynamic process. It involves multiple stakeholders who often lack an in-depth understanding of the context, competition and challenges that the organization faces. The art and science of strategic planning is an iterative and often complex process. It involves working with people and acquiring the trust, commitment and voluntary contribution of the employees of the organization toward the process. Making strategy difficult to replicate by competitors is greatly dependent on people factors and its customizable local implementation options.

In line with Roth (2015), we recommend that companies that want to survive the increasingly complex environment structure their options around the following three procedures: (i) find a strategy to slow the rate of change, (ii) come up with a strategy that would predict where the change is leading, and prepare for it, and (iii) design their organization so that it is capable of monitoring change both internally and externally and adapting rapidly, or even shaping it. The last option appeals to a growing number of organizations as it does not only make the most sense but is also implementable.

We hope this chapter will provide practicing managers with the context, approaches, tools and frameworks that are relevant for undertaking a strategy-planning session or for stimulating strategic thinking and analysis for their organizations. With the dynamic nature of the global market, continuous scanning, and adaptation of the factors that affect an organization's line of business, should be the order of the day. This chapter is not prescriptive in the way that strategic planning should be approached as there is no prescribed approach or sequence of events. Rather, we intend to convey that future strategic planning success will depend on the ability of practitioners to effectively analyze their internal and external contexts, deploy the right tools and frameworks and leverage human capital in their planning efforts.

## References


Blythe, J., & Zimmerman, A. (2004). Strategic planning for global markets. *The Marketing Review, 4*, 369–384.

Broderick, M. (2011). *The art of managing professional services: Insights from leaders of the world top firms* (1st ed.). Upper Saddle River, NJ: Prentice Hall.

Deloitte Human Capital (2014). *The global and local HR function: Balance scale and agility*. London: Deloitte. Retrieved from https://www2.deloitte.com/insights/us/en/focus/human-capital-trends/2014/hc-trends-2014-global-and-local-hr.html Accessed December 9, 2018.

Drucker, P. (1973). *Management: Tasks, responsibilities, practices.* New York: Harper & Row.

Evans, V. (2013). *Key strategy tools* (1st ed.). Harlow, UK: Pearson Education Limited.

Johansen, B. (2007). *Get there early: Sensing the future to compete in the present* (1st ed.). San Francisco, CA: Berrett-KoehlerPublishers, Inc.

Jowkar, A., Nia, M. B., & Far, S. K. (2015). A comparative analysis for organizations strategic planning using essential implications of strategic management within an organization (Case study: Organizations of Khorasan Razavi used organizational long term plans). *International Journal of Scientific Management and Development, 3*(1), 784–792.

III Kiechel, W. (2010). *The lords of strategy* (1st ed.). Boston, MA: Harvard Business Press.

Kim, C. W., & Mauborgne, R. (2005). *Blue ocean strategy* (1st ed.). Boston, MA: Harvard Business School Publishing Corporation.

Labib, A. (2014). *Learning from failures* (1st ed.). Oxford, UK: Elsevier Inc.

McGrath, R. G. (2013). *The end of competitive advantage* (1st ed.). Boston, MA: Harvard Business Press.

Petkovic, J. and Jasinskas, E. (2016). Significance of strategic planning for results of sport organization. https://doi.org/10.15240/tul/001/2016-4-005

Rajasekar, J., & Raee, A. A. (2014). Organizations' use of strategic planning tools and techniques in the sultanate of Oman. *International Business Research, 7*(3). https://doi.org/10.5539/ibr.v7n3p159

Roth, W. F. (2015). Strategic planning as an organization design exercise. *Performance Improvement, 54*(6), 6–13. https://doi.org/10.1002/pfi.21487

Roy, S., & Singh, S. N. (2015). Strategic planning for management of technology-an empirical study with indian steel sectors. *Vision: The Journal of Business Perspective, 19*(2), 112–131. https://doi.org/10.1177/0972262914567771

Siddique, C. M. (2015). A comparative study of strategic planning practices. *Strategic Change, 24*(6), 553–567 https://doi.org/10.1002/jsc

Turner, P. (2002). *HR forecasting and planning* (1st ed.). London, UK: Chartered Institute of Personnel and Development.

Van den Heijden, K. (2005). *SCENARIOS: The art of strategic conversations* (2nd ed.). West Sussex, UK: Wiley.

Varkey, B. P., & Bennet, K. E. (2010). Practical techniques for strategic planning in health care organizations. *Physican Executive, 36*(2), 46–48.

Weatherly, l. A. (2003). *Human capital—the elusive asset: Measuring and managing human capital.* Alexandria, VA: SHRM Research Department.

# 9

# Global Talent Management

*John D. Pessima*[1] *and Bart Dietz*[2]

[1] *The World Bank Group*
[2] *Erasmus University*

The business context in which organizations operate today has increasingly become global, highly unpredictable and competitive. This period has also been marked by the presence of multiple generations in the workplace and a shortage of talent with critical skills. In addition to these, other talent challenges (e.g., Guthridge, Komm, & Lawson, 2008) that global organizations continue to face have been identified. These include: (i) reducing and removing talents to lower the cost of operations, (ii) locating and relocating operations to cost competitive geographies, and (iii) acquiring competent talent anywhere in the world at cost-competitive salaries. These challenges have been named "global talent shortages" which can be addressed through HR policies referred to as "global talent management" (Schuler, Jackson, & Tarique, 2011). What has made talent management critical for many organizations is the fact that talent is not owned by organizations and there is no hidden pool of talent that organizations can tap into in case of urgent need.

Since the early 1990s, the demand for talent has exceeded supply, which has increasingly created more demand for talents than markets can supply ("talent," "workforce," or "employee" are used interchangeably in this chapter). This trend has resulted in global talent shortages (Chambers, Foulon, Handfield-Jones, Hankin, & Michaels, 1998; Michaels, Handfield-Jones, & Axelrod, 2001). Many global organizations have started to experience high turnover of talent with scarce critical skills. Consequently, the terms "talent retention" and "talent management" have become key to the growth and long-term survival of organizations (Guthridge et al., 2008).

Beechler and Woodward (2009) introduced the term "global talent management" to represent the challenge that global organizations face to attract, develop, deploy and retain talents. It also refers to the systematic use of specific HR policies to manage global talent. These include specific aspects related to location and relocation management, workforce planning, forecasting, attracting, selecting, retaining, reducing and removing, training and developing, and evaluating

*The Wiley Handbook of Global Workplace Learning*, First Edition.
Edited by Vanessa Hammler Kenon and Sunay Vasant Palsole.

employees consistently with a firm's strategic direction (Schuler et al., 2011; Scullion & Collings, 2011).

These external factors, with talent demand exceeding supply, are driving the ways that organizations compete and have precipitated several global challenges, leading to the "war for talent" (Beechler & Woodward, 2009). Multi-national corporations (MNCs) have recognized that talent represents a source of competitive advantage. In today's economy, MNCs need strategies to deal with increased talent mobility, for managing multiple generations at the workplace, and to manage the impact of technological change on work. These strategies will help gain and sustain competitive advantage and meet stakeholder needs. The deployment of integrated talent management (ITM)[1] has helped many organizations operating both locally and globally (glocal), to better understand their talent management challenges and to make needed adjustments to their talent management strategies and approaches.

Essential to any local or global organization is the ability to design, develop and execute an ITM strategy that connects critical talent processes, systems and departments to realize an optimal impact of their talent strategies. According to Deloitte Bersin, the successful realization of an optimal talent strategy requires the tremendous input and effort of more than one unit and stakeholders across the organization. It also requires stewardship from leaders across the organization to make it successful.

Workforces around the world have expanded both quantitatively and qualitatively to reflect economic growth demands. Local and global firms are affected by external factors, which impact talent demand and support or the availability of talent in their markets. However, global firms are impacted differently as they are exposed to the conduits of global talent forces and global competition which provide them with a global competitive advantage when they effectively manage their global workforce. A key challenge for many organizations is to look into future talent demands and develop the strategies to work against latent talent risk, which is one of the top threats faced by so called "people businesses."

Talent in most organizations is the biggest differentiator for business success (Beechler & Woodward, 2009; Collings & Mellahi, 2010; Iles, Chuai, & Preece, 2010). Attracting a disproportionate number of talented people contains a competitive advantage. Indeed, research by Bersin by Deloitte (2017) shows that a robust ITM strategy reflects in higher employee engagement (29%), higher leadership development (36%) and higher succession pipeline (41%). These results have a positive impact on organizational profitability as a 15% increase in employee engagement is known to result in a 2% growth in profitability through the retention of top performers, thus reducing recruiting costs and prioritizing of staff training and development needs.

## The Talent Concept

Many uses of the words "talent management" in organizational contexts not only refer to managing the individual capacity and capability to contribute toward corporate performance, but also to the strategic investment of organizations in terms of the identification, selection, development, planning, retention and outplacement of people, or "talent."

Talent is operationalized as human capital – term used by Farndale, Scullion, and Sparrow (2010) to refer to the stock of competencies, knowledge, social and personality skills embodied in the ability to perform labor and produce economic/social value. Lepak and Snell (1999) added a dimension to the definition by attributing value and uniqueness to human capital. Value refers to the potential to contribute to an organization's core competencies and advance its competitive position, while uniqueness refers to the extent that human capital is difficult to replace due to unique job or organizational requirements and labor market scarcities.

Employees rated high on both value and uniqueness are referred to as "talent" (Schuler et al., 2011), which supports the exclusive concept of talent as supported by Nijs, Gallardo-Gallardo, Dries, and Sels. (2014). Becker and Huselid (2006) argue that the value of talent depends on specific positions employees occupy and for which increments in quality or quantity would result in an above-average return on those strategic measures seen as pivotal (Boudreau & Ramstad, 2004), that talent should be allocated to high-value, high-uniqueness employees called "players."

Various philosophies exist about the definition of talent, though no consensus has yet been reached (Beechler & Woodward, 2009; Collings & Mellahi, 2010; Sparrow & Makram, 2015; Vaiman & Collings, 2013). Currently, there are two schools of thought broadly defined: the inclusive philosophy, which defines talent as every single person in the organization with the potential and capability to contribute to the objectives of the organization; and the exclusive definition of talent, which recognizes the top-performing individuals of that organization (Egerová, 2013; Iles et al., 2010; Vaiman & Collings, 2013). Global talent management is not only about HR activities and processes, but also a way of thinking and decision-making in which holistic and integrated approaches are used to gain competitive advantage (Beechler & Woodward, 2009; Iles et al., 2010; Lawler, 2009; Zula & Chermack, 2007) for the organization and its people. Such holistic and integrated approaches include the identification, development and redeployment of talented employees (Iles et al., 2010).

Globalization of the workforce is driving integration of talent management processes, increasing connectivity between processes such as career management and learning and development, strategic staffing, talent mobility and talent acquisition. Cloud-hosted technology applications are making such integration possible. With global career paths tightly knotted with learning and development strategy, Go-To-Market (GTM) organizations are improving the planning, recruitment, deployment and development of their staff, effectively building pipelines of global leaders and more efficient use of their talent management investments. Through global mobility, organizations are deploying skills in places and regions where they are most needed, helping to create highly responsive, high-performance, sustainable organizations that respond to current and future talent challenges.

## The Talent Life Cycle

The Talent Life Cycle (TLC) encompasses the chain of events between organizations and human capital (Schiemann, 2014). It ranges from effort to attract, hire, on-board, develop and manage talent to the moment when such talent either retires or moves to another organization. Activities within the talent cycle that are designed to have an impact on the bottom line of the organization either in terms of productivity or profitability, can be referred to as the talent value (Sparrow & Makram, 2015).

According to (Schiemann, 2014), TLC is the path which most people use to interact with the organization. TM is the way in which the TLC is managed, while the TLC is the value that is created for the talent and the organization when properly managed (Schiemann, 2014; Schuler, 2015; Sparrow & Makram, 2015). TLC is synonymous with the concept which Schiemann (2014) coined as talent optimization – the alignment of the TLC components such as talent acquisition, development, performance management and retention strategies, processes and policies to the extent that it maximizes the outcome of those talent investments – higher employee productivity, maximized customer outcome, higher quality, higher talent retention of desired employees, reduced regulatory or environmental risk and strong operational and financial performance.

These benefits impact both local and global organizations and current assessment of workforce challenges are not seen from a TLC perspective, but from the individual perspective of the components of the TLC.

Figure 9.1 illustrates the levels of talent management integration maturity.

- Level 1, the organization is yet to explore connecting the talent processes and systems and still operating at the individual process level.
- Level 2, a decision is made to integrate talent management processes but processes are not optimized.

**Figure 9.1** Levels of Talent Management Integration Maturity. *Source:* Bersin and Associates (2012)

- Levels 3 and 4, talent management strategy is fully integrated with business strategy and the talent technology to support collaboration across processes.

Research by Deloitte and Bersin shows that organizations at level 2 have double the turnover of high performers when compared to organizations at level 4 with more strategic, business-driven talent management strategies, processes and systems.

The framework illustrated in Figure 9.2 shows how critical alignment of talent management processes through ITM can help in planning and realization of critical TM outcomes. Linking strategic staffing of talent with the identifications of the right skills from the strategic staffing exercise supports "ahead of the curve" recruiting (proactive sourcing) either from internal or external talent pools. With integration of talent acquisition with talent pools from talent review, it helps with the internal movement of skills to places they are needed most at the right time to support business continuity and to deliver on strategy. Aligning talent pools from talent reviews with career development also helps to recommend a training and learning curriculum needed to support staff for their next assignment(s) or their next career move. The alignment between strategic staffing, career development and talent acquisition helps organizations to best manage demand and supply gaps either through proactive recruitment strategies or innovative learning and leadership training to meet critical skill gaps.

The following section will look into processes and proposed new insights for looking at future workforce challenges.

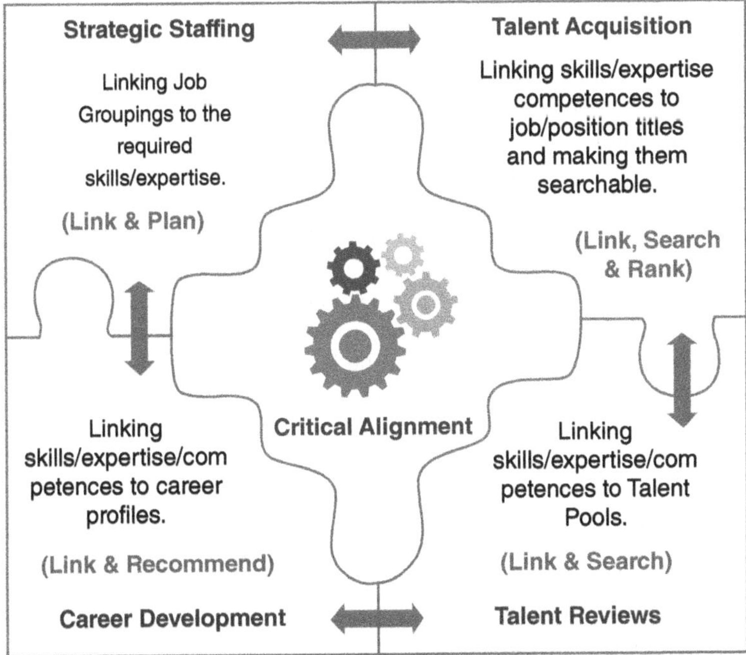


**Figure 9.2** An Integrated Talent Management Framework

## Talent Value Chain

This section explores components of the TLC in terms of the values inherent in each segment of the life cycle and how they engender new perspectives to TM. Disintegration of TM processes to evaluate its impact and efficiency leads to silorization of the Talent Value Chain (TVC), which undermines the linkage between talent management processes. Understanding how organizations create value and differ from their peers is a central challenge for both the theory and practice of strategic management. TVC research is particularly useful in understanding issues of sub-value chains such as the tactical and operational activities that feed into the value components (primary talent management activities) or segments (support processes or infrastructure).

In a rapidly changing business context, creating value through innovative linkages of primary talent management activities and support process or infrastructure is becoming a stronger determinant of competitive advantage. A complete but parsimonious typology of the alternative forms of value created is a prerequisite for expressing and exploring how firms differ in a competitive sense (Koc & Bozdag, 2017; Stabell & Fjeldstad, 1998).

The Porter Value Chain Framework of 1985is the most commonly accepted framework for representing and analyzing the logic of firm-level value creation (Stabell & Fjeldstad, 1998). Analyzing an organization value chain involves decomposing the firm into strategically important value activities and understanding their impact on cost and added value contribution. Given the context of volatility, uncertainty, complexity and ambiguity (VUCA) in which businesses operate today, agility and efficiency of how they deliver such value has become a critical success factor. The entire value-creation logic of the Porter value chain with its generic categories of activities remains valid in all industries (Stabell & Fjeldstad, 1998). The Porter value chain model, when adapted to talent management, resulting in the creation of the talent value chain, holds the same relevance and applicability to different industries. The activities in the value chain that are vital to the firm's competitive advantage are industry-dependent.

Historically, the term value chain is defined as the collaborative relationship between business and consumers (Koc & Bozdag, 2017; Stabell & Fjeldstad, 1998; Zamora, 2016). This definition has been criticized for lacking specificity in also defining the inherent linkages between causal linkages of the value-creation process. The talent value chain is adapted from the Porter value chain and forms a collaborative network of talent management processes and decision points inherent in the day-to-day management of talent in organizations. Key characteristics of the value chain are the TM activities and actors involved in delivering TM services, which provides value added benefits for the talent and the organization. The talent value chain concept is a new field of study with limited or no extant literature, which precludes a comprehensive understanding of the opportunities and vulnerabilities within the value chain. Figure 9.3 represents the talent value chain adapted from the Porter Value Chain. It illustrates the primary and support activities and processes required to drive efficiency and value in local and global talent management.

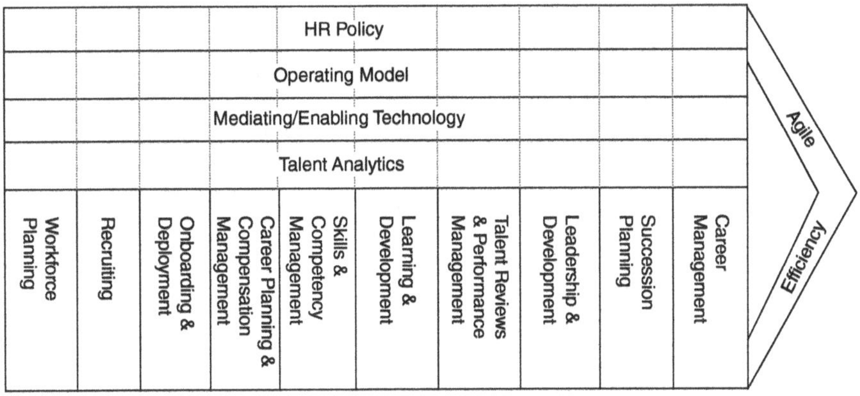

HR Policy
Operating Model
Mediating/Enabling Technology
Talent Analytics
Workforce Planning
Recruiting
Onboarding & Deployment
Career Planning & Compensation Management
Skills & Competency Management
Learning & Development
Talent Reviews & Performance Management
Leadership & Development
Succession Planning
Career Management
Agile
Efficiency

**Figure 9.3** The Talent Value Chain

The TVC utilizes the vertical linkages when the firm seeks to leverage its competitive advantage using internal resources and strategies inherent in its value chain components. Configuration of the value chains depends on the firm's talent strategies, the TM approach it is pursuing and its associated defined processes. This explains why no two organization can have the same talent value chain. Re-engineering the value logic to deliver TM activities can lead to significant cost savings and boost operational efficiency for organizations with the insight to pursue such path.

What constitutes value within the value chain is the inherent ability of each constituent part of the chain to build on the value of the component it precedes or succeeds. Delivering value within TM would require an integrated and collaborative network of talent value components developed in line with the conceptualization of TM as implemented by the organization. This understanding has led to the concept of ITM. Therefore, TM vulnerabilities that organizations struggle with on a regular basis are issues impeding the management of each TM process from talent identification, talent development, talent retention, talent mobility or talent replacement.

The strength or success of an organization's talent strategy is only as good as the weakest link of the talent processes in the TVC and its relevance to its business strategy. Each process vulnerability threatens the value chain sustainability, impact and efficiency. Therefore, it is imperative that firms invest resources toward an ongoing process of identifying weaknesses in the value chain and making the necessary adjustments to maintain the robustness and sustainability of the talent strategy and its implementation. Furthermore, talent strategy should be constantly aligned with competitive market forces to help maintain relevance in a constantly changing business environment.

## Talent Analysis

The starting point in managing talent management challenges whether at the local or global level is to consider inefficiencies in the talent value chain either at the individual processes level or in the entire chain itself. A value chain approach to managing TM challenges holds the potential of unearthing latent TM issues often caused by fragmentation in the value chain which, undermines effort to fully address critical TM challenges that often impact the business negatively. This approach to TM which, involves managing the constituent parts of the value chain, is made possible by advances in technology and the availability of a plethora of data to support talent decisions. The value chain analysis of talent management helps determine areas of critical value creation and to develop an understanding of the current competitive position of the firm and how such a position can be maintained and strengthened.

**Primary Talent Management Activities**—these relate directly to the process that is performed to plan, identify, acquire, develop and retain, reward or retire/outplace talent in the organization (see Table 9.1).

**Support processes/infrastructure** – these are activities that support the TM processes that the organization undertakes. In Porter's model, the dotted lines show that each support activity is relevant to all primary activities. For example, policy is needed for each of the TM processes to guard the management and implementation.

- Policy – this refers to the specific HR or talent management policy that supports a given talent management component in the value chain and its application to varying talent scenarios.
- Operating model – a model of the talent management process including what will be offered and how it has been delivered and/or integrated with the other talent management processes in the TLC or TVC.
- Technology – the use of innovative and mediating technologies to support primary talent management activities will help align the value chain components to gain synergies, which is critical for a firm to realize its value chain impact. Some mediating/enabling technologies include: Learning Management System, Employee or Manager Self-Service, Workforce Dashboards, Compensation System, Recruitment Management System, etc.
- Analytics – With the datafication of talent management, use of (applied) analytics in understanding the value chain components can help to significantly strengthen talent strategies while cementing a firm's competitive advantage in its implementation of its talent management programs. Such analytics focus on tracking and trending data over time to help answer critical talent management questions. It also helps to better formulate talent management problems which are effectively addressed by the organization.

## Global Talent Management Challenges

Various organizations have approached TM differently and, therefore, experienced different talent management outcomes. There is not a single approach to talent management. The concept is precipitated by varying definitions of talent management and the notion of what talent is; although all approaches involve decisions about attracting, selecting, developing, and retaining people with the right skills needed to meet the objectives of the institution at the right time. The talent

**Table 9.1** Primary Talent Management Services

| | |
|---|---|
| Workforce planning | Business processes that analyze the supply and demand of talent within the organization. This core talent management activity helps the organization understand the current state of its human capital, forecast talent and skills gaps and suggest the necessary actions to close the gaps. |
| Talent acquisition | Talent management activity that supports a strategic approach to identifying, and attracting top talents into the organization. This is a critical activity in the talent life cycle. |
| Onboarding and deployment | Talent management activities that involve providing critical support to employees new to the organization helping to facilitate their orienting and immersion into the corporate culture while also helping to shorten their time to productivity. |
| Compensation management | Services that manage the payment of salaries and benefits of employees and contractors within the organization. This activity also includes other organizational rewards and recognition arrangements. |
| Skills and competency management | Talent management activities that help identify, optimize and manage the skills and competence required to deliver on the business strategy and align with stakeholder demands. It also provides the foundational data to support other talent management processes. |
| Learning and development | Talent management activities that support organizational interventions aimed at improving the performance of individuals and teams within the organization focused on addressing the skills, knowledge and competence gaps identified through workforce planning. |
| Talent reviews and performance management | Talent management activities involving managing employee objective setting, performance and (bi)annual reviews and evaluation. This process provides critical input into employee career management, leadership development, and succession planning. |
| Leadership and development | Talent management activities that support the systematic processes that assesses, develop and grow talent at management and professional levels. It integrates closely with performance management and succession planning. |
| Succession planning | Talent management activities that support the organizational processes for identifying, selecting, and managing successors. It also involves career planning, talent reviews and talent mobility of critical staff to fill critical roles within the organization. |
| Career management | Talent management activity geared at supporting employee progression within the organization through a logical sequence of jobs (individual and teamwork) requiring the development of new skills sets/expertise that are gained through advanced or diverse assignments resulting in greater influence and responsibility. |

*Source:* Definitions adapted from Deloitte and Bersin.

management approaches which an organization adopts reflect the particular organization's objective that it plans to meet in the context of the strategic constraints, which it faces, the geographies in which it operates, and the products/ services it offers. The different programs and designs of talent management can lead to different outcomes. Although talent is of critical importance to most organizations, representing one of the highest-cost items on the balance sheet and which also serves as a source of competitive advantage for many people organizations (Meyers & van Woerkom, 2014); many organizations continue to struggle to develop and implement robust talent management programs and practices that will optimize the benefit of their talent value chain while enhancing their TLC.

## New Mindset to Addressing Talent Management Challenges

Workforce planning models developed in the post-war era to effectively manage the workforce are typically not fitted to the talent management challenges organizations are facing today. The traditional approach to analyzing, diagnosing, and addressing current talent issues in organizations is exposing many organizations to emerging talent risks. Talent risk reporting is a new concept for most organizations and many organizations considering the concept are failing to approach talent risk measurement from an integrated perspective that will capture the risk between talent management processes. The concept of ITM was introduced to optimize talent management sustainably and to identify latent talent management risks that might undermine the organizational approach to talent management.

Many organizations fail to manage their talents effectively and measures of performance in this area remain underdeveloped (Tarique & Schuler, 2010). The new paradigm to talent management is asking for evidence-based management requiring readiness to put aside past beliefs and wisdom in place of informed and intelligent decisions (Pfeffer & Sutton, 2006). It requires the ability to re-imagine future talent management challenges through asking tough questions, critically evaluating talent management planning initiatives, reviewing talent management technologies, processes and strategies; embracing design thinking in the design of Human Resources/ Talent Management processes for optimal impact. Moving beyond vacancy-led recruitment to recruiting “ahead of the curve” by attracting people with high value and unique skills into global talent pools (irrespective of the existence of vacancies for this skill) which can be mined when the need arises, will be a key part of the future of TM. The following section will present an alternative lens on how to look at some key talent management challenges organizations are facing.

## Attrition of Skills/Expertise and not Headcount or Diversity Attributes

Many organizations today are reporting attrition numbers based on the number of staff who left within a given period. They are also looking at exits per geographies, gender, age group, and product-line and diversity indices. Very few organizations are analyzing attrition in terms of the skills/ expertise leaving the organization or unit, which may induce the adverse effect of forcing organizations into faster attrition of competencies, skills and expertise which are not measured by current diagnostic tools. It will, therefore, be challenging to diagnose skills and expertise turnover using current diagnostic approaches (which have remained unchanged and focus on attrition of employees not skills) to uncover which skills and expertise are leaving the organization. This makes it difficult for such organizations to target which replacement skills/ expertise they should go-to-market for today and in the future.

The implication for such an organization would be that its staffing levels would be in place but its in-house capabilities needed to deliver on its business strategy or to remain competitive will unnoticeably diminish over time. Many organizations have adopted tools to help minimize attrition, through staff turnover, external hires, promotion, and employee morale, which have proven to be invaluable for leading practices in the workforce-planning domain (Cappelli, 2009). However, such tools further need to be redefined to track, monitor and report which capabilities (skills/ expertise) are leaving or needed in the organization.

## Retention of Productivity, or Growth Instead of People

The link between people and budget used as a measure of productivity and growth is in many organizations computed from headcount/ full time equivalent perspective. Retention/ growth of productivity is done from the same perspective. Although academic research into this phenomenon is scarce, we advocate a different perspective: essentially, the retention of critical personnel and not the retention of critical skills and capabilities needed to grow the business; a process which, when well-managed, would lead to higher talent retention. (This may not necessarily lead to retention or growth of corporate/ business unit productivity or revenue due to misalignment of the two indicators.) Building on research in I/O psychology that has long documented the complexity of the job satisfaction–productivity relationship (Judge, Thoresen, Bono, & Patton, 2001), we would recommend a more nuanced perspective than the narrowly focused "productivity" one.

By integrating skills and expertise into vacancies, the talent review, career development, strategic staffing and performance management segments of the TLC will help to capture, monitor and report skills flows within the organization from a demand and supply perspective. Organizations applying this procedure would be agile in adapting to global demands and changes to their talent configuration and deployment. A focus on retention from this perspective could also help HR to better link their outcomes and analytics with those from other colleagues in the business (e.g., Finance).

## Technology That Drives Value Within the TLC

Although talent management solutions have become pervasive on the market, many organizations are not taking a coordinated approach to managing their workforce (Farndale et al., 2010) leading to a disconnect in HR processes. Many organizations are failing to adopt robust mobile productivity technologies that would deliver significant benefits to what is becoming an increasingly mobile workforce (Hughes, 2010). Such technological capabilities are known to support work–life integration, facilitate flexibility in working arrangements which is now a requirement for most new hires. Misalignment of integrated talent management technology with strategy has resulted in many organizations potentially underutilizing such technological solutions or paying for delivered functionalities that they are not using.

## Staffing Model Not Aligned to Budget

Many organizations have not adequately adopted innovation in staffing models, or considered the cost implications of HR instruments for managing their workforce. Such organizations are failing to benefit from disproportionate cost savings or an increase in employee productivity and associated engagements. These changes in understanding workforce challenges are leading to a seismic shift in the way organizations around the globe manage their talents/ workforces, leaving them less prepared, unable to compete or to maximize the benefits of their talent strategies. Using simulation tools, leading organizations in workforce planning have demonstrated the link between project sales, compensation impact and talent demand (Cappelli, 2009). Linking staffing with budget helps to support evidenced-based planning and management (Becker & Huselid, 2006), forecast revenue from a new product launch, or the impact of critical business development or reorganization initiatives.

## Talent Metrics and Measurements That Support Evidenced-based Decision-making

With the evolution toward a service-driven economy, there is a continuing reliance on talent and human capital as sources of competitive advantage and therefore the need for measurement systems to help manage talent resources (Pfeffer & Sutton, 2006; Zula & Chermack, 2007). The emergence of ITM platforms on the market, people analytics tools, and robust data-visualization software is all helping organizations to make informed data-driven decisions, integrating multiple data points along the TLC. According to Zula and Chermack (2007), Human Capital Measurement Systems (HCMS) when designed and implemented effectively, will help organizations focus on prediction and feedback on the firm's people-related assets.

Talent capacity and capability forecasting would demand a complete re-engineering of the TLC into its value constituents connecting critical decision data points, cutting through the departmental silos (Zula & Chermack, 2007), which serve as an effective barrier to innovative and accurate workforce planning and effective talent management. These challenges get amplified for many global organizations faced with different systems integration challenges and the equitable spread of the right skills needed to manage such an approach.

## Workforce Planning Without Scenarios or Alignment of Planning Outputs with Inputs

The proliferation of workforce-planning solutions and the use of big data capabilities have offered organizations innovative ways of exploring future workforce challenges in the form of advanced scenario planning (Cappelli, 2009; Schwartz, 1996; van den Heijden, 2005). This emergence of these capabilities is requiring many organizations to rethink their business models of tomorrow to remain competitive. In addition, many organizations operate a 3–5-year planning horizon as part of their strategic workforce planning cycle. Often, such exercises fail to align the people and skills that would be needed during that time horizon with the projected business outcomes. The mismatch between business outcome in profitability and the capabilities needed to deliver on that goal is often due to business planning not being aligned with skills demand, thereby failing to sufficiently close the future talent/ skills gaps.

## Conclusion

This chapter has explored "talent" or "workforce" challenges precipitated either by factors external to the organization such as competition, scarcity of the right talent, globalization affecting the availability of talent to meet increasing skill demands or rapid technological changes substituting the need for talent or providing added capabilities to better understand the talent management challenges holistically. Factors internal to the organization could also play a role – organizational culture and capability to attract, select, motivate, engage and retain talents, technological capabilities to effectively support the talent management processes and administration, or the existence or absence of a "talent" mindset in the organization. In both areas, there are still substantial gaps in our understanding either practical or theoretical, and of the dynamics and interplay between these two areas of talent threats and opportunities.

Also, the desire for organizations to find the right talent with the right skills at the right time in the right place remains an ongoing conceptual and complicated logistical challenge for many global organizations. It requires an integrated forward looking succession planning to ensure that the right selection, development, and pipeline management is in place to support the realization of this goal. Organizations that continue with a silo approach to talent management or discuss talent issues in a vacuum, will struggle to attract, select, engage and retain their talents (Beechler & Woodward, 2009).

Many global organizations implementing global talent management initiatives have faced the global challenges highlighted earlier. However, as part of their efforts to make talent management a key part of their strategic priorities, they have adopted the right talent definitions that support their global as well as local interests; the right talent infrastructure that encompasses the right skills/expertise and competences as the foundation for integration; developed the different building blocks of their talent management framework – compensation and reward, performance management, learning, career management, talent acquisition and succession planning and leadership development and, lastly, they have effectively developed the core competency to optimize value within their talent management talent value chain – representing a chain of interconnecting building blocks in their talent management framework.

Many global organizations have also taken a cooperative and integrative approach to planning and managing talent and have adopted ITM as a precursor to optimizing their talent benefit along the talent value map. The process to optimizing the talent value map is one that encompasses multiple stakeholders and departments within the institution and the roadmap to such a framework varies from one organization to another. Technology is not only an effective ingredient for integrating talent management and optimizing the talent value map, but it also serves as an enabler for knitting the various building blocks which will allow HR teams to build robust talent management processes and deliver the capability to interact in ways that would enhance the ability of organizations to maximize the benefit of their overall talent management strategy. This raises the bar for HR professionals, and for HR –business partnership.

Beechler and Woodward (2009), argue that organizations' responses to these new and innovative trends have been slow due to organizational inertia, existing business and mental models developed for a different generation/ age, resistance to change, cognitive biases to decision-making, and the knowledge–doing gap.

## Note

1 "Integrated talent management" is the seamless integration of three or four organizational processes within the talent life cycle designed to attract, manage, develop, engage, motivate and retain key people or talents. These processes include activities such as performance management, career development, total reward and talent acquisition. Such integration happens either through data platforms, workflow or across-process reporting and analytics (Bersin and Associates, 2012).

## References

Becker, B. E., & Huselid, M. A. (2006). Strategic Human Resources Management: Where Do We Go From Here? *Journal of Management, 32,* 898–925.

Beechler, S., & Woodward, I. C. (2009). The global "war for talent.". *Journal of International Management, 15*(3), 273–285. https://doi.org/10.1016/j.intman.2009.01.002

Bersin and Associates (2012). *Integrated Talent Management: A Roadmap for Success.* Research Bulletin 2012. Oakland, CA: Bersin and Associates.

Bersin by Deloitte (2017). *Rewriting the rules for the digital age.* London: Deloitte University Press.

Boudreau, J. W. and Ramstad, P. M. (2004). Center for Effective Organizations. Talentship and the Evolution of Human Resource Management: From "Professional Practices" to "Strategic Talent Decision Science." CEO Publication G 04–6 (458).

Cappelli, P. (2009). A supply chain approach to workforce planning. *Organizational Dynamics,, 38*(1), 8–15. https://doi.org/10.1016/j.orgdyn.2008.10.004

Chambers, E., Foulon, M., Handfield-Jones, H., Hankin, S., & Michaels, E. (1998). The war for talent. *The McKinsey Quarterly, 3,* 44–57.

Collings, D. G., & Mellahi, K. (2010). Strategic talent management: A review and research agenda. *Human Resource Management Review, 19*(4), 304–313. Retrieved from http://vmserver14.nuigalway.ie/xmlui/bitstream/handle/10379/683/Clean_for_submission_REVISION_FINAL.pdf\npapers3://publication/uuid/1220E2F7-F014-4BFD-932A-4C82405616E9

Egerová, D. (2013). Integrated talent management – A challenge or necessity for present management. *Problems of Management in the 21st Century, 6*(2006), 4–6.

Farndale, E., Scullion, H., & Sparrow, P. R. (2010). The role of the corporate HR function in global talent management. *Journal of World Business, 45,* 161–168.

Guthridge, M., Komm, A. B., & Lawson, E. (2008). Making talent a strategic priority. *The McKinsey Quarterly, 1,* 3–6. Retrieved from http://www.dnlglobal.com/includes/repository/newsitem/TheMcKinseyQuarterly01_08.pdf

Hughes, C. (2010). "People as technology" conceptual model: Toward a new value creation paradigm for strategic human resource development. *Human Resource Development Review, 9,* 48–71. https://doi.org/10.1177/1534484309353561

Iles, P., Chuai, X., & Preece, D. (2010). Talent management and HRM in multinational companies in Beijing: Definitions, differences and drivers. *Journal of World Business, 45*(2), 179–189. https://doi.org/10.1016/j.jwb.2009.09.014

Judge, T. A., Thoresen, C. J., Bono, J. E., & Patton, G. K. (2001). The job satisfaction-job performance relationship: a qualitative and quantitative review. *Psychological Bulletin, 127,* 376–407.

Koc, T., & Bozdag, E. (2017). Measuring the degree of novelty of innovation based on Porter's value chain approach. *European Journal of Operational Research, 257,* 559–567.

Lawler, E. E. (2009). Make human capital a source of competitive advantage. *Organizational Dynamics, 38*(1). https://doi.org/10.2139/ssrn.1311431

Lepak, D. P., & Snell, S. A. (1999). The Human Resource Architecture: Toward a theory of human capital allocation and development. *Academy of Management Review, 24,* 31–48.

Meyers, M. C., & van Woerkom, M. (2014). The influence of underlying philosophies on talent management: Theory, implications for practice, and research agenda. *Journal of World Business, 49*(2), 192–203. https://doi.org/10.1016/j.jwb.2013.11.003

Michaels, E., Handfield-Jones, H., & Axelrod, B. (2001). *The War for Talent.* Cambridge, MA: Harvard Business Review Press.

Nijs, S., Gallardo-Gallardo, E., Dries, N., & Sels, L. (2014). A multidisciplinary review into the definition, operationalization, and measurement of talent. *Journal of World Business, 49,* 180–191.

Pfeffer, J., & Sutton, R. I. (2006). Evidence-based management. *Harvard Business Review,* January, 40–January, 41. Retrieved from http://ezproxy.library.capella.edu/login?url=http://search.ebscohost.com/login.aspx?direct=trueanddb=bthandAN=43328611andsite=ehost-liveandscope=site

Schiemann, W. A. (2014). From talent management to talent optimization. *Journal of World Business, 49*(2), 281–288. https://doi.org/10.1016/j.jwb.2013.11.012

Schuler, R. S. (2015). The 5-C framework for managing talent. *Organizational Dynamics, 44*(1), 47–56. https://doi.org/10.1016/j.orgdyn.2014.11.006

Schuler, R. S., Jackson, S. E., & Tarique, I. (2011). Global talent management and global talent challenges: Strategic opportunities for IHRM. *Journal of World Business, 46*(4), 506–516. https://doi.org/10.1016/j.jwb.2010.10.011

Schwartz, P. (1996). *The art of the long view.* New York, NY: Doubleday.

Scullion, H., & Collings, D. G. (2011). *Global talent management*. Madison, WI: Routledge.

Sparrow, P. R., & Makram, H. (2015). What is the value of talent management? Building value-driven processes within a talent management architecture. *Human Resource Management Review*, *25*(3), 249–263. https://doi.org/10.1016/j.hrmr.2015.04.002

Stabell, C. B., & Fjeldstad, Ø. D. (1998). Configuring value for competitive advantage: On chains, shops, and networks. *Strategic Management Journal*, *19*, 413–437.

Tarique, I., & Schuler, R. S. (2010). Global talent management: Literature review, integrative framework, and suggestions for further research. *Journal of World Business*, *45*(2), 122–133. https://doi.org/10.1016/j.jwb.2009.09.019

Vaiman, V., & Collings, D. G. (2013). Talent management: Advancing the field. *The International Journal of Human Resource Management*, *24*(9), 1737–1743. https://doi.org/10.1080/09585192.2013.777544

van den Heijden, K. (2005). *Scenarios: The art of strategic conversations*. Chichester, UK: Wiley.

Zamora, E. A. (2016). Value Chain Analysis: A Brief Review. *Asian Journal of Innovation and Policy*, *5*, 116–128.

Zula, K. J., & Chermack, T. J. (2007). Human capital planning: A review of literature and implications for human resource development. *Human Resource Development Review*, *6*(3), 245–262. https://doi.org/10.1177/1534484307303762

# 10

# The Confucius Institute Teachers' Workplace Training

*Xiaonan Wang and Wan Xiang Yao*

*University of Texas at San Antonio*

As a consequence of the dramatic growth of the Chinese economy and its economic exchanges with other parts of the world, the demand for learning about Chinese language and culture around the world has increased sharply (Hartig, 2012a, b). China's connection and representation in the world, Barabantseva states (2009), "have become matters of concern among scholars, the media, and policymakers" (p. 131). In responding to such a growing demand, the Chinese government decided to found Confucius Institutes to promote the study of both Chinese language and culture, and established the first Confucius Institute in Seoul, Korea, in 2004 as a result of the decision (Lien, 2013). Since then, over 400 Confucius Institutes have been established around the world today (About Confucius Institute/ Classroom, 2017a). Much of China's inspiration for the Confucius Institute was borrowed from Germany's Goethe Institut (see the Hanban Official Website: http://english.hanban.org). Founded in 1951 as a successor to the Deutsche Akademie, the Goethe Institut's goal is to promote German language learning and to enhance exchange relationships around the world (Goethe Institut, n.d.). The success of the Goethe Institute encouraged the decision to establish the Confucius Institutes (Hanban Official Website, n.d.).

There are three types of Confucius Institute: those managed by the Confucius Institute Headquarters, alone; those controlled by the country in which they exist; and those that operate through cooperation between a Chinese university, a university in the host country, and the Confucius Institute Headquarters (Gil, 2009, pp. 62–63). The latter is the most common form, Gil reasons (2009), as it offers "the advantages of sharing establishment and operation costs and the prestige derived from association with host universities" (pp. 62–63).

As part of the family of the Confucius Institutes, the Confucius Institute (CI) at the University of Texas at San Antonio (UTSA) was founded in 2009 (UTSA–Confucius-Institute, 2009). One of UTSA's goals is to prepare students for work in a global environment. With this increasing economic tie between the United States and China and the growing role San Antonio plays in the global economy,

*The Wiley Handbook of Global Workplace Learning*, First Edition.
Edited by Vanessa Hammler Kenon and Sunay Vasant Palsole.

the demand for learning the Chinese language and understanding Chinese culture at UTSA and the San Antonio area has also increased.

Thus, UTSA, in collaboration with Hanban (the headquarters of Confucius Institutes), decided to establish its Confucius Institute to better meet this increasing demand and UTSA's goal. The mission of the CI is to promote Chinese language instruction, appreciation of Chinese culture, and understanding of Chinese history and society. The CI helps build a bridge between China and the U.S., especially at UTSA and in Texas in terms of promoting awareness of multiculturalism and cultural and educational exchange, and strives to create the best environment for students of all ages to learn Chinese language and culture (UTSA–Confucius-Institute, 2009).

## The Significance of Workplace Training for Chinese Teachers in the CI

There are approximately 50 Chinese-language instructors in San Antonio, Texas. Among them, only a few have received undergraduate and/or graduate degrees in the major of teaching Chinese as a second language. Thus, the need and demand for workplace training is sizable, and significant in the city. The professional quality of teachers is the foundation of the development of the Confucius Institute. Therefore, the Confucius Institute at UTSA has been focusing on personal career development for the teachers in the city and in the state of Texas.

The CI at UTSA focuses on the personal career development of every teacher and hopes to realize the common development of the CI through teachers' personal development. The CI provides teachers with professional guidance and support to continuously improve their professional accomplishments and all-round ability, so as to provide a lasting impetus to the long-term sustainable development of the CI (Illeris, 2003). The CI at UTSA is constantly improving the standard of teacher training, and offers different levels of training to meet the different needs of Chinese teachers. The goal of the training is to enhance the professional quality and sense of mission of Chinese teachers, to improve their second-language teaching skills, classroom management ability, Chinese cultural communication ability (Lei, 2016), and intercultural communicative competence. Qualified Chinese teachers can adjust their teaching contents to suit different situations and promote the influence of the CI through public diplomacy as a friendly bridge between China and the outside world (Confucius Institute Readers Club, 2015).

## Criteria for the Selection of Chinese Teachers

In selecting Chinese teachers, Hanban (the headquarters of Confucius Institutes) has developed strict selection criteria and procedures so as to recruit teachers who meet the requirements of Confucius Institutes (Hanban-News, 2013).

### Basic Requirements

- A passion for international Chinese education and the CI, high moral standards, and good team spirit.
- Undergraduate degree (or higher). A master's degree or higher is essential for teaching in universities
- Mandarin proficiency to be at and/or above the level of second-class (inclusive).
- Fluency in English.
- More than two years' teaching experience in the past eight years. Candidates with the International Certificate of Chinese Language Teaching from Hanban, and have teaching experience and foreign-related work experience are preferred.

### Eligibility

Hanban employs experts to review the qualifications of applicants to determine their eligibility (Hanban. Government-Sponsored Teacher Program, n.d.). Basic qualifications are listed below:

1) He/she shall be of Chinese nationality, be physically and mentally healthy, younger than 50 (although for those offering less commonly used languages, the age limit can be extended to up to 55);
2) He/she shall be decent and well-behaved, and have no criminal or negligence record;
3) He/she shall love to popularize Chinese language to other countries, have a strong sense of mission, glory, and responsibility and be conscientious and meticulous in work. Self-discipline and devotion are desired;
4) He/she shall be competent in teaching, administration and coordination;
5) He/she shall be capable of adapting to and communicating while set against a cross-cultural background;
6) He/she shall have foreign language proficiency, and be capable of skillfully using English or the native language for teaching and communication;
7) He/she shall have Chinese Putonghua proficiency with standard Putonghua pronunciation, and his/her Mandarin test result shall be above Band Two;
8) He/she shall have a teaching history longer than two years and an academic diploma above a Bachelor's degree, and be a teacher in service at a university, middle or primary school engaging in the subjects of teaching Chinese as a foreign language, or teaching Chinese language, foreign language or pedagogy. Experience of teaching Chinese as foreign language in other countries shall be a plus.

### Selection Examination

Applicants are required to participate in a selection examination organized by Hanban. The examination mainly covers the areas of Chinese language knowledge, teaching skills, Chinese cultural communication and intercultural communication ability, English level, and psychological quality (Hanban.

Government-Sponsored Teacher Program, n.d.). It consists of four different elements: a written examination, a Chinese teaching interview, an English interview, and a psychological computer test.

## Training Methods for Confucius Institute Chinese Teachers

### Pre-job Training Organized by Hanban

Teachers who have passed the selection test are then required to participate in pre-job training. The training period is from the end of July to early August, which is about 20 days and 210 hours (Hanban-News, 2011).

### Training Objectives and Principles

In accordance with the CI teacher training program, workplace training is dominated by solving practical problems and focusing on case teaching, and uses network practice as a platform (Hanban-News, 2017). Hanban tries to improve the professional quality of teachers and their ability to solve problems encountered in the future workplace.

### Training Experts

The training team consists of experts with rich experience in teaching Chinese in the U.S., CI/classroom directors, or local school educators teaching Chinese as a foreign language.

Course Module Arrangement (Hanban. Teacher Education and Training, n.d.)

Course Module Color Distinction

| *Lectures* | *Chinese Teaching Class* | *English Learning Class* | *Chinese Arts & Crafts Class* | *Discussion Class* | *Independent Study* | *Group Activities* |
|---|---|---|---|---|---|---|
| **All** | **Divided** | **Divided** | **Divided** | **Divided** | **All** | **All** |

*Note:* Data adapted from Hanban. Teacher Education and Training (n.d.).

*Lectures*: Topics covered include CI online classroom resources; the development situation of the CI; overview of the international Chinese teaching program; reflection and prospect of the North American Chinese teaching method; Chinese teaching development and differences between Chinese and English education; American teaching and classroom management skills; Chinese and Western cross-cultural communication; American education culture; Chinese pronunciation and grammar, Chinese language and culture; vocabulary and Chinese character teaching; Chinese classroom teaching principles, skills and materials selection and how to develop a syllabus (Teaching Materials, 2012).

*Chinese Teaching Class*: normally has ten trainees in a class who are mentored by experienced Chinese teachers and learn teaching skills and how to prepare lessons.

*English Learning Class*: designed to improve proficiency in English. The class aims to teach how to write a syllabus, set up class rules, evaluate students and communicate appropriately with colleagues, students, and parents by email all in English.

*Chinese Arts & Crafts Class*: designed to train teachers in Chinese paper cutting, calligraphy, Chinese painting, Chinese knotting, and other talents related to Chinese arts. Teachers are trained to be able to carry out overseas Chinese cultural promotion activities.

*Discussion Class*: experienced teachers will share teaching and life experiences with the trainees.

*Independent Study*: self-learning including studying reading materials and watching video materials provided by CI online learning.

*Group Activities*: designed to learn how to teach Tai Chi, to provide safety education and outreach training, to be aware of overseas security and to improve teamwork ability.

### Teaching Methods

The instructors apply approaches such as problem-oriented teaching, case teaching, interactive discussion and experience exchange.

## CI's Role in Organizing Workplace Training

With the dramatic growth in the demand for teaching Chinese as a foreign language, relying solely on Hanban for the teaching force has proved to be insufficient to meet the huge market demand (Yang, 2010). To meet the challenge, all CIs have to strengthen the presence of Chinese teachers and to establish a localized Chinese teacher training system. In addition, the CIs need to carry out the training of teachers' professional development. To this end, the CIs have established their own workplace training programs, including both long-term personnel training and short-term intensive training to carry out customized training to meet the actual needs of the various types of teachers and to develop the career of Confucius Institute teachers (Hanban. Teacher Education and Training, n.d.).

The CI's training implements case-centered, task-oriented methods to solve practical problems. The training features small class sizes to ensure high quality. According to the different characteristics of the teaching object, teaching conditions, teaching environment, teacher's role, American culture and other factors, the training focuses on combining theory and practice, classroom training and independent learning/cooperative research, teacher teaching and case analysis, classroom discussion, micro-teaching, and supervised teaching. There are lectures, open classes, workshops, seminars, interactive classes in the form of training (Hanban. Teacher Education and Training, n.d.).

## The CI at UTSA and the Chinese Teachers Association of Texas Active Cooperation in Building a Platform for Teacher Training

On August 6, 2016, the CI at UTSA hosted the 2016 Chinese Teachers Training Conference to establish a platform for Chinese teachers to learn from each other by sharing resources and experiences. The theme of the annual meeting was "21st Century Survival Skills and Chinese Learning." More than 70 Chinese teachers from all over Texas participated in the conference (CLTA-TX Annual Conference, 2016).

Dr. Youmei Ren, the Director of the CI of the University of Hawaii at Manoa, gave a keynote speech and hosted the teaching workshop for the participants. Dr. Ren introduced the task-based teaching method and advocated the use of real language materials. She suggested creating a learner-centered classroom that allowed students to maximize their output in the form of stories. Dr. Ren showed how the language classroom was carried out under the task-based approach by teaching a junior Hindi class. Chinese teachers from the University of Texas, Texas A&M University, Oklahoma and other universities shared experiences of the subject management, jigsaw strategy teaching method (Qiao & Jin, 2010), Chinese tone teaching, and Chinese summer camp activities.

The CI at UTSA has made strategic plans with the Chinese Teachers Association of Texas for the enhancement of Chinese language learning. The two organizations will cooperate to provide assistance and guidance to enable Pre-K-12 schools and institutions of higher education to establish, strengthen, and sustain quality Chinese language programs in San Antonio. They will co-assist in the development of articulated curricula, pedagogy, materials and assessment tools that reflect students' needs and career goals. The CI at UTSA will also provide more opportunities, such as study abroad, exchanges and summer camps to enhance teachers' linguistic development, cultural understanding and professional experiences.

In addition, the CI at UTSA plans to cooperate with world-famous educational institutions and famous language departments of American universities to hold international conferences and conduct in-depth research on local Chinese teacher training syllabi, standards, models and teaching materials. They will carry out local teacher-qualification training projects to promote Chinese international education and international teaching standards.

## Adaptation of New Technologies in Chinese Teacher Training

The CI at UTSA will carry out a rich and flexible network of Chinese teacher training by using big data. It will cooperate with the Confucius Institute Online to obtain the data (Confucius-Institute-Online, 2016). Different virtual classrooms will open for different virtual communities, which will be established according to the age and identity of students. Virtual classrooms support online voice chat or real-time video conferencing, community-based curriculum design and display exchange (Misra, 2014). The CI at UTSA plans to establish a local Chinese-teaching resource library including excellent teaching cases and cross-cultural communication cases to create a communication platform. The platform will provide resource sharing, teaching guidance, and scientific research support to broaden the scope of teachers' research, expand the scope of teachers' communication, expand the professional competence of teachers, promote the development of Chinese teachers, and promote the rational flow of Chinese teachers (Hess, 2011).

## Encouraging Teachers to Participate in the STARTALK Program

STARTALK is a language education program at the University of Maryland, created under the National Security Language Initiative, a federal program which seeks to expand the teaching of strategically important languages in the United States. There are currently 12 languages taught under the STARTALK program, including Chinese, Arabic and Dari. STARTALK's mission is to increase the number of U.S. citizens learning, speaking and teaching critical foreign languages. STARTALK offers students (K-16) and teachers of these languages creative and engaging summer experiences that strive to exemplify best practices in language education and language-teacher development (STARTALK, 2016).

The CI at UTSA encourages in-service teachers to participate in the training program of the STARTALK Program. The CI at UTSA intends to join the STARTALK Program. It also plans to invite well-known scholars, experts, professors and teachers to provide teachers with specific, practical and effective classroom teaching methods and strategies to provide multi-angle, deep-level learning opportunities to improve the quality of Chinese teachers, thus helping to solve the shortage problem of high-quality Chinese teachers and reserving a pool of qualified teachers. Additionally, the CI at UTSA also plans to use STARTALK Program funding to make the training courses open to all teachers who want to learn and to help more Chinese teachers get learning opportunities. Each teacher who participates in the training will receive a training certificate issued by the CI after completing all the training courses.

The Chinese teacher training program at CI at UTSA applies the "practice first" principle and pays attention to the standardization of teacher training (Hanban. Teacher Education and Training, n.d.). The CI provides different-level training programs according to the various needs of Chinese teachers. This kind of professional training method has achieved good results and greatly promoted local Chinese teaching (Confucius Institute Annual Development Report, 2016). There is a significant increase (11%) in the number of students learning Chinese at UTSA and other institutions. UTSA currently offers a new elementary Chinese course with a class size of 40. CI helped St. Mary's to establish Chinese culture promotion and opened an after-school Chinese class at the Keystone Charter School.

In summary, the Confucius Institute has been providing effective workplace training for Chinese instructors not only from UTSA but also from other schools in the State of Texas, to meet the demand for enhancing the professional quality and sense of mission of Chinese teachers, and for improving their second-language skills. Although workplace training in the past proved effective, the challenge of maintaining a high-quality teaching force remains, due to the frequent loss of trained Chinese instructors. To tackle it, the CI at UTSA will offer workplace training periodically and make it available online in the future.

## References

Barabantseva, E. (2009). Change vs. order: Shijie meets Tianxia in China's interactions with the world. *Alternatives: Global, Local, Political, 34*(2), 129–155. Retrieved April 17, 2017 from www.jstor.org.libweb.lib.utsa.edu/stable/40645263

CLTA-TX-ADMINISTRATOR. (2016). CLTA-TX Annual Conference. Retrieved April 17, 2017 from http://clta-texas.org/?p=808

Confucius Institute Annual Development Report. (2016). Retrieved April 17, 2017 from http://www.hanban.org/report/2016.pdf

Confucius-Institute-Online. (2016). Retrieved April 17, 2017 from www.chinesecio.com

Confucius Institute Readers Club. (2015). Confucius Institute around the world. Retrieved April 17, 2017 from http://confuciusmag.com/confucius-institute-around-the-world

Gil, J. A. (2009). China's Confucius Institute project: Language and soft power in world politics. *The Global Studies Journal, 2*(1), 59–72.

Goethe Institut-History of the Goethe Institute.. (n.d.) Retrieved September 5, 2017 from https://www.goethe.de/en/uun/org/ges.html

Hanban. Government-sponsored Teacher Program.. (n.d.) Retrieved June 7, 2017 from http://english.hanban.org/node_7973.htm

Hanban. Teacher Education and Training.. (n.d.) Retrieved June 7, 2017 from http://english.hanban.org/node_9903.htm

Hanban-News. (2011). Training Program on Teaching Materials for Overseas Chinese Language Teachers. Retrieved April 17 2017 from http://english.hanban.org/article/2011-06/09/content_268835.htm

Hanban-News. (2013). Notice on the Application for 2014 Volunteer Chinese Language Teachers. Retrieved April 17, 2017 from http://english.hanban.org/article/2013-09/29/content_514645.htm

Hanban-News. (2017). About Confucius Institute/ Classroom. Retrieved June 7, 2017 from http://english.hanban.org/node_10971.htm

Hartig, F. (2012a). Confucius Institutes and the rise of China. *Journal of Chinese Political Science, 17*(1), 53–76. https://doi.org/10.1007/s11366-011-9178-7

Hartig, F. (2012b). Cultural Diplomacy with Chinese Characteristics: The Case of Confucius Institutes in Australia. *Communication, Politics and Culture, 42*(2), 256–276.

Hess, C. (2011). Using Technology in the Languages Classroom from the 20th to the 21st century: A literature review of classroom practices and fundamental second language learning theories. *Babel, 46*, 4–11.

Illeris, K. (2003). Workplace learning and learning theory. *Journal of Workplace Learning, 15*(4), 167–178. https://doi.org/10.1108/13665620310474615

Lei, Q. (2016). The difficulties and possibilities of cross-cultural communication: A case study of the global development of the Confucius Institutes. *Chinese Education and Society, 49*(6), 404–410. https://doi.org/10.1080/10611932.2016.1252220

Lien, D. (2013). Financial effects of the Confucius Institute on Chinese Language Acquisition: Isn't it delightful that friends come from afar to teach you *Hanyu? The North American Journal of Economics and Finance, 24*, 87–100.

Misra, P. K. (2014). Online training of teachers using OER: Promises and potential strategies. *Open Praxis, 6*(4), 375–385.

Qiao, M., & Jin, X. (2010). Jigsaw strategy as a cooperative learning technique: Focusing on the language learners. *Chinese Journal of Applied Linguistics (Bimonthly), 33*(4), 113–125 Retrieved from www.celea.org.cn/teic/92/10120608.pdf

STARTALK.. (2016). About STARTALK. Retrieved April 17, 2017 from https://startalk.umd.edu/public/about

UMN-Confucius-Institute.. (2012). Teaching Materials Training Program for Local Chinese Teachers from foreign countries 2012. Retrieved September 13, 2017 from http://confucius.umn.edu/teachers/pd/teaching_materials_program/index.html

UTSA-Confucius-Institute.. (2009). About the Confucius Institute. Retrieved April 17, 2017 from http://www.utsa.edu/confucius/about

Yang, R. (2010). Soft power and higher education: An examination of China's Confucius Institutes. *Globalisation, Societies and Education, 8*(2), 235–245.

# 11

# Navigating Generational Differences in the Workplace

*Khamael Al Safi*

*Middlesex University Dubai*

An article published in *The Huffington Post* in 2013 entitled "Why Generation Y Yuppies are Unhappy" by Tim Urban, shared the story of Lucy, a young woman who is part of Gen Y, the generation born between the late 1970s and mid-1990s. Lucy was brought up by her parents, who were born in the 1950s, and are part of the Baby Boomers generation. Lucy's parents were raised by Lucy's grandparents. Having witnessed the Great Depression and the Second World War, her grandparents were consequently obsessed with economic security and raising Lucy's parents to build secure and stable careers. Their priorities, when raising Lucy's parents, was to ensure that they instilled a sense of hard work and perseverance in their children so that they could achieve more prosperous career paths than their own. Lucy's parents were taught that if they put in enough effort and patience, there could be no obstacles to achieving stable careers.

Lucy's parents, after graduating, witnessed a period of unprecedented economic prosperity in the 1970s and 1980s, leading them to live a better life experience than expected. This inevitable optimism led Lucy's parents to bring up their Gen Y child to believe that he/she could be whatever he/she chose to be, and that he/she was unique and "special" in identity and ambition. As a result, a stable career was not enough for Gen Y. Lucy and her generation expected a career that was exceptional and that they would be passionate about.

There are several disappointments that Lucy faces today having entered the job market. While her parents anticipated that hard work and long hours would go into building a stable career, Lucy believes securing a job is a given and that it will only take a short time before she will be able to climb the career ladder to the top. On the other hand, Lucy is taunted by the social media world. If Lucy's parents were unhappy at any point in time, they were not always exposed to how others in their generation were doing. The social media world provides Lucy with a constant newsfeed of her peers – a distorted newsfeed to be specific. Most of Lucy's peers (and perhaps Lucy herself) present an inflated version of their lives on social media, often only highlighting the positive sides of their lives. Moreover,

*The Wiley Handbook of Global Workplace Learning*, First Edition.
Edited by Vanessa Hammler Kenon and Sunay Vasant Palsole.

it is likely that active social media users are usually those whose career situations are going well, and find their lives worthy of broadcasting (Urban, 2013).

Generation gaps are nothing new to organizations and the workplace, A magazine article in *Time* quoted an author in his 40s, "veteran teachers are saying that never in their experience were young people so thirstily avid of pleasure as now ... so selfish." The quote was sourced from a letter published in *The Atlantic* in 1911 (Stein, 2013). However, today's employers seem to be more concerned about managing various age groups with such differing attitudes and expectations. According to a survey by Ernst and Young, American professionals today view Baby Boomers, born between 1946 and the mid-1960s, as hard-working and productive. The perception of Gen X is also relatively positive, with most professionals viewing them as good team-workers. Gen Y, are viewed in accordance with the expected stereotype of being tech-savvy but truculent and relatively workshy (Stein, 2013). Understanding generational differences is core to organizational learning and informing managers about ways to enhance workplace learning for employees of different generations, each of them coming with his/her own expectations, attitudes and values.

## Managing Five Generations at a Time

Companies are soon going to roll out the red carpet for the Generation 2020er, born after 1997. On the other hand, in some developed countries, with advanced healthcare and longer life expectancies, employees from the Traditionalist generation, born prior to 1946, are reluctant to retire just yet. A typical company today may be bringing together the Traditionalist, the Baby Boomer struggling to cope with a fast-changing technological world, the Gen X employee who is "stuck in the middle between older workers who refuse to retire and younger ones who are treated far better than they ever were," the Gen Y employee who struggles to get her eyes off her phone, and will soon be joined by fresh graduates from Gen 2020 or already welcoming them on board as interns (*The Economist*, 2013).

Older employees are often disappointed to find that years of service no longer guarantee promotions, and as companies emphasize the value of innovation and digital skills, younger staff are rapidly climbing ahead. At the same time, many researchers stress that there is an intergenerational "sweet spot" that organizations and employees should aim for – a maximum learning and engagement point for all employees (Knight, 2014). However, it is important for organizations, managers and employees to first understand generational differences in the workplace, in order to comprehend how they would impact organizational and workplace learning.

### The Traditionalist Generation (Born Before 1945)

The Traditionalist Generation refers to the generation of men and women born between 1922 and 1945. Literature has also referred to this generation as The Silent Generation, World War II Generation or Industrialists. Most traditionalists today have aged out of the workplace, making up only 5% of today's workforce.

According to *Statistics Canada*, only 518,300 traditionalists were still in the workforce in 2010. Having barely survived the Great Depression, most traditionalists kept their "nose to the grindstone" with commitment and loyalty being primary attributes, shaping their work ethics and approach to organizational performance. This is a time where Taylorism witnessed a prevalence in organizations – this approach, also called Scientific Management, was proposed by Frederick Taylor as a way of improving economic efficiency, particularly labor productivity, through elements such as standardization, elimination of waste and mass production (Drury, 1915). The most enlightened companies Traditionalists could find were embracing bureaucratic approaches to management that enforced rigid hierarchies and clear top-down chains of command. With the impersonal nature of the organizational and social environments at work, Traditionalists valued the separation of personal and professional lives. Having said this, most employees viewed work as a means for survival, and were generally motivated by money and position. Traditionalists took pride in independence and generally preferred tangible forms of reward such as trophies or certificates.

## Baby Boomers (Born 1946–mid 1960s)

The Baby Boomer generation is described as the generation of individuals born in the post-World War II period, where the fertility rates in most countries, particularly in the Western world, rose significantly. In the United States, the General Fertility Rate (GFR) rose from 75.8 children per 1,000 women of child-bearing age in 1936 to a high of 122.7 in 1957, and then fell to a new all-time low of 65.0 in 1976. Following the boom in 1965, 38% of the total U.S. population were Baby Boomers, but by 2050, their share is projected to drop to only 5%, with 18 million surviving at age 85 or older in that year. Baby Boomers have always had an outsized presence compared with other generations. They were the largest generation and peaked at 78.8 million in 1999. There were an estimated 74.9 million Boomers in 2015.

The Baby Boomers have been characterized as individuals who believe that hard work and sacrifice are crucial requirements for success. They started the "workaholic" trend and marked the first generation to emphasize the contribution of teamwork, collaboration and group decision-making to organizational success.

Female labor force participation soared among the Boomers, and young women began moving into previously male-dominated professions, while marriage rates declined and cohabitation and divorce rates increased significantly. Simultaneously, this generation witnessed a prevalent income inequality at first hand, in contrast to its parents. One study suggests that inequality among the Boomers is nearly 15% greater than it was among their parents at the same age. In the mid-1990s, the median income of white Boomer families was nearly twice that of black Boomer families.

In contrast to their parents, the vast majority of people aged between 50 and state pension age are in employment and many Baby Boomers are hesitant to retire at the same age as their Traditionalist generation counterparts (Wiedmer, 2015).

### Generation X (Born 1965–1981)

Gen X grew up during the computer revolution, as well as a time of corporate downsizing and massive layoffs compared to the days when the Baby Boomers were entering the workplace. Employers also witnessed a relative shortage of candidates when Gen X entered the workplace, due to many Baby Boomers deciding to have smaller families. At the same time, loyalty to employers began to become less crucial to employees and job-hopping became more common and accepted as a method for career advancement.

Due to the scarcity of candidates, the criteria for job satisfaction and job selection changed too, with money being the main motivating factor, and stock options being more common as currencies. However, Gen X introduced the importance of work–life balance, and learning and lifestyle issues grew more valuable. With this came the need for flexibility of work that demanded continuous learning and advancing skill-sets. Having a secure job was no longer enough; opportunities for self-development and organizational learning became one of the main criteria for job selection (Bova & Kroth, 2001).

### Generation Y (Born 1982–2000)

A relatively younger generation today is Gen Y, also referred to as Millennials. In 2014, Millennials represented a quarter of the world's population and are expected to dominate the workforce by 2024. Studies have shown that Millennials are comfortable with technology, and tend to use this as an enabling factor for their social activity. Most Millennials are found to be keen on skill development and taking on new challenges at work. In comparison to Gen X, Millennials seem to put more emphasis on the potential that work content and flexibility can have in motivating employees. On the other hand, like Gen X, most Gen Y individuals prioritize the need for learning and development in the workplace, and value the need for a work–life balance. Gen Y has added the aspect of work community to the list of preconditions for work motivation and job satisfaction, where pleasant colleagues who are motivated and supportive are valued (Kultalahti & Vitala, 2014).

In contrast to its grandparents, Gen Y hardly appreciates the significance of job security and seems to consider a lack of change as threatening. Rather than focusing on formal roles or status symbols, Gen Y hold valuable the variance and challenge presented in job tasks. Motivation and demotivation are primarily determined by how mundane job tasks are perceived to be (Martin, 2005).

### Generation Z (Born Early 2000s–2010)

Not enough is known about this youngest generation yet. However, a lot is known about the environment in which Gen Z, also known as Generation 2020, iGeneration, Gen Tech, or Digital Natives, has grown up. Gen Z currently fills educators' classrooms, a critical point that employers and organizations need to remember as instruction is designed and delivered for today's Gen Z students. Most defining characteristics for this generation are yet to be established unambiguously; however, one certain dominating aspect is that of being highly connected, with a lifelong use of communication and technology such as the World Wide Web, instant messaging, text messaging, MP3 players, mobile phones and tablets.

Generally accepting of diverse populations, Gen Z is communicating in a "real" way with individuals who do not occupy the same physical space, thanks to Facebook, Skype, FaceTime and other applications. This has led to the need for Gen Z to be constantly updated with real-time dialog and news. Research in the U.S. has found that this generation is the most home-schooled generation in the modern public school era, since 1920, which may enable it to develop digital tools for independent thinking, which may also lead it to resent continuous supervision or direction.

According to academic research, Gen Z is accustomed to seeking alternative ways to conventional pathways to education and work. Consequently, 65% of grade-school students today will work in jobs that do not currently exist, with most of them being freelance contractors appreciating flexibility, rather than 40-hour per week cubicle workers (Wiedmer, 2015).

## Generational Approaches to Workplace Learning

Generational attitudes and approaches to work are difficult to fully understand. It is only in recent years that, with the prevalence of technological factors emphasizing generational differences, more substantial empirical research has been made into the variance of career expectations and employee attitudes among generations. Despite this, most of the knowledge we have today of generational differences in the workplace is anecdotal or based on extrapolations derived from different generations' life experiences. For the few systematic or cross-sectional studies that exist, it is unclear whether measurements and assessments of work values are due to generation or merely career stage. However, despite these complexities, it is important that employers and relevant stakeholders are at least made aware of reported or observed work attitudes of different generations, regardless of the causal factors (Twenge, Campbell, Hoffman, & Lance, 2010).

## Career Expectations and Attitudes to Work

The understanding of career expectations and work values of different generations helps employers and organizations appreciate how to optimally structure jobs, working conditions, reward and remuneration packages and human resource policies to accommodate for and attract different potential employees of different generational cohorts. What a Baby Boomer or Gen Xer expects from an employer or manager may be different from what a Gen Yer or Gen 2020er expects when coming into the workplace. Generalizing management strategies and organizational design in a "one-size-fits-all" manner may not yield employee satisfaction and motivation.

Popular stereotypes of Traditionalists and Baby Boomers "living to work," in contrast to Gen Xers and Gen Yers who "work to live," have been proven correct, with a 2004 survey by the Society of Human Resource Management finding younger generations "seek work/life balance" and to appreciate informality at work. Baby Boomers were found to prioritize careers and employment since their younger years, while younger workers in today's workplace, particularly Gen Yers, are more attracted to jobs that accommodate their family and personal lives. Some researchers argue that work–life balance is almost fundamental for Gen Xers and Gen Yers, and others have emphasized this, finding a decline in work centrality and work ethic between 1974 and 1999, simultaneous with a rise in leisure values in the same period. Given this, the younger the generation an employee is from, the more likely he/she is to seek career opportunities that promote personal life goals rather than merely organizational goals (Chao, 2005).

When shedding light on the expectations that different generations have from employers, it is important to distinguish between extrinsic and intrinsic rewards and values. "Extrinsic work values focus on the consequences or outcomes of work" (Twenge et al., 2010). In other words, these are the tangible rewards external to the individual, such as income, advancement opportunities and status. In contrast, intrinsic work values focus on "the process of work, that is the intangible rewards that reflect the inherent interest in the work, the learning potential, and the opportunity to be creative" (Twenge et al., 2010).

Extrinsic rewards are generally believed to be more valued when a generation has lived through a depression where financial security is scarce. For instance, most non-empirical reports have found that Traditionalists prioritized salaries and monetary rewards and encouraged their children, the Baby Boomers, to take on career opportunities that guaranteed such financial security (Keelan, 2014). In contrast, many organizations assume that younger generations, such as Gen X and Y, are more enlightened when it comes to intrinsic expectations of rewards and motivation, valuing "interesting" jobs and are encouraged to "do what they love." However, empirical evidence has shown that this has not resulted in younger generations placing lower value on extrinsic rewards and expectations, in comparison to Baby Boomers or Traditionalists. In fact, Gen Yers are found to prioritize extrinsic rewards just as much as their older counterparts, together with a combination of not wanting to work too hard – re-emphasizing the sense of entitlement that Gen Y relatively has (Twenge et al., 2010). Additionally, Gen Yers are found to value personal time (e.g., not wanting to work overtime, etc.), and yet still expect more status and compensation, illustrating what some studies have described as a disconnection between expectations and reality (Twenge et al., 2010).

On the other hand, the importance of intrinsic values and rewards has declined slightly over the past generations, despite popular belief that newer generations are more likely to be motivated by intrinsic rewards such as job satisfaction and meaning at work. While it is true that today's Gen Y employees feel an entitlement to work that is challenging and "interesting," that provides opportunities for growth, Gen X and Gen Y employees are also found to be more likely than previous generations to be motivated by relatively higher salaries and monetary benefits, together with a high rating for intrinsic values (Cennamo & Gardner, 2008).

## Who Works the Most Hours?

Since the 1960s and the rise of more organizational studies on employee behavior, the concept of "work–life balance" has been popular among academics and practitioners. An organization purchases an employee's time at a designated place, and consequently, employees need to "self-negotiate" approaches to coordinate their personal and professional lives.

For the Traditionalists and Baby Boomers, job security and financial guarantees were highlighted in importance given the cultural and societal impacts of the Great Depression and the aftermath of World War II. In contrast to this, Gen X and Y have focused more on more "higher" needs of motivation, such as social factors at work and home, which go beyond merely securing a job. For Gen Y, in particular, employees are significantly less likely to be work-centric than previous generations. This means that they view work–life balance as a basic expectation from a work opportunity and position. In a study on Gen Y nurses, Jamieson, Kirk, and Andrew (2013) found that 89.9% stated that work-life balance was of high importance to them, with 86% of these nurses providing free text comments when asked to describe what work–life balance meant to them, indicating the importance of this concept for them.

Gen Y job candidates consider work–life balance to be important in making career decisions where work–life balance is perceived as a determinant of job satisfaction, job performance and ethical decision-making, particularly for female job candidates in Generation Y (Smith, 2010). In a survey, 87.3% of Gen Y employees were found to decline extra pay and instead choose either more vacation or flexibility in working hours (Smith, 2010).

Ironically, despite this growing importance of work–life balance with generation, expectations that employers and organizations have from their employees, as well as the social nature of work in recent years, work–life balance management is actually becoming more difficult by the generation. For instance, the notion of 40-hour work weeks is gradually becoming more uncommon with approximately half of managers (46%) surveyed by Ernst and Young working 40-plus hour weeks, and four in ten managers reporting that their hours had increased over the past five years.

In the United States, a majority of full-time employees (62%) had a spouse or partner who worked at least full-time; however, the likelihood of this happening is much higher for Gen X (73%) and Gen Y (78%), than Baby Boomers (47%). Additionally, Gen Y employees are more likely to sacrifice their jobs or careers for parental responsibilities, than Gen X employees or Baby Boomers. In a survey by Ernst and Young, more than one-third of Gen Y employees said they would "move to another country with better parental leave benefits," as opposed to 28% of Gen X employees and 11% of Baby Boomer employees. However, simultaneously, Gen Y employees (50%) are much less likely to take a career break after having children, than Gen X employees (75%) or Baby Boomers (67%) (Ernst & Young, 2015).

For retaining employees, and particularly those from Gen Y, organizations today offer flexible work arrangements, such as special holiday hours, flex-time or telecommuting. Many firms and companies are yet to compromise on their expenses and costs to accommodate work–life balance requirements of millennial employees; however, organizations that do offer such benefits are found to attract younger people who are making career choices.

## Generational Differences in Soft Knowledge Situations

In organizations today, knowledge has become increasingly important in ensuring competitiveness and survival. Knowledge capital is primarily focused on deriving soft knowledge or "tacit" knowledge, which resides in the minds of employees. In most typical organizations, experienced employees take on management positions, and more junior employees learn from experienced colleagues and develop their own knowhow through addressing workplace challenges (Busch, Venkitachalam, & Richards, 2008). Having said this, employees who work for many years in an organization have greater opportunities for soft knowledge accumulation. This implies that employees have variations in experiences and these must be comprehended to understand the handling of soft knowledge situations by employees from different generations (Field, Burke, & Copper, 2013).

Soft knowledge, despite its broad scope, can be defined as knowledge that is implicit. In organizations, this soft knowledge is generally associated with the ability to manage oneself, others and one's career. In this aspect, employees from younger generations such as Gen Y and Gen X, are found to have more idealistic views on what a workplace should provide and accommodate, as opposed to the Baby Boomer generation, where employees are more likely to accept the workplace for what it is. This provides useful indicators for managers and organizations on what expectations different employees from these generations would have (Busch et al., 2008).

Additionally, younger employees of Gen Y and Gen X, are likely to feel a sense of ownership of projects more acutely than older peers, who are found to be more ambivalent about the ownership of projects on which they've worked. Ironically, older employees of the Baby Boomer generation, saw workplace learning more positively than younger employees of Gen Y and Gen X. Despite this, Baby Boomers have a lower tendency to be interested in gaining formal recognition awards when compared to Gen X and Gen Y employees.

Gen X and Gen Y employees are motivated by recognition and find it important to have the opportunity to apply their ideas into their work routines, in contrast to Baby Boomer employees who have the tendency to refrain from applying their own ideas in the workplace. With regards to alternative views and others' opinions, Baby Boomer employees are more interested in listening to alternate ideas, with younger employees being less interested in opening up to others' ideas. At the same time, Gen X and Gen Y employees have been found to appreciate change in employment and view it favorably, as opposed to Baby Boomer employees, who view employment turnover negatively (Lyons & Kuron, 2013).

As most studies would theorize, research has found that older employees, who are more experienced, make greater use of their tacit knowledge, which is less common among employees at entry level. Younger generations are found to be more interested in career advancement and the opportunity to gain more experience, so long as they find work challenging and stimulating (Busch et al., 2008).

Managers, from the Baby Boomer generation, in light of the implications of the above, should encourage younger employees through fostering recognition of achievements. These managers are also in a position to aid younger Gen X and Gen Y employees to view organizational learning positively and to understand the consequences of responsibilities in the workplace (Arsenault, 2004; Busch et al., 2008). On the other hand, younger employees of the Gen X and Gen Y can instill in older generations such as the Baby Boomers, or even the Traditionalists still working in organizations, their work-related enthusiasm and ambitions. Viewing the Gen Y idealism as a gateway to more innovative ideas could bring Baby Boomer managers and employees the benefits of creative organizational cultures. This, however, would require a flexible attitude and the provision of opportunities for younger employees to voice their opinions and ideas (Busch et al., 2008).

## Generational Attitudes to Teamwork

When exploring generational differences, a question that is often posed is whether differences in working preferences between generations are due to actual generational differences or simply artifacts of the era and the age in which an employee lives. An employee's work habits are formed and developed in the adolescence age period, where economic, political and social factors may influence an individual's work values and expectations. Although these may change naturally as an individual grows in age, generational experiences have been shown to influence work values perhaps more than age or maturation, which suggests that generational differences in working preferences are significant.

Differences between generations are often viewed as an expected occurrence resulting from the different influential factors individuals in different generations may witness. However, what may lead to problems in the workplace is when these differences hold a high potential for conflict to erupt when working together in groups and teams in organizations. Research and literature point out that Baby Boomers, Gen X and Gen Y hold differences in work values that may lead to clashes, causing tension in organizations and their work environments. Particularly in today's team-oriented, "work hard and play hard" aggressive corporate cultures, these generational differences appear to be more significant (Sirias, Karp, & Brotherton, 2007).

In today's environment, cooperation among employees, particularly where teamwork is central to achieving goal's objectives, is essential. One way of understanding how individuals from different generations view groups and teams is through measuring their acceptance of others. It is theorized that high levels of acceptance of others may indicate being more comfortable with working with others and therefore, favoring group work.

A study exploring differences between generations in acceptance of others found that Baby Boomers were significantly higher than Gen X in acceptance of others, and that at the same time, Baby Boomers were low compared to the

Traditionalists. This was interpreted as correlating with the general suggestion that trust and acceptance in American societies are declining over time as society is itself perceived as less "civil." Additionally, over time, Baby Boomers were found to "like being with others" more than Gen X, supporting the notion posed by popular culture and literature of Gen X valuing independence more than earlier counterparts (Yrle, Hartman, & Payne, 2005).

On the other hand, other literature has quoted research finding that Gen X and Y tend to have more respect for those who share their own values, which could present an opportunity for group assignments that capitalize on common values between employees of different generations. Additionally, Gen Y individuals have been found, in contrast to expectations from previously mentioned studies, to be involved in teamwork since their early years, building confidence about working with others (Barton & Skiba, 2006).

To capitalize on team potential with Gen Y in particular, Microsoft built teams made up of Gen Y employees, particularly those with two years of working experience or less, to provide feedback. New hires recruited at Microsoft usually have distinguished profiles, but also feel that they are given little opportunity to share their ideas due to being less experienced than employees of older generations. To address this, Microsoft launched the 42New forum that allows for teams of Gen Y employees to share their ideas, with no managers present. Managers at Microsoft found that these employees had fresh perspectives to present, and were more willing to hear the opinions of older employees in the firm and to learn about the history of Microsoft's projects when it was stripped of fancy jargon or complex presentations. This has allowed for information flow in both directions and has also helped managers understand new hires better, having even used gaming to engage employees in team meetings and discussions at 42New. Others may argue that such an approach may further isolate generational groups of employees from each other. However, Microsoft claims that if managed well and adopted with an open mindset, this approach can help in accommodating opinions and ideas of different employees from different generations. It could potentially allow for different generations in the workplace to better understand each other's' perspectives so that more cooperative and collaborative cross-sectional teamwork between employees from different generations is established (Birkenshaw & Crainer, 2008).

## Generational Differences across the Globe

Generational variation in collectivist and individualist cultures are yet to be fully understood. While most studies and research have focused on Western societies, relatively little research has explored whether these generational categorizations apply cross-culturally. Generational categorizations are theorized based on the collective memory embedded within an age group of individuals, particularly location, age, major life events, social, political, economic and technological changes at their development periods. This collective memory influences the values, attitudes, and therefore behaviors in everyday life and in the workplace at later stages of life.

## Generation Variation in Collectivist and Individualist Cultures

A certain age group or generation can be viewed as a reflection of that group's value orientations emphasized during a particular time period in the country in which they live. As a result, generation categorizations differ in various countries and cultures. For instance, in Chinese society, generations are usually labeled by birth decade, that is "Born in the 1960s," "Born in the 1970s," and "Born in the 1980s." Other labels define these age groups by events such as the Cultural Revolution (born 1961–1966), Social Reform (born 1971–1976), and Millennials (born 1981–1986). The Cultural Revolution generation, or "Born in the 1960s," experienced the Cultural Revolution (1966–1976) and extreme poverty in its youth, where it was the first generation to witness a deregulated economy; therefore it holds financial security in high esteem. The Social Reform generation, or "Born in the 1970s," experienced drastic economic development in China during its formative years, and so witnessed an increase in material prosperity. This is in comparison to the Millennials generation, also known in China as the "One-Child Generation" a few years after the One Child Policy was launched in 1979 permitting urban families to have only one child. This generation has been stereotyped as being self-centered and spoilt, as a result of being the only child. However, it is also characterized as having strong self-confidence, diverse interests and a strong drive for self-improvement (Yi, Ribbens, Fu, & Cheng, 2015).

According to research, Americans are found to demand and expect more from their managers than Chinese employees. Contrary to popular belief, Chinese employees today are more likely to make career changes or moves than Americans, indicating that paternalistic cultural characteristics are being diluted in Chinese societies and younger generations are beginning to take more control of their careers (Yi et al., 2015).

Most literature on generational differences in Western societies has found distinct differences between generations. However, generational differences in the U.S. have been found to be generally greater than such differences in the Chinese society. This highlights the significance of strong traditional culture and its influence on work-related perceptions and that these are relatively stable across generations in China (Yi et al., 2015).

A more inclusive and applicable way of looking at generations is that even though individuals from different countries are born in the same time period, they are not shaped in the same way since they are not brought up in environments that witness the same historical and cultural events. It has been argued that consequently, individuals born in the same time period, from different countries, cannot be classified as the same generation (Yi et al., 2015).

In terms of values, individuals born in the same age period have been found to have differing values, when they come from different cultural backgrounds, even when they live in the same country. A study on immigrant cultural groups in Canada found that these groups were different to Canadians and to other immigrant groups in their perspectives on family relations and dynamics. Other aspects such as openness to change were also found to be different for people of the same age group belonging to different immigrant communities. For instance, people belonging to the Gen Y age group were found to hold views about family obligations similar to their parents, when they came from Asian communities, when compared to Anglo-Celtic families in Canada (Kwak & Berry, 2001).

Within Asian immigrant groups in Canada, more differences are prevalent between generational age groups. In East Indian and Korean communities, families, old and young generations alike showed a preference to maintain core elements of language and family relations. However, parents belonging to Gen X and Baby Boomer age groups show this preference more strongly than their children. In contrast, both Gen X and Y in Vietnamese families in Canada were found to be more inclined to foster group memberships that adapt to new societal expectations. These differences in preferences indicate that generational expectations and characterizations cannot be generalized cross-culturally, even for ethnic groups living in the same country (Kwak & Berry, 2001).

- A study on U.S. generations indicated that all three generations of Baby Boomers, Gen X and Gen Y, ranked in their top-five value of importance the terminal values of family security, freedom and health, and instrumental values of honesty and responsibility, and in their bottom five of importance the terminal values of a world at peace, a world of beauty, national security and social recognition, and the instrumental values of cleanliness, forgiveness, imaginative, obedience and politeness.
- A similar study in Thailand found Boomers to highly value terminal values of a sense of accomplishment, equality, pleasure and salvation, and the instrumental values of loyalty and obedience. Across all three generations in Thailand, the terminal values of family security and health and instrumental values of honesty and responsible were ranked in the top five of importance (ranked 1–5) across the generations. Furthermore, the terminal values of an exciting life, a world of beauty, national security and social recognition and the instrumental values of cleanliness were ranked as not important (ranked 14–18) by all three generations.
- In Latin America, Monserrat et al.'s (2009) study suggested that the most important terminal values across the generations were a comfortable life, health, self-respect and family security, and the instrumental values were honesty and responsibility. Monserrat et al.'s study also indicated that all three generations rated as unimportant the terminal values of an exciting life, a world of beauty, national security and social recognition, and instrumental values of imaginative, forgiving, obedience and politeness. Such findings shed light upon the fact that some values between generations from different countries may be shared.

To add support to this indication is the fact that Gen Y in Thailand ranked ambition as more important than capability, while Gen X and Boomers ranked capability as more important than ambition. This suggests that Gen Y appreciates recognition and promotion early on in its careers, as opposed to Gen X and Baby Boomers in Thailand, who believe that experience and knowledge are prerequisites for promotions and recognition. These values ranked by Gen Y in terms of ambition are contrary to the Thai cultural value of hierarchy and the Buddhist concept of "accepting your current status," promotions are earned through time, experience and training, and over a long period of time, suggesting that the younger generation in Thailand may be marking a slight diversion in career expectations and a convergence with Western Gen Y expectations.

In individualist cultures, obedience is often ranked as unimportant for all generations X, Y, and Baby Boomers. In collectivist cultures such as Thailand, obedience is often regarded as crucial, particularly to Gen X and Boomers. However, a potential intergenerational conflict arises as a result of Gen Y holding a relatively lower importance for obedience as a value – a characteristic of Gen Y in Thailand that is more individualist than collectivist (Murphy, Mujtaba, Manyak, Sungkhawan, & Greenwood, 2010).

In the Middle East, studies on intergenerational differences are also relatively fewer than in the West. According to research conducted in the Middle East, it is possible that social desirability plays a more significant role than in other cultures on the attitudes and opinions of individuals in the Arab world, including younger generations X and Y. Social desirability biases involve conscious or unconscious attempts to create a certain impression and play an important role in Arab culture, due to its collectivist nature of "saving face." This involves the reluctance to say "no" and to avoid giving an answer that others do not wish to hear. Despite its continued prevalence among younger people in Arab generations, this has been found to be relatively more diluted compared to older counterparts. In the United Arab Emirates (UAE), younger UAE nationals have been found to have higher levels of individualism than older UAE nationals. This may also indicate that modernization and Westernization of the Arab region may be having an important influence on the values of UAE nationals.

At the same time, certain aspects of society still exist in similar levels of importance for younger UAE nationals. An example of this is the utility of *wasta*. The term wasta describes a form of networking and a type of social capital in the Arab world. It refers to a process of mediation between two parties by a third person, called the *waseet*. In Arab societies, wasta is still considered as a backbone of social organization, either in interacting with government authorities, business relations or job searches (Ramady, 2015). Given the increasing individualism in Arab societies with younger generations in particular, it has been proposed that UAE nationals over age 30 would believe in the utility of wasta more than underage 30 UAE nationals. Research has shown that this is not the case. Some research has implied that younger UAE nationals see the utility of wasta as more important than their counterparts from older generations. This could be due to the perceived increasing difficulty in having a great deal of access to wasta and; therefore, they may fear being at a disadvantage because of the wasta of others. Older generations are generally part of more small, tight-knit communities than younger generations in the UAE, which promotes closer connections and more access to wasta. Today's competitive job market and multinational work environment may increase the perceived need for wasta that younger generations may not easily access when compared to their parents and grandparents (Whiteoak, Crawford, & Mapstone, 2006).

Studies have shown that generations in the Arab region are more similar than different in their values. Yet to identify differences that do exist between generations, Booz and Company categorized generations in the Arab region differently than the general global categorization theorized. This approach classified the working population in the Middle East into three categories:

- Arab National Generation (ANG): This demographic cohort was born between 1948 and 1964 (ages 49 to 65). The key socioeconomic event that shaped this era was the rise of Pan Arabism.
- Arab Regional Generation (ARG): Born between 1965 and 1977 (ages 36 to 48), this group grew up during the expansion of oil wealth in some countries, especially in the 1970s and 1980s.
- The Arab Digital Generation (ADG): Born from 1978 onward, with the research including only those ages 15 to 35, this age cohort experienced the onset of digital technology, along with economic globalization.

Their study found that values such as generosity and hospitality were shared across these generations, but seem to be declining with generations. Additionally, satisfaction with life achievements, particularly career-wise, was found at its lowest among the ADG, and highest among the ANG, reflecting the recent high unemployment rates, together with the increasing cost of living, and reduced economic opportunities. These three generations were distinguished by what they associate with: with the ADG associating itself more with adventure and extravagance than older counterparts, and ANG associating itself with achievement (Strategyand, 2013).

These similarities and differences between generations in different countries have practical implications for managers, especially those from MNCs that have operations in both Western and Eastern countries. The most important of these being that human resource managers should ensure that admired "best practices" are adopted with considerations of people in different generations. Having said this, it is also important that managers should be aware that these practices proven to work in Western contexts such as the U.S. may not work in collectivist cultures such as China or the Middle East. For example, the younger generations in the USA are often considered to be more aggressive, dynamic, and demanding than the older generations. On the other hand, the values of people in collectivist societies are relatively more stable across generations than in individualist societies. This implies that the focus of managers in different cultural contexts should be customized as to whether different approaches should be taken for different generations or not, and to what extent. In the USA for instance, managers may focus more on challenging and engaging younger employees to retain them. In China, managers may focus less on such aspects and more on the Chinese culture and its influence on work attitudes and perceptions of younger and older employees. Furthermore, managers should be aware of employees' expectations of them, whether these may be more demanding in American cultures or more obedient in Chinese or collectivist cultures. Research in various cultural contexts emphasizes the fact that between-culture differences in values are larger than within-culture differences (Yi et al., 2015).

## The "Intergenerational Sweet Spot"

Comparative research has shown that there are more similarities than differences between generations in the workplace, in terms of job attitudes and values. Some argue that these differences are due to factors other than generational factors. An example of this is the common perception that Gen Y employees are more likely to switch jobs more frequently than older generations. However, research has shown people who have worked longer for an employer are less likely to quit, thereby suggesting that Gen Y employees may be switching jobs simply because they have been working for fewer years (Valcour, 2013).

To reach an intergenerational sweet spot, it is crucial that correlations are not mistaken for causations, which could contribute to forming stereotypes about different generations. This intergenerational sweet spot can be defined as a point of maximum engagement for all employees, a concept that could help managers tap into the potentials of employees of different ages.

## Intergenerational Differences: A Challenge Far from Novel to Organizations

As the 1911 letter to *The Atlantic* cited earlier shows, differences that frustrate employees of different generations, believed to be a source of conflict, are behaviors portrayed by probably most individuals or employees of a certain age group. Every generation has been found to be puzzled by the behaviors of the succeeding one or have at least questioned the beliefs and priorities of succeeding and preceding generations.

Looking at differences in expectations from different generations in the workplace, some research has found that Gen Y employees, more or less, want similar things from their organizations as Gen X and Baby Boomer employees. This is in terms of meaningful work, opportunities for learning, fair treatment, and competitive pay. Moreover, employees from these three generations agree on the characteristics of an ideal leader – someone who leads by example, acts as a mentor, helps employees see how their roles contribute to the organization and holds them accountable for their roles (White, 2011).

## Rethinking Generation Y

Gen Y is often tagged with being a generation of smartphone addicts who live on praise and feedback, feel entitled to rapid advancement and promotion without being willing to fulfill the requirements this advancement entails, prioritize work–life balance over employers' needs and think that they could work wherever, however, whenever and whatever they want. Despite the importance of understanding such characteristics, the exaggeration of differences between generations may lead to biases in the workplace and a misalignment in expectations.

A popular perception is that the past decade has involved a rise in the culture of egoism and self-worth, a decline in social and family relations, and an unrealistic set of expectations of the future and career paths. A "60 Minutes" episode described Gen Y or Millennials as a new breed of "American workers about to attack everything you hold sacred." However, research has shown that there seems to be a trend in every age that the members of the current, younger generation are viewed as different from previous generations, usually in a negative way. Studies have also shown that contrary to popular belief, the differences between Gen Y and other generations are often over-hyped. For instance, Gen Y employees are less interested than other generations X and Baby Boomers in keeping up with materialistic trends; however, they are more tolerant of consumerism and marketing of unnecessary material goods. Additionally, the importance of having money has declined since its peak in the 1990s. One study found that the effects for or of self-enhancement and self-esteem among Gen Y were actually negative, where younger generations had lower scores on these variables than older generations. Also, the effects for happiness and life satisfaction were positive, with younger generations having higher scores on these variables than older generations.

Gen Y, or as some call them "Generation Me," may not be as dramatically different from members of other generations, as many managers or organizations may assume. Empirical research has found today's youth to be no more egotistical than previous generations and just as satisfied as previous generations. However, research has also found that, in line with popular belief, Gen Y employees do have higher expectations for their careers and are more cynical and distrusting than previous generations. This implies that it is important that managers understand new recruits from Gen Y but also that stereotypes and misconceptions about this generation be evaluated as they have important implications for how a generation views itself and how it is viewed by society at large (Trzesniewki & Donnellan, 2010).

While most employers are focused on Gen Y employees as the youngest and upcoming of the labor market, Gen 2020 or Gen Z, described earlier is this chapter, is the newer game in town. Despite not being in the labor market yet, some Gen Z kids are beginning to join organizations through work experience or internships. Interestingly, a study by Future Workplace and Randstad found that the percentage of Gen 2020 individuals preferring to work in an office has surged, with an increase from 16% in 2014 to 36% in 2016. In contrast to this, this preference is becoming less popular with Gen Y employees, with 37% of employees choosing to work in an office, a 10% drop from 2014.

Despite the popularity of social media among Gen Y and 2020, their preferred mode of communication was in-person, where both groups found that communicating with managers was more effective face-to-face. Additionally, 48% of Gen Y employees in 2016 still wanted to be mentored by their bosses. Although Gen 2020 is younger, with less experience, it seems to be spreading its wings more quickly; in comparison to 2014 where 64% of Gen 2020 wanted mentoring, only 49% today want the same. This emphasizes the fact that younger generations may be gradually reverting to workplace habits of earlier generations of Baby Boomers or Gen X (White, 2016).

## A Four Generational Workplace: Tomorrow's Ideal Environment for Organizational Learning

Some theorists have gone as far as to propose that all generations have similar values, they just express them differently and therefore, all generations have similar expectations in terms of having a credible and trustworthy leader (Deal,

2007). Despite this being debatable to an extent, it is agreed that managers improving their ability to relate to Gen Y employees and employees of other generations will make them better managers to all employees. Engaging employees of different generations does not involve letting employees use social media at work or bring their pets. It is about providing challenging, meaningful work, communicating effectively, and helping employees to see their contributions. The optimal manager for all generations of Baby Boomers, Gen X, and Gen Y, is a person with a coaching orientation, who is aware of employees' expectations, attitudes, talents and interests, whether these reflect generational trends or not. This involves the judgment to provide support and coaching when needed and to accommodate for independence and autonomy when needed too.

A new model proposed to manage intergenerational teams effectively places value on how individuals are different, through particularly capitalizing on the best contribution that each individual can make to the group. In other words, this would entail work with individual boundaries, rather than group boundaries, so that each member of the group is more accepting of how he/she views the environment. Once these individual boundaries are understood, group members become clear and non-defensive about their respective viewpoints and values. When emphasizing individuality and de-emphasizing normative values, there is no pressure for anyone to present a different face than the one that shows who he or she actually is (Sirias et al., 2007).

To understand these individual boundaries, managers should strive to understand what factors determine employee behavior, and whether employee behavior is due to generational factors or not. Reaching the intergenerational sweet spot primarily involves understanding the behavioral and attitudinal differences managers perceive among generations (Valcour, 2013).

## References

Arsenault, P. (2004). Validating generational differences: A legitimate diversity and leadership issue. *Leadership and Organization Development Journal, 25*(2), 124–141.

Barton, A. J., & Skiba, D. J. (2006). Adapting your teaching to accommodate the next generation of learners. *Online Journal of Issues in Nursing, 11*(2), 15–25.

Birkenshaw, J. and Crainer, S. (2008). Game on: Theory Y meets Generation Y. *Business Strategy Review*, London Business School.

Bova, B., & Kroth, M. (2001). Workplace learning and generation X. *Journal of Workplace Learning, 13*(2), 57–65.

Busch, P., Venkitachalam, K., & Richards, D. (2008). Generational differences in soft knowledge situations: Status, need for recognition, workplace commitment and idealism. *Knowledge and Process Management, 15*(1), 45–58.

Cennamo, L., & Gardner, D. (2008). Generational differences in work values, outcomes and person-organization values fit. *Journal of Managerial Psychology, 23*(8), 891–906.

Chao, L. (2005). For Gen Xers, it's work to live: Allowing employees to strike balance between job and life can lead to better retention rates. *Wall Street Journal,* Eastern ed., B6.

Deal, J. J. (2007). *Retiring the generation gap: How employees young and old can find common ground.* San Fancisco: Jossey-Bass.
Drury, H. B. (1915). *Scientific management: A history and criticism.* New York: Colombia University Press.
Ernst and Young. (2015). *Global Generations Study.* Retrieved from http://www.ey.com/Publication/vwLUAssets/EY-global-generations-a-global-study-on-work-life-challenges-across-generations/$FILE/EY-global-generations-a-global-study-on-work-life-challenges-across-generations.pdf
Field, J., Burke, R. J., & Copper, C. L. (2013). *The Sage handbook of aging, work and society.* Thousand Oaks, CA: Sage.
Jamieson, I., Kirk, R., & Andrew, C. (2013). Work-life balance: What generation Y nurses want. *Nurse Leader, 11,* 36–39.
Keelan, E. K. (2014). Organising generations – What can sociology offer to the understanding of generations at work? *Sociology Compass, 8*(1), 20–30.
Knight, R. (2014). Managing people from 5 generations. Retrieved May 3, 2016, from Harvard Business Review, https://hbr.org/2014/09/managing-people-from-5-generations
Kultalahti, S., & Vitala, R. L. (2014). Sufficient challenges and a weekend ahead – Generation Y describing motivation at work. *Journal of Organizational Change Management, 27*(4), 569–582.
Kwak, K., & Berry, J. W. (2001). Generational differences in acculturation among Asian families in Canada: A comparison of Vietnamese, Korean, and East-Indian groups. *International Journal of Psychology, 36*(3), 152–162.
Lyons, S., & Kuron, L. (2013). Generational differences in the workplace: A review of the evidence and directions for future research. *Journal of Organizational Behavior, 35*(1), 139–157.
Martin, C. A. (2005). From high maintenance to high productivity. *Industrial and Commercial Training, 37*(1), 39–44.
Monserrat, S. et al. (2009). Democracy's children: Changing values in Argentina and Brazil? *Proceedings of the Eastern Academy of Management,* Rio de Janeiro, June 21–25, 2009.
Murphy, E. F., Mujtaba, B. G., Manyak, T., Sungkhawan, J., & Greenwood, R. (2010). Generational value differences of Baby Boomers in Thailand. *Asia Pacific Business Review, 16*(4), 545–566.
Ramady, M. A. (2015). *The political economy of Wasta: Use and abuse of social capital networking.* New York: Springer.
Sirias, D., Karp, H. B., & Brotherton, T. (2007). Comparing the levels of individualism/collectivism between Baby Boomers and generation X. *Management Research News, 30*(10), 749–761.
Smith, K. T. (2010). Work-life balance perspectives of marketing professionals in generation Y. *Services Marketing Quarterly, 31*(4), 434–447.
Stein, J. (2013). Milennials: The Me Me Me Generation. Retrieved May 3, 2016, from Time, http://time.com/247/millennials-the-me-me-me-generation/#paid-wall
Strategyand. (2013). *The Arab World Today: Generational Differences Must Inform Policy.* Retrieved from http://www.strategyand.pwc.com/me/home/press_media/management_consulting_press_releases/article/52947583

The Economist. (2013). Generations in the Workplace: Winning the generation game. Retrieved May 3, 2016, http://www.economist.com/news/business/21586831-businesses-are-worrying-about-how-manage-different-age-groups-widely-different.

Trzesniewki, K. H., & Donnellan, M. B. (2010). Rethinking generation "me": A study of cohort effects from 1976–2006. *Perspectives on Psychological Science, 5*(1), 58–75.

Twenge, J. M., Campbell, S. M., Hoffman, B. J., & Lance, C. E. (2010). Generational differences in work values: Leisure and extrinsic values increasing social, and intrinsic values decreasing. *Journal of Management, 36*(5), 1117–1142.

Urban, T. (2013). Why Generation Y Yuppies Are Unhappy. Retrieved May 3, 2016, from The Huffington Post, https://www.huffingtonpost.com/entry/generation-y-unhappy_b_3930620.html

Valcour, M. (2013). Hitting the Intergenerational Sweet Spot. Retrieved 14 January 2017 from Harvard Business Review, https://hbr.org/2013/05/hitting-the-intergenerational

White. (2011). *Rethinking Generation Gaps in the Workplace: Focus on Shared Values*. Retrieved from University of North Carolina Kenan Flagler Business School http://www.kenan-flagler.unc.edu/executive-development/about/~/media/C8FC09AEF03743BE91112418FEE286D0.ashx.

White. (2016). Here's What Makes Gen Z and Millennials Happiest in the Workplace. Retrieved January 3, 2017 from Time, http://time.com/money/4476832/millennials-generation-z-workers

Whiteoak, J. W., Crawford, N. G., & Mapstone, R. H. (2006). Impact of gender and generational differences in work values and attitudes in an Arab culture. *Thunderbird International Business Review, 48*(1), 77–91.

Wiedmer, T. (2015). Generations do differ: Best practices in leading traditionalists, boomers, and generations X, Y and Z. *Delta Kappa Gamma Bulletin, 82*(1), 51–58.

Yi, X., Ribbens, B., Fu, L., & Cheng, W. (2015). Variation in career and workplace attitudes by generation, gender and culture differences in career perceptions in the United States and China. *Employee Relations, 37*(1), 66–82.

Yrle, A. C., Hartman, S. J., & Payne, D. M. (2005). Generation X: Acceptance of others and teamwork implications. *Team Performance Management: An International Journal, 11*(5/6), 188–199.

# 12

# Multicultural Curriculum and Cross-Cultural Workplace Learning

*Ana Ivenicki*

*Federal University of Rio de Janeiro*

This chapter discusses a curriculum initiative in municipalities in Rio de Janeiro, Brazil, from a multicultural perspective and reviews possible challenges and potentials in its implementation, particularly linked to the presence (or absence) of multicultural leaderships at the workplace. The initiative was taken by local educational authorities, who approached the researcher so that primary school municipal curriculum guidelines could reflect the valuing of diversity, and the challenging of racism and stereotypes.

The main argument that informed the construction of the curriculum guidelines was that identity building is inherent to curriculum proposals, and that identity should be viewed as hybrid, transitory and fluid (Banks, 2004; Canen and Peters, 2005; Hall, 2003; Ivenicki, 2015; Warren and Canen, 2012). In that sense, the relevance of such a perspective was justified in that de-essentializing identities should likely help teachers and pupils understand the need to challenge dichotomized approaches that freeze "I" and "the other." It is the cornerstone of a multicultural approach that intended to problematize hegemonic, homogenized and monocultural curricular discourses, so as to value equity and minority education.

On the other hand, revisiting that experience through the discourses of educational actors responsible for its implementation show that the lack of multicultural leaderships can have deleterious effects on the workplace and, as a consequence, on the implementation of the very multicultural curriculum itself. The chapter argues for the need for multicultural leadership in the workplace, so that the cross-cultural dimension can be learned and reinforced in the everyday institutional environment, as well as in the curriculum development.

*The Wiley Handbook of Global Workplace Learning*, First Edition.
Edited by Vanessa Hammler Kenon and Sunay Vasant Palsole.

## Theoretical Framework, Methodology and Background to the Study

### Discussing Multi/ Interculturalism

When discussing a multicultural curriculum, it should be noted that the terms multiculturalism and interculturalism have been used in different contexts, the first one more common in European and Latin American literature, and the second one in Anglo-Saxonic texts. Even though some discussions concerning differences between them have been in place, the present chapter has opted to use the term multi/ interculturalism so as to avoid getting into metalinguistic discussions and focus on what seems to be a general perspective underlying that thinking. In fact, multiculturalism or interculturalism have been two terms to refer to a set of theoretical and political answers to cultural diversity, including the array of paradigms, efforts and reflections about ways of ensuring non-discriminatory and inclusive perspectives within the diverse social practices, including the educational ones.

As posited by Ng and Bloemroad (2015), multiculturalism has strengths, inasmuch as it fosters national identity (as probably the referred authors believe that to the extent cultural groups feel they are represented, they refrain from promoting disruptive movements that challenge identity), promotes cultural tolerance, and assists with the incorporation of cultural minorities. However, the referred authors also point out that its weaknesses come insofar as it may create "faultlines" along cultural and religious groups; could promote separate and parallel lives; and could pose a challenge to equality in liberal societies. According to them, sometimes it could even be perceived as a threat, as incompatible with Western, liberal values, burdening the state welfare and challenging existing identities. Nevertheless, it could be seen as providing opportunities, since multi/ interculturalism could be seen as having potentials to be used as a tool for attracting talents, a source of competitive advantage for nations, and even a discourse for politicians to score political gains.

It is important to note that Ng and Bloemroad (2015) contend that much of the rhetoric and debates surrounding multi/ interculturalism can be attributed to how it is understood and implemented, and whether it is successful in achieving its explicit or implicit objectives. In fact, I argue that even though a general meaning can be attributed to multi/ interculturalism, it does get more blurred when getting to different interpretations that underpin diverse policies and practices.

As argued elsewhere (Canen, 2005, 2009, 2012; Ivenicki, 2015; Ivenicki and de Xavier, 2015), diversity is generally perceived as moving within a continuum from more folkloric approaches (in which multiculturalism is understood as the valuing of cultural diversity that tends to emphasize holidays, black consciousness days and recipes and rituals from diverse cultures, for instance), up to more critical perspectives (those that stress the need for interrogating prejudices and unfair power relations that marginalize identities on the lines of race, gender, social class, religion, culture, language and other markers of identity).

More than mere rhetoric, I have argued that such differences in meanings do get different implications when talking about educational policies and practices. It seems to be clear that reducing multiculturalism to scattered events that essentialize identities on the lines of festivities and rituals could not be the same as fighting within everyday teaching practices in gearing educational practices and curriculum toward questioning unfair relationships that marginalize Black people, indigenous people, women and other identities, so as to challenge stereotypes and discriminatory practices.

### Designing a Curriculum in a Multicultural Perspective

Multiculturalism should arguably provide possible roads ahead toward a transformative higher education that not only challenges prejudices and stereotypes, but also attempts to take both cultural plurality and academic excellence onboard. Based on a multi/ intercultural theoretical framework (Banks, 2004; Hall, 2003; Ivenicki, 2015; Ivenicki and de Xavier, 2015; Warren and Canen, 2012), I argue that curriculum and teacher education in a multi/ intercultural perspective could contribute to a more equity-oriented process of schooling inasmuch as it offers possible ways toward promoting the inclusion of marginalized groups, in addition to the education of new generations that challenge stereotypes and discriminations. I also contend that a *critical, post-colonial multicultural perspective* in curriculum and in teacher continuing education may have a positive impact in shaping new outlooks and avenues in order to combat prejudices and transform schools into more inclusive, plural, and equity oriented sites. Such a perspective should arguably highlight the provisionary and fluid nature of identity construction, as well as work out the relevance of unsettling hegemonic discourses that ideologically construct the very concept of otherness (Banks, 2004; Warren and Canen, 2012), imbuing the curriculum with an equity and an approach oriented toward social justice.

## The Case of University Partnerships in Brazil

In the Brazilian context, the building of multicultural curricula came in the context of government moves toward national guidelines for curriculum and assessment of educational institutions. In fact, from the end of the 1990s onwards, the Brazilian government has presented national moves toward curriculum guidelines and large-scale assessment, in response to a general trend of large-scale control and measurement of educational quality. However, even though acknowledging the presence of those intentions, it should be noted that those moves have had impacts in processes of discussions and rethinking of curriculum, such as the need for it to take into account cultural, racial and ethnic Brazilian diversity. Brazilian municipalities were asked to incorporate those principles and create their own curriculum designs, taking into account their local cultures, needs and perceived curricular emphases. In that sense, higher education scholars have been invited to help local authorities produce those guidelines, through a collective endeavor involving municipal/ local teachers, school administrators and other educational actors' representatives.

In that context, local municipal guidelines were produced in partnership between an HEI and local educational authorities. They were underlined by multicultural concerns, so as to incorporate equity and minority education perspectives. Challenges involved in the construction of the mentioned local curricular guidelines have touched directly on multicultural tensions, among which have been: (i) the very idea of the possibility of the construction of a multicultural, transformational curriculum design; (ii) the kind of research methodology that could be coherent with the multicultural, transformational perspective and actively involve educational actors in a partnership that could legitimize the whole process; and (iii) the main axes to support the curriculum design narrative, so that the tensions between unity and cultural sustainability should be dealt with in a way as to challenge homogeneity and essentialization of identities.

Concerning the first mentioned tension, Ball (2012) argues that educational researchers should move away from research designed as mere demonstrations of knowledge toward what she calls "generative research"—"the one that has the power to close the knowing–doing gap in education, research that is designed to inform others, influence others' thinking, and inspire others to action" (Ball, 2012, p. 283).

Elbaz-Luwisch (2010) calls attention to the pitfalls of qualitative research methodologies that involve partnership between researchers and school actors, among which are: teachers lead busy and complex lives and participation in research may not be perceived as serving their purposes; in different settings, researchers may be more or less welcome in schools, and more or less able to form productive research relationships. Whilst these factors were present in the development of the present study, it should be pointed out that others linked to political challenges could have also been pinpointed, particularly in a context in which school actors seem to be wary of perceived outside political initiatives that are likely to interfere with their work.

A further tension referred to the content of the municipal guidelines themselves, in terms of the multicultural perspective to underlie it. In fact, from the outset, the idea was that the construction of the local municipal guidelines should represent an opportunity in which all should grow in their understanding of diversity in the road toward contributing to a more inclusive, equitable, and supportive learning environment. It was stressed that the construction of municipal local curricular guidelines had to involve a collective effort so that researchers and local educational actors acted as partners and politically legitimized the whole process, in coherence with the multicultural, decolonized perspective embraced by the study.

In fact, Sleeter (2010) suggests that "to decolonize curriculum is to critically examine the knowledge and its relationship to power, re-centering knowledge in the intellectual histories of [marginalized groups, among which] indigenous people," (as well as) … "theorizing the histories and experiences of nontribal, detribalized, and mixed-blood peoples."

Based on that, meetings and workshops were geared toward the discussion of case studies, texts, and ideas generated from school actors, in dialog with the multicultural approach.

Principles were presented that were considered key to underlie the municipal guidelines, among which were:

- to promote diversity of knowledges, dialogs and coherence of school actions with those;
- to promote teacher continuing education in a way as to respect teachers' identities and those of the schools;
- to strengthen teachers, students and other school actors in their citizenship processes and identity construction;
- to foster global, national and local perspectives to curriculum development, so as to respect diversity but also to help prepare students for the world of the market;
- to develop a differentiated perspective that values inclusion, cultural diversity and local municipal cultures;
- to respect and value the various languages, learning styles and family arrangements in school and teaching activities (from the workshops in the municipality, 2011).

Following these events, documents were produced in which general curriculum guidelines were issued, which consisted of:

i) An introduction, in which cultural diversity of the municipality was acknowledged and a cursory view of its history, as well as the rationale and the process of the construction of the guidelines were presented.
ii) A second part, in which the interplay between global and local perspectives, as well as between provisionary individual, collective and institutional identities was discussed.
iii) A third section, in which a multiculturally oriented set of ideas and principles was presented that should underlie future curriculum developments in the various disciplines, areas and syllabi.
iv) A fourth and last part, containing some conclusions and suggestions as ways ahead for the ongoing assessment and development of those municipal curriculum guidelines.

Focusing on the third part, it is important to note that a format was agreed in which the multiculturally oriented ideas discussed in the previous sections should be translated in a set of simple sentences, similar to a set of competencies, intended to provide several school actors with a basis upon which to propose future discipline-based year programs that incorporated multicultural concerns in their contents and methodologies. In addition to those above-mentioned statements, which were considered crucial for the curriculum design, the following statements were collectively produced. They further illustrate what came to be named by the group as "integrative multicultural curricular dimensions," which were the basis of the municipal curriculum design:

> value cultural diversity and sustainability; proactively and reactively work towards challenging discriminations; value global, national and municipal assets and cultures, so as to promote individual and collective growth; critically and autonomously relate to knowledge building; have a clear and integrated vision of curriculum contents and knowledges;

> perceive ethical implications of attitudes in everyday schooling; understand knowledge as culturally produced and located. *(From the final Niteroi Municipal Curricular Guidelines, 2010)*

It should be pointed out that identity was key to the municipal guidelines, so that the multicultural perspective would go beyond a mere celebration of cultures and indeed allow for the interrogation of racism and the challenge of essentialized identity construction, so as to promote what Sleeter (2010) calls the decolonization of the curriculum. Municipal school actors not only recognized cultural diversity in the municipalities, but pinpointed issues related to discrimination and low performance of groups of pupils, leading them to embrace a multicultural approach and indeed suggest ways in which the curriculum could help build transformational identities. In this way, a set of positive expectations had been made and the research design-based research was successful in the three cases.

Focusing on the contents of the curricular documents produced, some observations can be made. In all the cases, the option was to have a document in which the introduction dealt with the history of the municipality, its cultural diversity, and the rationale for the multicultural approach to curriculum, explicating some theoretical concepts related to it. Also, there was a common trend in specifying some multicultural axes or dimensions that should underpin all areas of the curriculum, as can be illustrated by the following excerpts:

> Two dimensions constitute the curriculum in Niteroi, namely: the specific one of the curriculum themes; the citizenship dimension, geared towards cultural diversity, which will integrate all the levels of schooling. The first dimension comprises the curricular contents; the second comprises abilities that should underlie those contents and give them coherence in terms of citizenship in a multicultural perspective, namely: value ethnic, cultural, racial, gender, religion, linguistic, sexual orientation and other plural identities, pinpointing their contributions to society at a local, national and global levels; challenge prejudices, discriminations, bullying and any form of intolerance and violence against the others, trying to recognize their origins and denounce its manifestations; recognize and value the history and cultures of the communities of the municipality of Niteroi, emphasizing their dialogues with other Brazilian cultures, in a multicultural context; understand the construction of knowledge as historically and culturally situated, being directly linked to the research practices and the problem resolutions, liking curricular contents to the everyday; critically and creatively develop the relationship with the technologies, using them as resources for the advancement of knowledge, research and the adaptation to a contemporary and plural world; participate in activities that stimulate ethical, cooperative, respectful and empathic attitudes towards the other. (Niteroi, Curricular Guidelines, 2010)

> The integrating multicultural dimensions of the curriculum translate behaviors and abilities that can be developed in the curriculum, namely: value diversity and sustainability; proactively and reactively work towards

> the challenge of prejudices; value the culture of the municipality of Macaé and of other localities, so as to promote personal and collective growth; develop critical and autonomous positioning related to knowledge building; articulate and integrate the curricular contents among themselves, including the technological ones; perceive ethical implications of attitudes in everyday schooling; understand the construction of knowledge as historically and culturally situated. (Macaé, Pedagogical Proposal, 2012)

> The curriculum will be developed around five principles: diversity, citizenship, ethics, ecology and sustainability, science and technology. [In the principle of diversity, some dimensions and indications for pedagogical practices can be pinpointed]. Dimensions: work towards education for cultural diversity that challenges prejudices, stereotypes, discriminations, silences and social exclusions; (...) understand that there is no homogeneity of identities, towards which the critical post-colonial multiculturalism can give important inputs (...). [Pedagogical actions include]: Include and guarantee, in the curriculum, in an interdisciplinary approach, themes related to gender, gender identity, race, ethnicity, religion, sexual orientation, mental and physical disabilities, family diversity, as well as all forms of discrimination and violation of rights; implement cultural and educational projects geared towards challenging all forms of discrimination. (Mesquita, Curricular Guidelines, 2016)

As can be noted, in all the curricular proposals, a mix of folkloric, critical and post-colonial multi/ intercultural perspectives could be pinpointed, which seems to reinforce the idea that multi/ interculturalism can be developed in the curriculum in many perspectives, even though they should not be limited to a harmonized approach that does not face the challenge of fighting against discrimination and prejudice.

Also, in terms of the structure of the three proposals, it should be pointed out that the level of detailing and prescription was kept to the minimum, so as to allow for cultural diversity in the municipalities to flourish in the actual everyday implementation of the curriculum. Even in the Niteroi curriculum, in which a detailed presentation of tables referring to the different areas of the curriculum and possible linkage of their contents to a multi/ intercultural perspective was presented, such a presentation was offered as possible suggestions and not as a final proposal to be worked out in schools. In the case of Macaé and Mesquita, the way the multi/ intercultural principles could be linked to the curricular contents was presented in a more discrete way, as illustrations of possibilities of translating intentions into actual curricular areas. The following extracts may illustrate that point:

> Content knowledges of Sciences for Primary education: theme: origin of life, biodiversity, ecology. Multicultural perspective for that content: recognize the diverse discourses by which the origin of life has been interpreted by plural religions, cultures and world visions, challenging prejudices; discuss and position oneself in relation to ethical aspects involved in issues of science and technology; understand that systems of biological classification are attempts to understand diversity in a controlled way. (Niteroi, Curricular Guidelines, 2010)

> Content knowledges of Mathematics for Primary education: to group people, facts and objects by classes, following different criteria; multicultural perspective for that content: identify similarities and differences in the diverse groups by gender, ethnicity, culture, social class and other identity markers, so as to value diversity and allow for the interaction with other children from different cultural groups. (Mesquita, Curricular Guidelines, 2016)

> Content knowledges of Mathematics for Primary education: percentage. Multicultural perspective for that content: identify the percentage of illiteracy in Brazil and more specifically in the municipality of Macaé; relate the concept of percentage to the integrating dimensions, including the diversity ones, of the curriculum. (Macaé, Curricular Guidelines, 2012)

Even though the focus of the study is on the way multi/ intercultural sensitivities have been translated into municipal curricular contents, some cursory look at informal opinions of educational actors that took part in the process showed the importance of a multi/ intercultural perspective in curriculum initiatives, as can be noted below:

> It is good that we helped build and adopt a curriculum that should be based on the valuing of the dialogue among the differences; that should be democratic; and that should challenge that view of the modernity related to science being the only valid knowledge. The curriculum should recognize the many forms of knowledge and value them (from a teacher, as a written answer to a question asking how they felt about the process of collectively building municipal curricular guidelines. (Mesquita, 2016)

The pitfalls of qualitative research carried out in partnership between researchers and school actors, as cited by Elbaz-Luwisch (see p 204 above) were present in the development of the present study. However it should be pointed out that the three documents were formally approved at the legislative instances of the municipalities and have been informing schools in the three municipalities ever since.

Our research is an ongoing project. As part of that project, there is a possibility that, in the future, other partnerships could be made between the university and those local authorities in order to gauge how actual teachers translated guidelines into lesson plans. Equally importantly, it may be possible, in the future, to glean what kind of differences the curriculum construction actually made to the attitudes and behaviors of students, especially if it could be compared to those who had not experienced that kind of curriculum. However, it should be noted that such aspects were not part of the partnerships developed, and they would have to be negotiated, in the future, with local authorities. That would be central to understanding how multicultural guidelines should actually impact everyday school lives and school actors.

## The Role of Leadership

The previous experiences resulted in the construction of multiculturally oriented curricular guidelines. However, we argue that the presence of a document is not enough in order for a multicultural environment to be fostered and for a cross-cultural learning workplace to be developed. In fact, students and teachers should likely perceive themselves as co-responsible for supporting identity construction that fosters their potential and go beyond essentialized dichotomic approaches that separate "I" and "the other." Institutions and organizations are urged to look and value the diversity within broad categories of collective identities, such as racial, ethnic, sexual orientation and so forth.

In a study by Canen and Canen (2008), it was clear that a monocultural leader can be detrimental to the development of a transformative curriculum in the everyday institutional life. Cox (2001) suggests some characteristics a leader should have, such as: intervening to stop others from using slurs, telling offensive jokes, or displaying other inappropriate behaviors; openly expressing support for diversity-related goals of the organization; inviting feedback from colleagues on behavior that is related to diversity competency; seeking persons who are culturally different for informal contact (for example, for lunches or for break-time or after-work activities); bringing diversity-related problems or opportunities to the attention of higher levels of management; mentoring people that are culturally different from himself or herself; participating enthusiastically in diversity-related education activities.

Canen and Canen (2008) posit that whilst a monocultural leader lets tensions increase, a multicultural one handles them, without letting them become real conflicts, and without losing control. Furthermore, whilst a monocultural leader presents responses that tend to silence cultural diversity and reinforce hegemonic voices, a multicultural one values cultural diverse voices and makes sure all are respected.

In order to do so, HEIs should be viewed as multicultural organizations themselves, not only in terms of developing multicultural curricula, but also in reviewing institutional practices and leadership impacts on organizational climate. Leaders should be ethically and multiculturally accountable for ensuring an institutional identity open to cultural plurality and to the challenge of the institutionalization of differences.

Organizational climate and the extent to which it has been valuing cultural diversity and building on it for tapping creative resources, original problem-solving and enhancing each and every individual's potential can add value to and make a strong impact on organizations. We have been arguing that multiculturalism – a theoretical, practical and political framework that values cultural diversity and tries to offer paths in order to translate such valuing into actual responses to cultural plurality and to challenging prejudices and stereotyping against cultural, ethnic, racial, gender, religious and other identities – can play a key role in changing institutions into ethical, multicultural organizations.

Based on those ideas, Canen and Canen (2008) consider HEIs as multicultural organizations, if and when they offer answers that value cultural plurality both in curriculum approaches and in their everyday policies and practices. Considering their critical role in promoting critical thinking and challenging stereotypes and dogmas, multicultural thinking should be embedded in such organizations.

HEIs as multicultural organizations directly refer to the degree everyday institutional policies and practices offer support to cultural plurality. In order to achieve that, the role of leadership is crucial not only in dealing with the cultural identities that are inherent in HEIs' everyday lives, such as students and general staff, but also to ensure an ethical organizational climate and a solid institutional project open to cultural diversity. In fact, the role of leadership in promoting multiculturalism in the institutional identity cannot be stressed enough. In order to effectively face up to their mission, HIEs should capture the power and potentialities of group and individual identities. In order to do so, their leaders should be involved so as to boost an institutional climate in which all feel valued and where trust is the key element.

Literature dealing with organizational cultural diversity and leadership offers important insights about both aspects, but there is still a need for further studies that articulate them in a multicultural framework for organizational success. Talking about the benefits of well-managed diversity, Cox (2001) contends that it can add value to an organization by improving problem-solving, increasing creativity, innovation and organizational flexibility, as well by improving its services to cultural plural audiences. Some key elements are proposed in order to evaluate diversity climate in an organization, both at the individual and organizational levels. At the individual level, some of them are: amount of identity – group prejudice; amount of stereotyping; amount of ethnocentrism; diversity-relevant personality traits; level of intergroup conflict; group identity strength; quality of intergroup communication and cultural differences and similarities.

At the organizational level, some key measures are: the identity profile of the workforce; the mode of acculturation; the content of organization culture; power distribution among groups; people management practices and policies; and openness of informal networks. Cox's (2001) remarks about leaders' behaviors affecting the development of a transformative curriculum and of values diversity are invaluable (see above, p. 000).

As argued by Canen and Canen (2008), such qualities are good indicators to assess a multicultural leader. Some characteristics are suggested in order to evaluate effective diversity respondents, such as: they accept personal responsibility for enhancing their own and their organization's effectiveness; demonstrate contextual knowledge; they understand key diversity concepts and definitions; they are clear about requirements and base include/ exclude decisions about differences on how they impact the ability to meet these requirements; they understand that diversity is accompanied by complexity and tension and are prepared to cope with these in pursuit of greater diversity effectiveness – which means that they handle tensions, without losing control and without letting them become real conflicts. Further, they are willing to challenge conventional wisdom and endorse and engage in continuous learning.

This involves respecting diverse singular and group identities, and being open to diversity not only of identity attributes (such as gender, race, sexual options, ethnicity, religious beliefs and others) but also of identity behaviors, which means the plurality of opinions that may arise concerning organizational issues. It should be noted that a highly monocultural leadership approach means the opacity to cultural plurality and the development of a toxic, ethnocentric organizational ethos, considered unethical from a multicultural perspective that we embrace. Many times, such an extreme monocultural leadership mirrors personality disorders, as analyzed by Goldman (2006), who examines two case studies of leaders who clearly exhibited personality disorders within their respective organizational contexts. The leader that showed a "narcissistic personality disorder" was the head of the department taken as a study by the referred author, who was never satisfied with doing a good job but "had to be ignoring and emotionally abusing her colleagues" while she herself "was busy shattering surgical precedent" and exploiting others "in order to achieve her personal goals" (p. 397). Likewise, the leader that showed an "antisocial personality disorder" was a senior manager who was involved in repeated incidents of abuse against subordinates in the workplace.

Those traits and patterns of behavior fundamentally represented self-centered leadership approaches that ignored plurality and were blind toward other identities and group feelings and cultures. The important point to note here is that the main results of such disruptive and pathological leaders were the impairment of interpersonal relations and organizational ethos, chiefly by the widespread mimicking and mirroring of aspects of the leaders' traits and behaviors throughout the organization, to the detriment of the construction of a respectful, positive and multicultural institutional identity.

Multicultural leaders should arguably be role models to ensure the presence of multicultural organizations. It should be pointed out that the dangers of the lack of a multicultural leadership include the prevalence of hegemonic thinking, the opacity to plural voices and, in the limit, the condoning of bullying. Canen and Canen (2008) consider multicultural competence as the ability and flexibility to deal with the tensions of cultural differences by: valuing staff's cultural diversity and clearly recognizing organizational cultural identity; understanding cultural diversity of suppliers and customers (in the case of HEIs, we could translate this last dimension in terms of students and other social actors involved in HIE activities).

Such multiculturally imbued leaders can be responsible for an organizational environment with the potential to foster the growth of the institution and of all its human components. They make for the appropriate organizational climate for the continuing professional development of educational actors, providing the coherent scenario in which multicultural curricula can flourish.

## Conclusion

This chapter drew on data from previous studies. One discussed the process of construction of curricular guidelines in municipalities in Brazil, geared toward the valuing of diversity, and the challenge of racism and stereotypes. The other supported the idea that a monocultural leader can be detrimental to the development of multicultural curriculum guidelines and to the very institutional climate.

As discussed above, I have contended that many debates surrounding multi/interculturalism beg for the analysis of how those concepts have been understood and implemented, and whether it is successful in achieving its explicit or implicit objectives. Even though a general meaning can be attributed to multi/interculturalism, it gets more blurred when getting to different interpretations that underpin diverse policies and practices. That way, the chapter initially discussed the meanings of multicultural thinking, ranging from folkloric, liberal approaches that value diversity in terms of cultural rituals, festivals and food, up to more critical ones, which highlight the construction of differences and the need to challenge stereotypes and prejudices.

The analysis of curricular guidelines developed in partnership between the university and municipal educational authorities in Brazil showed that it is possible to engage educational actors in the construction of curriculum and pedagogy attuned to multicultural sensitivities. Such processes arguably represent ways to promote professional educational development of teachers and educational administrators toward incorporating multicultural issues into their curricular contents and didactics.

I have argued that organizational cultural diversity and multicultural leadership can add value to an organization by improving problem-solving, increasing creativity, innovation and organizational flexibility, as well as by improving its services to cultural plural audiences.

The extent to which the integrative multicultural curricular dimensions in the curriculum construction should indeed provide a decolonizing, non-essentialized approach to identity construction should likely depend on the future actions to be taken, in those municipalities and elsewhere.

It is widely recognized that curriculum design represents a set of statements of intents, which should come to life in school actors' construction of their course and lesson plans, as well as in their enactments of those intentions in real classroom situations. Above all, they should flourish in an environment in which multicultural leaders should respect actors' diversity, turning the workplace into a multicultural, continuing transformative professional development experience.

## References

Ball, A. F. (2012). To know is not enough: Knowledge, power and the zone of generativity. *Educational Researcher, 41*(8), 283–293.

Banks, J. A. (2004). Introduction: Democratic citizenship education in multicultural societies. In J. A. Banks (Ed.), *Diversity and citizenship education* (pp. 3–15). San Francisco, CA: John Wiley and Sons.

Canen, A. (2005). Multicultural challenges in educational policies within a non-conservative scenario: The case of the emerging reforms in higher education in Brazil. *Policy Futures in Education, 3*(4), 327–339.

Canen, A. (2009). *Teacher education and competence in an intercultural perspective.* Köln, Germany: Lambert Academic Publishing.

Canen, A. (2012). Brazil: Lifelong learning and the role of the university in Brazil, some reflections. In M. Slowey, & H. G. Schuetze (Eds.), *Global perspectives on higher education and lifelong learners* (pp. 266–278). Abingdon, UK: Routledge.
Canen, A. G., & Canen, A. (2008). Multicultural leadership: The costs of its absence in organizational conflict management. *International Journal of Conflict Management, 19*, 4–19.
Canen, A., & Peters, M. (2005). Editorial: Issues and dilemmas of multicultural education: Theories, policies, and practices. *Policy Futures in Education, 3*(4), 309–313.
Cox, T. Jr. (2001). *Creating the multicultural organization*. San Francisco, CA: John Wiley and Sons.
Elbaz-Luwisch, F. (2010). Narrative inquiry: Wakeful engagement with educational experience. *Curriculum Inquiry, 40*(2), 263–279.
Goldman, A. (2006). Personality disorders in leaders. *Journal of Managerial Psychology, 21*(5), 392–414.
Hall, S. (2003). *Da Diáspora: identidades e mediações culturais*. Belo Horizonte, Brazil: UFMG.
Ivenicki, A. (2015). Adult education and cultural diversity in Brazil: National policies and contributions of higher education. In M. Milana, & T. Nesbit (Org.) (Eds.), *Global perspectives on adult education and learning policy* (1st ed.) (pp. 60–72). Basingstoke, UK: Palgrave MacMillan.
Ivenicki, A., & de Xavier, G. P. M. (2015). Currículo Multicultural e Desafio às Fronteiras de Exclusão: reflexões e experiências de construção docente coletiva. In A. Nascimento, & J. L. Backes (Eds.), *Inter/Multiculturalidade, Relações Étnico-Culturais e Fronteiras da Exclusão* (pp. 195–210). Campinas, Brazil: Ed. Mercado de Letras.
Ng, E. S., & Bloemroad, I. (2015). A SWOT analysis of multiculturalism in Canada, Europe, Mauritius and South Korea, special issue: Multiculturalism during challenging times. *The American Behavioral Scientist, 54*(6), 619–636.
Sleeter, C. (2010). Decolonizing Curriculum. *Curriculum Inquiry, 40*(2), 193–204.
Warren, J., & Canen, A. (2012). Racial diversity and education in Brazil. In J. A. Banks (Org.) (Ed.), *Encyclopedia of diversity in education* (1st ed., Vol. *1*) (pp. 262–264). Thousand Oaks, CA: Sage.

# 13

# Employee Learning Disabilities and Workforce Learning

*Damian Andreas Riviez*

*Abu Dhabi School of Management*

> "Everybody has a plan until they get punched in the mouth"
> – *Mike Tyson, former world heavyweight boxing champion.*

The condition of learning disabilities (LD) does not discriminate. LD does not consider aspects of skin color, religion, gender, societal status, ethnic background, educational attainment, or economic means. Learning disabilities do not care about the social clubs you engage in, the significance of your surname or your family heritage. Learning disabilities have the perfect characteristics of indifference, and are a near-perfect example of non-discrimination. Unfortunately, our society does not have these characteristics. Discrimination today takes on a plethora of issues and demonstrates itself in a plethora of means on a daily basis in almost every aspect of our environment. We can see such on the global landscape; in our places of employment, our educational system(s), in our communities; in business enterprises; in our social and political institutions and in our own families. From the second we arrive on this earth, from the inception of birth, evaluation and discrimination begins. In theory, humans should be non-discriminating toward people with learning disabilities; however, the opposite behavior is demonstrated in our society and consequently in the workplace. We humans do care and have bias about all aspects mentioned above; and we make professional and personal judgments based on these aspects. This is might be considered a universal societal norm.

My son was born with an extensive immune system difficulty that affects his learning development. Specifically, he has been assessed, evaluated, diagnosed, misdiagnosed, re-assessed, tested, re-diagnosed and further tested and diagnosed to the present. He is 6 years old. Based on what we know of his condition, at the moment, he has been diagnosed with Autism Spectrum Disorder (ASD).

This chapter is dedicated to all those in the workplace who are "different".

*The Wiley Handbook of Global Workplace Learning*, First Edition.
Edited by Vanessa Hammler Kenon and Sunay Vasant Palsole.

My wife and I are still unclear about the accuracy and significance of this classification and we are researching and practicing all means to assist in my son's development, regardless of classification. However, we do all we can to avoid broadcasting this to the society as a whole. Why? It is not that we are ashamed or disgraced by our son: he is immensely intelligent, is learning every-day, and is the unique, loving and eclectic individual we always aspired to have as a child. Honestly, I can't say we envisioned this prior to his birth, but he is a perfect example of the challenges a human faces if they are "at all" different. The reason we don't broadcast his challenges is because in five very short years, we as a family have been scoffed at, pointed at, stared at, told he would never progress, had our parenting skills scrutinized; and have been discriminated against for therapeutic, educational, medical and learning services.

The good news is that we have been able to overcome this type of human and societal insecurity, by being open to learning and discovery, understanding the magnitude of typical human flaws, working on ourselves as people and being nurturing toward the holistic development of our son. Make no mistake, this has not been easy. Patience, perseverance, love, a healthy sense of humor, and reflective practice in our mantra keeps us growing as a unified family. It has been painful, joyful, traumatic and elating; and most fulfilling, in every aspect of human progression. To date it has made us better people.

I am not presenting my individual story so the reader takes pity on me or my family; on the contrary. My son is the most precious gift that could have been bestowed upon me and I know he will be so successful in his life. However, I know the "system" will never help him and he will be enabled through his own hard work and ours to develop into a highly purposeful and valuable human being. He has challenged my leadership capacity as an educator, a writer, a father, a husband and as a man. His presence in my life has challenged the ideal of normalcy. I am very grateful for his being a significant part of my life, providing amazing life learning lessons; as well as great purpose and focus. I thank him every-day for his presence and remind him of his essence.

However, I am using this individual story as a platform for what you are about read. My experience has provided me with the motivation and ambition to research learning disabilities in the workforce. Because, I know what awaits my son, I need to prepare him and others like him for future involvement with the workforce. I also know that I am not alone in my journey and there are many people who experience similar challenging scenarios. Additionally, it is my intent to help others by sharing experience through research and the dissemination of information relevant to those who are interested, so we may envision genuine equity, diversity and purposeful inclusive learning development in the workplace. Innovation is an idea that most organizations espouse and strive to achieve. Learning differences and the application of those differences are an aspect of organizational life worth pursuing. It would seem a paradox that we aspire toward the great differences that the human can bring to society and the workplace while our living and operating systems erect barriers, apply constraints and impose ideological processes in condemning those differences.

The ensuing chapter is a multidisciplinary approach to investigating learning disabilities in the workforce and the effects on workforce and organizational learning. It is the intent, by providing links toward a systems approach to learning disabilities, that the reader will be better informed as to the complexities of the topic and are able to act with intelligence in enacting a strategy of tolerance and advancement toward a more compassionate and professional approach to affected individuals. Moreover, it is not out of pity or charity that organizations should consider the engagement of individuals with learning disabilities; but rather out of consideration of the value the individual brings to the organization. Research has shown advantages in the view that those with learning disabilities see life in ways that can have tremendous creative and innovative benefit for organizations.

The format of the chapter consists of a brief overview of diversity, a survey discussion about disabilities, followed by inclusive learning developments in organizations. Finally, a summary of thoughts is presented about learning disabilities and their relationship to organizational learning.

## Diversity

"Diversity: the art of thinking independently together."
– *Malcolm Forbes, founding publisher of Forbes Magazine*

Diversity is not a program. It is a belief. It is a choice. It is intentional. It is a value system, ingrained in the cultural environment of any society, community, and organization. Diversity can be purposefully constructed and designed into the very fabric of any organization. Merriam Webster's dictionary defines diversity as "the condition of having or being composed of differing elements: variety, especially in the inclusion of different types of people (e.g., race, culture) in a group or organization" (Diversity, n.d.). Further, diversity can be stated as "being in a state of different components, elements and qualities." Additionally, at the very least, there must exist within the environment a notion of tolerance for such variability within these definitions. Moreover, workforce diversity is considered one of the main challenges for human resource management in modern organizations (Alcázar, Fernández, & Gardey, 2013). At the very core in challenging diversity and the biggest inhibitor of practical and successful integration at any level is the issue of prejudice.

According to the Oxford Dictionary (Prejudice, n.d.), prejudice is defined as "a preconceived opinion that is not based on reason or actual experience." As a result and in many instances, prejudice produces a dislike, hostility, or unjust behavior between individuals at the organizational, individual and societal levels of life, deriving from bias, assumptive and unfounded opinions. Moreover, the essence of diversity is a base tolerance among group members at any level in cooperative living and working toward common goals and objectives.

Gordon Allport (1954) initiated a significant social psychological event of the twentieth century; stating that contact between members of diverse groups can work to reduce prejudice and intergroup conflict. His hypothesis was the idea of contact among different groups can assist to reduce prejudice and enhance social relations.

The intergroup contact hypothesis proposed by Allport (1954) suggested that positive effects of intergroup contact occur in contact situations characterized by four key conditions: equal status, intergroup cooperation, common goals and support by social and institutional authorities (See Table 13.1). According to

**Table 13.1** Four Key Conditions of Intergroup Contact

| Condition | Meaning | Example | Evidence |
|---|---|---|---|
| Equal Status | Members of the contact situation should not have an unequal, hierarchical relationship. | Members should not have an employer/ employee, or instructor/ student relationship. | Equal status is important both *prior* to (Brewer & Kramer, 1985) and *during* (Cohen & Lotan, 1995) the contact situation. |
| Cooperation | Members should work together in a non-competitive environment. | Students working together in a group project. | Aronson's "jigsaw technique" structures classrooms so that students strive cooperatively (Aronson & Patnoe, 1967), and this technique has led to positive results in a variety of countries |
| Common Goals | Members must rely on each other to achieve their shared desired goal. | Members of a sports team. | Hu and Griffey (1985) have shown the importance of common goals in interracial athletic teams who need to work together to achieve their goal. |
| Support by Social and Institutional Authorities | There should not be social or institutional authorities that explicitly or implicitly sanction contact, and there should be authorities that support positive contact. | There should not be official laws enforcing segregation. | Landis's (1984) work on the importance of institutional support in reducing prejudice in the military. |

*Source:* Everett (2013).

Allport, it is essential that the contact situation exhibits these factors in some way. These factors do appear to be significant in reducing prejudice, as shown by the distinctive importance of cross-group friendships (Pettigrew, 1998). Most friends have equal status, work together to achieve shared goals, and friendship is usually absent from strict societal and institutional limitation that can particularly limit romantic relationships (e.g., laws against intermarriage) and working relationships (e.g., segregation laws, or differential statuses) (Everett, 2013).

Overall, Allport's (1954) theoretical perspective became a framework and a foundational aspect of structure in policy-making all over the world. More recently, ample work has confirmed the essence of contact in reducing prejudice. Critically, positive contact experiences have been shown to reduce self-reported prejudice (the most typical method of assessing intergroup attitudes) toward black individuals, the elderly, gay men, and the disabled – to name a few categories (Caspi, 1984; Vonofakou, Hewstone, & Voci, 2007; Works, 1961; Yuker & Hurley, 1987). Furthermore, in a wide-scale meta-analysis (i.e., a statistical analysis of a number of published studies), it has been found that while contact under Allport's conditions is significantly effective at reducing prejudice, even unstructured contact reduces prejudice (Pettigrew & Tropp, 2006). This seems to suggest that Allport's proposed conditions should be best viewed as optimal, rather than essential. Moreover, this further demonstrates that prejudice is the single or at the minimum, most challenging aspect of diversity.

Moreover, numerous research and studies have been conducted into diversity (Bandura, 1977; Bell, 2012; Cox, 1993; Dovidio & Gaertner, 1986; Robinson, 2002; Shore et al., 2009). Further studies have suggested the absolute need for diversity in the challenging context of industry competition and survival, concluding that diversity is a comprehensive advantage and essential for organizational achievement and success (Koonce, 2001; Loysk, 1996; Roosevelt Jr., 2001; Society for Human Resource Management [SHRM], 1998). None the less, despite the importance of workforce diversity, the majority of models used to describe and investigate the field of human resources consider the workforce as generic and homogeneous. Essentially, cultural differences are ignored in studying and implementing diversity in organizations (Alcázar et al., 2013). The world's increasing connection through globalization requires more engagement among people from various and divergent backgrounds.

People no longer live and work in isolation; they are part of an interconnected system in a worldwide economy competing within a global framework. For this reason, organizations of all types (e.g., business, community, societal) would seem to need diversification to remain competitive and viable. Addressing, managing, maximizing and capitalizing on workplace diversity are an important issue for organizations today (Green et al., 2015). Diversity is beneficial to both employees and employers. Although employees are interdependent in the workplace, respecting individual differences can increase productivity. Diversity in the workplace can reduce legal liability and increase marketing opportunities, recruitment, creativity, and business image (Esty, Griffin, & Schorr-Hirsh, 1995).

In contrast, diversity may present challenges in decision-making about allocation of resources across the organization, which creates inefficiency in operating firm objectives and overall investment (Rajan, Servaes, & Zingales, 2002). Further, taking into consideration the potential challenges in employee relations of a diversified workforce, management is faced with the potential disruption that diversity can bring to the organization (e.g., communication, moral, teamwork, etc.) (Ricco & Guerci, 2014). In an era when flexibility and creativity are keys to competitiveness, managing diversity is critical for an organization's success. Adhering to the status quo seems like an inadequate approach to organizational success.

In attempting to provide a framework to a theoretical perspective of diversity, Marilyn Loden (1996) created a model called the Diversity Wheel. This tool was introduced in order for people to better understand how group differences contribute to people's social identities (See Figure 13.1).

This model was initially developed to illustrate the various dimensions that can contribute to the complexity of diversity. Additionally, the model illustrates both the primary and secondary dimensions of diversity that exert an impact on individuals at home, work and in society. While each dimension adds a layer of complexity to individual identity, it is the dynamic interaction among all the dimensions that influences self-image, values, opportunities,

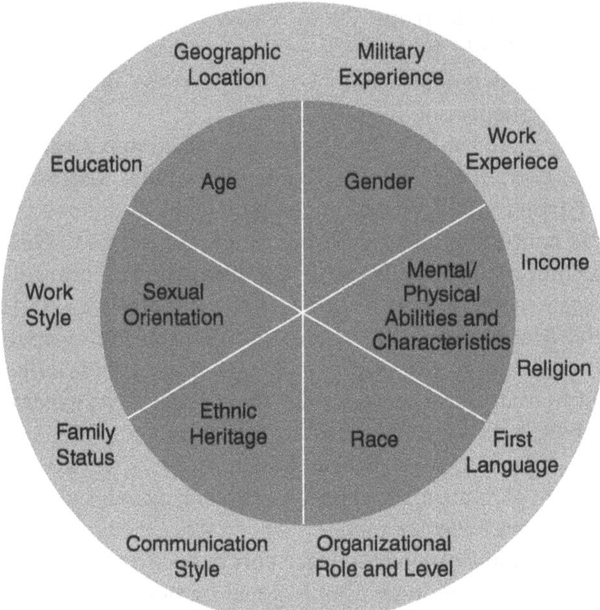


**Figure 13.1** Diversity Wheel. *Source:* Loden (1996)

and expectations. Together, the primary and secondary dimensions of diversity give definition and meaning to our lives by contributing to an integrated whole – the diverse person. Primary dimensions of diversity include age, ethnic heritage, gender, mental/ physical abilities and characteristics, race and sexual orientation. These six differences are termed core dimensions of diversity because they exert an important impact on our early socialization and a powerful, sustained impact on our experiences, values, assumptions and expectations throughout every stage of life. Secondary dimensions of diversity include but are not limited to elements, as illustrated by the outer circle. Generally, secondary dimensions are less visible, and many contain a greater element of choice (Loden, 1996).

Additionally, The Four Layers of Diversity model (Gardenswartz & Rowe, 2003) has prompted and extended the discussion on diversity. This model is an adaptation from Loden and Rosener (1991) that further establishes a case for inclusion by reflecting each person's reality in the organization (See Figure 13.2). The usefulness of this model is that it includes the dimensions that shape and impact both the individual and the organization itself.

The Diversity Wheel shows the complexity of diversity filtering through which all of us process stimuli and information. This process leads to the assumptions that we make (usually about the behaviors of other people), which ultimately drive our own behaviors, which in turn have an impact on others. From an organizational perspective, while the internal dimensions receive primary attention in successful diversity initiatives, the elements of the external and organizational dimensions often determine the way people are treated,

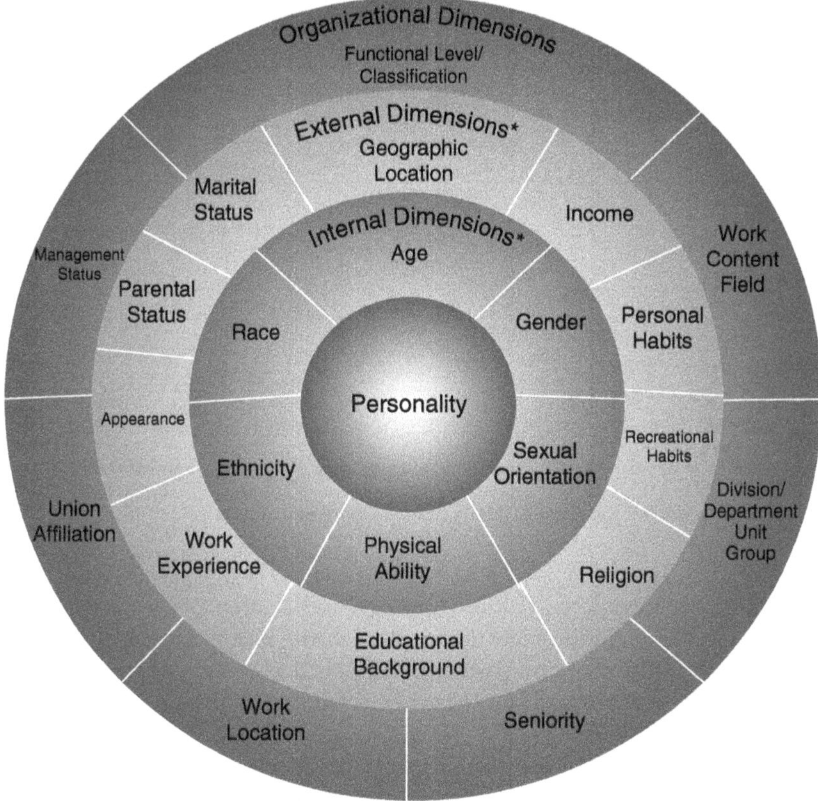


**Figure 13.2** Four Layers of Diversity Model. *Source:* Gardenswartz and Rowe (2003)

who fits or not in a department, who gets the opportunity for development or promotions, and who gets recognized.

Further to the discussion on diversity, Shore et al. (2009) aligned with the work of Loden (1996) and provides an overview of diversity research, studying six dimensions of diversity: race, gender, age, disability, sexual orientation and national origin. The overall purpose of the investigation was to assess the appropriateness of diversity and provide a more integrative view of how it fits in organizations (See Figure 13.3). There appear to be contextual elements both outside and inside the organization that may influence the prevalence and impact of diversity. Some external aspects of context are expressed by national culture (Stone-Romero & Stone, 2007), occupation (Heilman & Okimoto, 2007), industry (Blum, Fields, & Goodman, 1994; Goodman, Fields, & Blum, 2003; Kochan et al., 2003), legal context (e.g., a Title VII lawsuit; Kalev, Dobbin, & Kelly, 2006), economy (e.g., labor market; Fields, Goodman, & Blum, 2005), and family and community in which the organization and its employees are embedded (Ragins, 2008). Each of these aspects of the context may have separable effects with broad (e.g., the economy) or narrow (e.g., the employee's family) implications for individuals, groups and organizations. Likewise, internal organizational contextual

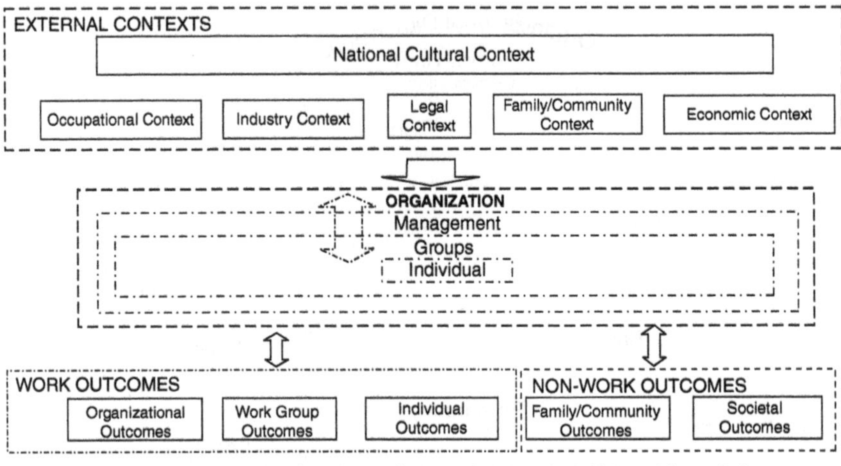


**Figure 13.3** An Integrative Model of Diversity. *Source:* Shore et al. (2009)

effects include organizational culture, strategy, and human resource practices (Kochan et al., 2003). Additionally, depending on the size of the organization, there may be many different groups and individuals that determine the extent to which the workforce is diverse, and whether diversity has positive, negative or neutral effects.

Diversity has also been studied at multiple levels, including the individual, the individual within the work group, the individual relative to the manager, the work group, the management team, and the organization. In Figure 13.3, the dashed double-headed arrow signifies the variety of potential ways to assess diversity within organizations, including across levels and within levels of organizational structure. Upon the basis of this notion, it would appear that such an effort of understanding diversity within organizations requires a reflection of the human experience. It is clear from the literature that there are core human issues and concerns embedded in life in the workplace that require attention to the human elements of organizational and managerial messages regarding respect, dignity and a clear value placed on dismantling barriers to a genuinely diverse workforce.

For example, Scheid (2005) found that employers with a coercive (fear of lawsuit) as opposed to normative (belief that it is the right thing to do) rationale for compliance were more likely to hold stigmatized attitudes toward those with disabilities. The range of philosophies toward diversity at these levels of analysis is captured well by Ely and Thomas's (2001) qualitative study highlighting customer–market, compliance, and learning perspectives toward diversity in groups. Currently, if the notion of diversity is such a challenge to embrace and implement in organizations, one can imagine the difficulty in staffing and training those who are different and have learning disabilities within the workforce. Yet, typical understanding of the basic terminology in disabilities is minimal at best and further increases the complexity and difficulty in addressing development needs of the individual and organization.

## Disability

"I am different. Not less." Dr. Temple Grandin – noted educator with autism spectrum disorder; author, speaker, and cited expert in many publications.

The term disability has taken on many connotations over time. One could argue that one's disability can be another individual's strength and competitive advantage. Merriam-Webster's dictionary defines learning disability as "any of various conditions (as dyslexia) that interfere with an individual's ability to learn and so result in impaired functioning in language, reasoning, or academic skills and that are thought to be caused by difficulties in processing and integrating information – also called *learning difference*" (Learning Disability, n.d.).

As a foundation for understanding the challenges of disabilities in society, one could approach the topic using von Bertalanffy's (1968) concept of general systems theory, as a conceptual framework that seems to capture the complexity of the topic. Von Bertalanffy (1956) defined a system as a complex of interacting elements. General Systems Theory (GST) (See Figure 13.4) is the notion that components in any system interact with each other, and such, metamorphose into something that is greater than the sum of its parts. This interaction is typically non-linear, as living systems evolve to open systems of importing and exporting and sharing components to produce new systems. Knowing one part of a system allows us to know another part of the system (Kuhn, 1974). Thus, an open systems theory perspective has evolved from the GST premise. An open system imports energy, transforms it, and exports a product to the environment that is the source for re-energizing the cycle (Katz & Kahn, 1978, p. 55.). In understanding the theoretical underpinning of GST, this allows us to grasp the complexity in addressing the multivariable issues in a global learning disability inquiry. Hence, we can align our comprehension of presented scaffold models,

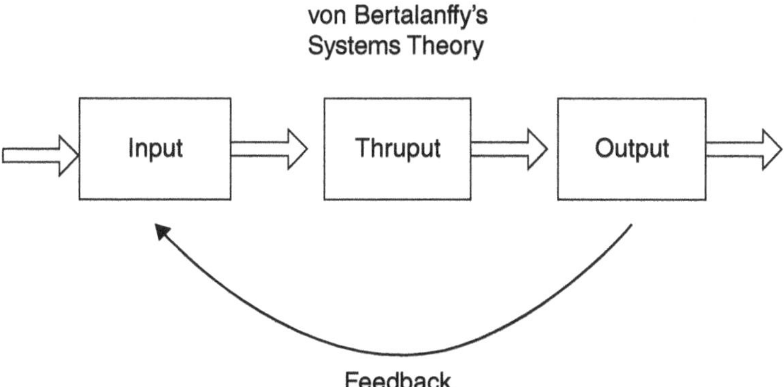


**Figure 13.4** General Systems Theory

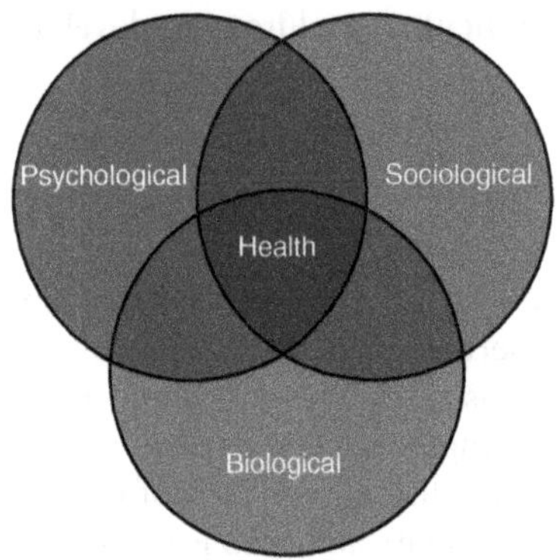


**Figure 13.5** Biopsychosocial Model

linking them by the very definition of their development, toward a discerning, thoughtful assessment of belief. Therefore, we can consider the theoretical framework above as relevant in furthering our discussion on learning disabilities in the workplace. Specifically, variability in perception of input is going to create inaccuracies in throughput and the resulting output. This will be further examined.

In many instances, disability and disease are often interchanged, misinterpreted or pronounced in similar settings when describing the challenges of individuals who exhibit atypical symptoms or various human behaviors. Engel (1977) demonstrated the need for a new medical model to challenge the traditional biomedical model to understand disease. The Bio Psycho Social Model (BPSM) (See Figure 13.5) is a broad view that attributes disease outcome to the intricate, variable interaction of biological factors (genetic, biochemical, etc.), psychological factors (mood, personality, behavior, etc.), and social factors (cultural, familial, socioeconomic, medical, etc.) (Santrock, 2007). The biopsychosocial model differs from the biomedical model, which attributes disease to only biological factors, such as viruses or genes (Engel, 1977). The model applies to disciplines ranging from medicine to psychology to sociology, and its acceptance and prevalence vary across disciplines (Penney, 2010) and across cultures (Santrock, 2007).

The biopsychosocial model is both a philosophy of clinical care and a practical clinical guide. Philosophically, it is a way of understanding how suffering, disease, and illness are affected by multiple levels of organization, from the societal to the molecular. At the practical level, it is a way of understanding the patient's subjective experience as an essential contributor to accurate diagnosis, health outcomes and humane care (Borrell-Carrió, Suchman, & Epstein, 2004). By and large, society has provided carte blanche to the medical community in the diagnosis and treatment of disability-related care. Specifically, in learning disability prognosis, so much has yet to be uncovered and understood about many conditions and syndromes that exist. Moreover, once the medical industry has placed a stamp of "understanding" on such issues, it is very hard for society to backtrack and correct any discrepancies that may have occurred along the way in research, diagnosis, treatment and protocol. The concept of "understanding" is another acronym for "assumptions" and or "untruths" regarding learning disabilities. This is the reason the biopsychosocial model is very important as a foundation of understanding and as a framework to assist in comprehending the complexity that is presented by challenges in the human condition.

In applying an adaptation of the biopsychosocial model in a holistic method of understanding disabilities at the macro and micro levels (See Figure 13.6), one can see the parameters by which individuals with learning disabilities have to

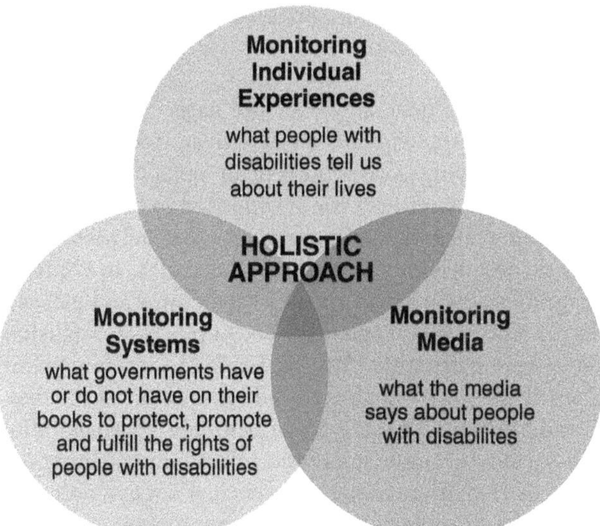


**Figure 13.6** Holistic Model of Understanding Disabilities

contend and surpass in living a "typical" life. As can be seen below, there are three spheres to the Holistic Model of Understanding Disabilities:

- Monitoring individual experiences – what do people with disabilities tell us about their experience and how do we respond?
- Monitoring systems – what tools are available to governments to fulfill the rights of people with disabilities and how do they implement, enforce and manage compliance mandates?
- Monitoring media – what does the media say about people with disabilities and how does this influence society?

In the above model, we can see interaction, influence and intersection of society "perception" regarding individuals who have learning disabilities. Research conducted on attitudes of the general public toward people with disabilities concluded that the public verbalizes favorable attitudes toward people with disabilities but actually hold deeper, unverbalized feelings which are frequently rejecting (Daruwalla, 1999). Further, Yuker (1977) and Gellman (1960) have indicated that attitudes, both positive and negative, are learned and that the disability itself has little bearing on these attributions and prejudices. Therefore, in the case of positive prejudice, people are glorified as being selfless, brave, and so forth. In the instance of negative prejudice, the individual with a disability may be perceived as helpless, dependent, ungrateful, selfish, freakish, evil, deranged, tragic, depressed, or special (Hume, 1995). Wright (1980, 1983) termed this a form of prejudice "spread." These stereotypical views of disability also include the assumption that one disability includes the characteristics of other impairment groups. For example, a service provider who assumes a wheelchair user is unable to communicate does not address the person in the chair directly but talks to the companion instead. Lack of information, knowledge, and fear generally experienced by wider society contribute toward negative attitudes (Daruwalla & Darcy, 2005).

Additionally, conceptualizations of "normalcy" are the basis of the medical model in singularity and espouse its framework of beliefs (Oliver, 1990). Disability, impairment and handicap are underlying assumptions of an "objective scientific" construct of the normal. As such, these concepts are supposed to be objectively measurable. However, Barnes, Mercer, and Shakespeare (1999), Chadwick (1994) and Linton (1998) challenged these notions of scientific normalcy. In contrast, the social model views disability as the product of social structures and places it firmly on the social, economic, and political agendas. The oppression, exclusion, and segregation of people with impairments from participation in mainstream activities are not a result of the person's impairment but a function of the disabling social environments and prevailing "hostile social attitudes" (Barnes, 1996). In other words, society's incapacity to understand and tolerate impairment differences is at the core of problem identification. In essence, if society perceives disability or human differences as a problem, then it becomes one. As suggested by Alexander (1994), the industry holds the same negative attitudes and stereotypes as the rest of society.

Further in understanding the disability perspective that has been shaped by such traditional notions as described above, there are many misperceptions and a lack of educational awareness regarding disabilities. For example, in contrast to the numerous studies on employment levels, little research has examined the experiences of people with disabilities who are currently working (e.g., Bruyère, Erickson, & Ferrentino, 2003; Colella, 1996; Schartz, Hendricks, & Blanck, 2006; Schartz, Schartz, Hendricks, & Blanck, 2006; Stone & Colella, 1996; Yelin & Trupin, 2003). Morgan and Alexander (2005) studied perceptions of employers with and without experience in hiring people with developmental disabilities. What is interesting, is that most employers with experience identified advantages consistent with typical organizational norms: consistent attendance, long term commitment, and high co-worker relationships. Those employers who did not have experience seemed to be receptive, albeit cautiously. Safety seemed to be an issue with both groups.

While one cannot ascertain and state with absolute certainty the perceptions, attitudes and behavior of all individuals in society, as well as the action of particular industries, prejudice against people with disabilities is prevalent when identifying business employment practices. Nishii and Bruyere (2013) provided research findings in identifying factors influencing the engagement of individuals with disability. The intent of the research was to address the issue of disability discrimination and discover ways to maximize disability inclusion. Results demonstrated that across the sample there were significantly low levels of awareness about organizational disability practices in the following areas: targeted recruiting of people with disabilities; a centralized source of funding for accommodation; formal decision-making process for case- by-case provision; a regular review of the accessibility of the organization's job application system; and whether there was regular training of HR staff and hiring managers in effective interviewing techniques of people with disabilities. As the research shows, prejudice can take the form of negligence, whether intended or not, in business priorities, processes and practices. The notion of prejudice, addressed earlier in a different context, can be related to human perceptions in decision-making.

The persistent lack of understanding of learning challenged behaviors in the workplace seems to pervade cultural and global contexts. Many managers and leaders do not recognize the symptoms of the learning disabled individual. And since disclosure is problematic, due to a reluctance to come forth, learning disabled individuals fear that they will be categorized as having inferior intelligence or a lack of education. Neither of these issues are the cause of a learning disability. Additionally, non-disclosure results from an employee feeling at risk due to historical prejudice and discrimination, and the resulting actions taken against employees by employers. Therefore, many organizations are not explicitly aware of the challenges brought by the employee. The following are a few common symptoms of learning disabilities reported by affected individuals (Reisman, 1996)

- The "unfocused or rude" employee, who continually repeats things, speaks at inappropriate times or spends unnecessary time at one task may not be doing so by choice. These characteristics can be signs of perseveration or impulsivity, both learning disabilities.
- The employee who "refuses" to follow instructions may not be insubordinate. Many learning disabilities prohibit people from retaining instructions. They simply cannot remember the order in which to do things; they cannot "sequence."
- The employee who has "poor judgment" may just have trouble understanding directions that are not concrete or specific. For instance, telling these employees they may take a break when they have a reasonable amount of tasks completed will not work – you may have differing definitions of "reasonable."
- The employee who cannot take a hint may not be overly persistent or aggressive. Many people with learning disabilities have trouble picking up social cues. For instance, saying "How have you been?" may not be interpreted as a greeting, but rather an actual question to be answered (Reisman, 1996).

Additionally, the need for repetitive activity, a focus on only one thing at time and a meticulous attention to detail are all characteristics that may be typical of learning disabilities. Certain job functions within the organization may be an exact fit. Most experts state that managing employees with learning disabilities is just like managing any other workers, just with more intensity. A reasonable accommodation of variability is necessary, managed with a blend of understanding, creativity and patience. These are the same characteristics demonstrated by most individuals who live with learning challenges. It would seem that there is commonality and alignment that could reasonably be realized by both organization and individual.

There may be some positive movement toward a clearer understanding and agenda of worker disabilities. For example, in the United Kingdom, and according to Penny Mordaunt (2017) Minister for Disabled People, Work and Health in the Department of Work and Pensions (DWP), "Disabled people make up a significant proportion of the potential workforce, and employers must ensure they don't miss out on some of the best talent in their community" (p. 2).

Additionally, Department of Work and Pensions (DWP, 2017 reports almost one-fifth of the working-age population is disabled, and the vast majority of these people will develop their condition or impairment during their working life. Over the last four years almost 600,000 disabled people have entered the UK workforce. This has been made possible by increasing the number of Disability Employment Advisers in Job Centre Plus offices and raising awareness of programs like Access to Work and Disability Confident, a program that provides employers with the skills, examples, and confidence they need to recruit, retain and develop disabled employees. This shows one way that governments can lead the charge in promoting a disabled person, not as an anomaly, but as a norm within strategic organizational management and leadership.

## Inclusive Workplace Development

"Diversity is the mix. Inclusion is making the mix work."

*–Andres Tapia, Senior Client Partner and Solutions Leader in Workforce Performance, Inclusion and Diversity Practice at Korn-Ferry.*

Human resources are the heart of any successful organization. It takes the effective and efficient coordination and cooperation of a multiply variable labor force to accomplish organizational goals and objectives. Human resource departments focus on human resource development (HRD) needs and the specific criteria of human capital in order to assist the organization in reaching its goals. Hence, HRD can be defined as "the process of facilitating organizational learning, performance, and change through organized interventions and initiatives and management actions for the purpose of enhancing an organization's performance capacity, capability, competitive readiness, and renewal" (Gilley & Maycunich, 2000, p. 6).

As can be seen in Figure 13.7, human resource components can be segregated and included in overall HRD development.

It is pertinent to demonstrate that HR departments have a breadth of responsibilities in ensuring that human engagement with the organization is at its optimal level, beyond strictly attaining financial results. Moreover, within this model, two key functions emerge as relevant when discussing the relationship between learning management's role in HR functions of training and staff development and organizational development. Hence when contemplating the prior discussion of diversity, disabilities and inclusion, one can infer that these particular mandates in the organization would share a significance relationship in optimal organizational achievement and outcomes.

Additionally, in the study of HRD, conventional HRD literature recognizes three main disciplines as the foundation of the field: psychology, economics, and systems theory (Swanson & Holton III., 2001). It is generally believed that within these disciplines of convention in HRD, a process of ethics and ethical behavior is at the forefront of practice. While the notion of ethics is espoused in organizational achievement, there are many examples in contradiction.

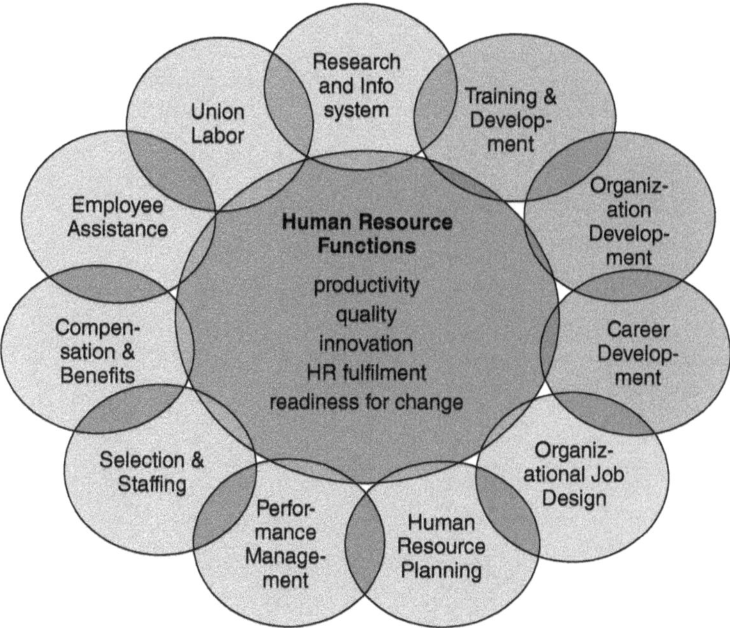


**Figure 13.7** Typical Human Resource Functions

Further, there has been persistent debate on whether performance or learning is most important for the field (Swanson, 1995; Watkins & Marsick, 1995). The performance view argues that the purpose of HRD is to improve organizational performance (Swanson & Arnold, 1996), whereas the learning view contends that HRD should develop individuals who ultimately contribute to organizational prosperity (Bierema, 1996). Nevertheless, the majority seem to agree that learning should be a vital component of HRD research and practice (Yang, 2004). A new conception of HRD views the field as including learning, performance and change (Gilley & Maycunich, 2000). Because HRD as a professional field has to work with all types of adults in various organizations for the purpose of facilitating learning, performance and change at both individual and organizational levels, it would seem relevant that diversity would be key driver within the landscape of HRD. Furthermore, if change and innovation are two particular activities that most organizations aspire, then it would seem strategically advantageous to harness diversity as the engine behind organizational development.

In developing the discourse on HRD and the relevant links to diversity, there seems to be a common agreement about the critical importance of workplace learning in organizations (Clarke, 2005; Jacobs, 2003; Lohman, 2005). As such, the topic has received much attention among HRD researchers and practitioners alike, mostly focusing on two major components: formal training and informal learning. In effect, these components have become the defining features of workplace learning (See Figure 13.8). This ideal proposes a framework of workplace learning that comprises the interaction of three variables: the location of the learning, the extent of planning that has been invested in developing and

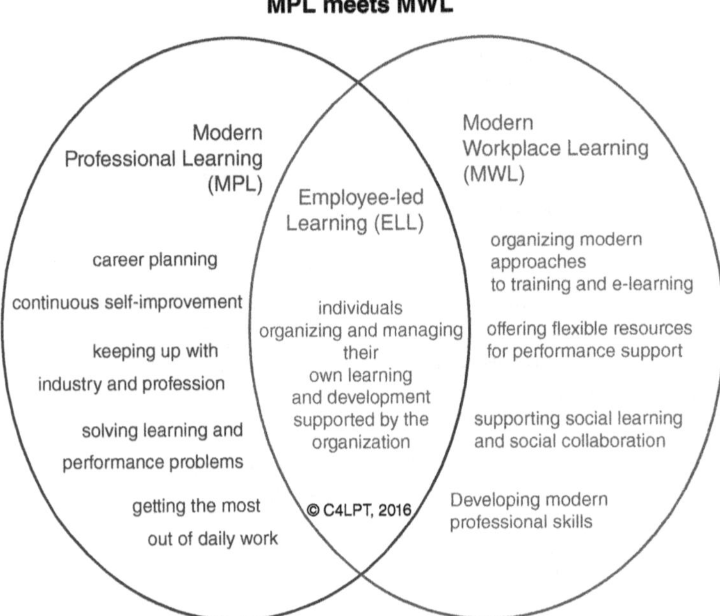


**Figure 13.8** Modern Professional Learning and Workforce Learning

delivering the learning experiences, and the role of the trainer, facilitator, or others during the learning process. The need for the framework stems from two concerns. First, formal training and informal learning represent incompatible levels of discourse, making it difficult to have a cohesive understanding of workplace learning. Second, definitions of workplace learning appear to exclude a large segment of HRD practice, particularly when formal training programs occur in the work setting (Jacobs & Park, 2009). This would seem to contradict the very essence of HR practices within the organizational framework on the overall intent of growth and development. Moreover, this misalignment of learning management with human resources creates barriers and gaps in organizational outcomes that become evident with conflicts and tension within organizational departments.

Workplace learning can be defined as the process used by individuals when engaged in training programs, education and development courses, or some type of experiential learning activity for the purpose of acquiring the competence necessary to meet current and future work requirements. The definition assumes the need to balance, though not always equally, the needs of organizations which provide the context for the learning, with the needs of individuals who may undertake the learning to advance their own work-related interests and goals (Jacobs, 2001; Muhamad & Idris, 2005; Swanson & Holton III., 2001). Workforce learning may be the most inclusive term used to describe the many ways that employees learn in organizations. Training typically refers to a single program of some kind. Employee development has come to represent a range of learning opportunities that focus on accomplishing broad career or professional goals (Jacobs & Washington, 2003; Noe, 2008). Similarly, talent development involves learning through multiple programs and experiences, often involving role-play and simulation, with an emphasis on acquiring the underlying competencies required for a position (Thorne & Pellant, 2007). In identifying specific areas of influence upon the organization that traditional human resources departments have on organizational outcomes, it becomes apparent the importance of an ideological shift among HR departments regarding disability engagement within the organizational structure.

The concept of learning and development is a concept that has been drawn out of traditional HR practices by practitioners over the years and, in some cases, applied in lieu of the term "human resources." Learning and development is defined as the process of ensuring that the organization has the knowledgeable, skilled and engaged workforce it needs. (Armstrong & Taylor, 2014). Harrison (2009) defined learning and development as an organizational process to aid collective progress through the collaborative, expert and ethical stimulation and facilitation of learning and knowledge that support business goals, develop individual potential, and respect and build on diversity. The components of L and D are as follows:

- *Learning* – the process by which a person acquires and develops knowledge, skills, capabilities, behaviors and attitudes. It involves the modification of behavior through experience as well as more formal methods of helping people to learn within or outside the workplace.
- *Development* – the growth or realization of a person's ability and potential through the programming of learning and educational experiences.
- *Training* – the systematic application of formal processes to impart knowledge and help people to acquire the skills necessary for them to perform their jobs satisfactorily.
- *Education* – the development of the knowledge, values and understanding required in all aspects of life rather than the knowledge and skills relating to particular areas of activity (Armstrong & Taylor, 2014).

Additionally, it is important to distinguish learning from training. "Learning is the process by which a person constructs new knowledge, skills and capabilities, whereas training is one of several responses an organization can undertake to promote learning" (Reynolds, Caley, & Mason, 2002). Learning is what individuals do; training is what organizations do to individuals. Moreover, from an organizational structure perspective, many organizations have decided to separate the learning development aspect from the purview of HR. This decision typically happens for a variety of reasons, though shared development responsibilities, control, cost management and autonomy in training design seem to be prevalent (O'Toole, 2010). The key point is that departments of HR and LD must work collaboratively to realize organizational success. This is not always the case, as political and organizational conflict arises out of the need for status, control and budgeting issues.

## Organizational Learning

"Where my reason, imagination or interests were not engaged, I would not or could not learn." – Sir Winston Churchill

Sir Winston Churchill, prime minister of Great Britain during most of the Second World War, had a lisp that prevented him pronouncing the letter S. He made this a distinct part of his oratory and worked to turn a disability into an asset

Organizational learning is the brain or the intelligence by which organizations can change current behavior with desired or more preferential behavior. Additionally, an organizations ability to reflect and act upon their past experiences is what stimulates a contrast between success and failure. Organizations cannot stand on their laurels; all must engage in real change processes. In essence, an organization is either growing and developing or it is regressing toward failure. Organizations learn by encoding inferences from past experiences into routines that guide behavior (Levitt & March, 1988). This process of learning involves knowledge acquisition, information distribution, information interpretation and development of an organizational memory (Huber, 1991). In many instances, organizational learning results from a detection or correction of errors (Argyris, 1977). When an organization has a problem, members actively engage in knowledge acquisition and searching for a strategy to resolve the problem (Argyris & Schon, 1978).

By and large, successful problem resolution and organizational learning is dependent upon the organization's ability not only to acquire knowledge, but also to respond and adapt its behavior. Organizational learning requires the organization to adapt continuously to a changing business environment by drawing on knowledge – a repertoire of skills and routines – that influences decision-making (See Figure 13.9).

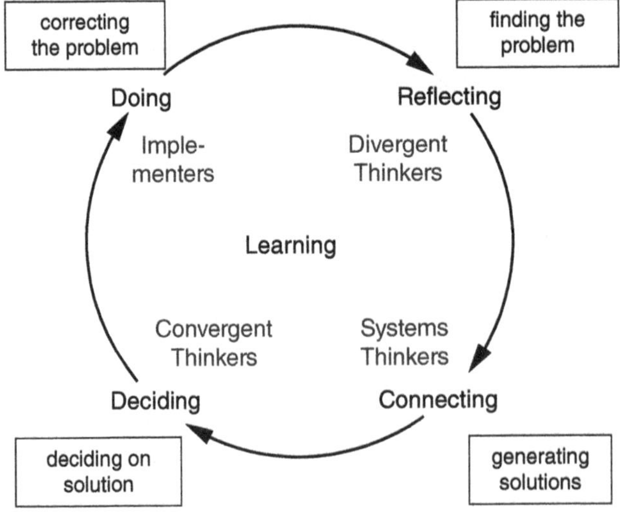


**Figure 13.9** Model of Organizational Learning

In this sense, learning relates to an organization's ability to encompass both processes and outcomes into its mental model – a set of ingrained assumptions defining how leaders and managers understand the world and respond to problems (Dodgson, 1993; Senge, 1990).

Organizations learn from their mental models as they become a part of the organization's memory and routines. Senge (1990) defines mental models as the reflection of individuals to continually clarify and improve the internal vision of the world and how this vision shapes personal action and decision making. Mental models stimulate and support a collective reflective practice of thinking and developing awareness in organizations. Mental models can be tacit or explicit and evident in an organization's culture, policies, behavior and practices. For example, some organizations develop mental models that handle discriminatory behavior and harassment of disabled employees through accepting the status quo and not changing the situation (James & Wooten, 2000). This was the case in an Olive Garden Restaurant lawsuit where management's mental model entailed ignoring incidents when an employee was subjected to almost daily physical and verbal abuse relating to his disability (Wooten & James, 2005).

Organizational learning strategies aim to improve organizational effectiveness through the acquisition and development of knowledge, understanding, insights, techniques and practices. This is in accordance with one of the basic principles of HRM, namely that it is necessary to invest in people in order to develop the human capital required by the organization and to increase its stock of knowledge and skills. As stated by Ehrenberg and Smith (1994, pp. 279–80), human capital theory indicates that: "The knowledge and skills a worker has – which comes from education and training, including the training that experience brings – generate productive capital." This human capital becomes a tremendous asset for the organization.

Moreover, management scholars have identified two specific types of organizational learning (Argyris & Schon, 1978; Senge, 1990) (See Figure 13.10).

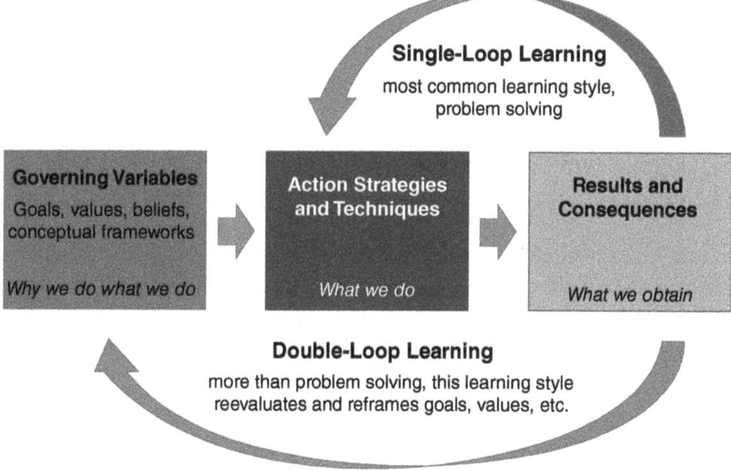


**Figure 13.10** Single-Loop and Double-Loop Organizational Learning

In single-loop learning, the organization adapts to a situation by taking corrective actions for a problem (e.g., accommodation for a single individual) without questioning or changing the present policies (e.g., universal design of the facility). Single-loop learning is the short-term, reactive viewpoint of organizational learning that does not examine the appropriateness of current behaviors (Yogesh, 1998). In double-loop or reflective learning, the organization's solution involves identifying, considering, and modifying underlying norms, policies, and objectives. This type of organizational learning demands a re-examination of and reflection upon fundamental organizational core values that influence such behavior.

Therefore, many organizations when confronted with the discrimination of a disabled employee adopt a single-loop learning strategy. For example, when this basic strategy of learning is applied, monetary settlements are paid, jobs are reinstated, or changes are made to accommodate the disabled employee. However, few organizations examine the underlying cause of the discriminatory behavior in resolving such issues. This requires an organization to take the time and make the effort in the gaps that exist in organizational processes and procedures. Additionally, this may demand a change in human resource management practices, instilling new cultural values. Apparently, organizations struggle with such efforts in expending the effort and energy toward identifying the core problem in solving the issue, as opposed to appeasing each individual case. As a result of this repetitive process and single-loop learning strategy, the same problem repeats itself infinitely and organizations are constantly seeing the issue as a chronic problem, rather than a "normal" operating issue. Moreover, the organization will eventually become intolerant with the persistence of such events and take measures to completely eradicate a problem they refuse to address by developing policies to discourage and/or eliminate conditions considered to be problematic. Hence, one can see the thought process behind unintended discrimination and prejudice perpetuation, as outlined prior.

## Conclusion

> "The only thing worse than training your employees and having them leave is not training them and having them stay"
>
> – *Henry Ford. The founder of the Ford Motor Company: he struggled mightily to read.*

In summarizing and aligning the framework of discussion within this chapter, one can see the complexity of connections and the disparity between aspiration and reality in the workforce in regards to diversity and learning disabled individuals in organizations. The tenets of diversity, prejudice, disability, inclusive workplace development and organizational learning were presented as a guide in understanding the challenges that confront leaders and managers across the globe. Moreover, an underlying aspect of the human condition has been explicitly implied as well. Many conditions encountered by leaders and managers in organizations are a direct result of human relations on a broader, sociological scale.

The topic of disabilities in the workforce is not an easy topic, with simple solutions for improvement. It is important to recognize that in order to comprehend such complexity in what would seem disparate notions one cannot think about the workforce in absence of socially accepted norms in our everyday lives. In our discussion of learning disabilities in the workforce, theoretical definitions, models and programs abound; however, implementation has proven to be very difficult, with business, societies and communities unable to reconcile diversity as a genuine norm in organizational life. This is not surprising, as our societal norms have not achieved such a reconciliation either.

The organizational approach that seems to persist in regard to the engagement of learning disabled individuals is combative and divisive. The organization, as a mirror of society, shows the tendency to ignore and place barriers of entry to those individuals who could actually help the company reach its innovation, creativity and stated objectives within the corporate mandate. Managing an effective, and diverse workforce in the organization, takes vision, persistence, fortitude and, above all, leadership. The leadership required in this scenario is an understanding of the urgent and essential need to transform societal norms toward effective human resource strategies.

One has to ponder as to who – the organization or the "disabled" individual – is really demonstrating attributes of learning challenges within this context. It would seem apparent that until the restrictions imposed by the dominant mental models are abandoned for more holistic and systemic thinking, discrimination and prejudice will perpetuate. And that would be such an injustice to both the individual and the organization as such repetitive and ineffective thinking erects barriers to growth in the path of all stakeholders.

## References

Alcázar, F. M., Fernández, P. M. R., & Gardey, G. S. (2013). Workforce diversity in strategic human resource management models: A critical review of the literature and implications for future research. *International Journal of Cross Cultural Management, 20*(1), 39–49. https://doi.org/10.1108/13527601311296247

Alexander, R. (1994). *Attitudes towards the disabled in destination marketing organizations.* Doctoral Dissertation. Virginia Polytechnic Institute and State University.

Allport, G. W. (1954). *The nature of prejudice.* Reading, MA: Addison-Wesley.

Argyris, C. (1977). Double-loop learning in organizations. *Harvard Business Review, 55,* 115–125.

Argyris, C., & Schon, D. A. (1978). *Organizational learning: A theory of action perspective.* Reading, MA: Addison-Wesley.

Armstrong, M., & Taylor, S. (Eds.) (2014). *Armstrong's handbook of human resource management practice.* London, UK: Kogan Page.

Aronson, E., & Patnoe, S. (1967). *The jigsaw classroom: Building cooperation in the classroom.* New York: Longman.

Bandura, A. (1977). *Social learning theory.* Englewood Cliffs, NJ: Prentice Hall.

Barnes, C. (1996). Theories of disability and the origins of the oppression of disabled people in western society. In L. Barton (Ed.), *Disability and society: Emerging issues and insights* (pp. 43–60). New York: Longman.

Barnes, C., Mercer, G., & Shakespeare, T. (Eds.) (1999). *Exploring disability: A sociological introduction*. Malden, MA: Polity Press.

Bell, M. P. (2012). *Diversity in organizations* (2nd ed.). Boston, MA:: South-western, Cengage Learning.

Bierema, L. L. (1996). Development of the individual leads to more productive workplaces. In R. W. Rowden (Ed.), *Workplace learning: Debating five critical questions of theory and practice*, (pp. 21–28). San Francisco, CA: Jossey-Bass.

Blum, T. C., Fields, D. L., & Goodman, J. S. (1994). Organization-level determinants of women in management. *Academy of Management Journal, 37*, 241–268.

Borrell-Carrió, F., Suchman, A. L., & Epstein, R. M. (2004). The biopsychosocial model 25 years later: Principles, practice, and scientific inquiry. *Annals of Family Medicine, 2*(6), 576–582.

Brewer, M. B., & Kramer, R. M. (1985). The psychology of intergroup attitudes and behavior. *Annual Review of Psychology, 36*(1), 219–243.

Bruyère, S., Erickson, W. A., & Ferrentino, J. T. (2003). Identity and disability in the workplace. *William and Mary Law Review, 44*(3), 1173–1196.

Caspi, A. (1984). Contact hypothesis and inter-age attitudes: A field study of cross-age contact. *Social Psychology Quarterly*, 74–80.

Chadwick, A. (1994). For disabled people the body is the principal site of oppression, both in form and what is done to it. *Australian Disability Review, 4*, 36–44.

Clarke, N. (2005). Workplace learning environment and its relationship with learning outcomes in healthcare organizations. *Human Resource Development International, 8*, 185–205.

Cohen, E. G., & Lotan, R. A. (1995). Producing equal-status interaction in the heterogeneous classroom. *American Educational Research Journal, 32*(1), 99–120.

Colella, A. (1996). Organizational socialization of newcomers with disabilities: A framework for future research. *Research in Personnel and Human Resources Management, 14*, 351–417.

Cox, T. (1993). *Cultural diversity in organizations: Theory, research and practice*. San Francisco, CA: Berrett-Koehler Publishers.

Daruwalla, P. (1999). *Attitudes, disability and the hospitality and tourism Industry*. Doctoral dissertation, University of Newcastle, Australia.

Daruwalla, P., & Darcy, S. (2005). Personal and societal attitudes to disability. *Annals of Tourism Research, 32*(3), 549–570.

Diversity. (n.d.). Retrieved January 9, 2017, from https://www.merriam-webster.com/dictionary/diversity. Web. 22.

Dodgson, M. (1993). Organizational learning: A review of some literature. *Organization Studies, 14*, 375–394.

Dovidio, J. F., & Gaertner, S. L. (1986). *Prejudice, discrimination, and racism*. San Diego, CA: Academic Press.

Department of Work and Pensions. (2017, September). *Five thousand UK employers are now disability confident*. London, UK: Caxton House.

Ehrenberg, R. G., & Smith, R. S. (1994). *Modern labor economics*. New York, NY: Harper Collins.

Ely, R., & Thomas, D. (2001). Cultural diversity at work: the effects of diversity perspectives on work group processes and outcomes. *Administrative Science Quarterly, 46,* 229–273.

Engel, G. L. (1977). The need for a new medical model: A challenge for biomedicine. *Science, 196,* 129–136.

Esty, K., Griffin, R., & Schorr-Hirsh, M. (1995). *Workplace diversity. A manager's guide to solving problems and turning diversity into a competitive advantage.* Avon, MA: Adams Media Corporation.

Everett, J. A. C. (2013). *Intergroup contact theory: past, present, and future. The Inquisitive Mind, 2*(17). Retrieved from http://www.in-mind.org/article/intergroup-contact-theory-past-present-and-future

Fields, D. L., Goodman, J. S., & Blum, T. C. (2005). Human resource dependence and organizational demography: a study of minority employment in private sector companies. *Journal of Management, 31,* 167–185.

Gardenswartz, L., & Rowe, A. (2003). *Diverse teams at work* (2nd ed.). Alexandria, VA: Society of Human Resource Management (SHRM).

Gellman, W. (1960). Attitudes toward rehabilitation of the disabled. *Journal of Occupational Therapy, 14,* 188–190.

Gilley, J. W., & Maycunich, A. (2000). *Organizational learning, performance, and change: An introduction to strategic human resource development.* Cambridge, MA: Perseus.

Goodman, J. S., Fields, D. L., & Blum, T. C. (2003). Cracks in the glass ceiling: In what kinds of organizations do women make it to the top? *Group and Organization Management, 28,* 475–501.

Green, K., López, M., Wysocki, A., Kepner, K., Farnsworth, D., and Clark, J.L. (2015, Oct.). *Diversity in the workplace: benefits, challenges, and the required managerial tools.* The Institute of Food and Agricultural Sciences (IFAS), University of Florida, USA. (UF/IFAS extension (HR022).

Harrison, R. (2009). *Learning and development* (5th ed.). London, UK: CIPD.

Heilman, M. E., & Okimoto, T. G. (2007). Why are women penalized for success at male tasks: the implied communality deficit. *Journal of Applied Psychology, 92,* 81–92.

Hu, D., & Griffey, D. (1985). The contact theory of racial integration: The case of sport. *Sociology of Sport Journal, 2*(4), 323–333.

Huber, G. (1991). Organizational learning: The contributing processes and the literature. *Organization Science, 2,* 88–115.

Hume, J. (1995). *Media guidelines.* Sydney, Australia: Disability Council of NSW.

Jacobs, R. L. (2001). Managing employee competence in global organizations. In J. Kidd, X. Li, & F. Richter (Eds.), *Maximizing human intelligence deployment in Asian business,* (pp. 44–56). New York, NY: Palgrave.

Jacobs, R. L. (2003). *Structured on-the-job training: Unleashing employee expertise in the workplace.* San Francisco, CA: Berrett-Koehler.

Jacobs, R. L., & Park, Y. (2009). A proposed conceptual framework of workplace learning: Implications for theory development and research in human resource development. *Human Resource Development Review, 8,* 133.

Jacobs, R. L., & Washington, C. (2003). Employee development and organizational performance: A review of literature and directions for future research. *Human Resource Development International, 6,* 343–354.

James, E. H. and Wooten, L. P. (2000). Being in the spotlight: How firms respond to public diversity crises. Paper presented at the *Academy of Management* meeting, Toronto, BC.

Kalev, A., Dobbin, F., & Kelly, E. (2006). Best practices or best guesses: assessing the efficacy of corporate affirmative action and diversity policies. *American Sociological Review, 71*, 589–617.

Katz, D., & Kahn, R. L. (1978). *The social psychology of organizations* (2nd ed.). New York, NY: John Wiley and Sons.

Kochan, T., Bezrukova, K., Ely, R., Jackson, S., Joshi, A., Jehn, K., et al. (2003). The effects of diversity on business performance: report of the diversity research network. *Human Resource Management, 42*(1), 3–21.

Koonce, R. (2001). Redefining Diversity: It's not just the right thing to do; it also makes good business sense. *Training and Development*, 12, 22–32.

Kuhn, H. (1974). *The logic of social systems*. San Francisco, CA: Jossey-Bass.

Learning disability. (n.d.). Retrieved January 9, 2017, from https://www.merriam-webster.com/dictionary/learning disability. Web. 22

Landis, D., Hope, R. O., & Day, H. R. (1984). Training for desegregation in the military. In N. Miller, & M. B. Brewer (Eds.), *Groups in contact: The psychology of desegregation* (pp. 257–278). Orlando, FL: Academic Press.

Levitt, B., & March, J. (1988). Organizational learning. *Annual Review of Sociology, 14*, 319–340.

Linton, S. (1998). *Claiming disability: knowledge and identity*. New York, NY: New York University Press.

Loden, M. (1996). *Implementing diversity*. Toronto: Irwin Publishing.

Loden, M., & Rosener, J. (1991). *Workforce America*. Toronto: Business One Irwin Publishing.

Lohman, M. C. (2005). A survey of factors influencing the engagement of two professional groups in informal workplace learning activities. *Human Resource Development Quarterly, 16*, 501–527.

Loysk, B. (1996). *Managing a changing workforce: Achieving outstanding service with today's employees*. Davie, FL: Workplace Trends Publishing.

Mordaunt, P. (2017, September). *Five thousand UK employers are now disability confident*. Department of Work and Pensions. London, UK: Caxton House.

Morgan, R. L., & Alexander, M. (2005). The employers' perception: Employment of individuals with developmental disabilities. *Journal of Vocational Rehabilitation, 23*(1), 39–49.

Muhamad, M., & Idris, K. (2005). Workplace learning in Malaysia: The learner's perspective. *International Journal of Training and Development, 9*, 62–78.

Nishii, L. and Bruyere, S. (2013, October). Inside the workplace: Case studies of factors influencing engagement of people with disabilities. *Research brief in the proceedings of the State of the Science Conference, Washington, DC* (pp. 1–7). Cornell University ILR School, Employment and Disability Institute.

Noe, R. A. (2008). *Employee training and development*. New York, NY: McGraw-Hill.

Oliver, M. (1990). *The politics of disablement*. Basingstoke, UK: Houndsmills Macmillan.

O'Toole, S. (2010, July). Training, LandD, OD, HRD: What's in a name? *Australian Journal of Adult Learning, 50*(2), 419–426.

Penney, J. N. (2010). The biopsychosocial model of pain and contemporary osteopathic practice. *International Journal of Osteopathic Medicine, 13*(2), 42–47.

Pettigrew, T. F. (1998). Intergroup contact theory. *Annual Review of Psychology, 49*(1), 65–85.

Pettigrew, T. F., & Tropp, L. R. (2006). A meta-analytic test of intergroup contact theory. *Journal of Personality and Social Psychology, 90*(5), 751.

Prejudice. (n.d.). Retrieved January 9, 2017, from https://en.oxforddictionaries.com/definition/us/prejudice. Web.45.

Ragins, B. R. (2008). Disclosure disconnects: antecedents and consequences of disclosing invisible stigmas across life domains. *Academy of Management Review, 33*, 194–215.

Rajan, R., Servaes, H., & Zingales, L. (2002, December). The cost of diversity: The diversification discount and inefficient investment. *The Journal of Finance, 55*(1), 35–80.

Reisman, E. (1996, January). Get the best from employees with learning disabilities. *The Personnel Journal, 75*(1), 76–84.

Reynolds, J., Caley, L., & Mason, R. (2002). *How do people learn?*. London, UK: CIPD.

Ricco, R., & Guerci, B. (2014, March–April). Diversity challenge: An integrated process to bridge the "implementation gap". *Business Horizons, 57*(2), 235–245.

Robinson, K. S. (2002). *U.S. must focus on diversity or face decline in competiveness.* Alexandria, VA: The Society of Human Resource Management (SHRM).

Roosevelt, T.R. Jr. (2001). Elements of a successful diversity process. *The American Institute for Managing Diversity.*

Santrock, J. W. (2007). *A topical approach to human life-span development* (3rd ed.). St. Louis, MO: McGraw-Hill.

Schartz, H., Hendricks, D. J., & Blanck, P. (2006). Workplace accommodations: Evidence-based outcomes. *Work, 27*, 345–354.

Schartz, H., Schartz, K. M., Hendricks, D. J., & Blanck, P. (2006). Workplace accommodations: Empirical study of current employees. *Mississippi Law Journal, 75*, 917–943.

Scheid, T. L. (2005). Stigma as a barrier to employment: mental disability and the Americans with disabilities act. *International Journal of Law and Psychiatry, 28*, 670–690.

Senge, P. (1990). *The fifth discipline.* New York, NY: Doubleday.

Shore, L. M., Chung-Herrera, B. G., Dean, M. A., Ehrhart, K. H., Jung, D. I., Randel, A. E., & Singh, G. (2009, June). Diversity in organizations: where are we now and where are we going? *Human Resources Management Review, 19*(2), 117–133. https://doi.org/10.1016/j.hrmr.2008.10.004

Society for Human Resource Management. (1998). SHRM survey explores the best in diversity practices: Fortune 500 firms outpace the competition with greater commitment to diversity. *The Society for Human Resource Management* (SHRM), http://www.shrm.org.

Stone, D., & Colella, A. (1996). A model of factors affecting the treatment of disabled individuals in organizations. *Academy of Management Review, 21*, 352–401.

Stone-Romero, E. F., & Stone, D. L. (2007). The influence of cultural, cognitive, and affective processes on stigmatization in organizations. In J. Martocchio

(Ed.), *Research in personnel and human resource management* (Vol. *26*) (pp. 117–167). New York, NY: Elsevier.

Swanson, R. A. (1995). Human resource development, performance is key. *Human Resource Development Quarterly, 6*, 207–213.

Swanson, R. A., & Arnold, D. E. (1996). The purpose of human resource development is to improve organizational performance. In R. W. Rowden (Ed.), *Workplace learning: Debating five critical questions of theory and practice* (pp. 13–20). San Francisco, CA: Jossey-Bass.

Swanson, R. A., & Holton, E. F. III. (2001). *Foundations of human resource development*. San Francisco, CA: Barrett-Koehler.

Thorne, K., & Pellant, A. (2007). *The essential guide to managing talent: how top companies recruit, train and retain the best employees*. Philadelphia, PA: Kogan Page.

Von Bertalanffy, L. (1956). General System Theory. In F. E. Emery (Ed.), *General systems, the yearbook of the society for the advancement of general systems theory* (pp. 1–10). York, UK: ISSS.

Von Bertalanffy, L. (1968). *General system theory: Foundations, development, applications*. New York, NY: George Braziller.

Vonofakou, C., Hewstone, M., & Voci, A. (2007). Contact with outgroup friends as a predictor of meta-attitudinal strength and accessibility of attitudes towards gay men. *Journal of Personality and Social Psychology, 92*, 804–820.

Watkins, K. E., & Marsick, V. J. (1995). The case for learning. In E. F. Holton (Ed.), *Academy of human resource development conference proceedings, 1–10*. Austin, TX: Academy of Human Resource Development.

Wooten, L. P., & James, E. H. (2005). Challenges of organizational learning: perpetuation of discrimination against employees with disabilities. *Behavioral Sciences & The Law, 23*(1), 123–141.

Works, E. (1961). The prejudice-interaction hypothesis from the point of view of the Negro minority group. *American Journal of Sociology, 67*, 47–52.

Wright, B. (1980). Developing a constructive view of life with a disability. *Rehabilitation Literature, 41*(1980), 274–279.

Wright, B. (1983). *Physical disability: A psychosocial approach*. New York, NY: Harper and Row.

Yang, B. (2004, May). Can adult learning theory provide a foundation for human resource development? *Advances in Developing Human Resources, 6*(2), 129–145. https://doi.org/10.1177/1523422304263325

Yelin, E., & Trupin, L. (2003, May). Disability and the characteristics of employment. *Monthly Labor Review*, 20–31.

Yogesh, M. (1998). Deciphering the knowledge management hype. *Journal for Quality and Participation, 21*, 58–60.

Yuker, H. E. (1977). *Attitudes of the general public toward handicapped individuals*, In *Awareness Papers*, 1. Albertson, NY: Human Resources Center.

Yuker, H. E., & Hurley, M. K. (1987). Contact with and attitudes toward persons with disabilities: The measurement of intergroup contact. *Rehabilitation Psychology, 32*(3), 145.

# 14

# Digital Education in Career and Technical Education and the Support of Creative Professional Development

*Antje Barabasch and Alberto Cattaneo*

*Swiss Federal Institute of Vocational Education and Training*

## Creativity Development Through Digital Technologies

There has been growing recognition that nurturing students' creative potential is a valuable, yet often unrealized, educational goal. The increased interest in creativity education results from the need for innovation in the workplace, which requires more than the general skills that education is mainly promoting. Much of the research focusing on creativity is concerned with the individuals' intellectual skills stimulating creativity, such as divergent thinking, collaborative problem-solving, imagination, or empathy. In career and technical education (CTE) (USA) or similarly vocational education and training (VET) there is little research done so far on creativity development as a competence that supports innovation at the workplace.

Also, not much is known yet about how to incorporate creativity in everyday teaching in VET and how students learn to be creative in the workplace. Modern workplaces increasingly rely on team effort, which requires from an individual an understanding of a variety of social practices and their relevance for creative endeavors within the team. Such an understanding can be developed within VET at school, in training centers as well as with the apprenticeship at work by providing team work experiences that are supportive of creative processes and innovative practice.

Through the increasing introduction of computer-based and web-based applications students are coming of age as digital natives[1] who are expected to significantly transform many workplaces. At this time digital technologies have entered workplace learning in many different forms, especially as production or design tools (e.g., numerical control machines, electronic measurement devices, and computer-aided design software), but their use as a training tool within VET remains under-exploited. Digital technologies usually rise up in different contexts and for different aims than educational ones. Most of the times, they are then declined for educational purposes too. Educational or instructional technology

*The Wiley Handbook of Global Workplace Learning*, First Edition.
Edited by Vanessa Hammler Kenon and Sunay Vasant Palsole.

is a broad field of investigation however, specifically defined as "the study and ethical practice of facilitating learning and improving performance by creating, using, and managing appropriate technological processes and resources" (Januszewski and Molenda, 2008, p. 1).

In this paper, we will focus in particular on the last word of this definition and consequently on those technologies that can constitute tools to foster learning and instruction. Given what we already said about the typical genesis of digital technology, it is not easy to give a comprehensive view on what "learning technologies" include. For example, just concentrating on "Web 2.0" technologies, Bower (2016) could review and document 37 different types of them, then arranged in 14 clusters. Analogously, reviewing 343 papers on "e-learning technologies," Purarjomandlangrudi, Chen, and Nguyen (2015) derived nine main categories of such tools. To make it simpler, we include within the term "digital learning technologies" all those tools, devices, materials that can intervene in a process of teaching and learning process to foster knowledge acquisition and competence development.

Examples range from all different kinds of cognitive tools for individual or collaborative productivity and instruction (word processing, spreadsheets, database, but also multimedia materials, self-assessment quizzes,...), for information retrieving (search engines, repositories, folksonomies,...) for knowledge graphical representation, organization and visualization (mind-mapping, computer-aided design, graphical organizers, graphs, 3D visualizers,...) for modeling/simulation (videos, hypervideos, simulation environments, augmented reality, virtual reality, programming tools, interactive apps,...) for collaboration and communication (forum, weblogs, wikis, web conference systems, presentation software,...), also including specific management systems (Learning Management Systems, Learning Content Management Systems, Virtual Learning Environments,...) and different pieces of hardware (from tablets to smartphones, from interactive tabletops to Interactive Whiteboards, from beamers or visualizers to 3D printers).

The subject of inquiry in this chapter is to elaborate on the questions of creativity unleashing and enhancement in the field of VET by introducing learning technologies in the school context. We will specifically focus on visual learning, meant as the use of static and dynamic visual aids to support teaching-and-learning processes. The driving research question to be answered is: How can schools provide opportunities for choice, imagination and exploration as a collaborative endeavor within their curricula by applying information and communications technology (ICT)? Imagination and exploration are inherent in creative processes and we therefore establish a connection between research on creativity, the idea of supporting the creative development of VET students and the application of visualization tools. We will discuss creativity first from a theoretical point of view, then with a particular emphasis on VET in Switzerland and eventually as an embedded pedagogical goal within the didactic approach of using visualization tools to bridge learning between school and workplace in the Swiss context of VET.

## The Age of ICT in VET

The industry proclaims the age of industry 4.0 pointing to the digitalization of workplaces and the need to train workers accordingly. A study of the German chamber of industry and commerce in which 1849 enterprises participated revealed that a total of 94% of the entrepreneurs expect an impact of digitalization on their work processes (Schumann, Assenmacher, Liecke, Reinecke, and Sobania, 2014). The Swiss Federal Council published a report at the beginning of 2017 pointing to the urgency of skilling workers according to new workplace requirements (Swiss Confederation, 2017). A survey launched nationally to address political priorities for the next years similarly identified the topic "digitalization" as the most important trend to cope with (Ecoplan, 2017). At the Swiss Federal Institute of Vocational Education and Training a study is currently conducted to determine the skills needed in a changing economy with an emphasis on digitalization (Eidgenössiches Hochschulinstitut für Berufsbildung [EHB], 2016) in order to inform VET providers as much as teachers colleges, who need to adjust their educational provision.

The Organization for Economic Co-operation and Development (OECD, 2016) outlines in its interim report on the production revolution how a confluence of technologies ranging from a variety of digital infrastructures (e.g., 3D printing, Internet of Things, advanced robotics) to new materials (e.g., bio-or nano-based) to new processes (e.g., data driven production, artificial intelligence, synthetic biology) will have a major impact on the production and distribution of goods and services. Therefore, far-reaching consequences for productivity, skills development and the shaping of the work-life-balance are expected. An Austrian report comes to the conclusion that a dual training system as it exists in Switzerland, Germany and Austria prepares most adequately for the industry 4.0 age, because employers react more quickly to training their staff on and for the new technologies – knowledge and knowhow that feeds back into the schools (Pfeiffer, 2015).

In Germany, a country with many large enterprises consisting of more than 250 employees, political initiatives have been started in order to spread awareness about the need for building ICT competence and nurture workers creativity to prepare the future workforce to adapt to the newly developed technologies (Bundesinstitut für Berufsbildung, 2016). Government-funded support programs target the development of pilot projects in vocational training centers and pay for technical equipment in public schools. A highly relevant question addressed to researchers in this respect is how vocational teachers and trainers use digital media when training apprentices as well as adults attending further training courses? Embedded in this question is the inquiry into:

- media didactics in terms of shaping and using media in the classroom in order to achieve educational goals and
- media education in terms of a critical mindset toward evaluating the usefulness of media and in order to use media in a reflective and goal-oriented way.

Research provides more and more evidence that technology per se is not beneficial to learning (OECD, 2015) and that its effectiveness relies on educators' didactical competence (Hattie, 2009; Higgins, Xiao and Katsipataki, 2012). Under this assumption, other scholars showed through meta-analysis that digital technologies improve learning, from primary (Chauhan, 2017) to higher education (Bernard, Borokhovski, Schmid, Tamim and Abrami, 2014) and for different subject matters (Johnson and Johnson, 2006; Tamim, Bernard, Borokhovski, Abrami and Schmid, 2011), including mathematics (Qing and Xin, 2010), statistics (Larwin and Larwin, 2011) and language learning (Grgurović, Chapelle and Shelley, 2013). Within this framework, Wilbers (2016) also takes sides for digital learning as well as augmented learning. He claims that video technologies and additional information provided within computer-based environments combining pictures and audio – in compliance with multimedia learning theory (Mayer, 2005, 2009) – enhance the learning experience and support the adaptation to more professional interaction with digital applications. Given that vocational teachers have received training regarding media competence and media didactics and a school as well as workplace environment nurtures media literacy, Wilbers' claim has relevance for vocational education and training.

> Competences that are increasingly sought at workplaces include in addition the mastery of systems with decentral intelligence, processing of data and their analysis as well as the ability to ensure continuity in computer-driven work processes (Spöttl, Go, Windelband, Grantz and Richter, 2016).

Vocational education and training needs to respond to these needs and increasingly emphasize media didactics not just as a singular subject but as an integrated part of all subjects. Although technologies transform the production system in many professions, research on digital technologies in VET is limited. What has been addressed so far concerns 3-D applications in technology learning, the integration of tangible objects, the use of augmented reality, computer-supported collaborative learning solutions, gamification as well as e-learning environments. This chapter will specifically focus on creativity development among VET students and the approach of using visualizations for training purposes. The chapter will now summarize research on creativity and the theoretical foundations for creativity research. Afterwards we will outline how visualizations can be applied within VET to connect workplace and school based learning.

## Unleashing the Creative Potential of VET Students – Theoretical Approaches

### Creativity as a Skill

What does creativity development have to do with new technologies and why is VET more concerned with it? Being able to use or apply technologies for learning and at work or develop them requires new skills, such as transversal thinking, imaginative learning and working, recognizing good ideas, and the persistence to work on something new until it is done. Next to styles of thinking, creativity also requires skills, such as concentration ability and discipline (Dyer, Gregersen and Christensen, 2011). What are the conditions under which creativity and creative work with new technologies can prosper?

Torrance (1965) claims that creativity is the process of becoming sensitive to problems, deficiencies, gaps in knowledge, missing elements, or disharmonies.

It is about identifying difficulties, searching for solutions, making guesses or formulating hypotheses about deficiencies, testing and retesting them, and finally communicating the results. Creativity as an unconscious process (Poincaré, 1913 in Brown, 1989, p. 5) refers to a relaxation period of the mind in which a large variety of options are thought through. While many might not lead to anything, some eventually do arrive in our consciousness and support meaningful results. This has implications for the ways in which VET must be shaped.

While the claims above lead to advocating for material and mental space for exploration, exchange and relaxation as a creativity-supporting environment, for Poincaré a solid knowledge base is highly important for ideas to grow. Thus the learning of facts, theories and processes, in general acquiring a broad as much as a specific knowledge base, is highly relevant for creativity. Next to knowledge-acquisition, endurance in working on a task is essential. Ericsson (2006) speaks about deliberate practice and argues that creative endeavors require many hours of practice. Cropley (2001) adds to it that experimenting and playing with materials or as Tanggaard (2008) calls it "fooling around" unleashes the creative potential in students.

The construct of problem-solving is also often used as a synonym for creativity (Newell, Shaw and Simon, 1962). Problem-solving refers to the creation of new combinations of objects and actions in order to arrive at a good solution (Proctor, 1999, p. 2). Gestalt therapy, applied in psychoanalysis, is based on this approach and postulates a restructuring of problems (e.g., Wertheimer, 1945). According to Wertheimer when something is done in a different context, it needs to be done differently. To understand the forces that provide an inherent structure in a situation, process or event is decidedly important. In innovation research this approach to *gestalten* is highly relevant within productive thinking or within the production of prototypes. The reorganization of objects or artifacts requires somewhat of a detachment from prior experiences and the viewing of the new problem as a new experience. It needs to be carefully observed and clearly framed to be worked on. There is not necessarily a straight forward way, but instead a trial-and-error phase is necessary. In VET this can be a challenge at the workplace. However, space and time for experimentation can be provided both in training centers and within VET schools.

## Creativity Development in VET

In relation to the development of creativity in VET, the following aspects are decisive: the learning environment, coaching and didactics. In terms of the learning environment, schools experiment with a variety of different settings to help students learn best. It has been recognized that creative tasks have a tendency to be more unstructured, although the different learning needs among students require a balanced mix of structured and unstructured tasks. For VET, the learning environment includes not just the school, but also a (real or simulated) workplace and often a workshop in which practical skills are acquired.

The role of the teacher increasingly includes working as a coach and mentor. From teachers it is expected that more than ever they help students to discover their potential and develop flexible thinking skills. Students need to be able to know about their own capacities, critically reflect upon them and take on a particular role within a team accordingly. Teachers can help students in becoming experts at what they are good at, because modern workplaces do not require generalists, but instead compose teams who can work harmoniously together, because their skills and competencies substitute each other. In order to do so a variety of didactical tools are available to the teacher. Many scholars have pointed out that teachers willing to experiment with new ideas and new ways of teaching provide favorable conditions for the development of creativity among their students (Craft, Gardner and Claxton, 2008; Schön, 1987; Tanggaard, 2010).

The idea that groups solve problems more effectively and efficiently is increasingly taking hold; it leads to new forms of classroom instruction or flipped classroom settings. They all respond to the idea that different ways of thinking exist and that they need to be mixed to achieve the best possible results. Increasingly, schools and enterprises experiment with different group constellations in order to unleash what Glăveneau (2010) terms "we-creativity," referring to the creativity of a community. In a school context the "we-creativity" includes the teacher. Tanggaard Pedersen (2016) claims that the creative person "is a social actor able to (and in today's work compelled to) co-construct one's sense of creative value in communication with others..." (p. 377).

Summing up, creativity-supportive practices include: establishing a creativity-supportive learning environment; encouraging students' intrinsic motivation; explicitly teaching creative thinking; providing opportunities for choice and discovery; and providing opportunities for students to use their imagination while learning to develop aspirational commitment (Beghetto and Kaufman, 2014). In order to support this practice, VET institutions are challenged to strike the balance between providing structure and freedom so that students feel supported and encouraged to take the risks that exploration entails. In addition, the learning environment in vocational schools like the learning culture at the workplace needs to support creative expression.

## Creativity Development in VET

Another dimension of creativity regards it as an associative process. According to Spearman (1931 in Brown, 1989, p. 5) the generation of new ideas is explainable by three principles: "principle of experience," where an individual relies on one's own imaginations, feelings and efforts; "principle of relationships," in which a person perceives different items in different ways; and "principle of interrelationships," related to the consciousness about existing items and their influence on the creation of new ones. These experiences are the foundation for mental models, which are a subjective representation of a person's thought process about something that works in the real world. Ward, Smith and Vaid (1997) state that mental models are highly relevant for creative processes because they are the foundation for new discoveries.

In order to incorporate creativity in everyday teaching in VET and support students to learn how to be creative at the workplace, new VET didactics need to be developed. This requires using activities that lead to the development of multiple ideas, problem definition, the use of analogies and evaluating ideas and products that students generate.

One approach to be introduced is to offer students the possibility to collect their experiences at the workplace in the form of pictures, videos or sketches and to transform them – with the help of their vocational teachers – into structured learning materials on which to activate reflective processes (Schwendimann et al., 2015).

Pedagogical research on creativity focused on art as experience and subject of creative expression. Visual art is for many people the paradigmatic domain of creativity not least due to the fact that humans are to a great extent visual creatures. Large parts of our brains are either dedicated to or involved in processing visual information (Kozbelt, 2016; Medina, 2008). Working with visual representations of reality, as further outlined in the next paragraph, also has an effect on human esthetic sense. The study of neuroaesthetics is concerned with the understanding of the neural substrate of esthetic experience, preference and judgment (Cela-Conde, Agnati, Huston, Mora and Nadal, 2011; Chatterjee and Vartanian, 2014; Skov and Vartanian, 2009; Zeki, 1999). Studying the esthetic development in relation to digital technologies with an emphasis on visualization can be expected to become increasingly important. Not least, it is one aspect that humans will continue to have largely under control and it will shape the ways in which workplaces are viewed and further developed. Enhancing students' sense of esthetics can be expected to have an impact on their creativity as well. When introducing the possibility of working with visualizations of workplace practice students not only develop and work with tools for reflection; they also create and re-create through the art of producing images what workplace practice means to them. The ways in which visuals support teaching and learning while also encouraging students to be creative is further elaborated in the next section.

## How Visuals Transform Teaching and Learning

A visual display in education – sometimes referred to as "instructional visual display" or simply as "visuals" – is any visual or graphic representation of information intended for communication with a learner – and used to convey a set of relationship (Schraw, McCrudden and Robinson, 2013; Mayer, 2013; Schraw and Paik, 2013). According to Schraw et al. (2013), the main reason for including a visual display in an instructional message is "to increase cognitive efficiency by reducing information processing load, distributing the load over multiple channels, and to highlight salient information" (Schraw et al., 2013, p. 4; see also Hoffman and Schraw, 2010). Visuals can be an effective means of transforming teaching and learning, both in their static and dynamic form.

Research results to be introduced here show that mobile learning and video-based technologies can constitute interesting opportunities to unleash creativity in VET. The combination of the use of such tools allows the learners to take on a primary role as authors. The teacher, acting as an orchestrator (Dillenbourg, Nussbaum, Dimitriadis and Roschelle, 2012), can exploit at school the use of pictures or videos provided by the students and engage them in a reflexive conversation about the representations of their experience. In this section we will first introduce the context of VET/PET in Switzerland and then two cases of individual and collaborative creative use of visuals to support teaching-and-learning.

## The Swiss Vocational System

The particular context in which the application of visuals has been researched is VET in Switzerland. The VET system – including about 230 occupations and corresponding curricula – is the choice that two out of three teenagers follow at the secondary level (State Secretariat for Education Research and Innovation [SERI], 2016; Strahm, Geiger, Oertle and Swars, 2016). The system is organized across three different learning locations, similarly to what happens in other European "dual systems" – it is the case, for example, in Germany (Deissinger, Heine and Ott, 2011), Austria (Lassnigg, 2011) and Denmark (Juul and Jørgensen, 2011). Apprentices sign an apprenticeship contract with a training company, where an in-company trainer takes care of their professional skills acquisition and where they work – depending on the curriculum – 3–4 days per week. This work-based track is alternated with a school-based track in the rest of the week (1–2 days).The apprentices follow courses in a vocational school, attending both LCS (Language, Communication and Society) lectures and job-related theoretical subjects (Professional Knowledge lectures). Since 2002, when the Swiss law on VET came into force, a third learning place constitutes the peculiarity of the Swiss system: the so-called branch courses, often organized directly by corporate associations in specific training centers and lasting approximately 15 days per semester.

This additional training segment includes both theoretical and practical aspects and is intended to "complement the work-based and school-based segments" (Swiss Confederation VPETA, art. 16, par. C) aiming to allow apprentices to exercise the fundamental, essential and employer-specific competences and skills of the profession. We can say that each learning location has a complementary role concerning the development of apprentices' professional knowledge: in the training company apprentices are mainly confronted with concrete situations and implicit knowledge; at school, they are exposed to disciplinary explicit knowledge; at the intercompany courses they can pass directly from one epistemological function to the other, connecting and mediating explicit and implicit learning (Landwehr, 2002).

Against this background, it is not always easy for apprentices to connect experiences happening across learning locations, which is one major challenge for any learner today (Ludvigsen, Lund, Rasmussen and Säljö, 2011) and especially for VET students. The cooperation among the three VET learning locations (also known in German as "Lernortkooperation," Euler, 2004) can be enhanced by a specific use of technologies (Schwendimann et al., 2015). The Swiss Federal Institute for Vocational Education and Training (SFIVET), the Swiss expert organization in charge of qualifying VET practitioners, providing VET research, and developing careers and vocational curricula, contributed as main partner[2] to the development and assessment of research programs seeking to understand how technologies can become useful means to promote an effective *Lernortkooperation.*

## Using Mobile Learning with Apprentice Chefs

Connecting learning experiences happening in different locations is also one of the main benefits offered by mobile learning. Although, a precise, generally agreed definition of mobile learning is still being debated, we can start from the assumption that m-learning is "learning across multiple contexts, through social and content interactions, using personal electronic devices." (Crompton, 2013, p. 4). Such a definition highlights at least two important components of m-learning that are relevant for our discourse: the technological and the human components.

Advantages of m-learning have been repeatedly underlined along time as the distinctive trait of this approach (Lai, Yang, Chen, Ho and Chan, 2007; Pachler, Bachmair and Cook, 2010; Pea and Maldonado, 2006; Sharples, 2000; Song, 2011; Wright and Parchoma, 2011). They include – inter alia – availability beyond time and space, portability, computing power, ease-of-use, accessibility, multimedia convergence, connectivity, social interactivity, and more. We could summarize these affordances by saying that whenever and wherever needed, users can rapidly access mobile interfaces for note- and photo-taking and sound- and video-recording. However, scholars agree nowadays that m-learning is not just including the mobile device; rather, m-learning works best when a combination of mobile devices and desktop or cloud solutions is available (Parsons, 2011). The resulting "learning hub" (Wong, 2012) will constitute a technological solution easily supporting cross-boundary learning.

On the other side, the human component is fundamental to catch the real nature of mobile learning: "Learners are continually on the move. We learn across space, [...] across time, [...] we move from topic to topic, [...] in and out of engagement with technology" (Sharples, Taylor and Vavoula, 2007, p. 222). Exploiting the above-mentioned features of technology, learners can thus connect formal and informal occasions of learning, school and workplace contexts, theory and practice, and create authentic "seamless learning" experiences across locations (Pachler, 2009; Wong, 2012). Even more, working on their own experiences or bringing their own experiences in a digitalized form from one context to the other (e.g., through the use of pictures), learners have the chance to actively engage – both individually and collaboratively – in meaning-making processes.

Such "user-generated contexts" (Cook, 2007; Cook, Pachler and Bachmair, 2011) emphasize mainly the role learners take, and the fact that learners' creativity, collaboration and communication is much more important than simply delivery of information (Kukulska-Hulme, Sharples, Milrad, Arnedillo-Sànchez and Vavoula, 2011). To such extent, scholars have repeatedly underlined that an inspired use of mobile devices can really empower creativity within mobile learning experiences (e.g., Buchem, Jahnke and Pachler, 2013; Stevenson, Hedberg, Highfield and Mingming, 2015), allowing students to create their own content as well as to share it. For example, Petersen, Procter-Legg, and Cacchione (2013) showed how mobile devices can foster language learning via three different creative perspectives, emerging respectively from the situated context, collaborative construction of content and original use of language. Similarly, Ranieri and Bruni (2013) show how mobile devices easily allow learners to create digital artifacts that serve as cultural resources used for meaning making and transformation. On the other side, authors like Jahnke (2013) and Master (2013) emphasize the important role of well-designed and innovative teaching scenarios and strategies able to facilitate creative learning.

Based on this framework, and also considering that for an effective mobile pedagogy guidance and support are needed within specifically designed learning activities (Passey, 2010), apprentice chefs were given the opportunity to use their smartphones in order to collect traces of workplace experiences through pictures, short movies or audio-notes.

These traces serve a multi-faceted function:

- Apprentices can use them to build their own recipe book; this has to be presented to the final exams and can also be used in certain assessments as a documentation tool.
- In-company trainers can use them to discuss with apprentices their professional development, including skills still to be trained and better mastered.
- Professional knowledge teachers can use them in class to link theoretical knowledge with practice experience, to promote comparisons on how the same procedure takes place in qualitatively different workplaces (e.g., a canteen, a high-ranked restaurant, a cafeteria,…), to train professional vision, and more.

Through a specific application, the collected traces can be sent to a web-based environment. Here, each apprentice has his/her own profile and can develop his/her book of recipes. Each recipe also contains a reflective section, where apprentices can analyze their own practice thanks to specific prompts, as well as receive their supervisor's feedback and assessment. In fact, the environment is also accessible to other stakeholders, configuring itself as a boundary object (Akkerman and Bakker, 2011; Star, 1989): while supervisors can see their apprentices' documentation, the teacher can access the pages of all of their students.

From the beginning, the implementation has been monitored, taking into consideration the three main dimensions on which m-learning evaluation can be done (Sharples, 2009): usability, satisfaction and effectiveness. Usability was not a concern for all the involved users, and in particular for apprentices, the number of whose recipes constantly increased over time (Motta, Cattaneo and Gurtner, 2014). Satisfaction also scored high: apprentices perceived the system as useful for both learning and professional practice, and, which is almost more important, even for improving and fostering the connection between work-based and school-based activities. Such an impression was also shared by the other stakeholders who took part in the experience. Research also showed that the tool is effective due to the declarative learning acquisition taking place.

Additionally, students' familiarity with reflective prompts revealed significant improvement in their metacognitive skills in comparison with the control group. Finally, their professional practice benefitted, as shown by a study where they prepared a real recipe (Cattaneo, Motta and Gurtner, 2015; also see Mauroux et al., 2016; Mauroux, Könings, Dehler Zufferey and Gurtner, 2014 for a similar experience with bakers).

Conclusively, the study indicated that apprentices profit from mobile learning by adopting a creative and generative role with respect to the content of the curriculum. They chose autonomously which kind of recipes to cook and to report on, and depending on the openness of their workplace culture, they could also freely experiment with variations of given recipes. In class, they also collaboratively created original and innovative learning materials based on their productions. In this way apprentices became the protagonists within their school lectures, in which their authentic workplace experience enabled realistic insights into their learning processes. The teacher was able to build classroom instruction around these visuals and provide a more interactive and authentic learning experience (see also Hämäläinen and Cattaneo, 2015).

## Using Hypervideo to Foster Procedural Learning with Surgery-Room Technicians

Hypervideo (see Sauli, Cattaneo and van der Meij, 2017) is a non-linear video, which: offers differentiated video control and navigation functions (including both the conventional play, pause, stop, rewind/fast forward buttons, plus more complex features like indices or summaries); includes spatially and temporally defined markers that hyperlink to additional material (documents, graphics, Webpages, audio files, etc.); and is provided with specific options enabling interaction, like individual and collaborative video annotation or embedded quiz buttons.

Given these features, hypervideo is a promising instructional tool to overcome some of the well-known limitations in using videos, like the passive attitude of the viewer and the many misuses in classroom settings (Hobbs, 2006). Further, it is a powerful means especially in vocational education, where work processes have to be learned (Höffler and Leutner, 2007) and can be easily shown for the learner to observe and reproduce them (see observational learning and demonstration-based training, Rosen et al., 2010).

From an instructional design point of view hypervideo can support a large variety of instructional approaches (Cattaneo, Nguyen and Aprea, 2016), from the more supplantive and teacher-centered to the more generative and learner-centered ones (Smith and Ragan, 1999). With respect to our interest here, the latter are the most interesting, as they support the learners' creative attitude. According to this, the hypervideo can be conceived within a socio-cognitive perspective as a tool for enculturation and collaboration (Zahn, Krauskopf, Hesse and Pea, 2012;

Zahn, Pea, Hesse and Rosen, 2010), providing the opportunity for people to engage in the discourse, practice and thinking of a community (Lave and Wenger, 1991). Such participation can lead to distributed and shared knowledge (e.g., in knowledge-building communities; Scardamalia and Bereiter, 2006); it can sustain the development of reflective skills, particularly through learning by design tasks where learners have to assume an active role of designers, collaborating and negotiating meaning, finding a way to resolve cognitive conflicts, looking for additional information, and building conceptual convergence toward problem-solving. Collaborative dynamics like these lead to a better understanding of the topic and to more extended creative, social, cognitive and meta-cognitive competences (Stahl, Finke and Zahn, 2006).

This was the case, for example, for a group of perioperative nurse students. Perioperative nurses are trained in specialized professional schools (tertiary level A) and also attend a dual-training curriculum: they practice in hospitals each semester. In addition they profit at school from surgical rooms where professional skills are acquired by simulated procedures in pseudo-real environments. This context became a research environment in which a teacher implemented a learning-by-design activity with hypervideo on a specific surgical operation (adenotonsillectomy).

First, learners received a lecture on the procedure to be performed, focusing on technical terms and using static images and "guidelines" on how to carry out the procedure. Then, they were assigned to four groups of four, each group handling a specific part of the procedure (1. patient positioning, 2. transtympanic paracentesis, 3. instruments for the ear, 4. antisepsis and drainage). The teacher asked them to identify possible questions on the assigned topic. Where possible, learners found answers through comparison and discussion. Unresolved questions were used for subsequent discussion in the classroom. Afterwards, learners created a storyboard to illustrate the different steps that would be followed in order to produce a video (the learners took on the role of actors). One week later the simulation phase in the operating room took place. The procedure was staged and filmed. All learners, who were not actively involved in the simulation, carefully observed and took notes, making sure that the various steps had been properly carried out. These notes were added to the hypervideo. A few days later the edited videos were watched in the class. Comments were added to the videos by the students, highlighting mistakes and drawing attention to key aspects. The discussion on the work processes showcased in the video continued at a distance when the collaborative video-annotation tool was used by the students to insert comments. The results of this reflection process served as the starting point for the final phase, in the classroom, when each group of students built its own hypervideo starting from the raw video it previously produced.

In such a scenario, the students are directly involved in the creative production of the material. This helps them to deepen their understanding of the topic, from the design phase and concrete implementation to subsequent analysis, discussion, and negotiations for decision-making, both within the small group and the whole class. Although, this learning-by-design approach to teaching requires more time in order to be effective, it has shown to be highly beneficial to learners and teachers. It helped the students to develop their ability to select information and materials and to deeply reflect upon what they are doing. Both the students and the teachers were highly satisfied and motivated when working within this setting.

One teacher in the study pointed out:

> People interact and participate actively and with motivation. [...] The result obtained by the learners' activity and production, not tied to the footage but to this kind of teaching method, went really far beyond the expectations! [The students] also used their spare time for this task and they did so gladly because they are active protagonists [...] [The tool] assumed the function to make the students reflect on what was performed, and consequently the multimedia was a great support [...] to use your head, to provide documentary evidence, to deepen, to make plans, to design – all indispensable skills today for one to become a good professional.

In this chapter we reported on two experiences exploiting the opportunities technology offers to promote creative learning within vocational education. Neither mobile learning or interactive videos are the latest technologies. However, their innovative potential is still underexploited in educational contexts. Their intrinsic affordances allow them to easily and effectively contribute to some important challenges in the field, as for example the need to further improve the articulation among learning locations in the case of m-learning, and the need to facilitate the awareness of the links between the theoretical and practical aspects of the same content in the case of interactive videos. Moreover, shifting the teaching-and-learning process toward a more generative instructional strategy (Smith and Ragan, 1999) enables creative action within the school activities. If teachers are open to new technologies these tools can be a valuable enrichment of the didactic tools available to them (Bauer, 1995; Mumtaz, 2000; Rogers, 2003). It further indicates that teachers need to acquire additional sets of pedagogical and instructional skills to apply technologies in a way that makes digital learning an added value in the classroom (OECD, 2015).

## Future Outlook

While technology will increasingly substitute manual work in various workplaces, its design and reflective use in the interest of innovation will be required from the future workforce. Policy has recognized the need for all to learn to work with technologies and prepare for the age of digitalization. If technologies are not further developed and applied in a responsible manner they might not support the improvement of life and work conditions,. In order to be a critical innovator creativity is essential. The development or unleashing of individuals' creative potential might need to become a more prominent task for educators to focus on. Creative development can be connected to technologies in manifold ways. For schools and workplaces to achieve this, theyneed to provide learning experiences with new technologies and also prepare the future workforce to critically develop and shape digital applications to work within the interest of social and environmental sustainability.

For vocational education and training it is highly important that school and workplace learning is intertwined, a connection that can be didactically supported by the implementation of technologies, such as the herewith introduced, tools, interactive videos or hypervideos. These and other technologies will eventually shape learning environments, in which new approaches to teaching or generally new didactical tools are needed. It may be observed that learning with visuals or the visualization of learning takes on an increasingly important role vice versa the learning solely based on text. Videos and technologies that enable the critical work with photos as another representation of reality will become a crucial tool to work with and most certainly support creativity development. In addition it requires teachers taking on the role of coaches and mentors to support students in navigating their learning processes more independently.

Changing perspectives in viewing the world around us can be enhanced just as much as technologies can augment critical reflection. Schools and workplaces will increasingly change, which requires that students and teachers are provided with space for the playful development of ICT literacy as well as visual esthetics among other qualities. They can become proactive shapers of these new developments instead of mainly following up on skills requests by the industry. In countries which are at the forefront of innovation, such as Switzerland, and in which VET is the main educational pathway for the majority, the aspects mentioned above are essential requests for a meaningful and fruitful collaboration of the learning venues workplace and school.

## Notes

1 Despite the evidence provided by neuroscience that digital natives do not exist if the term is intended to mean people whose intensive use of technologies has modified their brain structure, we will use this term as it is commonly understood: young people who are very familiar with the use of technologies such as PC, tablet and smartphones.

2 The partnership includes the EPFL (Federal Technical University of Lausanne), which also coordinates the leading house, the University of Fribourg, and SFIVET. Formerly, the University of Geneva was part of the project.

## References

Akkerman, S. F., & Bakker, A. (2011). Boundary crossing and boundary objects. *Review of Educational Research, 81*(2), 132–169.

Bauer, M. (1995). *Resistance to new technology*. Cambridge, UK: Cambridge University Press.

Beghetto, R. A., & Kaufman, J. C. (2014). Classroom context for creativity. *High Ability Studies, 25*, 53–56.

Bernard, R., Borokhovski, E., Schmid, R., Tamim, R., & Abrami, P. (2014). A meta-analysis of blended learning and technology use in higher education: From the general to the applied. *Journal of Computing in Higher Education, 26*(1), 87–122.

Bower, M. (2016). Deriving a typology of Web 2.0 learning technologies. *British Journal of Educational Technology, 47*(4), 763–777. https://doi.org/10.1111/bjet.12344

Brown, R. T. (1989). Creativity: What are we to measure? In J. A. Glover, R. R. Ronning, & C. R. Reynolds (Eds.), *Handbook of creativity* (pp. 3–32). New York: Plenum Press.

Buchem, I., Jahnke, I., & Pachler, N. (2013). Special issue on mobile learning and creativity: Current concepts and studies. *International Journal of Mobile and Blended Learning, 5*(3), iv–ix.

Bundesinstitut für Berufsbildung. (2016). Förderung von Digitalisierung in überbetrieblichen Berufsbildungsstätten (ÜBS) und Kompetenzzentren. [Supporting digitalization in VET institutions and competence centres.]. Retrieved from: https://www.bibb.de/de/36913.php (5.3.2017)

Cattaneo, A., Motta, E., & Gurtner, J.-L. (2015). Evaluating a mobile and online system for apprentices' learning documentation in vocational education: Usability, effectiveness and satisfaction. *International Journal of Mobile and Blended Learning, 7*(3), 40–58.

Cattaneo, A., Nguyen, A. T., & Aprea, C. (2016). Teaching and learning with hypervideo in vocational education and training. *Journal of Educational Multimedia and Hypermedia, 25*(1), 5–35.

Cela-Conde, C. J., Agnati, L., Huston, J. P., Mora, F., & Nadal, M. (2011). The neural foundations of aesthetic appreciation. *Progress in Neurobiology, 94*, 39–48.

Chatterjee, A., & Vartanian, O. (2014). Neuroaesthetics. *Trends in Cognitive Sciences, 18*, 370–375.

Chauhan, S. (2017). A meta-analysis of the impact of technology on learning effectiveness of elementary students. *Computers and Education, 105*, 14–30. https://doi.org/10.1016/j.compedu.2016.11.005

Cook, J. (2007). Generating new learning contexts: Novel forms of reuse and learning on the move. In C. Montgomerie, & J. Seale (Eds.), *Proceedings of world conference on educational multimedia, hypermedia and telecommunications 2007* (pp. 2766–2779). Chesapeake, VA: Association for the Advancement of Computing in Education (AACE).

Cook, J., Pachler, N., & Bachmair, B. (2011). Ubiquitous mobility with mobile phones: A cultural ecology for mobile learning. *E-Learning and Digital Media, 8*(3), 181–195.

Craft, A., Gardner, H., & Claxton, G. (2008). Nurturing creativity, wisdom, and trusteeship in education – exploring the role of education. In A. Craft, H. Gardner, & G. Claxton (Eds.), *Creativity, wisdom, and trusteeship: Exploring the role of education* (pp. 1–3). Thousand Oaks, CA: Corwin Press.

Crompton, H. (2013). A historical overview of mobile learning: Toward learner-centered education. In Z. L. Berge, & L. Y. Muilenburg (Eds.), *Handbook of mobile learning* (pp. 3–14). Florence, KY: Routledge.

Cropley, A. J. (2001). *Creativity in education and learning. A guide for teachers and educators*. London, UK: Routledge.

Deissinger, T., Heine, R., & Ott, M. (2011). The dominance of apprenticeships in the German VET system and its implications for Europeanisation: A comparative view in the context of the EQF and the European LLL strategy. *Journal of Vocational Education and Training, 63*(3), 397–416.

Dillenbourg, P., Nussbaum, M., Dimitriadis, Y., & Roschelle, J. (2012). Design for classroom orchestration. *Computers and Education*. https://doi.org/10.1016/j.compedu.2012.10.026

Dyer, J., Gregersen, H., & Christensen, C. M. (2011). *The innovators DNA: Mastering the five skills of disruptive innovators*. Boston, MA: Harvard Business Review Press.

Ecoplan. (2017). Berufsbildung2030.ch – Auswertung des Forums Megatrends. Retrieved from: http://berufsbildung2030.ch/wsp/site/assets/files/1/bb2030_ch_ergebnisse-forum-megatrends_170116.pdf

Eidgenössiches Hochschulinstitut für Berufsbildung. (2016). Digitalization study. Retrieved from: http://www.sfivet.swiss/sfivet-and-infras-awarded-contract-digitisation-study

Ericsson, K. A. (2006). The influence of experience and deliberate practice on the development of superior expert performance. In K. A. Ericsson, N. Charness, P. J. Feltovich, & R. R. Hoffman (Eds.), *The Cambridge handbook of expertise and expert performance* (pp. 683–703). New York, NY: Cambridge University Press.

Euler, D. (2004). *Handbuch der Lernortkooperation. Band I: Theoretische Fundierung. [handbook of cooperation between learning places. Volume I: Theoretical foundations.]*. Bielefeld, Germany: Bertelsmann.

Glăveneau, V. P. (2010). Paradigms in the study of creativity: Introducing the perspective of cultural psychology. *New Ideas in Psychology, 28*(1), 79–93.

Grgurović, M., Chapelle, C. A., & Shelley, M. C. (2013). A meta-analysis of effectiveness studies on computer technology-supported language learning. *Journal of Eurocall, 25*(2), 165–198. https://doi.org/10.1017/S0958344013000013

Hämäläinen, R., & Cattaneo, A. (2015). New TEL environments for vocational education – teachers' instructional perspective. *Vocations and Learning, 8*(2), 135–157.

Hattie, J. A. C. (2009). *Visible learning. A synthesis of over 800 meta-analysis relating to achievement*. London, UK and New York, NY: Routledge.

Higgins, S., Xiao, Z., & Katsipataki, M. (2012). *The impact of digital technology on learning: A summary for the education endowment foundation*. Durham, UK: Durham University and Education Endowment Foundation.

Hobbs, R. (2006). Non-optimal uses of video in the classroom. *Learning, Media and Technology, 31*(1), 35–50.

Höffler, T. N., & Leutner, D. (2007). Instructional animation versus static pictures: A meta-analysis. *Learning and Instruction, 17*(6), 722–738.

Hoffman, B., & Schraw, G. (2010). Conceptions of efficiency: Applications in learning and problem solving. *Educational Psychologist, 45*, 1–14.

Jahnke, I. (2013). Teaching practices in ipad-classrooms: Alignment of didactical designs, mobile devices and creativity. *International Journal of Mobile and Blended Learning, 5*(3), 1–16.

Januszewski, A., & Molenda, M. (2008). *Educational technology. A definition with commentary*. New York, NY: Routledge.

Johnson, G. M., & Johnson, J. A. (2006). Computer technology and human learning: Review of recent quantitative syntheses. *Technology, Instruction, Cognition and Learning, 4*(3/4), 287–301.

Juul, I., & Jørgensen, H. (2011). Challenges for the dual system and occupational self-governance in Denmark. *Journal of Vocational Education and Training, 63*(3), 289–303.

Kozbelt, A. (2016). Creativity and culture in visual art. In V. P. Glăveanu, & B. Wagoner (Eds.), *The Palgrave handbook of creativity and culture research* (pp. 573–594). London, UK: Palgrave Macmillan.

Kukulska-Hulme, A., Sharples, M., Milrad, M., Arnedillo-Sànchez, I., & Vavoula, G. (2011). The genesis and development of mobile learning in Europe. In D. Parsons (Ed.), *Combining e-learning and m-learning: New applications of blended educational resources* (pp. 151–177). Hershey, PA: Information Science Reference (an imprint of IGI Global).

Lai, C.-H., Yang, J.-C., Chen, F.-C., Ho, C.-W., & Chan, T.-W. (2007). Affordances of mobile technologies for experiential learning: The interplay of technology and pedagogical practices. *Journal of Computer Assisted Learning, 23*, 326–337.

Landwehr, N. (2002). Der dritte Lernort. [the third learning location.]. In W. Goetze, P. Gonon, A. Gresele, S. Kübler, H. Landolt, R. Marti, et al. (Eds.), *Der dritte Lernort. Bildung für die Praxis, Praxis für die Bildung.* [The third learning location. Education for practice, practice for education] (pp. 37–71). Bern, Switzerland: hep Verlag.

Larwin, K., & Larwin, D. (2011). A meta-analysis examining the impact of computer-assisted instruction on postsecondary statistics education: 40 years of research. *Journal of Research on Technology in Education, 43*(3), 253–278.

Lassnigg, L. (2011). The "duality" of VET in Austria: Institutional competition between school and apprenticeship. *Journal of Vocational Education and Training, 63*(3), 417–438.

Lave, J., & Wenger, E. (1991). *Situated learning. Legitimate peripheral participation.* New York, NY: Cambridge University Press.

Ludvigsen, S., Lund, A., Rasmussen, I., & Säljö, R. (2011). *Learning across sites. New tools, infrastructures and practices.* New York, NY: Routledge.

Masters, J. (2013). Creative teaching and learning strategies for novice users of mobile technologies. *International Journal of Mobile and Blended Learning, 5*(3), 68–79.

Mauroux, L., Dehler Zufferey, J., Rodondi, E., Cattaneo, A., Motta, E., & Gurtner, J.-L. (2016). Writing reflective learning journals: Promoting the use of learning strategies and supporting the development of professional skills. In G. Oroleva, M. Bétrancourt, & S. Billett (Eds.), *Writing for professional development* (pp. 107–128). Leiden, The Netherlands: Brill.

Mauroux, L., Könings, K. D., Dehler Zufferey, J., & Gurtner, J.-L. (2014). Mobile and online learning journal: Effects on apprentices' reflection in vocational education and training. *Vocations and Learning, 7*(2), 215–239.

Mayer, R. E. (2005). *The Cambridge handbook of multimedia learning.* New York, NY: Cambridge University Press.

Mayer, R. E. (2009). *Multimedia learning* (2nd ed.). Cambridge, UK: Cambridge University Press.

Mayer, R. E. (2013). Fostering learning with visual displays. In G. Schraw, M. T. McCrudden, & D. Robinson (Eds.), *Learning Through Visual Displays* (pp. 47–74). Charlotte, NC: Information Age Publishing.

Medina, J. J. (2008). *Brain rules: 12 principles for surviving and thriving at work, home, and school.* Seattle, WA: Wash.

Motta, E., Cattaneo, A., & Gurtner, J.-L. (2014). Mobile devices to bridge the gap in VET: Ease of use and usefulness as indicators for their acceptance. *Journal of Education and Training Studies, 2*(1), 165–179.

Mumtaz, S. (2000). Factors affecting teachers' use of information and communications technology: A review of the literature. *Journal of Information Technology for Teacher Education, 9*(3), 319–342. https://doi.org/10.1080/14759390000200096

Newell, A., Shaw, J., & Simon, H. (1962). The processes of creative thinking. In H. Gruber, G. Terrell, & M. Wertheimer (Eds.), *Contemporary approaches to creative thinking* (pp. 63–119). New York, NY: Atherton.

Organization for Economic Co-operation and Development. (2015). Students, computers and learning: making the connection. *PISA*. Retrieved from: http://dx.doi.org/10.1787/9789264239555-en

Organization for Economic Co-operation and Development.. (2016). Enabling the next production revolution: The future of manufacturing and services-interim report. Retrieved from: http://www.oecd.org/sti/enabling-the-next-production-revolution-implications-for-industry-and-policy.htm

Pachler, N. (2009). Research methods in mobile and informal learning: Some issues. In G. Vavoula, N. Pachler, & A. Kukulska-Hulme (Eds.), *Researching mobile learning. Frameworks, tools and research designs* (pp. 1–15). Bern, Switzerland: Peter Lang.

Pachler, N., Bachmair, B., & Cook, J. (2010). *Mobile learning. Structures, agency, practices.* New York, NY: Springer.

Parsons, D. (2011). *Combining e-learning and m-learning: New applications of blended educational resources.* Hershey, PA: Information Science Reference (an imprint of IGI Global).

Passey, D. (2010). Mobile learning in school contexts: Can teachers alone make it happen? *IEEE Transactions on Learning Technologies, 3*(1), 68–81.

Pea, R., & Maldonado, H. (2006). WILD for learning: Interacting through new computing devices anytime, anywhere. In R. K. Sawyer (Ed.), *The Cambridge handbook of the learning sciences* (pp. 427–441). Cambridge, UK: Cambridge University Press.

Petersen, S. A., Procter-Legg, E., & Cacchione, A. (2013). Creativity and mobile language learning using LingoBee. *International Journal of Mobile and Blended Learning, 5*(3), 34–51.

Pfeiffer, S. (2015). Effects of industry 4.0 on vocational education and training. Retrieved from: http://epub.oeaw.ac.at/ita/ita-manuscript/ita_15_04.pdf

Poincaré, H. (1913). *The foundations of science.* Lancaster, PA: Science Press.

Proctor, T. (1999). *Creative problem solving for managers: Developing skills for decision making and innovation.* London, UK: Routledge.

Purarjomandlangrudi, A., Chen, D., & Nguyen, A. (2015). A systematic review approach to technologies used for larning and education. *International Journal of Learning and Change, 8*(2), 162–177.

Qing, L., & Xin, M. (2010). A Meta-analysis of the effects of computer technology on school students' mathematics learning. *Educational Psychology Review, 22*(3), 215–243.

Ranieri, M., & Bruni, I. (2013). Empowering creativity in young people through mobile learning: An investigation of creative practices of mobile media uses in and out of school. *International Journal of Mobile and Blended Learning, 3,* 17–33.

Rogers, E. M. (2003). *Diffusion of innovations* (5th ed.). New York, NY: Free Press.

Rosen, M. A., Salas, E., Pavlas, D., Jensen, R., Fu, D., & Lampton, D. (2010). Demonstration-based training: A review of instructional features. *Human Factors, 52*(5), 596–609. https://doi.org/10.1177/0018720810381071

Sauli, F., Cattaneo, A., & van der Meij, H. (2017). Hypervideo for educational purposes: A literature review on a multi-faceted technological tool. *Technology, Pedagogy and Education, 27*(2). https://doi.org/10.1080/1475939X.2017.1407357

Scardamalia, M., & Bereiter, C. (2006). Knowledge building: Theory, pedagogy, and technology. In K. Sawyer (Ed.), *Cambridge handbook of the learning sciences* (pp. 97–118). New York, NY: Cambridge University Press.

Schön, D. A. (1987). *Educating the reflective practitioner.* San Francisco, CA: Jossey-Bass Publishers.

Schraw, G., McCrudden, M. T., & Robinson, D. (2013). Visual displays and learning. Theoretical and practical considerations. In G. Schraw, M. T. McCrudden, & D. Robinson (Eds.), *Learning through visual dysplays* (pp. 3–19). Charlotte, NC: Information Age Publishing.

Schraw, G., & Paik, E. (2013). Toward a typology of instructional visual displays. In G. Schraw, M. T. McCrudden, & D. Robinson (Eds.), *Learning through visual dysplays* (pp. 97–129). Charlotte, NC: Information Age Publishing.

Schumann, A., Assenmacher, M., Liecke, M., Reinecke, J., & Sobania, K. (2014). *Wirtschaft 4.0 – Große Chancen, viel zu tun -Das IHK-Unternehmensbarometer zur Digitalisierung. [Economy 4.0 – Big opportunities, a lot to do. The IHK enterprise barometer.].* Berlin, Brüssel: Deutscher Industrie- und Handelskammertag.

Schwendimann, B., Cattaneo, A., Dehler Zufferey, J., Bétrancourt, M., Gurtner, J.-L., & Dillenbourg, P. (2015). The "Erfahrraum": A model for exploiting educational technologies in dual vocational systems. *Journal of Vocational Education and Training, 67*(3), 367–396.

Sharples, M. (2000). The design of personal mobile technologies for lifelong learning. *Computers and Education, 34*(3–4), 177–193.

Sharples, M. (2009). Methods for evaluating mobile learning. In G. Vavoula, N. Pachler, & A. Kukulska-Hulme (Eds.), *Researching mobile learning. Frameworks, tools and research designs* (pp. 17–39). Oxford, UK: Peter Lang Publishing Group.

Sharples, M., Taylor, J., & Vavoula, G. (2007). A theory of learning for the mobile age. In R. Andrews, & C. Haythornthwaite (Eds.), *The SAGE handbook of e-learning research* (pp. 221–247). London, UK: Sage.

Skov, M., & Vartanian, O. (2009). *Neuroaesthetics.* Amityville, NY: Baywood.

Smith, P. L., & Ragan, T. J. (1999). *Instructional design* (2nd ed.). New York, NY: Wiley.

Song, Y. (2011). Investigating undergraduate student mobile device use in context. In A. Kitchenham (Ed.), *Models for interdisciplinary mobile learning: Delivering information to students* (pp. 120–136). Hershey, PA/London, UK: IGI Global.

Spearman, C. (1931). *Creative mind.* New York, NY: Appleton.

Spöttl, G., Gorldt, C, Windelband, L., Grantz, T. and Richter, T. (2016). Industrie 4.0 - Auswirkungen auf Aus- und Weiterbildung in der M+E Industrie. Retrieved from: https://www.baymevbm.de/Redaktion/Frei-zugaengliche-Medien/Abteilungen-GS/Bildung/2016/Downloads/baymevbm_Studie_Industrie-4-0.pdf (04.03.2017)

Stahl, E., Finke, M., & Zahn, C. (2006). Knowledge acquisition by hypervideo design: An instructional program for university courses. *Journal of Educational Multimedia and Hypermedia, 15*(3), 285–302.

Star, S. L. (1989). The structure of ill-structured solutions: Boundary objects and heterogeneous distributed problem solving. In L. Gasser, & M. Huhns (Eds.), *Distributed artificial intelligence* (pp. 37–54). San Mateo, CA: Morgan Kaufmann.

State Secretariat for Education Research and Innovation. (2016). *Vocational and professional education and training in Switzerland. Facts and figures 2016.* Bern, Switzerland: SERI.

Stevenson, M., Hedberg, J., Highfield, K., & Mingming, D. (2015). Visualizing solutions: Apps as cognitive stepping-stones in the learning process. *Electronic Journal of E-Learning, 13*(5), 366–379.

Strahm, R. H., Geiger, B. H., Oertle, C., & Swars, E. (2016). *Vocational and professional education and training in Switzerland. Success factors and challenges for sustainable implementation abroad.* Bern, Switzerland: hep Verlag.

Swiss Confederation (2017). *Rapport sur les principales conditions-cadre pour l'économie numérique.* Bern, Switzerland: Federal Council.

Tamim, R. M., Bernard, R. M., Borokhovski, E., Abrami, P. C., & Schmid, R. F. (2011). What forty years of research says about the impact of technology on learning: A second-order meta-analysis and validation study. *Review of Educational Research, 81*(1), 4–28.

Tanggaard, L. (2008). *Kreativitet skal læres – når talent bliver til innovation. [creativity and learning – When talent turns into innovation.].* Aalborg, Denmark: Aalborg Universitetsforlag.

Tanggaard, L. (2010). *Fornyelsens kunst. At skabe kreativitet I skolen. [the art of change: Creativity in school].* København, Denmark: Akademisk Forlag.

Tanggaard, L. (2016). Creativity with a Danish edge. In V. P. Glăveanu, & B. Wagoner (Eds.), *The Palgrave handbook of creativity and culture research* (pp. 357–390). London, UK: Palgrave Macmillan.

Torrance, E. P. (1965). *Rewarding creative behavior.* Englowood Cliffs, NJ: Prentice-Hall.

Ward, T. B., Smith, S. M., & Vaid, J. (1997). Conceptual structures and processes in creative thought. In T. B. Ward, S. M. Smith, & J. Vaid (Eds.), *Creative thought* (pp. 1–27). Washington, DC: American Psychological Association.

Wertheimer, M. (1945). *Productive thinking.* New York, NY: Harper and Brothers.

Wilbers, K. (2016). Berufsbildung 4.0: Berufsbildung im Zeitalter der grossen Digitalisierung. [vocational education 4.0: Vocational education in the age of grand scale digitalization.]. *Berufsbildung, 70*(159), 7–10.

Wong, L.-H. (2012). A learner-centric view of mobile seamless learning. *British Journal of Educational Technology, 43*(1), E19–E23.

Wright, S., & Parchoma, G. (2011). Technologies for learning? An actor-network theory critique of "affordances" in research on mobile learning. *Research in Learning Technology, 19*(3), 247–258.

Zahn, C., Krauskopf, K., Hesse, F. W., & Pea, R. (2012). How to improve collaborative learning with video tools in the classroom? Social vs. cognitive guidance for student teams. *Computer-Supported Collaborative Learning, 7*(2), 259–284.

Zahn, C., Pea, R., Hesse, F. W., & Rosen, J. (2010). Comparing simple and advanced video tools as supports for complex collaborative design processes. *The Journal of the Learning Sciences, 19*(3), 403–440.

Zeki, S. (1999). *Inner vision: An exploration of art and the brain.* Oxford, UK: Oxford University Press.

# 15

# Professional Development Meets Personal Development

## Impact of a Master's Program on Alumni

*Yvonne Crotty, Margaret Farren, and Laura Kilboy*

*Dublin City University*

Jeannot, Stoll and Chastonay (2013) claim that many program evaluations are limited to the perception of students, whereas extending evaluations to include alumni could be more beneficial as their viewpoints of a program are often based on or shaped by their own professional contexts. A study into the effects of an MEd program on teachers' professional development (Trumper & Eldar, 2014) highlighted how teachers' participation in a program of study influenced their teaching and perceptions, but yet they felt restricted when trying to apply new ideas acquired from the program to their workplace. It is evident that the sustainable impact of educational programs remains under-researched (Zehetmeier, Andreitz, Erlacher, & Rauch, 2015).

Our research study focuses on mature learners on a Master's program who bring with them a wealth of practical knowledge from their own life and work experience (Tiffin & Rajasingham, 2003). We share Tosey and Marshall's (2017) view that it is important to document the value of action-based postgraduate programs especially in light of observations that a number of postgraduate programs in the UK whose pedagogies were characterized by inquiry-based, action-oriented experiential learning, which were thriving 20 years ago, have closed over the past few years.

This research study aims to explore the characteristics of students applying for a Master of Science (MSc) in Education and Training Management (eLearning) at Dublin City University (DCU) and the impact of the program on their professional and personal lives. An online survey was developed and distributed (see Methods) and responses were analyzed using thematic content analysis. A notable finding is that alumni referred to the role that a supportive learning environment played to facilitate growth and transformation. From a professional perspective, alumni felt empowered and equipped to improve their workplace situation.

*The Wiley Handbook of Global Workplace Learning*, First Edition.
Edited by Vanessa Hammler Kenon and Sunay Vasant Palsole.

## Philosophical Underpinnings of the MSc

The MSc is a two-year, part-time program, which was established at DCU in 2002. Participants are drawn from a range of disciplinary and professional backgrounds and work in the widely varying fields of education, industry, health, community, creative arts, NGOs, government departments and state agencies. The program is offered through a blended approach whereby participants benefit from synchronous web conferencing and face-to-face settings. There is an understanding that participants need to develop technical skills within a critically reflective framework if they are to creatively design and use technology to transform educational practice. The MSc is underpinned by an action research approach where practitioners are encouraged to conduct research in their practice with the intent to bring about a change or improvement, aligned with values that are rational and just, and specific to the situation. The philosophical underpinnings of the program emerged from the individual doctoral research studies conducted by Crotty (2012) and Farren (2006) as they clarified the meaning of their educational values in the course of their emergence in practice.

In her doctoral research Crotty (2012) clarifies and explains what it means to have an educational entrepreneurial spirit. This explanation includes acknowledging her values of passion and care, safety, creativity and excellence within her practice. The communication of these values required her to move beyond text-based accounts to include multimedia forms of representation (Eisner, 1997). She emphasizes the importance of creating safe environments to enable meaningful, enjoyable, and creative learning to take place. Farren demonstrates how her values were transformed into living standards of judgment that include a web of betweenness and pedagogy of the unique. The web of betweenness (Farren, 2006; O'Donohue, 2003) draws on ideas of Celtic spirituality to emphasize how we learn in relation to one another and how ICT can enable us to get closer to communicating the meaning of our values in the course of their emergence in practice. Pedagogy of the unique (Farren, 2006) respects the unique constellation of values and standards of judgment that each practitioner-researcher contributes to a knowledge base of practice. Pedagogy of the unique involves systematic processes of action and reflection and inspires thinking toward developing one's own pedagogy.

Since the start of their work in higher education, Farren and Crotty have supported postgraduate students to recognize and examine the values that guide their practice, and in doing so enhance their personal knowledge base for professional practice. In agreement with Barnett's (2000) call for a higher education that embraces knowledge, self-identify and action in its pedagogies (2000, p. 164), program participants are encouraged to take time out of their busy schedule to "stop and think" (Arendt, 1998) and to reflect on action (Schön, 1987). They are guided to enquire into their pedagogical practice, create educational multimedia resources that relate to that practice and reflect on the process. They are given space to explore and articulate their values and provide evidence of how they are living these values in practice. In this way they are taking responsibility for their own personal and professional development. In the words of Carl

Rogers "the only learning which significantly influences behavior is self-discovered, self-appropriated learning" (Rogers, 1969, p. 153).

Teaching on postgraduate degree programs pose a challenge as the students are part-time and may not have been in formal education for some time. While participants entering the MSc may feel competent in their work context, the challenge of returning to study, meeting new people from a range of work backgrounds, researching and writing assignments and entering the academic discourse can prove quite daunting at the start. Crotty's (2012) idea of a safe learning environment is to immediately name the students possible concerns and bring these to the fore in order to alleviate any initial fear. In this way, enthusiasm replaces anxiety; confidence replaces fear; and collaboration replaces reservation. She emphasizes the importance of having a vision for technology rather than focusing on technical skills alone. This led to the development of an entrepreneurial methodology – an Educational Entrepreneurial Approach (EEA) to action research–with its four steps: Exploring, Understanding, Creating and Transforming, which is designed to guide practitioner-researchers as they embrace digital technology to resolve an identified need in a workplace context (Crotty, 2014). Through the course of the MSc participants are actively engaged in carrying out research in their work context or in improving a social situation, using inquiry processes which involve critically reflecting on their learning through the use of online journals, engaging in assessment for learning tasks, experimenting with different forms of multimedia, collaborating with peers in group work, participating in peer validation meetings, and bringing new ideas and innovations into action.

The intention in supporting practitioners to research their own practice is primarily to enable them to grow in self-knowledge by critically reflecting on their own beliefs, values and professional practices, leading to new understandings of themselves and others in ways, which they experience as transformative. We agree with Steier (1991, p. 180) that with the observer situated within his or her research enquiry, there is the making of a reflexive methodology for research. Thus, theory is seen as situated in practice, explaining and energizing human exchanges in transforming social contexts (Farren, 2006; Farren & Crotty, 2014).

## Critical Reflective Practice and Action Research

Our approach to designing a continuing education program such as the MSc is influenced by ideas, over time, that have become key in the learning of professionals about changing and evaluating their practice. Some key terms include reflection (Dewey, 1933), reflective practitioner (Schön, 1987); community of practice (Lave & Wenger, 1991).

The philosopher John Dewey understood reflection as an "active, persistent, and careful consideration of any belief or supposed form of knowledge in light of the grounds supporting it and future conclusions to which it tends" (Dewey, 1933, p. 6). He understood that reflective thinking begins when one encounters a problem "an entanglement to be straightened out, something obscure to be cleared up" (Dewey, 1933, p. 6). He believed that before one could engage in reflection certain attitudes were required, these included open-mindedness, responsibility and wholeheartedness. Thus reflection is more than a skill, as it requires the person to have certain characteristics in order to reflect. For Dewey, thinking is an active process that involves constructing hypothesis and testing them out in practice. Dewey led the way for Schön's (1987) idea of reflection in professional practice. For Schön reflection happens when "knowing-in-action," or the knowledge that professionals depend on to carry out their work, spontaneously produces a surprise, which can lead to either "reflection-in-action" or "reflection-on-action." The former occurs immediately during the activity by thinking about possible ways to reshape the activity. The latter occurs following or by interrupting the activity. Both Dewey and Schön considered reflection as researching or experimenting in the field of practice.

Of particular relevance is Brookfield's (1998) suggestion that critically reflective practitioners constantly research their assumptions by seeing practice through four complementary lenses: 1) autobiographical, 2) the students'/ learners' eyes, 3) our colleagues' experiences, and 4) theoretical, philosophical and research literature.

Brookfield proposes that as well as reflecting on our own personal beliefs, we reflect through the lens of others, in order to bring in different perspectives including theory. The essential collaboration with others implied by Brookfield demands a professional practice that involves a continuous communication with fellow practitioners: a community of practice (Lave & Wenger, 1991).

Brookfield's Lens 1, the autobiographical lens, prompts us as educators to reflect back on our experience as a student/ learner as an important source of insight. In this way, we "become aware of the paradigmatic assumptions and instinctive reasonings that frame how we work" (Brookfield, 1995, p. 30). In applying lens 2, our students' eyes, we see ourselves through our learners' eyes in order to discover if the students are interpreting our actions in the way that is intended. For Brookfield the student lens reveals "those actions and assumptions that either confirms or challenge existing power relationships in the classroom." Lens 3 refers to our colleagues' experiences. Talking to colleagues about concerns and issues in our practice and gaining their perspective can provide useful insights. Further to the individual personal reflection, the sharing of individual narratives creates a sense of community. Through lens 4, an engagement with scholarly literature can help us to describe and understand the context of our practice and "the link between our private troubles and broader political processes" (1995, pp. 37–38).

Critical reflection therefore enables practitioners to enquire into their own practice in a systematic and scholarly way. Jarvis (1992), p. 180) claims that engaging in critical reflection enables practitioners to "continue to learn, grow and develop in and through practice." In the messy field of practice or the "swampy lowlands" (Schön, 1995) it is difficult to predict outcomes. Schön argued against the dominant model of technical rationality that is built into the modern university and proposed a new scholarship which he termed an epistemology of practice (1995). He suggested that this new scholarship would take the form of action research.

McTaggart's (1996) rightly points out that action research is not a "procedure" for research but is a series of commitments to observe and problematize through practice a series of principles for conducting social enquiry, it is also a departure from unengaged research as an inquiry path (Farren, 2006). The word "action" means that it is an approach that always involves participants making or implementing change, rather than just investigating an issue, and the word "research" is about making informed decisions about what and how participants are going to bring about change (Piggot-Irvine, 2006). The Educational Entrepreneurial Approach (EEA) to action research (Crotty, 2014) is a creative approach that engages students in the design and creation of an educational multimedia resource (for example, video, online educational resources) to bring about change.

## Methods

The MSc was evaluated using a mixture of closed and open-ended questions in the form of an online survey administered via Google forms. Open-ended questions were mostly used to gather data on the participants' perspectives, feelings and experiences. Close attention was paid to language used in the responses and emerging patterns and meanings of human experience were thus analyzed (Saldana, 2015). Analysis was carried out using thematic content analysis. Quotations from data collected are used in this report to illustrate key themes.

The survey was carried out in 2013. It was sent to past graduates of the MSc, since the program's inception in 2003. Participants of the course in 2013–2015 were excluded from the survey, as they had not completed the program. Therefore 157 surveys were sent online to past participants from 2003 to 2014, of which 105 responses were received, a 67% response rate. Data was gathered over a four-week period.

The purpose of the survey was to examine the characteristics of program graduates and their reasons for participating in the program. A further significant aim of the survey was to determine and subsequently analyze if and how the program may have impacted participants' personal or professional lives. A coding procedure was applied to the qualitative data gathered.

To correctly analyze qualitative responses, it was necessary to apply a correct coding procedure to the data gathered. Each response from the online survey results was read in detail. This followed an inductive, exploratory reasoning approach to the data gathered. Brief periods away from the data allowed time to reflect on the analysis to date and identify patterns emerging from the data. Open-ended questions were thus analyzed per question so that patterns could be identified accordingly. This technique follows an "immersion–crystallization" approach, which is an approach similar to the one used by Holmes, Zayas and Koyfman (2012).

Thematic analysis in qualitative research involves examining themes within the data. Due to the open-ended nature of questions used in this particular study, a large part of the data gathered focused on the human experience, perceptions and feelings with regard to participation on the program. Participants were asked to explain their thoughts on the program's impact on their personal and professional life. With respect to the professional impact of the program, participants were asked if they were able to bring about change in their organization and if so whether the MSc enabled this. The purpose of such questions was to determine if participants were able to apply the skills and knowledge from the course to the workplace.

## Findings and Discussion

Among the respondents 40% were male, 60% female. The majority of respondents (45%) were between 25 and 34 years of age at start of their participation on the program. 34% had between five and ten years' experience in their profession at the time of commencing the program, 31% had more than ten years' experience. At the time of beginning the program, respondents worked in a variety of contexts including:

- post-primary education (25%)
- primary education (14%)
- industry (9%)
- higher education (8%)
- further education (6%)
- adult education (7%)
- health (7%)
- state agency (5%)
- creative arts (5%)
- others such as voluntary sector, government organization, banking, Teaching English as a Foreign Language and community development

This variety of professional contexts was deemed useful to 94% of respondents' learning experience. Benefits included more interesting discussions, sharing of perspectives, skills and experiences, and exposure to fields outside one's everyday work context. A participant responded that "The mix of professionals helped me to step outside my own context. It is too easy to become defined by your personal day- to-day experience. In order to understand how things can change and improve within your own context, it was important to be exposed to experiences of others." Since completing the program, 66% of respondents have changed jobs. Expectations about the program had been fulfilled or surpassed: 95% confirmed that the program had met their expectations, the other 5% indicated that the "no" in this response was not negative in the sense that they had not expected the level of creativity and enjoyment unleashed during program:

> My answer of "no," in question 12 isn't a negative answer at all – there were a number of outcomes from the course that I really wasn't expecting! I wasn't expecting the course to have such a creative element to it. This was an unexpected and extremely welcome surprise. In that respect it surpassed my expectations. I also wasn't expecting to find myself so emotionally invested in my participation in the course. Identifying our values and the reason why we held those values forced me to face up to issues that I never knew I had!

Ninety-six percent of respondents acknowledged that the program enabled them to develop on a personal level. The majority reported an increase in confidence and self-belief.

Qualitative data from the survey responses offered a more in-depth and descriptive evaluation of their program experience. Five key themes emerged characterizing participants' reasons for applying to the program: 1) career development; 2) to obtain a formal qualification; 3) the further understanding of education and technology; 4) to upskill; and 5) personal development. These themes are elaborated on under "Reasons for Applying." The key findings regarding the impact of the program are summarized under "Professional Impact." Three findings significant to professional impact were identified: career development; application of skills; and confidence. With regard to the personal impact of the program, the themes identified were: increased confidence; increase in awareness through reflection and role of values. These findings are summarized under "Personal Impact."

## Reasons for Applying

The survey participants' reasons for applying for the program were categorized under five specific themes. Therefore, specific quotes are referenced to enable the reader to comprehend the reasons. The key thematic reason, which emerged is (1) career development. Participants wished to progress in their career. For example, a comment included, "I also wanted to undertake some professional development in an area that was of interest to me. I felt, at the time, that a master's would improve my chances of promotion within the school," as well as open up opportunities for change of career in the future "I also thought it would give me an option down the line if I wanted to get out of the classroom." A second reason for applying for the program was (2) to obtain a formal qualification. One participant said "I always wanted to attain a Masters Degree in education." Another thematic reason that emerged was: (3) THE further understanding of education and technology. While the program content appealed to many participants, their desire to enhance their understanding of learning and technology emerged, as a participant explained: "I wanted to focus on learning about how I teach and the theoretical background to teaching and learning." A fourth reason was (4) to upskill. Participants viewed the program as an opportunity to gain new skills to enhance their workplace: "I was interested in developing my technological skills to improve my skillset for the education sector in the 21st century." The final reason was (5) personal development. For example, participants expressed aspirations to achieve personal goals and challenge themselves: "I am passionate about lifelong learning and wanted to prove to myself I could rise to the challenge of studying on a Masters programme in my 40's."A common theme among reasons for applying for the program was the desire for career progression. A number of respondents stated that by acquiring a level nine qualification (Master's degree), they hoped it would open up more career opportunities in the future, for example, "Personal fulfilment and to increase my chances of acquiring a leadership role in my school."

## Professional Impact

The second part of the survey aimed to assess and evaluate the professional impact of the program. Ninety percent of alumni confirmed that the program had an impact on their professional role. Areas of the program which have proven useful in their careers include the e-learning component whereby participants are exposed to and utilize collaborative online environments, multimedia and the creation of online learning resources. The understanding and analysis of theory, such as management, pedagogy, learning styles and instructional design, was also considered to be significant, as respondents stated that they apply such theories in their current work contexts. The reflective framework of the program was mentioned as highly valuable, as participants stated how they are more conscious of improving their practice and the role of reflection in this process.

## Career Development

Sixty six percent of respondents have changed jobs since completing the program. The remaining 34%, while remaining in a similar role or position, highlighted extra responsibilities and involvement in workplace projects since completing the MSc:

> In an official sense my job in school is still the same ... So, while my job is officially unchanged it has unofficially changed in many ways. I run the student council, I co-created and now run the school website and I am the Erasmus+ coordinator in the school... Certainly my role in running the school website is a direct result of my participation in the eLearning MSc.

However, the most outstanding pattern that emerged from this category was that of career progression as a direct result of obtaining the qualification. This is evident in the sample of answers taken from the online survey related to the question "Has the MSc had an impact on your professional role?"

> I was offered a new post within my hospital based on my achievements as CPD [Continuing Professional Development] Officer. I attribute a large part of my success as CPD Officer to the Masters programme.
>
> I now work in education, specifically involving eLearning and Multimedia. This is as a direct result of completing the Masters. It opened my eyes to other possibilities and directions for me to go in my career.

As part of career progression, participants attributed work promotions to the MSc:

> Completing the MSc programme gave me a key advantage in comparison with other candidates when applying for various promotions within my organization.

Another participant stated:

> I have changed employers and am now employed at a more senior level with the new company.

## Application of Skills

Alumni also stated that they are practically applying various skills developed on the program to their place of work. This includes digital, reflective and research skills; all of which are enhancing the workplace:

> I have used the skills I learned from the programme in my own classrooms. I have increased the use of video in the classroom to supplement other tools I use such as PowerPoint presentations, discussions, research etc.
>
> I now develop any e-learning that I require myself, instead of having to hand over to a vendor or other team member. I'm also more willing to try new technologies-the "fear factor" was greatly reduced by my participation on this programme.

These responses highlight the application in the workplace of skills acquired on the program. There is evidence that participants are actively creating multimedia resources to improve the learning environment in their workplace, as well as enhancing workplace communication through better understanding of co-workers.

## Confidence

Another theme identified included increase in confidence as participants describe their increased ability to work effectively and contribute to workplace discussions and policy making:

> I am now working in an area that I love and am passionate about. The masters helped me realise what my passions were. It has also given me the confidence to pursue other interests professionally.
>
> The programme gave me more confidence to engage with my colleagues in relation to the required changes in our practice. The programme provided me with a lot of ideas and changed the way that I reflect on my own practice.

It is clear from the survey that the skills, knowledge and successes as a result of their participation on the MSc have impacted positively on alumni's professional lives. However, one respondent noted that they have been unable to utilize skills acquired on the program to impact the workplace due to external factors such as current education system restrictions.

## Personal Impact

Dadds (2014) asserts that it is important to acknowledge how personal growth is embedded in professional development and the complex relationship between knowledge and agency. Ninety-six percent of respondents said that the program has enabled them to develop on a personal level. Three significant themes related to personal development were identified: increased confidence, increased awareness through reflection and role of values.

### Increased Confidence

The most prominent theme emerging from the personal impact of the program was the sense of confidence and self-belief. Participants described their confidence in newly acquired skills and the transformative effect on their own attitudes:

> I feel more confident in the job I do today. I am also not afraid to make a mistake, which before the programme, this was something I dreaded.
>
> It was a life changing experience for me. It reawakened my creative abilities and helped me to believe in myself and become a more confident person.

There was a sense that participants were challenged to move beyond their comfort zone with a view to tap into their potential or otherwise hidden talents:

> The personal development and growth that happens during the programme is very powerful. The fact that it ignites new interests is brilliant. Forcing yourself to do something outside your comfort zone, while scary and risky, is ultimately exhilarating.
>
> I have gained considerable confidence and discovered that I have a considerable skill set that was previously untapped. I have learned my value in the workplace.
>
> It also has given me confidence in my opinions and in my ability to take on new challenges, move outside my comfort zone and succeed.

### Increased Awareness through Reflection

An important finding of the study highlights the level of self-reflection and understanding as a consequence of the reflective framework underpinning the program. Eighty-four percent of respondents agreed that the process of reflective journaling was beneficial for them. Seventy-seven percent said that they had no prior experience of reflective journaling prior to participating on the program. Respondents noted that they were challenged to think critically about past events:

> Again I think the course has helped me to be more reflective and taught me to think through why things have happened – in the past I may have been dismissive of events. My mindset is definitely one of growth and seeing the opportunity even in things that are difficult to deal with.

They developed an appreciation of their own knowledge and experiences and thereby have come to acknowledge the role that they play in their own learning process:

> I'm more self-reflective and have more trust in my own personal experience and value it rather than accepting other peoples' experiences as the norm.

This demonstrates the level of personal learning and self-awareness that emerged from participation. Participants have experienced changes in their mindsets, which have made them more reflective in their endeavors and have thus contributed to their personal growth.

There is further evidence to suggest that the MSc journey is one of growth and discovery, a good example is given at the end of the section "The Contribution of the Program to Personal Development."

### The Role of Values

A further pertinent theme is the role of values, as alumni referred to how they were challenged to critically think about their values.

> Being challenged to identify and name your values was a very thought-provoking exercise. It brought up a huge amount of unexpected emotions for me when I began to explore why I held the values I did. This was ultimately very beneficial to me personally.
>
> The values based aspect of the dissertation was quite personal and challenged me to consider these in both my professional and personal life and has led to a greater understanding of their role. I think the reflective aspect too is something that I have maintained.

All alumni who participated in this study stated how they changed, either personally or professionally, due to their participation in the program. From a professional perspective, they felt empowered and equipped to improve their workplace situations. From a personal perspective, they described the role that a supportive learning environment played in facilitating growth and transformation.

## The Contribution of the MSc

A central part of the program is its focus on action research. Tosey and Marshall (2017) warn that, "an increasing conformity to mainstream research and knowledge can result in a discounting of the legitimacy of certain types of research (e.g., action research) as well as types of knowledge (e.g., emergent, practical knowledge)" (p. 400). The findings from this study highlight the professional growth of participants as to skills gained and workplace competencies developed, it is also important to consider the changes, if any, that were brought to their workplace as a result.

Sixty-seven percent of respondents described how their participation in the program enabled them to bring about change in their workplace and improve their practice. These changes varied from the introduction of new projects to enhance learning to becoming leaders of change by contributing knowledge to ICT [information and Communications Technology] and workplace policies.

As an example, one respondent told how they introduced a challenging program in a primary school. "Since the program, I have started a High Achieving maths programme for senior students as well as the introduction of iPads. These two major changes are due to experiences and new learning I gained directly from my time in the programme." A number of responses also point to the championing role that alumnus have played in introducing online learning courses and professional development programs in their workplace, for example, "It has prompted me to set up a professional development programme in the school aimed at introducing teachers to different methods of teaching," as well as integrating the use of technology and online learning environments into the workplace. Another alumni referred to the "hugely increased web presence and use of e-learning tools organization-wide." And another, "I have introduced Moodle to my new organization also and is still running to this day." It is also important to note their confidence in contributing to policies and ICT planning in their workplace as a direct result of their experience on the program, "I have been involved in our schools ICT planning and development since embarking on the Masters. I do feel it has helped me bring about change because I felt empowered after the Masters to share my knowledge of the role ICT has in schools, not as a stand-alone subject but rather how it can aid the teaching of various subjects."

Although the evidence so far shows the increased confidence and personal growth of alumni, it is also fairly important to analyze the learning environment, which facilitated this process, as quoted in the survey. Noteworthy from the responses was the acknowledgement of the safe and supportive learning environment that was fostered on the program, which enabled participants to take risks and gain self-belief through their endeavors.

## Conclusion

The online survey results provided insights into the reasons that professionals choose to pursue a continuing education program such as the MSc. It showsthe level of professional and personal growth, which alumni gained through their engagement with program content and their application of skills and learning to changing or improving their own workplace situation. Alumni noted that they were challenged to think critically about past events, and they highlighted the level of personal learning and self-awareness as a result of participating in the program. They stated that they experienced changes in their mindsets, which have made them more reflective in their endeavors and contributed to their personal growth. The reflective framework and action research approach was highlighted, as alumni declared that they are more conscious of improving their practice and the role of reflection in the process.

The findings indicate that the learning on the program enabled participants to effect change in their organization; contrary to Trumper and Eldar's (2014) study, participants in the MSc course were able to apply new ideas acquired to their workplace. Findings indicate that learning on the MSc course is not isolated or removed from sociocultural contexts – quite the opposite. It is evident that the skills and understanding that the inquiry-based pedagogies promoted are needed more than ever in an increasingly complex, unpredictable, and fractious world characterized by 'wicked' problems (Tosey and Marshall, 2017).

## References

Arendt, H. (1998). *The human condition* (2nd ed.). Chicago: University of Chicago Press.

Barnett, R. (2000). *Realizing the university: In an age of supercomplexity*. Stony Stanton, UK: Open University Press.

Brookfield, S. (1995). *Becoming a critically reflective teacher*. San Francisco: Jossey-Bass.

Brookfield, S. (1998). Critically reflective practice. *Journal of Continuing Education in the Health Professions, 18*(4), 197–205. https://doi.org/10.1002/chp.1340180402

Crotty, Y. (2012). *How am I bringing an educationally entrepreneurial spirit into higher education?* PhD thesis, Dublin City University, Ireland. Retrieved from http://doras.dcu.ie/17540

Crotty, Y. (2014). Promoting a creative educational entrepreneurial approach in higher education. *International Journal for Transformative Research, 1*(1), 75–100.

Dadds, M. (2014). Continuing professional development: Nurturing the expert within. *Professional Development in Education, 40*(1), 9–16. https://doi.org/10.1080/19415257.2013.871107

Dewey, J. (1933). *How we think. A restatement of the relation of reflective thinking to the educative process* (Revised edn.). Boston, MA: D.G. Heath.

Eisner, E. (1997). The promise and perils of alternative forms of data representation. *Educational Researcher, 26*(6), 4–10.

Farren, M. (2006). How am I creating a pedagogy of the unique through a web of betweenness? PhD thesis, University of Bath, UK. Retrieved from http://www.actionresearch.net/living/farren.shtml

Farren, M., & Crotty, Y. (2014). Researching our own practice: An individual creative process and a dialogic-collaborative process. *International Journal for Transformative Research, 1*(1), 63–74. https://doi.org/10.2478/ijtr-2014-0004

Holmes, D., Zayas, L. E., & Koyfman, A. (2012). Student objectives and learning experiences in a global health elective. *Journal of Community Health, 37*(5), 927–934. https://doi.org/10.1007/s10900-012-9547-y

Jarvis, P. (1992). Reflective practice and nursing. *Nurse Education Today, 12*(3), 174–181.

Jeannot, E., Stoll, B., & Chastonay, P. (2013). Alumni evaluation of a community-oriented master of public health program. *Journal of Community Health, 38*(2), 357–359. https://doi.org/10.1007/s10900-012-9624-2

Lave, J., & Wenger, E. (1991). *Situated learning: Legitimate peripheral participation* ()Learning in Doing: Social, Cognitive and Computational Perspectives. Cambridge, UK: Cambridge University Press.

McTaggart, R. (1996). Issues for participatory action researchers. In O. Zuber-Skerritt (Ed.), *New directions in action research* (pp. 243–255). London, UK: Falmer Press.

O'Donohue, J. (2003). *Divine beauty: The invisible embrace*. London, UK: Transworld.

Piggot-Irvine, E. (2006). Sustaining excellence in experienced principals? Critique of a professional learning community approach. *International Electronic Journal for Leadership Learning, 10*(16), 1–19.

Rogers, C. (1969). *Freedom to learn*. Indianapolis, IN: Merrill.

Saldana, J. (2015). *The coding manual for qualitative researchers* (3rd ed.). Thousand Oaks, CA: Sage.

Schön, D. (1987). *Educating the reflective practitioner. Towards a new design for teaching and learning in the professions*. San Francisco, CA: Jossey-Bass.

Schön, D. (1995). Knowing in action: The New Scholarship requires a New Epistemology'. Change, November/December, 27–34. doi: 10.1080/00091383.1995.10544673.

Steier, F. (1991). Reflexivity and methodology: An ecological constructionism. In F. Steier (Ed.), *Research and reflexivity* (pp. 163–185). Thousand Oaks, CA: Sage.

Tiffin, J., & Rajasingham, L. (2003). *The global virtual university*. London, UK: RoutledgeFalmer.

Tosey, P., & Marshall, J. (2017). The demise of inquiry-based HRD programs in the UK: Implications for the field. *Human Resource Development International*, *20*(5), 393–402. https://doi.org/10.1080/13678868.2017.1329368

Trumper, R., & Eldar, O. (2014). The effect of an MEd program in science education on teachers' professional development: An Israeli case study. *Journal of Professional Development in Education*, *41*(5), 826–848. https://doi.org/10.1080/19415257.2014.958244

Zehetmeier, S., Andreitz, I., Erlacher, W., & Rauch, F. (2015). Researching the impact of teacher professional development programs based on action research, constructivism, and systems theory. *Educational Action Research*, *23*(2), 162–177. https://doi.org/10.1080/09650792.2014.997261

# Part III

# Culture and Language

# 16

# Competency in Globalization and Intercultural Communication

*Qin Guo*

*Macquarie University*

Globalization has increased exposures and interactions between different cultures around the world. The increase of intercultural encounters affords both opportunities as well as threats. On the one hand, intercultural exposures and interactions are opportunities for sharing and learning knowledge between different cultures. On the other, without appropriate communication, intercultural differences might cause misunderstanding and provoke conflicts. Intercultural competency is indisputably an imperative capability for optimizing the performance of individuals, as well as businesses, in the globalized society. This chapter focuses on the development of intercultural competency in the global workplace.

Intercultural communication capability lies at the core of intercultural competency. Communication is a process of creating, exchanging, and sharing meaning between participants within the process. Intercultural communication is essential for enhancing understanding and narrowing gaps between cultures. This chapter commences with a theoretical section concerning the conceptualization of intercultural communication. It discusses the definitions of the key concepts of intercultural communication study. This is followed by a discussion of the components of intercultural competency, exploring the strategies of building intercultural competency.

## Key Concepts and Theories of Intercultural Communication

The rapid advancement of information communication technology since the mid-twentieth century and the breakthrough in digital communication and network technology since the twenty-first century has changed the structure of human society, the relations between the systems and individuals within the societies, and the form and scale of human communication. The distinctive feature that separates the current stage of human society from previous ones is

*The Wiley Handbook of Global Workplace Learning*, First Edition.
Edited by Vanessa Hammler Kenon and Sunay Vasant Palsole.

the globalization process powered by digital communication technologies and global information network systems. The current globalization is a combination of the dual processes of convergence and fragmentation. Technically, the networked society is converged. It operates at the global level and links various civilizations around the world. Culturally, however, the global network society is fragmented. The integration of a multiplicity of cultures in a global network system did not create a cosmopolitan melting pot of the citizens of the world. Instead of generating a homogeneous global culture, the global network society holds a multiplicity of cultures. Therefore, the global network society is a society where diverse cultures, linked to fragmented histories and geographies, live and work interdependently in the converged global network. For the global network society to operate effectively and efficiently, the protocols of communication between different cultures is essential. Only communication can make possible the sharing of values, beliefs, and meanings of the diverse cultures. Without effective and efficient communication, the sharing of an interdependent global social structure will lead to systemic misunderstanding and conflicts, which will destruct the democratic foundation of the global network society (Castells, 2009, p. 37).

## Culture

Culture is a core concept in international communication studies because of its important role in communication: it shapes the contents, behaviors, and the process of communication. There are numerous definitions of culture, due to itsprevalence in all aspects of human life and its complex relation with society. Scholars have claimed that over 160 definitions of culture are in common use (Tuleja, 2005, p. 5), but in the context of intercultural communication, culture can be defined as a set of learned and shared values, beliefs, and norms that affect people's behavior (Castells, 2009; Lustig & Koester, 2003). This definition underscores three implications of culture in intercultural communication.

First, people are not born with the imprint of culture; instead, they learn about their cultures through various social interactions and activities. Culture is learned, therefore, a person's cultural association is not static. People's cultural association might change as their socialization experiences change. It is reflected in overt forms that can be seen and heard (e.g., dress, behavior, language, etc.) and covert forms that are less visible (e.g., value, belief etc.). Take myself as an example, I consider myself a Chinese Australian. I was born and grew up in China, and immigrated to Australia in my thirties. During the years of my living and social experiences in China and Australia, I have developed a hybrid cultural association comprising both the Chinese as well the Australian components in both overt and covert ways.

Overtly, for instance, during my childhood in China, I have learned the typical Chinese way of eating—to eat with a pair of chopsticks from a china bowl. In the years living in Australia, I have learned the Australian way of eating—to eat from a plate with a fork in one hand and knife in the other. In less visible forms, I identify my world views and values as a combination of the Chinese and Western systems. For example, on the equity/ hierarchy scale, I consider my tolerance of hierarchical divide as being higher than that of an average Australian, however, lower than a typical Chinese. Culture is dynamic, not only on an individual level, but also on a societal level. The values, beliefs, and norms upheld in a particular society evolve as social interactions and activities proceed within and beyond the society and members and memberships of the society change during these social processes.

Second, culture is shared values, beliefs, and norms. Values, beliefs, and norms form the essential components of patterns of cultures. Values are the desired characteristics of the culture; they define what is right, good, and worthy. Beliefs are the logical interpretations delineating right from wrong, true from false. Norms are the guidelines of appropriate behaviors in a specific culture. The generally shared values, beliefs, and norms of a group of people form its cultural patterns. The interpretation of culture as shared values, beliefs, and norms is twofold. On the one hand, culture represents the values, beliefs, and norms that are commonly approved by the members of the cultural group. Each cultural group has a set of unique cultural patterns, which distinguishes it from other groups. The differences between different cultures' values, beliefs, and norms may be enormous and contradictive.

What is considered as good and appropriate in one culture could be considered as wrong and inappropriate in another culture. For example, as far back as I can remember, I was repeatedly told by my parents and grandparents that the appropriate table manners were holding the rice bowl in the left hand and the chopsticks in the right hand. When eating, lift the rice bowl to the level of the mouth, and send the food from the bowl into the mouth with the chopsticks. It showed, as I was told by the older generations, laziness and therefore was shameful not to hold the rice bowl up when eating. It surprised megreatly when I was told by a colleague of mine that holding up the vessel and eating directly from it was considered rude in her country (The Philippines).

On the other hand, culture being the values, beliefs, and norms shared within the cultural group does not mean everyone belonging to the same cultural group will think and act in the same way. What people approve of is not necessary the same as what people actually act on. As Aristotle argued in his famous work *Rhetoric* more than 2000 years ago, the things people approve of openly are not those they approve of secretly. Openly, people's "chief praise is given to justice and nobleness; but in their hearts they prefer their own advantage" (Aristotle, 2001, p. 1424). Furthermore, some researchers contended that culture is not what people know, think, and feel about the world. Instead, culture is people's theory about what their fellows know, think and mean (Gudykunst & Lee, 2003, p. 8). Therefore, culture can be conceived as a system of subjective knowledge and understanding about what others think, believe, and act.

This system of knowledge and understanding is subjective because it is shaped and constrained by the individual's way of knowing. Cultural studies have revealed systematic variations between cultures as well as within cultures. In other words, within every culture there are individuals who vary from the common cultural patterns (Lustig & Koester, 2003, p. 91). Cultural patterns indicate the perceived standards, logics, and guidelines of what is desired, appropriate, and expected in a cultural group. However, they are not necessarily acted on by everyone of the cultural group all the time.

Third, culture informs and guides people's behavior. Culture not only shapes people's perceptions and attitudes, it also guides people in choosing solutions responding to the problems and making the decision of their actions. Cultural patterns that reflect the shared values, beliefs, and norms are materialized in people's behaviors in social activities. Therefore, culture provides expectations and predictability of human behaviors. In the context of communication, culture embodies a system of symbolic resources to be shared with and a system of communicative rules to be acted on.

While culture is a marker of human society, the interpretations of culture bear the imprint of the society. People's perception of culture is historically, politically, socially, and culturally constrained. In the nineteenth century, culture was constructed in alignment with the historical and political colonization processes. Most of the European anthropologists constructed the concept of culture under the assumption that the European way of life was the norm and the superior of all cultures. Cultures of the "others" (non-Europeans) were perceived as less civilized, or even non-cultural (Sorrells, 2016, p. 4). This discriminative perception of culture had influenced studies in other disciplines. For example, the modernization perspective of development theory shows a similar perception about culture. One of the assumptions on which the modernization perspective of development is based upon is the divide between societies: modern societies and traditional societies. The Western industrialized countries were considered modern societies, while the "diverse societies in the South, with different cultures, geographies, and histories" were considered as traditional and underdeveloped (Melkote & Leslie Steeves, 2001, p. 92).

The modernization perspective of development claims the universality of the Western world view and development experience, and thus conceives development as a modernization process whereby the Western political, economic and cultural models are distributed among the other societies. The Chinese perception of culture shows yet another example of the social, political, and cultural construction of culture's conceptualization. In China, the concept of culture (*wen hua*, 文化) is closely related with education (*jiao yu*, 教育). The term "*wen hua jiao yu*" (文化教育, literally meaning: cultural education) refers to intellectual education. Educated people are referred to as "*you wen huo*" (有文化, literally meaning: have culture), while less-educated people are referred to as "*mei wen huo*" (没文化, literally meaning: have no culture). In China, culture is generally defined as the aggregation of all the material and spiritual treasures that mankind created in the social practical activities throughout the human history (张念宏, 1988, p. 378). Despite the differences in their approaches (e.g., the anthropological approach in nineteenth-century Europe and the educational approach in China), there more or less exists a trend of taking a binary logic in identifying different cultures. Specifically, the binary division of the advanced and superior culture versus the backward or inferior culture (or even non-culture).

Cultural differences can be perceived differently. Many contemporary scholars propose to move away from thinking of culture as something that individuals or groups possess. It was suggested to conceive culture as "a way of referring to dimensions of situated and embodied difference" (Sorrells, 2016, p. 9). From this perspective, cultural differences form part of the global network society. They are to be recognized and appreciated instead of discriminated. Each culture in the world has its roots deep in the historical, geographical and societal contexts, which justifies its existence and value in the global network society. Every culture deserves an equal position in the globalized world. Culture bears the knowledge and wisdom produced by the people who are associated with it over the history of the particular civilization. In the global network society, culture becomes a resource to be shared between all connected societies.

Cultural diversity, therefore, is a precious wealth of mankind. This vision of cultural diversity as the common heritage of mankind to be recognized and affirmed for the benefits of the globalized world is articulated explicitly in the declaration on cultural diversity adopted by the United Nations Educational, Scientific, and Cultural Organization (UNESCO) in 2001. The *UNESCO Universal Declaration on Cultural Diversity* proposed that cultural diversity is embodied in the uniqueness and plurality of the identities of the groups and societies making up humankind. "As a source of exchange, innovation and creativity, cultural diversity is as necessary for humankind as biodiversity is for nature" (United Nations Educational, Scientific, and Cultural Organization [UNESCO], 2002, p. 4).

In the global network society, the traditional geographical boundaries dividing cultures begin to blur. Diverse cultures coexist in both cyberspace and geographical space. How cultures are identified is one of the fundamental questions in international communication studies.

## Identity

How are differences between cultures identified? By what means do we identify people's cultural association? When people meet for the first time, the acquaintance usually begins with exchanging information about "self" and the "others." The information identifies people's belonging to certain social and cultural groups. This information defining people's memberships within and without specific groups, form the identity of people. Identity is a way of knowing and constructing oneself (Guo & Waniganayake, 2016, p. 291) An individual's overall identity is built on his/her cultural, social, and personal identities. For example, each semester at my university, I will start the first class by introducing myself to the students. The first thing to tell the students about me is my name. I did not change my Chinese name after migrating to Australia. Therefore, my name is already clear enough for many people to figure out which nation I am originally from. I will then tell the students my ethnicity and provide brief information about my academic background and research interests, and my personal interest in gardening. The introduction gives a sketch of my identity in cultural, social and personal terms.

Cultural identity refers to one's sense of belonging to a particular cultural group. Social identity refers to the sense of belonging to a social group within one's culture. Personal identity is based on the unique characteristics of the individual (Lustig & Koester, 2003, p. 142).

Cultural identity is related with but not limited to ethnicity. On the one hand, it is expressed in learning and accepting language, religion, and various traditions of a culture. On the other hand, as it has been discussed previously, culture is learned. Therefore, personal experience and social environment also contribute to the formation of a person's cultural identity. It is possible that one's cultural identity is not consistent with his/her ethnicity or racial identity. For example, the cultural identity of many so called ABCs (American Born Chinese or Australian Born Chinese) might actually be closer to the culture of the society in which they grow up (i.e., the American culture or Australian culture), instead of the culture of their motherhood or their ethnicity. Although appearing like Chinese, many of them do not speak Chinese, accept the core values of the Chinese culture, nor act in the traditional Chinese way.

Social identity is developed as a result of one's memberships in particular social groups. "The characteristics and concerns common to most members of such social groups shape the way individuals view their characteristics" (Lustig & Koester, 2003, p. 141). The nature of these associations is diverse, including work and profession (e.g., doctor, teacher, accountant, etc.), location (e.g., neighborhood, region, nation, etc.), social class (e.g., migrant worker, blue collar, white collar, etc.), sport clubs, gender, age, and so forth. A person can assume a multiplicity of social identities at the same time, or take on different social identities in different contexts. Social identity is reflected in the sharing of the characteristics, interests and concerns that are common to the members of the group. Social identity shapes people's perceptions of their characteristics and world views, and thus affects people's behaviors.

Personal identity reflects the unique characteristics and interests of the individual. It "is based on people's unique characteristics, which may differ from those of others in their cultural and social groups" (Lustig & Koester, 2003, p. 141). The uniqueness of personal identity distinguishes a person from the others in the cultural and social groups, and thus sustains the individuality of human society. People belong to the same social group (e.g., of the profession of doctor) may differ in their characteristics (e.g., being sociable/unsociable, humorous/dull, optimistic/pessimistic, etc.) and interests (e.g., liking fishing, dancing, singing, photographing, etc.),

The classification of identity into cultural, social and personal dimensions was first proposed by psychologist Erik Erikson and subsequently adopted widely in other areas of study (Guo & Waniganayake, 2016, p. 290). It provides an effective framework for understanding the formation and construction of people's identity. However, the identification of the three dimensions of identity does not mean there is separation between them. On the one hand, cultural identity lies at the core of a person's identity and shapes the person's social and personal identity. On the other hand, individual characteristics, preferences, and interests affect the formation of one's cultural identity. Therefore, the identity of a person is the result of the interplay between the person's cultural, social, and personal identities.

## Intercultural Communication

Communication is a process of creating and exchanging meaning between all participants. Intercultural communication is communication that involves people of different cultural identities. From the perspective of cultural diversity as the common heritage and resource of mankind, intercultural communication constitutes the foundation of human's social activities in the global network society. The question about how to enable sharing of meaning between the diverse cultures of the global network society has attracted vast attention from various fields of studies. Among various theories and concepts proposed in response to this question, Manuel Castells' hypothesis of "global culture" offers a useful conceptual lens for understanding the nature of intercultural communication in the global network society. In his manuscript entitled *Communication Power*, Castells elaborated on the diffusion of the network society around the globe and the need for a global culture supportive to the effective operation of the convergent network in the existing culturally fragmented world (Castells, 2009). Castells argued that "the common culture of the global network society is a culture of protocols of communication enabling communication between different cultures not on the basis of shared values but of the sharing of the values of communication." In other words, the "global culture is a culture of communication for the sake of communication" (Castells, 2009, p. 38). This is a culture established on the common beliefs of cultural diversity as resources of mankind, the endorsement of the value of communication, and the norm of respecting, sharing and receiving these resources between all cultures in the world.

Intercultural communication and culture are tightly related with each other. Culture plays a crucial role in intercultural communication, while intercultural communication contributes to the formation of new culture. Culture affects intercultural communication by shaping the content and process of the exchanges and interactions between the participants. Intercultural communication enables the expression of cultures, supports the exchange of cultural resources, and facilitates the creation of new cultures.

## Intercultural Competence in the Global Network Society

Modern information communication technologies and the global network system have materialized the vision of "global village" (McLuhan, 1964) proposed by Marshall McLuhan more than 50 years ago. Humans are now able to reach every corner of the globe from home at a faster speed, better quality, and lower cost. Globalization is an inevitable trend of the history of human society. However, the actual consequences of the global network society are not determined by technologies, but by humans. Will cultural diversity become the common resource of mankind or cause more intercultural conflicts? Will the interconnection of diverse cultures result in exchanging and sharing the cultural resources of all the civilizations around the world, or lead to the destruction of the democratic foundation of the global society? The answers to these questions largely depend on the capability of people and societies of various cultures to interact appropriately and effectively with each other.

### Intercultural Competence

Intercultural competence broadly refers to people's capability for appropriate and effective intercultural interactions. In the contemporary human societies, intercultural competence is required for the constructive intercultural interactions that support the sharing of cultural resources for the benefits of mankind. Research on intercultural competence is widespread across various disciplines. One of the major research concerns of intercultural competence studies is the identification, assessment, and development of the capabilities required for successful intercultural interactions in various practical settings of human societal activities. Considerable studies have been carried out in the practical settings of education, health care, foreign aids, community services and development, and workplaces (Deardorff, 2006, 2011; Lustig & Koester, 2003; Paine, Jankowski, & Sandage, 2016; Peterson, 2004). Notwithstanding the disparities of the specific wordings, most of the theories agreed on the point that intercultural competence involves a complex set of interrelated capabilities. Two major approaches can be identified in the conceptualization of the intercultural competence: the process approach and the means approach.

The process approach underscores the embodiment of intercultural competence in the process of intercultural interactions. Intercultural competence is a developmental process of identifying our own cultural patterns, acknowledging the patterns of others and, eventually, learning to adapt across cultures (Bennett, 2009, p. 122). From this perspective, intercultural competence is not a static state of quality, but a process of effective and appropriate action and communication. The effectiveness and appropriateness of intercultural interactions are based on the development of the attitudes, knowledge and skills inherent in intercultural competence and specific to the practical setting (e.g., international education, international aid project, etc.). The process approach also implies that intercultural competence is a dynamic learning process. Intercultural competence is integrated with the process of learning between cultures. Actors involved in the intercultural interactions develop their intercultural competences in the processes of learning to know, learning to do, and learning to be (United Nations Educational, Scientific, and Cultural Organization [UNESCO], 2013, p. 9). Learning about other cultures is the first step of intercultural competence development. It is also a continuous process that exists throughout the lifetime of people living in the global networked society. Knowing about other cultures is fundamental to the interactions between cultures and to the development of intercultural competence. Learning to do is an active and productive aspect of intercultural competence development. While learning to do, people act on the existing knowledge and skills as well as gain more knowledge and skills. Learning to be is a reflective aspect of intercultural competence development. "Learning to be relies upon the reflective step of thinking about one's social self as having a place in the global world" (UNESCO, 2013, p. 9). This is the highest level in a circle of one's intercultural competence development, whereby the newly acquired knowledge and skills are internalized into one's existing system of knowledge and skill.

However, learning to be is not the end of the journey of intercultural competence development. Instead, learning to be signifies the commencement of a new cycle of intercultural learning. New intercultural encounters happen all the time in the contemporary globalized society. Therefore, intercultural learning is an ongoing circular process of development.

The Intercultural Competence Model proposed by Deardorff is an example of the process model of intercultural competence. On the basis of the body of the existing research, Deardorff proposed the Intercultural Competence Model to map the elements of intercultural competence and the relations between these elements (Deardorff, 2011). The Intercultural Competence Model identifies four interrelated elements of intercultural competence, namely attitudes, knowledge and comprehension, desired internal outcome, and desired external outcome. The process model defines the overall external outcome of intercultural competence as "effective and appropriate behavior and communication in intercultural situations" (Deardorff, 2011, p. 66). The process of intercultural competence begins with a set of appropriate attitudes (e.g., openness, curiosity, etc.).

It moves from the individual level (attitudes) to the interaction level (internal outcome and external outcome). The degree of intercultural competence, reflected in the interaction outcomes, depends on the acquired degree of attitudes, knowledge/comprehension, and skills (Deardorff, 2006).

In contrast to the perspective of intercultural competence as a process, some scholars conceptualize it as a means for successful intercultural interaction. For example, the conceptual framework of intercultural competences proposed by the United Nation Educational, Scientific, and Cultural Organization (UNESCO) conceived intercultural competences as a requisite response to the challenge of contemporary globalization, and a means to the achievement of the mankind's unity-in-diversity as well as unity beyond diversity through full participation in the infinite wealth of the cultures of the world (UNESCO, 2013, pp. 4–7). From the perspective of intercultural competences as a means of successful intercultural interaction, the term is defined as having adequate relevant knowledge, holding receptive attitudes, as well as having the required skills to draw upon both knowledge and attitudes when interacting with others from different cultures (UNESCO, 2013, p. 16). This definition emphasized the complex set of interrelated capabilities required for negotiating cultural boundaries in the globalizing world. To account for the multiplicity of the elements of intercultural competences, some researchers preferred to use the term in its plural form: competences (UNESCO, 2013, p. 16).

Most of the definitions about intercultural competence identified effectiveness and appropriateness as the key assessment criteria of intercultural interactions. Effectiveness refers to the degree of the achievement of the intercultural interactions' desired outcomes. It reflects the view of one's own performance in the intercultural interaction (Fantini, 2009, p. 458). Effective performance suggests "that people are able to achieve desired personal outcomes" (Wiseman, 2002, p. 209). Given a specific interaction, each individual might anticipate the desired outcomes differently. Effectiveness is measured from the perception of the individual, and thus mainly decided by the individual participants of the intercultural interaction. Appropriateness refers to the degree of meeting the intercultural expectations and ethical standards in a given situation. Appropriate performance entails the actions that meet the expectations and demands of the situation (Wiseman, 2002, p. 209). Appropriateness reflects how the "others" perceive one's performance (Fantini, 2009, p. 458). Therefore, appropriateness is measured from the perception of others. That is the appropriateness as perceived by people of other cultural backgrounds.

Therefore, it is decided by the participants of other cultures. The conceptualization of effectiveness and appropriateness implies the integrated measurement of intercultural interactions from the perceptions of all participating cultures. Spitzberg applied these concepts in the situation of communication and suggested that the combinations of the extremes of the effectiveness and appropriateness in the context of intercultural communication might result in four communication styles, namely minimizing communication, sufficing communication, maximizing communication, and optimizing communication (Wiseman, 2003). Minimizing communication is both inappropriate and ineffective. Sufficing communication is appropriate, but ineffective. Maximizing communication is effective in terms of achieving the goal of the individual but the achievement was reached at the cost of the appropriateness. Optimizing communication is the ideal style which is both appropriate and effective (Wiseman, 2003, p. 193). Similarly, by expanding Spitzberg's classification of intercultural communication into the general intercultural interaction, four types of interaction outcomes can be identified based on their effectiveness and appropriateness. This can be illustrated using the Cartesian Plane of Intercultural Competence (CPIC) as shown in Figure 16.1. In the CPIC, the x-axis indicates the appropriateness of the interaction outcome, and the y-axis indicates the effectiveness of the interaction outcome.

Any point on the plane represents a combination of the appropriateness and effectiveness of a particular intercultural interaction outcome. Quadrant I represents the desired outcomes of intercultural interactions, which are both effective and appropriate. These are the ideal situations of intercultural interactions. Quadrant III represents the undesired outcomes of intercultural interactions, which are both ineffective and inappropriate. These are the failed situations of intercultural interactions. Quadrant II and Quadrant IV symbolize the situations of limited success of the intercultural interactions. Quadrant II represents the situations where the interaction outcomes have met the desired objective(s) of one side of the participants, however, this has been achieved inappropriately. For example, to force people to take part in a family planning project is not a successful interaction outcome, because the objective of family planning is achieved in

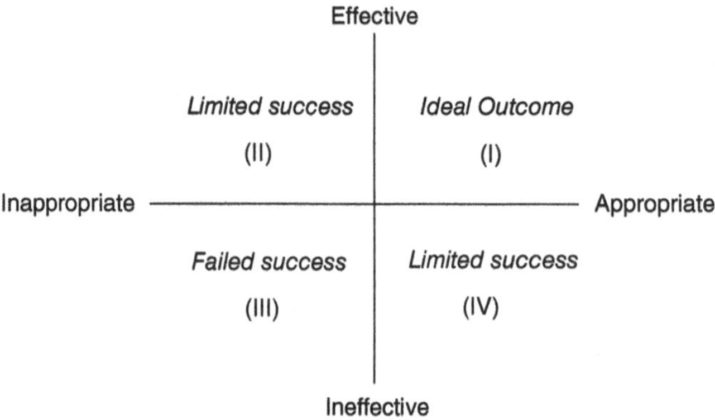


**Figure 16.1** Cartesian plane of intercultural competence

an inappropriate way. Quadrant IV represents the situations where the interaction outcomes fail to meet the desired objective(s), although the interactions have been carried out appropriately, meeting the cultural expectations and ethical standards.

The conceptualization of intercultural competence varies between different disciplines. There even exists disagreement on the terminology around the capability required to engage effectively in intercultural situations (Deardorff, 2011, p. 65). Alternative terms used to refer to the concept around intercultural competence include cultural competence, cultural intelligence (Peterson, 2004) and intercultural communication competence (Kotthoff & Spencer-Oatey, 2007; Wiseman, 2003). The term "intercultural competence" is used in this chapter for two reasons. First, "intercultural" is preferred for it underscores the interaction between cultures. Second, "intercultural competence" means various aspects of the capability that is needed for effective and appropriate intercultural engagement.

One of the obstacles hindering intercultural interactions originates from the differences between the cultures. The abilities of the actors involved in the interactions to discuss, explain and understand these cultural differences will determine the success of the interaction. Therefore, communicative capability lies at the core of intercultural competence. However, effective intercultural interaction demands a set of multifaceted capabilities. Apart from the ability to communicate intercultural differences, people's knowledge of and attitude toward intercultural differences affect the effectiveness of intercultural interaction as well.

### Components of Intercultural Competence

Intercultural competence involves a set of interrelated components. The three commonly recognized components are intercultural knowledge, attitude, and skill.

Intercultural knowledge refers to the information necessary for appropriate and effective intercultural interaction. Intercultural knowledge includes "the cognitive information you need to have about the people, the context, and the norms of appropriateness that operate in a specific culture" (Lustig & Koester, 2003, p. 68). Types of knowledge essential for effective and appropriate intercultural interaction include culture general knowledge, culture specific knowledge, and culture reflective knowledge.

Culture general knowledge consists of the awareness and understanding of the facts and traits of culture in general. Culture general knowledge provides insights into intercultural interactions abstractly and can therefore be a powerful tool in making sense of intercultural practices regardless of the cultures involved (Lustig & Koester, 2003, p. 69). This includes awareness and understanding of culture, cultural diversity, and cultural identity; and awareness and understanding of the impacts of culture, cultural diversity and cultural identity on intercultural interactions and their implications in the contemporary human society. Culture general knowledge establishes the essential foundation of intercultural competence. It enables one to gain insightful awareness and understanding of intercultural interactions.

Culture specific knowledge is knowledge concerning a particular culture. Culture specific knowledge includes knowledge about the culture of oneself and knowledge about a specific culture of "others." This includes information about the forces that maintain the culture's uniqueness and facts about the cultural patterns (Lustig & Koester, 2003, p. 69). Awareness and understanding of one's own culture is a stepping stone for the betterment of the knowledge of others' culture. Culture guides and shapes people's thinking and acting. However, people are seldom consciously aware of the guidance of culture when they think and act. Usually it is taken for granted, as if it is always there. Learning about one's own culture involves awareness and understanding of how and why one thinks and acts in that particular way. Culture specific knowledge about other cultures is related with the information about what, how, and why there are differences between one's own culture and the culture(s) of concern. This involves awareness and understanding of the facts and traits of the particular culture(s), its/their uniqueness, and the factors shaping its/their uniqueness. Important information contributing to culture specific knowledge includes that about the people (e.g., their beliefs and values), the context (the specific situations), and the norms (e.g., customs—what people usually do; and taboos—what people usually do not do). Culture specific knowledge about other cultures establishes the foundation to understand other cultures, predicts expected interaction tendency, and thus enhances the effectiveness and appropriateness of intercultural interaction.

Culture reflective knowledge is the information about the complex forces shaping the perceived uniqueness of a particular culture, including those which come from the knower. Culture reflective knowledge goes beyond the "conventional surface-level knowledge of foods, greetings, customs facts and so on to understanding the intricacies of" the historical, political and social contexts (Deardorff, 2009, pp. 479–480). In other words, culture reflective knowledge is the awareness and understanding of the complexity of the causes of the uniqueness of a culture and the status of one's understanding of the uniqueness. Culture reflective knowledge is an important component of intercultural competency for two primary reasons. Firstly, through explanation of the causes of the uniqueness of a culture, and reflection on the status of one's understanding of oneself, new knowledge of culture is produced. Secondly, through the reflection process the knower links and contrasts the newly acquired information with his/her existing knowledge. By doing so, the knower validates, sustains, and internalizes the new knowledge into his/her knowledge system. Culture reflective knowledge brings the knower's culture specific knowledge to a higher epistemic level. From an epistemic perspective, the quality of knowledge is determined by the degree of (a) how sure the knower is about what is known; (b) how safe it is that the knower's believing is correct (or how easily the knower might have been wrong); (c) how rationally justified the knower is in so believing; and (d) how reliably truth-conducive is the way in which the knower acquires or sustains the belief (Sosa, 2009, p. 136). Knowledge is considered of higher epistemic quality if it is more rationally justified and reliably acquired and sustained.

Intercultural attitude refers to complex characteristics directly associated with the values and beliefs concerning intercultural issues.

One of the most distinguishing features of intercultural encounters is the cultural disparities between people involved. Positive intercultural attitude is essential for two key reasons. Firstly, knowledge is the resource for competent action, but knowledge is not equal to the actual action. Appropriate and effective intercultural interaction requires adequate awareness and understanding of the facts and traits of these disparities as well as the willingness to actively and constructively apply this knowledge in designing and practicing intercultural actions. Secondly, a positive attitude is required for intercultural interaction participants to cope with uncertainty and ambiguity appropriately and effectively when knowledge is not yet available. Intercultural knowledge is fundamental to successful intercultural interactions. However, to interact on the basis of apt knowledge, where all interactions are predictable, is an ideal situation. This situation represents one extreme of intercultural interactions. The other extreme of intercultural interactions is when no knowledge is available at all. Everything of the interaction is unpredictable. In reality, intercultural interactions take place at some points between these two extremes. In other words, in ordinary human interactions, we have to deal with uncertainties and ambiguities occurring between the extremes of "predetermined order" and absolute "chaos" (Klyukanov, 2005, p. 35). Differences, unfamiliarity, uncertainty and ambiguity are inevitable in intercultural interaction, due to the complexity and fluidity of culture and the cultural heterogeneity of the setting. Competent intercultural actors are expected to value diversity of and inequality between cultures, and believe in the virtue of learning, sharing, and communicating between cultures in dealing with unfamiliarity, uncertainty and ambiguity in intercultural situations. Endorsement of these values and beliefs is essential to the formation of positive attitudes of intercultural issues, which is conducive to promoting the willingness to act appropriately and effectively in intercultural interactions. Lying at the heart of intercultural attitudes are the positive attitudes toward the differences, unfamiliarity, uncertainties, and ambiguities of the situations of intercultural interaction. Important attitudes for intercultural competent performance include intercultural respect, open-mindedness, curiosity, and tolerance.

***Intercultural respect*** is the characteristics of esteeming cultures of oneself and of others. Respectful attitude reflects in valuing other cultures and appreciating cultural diversity (Spitzberg & Changnon, 2009, p. 13). One can be aware of the existence of various cultures (of oneself and of others) and the differences between them, however disrespect the differences. With the attitude of intercultural respect, intercultural diversities are conceived as valuable wealth to be shared, learnt, and made use of for the benefits of the mankind.

***Intercultural open-mindedness*** is the characteristics of being flexible in confronting unfamiliar things and new situations (e.g., new ideas, opinions, practices, behaviors, etc.). Open-minded attitude reflects in withholding judgment and being open to intercultural learning and to people from other cultures (Spitzberg & Changnon, 2009, p. 13). Responding to unfamiliar experiences with an open mindset can strengthen one's willingness and consciousness to think alternatively and critically in intercultural interactions. Intercultural open-mindedness is helpful for enhancing intercultural adaptation and reflexivity.

***Intercultural curiosity*** is the characteristic of being interested and willing to learn different things, and to experience unfamiliar situations. Intercultural curiosity involves openness to new information, alertness to distinctions, sensitivity to different contexts, and willingness to understand other worldviews (Deardorff, 2009; Gudykunst, 2005a). Differences and unfamiliarity come with uncertainty. Uncertainty is defined as the cognitive inability to predict what people will do, or to explain why people do as they do (Klyukanov, 2005, p. 36). For effective and appropriate interaction, uncertainty needs to be minimized. Intercultural curiosity motivates reducing uncertainty through exploring and learning about the differences. There are three types of approaches to reducing one's level of uncertainty: passive, active and interactive (Lustig & Koester, 2003, p. 284). Passive approach of uncertainty reduction mainly relies on observation strategies. Active approach involves efforts to collect needed information by consulting other people or alternating the environment of interaction. Interactive approach deals with uncertainty by direct communication with other participants of the interaction.

***Intercultural tolerance*** is the characteristic of being willing and able to endure intercultural differences and ambiguity of intercultural situations. It contributes to the capacity of dealing with unfamiliar or unknown situations (Martin & Nakayama, 2007, p. 439). When interacting with other people, we usually make judgment based on our interpretations, which are established based on beliefs and value systems. Intercultural interactions involve people holding diverse beliefs and values and thus disparities of interpretation exist. Therefore, differences and ambiguity are unavoidable in intercultural interaction. One's tolerance for ambiguity affects his/her perception of ambiguous situations. Lack of tolerance for ambiguity involves perceiving ambiguous situations as threatening and undesirable (Gudykunst, 2005a, pp. 296–297).

Therefore, those with a lower degree of intercultural tolerance may respond to differences and ambiguity with fear and hostility, while those with a higher degree of tolerance are able to respond in a relaxing and an understanding manner. Depending on the degree of intercultural tolerance, there are generally three ways of dealing with differences and ambiguity: non-tolerant, limited tolerant, and tolerant. In the non-tolerant way, people are certainty oriented. They tend to think in terms of categories and stereotypes, and to base their judgment of the intercultural situation from their own perspective and on their first impressions (Gudykunst, 2005b, p. 432). In the tolerant way, people are uncertainty oriented. They tend to think beyond their own perspectives, and to seek out "objective" information about the situation (Gudykunst, 2005b, p. 432). The way of limited tolerant is located between the extremes of non-tolerant and tolerant. At non-tolerant level, differences and ambiguity are either rejected or ignored. People act without recognition of alternative interpretations and ambiguity of the situation. This is destructive to intercultural interaction that usually results in intercultural conflict or failure of intercultural interaction. At a the limited tolerant level, people recognize differences of interpretation and the ambiguity of the situation, and attempt to eliminate them by making assumptions on the basis of their beliefs. Despite the recognition of differences, people with limited intercultural tolerance usually underestimate the ambiguity that is rooted in intercultural disparities. Many intercultural misunderstandings and conflicts have originated from overlooking ambiguity, or attempting to eliminate ambiguity by making assumptions on the basis of the beliefs that are meaningful only to one's own culture. People who are tolerant of ambiguity can manage the nervousness and frustrations caused by ambiguity. They are able to adapt to the unfamiliar situation by making adjustments, instead of concealing the existence of ambiguity by making assumptions.

Intercultural skill refers to the ability to reflect on and act appropriately and effectively in intercultural settings. Exchanging and sharing information across cultural boundaries lies at the heart of intercultural interaction. Important intercultural skills can be classified into three aspects: information collecting (e.g., observing, listening, discovering, and learning, etc.); information processing (e.g., analyzing, evaluating, relating, and interpreting, etc.); and information communicating (e.g., verbal/non-verbal expressing, face-face/mediated expressing, and dialog, etc.).

## Development of Intercultural Competence in the Workplace

Development of intercultural competence is a lifetime process of learning, practicing, and reflecting. Because there are no identical intercultural encounters. Even with the same participants engaged in the same type of interaction setting, the actual interaction between these participants is determined by a complex of subjective and objective variables. Some of these variables may be more predictable (e.g., being able to speak the local language is conducive for the effectiveness of the interaction), while others are less predictable (e.g., the interpretation of meaning during the interaction). Therefore, it is safe to say that every intercultural encounter is a new intercultural encounter. While education and training are important ways of learning fundamental intercultural knowledge, attitude, and skill, intercultural interaction practice and one's self-reflection of the knowledge and practice are essential for making the learned knowledge, attitude and skill meaningful and useful. Development of intercultural competence at the workplace includes the system aspect and individual aspect.

### System and Individual Intercultural Competence

*System intercultural competence* is the capacity of an organization to perform appropriately and effectively in intercultural situations. System intercultural competence contributes to the success of an organization "an era of dynamic complexity" by enhancing its flexibility and synergy (Hogan-Garcia, 2003, p. 2). Intercultural interactions take place in a specific system. A system is a set of interrelated units engaged in a joint process to accomplish a common goal. Intercultural competence at the system level embodies the relational, institutional and contextual characteristics of the system where the interaction is carried out. Relational characteristics refer to the norms, values, and beliefs shaping the pattern of the relations between the units (individuals or sub-organizations within an organization) in a system (organization).

This includes establishing an environment that promotes respect, trust, and collaborative relations between people internal (e.g., employees, managers, supervisors, etc.) and external (e.g., clients, customers, etc.) to the organization (Hogan-Garcia, 2003, p. 92). Institutional characteristics are reflected in the regulations and policies governing the joint process (e.g.,: work responsibility designation, training and education, performance assessment policy, etc.). Contextual characteristics are related with the specific task, situation, and objective of the system (organization).

***Individual intercultural competence*** is the capacity of an individual to act appropriately and effectively in an intercultural situation. Individual intercultural competence provides the human infrastructure for developing system intercultural competence. An organization cannot be interculturally competent unless its employees at every level develop appropriate intercultural competence (Hogan-Garcia, 2003, p. 2). Although education and training can promote increasing knowledge and improving skills, meaningful and useful intercultural competence is mainly gained through the lifelong process of learning, practicing and reflecting. As intercultural issues become some of the major challenges of globalization, considerable studies have been conducted to explore strategies of intercultural competence. It is worth stressing that given the complexity and fluidity of human interactions, particularly those involving people of difference cultures, it is impossible to offer a ready-made panacea ensuring intercultural competence. The following capabilities indicate the minimal requirements of intercultural competence proved by existing research (Lustig & Koester, 2003; Peterson, 2004; Samovar, Porter, & EMcDaniel, 2006; Sarbaugh, 1988; Tuleja, 2005; UNESCO, 2013).

## Dialog

Dialog is a form of interaction whereby the participants exchange their knowledge and understanding. Dialog takes place "when participants, having their own perspectives, yet recognize the existence of other, different perspectives, remaining open to learning about them" (UNESCO, 2013, p. 14). Dialog occurs only when the two essential conditions exist. First, the participants are aware of the existence of both the perspectives of self and of other(s). On the one hand, dialoguers have their own views to express. On the other hand, they recognize the diversity of views. Second, the participants are aware of and respect the right to express the views of self and those of others. Intercultural competent dialog requires adequate intercultural knowledge (culture general, specific, and reflective knowledge) and skills (listening and expressing) to effectively articulate the views of self and understand those of others. Intercultural competent dialog also demands appropriate intercultural attitudes that motivate open and respectful interaction between the dialoguers. Dialog is a two-way information communication process. Unlike persuasion, dialog does not necessarily aim to change the opinion of others. "Dialogue requires comprehension, but not necessarily agreement" (UNESCO, 2013, p. 14).

## Sensibility

Intercultural sensibility is the ability to identify, appreciate, receive and accept cultural differences. One's level of intercultural sensibility is related with the level of awareness and understanding of intercultural differences, and reflected in the emotion and behavior in responding to intercultural differences. Intercultural sensitive participants are more competent in coping with the uncertainty and ambiguity of intercultural situations, and are therefore able to engage in intercultural interaction and respond to intercultural differences with confidence, respect, and enjoyment. The Intercultural Sensibility Scale (ISS), proposed by Chen and Starosta, identified five indicators of intercultural sensibility in intercultural interaction, namely interaction engagement, respect for cultural differences, interaction confidence, interaction enjoyment and interaction attentiveness (Chen & Starosta, 2000, p. 8).

### Humility

Humility is considered as a virtue conducive to intercultural competence. Intercultural humility is the willingness and ability to accurately appraise self and others, and to regulate emotion in intercultural situations. Humility is a construct relevant to intercultural competence since establishing meaningful relationships with culturally distinct others requires an appreciative receptivity to unfamiliar beliefs, values, and worldviews (Paine et al., 2016, p. 15). Intercultural humility is built on self-awareness and respect of intercultural differences. Contemporary researchers suggest that humility consists of five dimensions: a willingness to appraise the self accurately, an orientation toward others, interpersonal receptivity, the ability to regulate one's emotions, and appreciation of the value in things (Paine et al., 2016, p. 16). Accurate self-appraisement requires adequate knowledge of self as well as that of others, for only through critical reflection on the differences between self and others a comprehensive knowledge of self is developed. Another requirement of accurate self-appraisement is an ethno-relative approach to intercultural difference, which guides one in critically examining the self and others without prejudice.

Human interactions naturally involve two faces of one coin: the interconnectedness and the independence of the participants. People differ in their orientation toward the relation between the interconnectedness and independence in the interaction. Self-orientation tends to be interested in the independence of self. Research showed that "excessive self-focus associates with narcissism and shame" and tends to distort perception of one's own and another's culture (Paine et al., 2016, p. 16). Other-orientation is more interested in the interconnectedness between the participants of the interaction. Intercultural humility requires the other-orientation seeing self as a part of the interaction, instead of the superior one dominating the interaction.

This is the ability to balance the independence of self (individual concerns) and interconnectedness (needs for and concerns of others) in intercultural interactions.

Humility requires a mindset of openness. Humility originates from one's openness and receptivity to others. Intercultural competence is determined by cognitive, behavioral, as well as affective factors. Humility reflects the affective aspect of intercultural competence, as the result of one's emotion regulation. Finally, intercultural humility requires not only awareness of intercultural differences, but also the ability to discover and appreciate the values of unfamiliar things and values of intercultural diversity.

### Empathy

Intercultural empathy is the ability to understand and to feel from the perspectives of others. Intercultural empathy includes cognitive and emotional dimensions. Cognitive empathy is the ability to understand the perspectives of other cultures.

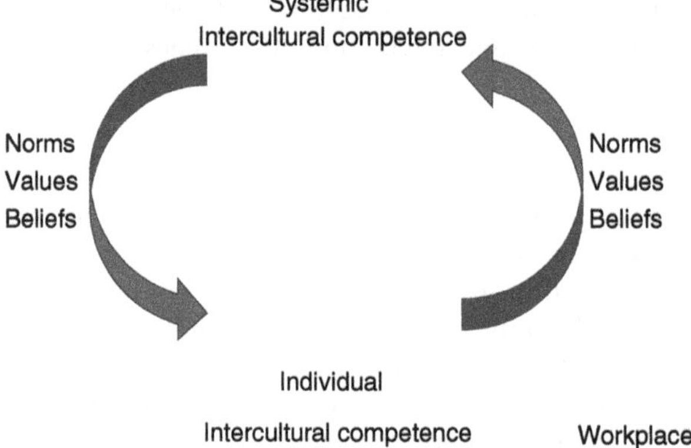


**Figure 16.2** Intercultural competence at the workplace

Emotional empathy is the "compassion-related emotions that arise from a feeling of concern" for the experience of others (Gudykunst & Lee, 2003, p. 121). Intercultural empathy is tightly related with intercultural awareness, sensibility and humility. On the one hand, people with a high level of intercultural empathy show a higher level of intercultural sensibility and humility, and are therefore able to gain better knowledge and understanding of other cultures. On the other hand, a high level of intercultural awareness, sensibility, and humility enable a higher level of intercultural empathy.

### Adaptation

Systemic intercultural competence and individual intercultural competence affect each other (Figure 16.2). The degree of intercultural competence of the individuals within an organization may affect that of the organization. Because the norms, values and beliefs commonly shared within an organization are shaped by the members of the organization and an organization's rules and regulations are implemented by the members of the organization. In turn, the degree of intercultural competence of an organization will affect that of the individuals within the organization, because intercultural competence norms, values and policies of an organization may encourage intercultural competent practices and behavior in the workplace of the organization and promote individual intercultural competence development, and vice versa.

## Conclusion

Cultural diversity and intercultural encounters are the characteristics of the contemporary human society. The degree of intercultural competence of the participants of intercultural interactions will determine whether and to what extent the value of cultural diversity as the wealth of mankind could be realized. Intercultural competence, consisting of knowledge, attitude, and skill, is required for optimizing the performance in the global networked society. Intercultural competence can be learned and developed. However, there is not a guaranteed prescription ensuring competence in intercultural interactions due to the complexity of intercultural interactions. Intercultural competence development is a continuing process of learning, practicing, and reflecting.

## Key References for Further Reading

Castells, M. (2009). *Communication power*. New York, NY: Oxford University Press.This book explores communication in the globalized society and the construction of power relationships through communication processes. It demonstrates a global culture of "communication for the sake of communication."

Deardorff, D. K. (2009). *The Sage handbook of intercultural competence.* Thousand Oaks, CA: Sage.This book is a collection of essays on intercultural competence. It covers theories, developments strategies and practical examples of intercultural competence.

Gudykunst, W. (2005). *Theorizing about intercultural communication.* Thousand Oaks, CA: Sage.This is a collection of essays about the key concepts and theories of intercultural communication. It covers theories on culture, communication, adaption, adjustment, and acculturation in intercultural interactions.

Lustig, M. W., & Koester, J. (2003). *Intercultural competence: Interpersonal communicaiton across cultures.* Boston, MA: Allyn and Bacon.This book systematically articulates the key concepts and theories of intercultural competence. It covers theories on communication and intercultural competence, cultural diversity and identity, verbal and noverbal communication in intercultural contexts, and communication in intercultural relationships.

## References

Aristotle (2001). Rhetorica. In R. McKeon (Ed.), *The basic works of Aristotle.* New York, NY: The Modern Library.

Bennett, J. M. (2009). Cultivating intercultural competence. In D. K. Deardorff (Ed.), *The Sage handbook of intercultural competence,* (pp. 121–140). Thousand Oaks, CA: Sage.

Castells, M. (2009). *Communication power*. New York, NY: Oxford University Press.

Chen, G. M., & Starosta, W. J. (2000). The development and validation of the intercultural sensitivity scale. *Human Communication, 1*(3), 15.

Deardorff, D. K. (2006). The identification and assessment of intercultural comeptence as a student outcome of internationalization at institutions of higher education in the United States. *Journal of Studies in International Education, 10,* 26.

Deardorff, D. K. (2009). Implementing intercultural competence assessment. In D. K. Deardorff (Ed.), *The Sage handbook of intercultural competence,* (pp. 477–491). Thousand Oaks, CA: Sage.

Deardorff, D. K. (2011). Assessing intercultural competence. *New Directions for Institutional Research, 149,* 15.

Fantini, A. E. (2009). Assessing intercultural competence. In D. K. Deardorff (Ed.), *The Sage handbook of intercultural competence,* (pp. 456–476). Thousand Oaks, CA: Sage.

Gudykunst, W. (2005a). An Anxiety/ Uncertainty Management (AUM) theory of effective communication. In W. Gudykunst (Ed.), *Theorizing about intercultural communication,* (pp. 281–322). Thousand Oaks, CA: Sage.

Gudykunst, W. (2005b). An Anxiety/Uncertainty Management (AUM) theory of strangers' intercultural adjustment. In W. Gudykunst (Ed.), *Theorizing about intercultrual communication,* (pp. 419–457). Thousand Oaks, CA: Sage.

Gudykunst, W. B., & Lee, C. M. (2003). Cross-cultural communication theories. In W. B. Gudykunst (Ed.), *Cross-cultural and intercultural communication,* (pp. 7–34). Thousand Oaks, CA: Sage.

Guo, Q., & Waniganayake, M. (2016). Building intercultural connections through technology-based play. In M. Ebbeck, & M. Waniganayake (Eds.), *Play in early childhood education,* (pp. 285–301). Melbourne, Australia: Oxford University Press.

Hogan-Garcia, M. (2003). *The four skills of cultural diversity competence.* Melbourne, Australia: Thomson Brooks.

Klyukanov, I. E. (2005). *Principles of intercultural communication.* Mexico City, Mexico: Pearson.

Kotthoff, H., & Spencer-Oatey, H. (Eds.) (2007). *Handbook of intercultural communication.* Berlin, Germany: de Gruyter Mouton.

Lustig, M. W., & Koester, J. (2003). *Intercultural competence: Interpersonal communicaiton across cultures.* Boston, MA: Allyn and Bacon.

Martin, J. N., & Nakayama, T. K. (2007). *Intercultural communication in contexts.* Boston, MA: McGraw Hill.

McLuhan, M. (1964). *Understanding media: The extensions of man.* London, UK: Routledge and Kegan Paul.

Melkote, S. R., & Leslie Steeves, H. (2001). *Communication for development in the third world: Theory and practice for empowerment.* New Delhi, India: Sage.

Paine, D. R., Jankowski, P. J., & Sandage, S. J. (2016). Humility as a predictor of intercultural competence: Mediator effects for differentiation-of-self. *The Family Journal, 24*(1), 8.

Peterson, B. (2004). *Cultural interlligence.* Yarmouth, ME: Intercultural Press.

Samovar, L. A., Porter, R. E., & EMcDaniel, E. R. (2006). *Intercultural commmunication: A reader.* Belmont, CA: Wadsworth.

Sarbaugh, L. E. (1988). *Intercultural communication.* New Brunswick, Canada: Transaction Publishers.

Sorrells, K. (2016). *Intercultural communication: globalization and social justice.* Los Angeles, CA: Sage.

Sosa, E. (2009). *Reflective knowledge.* New York, NY: Oxford University Press.

Spitzberg, B. H., & Changnon, G. (2009). Conceptualizing intercultural competence. In D. K. Deardorff (Ed.), *The sage handbook of intercultural competence* (pp. 2–52). Thousand Oaks, CA: Sage.

Tuleja, E. A. (2005). *Intercultural communication for business.* Toronto: Thomson.

United Nations Educational, Scientific, and Cultural Organization. (2002). Universal Declaration on Cultural Diversity. Paris: UNESCO.

United Nations Educational, Scientific, and Cultural Organization. (2013). *Intercultural competences: Conceptual and operational framwork.* Paris, France: UNESCO.

Wiseman, R. L. (2002). Intercultural communication competence. In W. Gudykunst, & B. Mody (Eds.), *Handbook of international and intercultural communication,* (pp. 207–224). Thousand Oaks, CA: Sage.

Wiseman, R. L. (2003). Intercultural communication competence. In W. B. Gudykunst (Ed.), *Cross-cultural and intercultural communication,* (pp. 191–208). Thousand Oaks, CA: Sage.

张念宏.. (1988). In 张念宏 (Ed.), 教育百科辞典 (pp. 664). Beijing: 中国农业科技出版社.

# 17

# Intercultural Communication in the Multilingual Urban Workplace

*Aditi Ghosh*

*University of Calcutta*

## Cultural Communication in the Multilingual Workplace

The significance of the study of intercultural communication lies in the fact that we do not live in a monolingual or monocultural world, but a highly multilingual and multicultural one. In recent times, there has been an increasing awareness and acceptance of this diversity. Endorsement of the ideology of monoculturalism, monolingualism and homogenization, which was the dominant ideology of the nineteenth-century nation states, now regularly encounters questions regarding its validity as well as viability. In spite of a sustained effort to enforce homogeneity in almost every social and cultural field, diversity survived as a natural state of humanity and it seems that it will not be obliterated in the foreseeable future. Further, it was seen that arguments in favor of homogeneity were largely based on the misconception that cultural differences are an inevitable threat to unity. However, research (cf., Fishman, 1968a, 1968b) has shown that this notion is unfounded. It is often seen that diverse cultures live in harmony whereas there is discordance even in communities which are culturally homogenous. Divisiveness, as Fishman points out, is an ideological position which can enhance and put negative value on even the most minor differences or even construct differences. Similarly, unification is also an ideological stance which can add positive values on even the greatest of differences or evaluate them as insignificant. To work successfully with diversity, a better understanding of the differences is required, along with a better understanding of successful processes of communication among diverse communities.

Cultural diversity is now among the central themes of a great number of academic discourses, as well as an issue of great concern to human rights organizations. UNESCO, for example, has taken a series of steps to promote and preserve cultural and linguistic diversity. In 2001, UNESCO adopted a resolution on the Universal Declaration on Cultural Diversity and the 21st of May was subsequently declared the World Day for Cultural Diversity for Dialog and Development. The celebration of cultural diversity is founded on the fact that

*The Wiley Handbook of Global Workplace Learning*, First Edition.
Edited by Vanessa Hammler Kenon and Sunay Vasant Palsole.

only through a deeper understanding and regular dialogs, can we envisage a dynamic future where human potential is fully realized.

Academically, focus on diversity and communication has become one of the central themes of sociolinguistics. The theme of communication across cultures has been approached from various points of view. A brief review of these will be presented in the course of this chapter. Before this some basic notions relevant to the discussion will be noted.

## Culture

Any study of intercultural communication requires a clear comprehension of two complex issues: culture and communication. Neither of these is easy to define, and "culture" is notoriously open to interpretation. Kroeber and Kluckhohn (1952, cited in Allwood, 1985, p. 1) talk about 200 different ways in which the concept of "culture" can be understood. Allwood (1985, p. 1) lists four primary factors that determine dimensions of culture, of which the first two involve direct human activity. These are –

1) Patterns of thought—including beliefs, values, norms and attitudes.
2) Patterns of behavior—which may be intentional, aware, individual or unintentional, unaware, and interactive.
3) Patterns of artifact—common ways of manufacturing things starting from pens to houses, such as commonly seen in museums.
4) Imprints in nature—as may be seen in agriculture, road, etc.

Of these, the first two are directly related to human activity. Other scholars recommend a more dynamic and constructivist view of culture. Urban (1996, cited in Coupland, 2003, p. 426) suggests that culture may be better seen, not as a known, stable set of values, norms and beliefs, but as repeated instances of textual construction—of distinctive styles, practices and rituals.

In all views of culture, language is seen as an essential factor constituting and maintaining cultural norms. Research in the field of linguistic relativity (Berlin & Kay, 1991; Whorf, Carroll, Levinson, & Lee, 2012) explores the connection between language and patterns of categorization of nature and construction of worldview. In such deliberations, culture can be seen as a thought process influenced by the native language of the speaker.

## Communication

The concept of communication may be less complex and less open to interpretation as compared to culture. Nonetheless, it has its own intricacies and has also been studied from multiple viewpoints. Communication may be verbal or nonverbal, but for this chapter the focus will be on verbal or linguistic communication. As already noted, one may perceive culture as a process constructed through linguistic communication. Linguistic communication, therefore, should not be seen only as a means of sending and receiving information. Through it, identity is constructed, categories and hierarchies are created and interlocutors are excluded or included in those categories. A number of forces come into play during the process of linguistic communication.

## Intercultural Communication

Intercultural communication is a specific type of communication process, which happens across perceived cultural differences.

Spencer-Oatey and Franklin (2009, p. 3) define intercultural communication as a communication situation where the interactants are conscious of their cultural differences in one way or another. "An intercultural situation is one in which the cultural distance between the participants is significant enough to have an effect on interaction/ communication that is noticeable to at least one of the parties."

Studies on intercultural communication mostly center on understanding how this distance impacts the process of communication, which factors become more salient than others in the process of communication, and what strategies the interactants adopt to handle the distance and promote mutual understanding. The study of intercultural communication is especially important, because during the course of intercultural communication, there is a lack of shared knowledge or norms or understanding, which is present during the intracultural communication process.

This asymmetry is emphasized by Allwood (1985) in the definition of intercultural communication

> [one may] briefly characterize communication as sharing information between people of different levels of awareness and control. I want especially to emphasize the latter since, in an intercultural context, this can become a problem particularly about features of awareness about which people have a low degree of awareness and find it difficult to control. Examples would include the way in which we show and interpret feelings and attitudes.

The term "cross-cultural communication" is used by some scholars in slightly different sense than "intercultural." According to Pym (2004, p. 1):

> Cross-cultural communication can be characterized by a relatively high degree of effort required to reduce complexity, by relatively high transaction costs, by relatively low trust between communication partners, and by relatively narrow success conditions that create points of high-risk discourse.

Gudykunst (2000) makes a distinction between the two terms based on the approach adopted by which the situation is studied:

> Cross-cultural research involves comparing behavior in two or more cultures (e.g. comparing self-disclosure in Japan, the USA and Iran when individuals interact with members of their own culture). Intercultural research involves examining behavior when members of two or more cultures interact (e.g. examining self-disclosure when Japanese and Iranians communicate with each other). ... Understanding cross-cultural differences in behavior is a prerequisite for understanding intercultural behavior. *(Gudykunst, 2000, p. 314)*

### Organization of the Chapter

The topic for this chapter is admittedly diverse and of very large scope—large enough, to have full length books and multi-author handbooks written on it. This chapter will try to provide an outline of the various angles which can be adopted to study the topic. The next section deals with some preliminary and basic theoretical approaches relevant to the study of intercultural communication. The following section gives brief accounts of prominent concepts and analysis for a better understanding of multilingual scenario in current globalized world. The penultimate section gives a few instances of intercultural communication in the workplace, followed by a final, brief, discussion of the issue.

## Theories Related to Intercultural Communication

### Communication Accommodation

Communication Accommodation Theory (CAT) developed as a theory of interaction during the 70s (Giles 1973, 1977; Giles, Bourhis, & Taylor, 1977) to explain the question of linguistic choices made by interlocutors during the course of a conversation. The theory also offers a critique to the studies that followed the Labovian paradigm (Labov, 1963, 1966) of interpreting variations in languages, which ranked shifts in speech styles in accordance with speakers' status in the society and with the contexts of the situation in which the conversation is taking place. In the Labovian framework of sociolinguistic analysis, speech variation in an individual is typically correlated with the level of formality of the conversation setting. An increase in the level of formality in conversation results in greater attention being paid to the speech, which in turn would cause a likely shift to a more "prestigious" variety of the language.

While accepting in principle the influence of the contextual and social factors in the modification of speech style, CAT proposes that one important factor was overlooked in the Labovian model—the influence of the participants in the interaction process. Giles (1973, p. 88) points out that in Labov's study the style shift of the interviewer was not analyzed. The class ≈ style or the context ≈ style norm may be relaxed during the interview as an influence of the interviewer. To address this issue, Giles proposed to offer an additional constraint to the social and situational constraints, i.e., the interpersonal constraint. This constraint requires that, in addition to the contextual cues, the speaker would access the speech style of the other participant(s) in the communication process and would modify their own speech to either converge with or diverge from the speech style of the interactant(s).

This modification is a strategy that the speaker adopts to facilitate the communication process. An "upward convergence," occurs when a speaker perceives the interactant's speech as that of a more prestigious style and tries to approach it; this is done to gain social approval. A "downward convergence" is also possible, where a speaker would approach a less prestigious speech style of the interactant to facilitate communication by reducing the social distance or tension.

In rarer cases the communication process may not aim toward integration. In such cases speech style of the speaker may shift in a way to diverge from that of the interactant(s). Like convergence, divergence is also a strategy adopted by the speaker with the aim of disassociation and the intention to minimize interaction.

Interactants in intercultural communication usually come together in long history of contacts between their culture groups, which may include conflict, prejudice, and rivalry. Accommodation based on group behavior is likely to reflect on language and language-related behaviors such as accent, register, etc. The studies of Coupland (1984), Bourhis and Giles (1976) Rickford and McNair-Knox (1994) show that a speakers' speech style shifts are indeed motivated by the desire to cooperate in the speech process.

CAT as a theory, therefore, is extremely useful in analyzing face-to-face interaction from social-psychological perspective; it can demonstrate how interactants in a conversation establish solidarity or create disassociation depending on a dynamic and complex organization of a number or interrelated factors. CAT is related to Tajfel's (1974, 1981) theory of intergroup relation and social change, which shows that social identity acquires meaning only in comparison with other groups, which motivates individuals to perceive and act in such a manner as to make their own group favorable and distinct from other groups. Together CAT and Social Identity Theory (SIT), as proposed by Tajfel are valuable in understanding intercultural communication (see Gallois, Giles, Jones, & Cargile, 1995; Giles et al., 1977).

## Communities of Practice

The concept of Communities of Practice (CofP) offers an alternative view of community. Instead of defining community in terms of a common cultural marker, it gives an understanding of community in terms of the collaborative work shared by a group of people. CofP adheres to a socially constructed view of community, where the understanding of the interrelationship among a group of people is based on "what they do together" rather than "what they are." The concept of a CofP was developed as part of the socially situated learning theory shaped by Lave and Wenger (1991). A situated approach is defined by Lave (1991, p. 67) as "situated social practice learning, thinking, knowing relations among people engaged in activity in, with and arising from the socially and culturally structured world." Citing Jordan's (1989) work on Yucatec Mayan midwives, it explains the non-classroom mode of learning, where learning happens as part of living the life. Participants in a CofP become masters in their own practices through apprenticeship rather than through a formal teaching–learning procedure. Learning happens as social practice in a group in the absence of a designated teacher. As may be apparent from the discussion so far, an individual can belong to a number of CofPs depending on their joint engagement in some areas, such as work, school, hobbies, etc. The concept is applicable to workplace communities where work groups often form a formally created or informally developed community which can be called a CofP as they are connected by the common work that they must do cooperatively, problems that they must address together and by things that are important to them. In the process, they construct a knowledge that is exclusive to them through joint participation in a common project. To quote Wenger (1998) -

> ... this kind of "knowing" that makes a difference in practice requires the participation of people who are fully engaged in the process of creating, refining, communicating and using knowledge. ... knowledge is created, shared, organized, revised, and passed on within and among these communities. In a deep sense, it is by these communities that knowledge is "owned" in practice.

Though a CofP is commonly formed in the workplace, it is different from other common forms of workgroups such as business units, teams, or networks. CofP has more flexible boundaries than a business unit and its members develop their own knowledge and understanding beyond the immediate business concern. CofP is different from teams as it is defined by knowledge rather than task and is different from networks as it is a joint practice rather than a set of relationships. CofP is constructed when a group of people approach a task together and form a new kind of organizational unit based on learning that people have done together rather than the unit they report to.

CofP is defined by three dimensions

1) Joint enterprise, which is defined, interpreted and negotiated continually by the members of the community
2) Mutual engagements—jointly participated pursuits that tie the members together
3) Shared repertoire—the common resources shared by the community, which may include routines, sensibilities, vocabulary, styles of language, etc.

CofP is an attractive and useful tool to analyze workplace communication, and it is even more engaging in intercultural contexts, since construction of a CofP regardless of cultural differences gives great insight to the process of workplace communication.

> CofP is useful in understanding how power and subordination in the workplace are created linguistically, through speakers' knowledge or lack of knowledge of the shared repertoire and locally shared history in the community of practice they are participating in. *(Corder & Meyerhoff, 2007, p. 457)*

Later developments in the field of CofP focus more on common interest and collaborative construction and sharing of knowledge rather than joint enterprise and mutual engagement. Here the CofP is interpreted as a formal or informal grouping of people who work on similar enterprises. The concept of CofP is redefined as "Groups of people who share a concern, a set of problems, or a passion about a topic, and who deepen their knowledge and expertise in this area by interacting on an ongoing basis" (Wenger, McDermott, & Snyder, 2002, p. 4). The new understanding of CofP, therefore, does not necessarily require a formal or geographical workplace and concentrates on collaborative production of knowledge. This helps us use the concept in global virtual communities.

## Power and Politeness

One of the most critical issues in the discussion of successful intercultural communication, especially in workplace context, is the strategy to avoid interpersonal discordances. Theories of politeness focus on such strategies. Most influential theories on linguistic politeness try to find out the universal commonalities in politeness strategies, even though they appear very diverse in different cultures and these theories draw from Grice's theory of conversational implicature (1975), where he deliberates on an overarching cooperative principle (CP) and four maxims of conversation, namely quantity, quality, relation and manner, which guide everyday conversations. In a regular conversation, the CP and the maxims would be followed intrinsically for maximal clarity and informative communication. However, successful communication does not depend only on the adherence of the maxims and the CP, but such communication may also be done by violating or flouting the maxims. In such cases, the interlocutors use interpretive procedures to ensure success in communication. The CP and the maxims show how people can communicate beyond the literal meaning of words spoken.

Lakoff (1990, p. 34) defines politeness as "a system of interpersonal relations designed to facilitate interaction by minimizing the potential for conflict and confrontation inherent in all human exchanges." Taken from Grice's (1975) theories of CP, it shows that politeness strategies involve apparent violation of the CP, which makes the hearer look for possible explanations in terms of politeness. The three politeness rules according to Lakoff (Lakoff, 1973, 1977, 1989) are—(a) don't impose, (b) give options, and (c) make the hearer feel good and friendly. Even though these three are universally applicable in politeness situations, the different cultures may choose different politeness strategies. They may either show (a) distance, (b) deference or (c) camaraderie.

Leech's (1983, 1980) theory of politeness also draws on Grice's (1975) theory of implicature, CP, and maxims of conversation. Leech proposes a new maxim called the "tact maxim." The apparent violations of semantic directness in utterances like—"can you pass the salt?"—can be explained by mapping the semantic interpretations of asking someone's ability to pass the salt to the pragmatic interpretation of a request.

> the direct and indirect interpretations of such utterances are respectively their semantic and pragmatic interpretations, and [...] the relation between the two, in the case of directives, requires the formulation of a "Tact maxim" in addition to the maxims of Grice's Cooperative Principle. The determination of pragmatic force, in this analysis, requires the placing of an utterance in relation to scales of politeness, authority, etc. in a multidimensional "pragmatic space." *(Leech, 1983, pp. 7–8)*

Apart from the tact maxim, Leech suggests five more maxims—the generosity maxim, the approbation maxim, the modesty maxim, the agreement maxim and the sympathy maxim. Adherence to the tact maxim minimizes cost and maximizes benefit for the other.

The functions of these maxims in creating a collaborative communication are as follows:

- Through the generosity maxim the speaker minimizes self-benefit, while maximizing the other's benefit.
- The approbation maxim requires that one minimizes dispraise of the other.
- The modesty maxim requires that one minimizes self-praise and maximizes self-dispraise.
- The agreement maxim is adhered when disagreement between self and other is minimized and agreement is maximized.
- The sympathy maxim ensures minimization of antipathy and maximized sympathy.

Leech also talks of situations of communication when adopting politeness strategies seem most useful. He categorizes communication situations in four types.

- Competitive situations where the illocutionary goal competes with social goal of ordering/asking
- Convivial situations, where the social goals are for thanking, etc.
- Conflictive situations, which involve threatening, etc.
- Collaborative situations involving asserting, announcing, etc.

Of these situations, adoption of politeness strategies is not required in collaborative or conflicting situations. The competitive situations require negative politeness strategy and convivial situations require positive politeness strategy. Leech's theory of politeness is often considered to be more applicable to intercultural communication situations, than the more influential theory of Brown and Levinson (1987), which takes a universalist approach (cf., Spencer-Oatey, Işık-Güler, & Stadler, 2012).

The potential for conflict and confrontation in regular everyday human communication is also the basic assumption of Brown and Levinson's (1987) theory of politeness, which defines politeness as a strategy to avoid Face Threatening Acts (FTA) in everyday communication. The concept of FTAs is based on Goffman's (1955, 1959, 1963) concept of "face" which can be understood as a social persona that every individual has during social/ cultural encounters. The "face," which is projected by the self can be maintained, lost or enhanced during the course of communication and is dependent on the self as well as the other. Regular everyday communications such as requests, orders, and apologies are potential FTAs either to the speaker or the hearer and the strategies adopted to minimize the FTA are the politeness strategies. They attend to either the "positive face wants"—the desire to be accepted and approved by others or the "negative face wants"—the desire to be free from impediments. The speaker adopts politeness strategies depending on three main factors—cost of imposition, social distance and power. Depending on the seriousness of the FTAs the speaker adopts several politeness strategies, such as avoiding the FTA, going off record (or hinting) and doing the FTA with either redressive action paying attention to either the positive or the negative face. Power is an important concept in most of the theories of politeness including Brown and Levinson's theory. Power here is defined as an asymmetric and vertical social relationship between two persons, where one can control the behavior of the other.

The theories of linguistic politeness discussed so far try to find the universal aspects of linguistic politeness, even though the expression of politeness may differ from culture to culture. Gu (1990), while discussing Chinese politeness norms, brings to attention the social differences in politeness phenomena, which cannot be understood in terms of universality. He points out that instead of individual strategizing to save face, politeness in Chinese context is about following prescribed social norms. Ide (1982) working on the use of Japanese honorifics, also emphasizes the social aspect rather than the individual wants and strategies for analyzing politeness. She points out "face" as conceptualized by Goffman and as used by Brown and Levinson is threatened when the socially prescribed norms are not adhered to. These theories of politeness are more culturally positioned, (than the others that are relatively socially neutral and based on an individual's free choice) moving away from the concept of politeness as a part of interpersonal communication to a more social phenomenon.

Eelen (2001) in his critique of politeness examines politeness as a dynamic social practice, rather than a prescriptive set of norms. Building on Bourdieu's (1987) concept of ***habitus***, which points out that those sociocultural norms are constructed through interaction, Eelen points out that politeness, as a social practice, is constructed and reconstructed through the process of evaluation during the course interaction by a group of a community of practice. This dynamic nature of evaluating and constructing politeness based on the interactional context, is also outlined by Watts (2003) who points out that politeness is evaluated in a social context, determined by social relationships including those of power and dominance through interaction.

Studies in politeness is extremely relevant in intercultural communication in global firms as it can help one take appropriate action to reduce conflicts and cultural tensions in workplaces.

## Intercultural Differences in Turn-Taking

Like CofP, social situatedness is also the basis of the theory of Conversation Analysis, which studies how face-to-face conversation is organized in turns by the participants. To quote Goffman (1983), "it is a fact of our human condition that, for most of us, our daily life is present in the immediate presence of others: In other words, that whatever they are, our doing is likely to be, in the narrow sense, socially situated." Goffman calls this domain of face-to-face interaction the "interaction order." The theory focuses on the fact that all interactions take place in the immediate presence of others and for this reason, for an interaction to be successful; one would require some cooperation such as a very well perceived joint focus of attention.

By paying attention to the maxims of conversations as propagated by Grice (1975) or by having a well-perceived joint focus of attention (Goffman, 1983) and preserving a conventional interaction order, the participants gain some advantages. They increase efficiency of communication by accommodating others by engaging in a collaborative exercise. Apart from looking at conversation from a linguistic point of view, face-to-face communication is also best looked at as a social action rooted in certain preconditions of social life with issues of personal and territorial prospects. Each participant in the communication process has their own cultural assumptions and prejudices. Through speech, the individual is also identified categorically (i.e., he/she is placed in one or more social or cultural categories, such as race, social status, etc.) as well as individually (i.e., depending on his/her style of speech, choice of vocabulary, tone, etc.)

The process of turn-taking, as expected, exhibits intercultural differences. For example, in some cultures, such as Navajo, silence of several minutes is acceptable, whereas in most western cultures such silence would be considered awkward. On the other hand, it is common in the course of African-American conversation, for several people to talk at the same time, which is also not acceptable in northwestern cultures (see Saville-Troike, 2003).

Sacks, Schegloff, and Jefferson (1974), in their proposed model of turn taking asserted that the allocation of term is managed interactionally and that it is a local management system. Analysis of organization of conversation in workplaces can throw light on the interpersonal relations, stratification, and hierarchical structure of the institutions. Analysis of conversation organization in specific workplaces may also reveal specific norms and practices of the workplaces in question.

## Contrastive Analysis

Contrastive Analysis as a field of interlingual study developed initially mainly to aid second language teaching. The work of Robert Lado (1957) is considered to have laid the foundation for using this method of comparing linguistic systems of two languages to understand, analyze and describe the nature of differences between the respective linguistics systems and using them to prepare language-teaching materials and device-teaching methods, which pay special attention to the differences between the languages, as it was assumed that it is the differences that create the most significant learning difficulties. However, even in the early days, contrastive analysis was envisaged as an effective tool to understand intercultural differences. Lado's work, though based within the tradition of descriptive linguistics, included a chapter on cultural analysis. He suggested that a contrastive analysis of culture is important for foreign language teaching. He suggested that "units" of culture should also be identified and contrasted for a successful language teaching. It is suggested that unless we understand and analyze these units cross-culturally we would not be able to understand how the same cultural forms may have different meanings. The most evident interference can be seen in the use of pronouns in different languages. Different languages make use of different number of pronouns, especially second person pronouns, for relevant purposes. People having a native language like English, which is characterized by a single second-person pronoun system, will surely find it difficult to understand the use of three-pronoun systems like Bengali. It will not be enough for them to learn the pronouns and their corresponding verbal forms but also the different use of them in different sociocultural contexts.

Even languages with a similar second-person pronoun system may have a different distribution. We can think of the different distribution of the pronouns in different Indian languages. Bengali and Hindi, for example, have a different distribution of "ap" forms.

The contrast between two cultures is made based on the same criteria of language—i.e., of form and meaning and distribution of those form and meaning. One may find that the same form has different meanings in different cultures. For example, the form of bullfighting has a complex meaning in Spanish culture. It is considered an entertainment, a sport and a display of bravery and triumph of art over the brute force of a bull. To a foreign observer the fighter, the spectators, and the whole event might appear cruel. But it is not that all the Spanish people enjoying the event are cruel, only that their culture does not attach the meaning cruelty to that particular event. Preconceived notions may constitute serious obstacles to the understanding of another culture. One of the main reasons, according to Lado, why the event of "bullfighting" is likely to be differently understood by a non-Spaniard is that in Spanish culture the distinction between animal and human being is far greater than in other linguistic cultures. To emphasize the importance of understanding differences Lado comments (1957, p. 4):

> A good hearted person, anxious to help toward unification of mankind wondered ... was it not better to ignore the differences ... were we not all the same fundamentally?
>
> ... Certainly ... but ... if we ignore these cultural differences we will misjudge our cultural neighbors ... as we constantly do at present.

Even before Lado, the possibility of comparing cultures to acquire a better understanding of language was being explored. Uriel Weinreich, Lado's mentor, recounted these possibilities in his celebrated *Languages in Contact* (1953) which was the first full-length work to explore the possibility of systematic comparison and contrasting of linguistic systems. Weinreich was one of the pioneers of the field and he also envisioned a broader applicability of the field of contrastive linguistics. Apart from its utility in language teaching, his focus was on bilingualism and language contact in its broadest sense. He was one of the first linguists to insist on going beyond the pure linguistic description of a language to include sociocultural factors. The use of social variables to study language change was later taken up by another one of his students, William Labov, and in many senses shaped the field of sociolinguistics as well as modern contact linguistics. Many current ideas in sociolinguistics can be traced back to Weinreich's work.

During the 1980s, contrastive analysis came to be used in various fields in addition to language learning. Some of the important ones are as follows:

- Contrastive pragmatics (Thomas, 1983) deals with the problem of differences in contextual meaning in different languages. What is polite in one culture is often rude in another, especially for languages which are linguistically and culturally widely separated, such as English and Japanese. Contrastive pragmatics often covers such subjects.

- Contrastive rhetoric (Purves, 1988) is concerned with the ways in which second-language learners of different language backgrounds produce written texts.
- Contrastive textology (Hartmann, 1980) is a cross-cultural comparison of text and the investigation of attitudes towards specific texts. The text, in this context, can be defined as connected and cohesive stretch of language either in writing or on discourse.
- Contrastive sociolinguistics (Hellinger & Ammon, 1996) criticizes the practice of contrastive linguistics for comparing and contrasting unspecified varieties of language and making generalizations based on those data. Instead, it advocates a systematic comparison of sociolinguistic patterns and developing a theory of language based on that (Jainicki, 1979).
- Similarly, cross-cultural pragmatics (Wierzbicka, 2003) also extends the basic principles of contrastive analysis. Languages or speech communities may differ in their degrees of directness, explicitness, etc., which may lead to intercultural misunderstandings (c.f., House, 1996).

Contrastive analysis, though initially utilized for language teaching/learning, can provide effective insight into different linguistic cultures and their communication patterns. Different new models of contrastive analysis, especially contrastive pragmatics, and their application in different levels of communication can be very useful in identifying potential problem areas in intercultural communication and avoiding possible miscommunication or dissonance.

## Ethnography of Communication

The field of ethnography of communication or ethnography of speaking developed as a critique of the Chomskyan concept of linguistic competence (Chomsky, 1965), which is defined as a system of intrinsic language knowledge that a native speaker has in order to be able to use the language. Competence is distinguished from performance, which is the observable use of language. This separation of language knowledge from its context was questioned by Hymes (1962, 1968, 1986), who pointed out that learning the grammatical rules of a language is only a part of learning how to speak a language. To be able to produce and understand grammatically correct sentences of a language, without any knowledge of the sociocultural norms about when and how to use them, is not enough to be a competent speaker. Languages exist for the purpose of communication and are always contextualized in a social-cultural setting. So to study language by separating it from the social world would be to not represent language in its entirety. Hymes calls the Chomskyan effort to separate competence from performance a "Garden of Eden" view, which does not fit any real human beings since the "perfect speaker–listener" envisaged in Chomskyan understanding is an abstraction. "...controlling image is that of an abstract, isolated individual, almost an unmotivated, cognitive mechanism, not, except incidentally, a person in a social world" (1972, p. 272).

He offered an alternative view of competence termed "communicative competence," suggesting that a theory of linguistics must be connected with a theory of communication or culture. He points out that language acquisition, which can only happen through social experience, is not just about learning grammatical rules of a language, but it is about when to speak, when not, what to talk about with whom, when, where, and in what manner. Communicative competence consists of four parts,

- Linguistic competence (whether and to what degree something is grammatical) is one. The other three are –
- Social appropriateness (whether and to what degree something is appropriate),
- Psycholinguistic limitations (whether and to what degree something is feasible).
- observing actual language use (whether and to what degree something is done)

Subsequently, to study communicative competence, Hymes proposes an alternative way to look into the "communication process in general." Linguistics as a tool to study of language is vitally important, but to study communication as a whole, one requires an ethnographic approach, where language can be studied within the framework of culture and society. The salient components of communication which can be studied by the ethnographers are—ways of speaking, fluent speaker, speech situation, speech event, speech act, components of speech events and acts, rules of speaking, functions of speech, and ways of speaking. Speech events and acts have 16 identifiable components, organized in a mnemonic acronym (SPEAKING) by Hymes: -

1) Setting—time and place of a speech act;
2) scene—psychological setting/cultural definition of an occasion;
3) (linked as components of act of Situation, *S*).
4) Speaker, or sender;
5) addressor;
6) hearer or receiver, or audience;
7) addressee;
8) (together Participants, *P*).
9) Purposes—outcomes
10) purposes—goals;
11) (grouped together as Ends, *E*).
12) Message form—how things are said;
13) message content;
14) (form and content jointly as components of "Act sequence," *A*).
15) Tone, manner or spirit in which an act is done (Key, *K*).
16) Channels—choice of medium—medium, oral, telegraphic, ...
17) forms of speech—language, dialect, register (channel and forms of speech can be linked as Instrumentalities, *I*).
18) Norms of interaction—implicate analysis of social structure, and social relationships generally, in a community;
19) norms of interpretation—implicate the belief system of a community (together, Norms, *N*).
20) Categories, such as poem, myth tale, proverb, riddle, curse (Genres, *G*).

The usefulness of ethnography of communication in understanding communications in different cultures is apparent. This effectiveness was demonstrated by Kiesling (2012), in his descriptive comparison of two extremely diverse meetings—a gathering of the Kuna community in Panama, (as reported in Sherzer, 1987) and a college fraternity meeting in Northern Virginia, USA.

## Communication in the Urban Multilingual Workplaces

### Multilingualism, Multiculturalism and Language Identity in Urban Spaces

Language-based identities, just like identities based on any other marker (such as ethnicity, gender, nationality, etc.) are dynamic, constitutive and highly negotiable. This nature of linguistic identity is the basic point of Le Page and Tabouret-Keller's acts of identity theory (1985) which presents linguistic identity as an act of negotiation which requires four main criteria to be fulfilled namely: (a) we can identify the desirable group; (b) we have both adequate access to that group, and the ability to analyze its behavior; (c) we have a strong enough motivation to "join" it, and this motivation is either reinforced or rejected by the group; and (d) we have the ability to modify our own behavior. The process and dynamics of negotiating identity in a multicultural, multilingual setting, also plays a pivotal role in Rampton's (1995) study of code switching as a strategic linguistic behavior through which individuals can negotiate identity, by either adopting someone else's ethnicity, or by getting together with them and creating a new one. This is done by an individual by switching into a language which "does not belong to them." Studying the interaction behavior of a group of multicultural adolescents, Rampton notes that the crossing of ethnic boundaries generally occurs when the constraints of social orders or norms are relaxed and in certain other contexts, they adopt the strategy of avoidance. "This kind of switching involves a distinct sense of movement across social or ethnic boundaries and it raises issues of legitimacy which, in one way or another, participants need to negotiate in the course of their encounter" (p. 485).

The negotiable nature of linguistic identity, especially in a modern, multilingual urban space, is also discussed by Otsuji and Pennycook (2009), who recommends the term "metrolingualism," as opposed to the more tradition labels like multilingualism, to capture the uniqueness of the linguistic dynamics of the urban space as which is "... a product typically of modern, urban interaction" (p. 245). Confirming its applicability even in rural and mobile settings, they define metrolingualism as a description of "the ways in which people of different and mixed background use, play with and negotiate identities through language." The focus here is on the fixity and fluidity of linguistic identity, keeping in mind the fact that borders seldom exist within languages. The concept of metrolingualism tries to throw light on how the highly mobile and dynamic social contexts witnessed in urban areas, create new linguistic and cultural identities. This is different from the traditional notions of multilingualism, which sees a similar contact situation as meeting of many fixed linguistic identities.

Another crucial aspect of identity formation is the process of construction, which involves a construction of self and subsequent exclusion of the other. The studies (Bhabha, 1994; Hall, 1997; Said, 1978) on "otherness," though varied and diverse in focus and approach, essentially agree that the construction of identity—be it cultural, national or linguistic—necessarily depends on the exclusion of an-other. Identity construction is an act of drawing boundaries and creating exclusion zones through the process of closure (Jaworski & Coupland, 2005, p. 672) and this process of othering, though based partly on discernible elements, is created largely by imposing subjective, socially constructed ideological significance on those elements. The construction of the "self" and the "other" almost always involves a negative evaluation of the "other.

Another closely related issue with that of "othering" is the construction of stereotypes, which can be understood as a stable and often decontextualized image of a social category made with a set of (often unsubstantiated) beliefs about its traits and characteristics and in studies of intercultural communication (be it research or teaching), cultural identity often refers to a localized national culture (Dervin, 2012). This becomes observable in almost all cases of intercultural contact. Othering of international students, especially Asian students, is discussed by Phan (2009), which shows how the stereotypes are constructed based on race and use of English language.

## Power, Dominance, Lingua Francas and World Englishes

One almost invariable outcome of interlinguistic contact situations is the emergence of a lingua franca. A lingua franca is by definition a communication language among individuals or groups with no common language. Often lingua francas develop as new languages out of contact situations, as may be seen in the cases in the development of pidgins and creoles in different parts of the world. In fact, the term originates from the name of the pidgin Lingua Franca—a mixed trade language used in the Mediterranean area during fifteenth to eighteenth centuries, having linguistic elements from most European languages as well as from Turkish and Arabic. However, in current urban multilingual situations in most cases a shared dominant language, which may or may not be a mother tongue of one of the interactants, functions as this communication language. In the modern global world, English has emerged as the most common international lingua franca, so much so, that English as Lingua Franca or ELF has emerged as a prominent subdiscipline of the research (Firth, 1996; Fishman, 1977; House, 2003; Jenkins, 2009; Ryan, 2012).

Knowledge of and degree of command over a dominant language, especially English may determine the nature of power or dominance of an individual in an intercultural communication situation. This in turn creates an asymmetric language situation, where the languages in non-dominant situations are in danger of falling into disuse (cf. Clyne, Fernandez, & Grey, 2004; Gundara, 1999; Thielmann, 2007).

The rise of English as an international lingua franca is considered to be one of the reasons for the position of great power and dominance of the English language in in the modern world. Knowledge of English holds diverse benefits for people of different cultures (cf, 2009; Meierkord, 2007).

Many international students confirmed that they felt comfortable and respected as international students who had a command of English in addition to their mother tongue. They clearly had taken advantage of the international role of English and presented themselves as having a certain authority with respect to this language. (2009, p. 202).

The widespread of the language also prompted another prominent field of enquiry- i.e., that of World Englishes or WEs (Crystal, 2003; Kachru, 1997; 2005; Kachru & Nelson, 1996; Kirkpatrick, 2010; Kirkpatrick & McLellan, 2012; Pennycook, 2003). Two most common discourses centering the discussion of ELF and WEs are as follows—first, the diversification of English into extremely distinct varieties which is indicated by the plural marker in the term "World Englishes" and second, the damaging effect of English as a lingua franca on other non-dominant languages and on multilingualism and linguistic diversity as a whole (Phillipson, 2008; Skutnabb-Kangas, 2008). Labels such as "killer language," "linguistic genocide," and "lingua frankensteinia" are given to English in such discussions.

## Cases of Intercultural and Interlinguistic Communication in Urban Workplaces

Studies of workplace interaction, especially in multilingual contexts have drawn the attention of scholars and large scale projects are undertaken to analyze this aspect of communication. Holmes and Stubbe's (2003) work on power and politeness in the workplace draws from the Language in the Workplace Project (LWP) which has a corpus of 2,000 interactions involving 700 people in more than 30 workplaces. Apart from descriptive analysis, workplace interaction is also analyzed for specific purposes. Holmes (2003) and Holmes and Fillary (2000) looked into the possibility of using such analysis to handle workers with intellectual disability. Stubbe and Brown (2002) explore strategies adopted for successful communication drawing on the LWP corpus. Newton (2007) discusses the importance of authentic data on workplace interaction for better understanding and training the employees for the communicative requirements of the workplace. Mak, Westwood, Ishiyama, and Barker (1999) studied the problems of social competence in short-term immigrant families despite their dedication and qualification and suggest how the sociopsychological barriers faced by this group can be addressed.

One important constituent of the study of interlinguistic communication in the workplace consists of the use of humor as a tool to build and maintain solidarity on the one hand and to exclude on the other. Studies have shown that humor contributes toward building an more overall conducive environment in the workplace and helps enhance the productivity of the employees (Caudron, 1992; Clouse & Spurgeon, 1995; Ehrenberg, 1995; Morreall, 1991).

Humor is also seen to be a part of workplace-specific culture, which differs from one workplace to another and can be understood as a part of the shared repertoire of a CofP. Holmes and Marra (2002) in their study of four different workplaces, find that each workplace has its own distinct culture of humor.

The fact that workplaces develop their own humor culture proves that humor is generally dependent on shared values and beliefs, which makes it relatable to the concept of CofP (See Section 2.2). It is not surprising; therefore, that humor is also highly culture specific. Consequently, humor often is used to create boundaries between cultures, while reinforcing the solidarity among in-group and excluding the out-groups (Holmes, 2007; Holmes & Hay, 1997; Kell, Marra, Holmes, & Vine, 2007; Lowe, 1986; Marra & Holmes, 2007). Holmes and de Bres (2012) in their analysis of Maori humor in workplace show how humor is used to mark group boundaries, to create in-group solidarity and establish and maintain Maori identity.

## Discussion

A discussion on intercultural communication in modern workplaces requires the examination of two very significant components of communication research—Communication in the workplace and communication in intercultural contexts. This makes the task appealing and challenging at the same time and asks for inputs from multiple perspectives, which requires a discussion on intercultural communication in a workplace context to be markedly diverse and interdisciplinary. Evidently, it is not possible to cover all the aspects of this topic within the scope of a single chapter. Certainly, there are aspects of this topic that have remained unattended in this chapter. However, it has demonstrated the vast range and scope of the topic, its importance in the current global scenario, its interdisciplinary nature and the several important contributions that the field can make in the general understanding of human interaction in the modern world.

## References

Allwood, J. (1985). Intercultural Communication. English translation of Tvärkulturell Kommunikation in *Tvärkulturell Kommunikation: Papers in Anthropological Linguistics, 12*. University of Göteborg, Department of Linguistics. http://sskkii.gu.se/jens/publications/docs001-050/041E.pdf>

Berlin, B., & Kay, P. (1991). *Basic color terms: Their universality and evolution.* Berkeley, Los Angeles, CA/ Oxford, UK: University of California Press.

Bhabha, H. (1994). The other question: Stereotype, discrimination and the discourse of colonialism. In B. Homi (Ed.), *The location of culture* (pp. 66–84). London, UK/New York, NY: Routledge.

Bourdieu, P. (1987). What makes a social class? On the theoretical existence of groups. *Berkeley Journal of Sociology, 32,* 1–17.

Bourhis, R. Y., & Giles, H. (1976). The language of cooperation in Wales: A field study. *Language Sciences, 42,* 13–16.

Brown, P., & Levinson, S. P. (1987). *Politeness: Some universals in language usage.* Cambridge, UK: Cambridge University Press.

Caudron, S. (1992). Humor is healthy in the workplace. *The Personnel Journal, 71*(6), 63–68.

Chomsky, N. (1965). *Aspects to the theory of syntax.* Cambridge, MA: MIT Press.
Clouse, R. W., & Spurgeon, K. L. (1995). Corporate analysis of humor. *Psychology: A Journal of Human Behavior, 32*(3/4), 1–24.
Clyne, M., Fernandez, S., & Grey, F. (2004). Languages taken at school and languages spoken in the community—a comparative perspective. *Australian Review of Applied Linguistics, 27*(2), 1–17.
Corder, S., & Meyerhoff, M. (2007). Communities of practice in the analysis of intercultural communication. In H. Kotthoff, & H. Spencer-Oatey (Eds.), *Handbook of intercultural communication,* (pp. 441–464). Berlin, Germany/ New York, NY: De Gruyter Mouton.
Coupland, N. (1984). Accommodation at work: Some phonological data and their implications. *International Journal of the Sociology of Language, 46,* 49–70.
Coupland, N. (2003). Sociolinguistic authenticities. *Journal of SocioLinguistics, 7*(3), 417–431.
Crystal, D. (2003). *English as a global language.* Cambridge, UK: Cambridge University Press.
Dervin, F. (2012). Cultural identity, representation and othering. In J. Jackson (Ed.), *The Routledge handbook of language and intercultural communication* (pp. 181–194). London, UK/New York, NY: Routledge.
Eelen, G. (2001). *A critique of politeness theories.* Manchester, UK: St Jerome Publishing, Routledge.
Ehrenberg, T. (1995). Female differences in creation of humor relating to work. *Humor—International Journal of Humor Research, 8*(4), 349–362.
Firth, A. (1996). The discursive accomplishment of normality: On 'lingua franca' English and conversation analysis. *Journal of Pragmatics, 26*(2), 237–259.
Fishman, J. (1968a). Nationality-nationalism and nation-nationism. In J. Fishman, C. Ferguson, & J. Dasgupta (Eds.), *Language problems of the developing nations,* (pp. 39–51). New York, NY: Wiley.
Fishman, J. (1968b). Some contrasts between linguistically homogeneous and linguistically heterogeneous polities. In J. Fishman, C. Ferguson, & J. Dasgupta (Eds.), *Language problems of developing nations,* (pp. 53–68). New York, NY: Wiley.
Fishman, J. (1977). English in the context of international societal bilingualism. In J. Fishman, R. L. Cooper, & A. Conrad (Eds.), *The spread of English,* (pp. 329–336). Rowley, MA: Newbury House.
Gallois, C., Giles, H., Jones, E., & Cargile, A. C. (1995). Accommodating intercultural encounters: Elaborations and extensions. In R. L. Wiseman (Ed.), *Intercultural communication theory. International and intercultural communication annual,* (pp. 115–147). Thousand Oaks, CA: Sage.
Giles, H. (1973). Accent mobility: A model and some data. *Anthropological Linguistics, 15*(2), 87–105.
Giles, H. (1977). *Language, ethnicity and intergroup relations.* New York, NY: Academic Press.
Giles, H., Bourhis, R. Y., & Taylor, D. M. (1977). Towards a theory of language in ethnic group relations. In H. Giles (Ed.), *Language ethnicity, and intergroup relations,* (pp. 307–348). London, UK: Academic Press.
Goffman, E. (1955). On face-work: An analysis of ritual elements in social interaction. *Psychiatry, 18,* 213–231.

Goffman, E. (1959). *The presentation of self in everyday life*. Edinburgh, UK: University of Edinburgh Social Sciences Research Centre.

Goffman, E. (1963). *Behavior in public places: Notes on the social organization of gatherings*. New York, NY: The Free Press.

Goffman, E. (1983). The interaction order. *American Sociological Review*, *48*(1), 1–17.

Grice, H. P. (1975). Logic and conversation. In P. Cole, & J. Morgan (Eds.), *Speech acts [syntax and semantics]*, (pp. 41–58). New York, NY: Academic Press.

Gu, Y. (1990). Politeness phenomena in modern Chinese. *Journal of Pragmatics*, *14*(2), 237–257.

Gudykunst, W. B. (2000). Methodological issues in conducting theory-based cross-cultural research. In H. Spencer-Oatey (Ed.), *Culturally speaking. Managing rapport through talk across cultures*, (pp. 293–315). London, UK: Continuum.

Gundara, J. (1999). Linguistic diversity, globalisation and intercultural education. In J. Lo Bianco, A. J. Liddicoat, & C. Crozet (Eds.), *Striving for the third place: Intercultural competence through language education*, (pp. 23–42). Melbourne, Australia: Language Australia.

Hall, S. (1997). The spectacle of the 'other.' In S. Hall (Ed.), *Representation: Cultural representations and signifying practices* (pp. 223–279). London, UK: Sage and Open University.

Hartmann, R. (1980). *Contrastive textology: Comparative discourse analysis in applied linguistics (studies in descriptive linguistics)*. Heidelberg, Germany: Groos.

Hellinger, M., & Ammon, U. (1996). *Contrastive sociolinguistics*. Berlin, Germany, New York, NY: Mouton De Gruyter.

Holmes, J. (2003). Small talk at work: Potential problems for workers with an intellectual disability. *Research on Language and Social Interaction*, *36*(1), 65–84.

Holmes, J. (2007). Humour and the construction of Maori leadership at work. *Leadership*, *3*(1), 5–27.

Holmes, J., & de Bres, J. (2012). Ethnicity and humour in the workplace. In J. P. Gee, & M. Handford (Eds.), *The Routledge handbook of discourse analysis* (pp. 494–508). London, UK/New York, NY: Routledge.

Holmes, J., & Fillary, R. (2000). Handling small talk at work: Challenges for workers with intellectual disabilities. *International Journal of Disability, Development and Education*, *47*(3), 273–291.

Holmes, J., & Hay, J. (1997). Humour as an ethnic boundary marker in New Zealand interaction. *Journal of Intercultural Studies*, *18*(2), 127–151.

Holmes, J., & Marra, M. (2002). Having a laugh at work: How humour contributes to workplace culture. *Journal of Pragmatics*, *34*(12), 1683–1710.

Holmes, J., & Stubbe, M. (2003). *Power and politeness in the workplace. A sociolinguistic analysis of talk at work*. London, UK: Longman.

House, J. (1996). Contrastive discourse analysis and misunderstanding: The case of German and English. In M. Hellinge, & U. Ammon (Eds.), *Contrastive sociolinguistics*, (pp. 345–361). Berlin, Germany/Boston, MA: de Gruyter Mouton.

House, J. (2003). English as a lingua Franca, a threat to multilingualism? *Journal of SocioLinguistics*, *7*(3), 556–578.

Hymes, D. H. (1962). The ethnography of speaking. In T. Gladwin, & W. Sturtevant (Eds.), *Anthropology and human behaviour* (pp. 13–53.). Washington, DC: Anthropological Society of Washington.

Hymes, D. H. (1968). The ethnography of speaking. In J. Fishman (Ed.), *Readings in the sociology of language* (pp. 99–119). The Hague, The Netherlands: Mouton.
Hymes, D. (1986). Models of the interaction of language and social life. In J. Gumperz, & D. Hymes (Eds.), *Directions in sociolinguistics: The ethnography of communication* (pp. 35–71). Malden, MA: Blackwell.
Hymes, D. (1972). On communicative competence. In J. B. Pride, & J. Holmes (Eds.), *Sociolinguistics. Selected reading* (pp. 269–293). Harmondsworth, UK: Penguin.
Ide, S. (1982). Japanese sociolinguistics: Politeness and women's language. *Lingua, 57*(2–4), 357–385.
Jainicki, K. (1979). Contrastive Sociolinguistics: Some Methodological Concerns. *Paper and Studies in Contrastive Linguistics,* 10, 33–40.
Jaworski, A., & Coupland, J. (2005). Othering in gossip: "you go out you have a laugh and you can pull yeah okay but like....". *Language in Society, 34*(5), 667–694.
Jenkins, J. (2009). English as a lingua franca: Interpretations and attitudes. *World Englishes, 28*(2), 200–207.
Jordan, B. (1989). Cosmopolitical obstetrics: Some insights from the training of traditional midwives. *Social Science and Medicine, 28*(9), 925–944.
Kachru, B. (1997). World Englishes and English-using communities. *Annual Review of Applied Linguistics, 17,* 66–87.
Kachru, B. B. (2005). *Asian Englishes: Beyond the canon.* Hong Kong: University of Hong Kong Press.
Kachru, B., & Nelson, C. (1996). World Englishes. In S. Mckay, & N. Hornberger (Eds.), *Sociolinguistics in language teaching* (pp. 71–102). Cambridge, UK: Cambridge University Press.
Kell, S., Marra, M., Holmes, J., & Vine, B. (2007). Ethnic differences in the dynamics of women's work meetings. *Multilingua, 26*(4), 309–331.
Kiesling, S. F. (2012). Ethnography of speaking. In C. B. Paulston, S. F. Kiesling, & E. S. Rangel (Eds.), *The handbook of intercultural discourse and communication* (pp. 77–89). Malden, MA: Blackwell Publishing Ltd.
Kirkpatrick, A. (2010). *Routledge handbook of world Englishes.* London, UK/New York, NY: Routledge.
Kirkpatrick, A., & McLellan, J. (2012). World Englishes and English as a lingua franca. In J. P. Gee, & M. Handford (Eds.), *The Routledge handbook of discourse analysis* (pp. 654–669). London, UK/New York, NY: Routledge.
Kroeber, A. L. and Kluckhohn, C. (1952). Culture: A critical review of concepts and definitions. *Papers. Peabody Museum of Archaeology and Ethnology, Harvard University, 47* (1). Cambridge, Massachusetts: the Museum
Labov, W. (1963). The social motivation of a sound change. *Word, 19*(3), 273–309.
Labov, W. (1966). *The social stratification of English in New York City.* Cambridge, UK: Cambridge University Press.
Lado, R. (1957). *Linguistics across cultures: Applied linguistics for teachers.* Ann Arbor, MI: Michigan University Press.
Lakoff, R. (1973). The logic of politeness,: or minding your p's and q's. *Papers from the Ninth Regional Meeting of the Chicago Linguistic Society,* 292–305.
Lakoff, R. (1977). What you can do with words: Politeness, pragmatics and performatives. In A. Rogers, B. Wall, & J. B. Murphy (Eds.), *Proceedings of the Texas conference on performatives, presuppositions and implicature* (pp. 79–105). Arlington, VA: Center for Applied Linguistics.

Lakoff, R. (1989). The limits of politeness: Therapeutic and courtroom discourse. *Multilingua, 8*(2/3), 101–129.
Lakoff, R. (1990). *Talking power.* New York, NY: Basic Books.
Lave, J. (1991). Situating learning in communities of practice. In L. Resnick, B. Levine, M. John, & S. Teasley (Eds.), *Perspectives on socially shared cognition* (pp. 2–63). Washington, DC: American Psychological Association.
Lave, J., & Wenger, E. (1991). *Situated learning: Legitimate peripheral participation.* Cambridge, UK: Cambridge University Press.
Le Page, R., & Tabouret-Keller, A. (1985). *Acts of identity: Creole-based approaches to language.* Cambridge, UK: Cambridge University Press.
Leech, G. (1980). *Explorations in semantics and pragmatics.* Amsterdam, the Netherlands: Benjamins.
Leech, G. (1983). *Principles of pragmatics.* London, UK/New York, NY: Longman.
Lowe, J. (1986). Theories of ethnic humor: How to enter, laughing. *American Quarterly, 38*(3), 439–460.
Mak, A., Westwood, M., Ishiyama, F. I., & Barker, M. (1999). Optimising conditions for learning sociocultural competencies for success. *International Journal of Intercultural Relations, 23*(1), 77–90.
Marra, M., & Holmes, J. (2007). Humour across cultures: Joking in the multicultural workplace. In H. Kotthoff, & H. Spencer-Oatey (Eds.), *Handbook of intercultural communication* (pp. 153–172). Berlin, Germany/New York, NY: Mouton de Gruyter.
Meierkord, C. (2007). Lingua franca communication in multiethnic contexts. In H. Kotthoff, & H. Spencer-Oatey (Eds.), *Handbook of intercultural communication* (pp. 199–218). Berlin, Germany/New York, NY: Mouton de Gruyter.
Morreall, J. (1991). Humor and work. *Humor: International Journal of Humour Research, 4*(3/4), 359–373.
Newton, J. (2007). Adapting authentic workplace talk for workplace communication training. In H. Kotthoff, & H. Spencer-Oatey (Eds.), *Handbook of intercultural communication* (pp. 519–536). Berlin, Germany/New York, NY: de Gruyter Mouton.
Otsuji, E., & Pennycook, A. (2009). Metrolingualism: Fixity, fluidity and language in a flux. *International Journal of Multilingualism, 7*(3), 243–254.
Pennycook, A. (2003). Global Englishes, Rip Slyme and performativity. *Journal of SocioLinguistics, 7*(4), 513–533.
Phan Le, H. (2009). English as an international language: International student and identity. *Language and Intercultural Communication, 9*(3), 201–214.
Phillipson, R. (2008). The new linguistic imperial order: English as a European Union lingua franca or lingua frankensteinia. *Unions: past-present-future. Journal of Irish and Scottish Studies, 1*(2), 189–203.
Purves, A. C. (Ed.) (1988). *Writing across language and cultures. Issues in contrastive rhetoric.* Beverly Hills, CA: Sage.
Pym, A. (2004). Propositions on cross-cultural communication and translation. *Targets, 16*(1), 1–28.
Rampton, B. (1995). Language crossing and problematisation of ethnicity and socialisation. *Pragmatics, 5*(4), 485–513.
Rickford, J. B., & McNair-Knox, F. (1994). Addressee and topic influenced style shift: A quantitative sociolinguistic study. In D. Biber, & E. Finegan (Eds.), *Sociolinguistic perspective on register* (pp. 235–276). New York, NY/Oxford, UK: Oxford University Press.

Ryan, P. (2012). The English as a foreign or international language classroom. In J. Jackson (Ed.), *The Routledge handbook of language and intercultural communication* (pp. 422–433). London, UK/New York, NY: Routledge.

Sacks, H., Schegloff, E., & Jefferson, G. (1974). A simple systematic for the organisation of turn taking in conversation. *Language, 50*, 696–735.

Said, E. (1978). *Orientalism*. New York, NY: Pantheon Books.

Saville-Troike, M. (2003). *The ethnography of communication: An introduction*. Oxford, UK: Blackwell.

Sherzer, J. (1987). *Kuna ways of speaking: An ethnographic perspective*. Austin, TX: University of Texas Press.

Skutnabb-Kangas, T. (2008). *Linguistic genocide in education or worldwide diversity and human rights*. New Delhi, India: Orient Longman.

Spencer-Oatey, H., & Franklin, P. (2009). *Intercultural interaction: A multidisciplinary approach to intercultural communication*. Basingstoke, UK: Palgrave Macmillan.

Spencer-Oatey, H., Işık-Güler, H., & Stadler, S. (2012). Intercultural communication. In J. P. Gee, & M. Handford (Eds.), *The Routledge handbook of discourse analysis* (pp. 572–587). London, UK/New York, NY: Routledge.

Stubbe, M., & Brown, P. (2002). *Talk that works. Communication in successful factory teams: A training*. Wellington, New Zealand: School of Linguistics and Applied Language Studies, Victoria University of Wellington.

Tajfel, H. (1974). Social identity and intergroup behavior. *Social Science Information, 13*(2), 65–93.

Tajfel, H. (1981). Social stereotypes and social groups. In J. C. Turner, & H. Giles (Eds.), *Intergroup behaviour* (pp. 144–165). Oxford, UK: Blackwell.

Thielmann, W. (2007). Power and dominance in intercultural communication. In H. Kotthoff, & H. Spencer-Oatey (Eds.), *Handbook of intercultural communication* (pp. 395–414). Berlin, Germany/New York, NY: Mouton de Gruyter.

Thomas, J. (1983). Cross cultural pragmatic failure. *Applied Linguistics, 4*(2), 91–112.

Urban, G. (1996). Entextualization, replication, and power. In M. Silverstein, & G. Urban (Eds.), *Natural histories of discourse* (pp. 21–44). Chicago: University of Chicago Press.

Watts, R. (2003). *Politeness*. Cambridge, UK: Cambridge University Press.

Weinreich, U. (1953). *Languages in contact: Findings and problems*. New York, NY: Linguistic Circle of New York.

Wierzbicka, A. (2003). *Cross-cultural pragmatics: The semantics of human interaction*. Berlin, Germany/New York, NY: Mouton de Gruyter.

Wenger, E. (1998). Communities of practice: Learning as a social system. *Systems Thinker, 9*(5), 2–3.

Wenger, E., McDermott, R. A., & Snyder, W. (2002). *Cultivating communities of practice: A guide to managing knowledge*. Boston, MA: Harvard Business School Press.

Whorf, B. L., Carroll, J. B., Levinson, C. S., & Lee, P. (2012). *Language, thought, and reality: Selected writings of Benjamin Lee Whorf*. Cambridge; MA: MIT Press.

# 18

# Internationalization of Higher Education in the United Arab Emirates

## Opportunities and Fears

*Sara AlAleeli*

*United Arab Emirates University*

> *Our grandfathers and ancestors have left a wealth of cultural heritage we are proud of. We shall conserve it and build on it, as it is the soul of this land and its future generations.*
>
> His Highness Sheikh Zayed Bin Sultan Al Nahyan (1918–2004), Founder of the UAE

In the last four decades, the United Arab Emirates (UAE) has experienced tremendous growth and development in its economy and infrastructure. The economic development the UAE has witnessed since the mid-1960s is mainly due to the discovery of oil, which brought affluence, growth and modernization to every aspect of the country. In a single generation, the UAE was transformed from a nomadic nation whose citizens lived in tents and depended on fishing and trading for a living to one of the wealthiest and most dynamic countries of the world. Telecommunications, modern construction, and accessible public and private utilities are among the many measures taken by the UAE government to provide a high standard of living and quality of life for its citizens in the twenty-first century. Accordingly, the UAE, as a relatively new "nation-state," has made remarkable strides in a number of areas, one of which is education.

Since 2000, the UAE Ministry of Education has been working on reforming the K-12 educational system through an ambitious plan entitled "UAE Education Vision 2020," which called for a "radical change in teaching/ learning concepts, practices, means" used in schools (UAE Ministry of Education and Youth, 2000). The UAE has also been investing in its higher education system by creating various educational organizations responsible for measuring and monitoring the progress and quality of public and private higher education institutions (Al-Nowais, 2004). In addition, the UAE government has allowed a substantial number of Western universities to set up branch campuses across the country. The increasing number of private education providers and foreign teachers in the UAE reflects a worldwide movement toward the internationalization of higher education. However, the effect the internationalization process

*The Wiley Handbook of Global Workplace Learning*, First Edition.
Edited by Vanessa Hammler Kenon and Sunay Vasant Palsole.

has on higher education institutions and academics' workplace learning in the UAE has not been extensively addressed. Accordingly, the purpose of this chapter is to examine the definition and rationale behind the internationalization of higher education programs worldwide and use such a conceptual framework to analyze the motives, opportunities, and implications for workplace learning that the internationalization movement might have on higher education in the UAE.

## Internationalization of Higher Education

Internationalization is a term that sheds light on the different ways nations respond to globalization, which "affects each country in a different way due to a nation's individual history, traditions, culture and priorities" (Knight & De Wit, 1997, p. 6). The prefix "inter" in the term "internationalization" means "between or among" nations, which reflects a reciprocal relationship between two or more nations. Hence, internationalization takes into account the international/intercultural exchange that takes place among nations. Such a perspective is crucial when looking at the reform decisions undertaken by different governments—as a response to the globalization process—because it acknowledges the nations' cultural and national identities as key elements in the internationalization process and, thus, reinforces the individuality of nations.

In educational research, internationalization is a term that is often used to describe the international dimensions of higher education around the world. Yang (2002) explained that even though there has been much talk about the internationalization of higher education since the 1980s, scholars have used the term to describe different practices that made it become difficult to have a "simple, unique or all-encompassing definition of internationalization" (p. 81). Knight (2004) added that there are different perspectives on the internationalization of higher education that make it difficult to construct a comprehensive definition of the term. The author demonstrated that some scholars perceive internationalization of higher education in terms of a series of international activities and programs that foster academic mobility for students and teachers, enhance international partnerships and research initiatives among various universities, and create new means for the delivery of education through distance techniques and branch campuses. Others give more emphasis to the intercultural dimension of the internationalization process and highlight that the term mainly reflects "the notion of between or among nations and cultural identities" (Qiang, 2003, p. 249), which reflects the importance of the national and cultural identity to the discussions of the internationalization process. Accordingly, internationalization of higher education can be viewed from different perspectives since "people use it in the way that best suits their purpose" (Yang, 2002, p. 83). Nations, thus, interpret the internationalization of higher education differently according to the different contexts, motives, and purposes for its use.

Yet, one important aspect that researchers have recently pointed out—when defining the internationalization of higher education—is to take into account the national (top-down), as well as the institutional (bottom-up) level of higher education. For example, Van der Wende (1997) introduced an early definition of internationalization that regarded it as a tool used by governments to restructure and improve the quality of their higher education systems. The author explained that the internationalization of higher education takes place when governments promote "any systematic effort aimed at making higher education responsive to the requirements and challenges related to the globalization of societies, economy and labor markets" (p. 18). Although this definition describes the role of governments in endorsing an internationalization stance—as an essential resource in the development of higher education—it lacks a contextualization of the internationalization process within the institutional levels (universities) and the implications such a process has on the education sector.

For that reason, a definition that considers both the national, as well as the institutional dimensions of the internationalization process is needed. Knight (2003) proposed a definition for the internationalization of higher education as "the process of integrating an international, intercultural or global dimension into the purpose, functions or delivery of post-secondary education" (p. 2). It is important to break down this definition in order to highlight how it encompasses both a top-down (national) and a bottom-up (institutional) perspective on the internationalization of higher education. In this definition, internationalization is described as a "process" to reflect the ongoing and continuous nature of this phenomenon. Nations adopting an internationalization approach toward their higher education system engage in an ongoing effort to adhere and be responsive to certain international standards and requirements, such as obtaining international accreditation. The "international, intercultural or global dimension" of internationalization reflects the richness of this process in conveying a sense of a reciprocal relationship among different nations and cultures. Accordingly, the goal of the internationalization of higher education is to integrate such an international/intercultural dimension into the "purpose, functions or delivery of post-secondary education" which is the second part of the above definition. The 'purpose' refers to the objectives and overall goals of higher education institutions. The 'function' reflects the elements that characterize a higher education system, which are usually "teaching/ training, research and scholarly activities, and service to the society at large" (Knight, 2004, p. 12). Finally, the delivery of education refers to the use of new methods, such as information and communication technologies and the provision of new institutional arrangements, such as international branch campuses. The above definition emphasizes the importance of looking at the national and institutional levels when assessing a nation's approach to the internationalization of higher education.

## The Context of the United Arab Emirates

The Gulf Cooperation Council (GCC) countries—the United Arab Emirates, Kuwait, Oman, Bahrain, Qatar, and Saudi Arabia—have put higher education reform and development at the top of their priorities. As a member in the GCC, the UAE has taken various actions to improve its higher education system, one of which is the internationalization of higher education.

Before discussing in more depth the internationalization initiatives the country has undertaken in the past decade to reform its higher education system, it is important to provide a brief history regarding the development of the UAE educational system.

## Brief History of the Educational Development in the UAE

The UAE is a federation of seven independent states located on the Arabian Peninsula. Prior to the discovery of oil, the UAE consisted of a group of low-income emirates under the protection of the British government. Leahy (2009) explained that the British involvement in the UAE was limited to "the management of external relations only. There was never any treaty concerning management of internal or domestic affairs...in educational terms, however, the internal infrastructure in the UAE was almost non-existent" (p. 528). Accordingly, the development of an educational infrastructure was largely left to the locals and neighboring Arab countries to develop.

Throughout the first half of the twentieth century, local traders funded Quranic schools that mainly provided religious and literacy instruction (Alhebsi, Pettaway, &Waller, 2015). In the 1950s, Kuwait, Egypt, and Qatar helped create schools in the UAE that offered subjects, such as social studies, science and geography, in addition to religious instruction (Al-Harbi, 1998). In addition to the help of neighboring Arab countries, the British government built the first school of commerce in 1958 (Al-Harbi, 1998). These schools were sponsored by their respective countries, which provided them with textbooks, curricula and staff. However, the type of education such schools provided was not systematic and greatly resembled that of the Quranic schools.

It was not until the discovery of oil and the independence of the Emirates in 1971 that a modern-like educational structure—which consisted of a four-tier system covering 14 years of education—was developed. The tiers included kindergarten (4–5 years old), primary (6–11 years), intermediate (12–14 years) and secondary (15–17 years) levels (Godwin, 2006). In addition, the UAE government took control over establishing and developing its national schooling system and maintained a policy of providing access and free education for all its citizens (Al-Abed, Vine, & Hellyer, 2005).

In order to nationalize the curriculum and foresee the subjects offered in schools, the government of the UAE established a central educational authority, the Ministry of Education and Youth (MOEY). Despite the establishment of such an educational ministry, the curriculum and textbooks of the secondary schools were still borrowed from neighboring countries (Farah & Ridge, 2009). In 1979 the MOEY launched its National Curriculum Project in order to create an Emirati curriculum, which came into full use in 1985 (Farah & Ridge, 2009). In addition, there is a private education system that caters for expatriates and is usually not segregated by gender at the school level. According to Starr (2010), the curricula used in the private schools mirrors that of the national curricula used in the foreigners' homeland, yet it is under the supervision of the Ministry of Education in the UAE to make sure that it adheres to national policy guidelines.

With respect to higher education, the first and oldest university was established in 1977 in Al Ain and titled the United Arab Emirates University (UAEU). The mission of UAEU, as stated on its website, is to "meet the educational and cultural needs of the UAE society by providing programs and service of the highest quality." Nowadays, UAEU is one of the most popular destinations for students seeking higher education, with over 15,000 students currently enrolled in its various departments (Starr, 2010). The Higher Colleges of Technology (HCT) were established in 1988 and grew into 11 campuses all over the country, followed by the all-women Zayed University, which was established in 1998 (HCT Fact Book, 2015). Currently, there are 27,262 national females in higher education, compared to 14,274 national men (Tanmai, 2005, p. 59), which has resulted in the expansion of public and private higher education institutions across the country. As a result of the increased numbers of students enrolled in secondary-level schools, higher education institutions, both public and private, expanded in the country.

In the context of the UAE, Emirati citizens constitute only 19 % of the country's population (Thomas, 2010), which makes them a minority in their own country. In 2003, the population of the UAE was estimated at 4 million people, of whom 670,000 are nationals with the remainder of the population being expatriate workers and their family (Heard-Bey, 2005). As a result of this unique situation, the UAE government has emphasized the role of higher education institutions in fostering students' sense of belonging to their nation and preserving the culture and traditions of the Emirate society. According to article 3 of Federal Law No. 4, the first goal of higher education in the UAE is "to emphasize the importance of the principles of Islam; to prepare schools to teach the cultures of Islam and the Arabs; to strengthen the originality and the development of the heritage; and to instill in students pride in the heritage, customs, and traditions of their society" (Al-Suwaidi, 1997). The UAE has a rich cultural heritage that is influenced by Islam and Arab traditions, and one way to ensure that the country's cultural traditions and values are passed on to future generations is by establishing a national education system. Accordingly, it is clear from the above history of the UAE educational development that upon its independence, the UAE was keen on building a national schooling and higher education system that is reflective of the culture and values of the nation.

## Education Reform in UAE

Since the unification of the seven emirates and the declaration of the UAE as an independent Arab state in 1971, the founder and late president of the UAE, Sheikh Zayed bin Sultan Al Nahayan recognized that education was at the heart of sustaining the progress and development of his country. In numerous speeches, H.H. Sheikh Zayed reiterated the importance of education and the need for preparing qualified generations who can use their skills and knowledge to preserve the wealth of the country as he declared:

> Unless wealth is used in conjunction with knowledge to plan for its use, and unless there are enlightened intellects to direct it, its fate is to diminish and to disappear. The greatest use that can be made of wealth is to invest it in creating generations of educated and trained people. *(Al-Abed et al., 2005, p. 20)*

Accordingly, upon its independence, the UAE government took control over establishing and developing its schooling system. Article 23 of the UAE constitution states that "Education shall be a fundamental factor for the progress of society. It shall be compulsory in its primary stage and free of charge at all stages within the Union" (Godwin, 2006, p. 2). The author explained that such a commitment to education has led to the building of 1,150 schools, which catered to 650,000 students by the year 2000. In addition, there are currently 116 higher education institutions that cater to 116,912 students, three of which are government universities—with campuses spread across the seven emirates—that provide free education exclusively to UAE nationals (Commission for Academic Accreditation, National Statistics Bureau, 2012). Thus, it is clear that education and human development have been viewed early on as major engines for nation building.

However, at the beginning of the twentieth century, concerns echoed regarding the quality of education in schools and universities and the extent to which such educational institutions prepared students for the global market. Mograby (1999) highlighted the challenges that the UAE education system faced:

> There is no doubt that the current education system is unable to sustain future development, cope with change, and realize desired national goals. The inability of the present curricula and structure to keep up with rapid technological development, new demands of labor market, modern communication, and the information age poses a serious threat to the future of UAE society and economy. (p. 302)

Accordingly, in 2004, the Minister of Education publicly announced the restructuring of the K-12 school system by reforming the curriculum and enhancing the teaching methods and assessment procedures carried out in schools. To that end, Godwin (2006) explained that the K-12 education reform was not only intended to enhance the quality of education, but also create a sense of affiliation to one's homeland as the Ministry of Education sought to "implement an advanced curriculum that will cover the study of modern subjects relevant to the UAE while including topics on Islamic and Arabic heritage" (p. 6). Furthermore, the UAE Ministry of Education issued a policy document in 2000 titled "Education Vision 2020." This document offers a comprehensive plan for the development of education in the UAE so that:

> By the year 2020 the Ministry of Education and Youth will have all graduate students from its schools equipped with the knowledge, skills, competencies,

> learning styles and commitment to national development that enable them to secure the future prosperity of the people of the United Arab Emirates. *(UAE Ministry of Education and Youth, 2000, p. 9)*

In addition, the above policy emphasized the importance of quality education and the integration of technology in schools in order to effectively prepare UAE citizens to compete in the global world. Principle 5 of Education Vision 2020 explained that:

> Education in essence is the making of the future. It prepares man for the future... It is the entry card to the world of the global economy which depends on knowledge and technology which enable man to compete efficiently and effectively. *(UAE Ministry of Education and Youth, 2000, p. 43)*

The UAE government, thus, regarded quality education and the development of human resources as key components for the progress and prosperity of the nation especially in a globalized and constantly changing world.Education reform was not limited to the K-12 schooling system, but extended to encompass the higher education system as well. In order to sustain the rapid economic and social development in the UAE, higher education institutions must produce well educated and highly qualified Emirate citizens who are not only able to compete against the foreign labor force who are currently present in the country, but can also compete successfully in the global marketplace (Nicks-McCaleb, 2005). Accordingly, higher education reform in the UAE has focused on two main goals: providing high-quality education and aligning the higher education system with the economic needs of the country. In 2007, the Ministry of Higher Education and Scientific Research published a policy plan entitled *Educating the Next Generation of Emiratis: A Master Plan for UAE Higher Education* that delineated the national goals of the higher education system in UAE (Fox, 2007). In order for the UAE to meet the economic and technological demands of the twenty-first century, diversify and sustain its economy, and reduce its reliance on oil revenues, the UAE higher education system must be able to: (a) promote access and educational opportunity for all Emiratis, (b) provide high quality education, and (c) contribute to UAE economic development (Ministry of Higher Education and Scientific Research, 2007). The policy also emphasized that, "maintaining the UAE commitment to offer Emiratis a place in a higher education system that reflects UAE values is part of the social fabric of the nation" (p. 10). Accordingly, the above national policy recognized the importance of reforming the UAE higher education system within a framework that honors and reflects the values of the UAE society.

Thus, the UAE government has taken various steps in order to reform and develop its higher education system. For example, the Minister of Education has authorized a program of international accreditation and quality assurance to ensure that UAE national higher education institutions are recognized internationally (Godwin, 2006). In addition, the government required public universities to use English as the medium of instruction and integrate information technology in the classroom though "the use of computer technology in improving learning, and through computers in instruction, networking, web based resources, and the use of laptops" (Fox, 2007, p. 9). In 2010, the UAE government announced an increase in higher education funding so that $1.3-billion will be invested in higher education reform by 2018 (Mills, 2010). Yet, the most prominent aspect of reform is reflected in the massive expansion of private higher education providers in UAE. In the last decade, overseas institutions—mostly from the United States—have begun to open branches in the UAE that are run by western academics and international faculty, such as the New York Institute of Technology, American University in Dubai, Boston University Institute for Dental Research and Education, Harvard Medical School, and Michigan State University in Dubai. A recent project took place in Dubai in 2003 called "Dubai Knowledge City" which is an educational free trade zone campus that allows higher education institutions from around the world to operate with 100 % foreign ownership in a tax-free environment (Godwin, 2006). Accordingly, it is clear the UAE government is dedicated to improving and developing the quality and standards of its higher education system through collaborating with international higher education institutions. Such efforts have resulted in the internationalization of UAE higher education system; a phenomenon the UAE is currently experiencing.

## Internationalization and Workplace Learning in Higher Education in the UAE

Internationalization is one of a county's strategic responses to the impact of globalization. In the context of UAE, internationalization is considered a crucial reform strategy undertaken by the government to develop and innovate its higher education system and, hence, meets the increasing demands of the global market. In order to take advantage of the possibilities that internationalization offers higher education institutions, it is important to examine the rationales that derive such a process and highlight the several implications they have on workplace learning and development in the UAE.

### Political rationale

The political rationale for adopting an internationalization perspective on higher education varies from one country to another. Some of the political motivations for integrating an international dimension to higher education include issues of enhancing national security and stability and fostering of national identity. In order to understand the UAE's political rationale for the internationalization process, it is important to examine the political position of the UAE globally and within the Arab region. The UAE is classified as a developing country with one of the world's highest per capita incomes, which refers to the personal income level of UAE citizens (World Fact Book, 2005). In addition, it is the thirteenth-largest producer of oil and has the fourth-largest natural gas reserves in the world (Burden-Leahy, 2009; Foley, 1990). Foley (1990) explained that the prestigious status of UAE among other Arab and gulf countries—due to the high level of national income, oil revenues, and its strategic geographic position (bordered by Iran, Oman, and Saudi Arabia)—has placed a security threat on UAE, mainly from

Iran. The author, thus, argued that in order for the UAE to maintain its security and stability, it would have to "reform its society, upgrade its education system, and develop collective and integrated security arrangements with its allies to maintain its security in the future" (Foley, 1999, p. 1). One of the important Western allies of the UAE is the United States since the UAE provided:

> $6.572 billion in assistance to the United States during the 1991 Gulf War, and permits that country to use its air bases and ports, which are the only harbors in the Persian Gulf deep enough to berth an aircraft carrier. (p. 1).

Accordingly, by collaborating with US universities and seeking the expertise of US and western academics to internationalize the UAE higher education system, the UAE government is enhancing its national security and stability in the region by strengthening its ties and foreign policy with the USA. To that end, Mills (2008) explained the deep involvement of US academics in the UAE higher education system:

> This month, Wyatt (Rory) Hume, a former provost of the University of California system, took over as provost at United Arab Emirates University, the most comprehensive of the country's three public institutions. Next month, Daniel M. Johnson, president emeritus of the University of Toledo, will become provost of Zayed University, which has branches in Dubai and Abu Dhabi. He is one in a series of Americans to hold that post. (p. 1)

Researchers examining the political rationale for the internationalization of higher education argue that the internationalization process it is not limited to ensuring the national security of a country, but extends to include aspects related to national identity. Since internationalization is seen as a counter-response to the impact of globalization, the internationalization of UAE higher education system could be seen as a way to strengthen and promote the UAE national identity.

De Wit (1999) highlighted that the internationalization of higher education plays an important role in strengthening the national identity of developing countries because:

> By becoming part of a global environment on more equal terms, higher education and society as a whole can move away from dependency and the dominance of Western technology, Western methods, and Western languages of instruction. This strategy would not involve the expansion of English as the language of instruction. (para. 9)

The author further explained that in the case of many Asian countries, replacing English with the national language in higher education institutions has been regarded as a strategic move in the internationalization process. However, this is not the case in UAE where there is a growing concern among the public (parents, teachers, and university faculty) regarding the impact of the internationalization of higher education on the national identity, culture, and language of the country (Thomas, 2010). Western educators have filled key positions in higher education institutions and have been supported by government officials to reform the higher education system to the extent that "the entire university system, from classroom instruction to institutional accreditation, is being overhauled to conform to American standards" (Mills, 2008, p. 1). Such a shift in the reform policies of the Ministry of Higher Education—that rely mainly on western expertise to develop an internationally recognized higher education system—has deeply troubled UAE local professors. Al-Roken, a former law professor in University of UAE voiced his concerns regarding the massive numbers of Western professors across higher education institutions in UAE, "The University is like the army, you cannot surrender it to foreign professors. We are not opposed to them because it is something to do with race, but it is culture. You cannot outsource identity" (as cited in Mills, 2008, p. 4).

In addition, English language plays an important role in the internationalization of higher education in the UAE. Clarke (2007) explains that the UAE has embraced "global English within a policy of linguistic dualism whereby English is associated with business, modernity, and internationalism, and Arabic is associated with religion, tradition, and localism" (p. 584). Given the large number of expatriates working in the private and public sectors of UAE, a growing need for the teaching and learning of English has been recognized by the government. Burden-Leahy (2009) illustrated that the recognition of English as a potential language for college instruction started in 1987 when the HCT were founded in UAE using a Canadian model of community college education and requiring English to be the medium of instruction. However, many UAE students had a low proficiency in English and were not able to do their college work successfully, which led to the introduction of the first English language entry test in higher education in 1995 (Burden-Leahy, 2009). If students did not meet the appropriate English proficiency level score that was required by the respective universities, then they were required spend at least 1 year taking English classes to get to a level that would enable them to undertake college work. Since then, English has become the medium of instruction in both public and private universities (Ministry of Higher Education and Scientific Research, 2007).

The initiatives undertaken by the Ministry of Higher Education and Scientific Research to promote English as the sole medium of instruction in public and private institutions have raised concerns regarding the social and cultural consequences of the spread of international education providers and the fate of the Arabic language. Ismail (2010) argued:

> Now there seems to be a generation of nationals with little or no experience of what it means to be Emirati, Muslim or Arab, with many getting by mostly on rumor and borrowed memories. They can't speak Arabic well, prefer English and in nearly all respects have lost their traditional character. (para. 6)

Even though the government tries to ease the anxiety of the public regarding its look to the West for educational development and ensuring them that learning a foreign language "does not contradict with our universities and colleges being genuine national institutions, because we are also concerned that graduates are well-versed in Arabic and the Arab and Islamic heritage" (Salama, 2010, para. 1), it seems that the public's main fear is that the internationalization of higher education in UAE is not in sync with the Emirate local culture and, thus, poses a threat to the community at large.

**Economic rationale**

The economic rationale often incorporates arguments related to the importance of developing a skilled national labor force that can effectively participate in the economic growth of UAE. Since its independence in 1971, the UAE government has come to realize that it could not rely solely on oil revenues and would have to diversify its economy in order to sustain the development and progress of the country. However, the lack of a qualified and skilled labor force has obliged the UAE to import foreign workers to build the economic and educational infrastructure of the country, which has led to an imbalance in the population ratio of nationals versus expatriates (Morris, 2005). For example, in order to enhance the quality of education and make up for the lack of qualified teachers, the UAE government started recruiting massive numbers of teachers from Arab and western countries to teach in the K-12 schools, as well as higher education. By year 2002, 5,540 teaching staff were employed in the public sector, 74% of whom were expatriates (Morris, 2005).

In response to this situation, the UAE government has promoted a policy of Emiratization (nationalization of the workforce/ teaching force) that aims at increasing nationals' involvement in the public and private sectors (Elhussein & Elshahin, 2008). According to the policy of "Education Vision 2020," the Emiratization of teaching staff is scheduled to reach 90% by 2020 (Al-Abed et al., 2005). However, in order to achieve this goal, UAE national teachers have to be as qualified and skilled as their foreign counterparts. Thus, the UAE government has been committed to taking all the necessary steps to develop and equip its human resources so that they can be able to take up the positions previously held by foreigners.

The economic motivation for the internationalization of higher education is usually linked to long and short-term economic benefits. The long-term benefit of the internationalization process lies in the impact such a process has on developing the quality of a national workforce and human capital in UAE. The UAE government sees the internationalization of higher education as a crucial step in better preparing UAE graduates to contribute to the economic development of the country and decreasing the employment of foreign workers who currently dominate the workforce. As part of a project that is responsible for financing top-class international institutions in UAE, such as Paris Sorbonne University in Abu Dhabi, the Department of Planning and Economy outlined its intentions for supporting such initiatives:

> One of the most important resources in any economy is the people that drive it. Through education, training and skills development, Abu Dhabi will develop and continue to attract a highly skilled and productive workforce to increase its economic might. *(MENAFN-Oxford Business Group, 2009, para. 4)*

To that end, Knight (2004) explained that nowadays "there is more attention being paid to enhancing the international dimension of teaching and research so that domestic students and academics can be better equipped to contribute to their country's effectiveness and competitiveness on the international stage" (p. 22). In the case of the UAE, the current Minister of Higher Education and Scientific Research, Sheikh Al Nahyan, has repeatedly emphasized the importance of internationalizing the higher education system to maintain a competitive edge with other countries and has regarded it as an investment in UAE human capital:

> Our leaders have consistently supported education as an important engine of economic growth and social development, and as a way to provide every citizen with the opportunity to develop his or her full potential. For our country to be successful, all of our students must have the education that will permit them to contribute to their society in line with their talents and their goals. The investment in human capital is a responsibility that rests on the shoulders of all segments of society. We must see ourselves as members of the Global Academic Community and understand the parameters for reaching international excellence in education. *(Srouji, 2010, para. 7)*

As a national leader, Sheikh Al Nahyan's words represent a commitment toward educational development not only for the good and prosperity of the nation-state, but also, for the good of the citizens themselves. In addition, the Minister's recognition that the country sees itself as a member of "the Global Academic Community" reflects the internationalization of higher education that UAE is currently experiencing and is also a part of.

The short-term benefits of the internationalization of higher education are more focused on the institutional level and the revenues generated from opening up branches of international universities within the UAE boundaries. The federally funded universities in UAE include United Arab Emirates University, Zayed University, and the HCT, which admit emirate students at no cost (Fox, 2007). Foreign higher education institutions, such as the American University in Dubai, Heriot-Watt University, and Wollongong University, were initially established to cater to the children of the expatriate community in UAE who were not allowed in public universities (Mahani, 2011). Coffman (2015) described the status of the foreign workers and their children in the Gulf region in general:

> Once considered temporary guest workers, these groups have gradually become more entrenched and have raised families in country. The first waves of thousands of their children coming out of secondary schools are now seeking university places in the Gulf. As they have usually been excluded from public universities as noncitizens, the private sector is their only option. (p. 17)

An increasing number of UAE nationals started filling up seats in the international higher education institutions, especially females who were not permitted by their families to study abroad (Coffman, 2015). Both expatriate and national students are expected to pay full tuition fees for enrolling in an international/private university, which is relatively high and, thus, generates financial benefits for the UAE government (Wilkins, 2010). Accordingly, Mahani (2011) explained that as UAE continues to strive toward internationalizing its higher education system and building partnerships with international universities and international accreditation programs, the UAE is "moving toward becoming a competitor to countries such as China, Singapore, and the Kingdom of Saudi Arabia which have each invested considerably in establishing top-tier research universities" (p. 2). By establishing itself as a leading educational hub in the gulf and the Middle East, the UAE government aims at sustaining and diversifying its economy, in addition to, promoting its national goals of creating a high quality higher education system that is recognized regionally and globally.

However, the massive number of international higher education providers in UAE has raised concerns regarding whether the economic rationale behind the internationalization process is jeopardizing the quality of higher education institutions. Knight (1999) argued that when considering the economic rationale for the internationalization of higher education, "it is essential to find the balance between income generating motives and academic benefits" (p. 19). In UAE, local media has criticized the speed at which international universities have been established across the seven Emirates and has referred to this phenomenon as "educational gold rush" (Lewin, 2008). For instance, in three years from 2006 to 2009, 49 international universities have established branch campuses in UAE (Becker, 2009). Such widespread establishment? of international universities has cast doubts on the motives of such institutions, especially since many of them had to shut down since they did not achieve standards of quality comparable to their home campuses (Wilkins, 2010). For this reason, a reevaluation of the impact of heavily adopting an economic rationale is necessary so as not to compromise the quality of UAE higher education system.

### Academic rationale

The main academic argument behind the internationalization of higher education is the perceived contribution it makes to the enhancement of the quality of higher education. However, in order for internationalization to have an impact on the quality of higher education, the integration of an international dimension to teaching, research and service has to be an essential goal and not an add-on feature of higher education institutions. Knight (1999) explained

> It is assumed that by enhancing the international dimension of teaching, research and service there is value added to the quality of our higher education systems. This premise is clearly based on the assumption that internationalization is considered to be central to the mission of the institution and is not a marginalized endeavor. (p. 20)

When looking at the mission statements of some of the higher education institutions in UAE, we can clearly see that they often refer to the importance of integrating an international aspect to the education of UAE citizens. For instance, the mission statement of the HCT in UAE states:

> HCT places significant emphasis on preparing students for a globalized workplace. Students are provided with opportunities to become conversant with international best practices in their professions and understanding of other cultures. Major international conferences such as Education Without Borders and Festival of Thinkers are organized by HCT to meet this objective. *(The Higher Colleges of Technology [HCT], 2012)*

The conceptual framework for Zayed University (ZU) emphasizes the importance of "Global Awareness" as a central learning outcome of the university. The university emphasizes ***global awareness*** as a learning outcome. For ZU, global awareness means:

> Respect and awareness of other cultural experiences, beliefs, and values and the ability to see connections among them. They also mean developing the ability to examine global issues within the local context, such as comparing various national systems of education and the ability to generate new understanding of a topic. Finally, global awareness means the ability to provide an informed response to a global concept or issue through conceptualization of a topic. *(Zayed University, 2010, p.14)*

Lastly, aside from its current vision and commitment to providing high-quality education for UAE students, the University of UAE described its future vision as, "The United Arab Emirates University will be an internationally distinguished comprehensive research university. While adhering to UAE values, it will become a world-class center for applied research, national and international outreach, innovation and outcome-based learning" (United Arab Emirates University [UAEU], 2012).

Even though the above mission statements reflect to an extent the commitment of UAE higher education institutions to internationalize their programs and prepare their students for a globalized world, there is an absence of research that describes how such institutions put their internationalization plans into action. Research that examines how UAE universities integrate an international dimension into their teaching, research, and service is needed in order to assess the success and failures of the internationalization of UAE higher education system.

The academic rationale also emphasizes the role of the internationalization process in addressing quality and accountability-related issues in higher education institutions. Meeting international academic standards for teaching and research is seen as one of the fundamental gains of the internationalization of higher education (De Wit, 1995, 2002; Knight & de Wit, 1999). In UAE, most universities seek recognition and the achievement of international academic standards through collaborating with professional bodies in the United Kingdom and the United States (Burden-Leahy, 2009). For example, one of the main goals for United Arab Emirates University is to "focus on international recognition of excellence through accreditation and external evaluation of all its activities"

(UAEU, 2012). In addition, Mills (2008) explained that it is imperative for higher education institutions in UAE to gain international accreditation because the government regards the meeting of international standards as essential for ensuring that their graduates would appeal to the international companies that exist in UAE. In addition, Fox (2007) described the link between international accreditation and quality of higher education in the context of UAE:

> A system that does not meet internationally accepted standards of quality—in its staffing, in its programs, in instructional technology and in its graduates—will not serve society well. Failure to maintain standards in all of these areas means that the job market will not welcome degree holders as readily, and this will in turn lead to students making other choices about their education. In order to certify quality, both the United Arab Emirates University and Zayed University are exploring accreditation from a United States regional accrediting body, and are receiving accreditation for specialized programs such as engineering and education. (p. 8)

Accordingly, UAE higher education institutions are constantly seeking international accreditation as part of their overall higher education reform and commitment to the internationalization process.

#### Sociocultural rationale

The sociocultural rationale reflects the national and institutional motivations for acknowledging cultural and ethnic diversity within and among different countries. Such rationale calls for the importance of promoting intercultural understanding and communication among individuals from diverse social, cultural and linguistic backgrounds. Knight (1999) explained that the sociocultural rationale "is considered by many academics as one of the strongest rationales for internationalizing the teaching/learning experience of students in undergraduate and graduate programs" (p. 20). In order to prepare students to participate effectively in an interdependent world, higher education institutions should demonstrate a commitment to promoting intercultural understanding and respect of cultural diversity. In the context of UAE, Emirati nationals live in a highly diverse nation, where foreigners and expatriate workers constitute about 80% of the population (Thomas, 2010). Accordingly, a sociocultural rationale to the internationalization of UAE higher education is important to cultivate in students a sense of pride in their own cultural heritage and traditions, as well as emphasize the importance of valuing and appreciating those of students from other culture.

Some of the UAE higher education institutions have taken an explicit stance toward integrating an intercultural aspect to their education. For example, Alhosn University in Abu Dhabi celebrated its fifth International Day, which called for "the importance of fostering respect and harmony across all cultures and nationalities" (Alhosn University, 2011). Zayed University integrated a "culturally responsive approach" in its conceptual framework in order to:

> Ensure that a student's prior knowledge, linguistic and cultural experience and abilities are seen as a "resource" and given value in the classroom

> curriculum, and to ensure that that teachers maintain high expectations of all their students (Moll, Amanti, Neff, & Gonzalez 1992; Gonzales, Moll and Armanti, 2005). This knowledge and focus is crucial in the multiethnic and multicultural society of the UAE. *(Zayed University [ZU], 2010)*

Accordingly, a sociocultural rationale ensures that the internationalization of UAE higher education system would not only serve economic, political, and academic goals, but would also help to build a climate of equity and tolerance among people from different ethnic and cultural backgrounds across the UAE. However, at the UAE national level, there seems to be a diminished importance of the sociocultural rationale to internationalization, which might be due to the dominance of the political and economic rationales.

Higher education institutions in the UAE are undergoing several policy changes as a result of the internationalization process, which has implications in regards to faculty workplace learning. Workplace learning refers to "all and any learning that is situated in the workplace or arises directly out of workplace concerns" (Lester & Costley, 2010, p. 562). Internationalization is reshaping the workplace for academics in UAE; thus, offering them new opportunities and challenges they have to adjust to. The changing educational policies—collaborating with US and international universities, using English as the language of instruction, integrating intercultural and exchange experiences—create a new learning environment for UAE academics. Changes to academics' practices in teaching, research, and service as a result of the new learning they are situated in due to the internationalization process should be examined.

## Conclusion

Realizing that oil is a finite commodity, the UAE government has been keen on diversifying its economy in order to sustain the development and progress of the country. However, the provision of a skilled and qualified workforce is a prerequisite for building a strong economy in UAE, which explains the UAE commitment to developing and reforming its higher education system since the 1970s. Nowadays, one way the UAE can maintain a competitive edge in a globalized world is by investing in its human resources through offering them the necessary knowledge and skills that would help them advance locally and globally. In this chapter, the concept of internationalization has been used as a lens to examine the initiatives undertaken by the UAE government to reform its higher education system and shed light on the cultural dimensions involved in such a process. By using the internationalization perspective to explain the expansion and transformation of UAE higher education institutions, one is able to understand and reflect on the different rationales that derive the higher education reform wheel in the UAE. The above analysis of the different dimensions of the internationalization of higher education in the UAE has several implications on workplace learning and development. Research that examines the impact of the internationalization process on academics' workplace learning in UAE's higher education institutions is needed amid the series of policy changes and education reform the country is undergoing.

## References

Al-Abed, I., Vine, P., & Hellyer, P. (2005). *United Arab Emirates yearbook.* Abu Dhabi, United Arab Emirates: Trident Press Ltd.

Al-Harbi, M. (1998). *Development of education in the UAE: A documentary introduction.* Dubai, United Arab Emirates: AlBayan Press.

AlHosn University. (2011). ALHOSN University emphasizes respect for national identity at 5th International Day. Retrieved from http://www.albawaba.com/alhosn-university-emphasizes-respect-national-identity-5th-international-day

Alhebsi, A., Pettaway, L., & Waller, L.R. (2015). A History of Education in the United Arab Emirates and Trucial Sheikdoms. *The Global eLearning Journal, 4*(1), 1–6.

Al-Nowais, S. (2004). Education system to get overhaul. *Gulf News Online.* Retrieved from http://www.gulfnews.com/Articles/print2.asp?ArticleID=141170

Al-Suwaidi, K. (1997). Higher education in the United Arab Emirates: History and prospects. In K. E. Shaw (Ed.), *Higher education in the Gulf: Problems and prospects,* (pp. 101–118). Exeter, UK: University of Exeter Press.

Becker, R. (2009). *International branch campuses: Markets and strategies.* London, UK: The Observatory on Borderless Higher Education.

Burden-Leahy, S. (2009). Globalization and education in the postcolonial world: The conundrum of the higher education system of the United Arab Emirates. *Comparative Education, 45*(4), 525–544.

Clarke, M. (2007). Language policy and language teacher education in the United Arab Emirates. *TESOL Quarterly, 41*(3), 583–591.

Coffman, J. (2015). Higher education in the Gulf: Privatization and Americanization. *International Higher Education, 33,* 17–19 Retrieved from https://ejournals.bc.edu/ojs/index.php/ihe/article/view/7393/6590

Commission for Academic Accreditation, National Statistics Bureau. (2012). Knowledge and Human Development Authority. Retreived from http://www.chea.org/pdf/Higher%20Education%20in%20Dubai.pdf

De Wit, H. (Ed.) (1995). *Strategies of internationalization of higher education. A comparative study of Australia, Canada, Europe and the United States.* Amsterdam, The Netherlands: European Association for International Education.

De Wit, H. (1999). Changing Rationales for the Internationalization of Higher Education, *International Higher Education.* Retrieved from https://ejournals.bc.edu/ojs/index.php/ihe/article/view/6477

De Wit, H. (2002). *Internationalization of higher education in the United States of America and Europe: A historical, comparative and conceptual analysis.* Westport, CT: Greenwood.

Elhussein, A. M., & Elshahin, A. (2008). Manpower Emiratisation in the United Arab Emirates federal government: An exploratory study from the perspective of civil service leadership. *Asia Pacific Journal of Public Administration, 30*(1), 83–95.

Farah, S. and Ridge, N. (2009). Challenges to curriculum development in the UAE. Retrieved from http://www.dsg.ae/PUBLICATIONS/PublicationDetail.aspx?udt_826_param_detail=760

Foley, S. (1999). The UAE: Political issues and security dilemmas. *Middle East Review of International Affairs, 3*(1). Available at http://www.rubincenter.org/1999/03/foley-1999-03-03/), Accessed October 18, 2018.

Fox, W. (2007). The United Arab Emirates: Policy choices shaping the future of public higher education. Berkeley Center for Studies in Higher Education, Research and Occasional Paper Series: CSHE.13.07, 1–15. Available at https://cshe.berkeley.edu/sites/default/files/publications/rops.fox.uae_he_policy.7.21.07.pdf Accessed October 18, 2018.

Godwin, S. (2006). Globalization, education, and emirtatization: A study of the United Arab Emirates. *The Electronic Journal of Information Systems in Developing Countries, 27*(1), 1–14.

HCT Fact Book. (2015). Retrieved from www.hct.ac.ae/content/uploads/HCT-Fact-Book-2015-2016-English-1.1.pdf

Heard-Bey, F. (2005). The United Arab Emirates: Statehood and nation building in a traditional society. *The Middle East Journal, 59*(3), 357–375.

Ismail. (2010, October 14). Westernised education is no substitute for national identity. *The National*. Retrieved from www.thenational.ae

Knight, J., & De Wit, H. (1997). *Internationalization of higher education in Asia Pacific countries*. Amsterdam, The Netherlands: EAIE.

Knight, J., & de Wit, H. (Eds.) (1999). *Quality and internationalization in higher education*. Paris, France: Organization for Economic Cooperation and Development.

Knight, J. (1999). Issues and trends in internationalization. In S. Bond, & J. Lemasson (Eds.), *A new world of knowledge: Canadian universities and globalization* (pp. 201–238). Ottawa, Canada: International Development Research Center.

Knight, J. (2003). Updated internationalization definition. *International Higher Education, 33*, 2–3.

Knight, J. (2004). Internationalization remodeled: Definition, approaches, and rationales. *Journal of Studies in International Education, 8*(5), 5–31.

Lester, S., & Costley, C. (2010). Work-based learning at higher education level: Value, practice and critique. *Studies in Higher Education, 35*(5), 561–575.

Lewin, T. (2008, February 10). U.S. universities rush to set up outposts abroad. *The New York Times*. Retrieved October 28, 2009, from http://www.nytimes.com/2008/02/10/education/10global.html

Mahani, S. (2011). Internationalization of higher education: A reflection on success and failures among foreign universities in the United Arab Emirates. *Journal of International Education Research, 7*(3), 1–8.

MENAFN-Oxford Business Group (2009). Abu Dhabi Education Reform. Retrieved from http://www.menafn.com/qn_news_story_s.asp?StoryId=1093240098

Mills, A. (2008). Emirates look to the west for prestige. The Chronicle of Higher Education, September 26, 2008. Retrieved from http://chronicle.com/article/Emirates-Look-to-the-West-for/8165

Mills, A. (2010). Abu Dhabi proposes ways to improve a higher education system that falls short. The Chronicle of Higher Education, June 20, 2010. Retrieved from http://chronicle.com/article/Abu-Dhabi-Proposes-Ways-to/65851

Ministry of Higher Education and Scientific Research (2007). Educating the next generation of Emiratis: A master plan for UAE higher education. Retrieved from

http://planipolis.iiep.unesco.org/upload/United%20Arab%20Emirates/United%20Arab%20Emirates_Higher_Education_plan.pdf
Mograby, A. (1999). Human development in the United Arab Emirates: Indicators and challenges. In J. S. Al Suwaidi (Ed.), *Education and the Arab world: Challenges of the next millennium* (pp. 279–308). Reading, UK: Ithaca Press.
Moll, L., Amanti, C., Neff, D., & Gonzalez, N. (1992). Funds of knowledge for teaching: Using a qualitative approach to connect homes and classrooms. *Theory into Practice, 31*(2), 132–141.
Morris, M. 2005, Organization, social change and the United Arab Emirates, Paper presented to the Social Change in the 21st Century Conference, Centre for Social Change Research, Queensland University of Technology.
Nicks-McCaleb, L. (2005). The impact of state funded higher education on neighborhood and community in the United Arab Emirates. *International Education Journal, 6*(3), 322–334.
Qiang, Z. (2003). Internationalization of higher education: Towards a conceptual framework. *Policy Futures in Education, 1*(2), 248–270.
Salama, S. (2010, October 6). Emphasis on foreign languages does not contradict UAE policies. *Gulf News*. Retrieved from http://gulfnews.com/news/gulf/uae/education
Srouji, S. (2010, June 03). 90% adult literacy rates in UAE. *Zawya*. Retrieved from www.zawya.com
Starr, J. (2010). United Arab Emirates. State University. Retrieved from http://education.stateuniversity.com/pages/1614/United-Arab-Emirates SUMMARY.html
Tanmai, T. (2005). *United Arab Emirates Human Resources Report*. Dubai, United Arab Emirates: UAE Ministry of Information and Culture.
The Higher Colleges of Technology, 2012. The HCT Advantage. Retrieved from www.hct.ac.ae/about/advantage
The United Arab Emirates University (2012). Future Vision. Retrieved from www.uaeu.ac.ae/about/vision.shtml
Thomas, J. (2010). Partnerships, collaborations, and international education in the UAE: The question of context and relevancy. Retreived from http://www.mei.edu/sites/default/files/publications/EducationVPVol.III_.pdf
United Arab Emirates University. Retrieved from www.uaeu.ac.ae/hr/eguide/docs/New_Emp_Guide_The_UAEU_v2.pdf
United Arab Emirates Ministry of Education and Youth. (2000). Education Vision 2020: Pillars, strategic objectives, projects and implementation programs for UAE education development. Abu Dhabi, United Arab Emirates.
Van der Wende, M. (1997). Missing links: The relationship between national policies for internationalisation and those for higher education in general. In T. Kalvermark, & M. van der Wende (Eds.), *National policies for the internationalization of higher education in Europe,* (pp. 10–31). Stockholm, Sweden: Hogskoleverket Studies, National Agency for Higher Education.

Wilkins, S. (2010). Higher education in the United Arab Emirates: An analysis of the outcomes of significant increases in supply and competition. *Journal of Higher Education Policy and Management*, *32*(4), 389–400.

World Fact Book. 2005. Rank order, oil production. Central Intelligence Agency. http://www.odci.gov/cia/publications/factbook/rankorder/2173rank.html.

Yang, R. (2002). University internationalization: Its meanings, rationales and implications. *Intercultural Education*, *13*(1), 81–95.

Zayed University, 2010. Precondition 4. 1–42 Retrieved from https://www.zu.ac.ae/main/en/colleges/colleges/__college_of_education/about_us/Framework.aspx Accessed October 18, 2018.

# 19

# Are We Teaching and Assessing the English Skills Needed to Succeed in the Global Workplace?

*Maria Elena Oliveri and Richard J. Tannenbaum*

*Educational Testing Services*

Globalization is increasing the need for English skills in the workplace. For example, over 60% of global companies surveyed in Educational Testing Service [ETS], 2015 identified English as a language used on a daily basis in written and spoken corporate communications, transforming English Language Proficiency (ELP) into a prerequisite for functioning in a global society (Institute for International Business Communication, 2009). This percentage suggests that to remain competitive in a global economy, businesses will likely need to pay increased attention to reinforcing ELP skills to keep up with the increased demands for ELP. However, a focus on ELP is not sufficient, ELP improvements also require greater awareness of which particular English skills may need more or less growth and development, so that limited time and teaching resources can be targeted to addressing the needed skills. Learners, teachers and employers should thus ask whether ELP improvements require studying more grammar, technical vocabulary or oral communication? Or should greater attention be applied to the development of pragmatic aspects of productive English communication? Whether language classrooms are aligned or not with the skills and competencies needed to satisfy workplace expectations? And, How can educators close the gaps?

English-language competency includes all four major skill areas: reading, writing, listening and speaking. It also includes interactive and dialogic skills. For instance, Gunnarsson (2009) and Myles (2009) suggest that oral proficiency includes the ability to participate in dialogs between two or more persons in face-to face interactions, online collaborations and presentations. Moreover, Duff (2008) also suggests the inclusion of how to interact with persons of other cultures or backgrounds in an ELP model. These skills play an increasingly important role as international organizations expand their global reach. Further, Duff highlights that a global expansion of businesses, accompanied by increased technological and societal changes, puts pressure on the development of new or the expansion of existing forms of English literacy and related communicative skills, which in turn, raises new demands and expectations for English language

*The Wiley Handbook of Global Workplace Learning*, First Edition.
Edited by Vanessa Hammler Kenon and Sunay Vasant Palsole.

learning. For example, in the following vignette, consider noting the skills needed for conducting a business transaction regarding a point of sale:

> A laptop might be ordered from a Web site, the order immediately transmitted to China managed by a Taiwanese firm that supplies computers to several large manufacturers [with] the final assembly completed in China, [where it is] shipped via FedEx to your home (O'Toole & Lawler III, 2015, p. 31).

This example highlights the complexities that may occur in a business transaction with respect to the number of countries, firms, communication forms and teams that an item passes through from the point of manufacture all the way through an online purchase.

The consequences of not reacting and adapting quickly to keep up with globalization coupled with increases in the need for English language proficiency may adversely impact businesses' ability to remain competitive. It also may reduce worker employability and companies' financial prosperity, or give rise to more companies investing in English-speaking nations (Stickel, 2010). The issue of an expanded English-language skillset thus becomes salient to multiple stakeholders (e.g., employers, employees, students and educators).

Because a failure to keep up with English demands can have significant negative consequences, one might reasonably expect language classroom settings to be a solution for assuring needed English proficiency. However, this cannot be taken for granted. In fact, research indicates that the simple duration of language instruction does not have a strong relationship to workplace readiness (Martin, 2004). Bhatia (2010) also points out that despite prolonged instruction, students often end up under-prepared for the communicative demands of the workplace. These results do not discount the importance of English-language instruction, per se, but rather reinforce the criticality of understanding and aligning the purpose of the instruction and the content of that instruction (e.g., what aspects of English proficiency need to be taught to support the intended language application?) rendering the substance of what is taught a more important component for increasing competency in English than the simple duration of what is taught.

In this chapter, we provide a general overview of the consequences related to ELP for various stakeholders, including employees, employers, international businesses and countries. As a first step to mitigating likely negative consequences of low ELP, we consider what English-related skills are essential to carry out workplace functions in international businesses. We examine this issue from a general perspective as described in the literature and from the employers' perspective as distilled from large-scale survey responses. As an example of the expanded English-language skillset needed, we describe the role of pragmatics, the use of language in context, as well as interactive and collaborative communication skills deemed critical for workplace success. Bolchover (2012) and Marra (2012) note the importance of sociopragmatics and cross-cultural communication for workplace readiness with an impact on business operations and instructional approaches, respectively. We conclude by suggesting that an expanded skillset has implications for educators who support English language learners, the learners themselves and for developers of language assessments. While we aim to contribute to this discussion by considering ways that classroom curricular and instructional materials may be revised to improve student learning, we suggest that much more research and collaborative efforts among stakeholders are needed to improve current preparation practices. This chapter is intended to provide an overview of these issues rather than an in-depth treatment, given the limitations of space. Our goal is to offer new insights and to foster continued discussion.

## Impact of Low ELP on Countries, International Businesses, Employers and Employees

Low ELP has a negative impact on various stakeholders including countries, businesses seeking to expand beyond national borders, employers seeking to run international businesses successfully and employees seeking greater job opportunities, higher salaries and promotions. In relation to an impact on non-English speaking countries, Stickel (2010) describes how low ELP negatively impacts nations wishing to remain globally competitive by reducing business growth opportunities. Worldwide, proficiency in English helps reduce gaps in employee preparation, providing enhanced opportunities for employees and enabling organizations to compete globally. Baker, Resch, Carlisle, and Schmidt (2001), for example, state that English-speaking employees earn 25 to 35% higher salaries than their non-fluent counterparts and have access to a greater number of higher-level jobs. The higher salaries and the concomitant increases in national investments in English-speaking nations or nations with high numbers of English-speakers has led to a steep increase in English language schools across Europe (Baker et al., 2001).

For international businesses, high ELP helps increase confidence that employees will successfully carry out key workplace functions (e.g., customer service, communications with clients and partners overseas) that bolster the company's reputation and brand (ETS, 2014). The results of a large-scale global survey conducted by the Economist Intelligence Unit (Bolchover, 2012) with 572 executives from over 250 international companies suggest that low ELP may lead to loss of revenue resulting from misunderstandings in communication, which prevents the completion of major cross-border transactions (Welch, Welch, & Marschan-Piekkari, 2001). More specifically, low ELP within an international organization likely has a negative impact on interactions with English-speaking clients, partners and customers. These interactions are central to business success, since poor communication may result in a lack of confidence, credibility and trust between the external client and the organization (ETS, 2014, 2015). Low ELP also leads to delays in phone call responses, emails and letters in English, as client inquiries must be re-routed to employees who are more proficient in English (ETS, 2015). Across such instances, employers may incur extra expenses and do incur lost productive time, as additional employees are needed to translate information across offices (Bolchover, 2012).

For employees, proficiency in English may help prepare them for higher-paying jobs, increase their marketability, and offer them opportunities for professional growth including travel overseas (Chiswick & Miller, 2010; Kassim & Ali, 2010; Ojanpera, 2014). To illustrate the impact of ELP on personal income, Chiswick and Miller (2010) used the 2000 US Census data and the Occupational Information Network (O*NET) database to examine the required English-language proficiency of occupations in the US labor market and to evaluate the value of English proficiency on earnings for men aged 25–64 years for both native- and foreign-born individuals in the 50 US states and the District of Columbia. The researchers found that for every standard deviation in change in the level of required occupational English, there was an associated increase in earnings by 15.9% (for native-born employees) and 19.7% (for foreign-born employees). The researchers noted that these changes "are the equivalent of the earnings effects associated with two years of schooling for the native-born and almost six years of schooling for the foreign-born" (p. 368). Marschan, Welch, and Welch (1997), Piekkari (2006) and SanAntonio (1987) point out that individuals who are competent in a key language of the organization may gain strategically important positions beyond their formal job status. Conversely, low ELP may lead to truncated opportunities for growth, employees stuck in dead-end positions involving simpler tasks, or employees feeling unrecognized for their work.

## English-Related Communicative Skills Necessary for the Global Workplace

Despite the importance attributed to the English language and the substantial national investments made to improve ELP, most attempts to increase it have been unsuccessful in preparing students for the demands of the workforce (Chew, 2005; Noguchi, 2010). For instance, Martin (2004) states that despite the time, effort and money spent in studying English in Japan, "it is rare to find a Japanese student who, after 6 years of English, is able to engage in even a marginal dialog with a speaker of English" (p. 50). This quote suggests that what is needed is not a focus on more studying time, but the identification of the key language skills required by employers to improve workplace readiness. Moreover, once such skills are identified, teacher preparation needs to follow to equip teachers with the pedagogical know-how for teaching the needed skills.

In this regard, Evans (2013) used case studies, interviews and surveys to investigate communicative tasks and key task characteristics expected of employees in an English-speaking workplace setting in Hong Kong and found the following communicative activities most prominently featured: writing and reading of e-mails and reports, formal and informal meetings, telephoning, conferences, seminars and presentations. Powers, Kim, Yu, Weng, and VanWinkle (2009) suggested the following forms of oral communication as relevant to professional contexts: meetings, telephone conversations and social talk (based on a survey conducted with 3,814 TOEIC® test takers who were asked to identify which tasks they were usually engaged in and able to do in their respective workplace settings).

To gain further insights into the relevant English-communicative skills needed for the workplace, we also conducted secondary data analysis both of responses to and follow-up interviews associated with the *Why English Matters* survey (ETS, 2014) to obtain information from employers. The survey responses came from 749 managers in 13 countries and the interviews were with 15 managers each from France, Mexico, Hong Kong, Japan and China ($N$ = 75). The survey responses provided general insights into communicative breakdowns in workplace functions such as attending meetings, networking events, conference presentations and project collaborations attributed to low ELP. Respondents reported that English speaking and listening proficiencies are necessary for employees to (a) express their ideas fluently, (b) reflect clearly back to the client what is being expressed by them, (c) deliver instructions and plans correctly, and (d) reduce how long it takes to understand a message. These analyses gave us insights on two skillsets, which we deem relevant and useful for further evaluation and assessment: (a) breakdowns in relation to face-to-face dialogs and (b) collaborative projects as highly relevant and desirable.

## Face-to-Face Dialogs

Examples of communication breakdowns were reported to occur in face-to-face conversations, such as when receiving and introducing international visitors to colleagues or traveling abroad for business to meet with partners and collaborators (Welch, Lawrence, & Piekkari, 2005). As suggested by a human resource manager in the *Why English Matters* survey (ETS, 2014):

> Last week, I was at a tourism symposium in Brussels, and I took a young collaborator with me. We met with our Dutch colleagues, who speak English perfectly, and my young collaborator was incapable of participating in the conversation, of participating with the group. So, during the 3 days of the symposium, I had to translate permanently for her. *(ETS, 2015)*

Respondents to the *Why English Matters* survey suggested that skills in social interactions would help ensure that conversations between employees and external (company) visitors feel natural and easy. Along the same lines, enhanced communication may involve easily contributing information in meetings. For example, one respondent noted, "it is a constant challenge to find staff who could participate [in meetings with Headquarters and other subsidiaries] because of [English] language issues ... the same persons tend to get overloaded by these duties" (Charles & Marschan-Piekkari, 2002, p. 18–19).

## Internal Communications and Collaborations

Low ELP may also negatively affect internal communications and work processes such as team-based projects, behavior in meetings or workshops and one-on-one interactions. Dialogs across units may become truncated and possible misunderstandings may arise (Charles & Marschan-Piekkari, 2002), which may negatively impact synergy in collaborations. Employees need to be able to ask for clarification if they do not understand the instructions or directions of their teammates. This includes checking their understanding of both basic messages and contextual nuances during meetings (Cowling, 2007). A lack of such clarification skills during collaborative projects could lead to errors or result in reduced productivity (Freihat & Al-Machzoomi, 2012). Collaborators also need to be able to explain their own thoughts clearly to avoid misunderstandings (Hart-Rawung, 2008). Additionally, when carrying out collaborative projects, employees need to be able to express their opinions and to present ideas and make suggestions for improvements upon carefully listening to information presented at meetings and one-on-one conversations (Cowling, 2007; Forey & Lockwood, 2007; Freihat & Al-Machzoomi, 2012).

The occurrence of breakdowns along conversational, face-to-face dialogs, collaborations, or other types of internal communications is well-supported by the literature. Clyne (1994), Marra (2012) and Timpe (2013) highlight that in part, these breakdowns relate to the sociopragmatic aspects of language and language used in context, thereby making knowledge and inclusion of such skills relevant for successfully carrying out work functions including interacting with colleagues, supervisors and clients. Research by Clyne suggests that although miscommunications due to pragmatic errors are a higher source of breakdowns in communication as compared to linguistic (phonological, lexical and morphosyntactic) features, the latter are more traditionally taught in the English learning classrooms leaving learners ill-equipped to succeed in transactions requiring knowledge of sociopragmatics. Along the same lines, Gumperz (1999) suggests that pragmatic misunderstandings may lead to more serious consequences than grammatical and lexical mistakes—with pragmatic errors often leaving the listener with negative impressions of the speakers (Holmes, 2000; Timpe, 2013; Washburn, 2001). As a result, Candlin (2002), Geluykens and Pelsmaekers (1999) highlight the need to focus on teaching and assessing discourse and pragmatics competence in the workplace. Thus, successful communication requires not only technical correctness, but also attention to socially contextualized aspects of language use (e.g., the status of each interlocutor and the means by which communication is conveyed). In professional settings, where conventions of appropriate social conduct are rigidly defined, pragmatics competence becomes especially important to avoiding breakdowns in communication making the teaching and assessment of these language skills relevant.

## Suggestions for Teaching and Assessing ELP

To curtail the shortcomings associated with low ELP and the breakdowns in workplace efficiency and productivity they might generate, we suggest that orchestrated efforts directed to stakeholders involved in the teaching and assessment of the English skills are needed to help enhance employee preparation.

## Focal Skills of Value

One suggestion for instructors and test developers is to focus on the teaching and assessment of pragmatics while maintaining an awareness of the complexities associated with such instruction. We suggest that such efforts start out by defining pragmatic competence more concretely (Crystal, 1997) along the various language (written, spoken, or hybrid) modes. Currently, as Laughlin, Wain, and Schmidgall (2015) highlight, few clear definitions exist and more foundational work on how to teach and assess pragmatics is needed. The researchers also point out that there are multiple complexities in teaching pragmatics. One difficulty is correcting students in pragmatic-related errors. For instance, Thomas (1983) and O'Keeffe, Clancy, and Adolphs (2011) outline discomfort with correcting such errors because, unlike grammatical errors, on which there is often agreement, pragmatic errors are often sociocultural in nature. Moreover, Bardovi-Harlig, Hartford, Mahan-Taylor, Morgan, and Reynolds (1991), Boxer and Pickering (1995), Gilmore (2004) and Usó-Juan and Ruiz-Madrid (2007) describe the limited number of rich and adequately contextualized learning materials needed to facilitate pragmatic learning. Further, the degree to which particular communication breakdowns occur due to the sociocultural nature of errors versus linguistic aspects may vary depending on the context of the workplace. Such nuances may also be contextually dependent, which further complicates the teaching, learning and assessment of pragmatic competence to nonnative English speakers (Elder & Davies, 2006).

## The Instruction of Generalizable English Skills

We suggest that improving classroom instruction and assessment to support workplace preparation should include focusing on content areas and skills that are generalizable across domains and contexts in which language will be used. Bhatia (2012) and Martin (2004) suggest that language instruction has focused too often on the teaching of technical vocabulary (e.g., words that are primarily associated with a professional field only) and grammar within domain-specific niches and the teaching of highly specialized vocabulary rather than frequently used words that generalize to broadly applicable professional contexts. A pedagogical approach that relies too heavily on the learning of technical skills loses sight of a systemic approach to language instruction, which includes learning how to write to diverse audiences in socially and organizationally appropriate ways. A more integrated approach goes beyond putting words together in grammatically coherent sentences. Instead, it explicitly considers audience, context and organizational norms, including the kinds of strategies employees use to negotiate meaning in the workplace. Neglecting to teach generalizable aspects of language may lead students to be ill-equipped to function in meetings, networking situations and other activities that require less formal or technical language (Bhatia, 2012). Future research on these questions should focus on identifying to what extent we can identify generalizable contexts without either diluting the language taught and assessed or losing sight of the role of language used in context.

## Pedagogical and Assessment Materials

Improvements in English language preparation for the workplace settings can also be addressed by careful selection of resources and pedagogical materials to use in the classroom (Bhatia, Jones, Bremner, & Pierson-Smith, 2013). Changes can be made to use learning materials that are more closely connected to the skills that need to be learned for workplace readiness, which require competence in oral communication, collaboration and negotiation with a wide-range of individuals of varied rank, expertise, and, more increasingly, from different cultures (Marra, 2012). Yet, despite the need for such competencies for workplace preparation, instructional material and course syllabi do not adequately address conversation and other communicative aspects relevant to workforce readiness, which may leave learners ill-prepared to successfully carry out workplace functions (Martin, 2004).

## Focal Classroom Tasks and Activities

Another set of issues to examine relates to adopting a more updated pedagogical model that introduces time for conversations, dialogs and collaborative projects. Bhatia (2010) discusses providing opportunities for students to engage in collaborative tasks in more authentic ways, which may have greater fidelity to the activities as they are carried out in the workplace. For instance, speaking and listening skills often are used concurrently and interactively in most workplace occasions; it therefore makes sense for the teaching of these skills to include dynamic verbal exchanges. Increased opportunities for collaborative projects, dialog and oral communication also may be useful and relevant to successfully navigate networking opportunities (such as those presented in conferences and workshops) to build collaborations with colleagues and build strategic relations with partners. Providing opportunities for students to practice such skills, such as through mentoring activities, workshops and seminar presentations, may be helpful to help improve workforce preparation. Additionally, Colen and Petelin (2004) point out that collaborative writing should be given time and attention because it represents the type of tasks that professionals do, as documents are often written collaboratively in the workplace. The authors suggest teaching students to be mindful of their audience when speaking and writing, given that collaborations (either in written or oral form, through activities including meetings, presentations and networking) typically occur with multiple clients and across diverse professionals with different types of expertise. They suggest that learners be given multiple opportunities to engage in and write in diverse genres, including client meetings, advertisements, press releases, or other types of written documentations. All of these exercises may help prepare learners to engage in the kinds of professional discourse they might encounter at work, in a job interview, or in a networking setting. Consequently, learners may be able to discuss their job and projects with increased ease and confidence, which may increase opportunities to build collaborations with international colleagues and leaders. These collaborations can lead to meaningful outcomes when properly carried out. If performed unsuccessfully, however, employees may be misinterpreted, make the wrong impression, or engage in tasks that are unnecessary or counter-productive.

### Implications for Future Research

Orchestrated efforts to improve English language teaching, learning and assessment are needed, given the increasing reliance on English as the lingua franca of international organizations, where employees may be non-native English speakers and may or not share the same or similar first language (Elder and Davies, 2006, Nickerson, 2005). In this chapter, we discussed the consequences of low ELP on various stakeholders including employers and employees in relation to workplace productivity, financial losses and relations across and within units. We suggested that to help mitigate negative consequences related to low ELP, an identification and analysis of relevant skills that matter for the global workplace are important. This analysis is needed to help narrow the gap between what is taught in English language courses and the skills needed in authentic workplace contexts. Besides skill identification, we suggested that pedagogical practices also be re-examined with the intent to revise curricula and resources used in instruction to better address the business-required expanded English-language skillset. Further research is needed, not only with employers to better understand the workplace context, but also with employees to understand the struggles they face to improve their English skills, as well as with teachers to help inform their curricula and instructional practices. Such efforts are important for our global society and economy to help reduce the reported gaps in employee ELP (Martin, 2004).

We suggest that further research on improving ELP be conducted using a multimethod approach to examine the organizational context in which English will be utilized. This suggestion is aligned with our views of language as complex and dynamic—presenting the need to integrate findings and views from diverse disciplines, units of analysis (students learning within classrooms, within schools and within organizations), and participants (students, instructors, employers and employees). Last, we suggest integrating findings from various disciplines and methods including discourse analysis, ethnography and interviews to inform a rich, contextual framework to define what English is in the workplace (what are its main constitutive components that should be taught and assessed to help learners gain competencies in ELP that generalize to the workplace contexts in which they will be used (Bhatia, 2010; Zhang, 2007). While we are unable to provide a full discussion of each of these main issues, as they might constitute research agendas on their own, we aimed to synthesize key issues of relevance to help guide future research and explorations on increasing ELP in international businesses.

## References

Baker, S., Resch, I., Carlisle, K. and Schmidt, K. (2001). The Great English Divide. *Bloomberg Business*. Retrieved from http://www.bloomberg.com/bw/stories/2001-08-12/the-great-english-divide

Bardovi-Harlig, K., Hartford, B. A. S., Mahan-Taylor, R., Morgan, M. J., & Reynolds, D. W. (1991). Developing pragmatic awareness: Closing the conversation. *ELT Journal, 45*, 4–15.

Bhatia, V. K. (2010). Interdiscursivity in professional communication. *Discourse and Communication, 4*, 32–50.

Bhatia, V. K. (2012). Critical reflections on genre analysis. *Ibérica, 24*, 17–28.

Bhatia, V. K., Jones, R. H., Bremner, S., & Pierson-Smith, A. (2013). Interdiscursive collaboration in public relations context. *Ibérica, 25*, 127–146.

Bolchover, D. (2012). The Economist Intelligence Unit. *Competing across borders: How cultural and communication barriers affect business*. Retrieved from https://www.jku.at/zsp/content/e273302/e273317/Competing_across_borders_ger.pdf

Boxer, D., & Pickering, L. (1995). Problems in the presentation of speech acts in ELT material: The case of complaints. *ELT Journal, 49*, 44–58.

Candlin, C. (Ed.) (2002). *Research and practice in professional discourse*. Hong Kong, China: City University of Hong Kong.

Charles, M., & Marschan-Piekkari, R. (2002). Language training for enhanced horizontal communication: A challenge for MNCs. *Business Communication Quarterly, 65*, 9–29.

Chew, K.-S. (2005). An investigation of the English language skills used by new entrants in banks in Hong Kong. *English for Specific Purposes, 24*, 423–435.

Chiswick, B. R., & Miller, P. W. (2010). Occupational language requirements and the value of English in the US labor market. *Journal of Population Economics, 23*, 353–372. https://doi.org/10.1007/s00148-008-0230-7

Clyne, M. (1994). *Inter-cultural communication at work: Cultural values in discourse*. Cambridge, UK: Cambridge University Press.

Colen, K., & Petelin, R. (2004). Challenges in collaborative writing in the contemporary corporation. *Corporate Communications: An International Journal, 9*, 136–145.

Cowling, J. D. (2007). Needs analysis: Planning a syllabus for a series of intensive workplace courses at a leading Japanese company. *English for Specific Purposes, 26*, 426–442.

Crystal, D. (Ed.) (1997). *The Cambridge encyclopedia of language*. Cambridge, UK: Cambridge University Press.

Duff, P. A. (2008). Language socialization, higher education, and work. In P. A. Duff, & N. H. Hornberger (Eds.), *Encyclopedia of language and education: Vol. 8. Language socialization*, (pp. 257–270). Boston, MA: Springer Science and Business Media.

Educational Testing Service (2014). *Why English Matters [PowerPoint slides]*. Princeton, NJ: Galloway, G. and Ipsos.

Educational Testing Service. (2015). Top 5 business benefits of English. In *Why English Matters Global Survey: English Language in the Workplace*. Retrieved from http://whyenglishmatters.com/facts/top-5-business-benefits-of-english

Elder, C., & Davies, A. (2006). Assessing English as a lingua franca. *Annual Review of Applied Linguistics, 26*, 282–304. https://doi.org/10.1017/S0267190506000146

Evans, S. (2013). Designing tasks for the Business English classroom. *ELT Journal, 67*(3), 281–293. https://doi.org/10.1093/elt/cct013

Forey, G., & Lockwood, J. (2007). "I'd love to put someone in jail for this": An initial investigation of English in the business processing outsourcing (BPO) industry. *English for Specific Purposes, 26*, 308–326.

Freihat, S., & Al-Machzoomi, K. (2012). The picture of workplace oral communication skills for ESP Jordanian business graduate employees. *International Journal of Business, 2*, 159–173.

Geluykens, R., & Pelsmaekers, K. (Eds.) (1999). *Discourse in professional contexts.* München, Germany: LINCOM Europa.

Gilmore, A. (2004). A comparison of textbooks and authentic interactions. *ELT Journal, 58*, 363–371.

Gumperz, J. J. (1999). *On interactional sociolinguistic method.* In S. Sarangi, & C. Roberts (Eds.), *Talk, work, and institutional order* (pp. 453–471). Berlin, Germany: Mouton de Gruyter.

Gunnarsson, B.-L. (2009). *Professional discourse.* London, England: Continuum.

Hart-Rawung, C. (2008). *Internationalizing English language education in Thailand: English language program for Thai engineers (unpublished doctoral dissertation).* Melbourne, Australia: RMIT University.

Holmes, J. (2000). Doing collegiality and keeping control at work: Small talk in government departments. In J. Coupland (Ed.), *Small talk* (pp. 32–61). London, England: Continuum.

Institute for International Business Communication. (2009). TOEIC Newsletter: 30 years of TOEIC (no.105). Tokyo, Japan: Public Relations Department.

Kassim, H., & Ali, F. (2010). English communicative events and skills needed at the workplace: Feedback from the industry. *English for Specific Purposes, 29*, 168–182.

Laughlin, V. T., Wain, J. and Schmidgall, J. (2015). Defining and operationalizing the constructof pragmatic competence: Review and recommendations (Research report 15–06). Princeton, NJ: Educational Testing Service.

Marra, M. (2012). *English in the workplace.* In B. Paltridge, & S. Starfield (Eds.), *The handbook of English for specific purposes*, (pp. 175–192). Malden, MA: Wiley.

Marschan, R., Welch, D., & Welch, L. (1997). Language: The forgotten factor in multinational management. *European Management Journal, 15*, 591–598.

Martin, A. (2004). The "katakana effect" and teaching English in Japan. *English Today, 20*, 50–55.

Myles, J. (2009). Oral competency of ESL technical students in workplace internships. *TESL-EJ, 13*, 1–24.

Nickerson, C. (2005). English as a lingua franca in international business contexts. *English for Specific Purposes, 24*, 367–380.

Noguchi, J. (2010). Exploring ESP frontiers: Systematic literacy, life-long learning, ESP bilingualism. *Annual Report of JACET-SIG on ESP* (Kanto Chapter), *12*, 3–13.

Ojanpera, M. (2014). *Effects of using English in business communication in Japanese-based multinational corporations.* (Master's thesis, University of Oulu, Oulu, Finland). Retrieved from http://jultika.oulu.fi/files/nbnfioulu-201402131106.pdf

O'Keeffe, A., Clancy, B., & Adolphs, S. (2011). *Introducing pragmatics in use.* London, UK: Routledge.

O'Toole, J., & Lawler, E. E. III (2015). *The new American workplace*. Basingstoke, UK: Palgrave MacMillan.

Piekkari, R. (2006). Language effects in multinational corporations: A review from an international human resource managemenet perspective. In G. Stahl, & I. Björkman (Eds.), *Handbook of research in international human resource management*, (pp. 536–550). Northhampton, MA: Edward Elgar.

Powers, D. E., Kim, H.-J., Yu, F., Weng, V. Z., and VanWinkle, W. (2009). *The TOEIC speaking and writing tests: Relations to test-taker perceptions of proficiency in English* (TOEIC Research Report No. 4). Princeton, NJ: Educational Testing Service. http://dx.doi.org/10.1002/j.2333-8504.2009.tb02175.x

SanAntonio, P. M. (1987). Social mobility and language use in an American company in Japan. *Journal of Language and Social Psychology, 6*, 191–200.

Stickel, G. (2010). *Language use in business and commerce in Europe*. Contributions to the Annual Conference 2008 of EFNIL in Lisbon. Frankfurt am Main, Germany: Peter Lang.

Thomas, J. (1983). Cross-cultural pragmatic failure. *Applied Linguistics, 4*, 91–112.

Timpe, V. (2013). *Assessing intercultural language learning. The dependence of receptive sociopragmatic competence and discourse competence on learning opportunities and input*. Frankfurt am Main, Germany: Peter Lang.

Usó-Juan, E., & Ruiz-Madrid, M. N. (Eds.) (2007). *Pedagogical reflections on learning languages in instructed settings*. Cambridge, UK: Cambridge Scholars Press.

Washburn, G. N. (2001). Using situation comedies for pragmatic language teaching and learning. *TESOL Journal, 10*, 21–26.

Welch, D., Lawrence, W., & Piekkari, R. (2005). Speaking in tongues: The importance of language in international management processes. *International Studies of Management and Organization, 35*, 10–27.

Welch, D. E., Welch, L. S., & Marschan-Piekkari, R. (2001). The persistent impact of language on global operations. *Prometheus, 19*, 193–209. https://doi.org/10.1080/08109020110072180

Zhang, Z. (2007). Towards an integrated approach to teaching business English: A Chinese experience. *English for Specific Purposes, 26*, 399–410.

# 20

# Bridging the Cultural Gap in the Global Workplace

## A Sociocultural Perspective

*Cynthia Carter Ching*[1] *and George Sellu*[2]

[1] *University of California*
[2] *Santa Rosa Junior College*

Over the past three decades, there has been an increase in trade partnerships between countries and an expansion of global markets. As a result of this growth, multinational corporations have faced the challenge of hiring staff with the cultural fluency, sensitivity and adaptiveness to work at different locations across the globe. In order to address this need, organizations have employed varied strategies, including corporate training and creating workplace environments that support learning. Initially, corporations focused on previous educational training as the most important factor in hiring. In some cases, these employees were then sent overseas to fill various onsite positions. During the early wave of globalization, candidates with prestigious educational credentials nevertheless sometimes failed to meet the complex job requirements in the global workplace. This skill gap led to a paradigm shift, with organizations moving away from hiring the candidates who seemed to possess the best a priori set of qualifications and toward candidates who were adaptable and willing to be trained in-situ and learn during practice (Illeris, 2011). A key challenge for success in global workplace learning, though, is defining the nature of what should be learned. What are some key features of workplace or organizational culture that can be challenging in a global context? What cultural variations can have impact on workplace learning? How does learning in practice differ from advance training, and how can it be most successful?

Identifying and adapting to workplace culture (situated within ethnic or national culture) and understanding learning in practice are both fundamental focal points within sociocultural theory (Lave & Wenger, 1991; Wertsch, del Rio, & Alvarez, 1995). In this chapter, we argue that sociocultural theory can provide helpful tools for those who study, create and manage global workplace learning. We identify some existing challenges in global workplace learning, offer a definition of organizational/workplace culture informed by sociocultural theory, and review some basic assertions of sociocultural theory. Then we identify three features of workplace culture from a sociocultural perspective—training versus

*The Wiley Handbook of Global Workplace Learning*, First Edition.
Edited by Vanessa Hammler Kenon and Sunay Vasant Palsole.

learning, artifacts of practice and technology-facilitated communication—and draw from existing published case studies across diverse contexts to illustrate each of these features.

## Setting the Stage: Challenges in Global Workplace Learning

Most conventional training programs initiated during the early era of the global workplace (1980s–1990s) focused more on frontloading training for international work, rather than adaptability, and learning-in-context. When workplace training was first introduced, it was designed to address the initial skill gap between previously domestically-based employees and the job expectations of multinational corporations (Schein, 1997). However, the models used for facilitating these trainings became extremely formalized, and workplace learning focused on individual training that did not take into account the interactions between employees and their environment. More importantly, workplace learning appeared to be out of step with real-life problems in the workplace (Orr, 1990a). Conventional corporate training provided abstract knowledge that was usually not applicable to real-world problems in the workplace (Lave & Wenger, 1991). In order to address some of the weaknesses of workplace trainings, some multinational organizations modified workplace training to include interactions between employees (Hofstede, 1991). Organizational learning built strong relationships and bonds between employees in particular workplace teams. Workplace teams were created by organizations, but they had boundaries for sharing knowledge or learning. As such, there was little or no interaction between teams within the same organization.

Some organizations have been strategic about creating teams to promote learning between individuals on a team. For example, IBM created organizational learning through three main models; (a) Learning in Organizations (LIO)—facilitated individual learning from experiences within the organization; (b) Learning by Organizations (LBO)—organizational behavior and processes based on experiences; and (c) Organizational Learning Mechanisms (OLM)—structured, intentional workplace learning processes that intentionally connect LIOs and LBOs (Hofstede, 1991). The implementation of OLMs across the globe may be different for organizations, and this might impact the success of organizational objectives. While OLMs have been used extensively, they can become formulaic, and they tend to make assumptions about the learning pathways of employees which may be misguided, depending on the particular setting in question. OLMs have been successful to a certain extent in some regions of the world. The variation in the effectiveness of OLMs could be attributed to the differences in social learning systems that encompass different cultures and subcultures within organizations (Reardon, 2010).

In communities or organizations that embrace hierarchy, bureaucracy and class systems, individuals can sometimes adapt their interpersonal practices to meet organizational expectations. Global transplant employees can sometimes thrive in such communities because they are guided by explicit rules and norms (Duguid, 2006). On the other hand, individuals in communities or organizations that are less hierarchical can also thrive because flexibility exists in rules and norms. Some researchers (Kim & McLean, 2014; Spencer, 2002; White & Thobo-Carlsen, 2002) have suggested that the failure of multinational organizations could be attributed to the fact that corporate executives assumed that employees in other countries were willing to adapt their personal values to meet the goals of their employer (standardization). Failure to achieve standardization across the globe led corporations to examine exogenous variables such as culture, history and governance that could affect the success of global organizations.

In order to fully understand workplace learning in multinational organizations, it is important to understand organizational/workplace culture and the culture of the social systems within which these corporations are situated.

## Definition of Organizational Culture

Organizational culture has been defined differently by various scholars and practitioners. Schein (1990) defines organizational culture as:

> a set of basic assumptions that a given group has invented, discovered or developed in learning to cope with its problems of external adaptations and internal integration that have worked well enough to be considered valid, and therefore, to be taught to new members as a correct way you perceive, think and feel in relation to these problems.

Porter, Lawler, and Hackman (1975) described organizational culture as:

> a set of customs and typical patterns of ways of doing things. The force, pervasiveness and nature of such models, beliefs and values vary considerably from organization to organization. Yet it is assumed that an organization that has developed some sort of culture and that this will have a vital impact on the degree of success of any effort to improve or alter the organization.

Based on the definitions above, organizational culture is dynamic and hence could be manifested differently with changes in the composition, size and location of employees in global organizations. Globalization, therefore, could engender somewhat different organizational cultures within the same organization across the world. Cameron and Quinn's Organizational Typology (1999) articulates four types of organizational culture as found in different locations around the globe: (a) market culture; (b) hierarchical culture; (c) adhocracy culture; and (d) clan culture. Most workplace learning theories and practices have been developed in western countries, based to some degree on market culture, but they have been implemented, and in some cases adapted and varied, across the world. Several researchers (for instance Felstead, Fuller, Jewson, & Unwin, 2009) have argued that workplace theories and practices cannot be effectively implemented without integrating cultural perspectives in different communities. In particular, McLean (2010) argued that most organizations experience a cultural gap in workplace learning when organizational objectives are implemented in global settings with different cultures. "Culture" is not a monolithic concept, however, and can mean different things, each of which are important to consider. The culture of the community within which the organization is situated may be different from the workplace culture. These two cultures could present barriers to the transfer of skills from one setting to another. In order to fully understand workplace culture, it is imperative that we conduct an examination of the local community culture and identify intersections and misalignment with workplace culture.

In communities or organizations where hierarchy and bureaucracy are pervasive, learning is stratified, compartmentalized, sequenced and guided by strict rules and policies. As such, learning experiences are shared based on cultural and social rules within these communities. Individuals who are socialized in hierarchical and bureaucratic social systems tend to bring their learning experiences from the larger social system into the workplace. Global organizations should understand how these nuances could affect organizational culture (Gannon, 2004). Such nuances are usually not captured in traditional learning and training programs in multinational organizations.

In the next sections, we articulate sociocultural theory as a useful tool for examining the role of culture, learning and practice in the global workplace, and we provide a few examples of studies of workplace learning from a sociocultural perspective.

## Sociocultural Theory as a Tool for Examining Global Workplaces

Sociocultural theory provides a useful lens through which to examine global workplaces and the potential cultural misalignment that can create barriers to learning and success. Wertsch et al. (1995) define the goal of a sociocultural approach as bringing together and explicating "the relationships between human mental functioning, on the one hand, and the cultural, institutional, and historical situations in which this functioning occurs, on the other," (p. 3). This definition creates a relationship that places equal weight on the contexts in which learning and workplace practices occur and on the individual meanings and understandings acquired by the learners in a given environment. In fact, even the concept of "learning" in sociocultural theory is multifaceted and draws on this relationship. Wenger (1998) articulates four components of a sociocultural theory of learning: Practice (learning as doing): Meaning (learning as experience): Identity (learning as becoming): and Community (learning as belonging). Each of these components has both individual and institutional/contextual aspects that work together to create its composition, in addition to the interplay across all the components that form a cohesive whole learning experience.

Because sociocultural theory always situates activity and analysis within broader contexts, these components relate not only to the workplace setting itself, but also to the surrounding culture in which individuals reside. These cultural contexts shape the existing identities and meanings employees bring with them when they are hired, and also shape the norms and values for practice and community within institutions (Wenger, 1998). For multinational corporations in a global workplace, however, applying a sociocultural theory of learning becomes even more complicated, because employees in different locations and different contexts may have radically different cultural influences that affect the construction of norms and learning at different local institutions.

In fact, one of the primary challenges of applying sociocultural theory to a global workplace is a traditional sociocultural emphasis on shared physicality and physical space: location, proximity, face-to-face discourse, concrete tool use, and immediate bodily action. Many of the early sociocultural models and key cases arose from anthropological studies of learning and doing in specific physical contexts such as grocery stores and kitchens (Lave, 1988), tailors' and butchers' shops (Lave & Wenger, 1991), blacksmiths' forges (Keller & Keller, 1993), and naval ships (Hutchins, 1995). In each case, a large part of what creates mutual practices and shapes learning for participants is the act of working together, shoulder to shoulder, as labor is shared and physical tools are demonstrated and manipulated. The layout of physical space is also critical in these cases, as some studies indicate that visual and physical access to supervisors, to more senior employees, and to other aspects of the work process that are beyond an individual's given level are important for creating a sense of shared practice, community, and identity as part of a whole (Lave & Wenger, 1991; Wenger, 1998). As Lefebvre (1991) argues, *the organization of physical space produces social space* and thus enables and constrains connection and communication across participants.

Within specific locations, multinational corporations can work to create physical and social spaces that allow access and shared meanings to emerge. Hierarchy and stratification norms may differ across cultural contexts, however, and this difference gives rise to the need for workplaces to be responsive to local meanings and values, even as they try to allow for workers to participate in a cohesive corporate identity. Additionally, in many global corporations, various phases of production and information processes may be spread out across distant locales, creating further challenges for meanings, practices and identities to be shared as a cohesive whole. In response to these challenges, global firms employ extensive trainings, distribute shared artifacts across locales, and use travel and technology to bridge distance. Each of the following sections provides cases from sociocultural workplace studies that can illuminate these efforts and suggest improvements.

## Training and Learning in a Global Workplace

Multinational firms have used corporate trainings as a means to address some of the challenges of global workplace learning. Global workplace trainings were initially designed to transfer explicit knowledge from experts or group of experts to employees at different regions across the world (Kim & McLean, 2014; Rylatt, 2000; Spencer, 2002). However, as trade and globalization expanded, corporations established training centers around the world based on western pedagogical models, which largely assumed that learning would take place prior to and separate from practice. Separation of work and practice could be counter-productive for employees and the overall success of an organization (Brown, Collins, & Duguid, 1989; Brown & Duguid, 1991). The training model that sequenced knowledge and practice was at best mediocre in preparing employees for the workplace. Supporting this perspective, Orr (1993) suggested that corporate trainings were too directive and failed to prepare employees to solve real-world problems.

The misalignment between knowledge acquisition and practice has been shown to be a source of failure for global corporations (Orr, 1990a, 1990b; Popper & Lipshitz, 1998). Studies have found that the majority of workplace problem-solving challenges could fall outside the scope of formal and directive trainings, which then could render employees incapable of troubleshooting and solving real-world problems (Boud & Garrick, 1999; Illeris, 2011). The inability of employees to solve problems could have severe economic consequences for global organizations. In order to better prepare employees for the global workplace, trainings should be coupled with practice.

## Case: Training and Learning in Practice

Xerox, which is one of the most recognized global organizations, has had to constantly make adaptations to its mission, vision, objectives and corporate training programs around the world. An examination of Xerox's corporate training trend shows the organization's initial training programs were based on the assumption that corporate values were insulated from the communities in which they operate. Specifically, corporate training programs did not incorporate the social, cultural and historical realities in communities where their organizations operated. The lack of attention to these exogenous factors (culture, social interactions and histories) posed the next set of unique challenges for the corporate training movement across the globe.

Xerox initially trained managers and technicians in western nations such as the United States and deployed them to work around the world. Researchers argued that the decoupling of learning and practice made the job of technicians extremely difficult because the abstract knowledge they acquired during their trainings were not applicable to actual problems in the workplace (Engestrom, 2001; Orr, 1996). In a nutshell, as Orr (2006) described, "... work is different from what management says it is," (p. 1806). The skills that technicians brought to the workplace from their personal schooling were mostly useful to obtain their jobs; however, those same skills were not always useful in addressing the real-world problems that Xerox technicians faced.

In addition to decoupled corporate trainings, Xerox managers assumed that technicians worked individually to solve service problems (Orr, 1996). Yet some technicians who worked individually across the world were unable to solve technical problems that clients faced in the field. Orr (1996) found that technicians who relied on collective knowledge and storytelling from sales representatives and other employees within the organization were more successful in solving unique problems. The lack of success of some technicians warranted a reevaluation of corporate training for technicians, and the company created opportunities and systems for technicians to share knowledge with one another on the job and during training.

Another challenge to advance training rather than learning in practice was around client use. In some global locations, clients used Xerox products differently than anticipated by Xerox manufacturing. As such, the technical problems that arose from such "misuse" of Xerox products created unique challenges for technicians that were not covered in their corporate trainings. (One such example is companies trying to save paper by running *all* copy jobs with the two-sided feeder, which would break down or cause jams repeatedly.) Sales representatives, however, who were in direct contact with clients, saw some of the "misuse" of Xerox products and could provide a perspective to help technicians better troubleshoot the problems they faced in the field. Widening the sphere of communication beyond the technician/manager loop was thus also important to learning in practice.

Other types of adaptations required of technicians in the field were due to cultural practices and norms that are unique to a particular region or area. For example, Orr (1996) described the disconnect in some Xerox repair locations between the "suit-and-tie" mode of dress deemed appropriate for some very formal corporate offices, and the inevitable "getting dirty" that everyday client troubleshooting of copy machines required, often involving toner smudges everywhere even for simple tasks like replacing cartridges or clearing paper jams. Clients were often reluctant to do these routine tasks, which would result in more frequent repair visits. These dress norms were then compounded when technicians would arrive in corporate-appropriate dress, but would then need to get out tools and work on the floor to access panels and the inner mechanisms of machines. Consequently, in addition to stories about the types of repairs particular to certain types of machines or regions, technicians also shared stories about the disconnects they experienced among the corporate image of Xerox, the formal style of some workplace cultures, and their "coveralls" type of everyday repair work (yet they were not allowed to wear coveralls). Learning in practice from other technicians thus also involved learning to negotiate their identities and perceptions relative to clients.

## Artifacts and Their Role in Learning

As a focus of explicit training or as a routine part of on-the-job learning in a particular location, workplace artifacts are key. While the general notion of cultural artifact is so broad as to include any and all forms that emerge from cultural and historical contexts, including foundational structures like language and number systems (Vygotsky, 1980), for the purposes of this chapter we focus on particular objects and/or structures that both convey meaning and guide and shape practices within and across levels of an organization. Examples include training manuals, order forms, procedure directives, reports and databases and so forth. In each of these examples, the artifacts in question both support and constrain the types of practices and meanings that can be conducted around each one (Rogoff, 2008). Further, the translation and migration of artifacts from one cultural workplace context to another can be problematic, since artifacts developed in one context carry with them the cultural and historical meanings of the contexts in which they arose, although this potential cultural mismatch may be less obvious to participants. As Lave and Wenger (1991) argue, "the activity system and social world of which an artifact is part are reflected in multiple ways in its design and use," (p. 102). The following case study of artifact misunderstanding across different levels of a single United States-based organization has strong implications for learning and practice in global organizations.

## Case: Meaning and Reification

In a sociocultural and ethnographic study of a large insurance corporation,[1] Wenger (1998) distinguishes between "participation" and "reification" as components of negotiating meaning in the workplace. Participation refers to "membership, acting, interacting, and mutuality" (p. 63) as important pieces of learning to work; this component comprises all the various social meanings and ephemeral moment-to-moment interactions involved in doing a job together. Reification, on the other hand, refers to all the heuristics and formalizations that organizations typically employ to structure, represent and (in some cases) simulate social participation. To understand their interplay, consider the example of a complex development project. Employees may have to work very closely together across departments and communicate regularly (participation) to accomplish a particular collaborative task. In terms of the final product, however, in this example, the prescribed format and system for filing the project report (reification) forces area managers to write up only how their respective departments functioned individually. In this case, not only does there exist a disconnect between the actual collaborative participation process and its reification into separate reports, but the structure of the final report itself also ends up shaping future action, such that departments are less likely to fluidly collaborate and more likely to focus more on their own internal processes, since separation and division of labor is what gets reported and evaluated.

Another example of a misalignment between participation and reification from Wenger's study was found in an insurance claims-approval process, wherein new claims examiners received too-hasty on-the-job training, rather than shadowing or deep collegial explanation (participation), on how to determine whether claims were approved or rejected, by using a procedure they called, "The C, F, and J Thing" (reification). A case history form would come to the claims department from another part of the company, examiners performed simple calculations on the form (line C—line F = line J) that yielded a decision of pay or deny, and then they passed the form on to the accounting department. In the majority of cases, this was the correct procedure. In a minority of cases, however, data contained on other lines of the form would provide information about the claim that could be used in making a different decision. When new examiners did not pay attention to this other data, incorrect claim decisions were often appealed by customers and required additional processing.

Artifacts that are transmitted within a global corporation from one cultural context to another risk even further misalignment than the examples above. Even when reification results in a workplace procedure that correctly reflects/represents the nature of accompanying participation in the culture of origin, when the procedure arrives in a different cultural context, participation norms in that location may not align. Language and cultural meaning translations can also pose challenges to reification, such that faulty heuristics in training (like the "C, F, and J Thing") rather than deep understanding become more likely. Close contact is helpful in identifying and rectifying such misalignments, and information technologies have allowed greater and more frequent contact across physically distant partners in the global workplace. Sociocultural theory is helpful in analyzing these kinds of global communications as well.

## Technology, Intercultural Communication and Support

Email, teleconferencing, video chat, online project management systems, cloud-based databases and virtual troubleshooting are all examples of technologies that can be used to create material and social connections across globally distant workplace locations. These technologies can be thought of as a bridge between social spaces. Yet from a sociocultural perspective, they each represent yet another type of social space in and of themselves, one that has its own context that includes people and their relations (Kutti, 2006), and is constantly evolving as technological possibilities, infrastructures, and norms change within and across cultures (; Kaptelinin & Nardi, 2006; Thorne, 2003). An examination of how technology can be used to bridge cultural gaps in a global workplace thus requires determining a starting assumption about the supportive or additive role of the technological environment in question.

Taking the perspective that technologies can be used as tools to support communities of practice, Hoadley (2012) describes four techniques that can be leveraged. First, technology can be used to link people with others who have similar practices, say for example across parallel departments at globally distant locations. Second, technology can be used to provide a repository for information resources. Note, however, that Hoadley is careful to point out that "while a simplistic view of knowledge might think that this repository is the knowledge of the community, the community of practice view sees such repositories simply as information that is used by the community in its practices (where the knowledge truly resides)," (p. 297). Third, technology can be used to support communication directly by providing tools (real time or asynchronous) for discussing with others. Fourth, technology can be used as an information resource to provide community members with awareness of similar contexts or problems they may be lacking (such as a "help" resource that links related topics together). These various techniques can be leveraged as tools for the global workplace.

### Cases: Technology in Context (or Not)

If, however, we consider that technology, rather than simply creating a bridge across cultural context and spaces, instead creates its own space and imparts the norms and assumptions of its design into the function it is supposed to serve (Kaptelinin & Nardi, 2006), then the picture becomes more complicated. In a case analysis he calls "The Wrong Tool for the Right Job," Thorne (2003) examines how generational shifts in meaning and norms of practice created a situation of disconnect between language instructors, who wanted their students to use email to facilitate written peer-to-peer communication (and thus practice communicative writing in the target language), and students, who found email stilted and unsuited to peer communication (which they preferred to conduct via texting and social media channels instead).

In a case of cross-cultural technological deployment in Nepal, Hoadley, Honwad, and Tamminga (2010) describe the social and economic disruption brought about by what seemed to be a benevolent and forward-thinking initiative to provide state-funded computers for rural schools, based on a western model of similar governmental initiatives like the United States' Goals 2000. The problem was, however, that remote Nepalese rural school villages then had to pay for the updating and installing of electricity and wiring in their buildings to make the computers function, and the ultimate benefit for the use of technology in the traditional curriculum paled in comparison to the community expense. Both these cases illustrate the importance of awareness of technological norms in a target context before recommending, designing, or deploying technological tools for use, whether the potential misalignment is generational or global (or both).

## Conclusion

As global markets continue to expand, the cultural gap in employee learning could widen and ultimately deter organizational success. However, organizations that understand and embrace cultural differences could learn to thrive as they enact global workplace learning. From the discussions in this chapter, we assert that organizational and national/ethnic culture plays a significant role in workplace learning and the overall success of global firms. In particular, in creating learning environments, workgroups and workplace learning communities that embrace social and cultural differences, both in the workplace and in local communities, are in a better position for success. Global organizations that enhance sociocultural learning in the workplace could improve learning, communication and problem-solving skills among employees. While the identification of effective workplace learning practices, artifacts and technologies is important, global workplace learning is dynamic and needs a fluid learning environment that is amenable to rapid changes in the workplace. We believe that a sociocultural perspective provides unique tools for global organizations to study, adapt, change and learn.

## Note

1 For his 1998 published book on learning in this insurance corporation, Wenger used a pseudonym company name, "Alinsu."

## References


Boud, D., & Garrick, J. (Eds.) (1999). *Understanding learning at work.* London, UK: Routledge.

Brown, J. S., Collins, A., & Duguid, P. (1989). Situated cognition and the culture of learning. *Educational Researcher, 18*(1), 32–42.

Brown, S. J., & Duguid, P. (1991). Organizational learning and communities-of-practice: Toward a unified view of working, learning and innovation. *Organization Science, 2*(1), 40–57.

Cameron, K. S., & Quinn, R. E. (1999). *Diagnosing and changing organizational culture. Based on the Competing Values Framework.* Reading, MA: Addison-Wesley.

Duguid, P. (2006). What talking about machines tells us. *Organization Studies, 27*(12).

Engestrom, Y. (2001). Expansive learning at work. Toward an activity—theoretical reconceptualisation. *Journal of Education and Work, 14*(1), 133–156.

Felstead, A., Fuller, A., Jewson, N., & Unwin, L. (2009). *Improving Working as Learning.* London, UK: Routledge.

Gannon, M. (2004). *Understanding global cultures: Metaphorical journeys through 28 nations, clusters, and continents* (3rd ed.). Thousand Oaks, CA: Sage.

Hoadley, C. (2012). What is a community of practice and how can we support it? In D. Jonassen, & S. Land (Eds.), *Theoretical foundations of learning environments* (pp. 287–300). London, UK, New York: Routledge.

Hoadley, C., Honwad, S. and Tamminga, K. (2010). Technology-supported cross cultural collaborative learning in the developing world. In *Proceedings of the 3rd International Conference on Intercultural Collaboration*, pp. 131–140. Association of Computing Machinery (ACM) Press.

Hofstede, G. H. (1991). *Cultures and organizations: Software of the mind.* New York: McGraw Hill.

Hutchins, E. (1995). *Cognition in the wild.* Cambridge, MA: MIT Press.

Illeris, K. (2011). *The fundamentals of workplace learning: Understanding how people learn in working life.* London, UK: Routledge.

Kaptelinin, V., & Nardi, B. A. (2006). *Acting with technology: Activity theory and interaction design.* Cambridge, MA: MIT Press.

Keller, C., & Keller, J. D. (1993). Thinking and acting with iron. In S. Chaiklin, & J. Lave (Eds.), *Understanding practice: Perspectives on activity and context* (pp. 125–143). Cambridge, UK: Cambridge University Press.

Kim, S., & McLean, G. N. (2014). The impact of national culture on informal learning in the workplace. *American Association for Adult and Continuing Education, 64*(1), 39–59.

Kutti, K. (2006). Activity theory, transformation of work, and information systems design. In Y. Engeström, R. Miettinen, & R. L. Punamäki (Eds.), *Perspectives on activity theory* (pp. 360–376). Cambridge, UK: Cambridge University Press.

Lave, J. (1988). *Cognition in practice: Mind, mathematics and culture in everyday life*. Cambridge, UK: Cambridge University Press.

Lave, J., & Wenger, E. (1991). *Situated learning: Legitimate peripheral participation*. Cambridge, UK: Cambridge University Press.

Lefebvre, H. (1991). *The production of space*. Oxford: Blackwell.

McLean, J. (2010). Communicating across cultures. *Manager* (Summer), 30–31.

Orr, J.E. (1990a). *Sound, feel, and practice: Some examples from diagnosis of machines*. Palo Alto, CA: Systems Science Laboratory, Xerox Palo Alto Research Center SSL Report SSL-90-42v.

Orr, J. E. (1990b). Sharing knowledge, celebrating identity: Community memory in a service culture. In D. Middleton, & D. Edwards (Eds.), *Collective remembering* (pp. 169–189). Thousand Oaks, CA: Sage.

Orr, J.E. (1993). *Ethnography and organizational learning: In pursuit of learning at work*. Palo Alto, CA: Systems Science Laboratory, Xerox Palo Alto Research Center SSL Report SPL-93-040.

Orr, J. E. (1996). *Talking about machines: An ethnography of a modern job*. Ithaca, NY: Cornell University Press.

Orr, J. E. (2006). Ten years of talking about machines. *Organization Studies, 27*(12), 1805–1820.

Popper, M., & Lipshitz, R. (1998). Organizational learning mechanisms a structural and cultural approach to organizational learning. *The Journal of Applied Behavioral Science, 34*(2), 161–178.

Porter, L. W., Lawler, E. E., & Hackman, J. R. (1975). *Behavior in organizations*. New York, NY: McGraw-Hill.

Reardon, R. F. (2010). The impact of learning culture on worker response to new technology. *Journal of Workplace Learning, 22*, 201–211.

Rogoff, B. (2008). Observing sociocultural activity on three planes: Participatory appropriation,guided participation, and apprenticeship. *Pedagogy and Practice: Culture and Identities, 1995*, 58–74.

Rylatt, A. (2000). *Learning unlimited: Practical strategies for transforming learning in the workplace of the 21st century* (2nd ed.). Warriewood, NSW: Business Publishing.

Schein, E. (1997). *Organizational culture and leadership*. San Francisco, CA: Jossey-Bass.

Schein, E. H. (1990). Organizational Culture. *American Psychologist, 45*(2), 109.

Spencer, B. (2002). Research and the pedagogies of work and learning. *Journal of Workplace Learning, 14*(7), 298–305.

Thorne, S. L. (2003). Artifacts and cultures-of-use in intercultural communication. *Language Learning and Technology, 7*(2), 38–67.

Vygotsky, L. S. (1980). *Mind in society: The development of higher psychological processes*. Cambridge, MA: Harvard University Press.

Wenger, E. (1998). *Communities of practice: Learning, meaning, and identity*. Cambridge,UK: Cambridge University Press.

Wertsch, J. V., del Rio, P., & Alvarez, A. (1995). Sociocultural studies: History, action, and mediation. In J. V. Wertch, P. Del Rio, & A. Alvarez (Eds.), *Sociocultural studies of mind* (pp. 1–34). Cambridge,UK: Cambridge University Press.

White, C. J., & Thobo-Carlsen, R. (2002). Cultural differences and managers' perceptions of work-related attributes. *Human Resource Development International*, *5*(2), 235–239.

# 21

# Compensating for the Lack of Physical Non-verbal Cues in a Virtual Team Context, Based on Cultural Background and Preferred Communication Style

*Yoany Beldarrain[1] and Karen Diehl[2]*

[1] *Reutlingen University*
[2] *Independent scholar*

Many researchers have explored the phenomenon of intercultural communication since Edward T. Hall first brought it to light in the late 1950s. Although the literature is quite extensive, the ongoing sociopolitical struggles are evidence that even in the twenty-first century, society has limited intercultural as well as intracultural communication competence. This limited understanding continues to bring about discord in every facet of life, including work.

The modern workforce is expected to possess certain knowledge, skills and attitudes that are inherently different from those expected from previous generations. Due to globalization, intercultural competence and highly effective communication skills are at the top of the list—a working knowledge of English as the lingua franca of today's business world can be considered a first step. Having a common language, though, is not sufficient for a workforce where the working environments and work organization of a team can be very diverse. One could argue that domestic organizations do not need to concern themselves with intercultural communication, but the reality is that the increased diversity in the domestic workforce makes it necessary for all types of organizations, regardless of operating markets, to invest resources into this topic.

For all practical purposes, organizations must rethink their processes and structures. Deployment, supervision and training of staff for example, are critical to an organization's success. As more companies embrace telecommuting, employees and employers alike are realizing that there is more to virtual teaming than meets the eye. If the constraints of digitally mediated communication (DMC) are not addressed, communication between individuals from different cultural backgrounds is consequently at stake. For the remainder of this chapter, the term DMC is used when referring to all communication facilitated by digital technology tools, including smart devices, mobile technologies, Web-based conferencing and so forth. The term DMC is also used to

*The Wiley Handbook of Global Workplace Learning*, First Edition.
Edited by Vanessa Hammler Kenon and Sunay Vasant Palsole.

replace computer-mediated communication (CMC), unless a particular literature source originally states CMC.

It is known that regardless of culture, individuals have the tendency to prefer one communication style to another (Gudykunst, 1998; Gudykunst & Ting-Toomey, 1988). In order to improve the communication between culturally diverse individuals who are also part of the same virtual team, it is necessary to first understand how each of them compensates for the lack of non-verbal cues that would otherwise help them derive meaning. One aspect here is how users from different cultures find ways to express non-verbal content through their use of virtual meeting tool(s) and the list of features offered thereby. Although experts generally agree with Mehrabian (1971) that about 55% of a message's meaning is derived from non-verbal communication in terms of body language and about 38% from the tone of voice and other paralinguistic nuances, there is little research on this topic in the context of communication styles and culturally diverse virtual teams. Therefore, the current gap in understanding presents a refreshing research opportunity.

This chapter explores how members of a virtual team, when using Web-based conferencing tools, might compensate for the lack of non-verbal communication. It also presents insights into the relationship between cultural background and the compensation method used. At the conclusion of the chapter, the authors make a case for implementing intercultural communication in virtual teams as an organizational strategy.

## What You Think You Understood Is Not What I Meant to Say

The potential for miscommunication in the workplace undoubtedly increased with the advent of DMC, where there are limited non-verbal cues or none at all. One clear example is e-mail, which for over 20 years has remained a favorite method of communication. It goes without saying that everyone who has used e-mails for communication has either felt misunderstood or has misunderstood someone's message at least once. Web-based conferencing tools offer more options for replicating face-to-face communication, but the reality is that many of the challenges remain the same.

Two decades of research indicate that gender, age and a person's status are all important factors that influence a person's communication, especially when using technology (Herring & Stoerger, 2014). As set out by Trompenaars and Hampden-Turner (2012) one source of error and failure to negotiate successfully is the clash of ascriptive versus performance-oriented cultures. In an ascriptive culture, age, gender, position and family are factors that determine who will automatically be assigned the more important positions. In a performance-oriented culture, the individual will receive more power and a higher position in terms of what he or she brings to the table in terms of knowhow or skills relevant to the virtual meeting (Trompenaars & Hampden-Turner, 2012).

## Verbal Versus Non-verbal Communication

According to one-way and two-way communication theory (Mead & Andrews, 2009), individuals will choose a one-way communication style for tasks that are urgent, simple, routine, and/or closed-ended. Conversely, they will choose two-way communication when the task lacks urgency, is complex, non-routine and/or open-ended. DMC is usually a hybrid communication interaction where the level of urgency depends on the timeline of the project as well as on the agenda of the meeting.

Research by Hollingshead (2004) indicates that without non-verbal cues, information is likely to be suppressed thus affecting the quality of the outcome or task, but as members of a virtual team get to know each other over time, the quality of the outcome is no longer an issue. Regardless of how well the virtual team members know each other, concern for the flow and accuracy of information remains, as members must still somehow compensate for the lack of non-verbal cues and make sense of the paralanguage. Although it falls under the umbrella of non-verbal communication, paralanguage helps members of a virtual team extract meaning from the verbal part of the interaction via the non-lexical components of communication such as tone of voice, intonation, pitch, speed, phonemes that indicate hesitation, confusion, agreement and so forth, hence impacting the trust and team dynamics (Lea & Spears, 1992).

The importance ascribed to verbal communication is evidenced by the fact that often a conference call is preferred to a virtual meeting (Maude, 2016). Studies have shown that in a communicative situation where non-verbal and verbal indicators send out opposing messages, the recipient tends to set the tone via verbal cues (Wallbott, 1990). Additionally, the behavior patterns in cross-cultural meetings show that individuals are more willing to adapt to other cultures because they see the necessity to make themselves understood and they do so by using voice as the most adaptable, flexible and natural instrument available (Bennett & Bennett, 2004).

Studies about trust within virtual teams also support the importance of non-verbal communication because the non-verbal cues convey interpersonal feelings and emotions (Walther, 1992, 1997). In addressing the role of trust and satisfaction in virtual teams, some social presence theorists (Gunawardena, 1995; Gunawardena & Zittle, 1997; Short, Williams, & Christie, 1976) however, did not consider how individuals in dispersed teams might actually compensate for the lack of non-verbal cues in terms of communication. Empirical studies show that individuals often self-categorize as insiders or outsiders of the team based on their perceived attributes of other team members, even if such attributes are based on stereotypes (Deaux, 1996; Lea & Spears, 1992; Walther, 1997). The Social Identity Model of Deindividuation (SIDE) as explained by Reicher, Spears, and Postmes (1995) further stipulates that the phenomenon of deindividuation minimizes the individual characteristics as well as the interpersonal differences within the group.

## Developing Trust

Based on some of the above-cited studies, as well as Meyerson, Weick and Kramer's (1996) concept of swift trust, Jarvenpaa and Leidner (1998) examined the communication behaviors that enable trust within temporary virtual teams.

According to the theory of swift trust, members of a newly formed virtual group such as a project team that is under time pressure, have the tendency to transfer expectations of trust from other familiar settings as well as stereotypes. This happens because the time pressure to complete the task limits their ability to gather information about the other team members and build a relationship (Jarvenpaa and Leidner, 1998). After looking at the initial level of trust in newly created teams versus the final level of trust, researchers identified certain behaviors that enabled some teams to be more successful than others in completing their task. More successful teams had clear responsibilities, a sense of purpose, clear and open communication and clear expectations. Although participants were indeed culturally diverse, the findings of the study did not fully take into account how cultural background might have played a role in these behaviors. Overall, Jarvenpaa and Leidner's study paves the way for understanding the development of trust in highly collaborative, highly dynamic global virtual teams.

Walther (1992, 1996, 1997) adamantly argues that CMCs slow the rate at which members of the virtual team develop relationships, but that ultimately members develop their own methods of filtering and interpreting individuation cues in order to minimize uncertainty (Tidwell & Walther, 2002). This could be true for teams that collaborate over a period of time or collaborate often, but it is not clear if this is the case for teams that have a limited lifespan, for example, short projects. To really understand how global virtual teams create trust, it would be important to differentiate between the longevity of the teams, as postulated under the concept of swift trust.

Eventually, members of the team will either hide behind the false sense of anonymity and portray a new persona or form an authentic bond with teammates (Baggio & Beldarrain, 2011). For this reason, Baggio and Beldarrain suggest that Walther's (1997) social information processing theory (SIP) should be applied to other forms of emerging DMC in order to determine if different technologies influence or facilitate certain behaviors. In doing so, more can be learned about why misunderstandings, lying and deceit not only tend to be more common in the early stages of virtual teaming, but overall more prevalent in DMC than face-to-face (Hollingshead, 2000; Hollingshead, Fulk, & Monge, 2002). The rate at which members of a virtual team filter cues and form relationships also depends on the cultural diversity of its members (Walther, 1997). Lying and deceit on the other hand, might be a matter of ethical/ moral relativism, which is outside the scope of this chapter.

## Intercultural Communication

In a synthesis of virtual team research spanning a period of ten years, Gilson, Maynard, Jones Young, Vartiainen, and Hakonen (2015) identified ten literature themes and ten new opportunities for research. One of the literature themes, globalization, highlights yet another factor that influences communication within a virtual team: cultural differences. When trying to ascertain the definition of culture however, one finds multiple perspectives that in turn influence the interpretation of intercultural communication.

Often referred to as cross-cultural communication, intercultural communication encompasses all of the elements and processes that enable cultural and social groups to communicate with each other as they negotiate shared meanings (Ting-Toomey, 1999). While earlier experts preferred a more narrow interpretation of culture that categorizes members according to common beliefs, knowledge, customs, morals and so forth. (Tylor, 1871) researchers today generally agree that groups negotiate shared meanings through their members′ interactions (intracultural communication), thus salient traits of the individual members contribute to the group identity (Gudykunst & Lee, 2003).

When focusing on in-group as well as across-group interactions, other researchers point out that true intercultural communication also takes place between religious, ethnic, regional subculture groups, as well as social groups that categorize themselves by sexual orientation, political views and so forth. (Martin & Nakayama, 2010; Samovar & Porter, 2004). Following those lines, a broader, more updated definition is required to understand intercultural communication in a virtual team context.

Samovar, Porter, and McDaniel (2009) define culture as a group of people who are part of the dominant culture in a society. Accordingly, they use the term co-culture when referring to smaller segments of society (subgroups) that share certain traits in particular. Their definition of intercultural communication is therefore appropriate for exploring the communication dynamics of intercultural virtual teams:

> ... intercultural communication occurs when a member of one culture produces a message for consumption by a member of another culture. More precisely, intercultural communication involves interaction between people whose cultural perceptions and symbol systems are distinct enough to alter the communication event. (p.12)

Samovar et al. (2009) stance supports Orbe's (1998) co-cultural communication theory, which stipulates that the dominant groups within society create the communication system and the rules that support and proliferate their own perceptions of the world. Interestingly, according to communication theory of identity (CTI) (Hecht, Warren, Jung, & Krieger, 2005) an individual's membership of a cultural group is not fixed, but it is, rather, dynamic. The authors contend that through interaction, individuals portray their cultural identities as reflected in their choice of non-verbal and verbal language, but also in their communication strategy. This is concurrent with the evaluation of Gilson et al. (2015), who identified virtual team adaptation as a research opportunity because a high level of adaptability would enable virtual teams to ride any wave of discord or environmental change. Due to the additional cultural factors involved, globally dispersed virtual teams are more likely to be successful if members engage in cross-cultural adaptations, although a higher level of cultural diversity might present a bigger challenge for the team (Anawati and Craig 2006; Zhang, Lowry, Zhou and Fu, 2007, as cited in Gilson et al., 2015).

When investigating intercultural communication in virtual teams, Hofstede (1997) cannot be ignored. The consensus among communication scholars is that dimensions such as individualism versus collectivism, and power-distance are extremely important to the study of intercultural communication (Samovar et al., 2009).

Likewise, E.T. Hall's work is of paramount importance. The more culturally intelligent members of a group are, the more adaptable they can become.

## High- Versus Low-Context Cultures

E.T. Hall, undoubtedly one of the most-cited researchers on the topic of cultural differences and communication, explored cultures through the lenses of context, time and space. Although his framework has not gone without criticism, it still offers viable points of reference. By looking at intercultural virtual communication through Hall's (1959, 1966, 1976, 1983, 1985) lenses, one can see that Hall's low- versus high-context cultural factors are still relevant today. Just as relevant are the factors differentiating monochronic versus polychronic time perceptions. All these factors contribute to the intercultural virtual team dynamics as previously mentioned (Gilson et al., 2015; Hecht et al., 2005) and should be further expanded by frameworks and models that specifically take into consideration cultural adaptations (Kim & Ruben, 1988). Furthermore, the space lens (proxemics) remains largely unexplored in the context of virtual teams.

The concept of virtual proxemics typically surfaces when discussing online behavior, especially avatars and virtual worlds but not virtual teaming. In order to study cross-cultural and intercultural communication patterns in connection to proxemics, Hasler and Friedman (2012) observed how pairs of Asian and European participants interacted as avatars. They noted that the interaction distance exhibited by the Asian participants was greater than the distance exhibited by the Europeans. Their findings were consistent with other similar face-to-face studies. When comparing European pairs with mixed pairs (Europeans and Asians), however, there was no significant difference in the interaction distance, an indicator that Asians might be more accepting of others′ influence and "invasion" of personal space (Hasler and Friedman, 2012). These findings support Hall's (1959, 1966, 1976, 1983, 1985) notion of Asian cultures being high-context and Hofstede's (1997) notion that Asian cultures prefer high power-distance, yet are more collectivist. One must keep in mind, nonetheless, that these are generalizations and that societies are becoming more culturally diverse. Therefore, Hall's and Hofstede's frameworks should be interpreted with scrutiny. Emergent applications such as virtual proxemics will help researchers gain new perspectives about the different factors that influence virtual team dynamics; further research in this area is therefore needed.

## Communication Styles Characterized by Certain Behaviors

The expression of thoughts, feelings and emotions is a natural part of communication. In face-to-face interactions, most of these elements are communicated non-verbally and, as already stated, most of the meaning of the message comes from non-verbal cues (Mehrabian, 1971). The literature reviewed thus far indicates that because individuals filter non-verbal cues based on a myriad of cultural and intercultural variables, the potential conflict in culturally diverse virtual groups is higher than face-to-face.

Traditional views of communication group observable behaviors into four basic categories: aggressive, assertive, passive and passive-aggressive. These categories draw from early interpretations of behaviorists such as Bandura (1971), Hartman (1963), Hull (1943) and Skinner (1971) who saw human behavior as a chain of actions and reactions that dictated human conduct with very little freedom of choice. These categories, however, are not useful for interpreting the complexities of intercultural communication, especially in virtual teams. Other commonly used communication style scales such as willingness to communicate (WTC) (McCroskey, 1997; McCroskey & McCroskey, 1988) or interpersonal communication competency scale (ICCS) (Rubin & Martin, 1994) are also not suitable for virtual contexts because some categories are more difficult to observe in a virtual context.

Widely known for its commercial use, the DiSCprofile (Personality Profile Solutions, 2017) offers additional insight into individual personality characteristics but it is also not ideal. By integrating some common elements from ICCS, behaviorism-based styles, as well as the DiSC dimensions, one can see some congruencies with the C.A.P.S. model (Controllers, Analyzers, Promoters and Supporters, see 1981) in terms of the categories analytical, amiable, driver and expressive. Not to be confused with the cognitive-affective personality system, also known as CAPS (Mischel & Shoda, 1995), the C.A.P.S. personal styles, aka social styles inventory, has its roots in social sciences and has gained wide acceptance in human resource management because it takes into account interaction and human relationships. Other commercial scales or models such as Communications Styles 2.0™ (Endress, 2016) make use of three labels that overlap with Merrill and Reid's (Merrill & Reid, 1981) model: labels Analyzer, Promoter, and Supporter, among others. The labels chosen for this study reflect the same definitions as Merrill and Reid's and are updated to reflect new approaches; Table 21.1 shows the labels and definitions used for this study. The descriptions shown are not exhaustive.

**Table 21.1** Labels and Working Definitions

| **Integrated Categories and Working Definitions for the Study** |
|---|
| Controller<br>• likes to know what others are doing, task-oriented<br>• results-driven<br>• provides input even when not asked<br>• easily upset or concerned if someone is not doing their share<br>• not afraid to confront others |
| Analyzer<br>• enjoys connecting ideas, information, people<br>• easily conceptualizes abstract ideas<br>• detail-oriented |
| Promoter<br>• readily expresses own views or pushes own agenda<br>• highly intuitive and communicative |
| Supporter<br>• more concerned with people than results<br>• values trust<br>• values collaboration and shared-decision making |

*Note:* Labels and definitions adapted from Merrill and Reid (1981) and Endress (2016).

Due to the communicative nature of the behaviors described under the C.A.P.S styles and the simplicity of application, C.A.P.S. is the model of choice for the study of intercultural communication in virtual teams as presented in this chapter. These behaviors are the basis of the survey designed for the study presented in subsequent sections of this chapter.

## A Research Imperative

Virtual teaming is here to stay. The technology tools will undoubtedly evolve, and with them the opportunities for interaction. The first step in implementing strategies that leverage the power of diversity is for organizations to understand how individuals from different cultural backgrounds communicate. This section presents a descriptive study (Glass & Hopkins, 1996) that aimed at gaining insight about intercultural communication in virtual teams by addressing the following research questions:

- *Primary RQ:* How do individuals who prefer a particular communication style compensate for the lack of physical non-verbal cues in a Web-based conference?
- *Secondary RQ1:* What compensation methods do individuals from different cultural backgrounds prefer?
- *Secondary RQ2:* What communication style do individuals from different cultural backgrounds prefer?

No hypotheses were formulated because the specific relationships or correlations between the variables were not tested. Instead, the objective was to describe the behaviors of the target population by looking at different variables: *communication style, compensation method* and *cultural background.* This descriptive approach is appropriate for gathering more information about the topic in order to develop correlational hypotheses for future studies (Borg & Gall, 1989; Glass & Hopkins, 1996).

### Target Population and Sampling Methods

The target population included everyone with prior experience with virtual teaming. Two distinct subpopulations were further defined using experience as the differentiating factor: power users and least experienced users. In doing so, experience became a quasi-control variable, but only for the univariate, descriptive analysis. Although the study did not directly aim at correlating experience with the other variables identified, the authors felt it was important to gain insight about experience because it could lead to further discussions.

Two sampling units were identified based on the researchers' accessibility to the potential respondents. Convenience sampling was chosen due to the simplicity of the process, but also because each potential respondent was part of the naturally occurring heterogeneous population (Borg & Gall, 1989) of either power or least experienced users. In the context of this study, it also included individuals from various cultural backgrounds. Below are the characteristics of these sub-populations and sample units.

### Power Users

Definition: *Power users* are working professionals who have experience working in virtual teams. They often collaborate with globally dispersed teammates. Age is not considered to be a factor in experience. Power users themselves do not necessarily live in their country of origin.

Sampling: The sample unit for *power users* was a group of professionals who met the above definition. The sample unit was a heterogeneous group of professionals across the globe. A unique survey link (SurveyMonkey) was sent to a sample size of 180 individuals via the researchers' professional networks. The response rate for this group was 9%.

### Least Experienced Users

Definition: *Least experienced users* are as those with less experience working in virtual teams. Their work experience is limited. Age is not considered to be a factor in experience. Least experienced users themselves do not necessarily live in their country of origin.

Sampling: The sample unit for *least experienced users* was two cohorts of international university students enrolled in a German public university. The sample unit was therefore a heterogeneous group of young individuals from across the globe. A unique survey link (SurveyMonkey) was sent to a sample size of 200 individuals via the university server. The response rate for this group was 23%.

### Data Collection Methods and Definitions of Variables

A structured, anonymous survey (Jackson, 2008) was designed using closed as well as open-ended questions. Filter questions were used to first determine if the participants were qualified to answer the survey. Anyone without experience using Web-based conferencing tools was removed from the sample. General demographical questions were asked in order to better desegregate the data. Other relevant demographical data such as job function, experience using Web-based conferencing, telecommuting, among others, were also gathered to capture additional descriptors about each sample unit.

A three-point ordinal Likert-type scale was used; the items ranged from strongly disagree, disagree, agree, to strongly agree, giving the most extreme, insignificant answer a value of zero. Items referring to *communication style* were randomly alternated as positive and negative statements. This was done to avoid acquiescent bias as well as extreme response bias (Kamoen, 2012; Smith, 2004). Reducing acquiescent bias in questionnaires designed for culturally diverse respondents is crucial to overall validity and reliability, as demonstrated by Smith (2004), who found that persons from high collectivist and high uncertainty avoidance cultures have high bias in responses to surveys that measure preferences.

Additionally, content validity for the entire survey was addressed via informal discussions with two small focus groups, one per sample unit. Each focus group included four to five individuals who were chosen randomly based on their availability. After considering their feedback and the main points in the literature, the final questions were piloted with two additional members of each sample unit.

The goal was to use the same questions for the two sample units in order to facilitate data analysis and gain as much insight as possible.

The key variables for this study were *communication style, compensation method* and *cultural background.* Due to the ambiguity of these variables, clear definitions were formulated.

When analyzing the data and discussing the findings, the user type (sampling unit) and cultural background were combined as follows:

- PL-power user/ low-context cultural background
- PH-power user/ high-context cultural background
- LL-least experienced user/ low-context cultural background
- LH-least experienced user/ high-context cultural background

## Communication Style

The labels *Controller, Analyzer, Promoter* and *Supporter* were used to categorize the communication tendencies of the participants. The categories were derived from the C.A.P.S. model (Merrill & Reid, 1981). For specific behaviors under each of these categories, please refer to Table 21.1. Participants were categorized based on their responses to survey items connected to each category. An ordinal Likert-type scale "strongly disagree" to "strongly agree" was used to rate the statements, for example: "I have difficulty conceptualizing abstract ideas," which was connected to the label *Analyzer.* A scale of 0–3 was used to assign values across the responses, but was inverted depending on the positive or negative statement as previously explained. In this case, an answer of "strongly agree" was assigned a value of 0 and interpreted as not contributing to the profile of an *Analyzer.* An answer of "strongly disagree" was assigned a value of 3, the highest indicator.

## Compensation Method

The different communication options available to members of a virtual team partaking in a Web-based conference were classified as: *visual, voice* and *chat.* Each of these represents a compensation method used by the participants in the absence of physical non-verbal cues (nodding head, yawn, etc.). The label *visual* includes any whiteboard content such as text, pictures, graphs and screenshots that helps the participant derive meaning visually. The label *voice* includes any adjustments to the voice quality (pitch, volume, tone, etc.), use of audible paralanguage elements ("aha," "hm"), and preference for using the microphone (adjustment of volume, switching it off/on, assigning it to other team members). The label *chat* captures the participant's preference for using the chat feature as a main source of communication via emoticons or text. Chat was considered a compensation style because it provides a clear alternative to speaking, thus facilitating communication for those who might otherwise feel inhibited.

Participants were categorized based on their responses to survey items connected to each category. Respondents rated statements using an ordinal Likert scale "strongly disagree" to "strongly agree" for example: "I find sounds with no verbal meaning (such as hm, ah, aha, etc.) useful when communicating in a virtual team/Web-based conference. This includes oral or written use thereof."

This statement in particular captures paralanguage elements as sounds but also as visual symbols. Instead of splitting the values between *voice* and *visual* or even *chat*, the authors counted it as an indicator of *voice* because the majority of focus group members (80 %) associated the visual symbols (such as hm, ah, sh, mmm in the chat box) with the auditory channel. Focus group members reportedly hear these sounds in their heads as they visually interpret the written non-verbals. Therefore, for the purpose of this study, these written non-verbals were categorized as audible paralanguage. This is a clear departure from the typology of textual paralanguage (TPL) and conceptual framework, as proposed by Luangrath, Peck, and Barger (2017).

A scale of 0–3 was used to assign values across the responses. In the example above, an answer of "strongly agree" was assigned a value of 3 points and interpreted as a strong indicator of *voice* as the preferred compensation method for the lack of physical non-verbal cues, while an answer of "strongly disagree" was assigned a value of 0; the lowest indicator.

### Cultural Background

For the sake of practicability and manageability, the labels of *high-context* versus *low-context culture* are used as per Hall's (1959, 1966, 1976, 1983, 1985) descriptors when referring to cultural background. It is clear that these terms are used here as generalizations about dominant cultural traits. Participants were categorized as low- or high-context based on their stated country of origin. This presents a limitation to the study, which can be overcome in future studies by additionally surveying the participants and homing in on particular individual traits.

### Limitations

As with any study, there are potential limitations in terms of transferability. Due to the small sample sizes and low response rates—especially for the power users, the findings cannot be confidently generalized to other samples of the population. Another potential limitation is the definition of experience. The working definitions of power users and least experienced users do not account for any gray areas such as a person's confidence level or the learning curve that organically takes place when learning how to do something new. To clarify this, the researchers should devise an experience rating scale to better select the samples and isolate experience as a variable.

Further studies in the field must also take the issue of generation into account, especially how digital natives approach DMC versus non-natives. This is not to assume that the digital natives are automatically more at ease with DMC, the findings suggest that the issue is more complex. Finally, as stated previously, the classification of cultural background solely using the labels high-context versus low-context do not take into account variations of subcultures.

## Making the Connection

The literature review provided a foundation for interpreting the findings of the study. Despite the caveats laid out in the limitations, the data gathered provide insight into the research questions and the overall phenomenon of intercultural communication in virtual teams. The findings are discussed using univariate analysis, thus examining each variable to first answer the secondary questions. The secondary RQs will provide overall conclusions for the primary RQ. Throughout the discussion, the terms "user group" and "sample unit" are used interchangeably to differentiate the level of experience as either power users or least experienced users.

The definition of experience, as stated earlier, did not include age as a factor. It is necessary to mention, however, that demographical data for the study shows that only 25 % of *power users* were between the ages of 20 and 25, while 76 % of *least experienced* users were in that same age group. Table 21.2 shows some of the key demographic comparisons.

As part of the survey, respondents were asked to answer a series of background questions to assess their experience using Web-based conferencing tools. The *power users* sample unit demonstrated having a wider knowledge of the different tools available such as Adobe Connect, GoToMeeting and so forth. Where the *power users* could list a number of tools, the *least experienced users* named Adobe as the main one. The most interesting divergence between the two sample units was concerning their different assessment of factors ensuring success in a virtual conference. For the *power users*, the most decisive factor here was *content knowledge* (50 %), whereas the *least experienced users* stated *cultural background* (41 %) as the most important factor. In both groups, *experience using the tool* came second; 27 % for *power users*, 31 % for *least experienced. Power users* named *previous contact with other VT Members* as third factor, while for the *least expe-*

**Table 21.2** Participant Characteristics per Sample Unit

| Characteristic | Power users | Least experienced users |
|---|---|---|
| Cultural diversity | Ten different nationalities<br>56 % currently living in the USA. | Ten different nationalities<br>85 % currently living in Western Europe, mainly Germany |
| Commuting | 50 % of all respondents | 0 % |
| Use of virtual teaming/ Web conferencing tools for DMC | 50 % use Web conferencing tools more than four times per month | 92 % use Web conferencing tools one or two times per month |
| Average age | 36 | 23 |
| Satisfaction with DMC/ virtual teams | 50 % very positive<br>50 % positive | 10 % very positive<br>71 % positive<br>20 % negative |

*Source:* The authors.

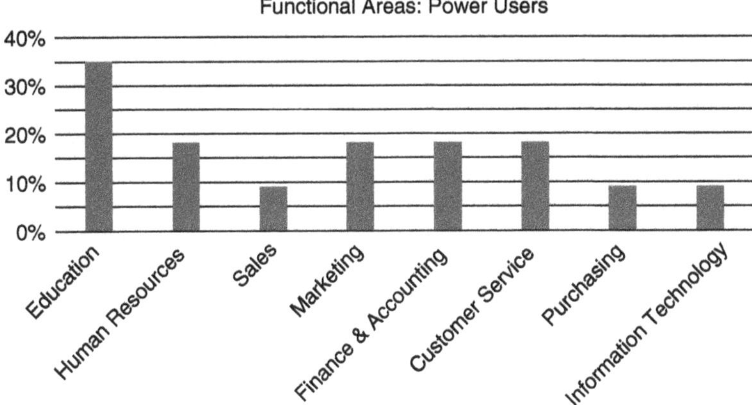


**Figure 21.1** Functional Areas Indicated by Power Users

*rienced* the factor *language proficiency* came third (with 28 %). Other factors such as gender, for example, were not regarded as important in DMC. With regards to professional experience, those working in education accounted for the 35 % of the *power users*, while the rest were equally distributed among the other different functional areas (see Figure 21.1).

## Secondary RQ1

An overwhelming percentage of respondents from both, low- and high-context cultures indicated *voice* as their preferred compensation method for the lack of physical non-verbal cues in a Web-based conference. *Voice* was the preferred compensation method for 100 % of respondents in the *power users* sample unit, regardless of cultural background or gender. Conversely, 50 % of respondents in the second sample unit, *least experienced*, indicated *voice* as their preferred compensation method, regardless of cultural background or gender. It should be pointed out that the low response rate among *power users* renders it problematic to extrapolate from the findings in this sample unit to a larger sample. It nonetheless seems significant that there is virtually no variation of compensation method among the respondents in this user group. Whether the respondents were male or female, from a high or a low context, and whichever communication style they preferred, the compensation method *voice* was preferred overall.

The second sample unit, *least experienced users*, indicated more heterogeneous preferences for a given compensation method. Here, *voice* was the preferred compensation method of 50 % of the respondents, while the others indicated preference for *visual* (39 %), and *chat* (11 %) as the least popular choice of compensation method.

Within the *least experienced users* group, the findings also show divergences on preference for a certain compensation method according to gender and cultural background. *Voice* was the preferred compensation method of all females (56 %), whereas 56 % of all males preferred *visual* as compensation method. Accordingly, the second-most preferred compensation method for *least experienced* males was *voice* (38 %) and visual with the female respondents (32 % of the females). Looking at the preferred compensation method according to both gender and cultural background, the high-context females show a marked preference toward *visual* as compensation method.

While the surveys yielded no data for the high-context, *least experienced* males, the *least experienced*, low-context males of this sample unit preferred *visual* as a compensation method (50 %) though not as marked as their female high-context counterparts. The low-context females, on the other hand, preferred *voice* as a compensation method (56 %). *Chat* was the least preferred compensation method among low-context, *least experienced* males (13 %) and females (12 %). It is significant to note that there is no evidence of chat being a preferred compensation method among high-context, *least experienced users*, and certainly not among any of the *power users*.

## Secondary RQ2

Findings indicate a trend for low-context individuals to prefer a Controller communication style, regardless of gender or experience. Overall, 77 % of *power users* indicated a preference for Controller, while 47 % of the *least experienced* participants indicated the same. The communication styles of high-context individuals were more heterogeneous regardless of experience. All communication styles except Promoter indicated similar preferences (see Figure 21.2).

Figure 21.2 illustrates the communication style by user type and context level. Among the *power users*, the overall preferred communication style was controller. When analyzed according to low or high context cultures (cultural background), the controller style is more prevalent in low context *power users* (PL) where 73% of the respondents were rated as controllers, versus only 33% of high context *power users* (PH) being rated as such. In the *least experienced* sampling unit, the low context respondents (LL) showed a marked preference for controller as communication style (47%), followed by supporter (34%), promoter (10%), and analyzer (9%). The high context respondents (LH) showed preferences that are more balanced with 36% in both categories, controllers and supporters. The remaining 28% were analyzers.

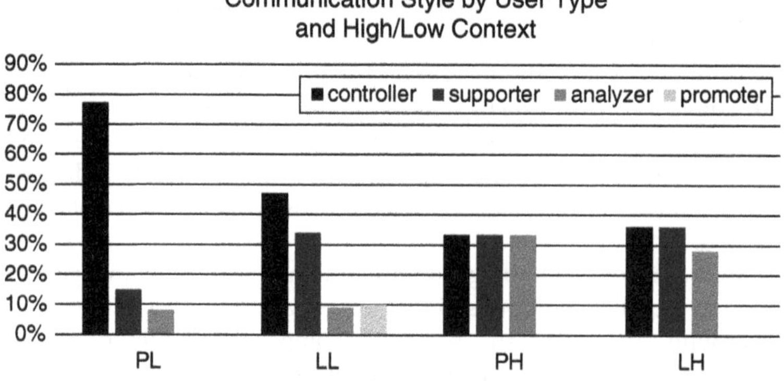


**Figure 21.2** Communication Style by User Type and Low-/High-Context Cultural Background

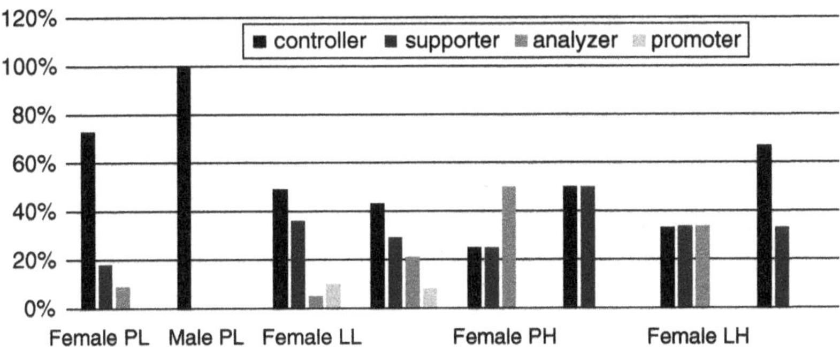


**Figure 21.3** Communication Style by User Type, Gender and Low-/High-Context Cultural Background

The preference for a particular communication style was also significantly determined by gender. Respondents from a low-context background indicated a tendency toward the Controller communication style. The low-context males were all Controllers, whereas 73 % of the low-context females were Controllers.

As shown in Figure 21.3, among the high-context *power users,* the female respondents were more likely to be Analyzers (50 %), whereas the high-context male *power users* were equally divided between Supporter and Controller (50 % in each category). The remaining female respondents were equally distributed between Supporter and Controller (25 % each). Albeit the respondent rate was very low for *power users,* it is significant to note that no *power user,* regardless of gender or cultural background, indicated Promoter as their preferred communication style.

Among the *least experienced users,* the respondents from low-context cultures show some similarities with those of the *power users from* low-context cultures. Almost half of the females from the low-context, *least experienced users* (49 %) sample unit indicated Controller tendencies compared to only 33 % among the high-context females of this user group. *Least experienced,* low-context females were therefore more likely to be Controllers than high-context females. High-context females were almost evenly distributed among three communication styles: Controller, Analyzer and Supporter. No high-context female indicated preference for the Promoter communication style. The high-context males indicated a marked preference for the communication style of Controller (67 %). Controller was also the predominant communication style among low-context males of the *least experienced users* (43 %), followed by Supporters (29 %) and Analyzers (21 %). *Least experienced,* low-context, males were the only respondents (8 %) with tendencies toward the Promoter communication style.

## Relevance of the Findings for RQ1 and RQ2

The key findings for voice support Maude's (2016) position that virtual teams prefer a conference call rather than a Web-based conference. This could be because voice offers the most variety of register and nuance, including the audible paralanguage elements that facilitate expression (Bennett & Bennett, 2004). The tone of voice and additional verbal cues (Wallbott, 1990) facilitate mutual understanding.

Web-based conferences, especially those related to a project with fixed deadlines, require that team members have functions assigned a priori and therefore individuals might be less pressured to assert status or power. This could be an explanation for the absence of the Promoter communication style in this study. Because the team members are only present in image, and sometimes even only as voice, the power relations become diffused, thus enabling individuals to assume new personae (Hollingshead et al., 2002). One the one hand, team members who might feel intimidated in a face-to-face meeting might become more assertive, on the other hand, team members who use their physical presence to assert themselves, compensate by being more aggressive. There is also indication that the low-context respondents from individualistic cultures are more likely to be assertive, concurrent with Trompenaars and Charles Hampden-Turner's (2012) position about ascriptive versus performance-oriented cultures.

Communication in a Web-based conference is a non-routine and complex task not only because of the element of technological mediation, but also because of the agenda and time constraints, thus it is two-way communication (Mead & Andrews, 2009). There was a more even distribution among the communication styles Controller, Analyzer and Supporter for high-context respondents from both sample units. One possible interpretation is that these individuals from high-context cultures can adapt to the challenges of two-way communication more easily than low-context individuals.

## Primary RQ

The findings for the secondary questions described the potential relationship between compensation methods and cultural background, and communication style and cultural background. The primary goal for this study revolved around overcoming the constraints of Web-based conferencing tools. Although modern Web-based conferencing tools offer a visual option via the camera interface, many users prefer to not use their camera. This is evidenced by the findings indicating that *voice* is the preferred compensation across *power users* and *least experienced* users alike. In fact, 100 % of *power users* across all communication styles preferred voice.

When desegregating the data by communication style and compensation method for the *least experienced* sample unit (Figure 21.4), there is clear indication that Controllers and Supporters were also more likely to prefer *voice* as a compensation method. This gives insight into the importance of verbal communication in Web-based conferencing, regardless of experience.

Because the overwhelmingly preferred compensation method for *power users* was *voice*, it is assumed that those with more experience are more likely to choose the compensation method that can be deployed with the least technological intervention. Both chat and visual are compensation methods that require a participant to make very specific technical use of the function, not to mention

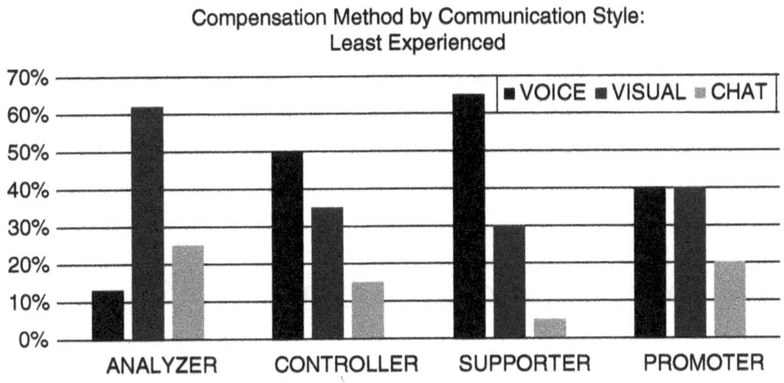

Compensation Method by Communication Style:
Least Experienced

70%
60%
50%
40%
30%
20%
10%
0%

VOICE VISUAL CHAT

ANALYZER CONTROLLER SUPPORTER PROMOTER

**Figure 21.4** Compensation Method by Communication Style: Least Experienced

that it requires focus to read something on the chat box or on the white board, and simultaneously listen to the speaker. The user would have to know how the chat function works in this tool, how to share images and so forth, and how to manage his/her own focus. The technological effort when engaging in spoken conversation is—even in DMC—comparatively low. Numerous aspects of voice as a compensation method are similar in face-to-face communication as in Web-based conferencing: speed, pitch, volume (if not regulated by microphone), tone and paralinguistic utterances.

One could draw the conclusion that *power users* are aware of different tools available, take over a variety of functions within the tool, and take part in virtual teaming with a higher frequency. In doing so, they might opt for the compensation method that ensures the maximum of communication across all tools and for all tool functions.

The *least experienced users,* on the other hand, seem to have more varied communication style compensation methods. Respondents with the communication styles Supporter and Controller both demonstrated a preference for voice, with visual preference coming second and chat as a third. The compensation methods for Controllers however, were distributed across voice (50 %), visual (35 %) and chat (15 %). Supporters and Analyzers showed a clear favorite communication style, with 62 % of the Analyzers choosing visual and 65% of the Supporters stating voice was the preferred compensation method.

An insight is that the communication styles among the low-context Promoters in the *least experienced group* were almost evenly distributed: voice and visual with 40 % each, and chat with 20%. The use of chat could be attributed to the fact that *least experienced users* were digital natives. Even if they might feel more comfortable and less inhibited using chat when reaching out to select team members during the Web-based conference, they still relied on voice and visual compensation to promote their contributions.

When comparing low- versus high-context *least experienced users* however, chat was not a preferred compensation method for high-context respondents. Interestingly, the majority of the *least experienced users* reported having the role of participant in Web-based conferences, which would lead to the impression that as digital natives, they should use the chat more often. *Least experienced users* might overall prefer to be participants instead of taking on a more active role. It is not clear how a participant's status within the team might influence their compensation methods. It can be inferred however, that low-context, *least experienced* individuals who have a low status might be more likely to compensate for low status by being more self-promoting.

## Intercultural Communication as an Organizational Strategy

Profit-making as well as not-for-profit organizations constantly strive to reinvent themselves in an ever-changing global economy. Their competitiveness is contingent upon the qualifications of their employees. Rethinking processes and structures is not enough; ultimately, those employees need to be able to communicate with internal and external stakeholders. In the post-industrial economy, where organizations are globally intertwined, virtual teaming is a necessity. One does not need to telecommute to be part of a virtual team, or to use DMC. DMC is part of everyday life, private and professional. Intercultural communication and virtual teaming skills, especially via the use of Web-based conferencing tools, must therefore be part of a sound organizational strategy.

### A Changing World

Current economic and sociopolitical factors have caused the displacement of millions of people across the world. While immigration/ emigration have been naturally occurring phenomena since the beginning of human societies, sudden and unforeseen demographical changes have a high level of impact on society. One of the biggest impacts is the psychological factor; whereas some individuals may be more culturally competent than others, the reality is that intercultural communication is crucial for cultural integration and assimilation. The long-term effects of demographic change can easily be seen in the workplace. According to a Pew Research Center report, the population in the United States is projected to reach 46 % White, 24 % Hispanic, 14 % Asian, 13 % Black and 3 % other by 2065 (Cohn & Caumont, 2016).

The American workforce is also more different than ever before in terms of age and gender. Millennials (born after 1980) are the most racially diverse generation in the history of America, with 43 % of millennial adults being non-white (and interestingly, millennials are the most-educated generation (Cohn & Caumont, 2016)). The role of women in the workforce is also more important than ever, as they were the breadwinners for 40 % of all households in 2011 (Cohn & Caumont, 2016). According to the same report, two of the most significant global trends are religious and age-related. Not only is the world's population rapidly aging, but also the number of Muslims will equal that of Christians by 2050. What does it all mean to employers? What does it all mean in terms of intercultural communication and geographically dispersed teams? The increased diversity in the domestic workforce as well as the global workforce cannot be ignored.

A competent communicator is able to convey a message appropriately and effectively across different cultural contexts (Ting-Toomey, 1999). Organizations need to ensure that employees are able to work in heterogeneous teams. Employees need to work with customers, suppliers, and a myriad of culturally diverse stakeholders that may have different political, social, linguistic, and religious views, just to name a few. Additionally, globalization, world trade and increased travel have all made the world smaller and more interconnected. Cross-cultural communication is inevitable. Expecting employees from a subculture to behave and think according to the expectations of the dominant culture is reminiscent of the far-fetched melting pot mindset, because it negates one's own cultural identity.

## Implications for HRD

The findings of the previously discussed study indicate that Human Resources Development (HRD) professionals must do more than just endeavor to promote intercultural communication in virtual teaming. They must also take steps toward training a more culturally competent workforce.

Some obvious implications for training and professional development are technical, such as learning how to use Web-based conferencing tools and other tools that facilitate DMC and virtual teaming. Learning the technical side of things is important, but employees must first engage in self-reflection in order to understand their own cultural background, and how this background may influence their behaviors and attitudes. Employees must also develop self-awareness of their cultural biases toward others. After all, intercultural communication competence does not have to be something abstract, it can actually be acquired (Varner & Beamer, 2010).

By understanding the different communication styles, coupled with intercultural communication competence, individuals will be better prepared to adapt to the demands of DMC. An individual's ability to interpret a message and adapt in regards to DMC has been shown in more recent studies to be paramount in the success of virtual teams (Lauring, 2011; Santillan & Horwitz, 2016; Trompenaars & Hampden-Turner, 2012). Importance should then be given to these variables when using Web-based conferencing tools.

A question arises however, as to how technology may influence self-identity (Colbert, Yee, & George, 2016). It might prove challenging, if not confusing, for individuals from a subculture to meet the expectations of the dominant culture, combined with one's own expression of cultural identity. Employers should therefore provide clear job expectations and anchor employee evaluation systems in objective, function-focused, non-biased behaviors, knowledge and skill-sets.

Industry experts have already sounded the alarm in terms of the war for talent and the skills gap. According to Bloomberg (2015), there is a high demand for individuals with good communication skills across all industries, but, surprisingly, adaptability seems to be a less desired skill. This presents a clear contradiction because current research in intercultural communication and the success of geographically dispersed virtual teams demonstrates otherwise. Experts agree that communication flexibility helps individuals select strategies that enable them to collect information about the situation before adapting their behavior, as required in intercultural negotiations for example (Gudykunst & Kim, 2003; Ruben & Kealey, 1979).

Why then this disconnect between research and practice? Organizations must bridge the gap between research and practice by integrating new methods, applications, techniques and knowledge to continuously improve HRD processes, policies, strategies and approaches. A culturally diverse workforce must be proficient in DMC.

## Considerations for Web-Based Conferencing

Key takeaways from this study indicate that whether it is a conscious or unconscious choice, participants in DMC may feel a need to take control of the communicative situation and/or to assert themselves more decisively. This could be due to the desire to make themselves understood and so they adapt to the new intercultural context.

The communication style of a Controller is most likely to ensure both of these goals, whereas the communication style of a Promoter—in order to be effective in DMC—requires a higher degree of mastering the DMC tool than most people may feel they confidently possess. If a Promoter is a person who is results driven and seeks influence, it is only logical that while overall only few of the respondents in this study were Promoters in their communication style, this small group was the one most likely the one to make most use of all compensation methods available.

When training individuals on using Web-based conferencing tools, the dangers of over-adapting to someone else's communication style and/or their low- versus high-context behaviors need to be made clear. The tendency for Promoters to use multiple compensation methods can be leveraged, as these individuals can become expert users of the technology tool and be a positive influence on those who might feel uncomfortable expressing their own identity. The Controller communication style on the other hand, can impair team cohesiveness if gone unchecked. In the case of low-context cultures, the likelihood of having more Controllers is increased, especially if they are also more individualistic.

Because Supporters tend to have a more intuitive style, a good role for them would be presenters. According to the results, Supporters preferred compensation method, by far, is voice. This indicates that they would not mind being more vocal, yet considerate of other's turns, opinions and so forth. Analyzers on the other hand, showed a marked preference for visual compensation. This means that visual support (pictures, graphs, larger text) is key to helping them infer meaning or even self-express. If the size of the virtual team is small, one consideration might be using the webcam to add more visual non-verbal cues. Analyzers as well as Promoters are more likely to compensate for the lack of physical nonverbal cues by relying on the chat feature. This means that the presenter should make the chat option available whenever the size of the group permits it.

According to the findings, the different factors regarded as being decisive for a successful DMC further contribute to the choice of compensation method and the individual's communication style. *Power users* regarded *content knowledge* as the most decisive factor, while *least experienced users* identified *cultural background* as the most important. It can be assumed that in the early life of a virtual team, members are preoccupied with getting to know one another so they can better adapt, consistently with the concept of swift trust (Jarvenpaa & Leidner, 1998; Meyerson et al., 1996). Furthermore, those with less experience are not as savvy using the tool and compensation methods, which may cause them to adapt more slowly. More experienced users on the other hand, might be able to achieve the same goal but faster, thus focusing earlier on content.

## Moving Forward

This study is but a first step toward a better understanding of DMC. Key findings indicate that regardless of experience using Web-based conferring tools, gender or cultural background, voice is an important compensation method for the lack of physical non-verbal cues. A hypothesis is that voice is the compensation method requiring the least technical adaptation, and imitates face-to-face interaction the most. This hypothesis should be tested in future studies.

Given the limitations put forth earlier, it can be assumed that there is a relationship between the compensation methods and the individual's communication style. This is evidenced by the variety of combinations of methods and styles found in the *least experienced* group, especially among participants from high-context cultural backgrounds. Due to the small response rate of the *power users*, it is not possible to make assumptions about this group. There is also a likely relationship between cultural background and communication style preference. Low-context participants indicated a tendency toward being Controllers. The relationships of these variables should be investigated using different research methodologies and approaches.

Another point for further exploration is the influence of experience using Web-based conferencing tools on an individual's compensation method. It should be made clear however, that experience is not always commensurate with age.

The insights gained are of high relevance to anyone involved in a virtual team. For organizations, it means bridging the gap between research and practice. The increasing diversity in the domestic as well as the global workforce make intercultural communication a necessity. Because DMC contributes to the success of any organization, it must be leveraged for collaboration in culturally diverse teams. Individuals who have intercultural competence and are self-reflective about their communication style are better prepared to adapt to the team dynamics as well as confidently compensate for the lack of physical non-verbal cues in Web-based conferencing. The awareness and knowledge gained might also curb the prevalence of Controller as the first choice of communication style, thus bringing about a balance of styles within a team.

Virtual communication is here to stay. Geographically dispersed teams need not only the right tools and technical knowledge, but also intercultural competence and communication strategies to be successful.

## References


Baggio, B., & Beldarrain, Y. (2011). *Anonymity and learning in digitally mediated communications: Authenticity and trust in cyber education*. Hershey, PA: IGI Global. https://doi.org/10.4018/978-1-60960-543-8

Bandura, A. (1971). *Social learning theory*. New York, NY: General Learning Press. Retrieved from http://www.jku.at/org/content/e54521/e54528/e54529/e178059/Bandura_SocialLearningTheory_ger.pdf

Bennett, J., & Bennett, M. J. (2004). Developing cultural sensitivity. An integrative approach to global and domestic diversity. In D. Landis, J. Bennett, & M. J. Bennett (Eds.), *Handbook of intercultural training* (3rd ed.) (pp. 147–165). Thousand Oaks, CA: Sage. https://doi.org/10.4135/9781452231129.n6

Bloomberg.. (2015). The skills gap. Retrieved February 14, 2017, from https://www.bloomberg.com/graphics/2015-job-skills-report

Borg, W. R., & Gall, M. D. (1989). *Educational research: An introduction* (5th ed.). New York, NY: Longman.

Cohn, D. and Caumont, A. (2016, March 31). Demographic trends that are shaping the U.S. and the world. Pew Research Center. Retrieved February 14, 2017, from http://www.pewresearch.org/fact-tank/2016/03/31/10-demographic-trends-that-are-shaping-the-u-s-and-the-world

Colbert, A., Yee, N., & George, G. (2016). The digital workforce and the workplace of the future. *Academy of Management Journal, 59*(3), 731–739. Retrieved from https://aom.org/uploadedFiles/Publications/AMJ/June_2016_FTE.pdf

Deaux, K. (1996). Social identification. In E. E. Higgins, & A. W. Kruglanski (Eds.), *Social psychology: Handbook of basic principles* (pp. 777–798). New York, NY: The Guildford Press.

Endress, P. (2016). *The magic of communication styles: Understanding yourself and those around you*. Harrisburg, PA: Cardinal House Press.

Gilson, L. L., Maynard, M. T., Jones Young, N. C. J., Vartiainen, M., & Hakonen, M. (2015). Virtual teams research: 10 years, 10 themes, and 10 opportunities. *Journal of Management, 41*(5), 1313–1337. https://doi.org/10.1177/0149206314559946

Glass, G. V., & Hopkins, K. D. (1996). *Statistical methods in education and psychology* (3rd ed.). Harlow, UK: Pearson.

Gudykunst, W. B. (1998). *Bridging differences: Effective intergroup communication* (3rd ed.). Thousand Oaks, CA: Sage. https://doi.org/10.4135/9781452229706

Gudykunst, W. B., & Kim, Y. Y. (2003). *Communication with strangers: An approach to intercultural communication* (4th ed.). Boston, MA: McGraw-Hill.

Gudykunst, W. B., & Lee, C. M. (2003). Intercultural communication theories. In W. B. Gudykunst (Ed.), *Cross-cultural and intercultural communication* (pp. 167–189). Thousand Oaks, CA: Sage.

Gudykunst, W. B., & Ting-Toomey, S. (1988). Verbal communication styles. In W. B. Gudykunst, S. Ting-Toomey, & E. Chua (Eds.), *Culture and interpersonal communication* (pp. 99–117). Newbury Park, CA: Sage.

Gunawardena, C. N. (1995). Social presence theory and implications for interaction collaborative learning in computer conferences. *International Journal of Educational Telecommunications, 1*(2), 147–166.

Gunawardena, C. N., & Zittle, F. J. (1997). Social presence as a predictor of satisfaction within a computer mediated conferencing environment. *American Journal of Distance Education, 11*(3), 8–26. https://doi.org/10.1080/08923649709526970

Hall, E. T. (1959). *The silent language*. New York, NY: Doubleday.

Hall, E. T. (1966). *The hidden dimension*. New York, NY: Doubleday.

Hall, E. T. (1976). *Beyond culture*. New York, NY: Doubleday.

Hall, E. T. (1983). *The dance of life: The other dimension of time*. New York, NY: Doubleday.

Hall, E. T. (1985). *Hidden differences: Studies in international communication*. Hamburg, Germany: Grunder and Jahr.

Hartman, F. (1963). A behavioristic approach to communication: A selective review of learning theory and a derivation of postulates. *Audio Visual Communication Review, 11*(5), 155–190 Retrieved from http://www.jstor.org/stable/30218492

Hasler, B. S., & Friedman, D. A. (2012). Sociocultural conventions in avatar-mediated nonverbal communication: A cross-cultural analysis of virtual proxemics. *Journal of Intercultural Communication Research, 43*(3), 238–259. https://doi.org/10.1080/17475759.2012.728764

Hecht, M. L., Warren, J. R., Jung, E., & Krieger, J. L. (2005). The communication theory of identity: Development, theoretical perspective, and future directions. In W. R. Gudykunst (Ed.), *Theorizing about intercultural communication* (pp. 257–278). Thousand Oaks, CA: Sage.

Herring, S. C., & Stoerger, S. (2014). Gender and (a)nonymity in computer-mediated communication. In J. Holmes, M. Meyerhoff, & S. Ehrlich (Eds.), *Handbook of language, gender and sexuality* (2nd ed.) (pp. 567–586). New York: Wiley. https://doi.org/10.1002/9781118584248.ch29

Hofstede, G. (1997). *Cultures and organizations: Software of the mind*. London, UK: McGraw-Hill Reprint from 1991.

Hollingshead, A. B. (2000). Truth and deception in computer-mediated groups. In M. A. Neale, E. A. Mannix, & T. Griffith (Eds.), *Research in managing groups and teams* (Vol. 3) (pp. 157–173.). Greenwich, CT: JAI Press. Retrieved from http://uscannenbergfaculty.org/andrea_hollingshead/research

Hollingshead, A. B. (2004). Communication technology, the internet and group research. Reprinted in M. Brewer and M. Hewstone (eds.), *Readings in Applied Social Psychology, Perspectives of Social Psychology Series*. Oxford, England: Blackwell. Retrieved February 14, 2017, from http://uscannenbergfaculty.org/andrea_hollingshead/research

Hollingshead, A. B., Fulk, J., & Monge, P. (2002). Fostering intranet knowledge sharing: An integration of transactive memory and public goods approaches. In P. Hinds, & S. Kiesler (Eds.), *Distributed work: New research on working across distance using technology*, (pp. 335–355). Cambridge, MA: MIT Press Retrieved from http://uscannenbergfaculty.org/andrea_hollingshead/research

Hull, C. (1943). *Principles of behavior. An introduction to behavior theory*. New York, NY: D. Appleton-Century Company, Inc. Retrieved from http://s-f-walker.org.uk/pubsebooks/pdfs/Principles%20of%20Behavior%20-%20Clark%20Hull.pdf

Jackson, S. L. (2008). *Research methods and statistics: A critical thinking approach* (3rd ed.). Mason. OH: Heinle Cengage Learning.

Jarvenpaa, S., & Leidner, D. E. (1998). Communication and trust in global virtual teams. *Journal of Computer-Mediated Communication.*, *3*(4). https://doi.org/10.1111/j.1083-6101.1998.tb00080.x

Kamoen, N. (2012). Positive versus negative. (Dissertation). Utrecht, Netherlands: LOT Publishers. Retrieved February 11, 2017, from http://vavi.wp.hum.uu.nl/files/2012/11/dissertatie_naomikamoen.pdf

Kim, Y. Y., & Ruben, B. D. (1988). Intercultural transformation: A systems theory. In Y. Y. Kim, & W. B. Gudykunst (Eds.), *Theories in intercultural communication* (pp. 299–321). Newbury Park, CA: Sage.

Lauring, J. (2011). Intercultural organizational communication: The social organizing of interaction in international encounters. *Journal of Business Communication*, *48*(3), 231–255. https://doi.org/10.1177/0021943611406500

Lea, M., & Spears, R. (1992). Paralanguage and social perception in computer-mediated communication. *Journal of Organizational Computing*, *2*(3&4), 321–341. https://doi.org/10.1080/10919399209540190

Luangrath, A. W., Peck, J., & Barger, V. A. (2017). Textual paralanguage and its implications for marketing communications. *Journal of Consumer Psychology*, *27*(1), 98–107. https://doi.org/10.1016/j.jcps.2016.05.002

Martin, J. N., & Nakayama, T. K. (2010). *Intercultural communication in contexts* (5th ed.). Boston: McGraw Hill.

Maude, B. (2016). *Managing cross-cultural communication. Principles and practice* (2nd ed.). London, UK: Palgrave.

McCroskey, J. C. (1997). Willingness to communicate, communication apprehension, and self-perceived communication competence: Conceptualizations and perspectives. In J. A. Daly, J. C. McCroskey, J. Ayres, T. Hopf, & D. M. Ayres (Eds.), *Avoiding communication: Shyness, reticence, and communication apprehension* (2nd ed.) (pp. 75–108). Cresskill, NJ: Hampton Press Inc. https://doi.org/10.1080/17513057.2013.769615

McCroskey, J. C., & McCroskey, L. L. (1988). Self-report as an approach to measuring communication competence. *Communication Research Reports*, *5*, 108–113 Retrieved from http://www.jamescmccroskey.com/publications/143.pdf

Mead, R., & Andrews, T. G. (2009). *International management* (4th ed.). Chichester, UK: Wiley.

Mehrabian, A. (1971). *Silent messages* (1st ed.). Belmont, CA: Wadsworth.

Merrill, D. W., & Reid, R. H. (1981). *Personal styles and effective performance.* Bradner, PA: Chilton Book Company.

Meyerson, D., Weick, K. E., & Kramer, R. M. (1996). Swift trust and temporary groups. In R. M. Kramer, & T. R. Tyler (Eds.), *Trust in organizations: Frontiers of theory and research,* (pp. 166–195). Thousand Oaks, CA: Sage. https://doi.org/10.4135/9781452243610.n9

Mischel, W., & Shoda, Y. (1995). A cognitive-affective system theory of personality: Reconceptualizing situations, dispositions, dynamics, and invariance in personality structure. *Psychological Review*, *102*(2), 246–268. https://doi.org/10.1037/0033-295X.102.2.246

Orbe, M. P. (1998). *Constructing co-cultural theory: An explication of culture, power, and communication.* Thousand Oaks, CA: Sage Publications. https://doi.org/10.4135/9781483345321

Personality Profile Solutions.. (2017). DiSC overview. Retrieved February 10, 2017, from https://www.discprofile.com/what-is-disc/overview

Reicher, S., Spears, R., & Postmes, T. (1995). A social identity model of deindividuation phenomena. In W. Stroebe, & M. Hewstone (Eds.), *European review of social psychology* (Vol. 6) (pp. 161–198). https://doi.org/10.1080/14792779443000049

Ruben, B. D., & Kealey, D. J. (1979). Behavioral assessment of communication competency and the prediction of cross-cultural adaptation. *International Journal of Intercultural Relations, 3*(1), 15–47. https://doi.org/10.1016/0147-1767(79)90045-2

Rubin, R. B., & Martin, M. M. (1994). Development of a measure of interpersonal communication competence. *Communication Research Reports, 11*(1), 33–44. https://doi.org/10.1080/08824099409359938

Samovar, L. A., & Porter, R. E. (2004). *Communication between cultures* (4th ed.). Belmont, CA: Wadsworth Press.

Samovar, L. A., Porter, R. E., & McDaniel, E. R. (2009). *Communication between cultures* (7th ed.). Belmont, CA: Wadsworth Press.

Santillan, C., & Horwitz, S. K. (2016). Application of collaboration technology to manage diversity in global virtual teams: The thinklet-based CE approach. In J. Prescott (Ed.), *Handbook of research on race, gender, and the fight for equality* (pp. 240–266). Hershey, PA: IGI Global. https://doi.org/10.4018/978-1-5225-0047-6.ch011

Short, J., Williams, E., & Christie, B. (1976). *The social psychology of telecommunications*. Chichester, UK: Wiley.

Skinner, B. F. (1971). *Beyond freedom and dignity*. Cambridge, MA: Hackett Publishing.

Smith, P. B. (2004). Acquiescent response bias as an aspect of cultural communication style. *Journal of Cross-Cultural Psychology, 35*(1). https://doi.org/10.1177/0022022103260380

Tidwell, L. C., & Walther, J. B. (2002). Computer-mediated communication effects on disclosure, impressions, and interpersonal evaluations: Getting to know one another a bit at a time. *Human Communication Research, 28*(3), 317 Retrieved November 2, 2018 from https://www.learntechlib.org/p/94063

Ting-Toomey, S. (1999). *Communicating across cultures*. New York, NY: The Guilford Press.

Trompenaars, F., & Hampden-Turner, C. (2012). *Riding the waves of culture. Understanding cultural diversity in business* (3rd ed.). New York, NY: McGraw-Hill.

Tylor, E. B. (1871). *Primitive culture: Researches into the development of mythology, philosophy, religion, art, and custom*. London, UK: J. Murray. Retrieved from https://catalog.hathitrust.org/Record/001274657

Varner, I., & Beamer, L. (2010). *Intercultural communication in the global workplace* (5th ed.). New York, NY: McGraw-Hill.

Wallbott, H. G. (1990). *Mimik im Kontext. Die Bedeutung verschiedener Informationskomponenten für das Erkennen von Emotionen [facial expressions. The importance of different information components for the recognition of emotions]*. Zürich, Switzerland: Verlag für Psychologie.

Walther, J. B. (1992). Interpersonal effects in computer-mediated interaction: A relational perspective. *Communication Research, 19*(1), 52–90. https://doi.org/10.1177/009365092019001003
Walther, J. B. (1996). Computer-mediated communication: Impersonal, interpersonal and hyperpersonal interaction. *Communication Research, 23*, 3–43. https://doi.org/10.1177/009365096023001001
Walther, J. B. (1997). Group and interpersonal effects in international computer-mediated collaboration. *Human Communication Research, 23*(3), 342–369. https://doi.org/10.1111/j.1468-2958.1997.tb00400.x

# 22

# Culture and Global Workplace Learning

## Foundations of Cross-Cultural Design Theories and Models

*Tutaleni Asino[1] and Lisa Giacumo[2]*

[1] *Oklahoma State University*
[2] *Boise State University*

The process of globalization has been ongoing since the beginning of human migration. Globalization is often driven by curiosity and necessity to explore and to improve processes, which in turn leads to a desire to figure out how to learn or better acquire the skills to advance. Brickman (1960), in his work on comparative education, references travelers' tales as exemplifying curiosity born out of human migration, whereby travelers come back to their place of origin to share about things they have seen and experienced. Crossley and Watson (2003) speak of the ancient Greeks and Romans who admired and wished to emulate Spartan education, and their fascination with Persian education, training and assessment of government employees. In other words, there has always been engagement with different peoples and attempts to learn from them.

What is novel is that the advancement of technology coupled with organizations having spread out globally has necessitated a workforce that is geographically dispersed and comprised of diverse persons originating from varied cultures, connected within departments of organizations in rapid, daily communication. Diversifying and harnessing the power of a workforce continues to be a concern for organizations (Zaballero, Asino and Briskin, 2012). However, this diversity is no longer limited to sensitivity training, or bringing employees to the headquarters of an organization for team-building. The nature of learning itself is changing; it is not merely sufficient to onboard employees to the culture of the organization, now it is also important to include and recognize the role of culture in workplace learning design, in order to achieve desired performance results.

While culture is recognized as a crucial ingredient in the design of learning and performance support systems in the workplace, the way that it informs learning strategy, performance improvement methods and instructional materials design is often not discussed in scholarly research, literature and graduate-level studies. That is to say, while there is focus and concern on recognizing the role that culture plays in globally distributed workplaces, the nexus of culture and workplace learning design is worthy of further exploration, and this will be the focus of this chapter.

*The Wiley Handbook of Global Workplace Learning*, First Edition.
Edited by Vanessa Hammler Kenon and Sunay Vasant Palsole.

This chapter addresses two important components (not the only important ones) in the globally-distributed workplace learning ecosystem: culture—both organizationally and geographically based; and performance improvement analysts and learning designers. Bates and Khasawneh (2005) suggest that an organization's learning culture is comprised of values, beliefs and norms, which inform employee development and management practices that facilitate performance improvement. However, Kang (2015) found that individuals also influence organizational culture and systems performance, and Katz, Swanson, and Nelson (2001) found that individuals working in multinational corporations carry expectations based in their local culture, which in turn influences organizational performance. Performance improvement analysts and learning designers are the individuals who partner with organizational members at all levels to codify organizational learning and performance needs, design strategies to meet them, and gather evidence of systematic employee development and systemic organizational systems performance improvement. Therefore, these two organizational components of the workplace-learning ecosystem have been chosen as significant factors for the focus of this chapter.

## What Is Culture?

Culture as a concept can be hard to explain or completely capture because it has many nuanced components; nonetheless, it is at the core of "what we do" and "who we are" (Eugene et al., 2009, p. 22). The notion of culture has not always been complicated to define. Early instances referenced by Katan (2009) illustrate a focus on examining people's way of life for the purpose of categorizing societies on a primitive to developed continuum. According to UNESCO (2017), culture is commonly defined as "that complex whole which includes knowledge, beliefs, arts, morals, laws, customs, and any other capabilities and habits acquired by [a human] as a member of society." Another definition by Branch (1997) frames culture as "the epistemology, philosophy, observed traditions, and patterns of action by individuals and human groups" (p. 38). The two definitions are complementary; one is useful in a very broad sense while the other is useful in instructional systems and educational technology communications research. However, neither seem to account for the merging of subcultures and evolution of practices found in multinational organizations. If we look to empirical research definitions of culture in economics, we find that authors agree on a definition that considers values as well as beliefs (Alesina & Giuliano, 2015). For example, the much-cited definition of culture by Guiso, Sapienza, and Zingales (2006) defines it as "those customary beliefs and values that ethnic, religious, and social groups transmit fairly unchanged from generation to generation." More recently, Guiso, Sapienza, and Zingales (2008) demonstrate how while individual beliefs are initially acquired from cultural transition from an earlier system of group beliefs, they can become slowly updated through experience and subsequently transmitted differently to the next generation. Therefore, we offer a novel definition of culture based upon this body of work: *the observed beliefs and values, demonstrated by patterns of action, that ethnic, geographic, religious and social groups transmit and evolve based on interactions with others.* Culture is crucial in the ecosystem, not just because it is integral to everyone's being, but also because as learning continues to be geographically dispersed, there are many more cultures that should more recently be considered when talking about learning in the global workplace. Regardless of the definition one adopts, the constant agreement in the literature is that culture influences the way we process information, how we communicate, how we learn (Matsumoto, 1996) and has been shown to influence the development of cognition (Bruner, 1973).

The second component, that of learning designers, is crucial because most of the systematic, intentional learning opportunities, whether formal or informal, that take place in the workplace are orchestrated by learning designers to meet various specific performance needs. Lee and Lai (2012) identified five trends in global workforce learning. The one that is of particular concern for this chapter is that participants and facilitators in global workplace learning are diversifying, and although collaboration between these diverse stakeholders should be continuously promoted, the diversification of a workplace "makes this field broader and more complex" (Lee & Lai, 2012, p. 3). To attend to this complexity, it is not just important for learning designers to be aware of the importance of culture, but it is necessary to provide tools that enable the design of workplace learning that is culturally aware and responsive to the communication norms of the target learner context.

There exist numerous models and guides that explore the role of culture in the design of learning, of which designers involved in global workforce learning initiatives, can and should be aware. Our chapter will include the following models as illustrations of what designers can look to when aiming to recognize and incorporate culture in the learning design process:

- Patricia Young's (2009)—The Culture Based Model (CBM);
- Edmundson's (2007)—Cultural Adaptation Process (CAP);
- Gunawardena, Wilson, and Nolla's (2003)—AMOEBA Design Framework;
- Hofstede's (1986; 2011)—National Cultural Dimensions (NCD);
- Henderson's (2007) Theorizing a Multiple Cultures Instructional Design Model for e-Learning and e-Teaching.

Through a review of pertinent literature, this chapter will explore the nexus of culture and global workplace learning by presenting different models that teach us how to integrate culture into global workforce learning. Our chapter will be guided by three main questions:

- What does global workplace learning look like and what does it involve?
- What is the role of culture in global workplace learning?
- How do organizations support workplace learning for a workforce that is globally distributed across a variety of geographically and globally dispersed cultures?

## Culture and Learning

The link between culture and learning is based on the understanding that learning is situated and context is critical to the learning process. Moreover, "the issues of culture and learning have been inseparable for centuries for the simple reason that one of the main goals of learning is the transmission of culture from generation to generation" (Kozulin, 2003, p. 13). This concept is perhaps easy to dismiss when the workplace seems predominantly culturally homogenous. Specifically, there is little motivation to be aware of differences or the need to take different perspectives in a place where everyone seems or appears to be the same. However, when differences do arise, culture becomes an issue. Our view aligns with that of Kozulin (2003) who argues that "In a monocultural environment culture remains mostly invisible," one only begins to paying attention to culture when two or more cultures are present in a space (p. 13).

Regardless of the theoretical perspective that one adopts, it is hard to deny that culture makes up each individual. Personal identity is a result of where a person was born, how and where they was raised, the language they speak and everything they have experienced. In other words, individuals bring all that they are with them to the workplace. They do not leave their identity at the door when they enter a workplace regardless of the strength of the current organizational structure. When learning occurs in the workplace, this learning is mitigated, consumed and integrated into the knowledge base of that individual. Therefore, culture is as important to learning in the workforce as it is to learning in many other contexts.

The theoretical support for culture and learning can be found in sociocultural learning theory, which is predicated upon the notion that an individual's nature and the environment in which they live plays a crucial role in their learning. Sociocultural theory, emerging from the works of Lev Vygotsky, a psychologist born in the Soviet Union, is based "on the concept that human activities take place in cultural contexts, are mediated by language and other symbol systems, and can be best understood when investigated in their historical development" (John-Steiner & Mahn, 1996. p. 191). Sociocultural theories, such as that advanced by Vygotsky, are appropriate for examining the role of culture in the workplace for three reasons: they reject the idea that the individual learner should be the focus, devoid of the components that make up the individual (we would argue this rejection supports the existence of a relationship between learning and culture); they emphasize learning as an ongoing process of participation in suitable activities and reject the primacy of learning as a product (we posit that this emphasis requires acceptance for the notion of knowledge construction that is situated within unique environmental inputs, including perceptions of the process and activities by the individual according to his/her socialized outlook); and they promote the understanding that learning cannot be divorced from context but rather workplace learning and performance are significantly shaped by social, organizational, cultural and other contextual factors (Hager, 2011, p. 23). Here, we further insist upon the importance of other individuals' and groups' influences upon the learner's environment and knowledge construction.

Culture is important to workplace learning. Perspectives from the three authors quoted below illustrate this well:

- "Human cultures emerge from people's struggles to manage uncertainties and to create some degree of order in social life" (Trice & Beyer, 1993, p. 1).

- "Culture is the way in which a group of people solve problems and reconcile dilemmas" (Trompenaars & Hampden-Turner, 1998, p. 6).
- "The culture of a group can be defined as the accumulated shared learning of that group as it solves problems of external adaptation and internal integration; which has worked well enough to be considered valid and, therefore, to be taught to new members as the correct way to perceive, think, feel, and behave in relation to those problems. This accumulated learning is a pattern or system of beliefs, values, and behavioral norms that come to be taken for granted as basic assumptions and eventually drop out of awareness" (Schein, 2017, p. 6).

These three examples illustrate that culture is integral to who an individual is, whether in the workforce or elsewhere. Furthermore, culture defines the rules of behavior, correct practices, how individuals are socialized and how they acquire resources, tools and strategies necessary for participating in and solving day-to-day problems (Alfred, 2002). Effective workplace learning cannot ignore culture and the role it plays in individuals.

Culture and learning are not only intersecting points, but intertwined elements. It is not an overstatement to say that understanding culture has been around since human existence. Hence, as long as humanity exists, and new fields of studies emerge, the concept of culture will continue to change in the human mind and a definition will continue to be sought (Salehi, 2012). Thus, in reflection of the process of influencing humans' minds and thoughts, cross-cultural learning design researchers and expert practitioners would acknowledge cultural to affect the way in which individuals process information, navigate organizations, build relationships and engage in workplace learning.

## Culture and Design

While culture is recognized as a crucial ingredient to systems within workplaces and support of learning, the way that it is integrated in the design of learning environments and experiences has often been glossed over. This oversight can have detrimental consequences especially when designers tend to have an ill-defined or even an incorrect understanding of their target audience, which can lead to decisions that merely fit with the designers' own viewpoints (Cooper, 1999). An explicit focus on including culture is a necessary component of design, as when designing for the "other" who differs in terms of cultural background, one risks the creation of an offensive or even exclusionary experience of said audiences.

Young (2009) argued that a link between culture and design is based on the idea that both are grounded in social acts, embedded in a social context and created to give meaning and order to lived experiences of the people. However, as discussed earlier, culture is a complex construct to define and, although there is general agreement indicating that each definition tends to focus on particular characteristics, a unified definition has eluded scholars for decades, resulting in varied lists of terms and definitions (see Kroeber & Kluckhohn, 1952; Spencer-Oatey & Franklin, 2009).

Similarly, the term *design* has been difficult to articulate. One of the broadest and most popular definitions of design is that advanced by architect Victor Papanek in his book *Design for the Real World* (1984). Papanek (1984) argued that we are all designers and are involved in the act of designing everyday:

> All that we do, almost all the time, is design, for design is basic to all human activity. The planning and patterning of any act towards a desired, foreseeable end constitutes the design process. Any attempt to separate design, to make it a thing-by-itself, works counter to the inherent value, of design as the primary underlying matrix of life. Design is composing an epic poem, executing a mural, painting a masterpiece, writing a concerto. But design is also cleaning and reorganizing a desk drawer, pulling an impacted tooth, baking an apple pie, choosing sides for a back-lot baseball game, and educating a child. Design is the conscious effort to impose meaningful order. (p. 3)

Therefore, to be a designer is to create meaning and order out of the information, tools and resources, available, to meet any given need. Consequently, if everyone is a designer when contributing within their own professional, community, or personal, roles and has a cultural vantage point that contributes to who they are, it is fair to argue that there is no one way to design, whether it is designing artifacts or designing workplace learning opportunities. The artifacts or workplace learning opportunities that are created by learning designers can include formal learning environments, training materials, professional development systems, incentives systems, job descriptions, selection criteria, onboarding systems, or informal learning program designs such as organizational communities of practice or facilitated internal mentoring, to name a few.

We argue that culture influences learning and hypothesize that designs of workplace learning must be aligned to cultural expectations if one expects to affect learning and performance outcomes. In short, culture has been shown to have significant effects on the outcomes of learning, knowledge transfer and performance (Frambach, Driessen, Chan, & van der Vleuten, 2012; Lucas, 2006; Zhang, De Pablos, & Xu, 2014). However, researchers and practitioners working to design learning environments across cultures are often unsure of how to accommodate different target audience needs. Therefore, we contend that research should focus on the design process and characteristics of design artifacts on learning and performance outcomes of individuals situated in ecosystems.

## Models for Incorporating Culture into Global Workforce Learning

The existence of terms such as organizational culture is proof that culture as a construct is of paramount importance to the workplace. It is easy to argue that the organization does not have to worry about accommodating other cultures, and that it is the employee who must adjust, but that is not true. In our experience, we do see employees adjusting but we also see organizations in certain sectors, such as banking, sales, high-tech and manufacturing, change their approach to workplace learning design when setting up new capacity in a foreign culture, when a direct relationship between performance and sales or productivity is found to be mediated by workplace learning design decisions that results in large profits or losses. Also, in the international non-governmental organization sector, one will find that individuals in headquarters often consider culture when making learning design choices for capacity development or civil society building in more remote areas. However, we believe these to be the few exceptions and smaller organizations with recent mergers or more inexperienced workplace learning designers are often unaware of when and how to make these decisions.

Culture is clearly important in workplace learning design, yet the glaring question that emerges is how? If practitioners, researchers and educators value culture and want to integrate culture holistically in the design process leading to workplace learning and performance improvement, then how do they do it? In this section we present four models that provide guidance on the process. We will provide a summary of each model and conclude by providing examples of their utility. It is, however; important to state here that these are not the only models that exist but are merely four illustrations.

## The Culture-Based Model (CBM)

There are few models that provide guidance on how to design with culture in mind. Hence, those interested in this pursuit are often left with the question of how to integrate culture into design. The CBM, developed by Patricia Young, provides an illustrative example. Young (2009) defines CBM as "an intercultural instructional design framework that guides designers through the management, design, development, and assessment process while taking into account explicit culture-based considerations" (p. 37).

CBM was created for practicing and researching designers interested in culture based Information Communication Technologies. The model emerged from studies of instructional products designed by and for African Americans, whose contributions to the history of instructional technology, as well as the contributions of other minority groups were often ignored. Young's (2009) research that led to the creation of CBM set out to further explore approaches to designing instructional products that were culturally and linguistically specific.

CBM is comprised of eight areas that form the acronym ID-TABLET: Inquiry, Development, Team, Assessments, Brainstorming, Learners, Elements and Training (Young, 2009), detailed in Table 22.1.

CBM is not a sequential model that needs to be followed from beginning to end. The designer or the team involved in the project determines if the whole cycle needs to be followed or if there is a specific area of CBM that fits the goal of that project.

### National Cultural Dimensions (NCD)

One of the most cited models when discussing culture is Geert Hofstede's NCD. NCD stem from an international study of IBM employees in the 1960s and 1970s as a way of explaining the differences between cultures. NCD posits that global

**Table 22.1** Eight Areas of CBM

| Area | Explanation |
|---|---|
| Inquiry | As the term indicates, this is about questioning, specifically the project and decisions as a way of monitoring for biases and ensuring focus on the targeted audience. |
| Development | Consisting of ten subcriteria, the development area provides a structure for solving problems. |
| Team | This area is concerned with the makeup of the team. It argues that to have a culturally sensitive/appropriate design, the team responsible for the decision-making must consist of cultural experts. |
| Assessments | The assessments area is concerned with the evaluation options of the project to uncover the effectiveness of the product and goals toward the targeted audience. |
| Brainstorming | This stage is concerned with ensuring that the project is headed in the right direction and aligned with the ideals of the design team. This is done in the pre-production stage and includes examining the financial status of the project to make sure that it can be completed. |
| Learners | This area is concerned with the learning in which learners engage by ensuring that the outcomes are in support of the learners' cultural prism. |
| Elements | This area addresses the development of content by making sure that the content produced is inclusive of all the cultures of which the project is comprised. |
| Training | This area deals with educating those who will utilize the product created. |

cultures can be divided into six dimensions (Figure 22.1), based on what elements a culture values. Hofstede (2012) states that the NCD represents the preference of one state over the other and stresses that the dimensions are relative, just as human beings themselves are unique and can change.

The first dimension, the power distance index (PDI), concerns inequality and power and how a society handles them. PDI is the extent to which the less powerful members of society (i.e., in institutions and organizations) accept that power is unequally distributed and the amount of authority one person has over others (Hofstede & Bond, 1984). The argument advanced in the PDI is that "People in societies exhibiting a large degree of Power Distance accept a hierarchical order in which everybody has a place and which needs no further justification. In societies with low Power Distance, people strive to equalize the distribution of power and demand justification for inequalities of power" (Hofstede, 2012).

The second dimension of the NCD model, individualism versus collectivism (INV), is a continuum of how individuals that comprise a society value the importance of individual goals versus those of the collective or society. INV groups cultures in terms of those who value the "I vs. we" as self-concept. When relating this dimension to family ties within a given society, on one side of the continuum is individualism, which is viewed as "a situation in which people are supposed to look after themselves and their immediate family only" (Hofstede & Bond, 1984, p. 419). On the other side of the continuum, perhaps as an opposite, people belong

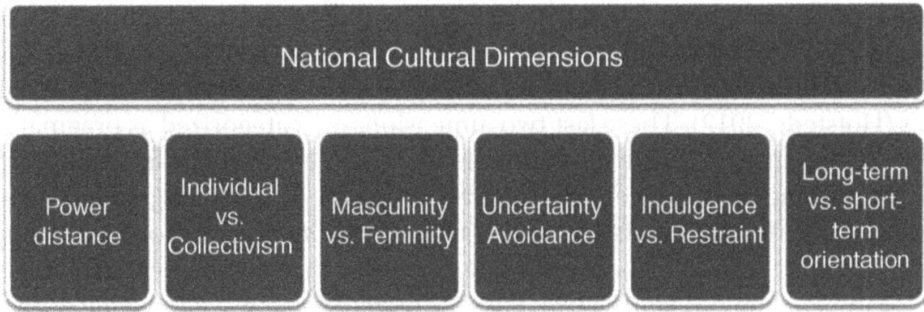


**Figure 22.1** A Representation of NCD Elements

to a group and as part of the collective they have a responsibility to look after each other as a larger collective community (Hofstede & Bond, 1984).

In the "masculinity versus femininity" (MAS) dimension of the NCD model, the emphasis is on which tendencies (masculine or feminine) are more powerful or valued within the community. This recognizes that men and women may have different values, whether those are naturally manifested or are a result of nurture. This dimension is based on long-established patterns of sex roles that exist in nearly all societies, whereby "boys are socialized toward assertiveness and self-reliance, and girls, toward nurturance and responsibility" (Hofstede, 1983, p. 55). One side of the continuum for this dimension is masculinity, which is defined as "a situation in which the dominant values in society are success, money, and things," while femininity, is regarded as "a situation in which the dominant values in society are caring for others and the quality of life" (Hofstede & Bond, 1984, p. 419). Viewing this dimension in terms of business contexts, a masculine society is regarded as more competitive, whereas a feminine society is consensus-oriented and tender (Hofstede, 2012).

Inspired by the work of Cyert and March (1964), the uncertainty avoidance (UAI) dimension of the NCD model is concerned with the extent to which members of a society place a premium on avoiding actions that could increase anxiety. Hofstede and Bond (1984) defined this as "the extent to which people feel threatened by ambiguous situations, and have created beliefs and institutions that try to avoid these" (p. 419). This dimension is fundamentally concerned with how a society assesses the future and "deals with the fact that the future can never be known: should we try to control the future or just let it happen? Countries exhibiting strong UAI maintain rigid codes of belief and behavior and are intolerant of unorthodox behaviors and ideas. Weak UAI societies maintain a more relaxed attitude in which practice counts more than principle" (Hofstede, 2012).

The last two dimensions of the NCD model, long-term orientation versus short-term normative orientation (LTO) and indulgence versus restraint (IVR), were not part of the original set of dimensions articulated by Hofstede (1984). Rather, they were added on in later years as validation of the research done and arguments from various researchers argued for an expansion (Hofstede & Bond, 1988; Hofstede, Hofstede, & Minkov, 2010; Minkov, 2007). In LTO, the focus is on how a society deals with its past, present and future. Societies that prefer honoring traditions and norms while at the same time being suspicious about change tend to score low on this dimension. The IVR continuum reflects a society's tolerance for individuals to freely indulge as a natural tendency versus suppressing gratification of needs and regulating them as a matter of strict social norms (Hofstede, 2012). These last two dimensions are categorized as pragmatic because a propensity to value modernity tends to score higher (Hofstede, 2012).

It is important to stress here that the NCD model was not originally established to study design. Hoefsted's work around national dimensions has been applied widely across disciplines, and one can argue that the dimensions "relate to very fundamental problems which face any human society, but to which different societies have found different answers," (Hofstede, 1983, p. 46). Perhaps Hofstede intended his work to be generalized beyond the discipline of organizational communication in which they originated. However, this model has been used to study participation in Massive Open Online Courses (Stager, 2016); to investigate the connection between culture, technology and learning (Vatrapu & Suthers, 2007), and the learner self-efficacy of success factors in online learning (Cortés & Barbera, 2009). Nonetheless, it is helpful to keep in mind that the original purpose of the research Hoefsted articulated (1983)—that the model was specifically created to understand the intricacies of organizations and communication of businesses. The six dimensions are used to explain different ways of structuring organizations, different motivations of people within organizations, and different issues people and organizations face within society (Hofstede, 1983, p.46).

## Cultural Adaptation Process (CAP)

The cultural adaptation process model (CAP) was intended to guide instructional designers who may need to redesign e-learning courses that exist in one culture so that learners in another culture can consume them. An example of this would be designing an e-learning course in the USA and wanting to redesign the same course for learners in Indonesia. The CAP model represents a matrix, in which steps are provided to modify any given e-learning course to address the needs of learners from another culture; for example from US culture to Chinese culture. Edmundson (2007) structures the steps into the following four levels: Level 1 is translation, where the designer determines if the course needs to be translated from one language to another; Level 2 is translation and localization; Level 3 is translation, localization and cultural learning objects; and Level 4 is origination (completely redesigning the course or starting from the beginning with something new). The model originates from synthesized research in industrial anthropology and education (Edmundson, 2007).

The CAP model guides an intricate analysis process that does not seek to rely upon or create cultural experts (Edmundson, 2007). Edmundson intended the model to represent a replicable, systematic process that would facilitate an instructional designers' decision-making approach about making changes to any given e-learning product to meet the needs of learners situated in a new target culture. He envisioned the users of the model to be faculty members of universities situated in a foreign country, or corporations with outsourced personnel or departments, as well as humanitarian aid or international development workers who may need to provide e-learning to underserved populations. However, in our search of peer-reviewed and scholarly publications we have not found any evidence that this model has been either implemented or tested and validated.

One assumption of the model is that product updates, operations or procedures are embedded in course designs that represent an instructivist–objectivist didactic approach and are aligned with precise behavioral objectives or focused goals. On the other end of the continuum, the model assumes that soft skills courses are presented via a constructivist approach and are aligned with cognitive objectives or unfocused goals. While this may be true for products created by formally trained instructional designers, the continuum cannot be observed universally in all e-learning products. In addition, this model focuses on the relationship between the design and the learners represented by national cultural norms, which are not likely to be present in all groups of people, especially those found in multinational organizations that move their employees around, or the cultural background of those who work in international non-governmental organizations. Therefore, instructional designers may need to consider a cultural context in which the e-learning product's design is not explicitly integrated into the model. Finally, Edmundson (2007) suggested that to in order to be able to use his model, it appears as though the instructional designer must first be aware of the research underlying Geert Hofstede's NCD model.

### AMOEBA Design Framework

Gunawardena et al. (2003) introduced the AMOEBA (Adaptive, Meaningful, Organic, Environmental-based architecture) design framework to drive the participatory negotiation and adaptations that they saw as essential to support learners and facilitators in a multicultural constructivist learning design. The AMOEBA metaphor represents the idea that any learning environment can be structured and then adapted as needed, to support the functions required by a facilitator and learners to accomplish their goals. An amoeba is after all, a single-cell organism, which adapts to its environment, and performs all processes required to function and maintain life without a definite shape yet still has structure.

The model was conceived as the result of a research project based on literature from cross-cultural psychology, intercultural communication and intercultural computer-mediated communication. The AMOEBA design framework includes components that the authors used to structure modifications they chose to make to a course offered to learners originating from different countries. The components of the model included the facilitator, learners, language, format, communication channel, activities, methods and knowledge. The entry point of the model begins with the two smallest components, which represent the instructor and the learners. These two components are linked by the language component to the rest of the model. Language links to the knowledge component, and all other components of the model are linked to the knowledge component, which is the largest component of the model and positioned as the belly of the AMOEBA. The other components are connected to and positioned above the belly, connecting to each other sequentially, from language to format, to communication channel, to activities and, lastly, methods.

Together, each of the components of the AMOEBA model make up the structure through which course design decisions should be made among the facilitator and learners as they work toward meeting relevant learning goals. For example, the language component can be used to guide conversations related to the language of the materials that should be provided based on the needs of the majority of the learners. Additionally, the authors suggest that as many other languages as resources will allow should be incorporated into the course design (Gunawardena et al., 2003). The format component was intended to focus group decisions apropos to the colors, icons, organization, navigation paths and other relevant decisions related to the course meeting-place, communications tools and document library (Gunawardena et al., 2003). The authors also intended that collaborative facilitator and learner decisions be made according to the synchronous and asynchronous communications tools that would be selected to support learning and exploration, as represented by the communications component (Gunawardena et al., 2003). The activity component was intended to represent the different ways the instructor and learners would choose to engage together in learning tasks, such as through individual work or group work, and the wide variety of deliverable formats available, which would allow demonstration of the learning goals and subject area, to meet the needs of the learning community (Gunawardena et al., 2003). Further, the authors also thought that the choice in roles available to learners and instructors should also be negotiated. These roles may include learner moderation of discussions or peer feedback mechanisms, instead of or in conjunction with promoting traditional instructor roles. Finally, the results of each of these collaborative decision points when combined with the completion of all course activities represent how the authors conceived of the overarching knowledge component (Gunawardena et al., 2003).

Gunawardena et al. (2003) also suggest that the participatory course design choices made by facilitators and learners in this framework would evolve over time. Further, they suggest that one of their goals would be for the instructor to push learners beyond their comfort zones and gradually build on learning activities that learners would have originally resisted or not been able to take on (Gunawardena et al., 2003). However, while it is good to push learners out of their comfort zone, we feel it is also important to avoid pushing learners to engage in activities that do not align with their educational and professional development goals. While encouraging the learner out of the comfort zone, the instructor must also ensure that they are developing relevant skills and workflows, which will align with the type of work he/she expects learners to perform upon completion of the course.

In addition to course design, Gunawardena et al. (2003), used this AMOEBA framework to conceptualize their research on perception, cognition and a constructivist learning process, in cross-cultural online education. Again, the theoretical constructs at the base of their research included language choice, format choices, communications channels choices, activity choices, methods choices and knowledge construction through interaction. Based on this framework and their experience with empirical cross-cultural research, they offered three recommendations: first, they suggest using a more comprehensive model for cross-cultural learning environment design and research; second, in any given project, researchers should be sure to include individuals who are a member and representative of each culture represented; third, considerable attention must be paid to the selected research methodology, in order to facilitate appropriate data collection and enable correct interpretation of the results. Further, Gunawardena et al. (2003) suggest incorporating the recommendations offered by Bhawuk and Triandis (1996), such as approaching empirical cross-cultural studies with a grounding in both emics and etics constructs and using a mixed methods approach because one cannot study differences without first uncovering similarities; and being deliberate with the level of data collected and analyzed, because cultures or nations as units of observation are capable of providing different insight from individual-level data.

While the participatory nature of this cross-cultural instructional design framework adds a unique approach to anticipating a cross-cultural learning community's needs, it may not provide enough guidance when working with employees who must each meet any given learning goal and yet still perform in separate organizational contexts located in different areas across the globe. Therefore, an important limitation is the disregard for the greater organizational cultural context within which learners are expected to engage and demonstrate their learning and/or performance outcomes. We would like to acknowledge that the authors did suggest that organizational factors would feed into design of the learning environment, such as the timeline, performance standards, completion value, costs and equipment. However, it is our experience that other organization-level systems components are missing and these may also affect the outcomes of any given workplace learning course or more informal learning program design. For example, there are systems components in organizations where we believe local culture would influence learning and performance expectations (Brethower, 2004). Other systems components, which may prevent a single successful course or program design may include organizational expectations, feedback mechanisms, information systems and organizational-level motives or extrinsic facilitators and barriers to desired performance (Chevalier, 2003).

## The Multiple Cultures Model of Instructional Design

The multiple cultures model of instructional design is a result of the dissatisfaction with instructional design models that fail in the matter of "promoting equity and inclusion among culturally diverse learners" (Smith & Ayers, 2006, p. 408). Henderson (2007) argued that a multiple cultures model to guide instructional design decisions was needed to provide access to learners from non-dominant cultures to participate in what she argues is currently a global academic culture rooted in western academic practices. Without providing opportunities for learners from non-dominant cultures to master various learning and publication activities traditionally reserved for western participants, designers may inadvertently prevent access or trivialize token components of instruction designed for various localized learner audiences. Therefore, to achieve sustainable global workplace learning outcomes a mix and match of dominant and non-dominant cultural affordances have to be implemented in the instructional design and learning processes.

The multiple cultures model of instructional design is a complex Venn diagram with five circles overlapping to make up the center point, where one might find the desired outcome of e-learning instructional design. Henderson (2007) represents this model with five circles which represent standpoint worldviews, including: global academic training, and entrepreneurial cultures; gender, religion, and class; indigenous and ethnic minorities' cultures; workplace cultures; and dominant global academic and training cultures. The multiple cultures model "strives for a coherent interplay among the various cultural logics: global academia or training cultures; the majority societal epistemologies of the e-learners and those of indigenous and ethnic minorities; issues of gender, class, religion, age, kinship, politics and various workplace cultures; and pedagogies" (p. 136). The purpose of recognizing each of the relevant worldviews held by learners originating from multiple cultures would be to provide access to knowledge, cultural histories and an understanding of multiple systems of power distribution, as well as the integration of various value systems when the intention is to optimize for equity (Henderson, 2007).

One assumption of this model of instructional design is that learners from the non-dominant culture want to access and participate in the dominant global academic culture and workplace learning culture. There is an inherent responsibility embedded in this model, which presupposes that learners from a culture other than the dominant one must also become versed in two cultures, that of their native origin and the global dominant culture. This is, of course, grounded in the assumption that those from the non-dominant culture must change and adapt to the dominant cultural ways of working.

## Discussion and Conclusions

In this chapter, we have discuss several models as illustrative cases for how culture can be included into the design process. Geert Hofstede's NCD provides for a way to classify culture across six different dimensions. It can provide guidance especially when designing a product to be consumed in multiple countries. Rather than simply choosing the dominant culture, this model provides guidance for grouping cultures if that is a requirement.

The AMOEBA Design Framework, is envisioned as a way of supporting a participatory approach in the design process. This framework provides a guide for how designers can create designs in partnership with their participants and in the environment in which the product is to be consumed, hence the reference to an amoeba, a single-cell organism which adapts to its environment. The next model, the CAP Model, is concerned with adaptation. It can serve as a guide for designers wishing to adapt their products to other cultures. This is especially significant in a culture of cross-cultural learning whereby, for example, a course is created in one culture and is adapted to another. It provides designers with ways of avoiding common mistakes such as simply changing colors or replacing an accent of a narrator when moving across cultures. The Culture Based Model (CBM) provides a systematic process of how to design with culture in mind. In the CBM, designers have options for how to integrate culture throughout the design process. The last model, the Multiple Cultures Model, explicitly provides guidance toward the complete assimilation of learners from a non-dominant culture into a dominant, globalized academic and workplace learning context. While the goal is to provide those from under-represented cultures access to widely accepted standards of learning and valued information sharing methods or outlets, the unintended consequences of overtly valuing one system over other ways of working should not be overlooked or rationalized away.

## Conclusion

Global workplace learning is invariably and inevitably diverse. It is and will continue to be diverse in terms of participants, diverse by way of means through which people learn, and diverse through the technology that is used, which changes continuously.

In this chapter our goal was to contribute to the conversation on the role of culture in the global workforce learning. As we have illustrated through varied research perspectives, culture is at the core of what it means to be human and as such, as humanity evolves and as we attempt to make sense of our world, the very understanding of culture will also shift. Yet, this challenge should not serve as latent permission to omit culture in the discourse or practice of workforce learning. In this chapter we provided examples of models that can be utilized in the integration of culture into workplace learning design.

We end our chapter as we began, arguing that the forces of globalization that began with early human migration will continue driven in large part by emerging and yet to be invented technologies. The workplace will be comprised of diverse people who are dispersed in terms of time and space, but who are all trying to meet the goal of the workplace. This will necessitate an approach to workplace learning that is aimed at facilitating equitable learning and performance outcomes for individuals across cultures. Standardized approaches to workplace learning are not sufficient in a globalized workforce, as the challenge is to not only recognize the importance of culture, but also make it an integral part in the formulation of workplace learning.

## References


Alesina, A. and Giuliano, P. (2015). Culture and Institutions. IZA Discussion Papers, No. 9246. Retrieved September 6, 2017 from https://www.econstor.eu/handle/10419/114123

Alfred, M. V. (2002). The promise of sociocultural theory in democratizing adult education. *New Directions for Adult and Continuing Education, 2002*(96), 3–14.

Bates, R., & Khasawneh, S. (2005). Organizational learning culture, learning transfer climate and perceived innovation in Jordanian organizations. *International Journal of Training and Development, 9*(2), 96–109.

Bhawuk, D. P. S., & Triandis, H. C. (1996). The role of culture theory in the study of culture and intercultural training. In D. Landis, & R. S. Bhagat (Eds.), *Handbook of intercultural training* (2nd. ed.) (pp. 17–34). Thousand Oaks, CA: Sage.

Brethower, D. M. (2004). Understanding behavior of organizations to improve behavior in organizations. *The Behavior Analyst Today*, *5*(2), 170.

Brickman, W. W. (1960). A historical introduction to comparative education. *Comparative Education Review*, *3*(3), 6–13.

Bruner, J. S. (1973). *The relevance of education*. New York, NY: Norton.

Branch, R. M. (1997, March–April). Educational technology frameworks that facilitate culturally pluralistic instruction. *Educational Technology*, *37*(2), 38–40.

Chevalier, R. (2003). Updating the behavior engineering model. *Performance Improvement*, *42*(5), 8–14.

Cooper, A. (1999). *The inmates are running the asylum*. Indianapolis, IN: Macmillan. https://doi.org/10.1007/978-3-322-99786-9

Cortés, A. and Barbera, E. (2009). Cultural Differences in Students' Perceptions Towards Online Learning Success Factors. In Academic Conferences International Limited (ed.), Conference on Factors in European e-Learning, pp. 555–565. London: Academic Conferences International Limited.

Crossley, M., & Watson, K. (2003). *Comparative and international research in education: Globalisation, context and difference*. London, UK: Routledge.

Cyert, R. M., & March, J. G. (1964). Organizational design. *New Perspectives in Organizational Research*. New York: John Wiley & Sons.

Edmundson, A. (2007). The cultural adaptation process (CAP) model: Designing e-learning. In A. Edmundson (ed.), *Globalized e-learning cultural challenges*, pp. 267–290. Hershey, PA: IGI Global.

Eugene, W., Hatley, L., McMullen, K., Brown, Q., Rankin, Y., & Lewis, S. (2009, July). This is who I am and this is what I do: Demystifying the process of designing culturally authentic technology. In *International conference on internationalization, design and global development*, (pp. 19–28). Berlin:: Springer.

Frambach, J. M., Driessen, E. W., Chan, L. C., & van der Vleuten, C. P. (2012). Rethinking the globalisation of problem-based learning: How culture challenges self-directed learning. *Medical Education*, *46*(8), 738–747.

Guiso, L., Sapienza, P., & Zingales, L. (2006). Does culture affect economic outcomes? *The Journal of Economic Perspectives*, *20*(2), 23–48.

Guiso, L., Sapienza, P., & Zingales, L. (2008). Social capital as good culture. *Journal of the European Economic Association*, *6*(2–3), 295–320.

Gunawardena, C. N., Wilson, P. L., & Nolla, A. C. (2003). Culture and online education. In M. Graham Moore (Ed.), *Handbook of distance education* (pp. 753–775). Mahwah, NJ: Lawrence Erlbaum Associates.

Hager, P. 2011. Theories of workplace learning: A critical overview. In M. Malloch, L. Cairns, K. Evans and B. N. O'Connor (eds.), The international handbook of workplace learning: Theory, research, practice, and issues, 17–31. London, UK: Sage.

Henderson, L. (2007). Theorizing a multiple cultures instructional design model for e-learning and e-teaching. In *Globalized e-learning cultural challenges* (pp. 130–154). Hershey, PA: IGI Global.

Hofstede, G. (1983). National cultures in four dimensions: A research-based theory of cultural differences among nations. *International Studies of Management and Organization*, *13*(1–2), 46–74.

Hofstede, G. (1984). *Culture's consequences: International differences in work-related values* (Vol. 5). Beverly Hills, CA: Sage.

Hofstede, G. (1986). The usefulness of the "organizational culture" concept. *Journal of Management Studies, 23*(3), 253–257.

Hofstede, G. (2011). Dimensionalizing cultures: The Hofstede model in context. *Online Readings in Psychology and Culture, 2*(1), 8.

Hofstede, G. (2012). National Cultural Dimension. Retrieved 09 February 2017, from http://geert-hofstede.com/national-culture.html

Hofstede, G., & Bond, M. H. (1984). Hofstede's culture dimensions an independent validation using Rokeach's value survey. *Journal of Cross-Cultural Psychology, 15*(4), 417–433.

Hofstede, G., & Bond, M. H. (1988). The Confucius connection: From cultural roots to economic growth. *Organizational Dynamics, 16*(4), 5–21.

Hofstede, G., Hofstede, G. J., & Minkov, M. (2010). *Cultures and organizations: Software of the mind* (Revised and expanded. New York, NY: McGraw-Hill.

John-Steiner, V., & Mahn, H. (1996). Sociocultural approaches to learning and development: A Vygotskian framework. *Educational Psychologist, 31*(3–4), 191–206.

Kang, I.-G. (2015). Empirical testing of a human performance model: Understanding success in federal agencies using second-order structural equation modeling (Order No. 3715873). Available from ProQuest Dissertations and Theses Global. (1701639415). Retrieved from http://ezproxy.lib.indiana.edu/login?url=http://search.proquest.com/docview/1701639415?accountid=11620

Katan, D. (2009). Translation as intercultural communication. In *The Routledge companion to translation studies* (pp. 88–106). London: Routledge.

Katz, J. P., Swanson, D. L., & Nelson, L. K. (2001). Culture-based expectations of corporate citizenship: A propositional framework and comparison of four cultures. *The International Journal of Organizational Analysis, 9*(2), 149–171.

Kozulin, A. (2003). Psychological tools and mediated learning. In A. Kozulin, B. Gindis, V. S. Ageyev, & S. M. Miller (Eds.), *Vygotsky's educational theory in cultural context* (pp. 15–38). Cambridge, UK: Cambridge University Press.

Kroeber, A. L., & Kluckhohn, C. (1952). *Culture: A critical review of concepts and definitions*. Cambridge, MA: Harvard University Press.

Lee, L. S., and Lai, C. C. (2012). Global trends in workplace learning. Paper presented at the International Conference on Complex, Intelligent and Software Intensive Systems (CISIS-2012) and the International Conference on Innovative Mobile and Internet Services in Ubiquitous Computing (IMIS-2012), Palermo, Italy, July 4.

Lucas, L. M. (2006). The role of culture on knowledge transfer: The case of the multinational corporation. *The Learning Organization, 13*(3), 257–275.

Matsumoto, D. (1996). *Culture and psychology*. Pacific Grove, CA: Brooks/Cole Publishing Company.

Minkov, M. (2007). *What makes us different and similar: A new interpretation of the world values survey and other cross-cultural data*. Sofia, Bulgaria: Klasika y Stil Publishing House.

Papanek, V. (1984). *Design for the real world*. New York, NY: Van Nostrand.

Salehi, M. (2012). Reflections on culture, language and translation. *Journal of Academic and Applied Studies, 2*(5), 82.

Schein, E. H. (2017). *Organizational culture and leadership* (5th ed.). New York: John Wiley & Sons.

Smith, D. R., & Ayers, D. F. (2006). Culturally responsive pedagogy and online learning: Implications for the globalized community college. *Community College Journal of Research and Practice, 30*(5–6), 401–415.

Spencer-Oatey, H., & Franklin, P. (2009). *Intercultural interaction: A multidisciplinary approach to intercultural communication.* Berlin: Springer.

Stager, S. J. (2016). *Exploring the relationship between culture and participation in an introduction to art MOOC* (Doctoral dissertation, The Pennsylvania State University).

Trice, H. M., & Beyer, J. M. (1993). *The cultures of work organization.* Upper Saddle River, NJ: Prentice Hall Adapted by permission of Pearson Education, Inc., Upper Saddle River, N.J.

Trompenaars, F., & Hampden-Turner, C. (1998). *Riding the waves of culture: Understanding diversity in global business* (2nd ed.). New York, NY: McGraw-Hill.

UNESCO. (2017). Cultural diversity. Retrieved September 7, 2017 from http://www.unesco.org/new/en/social-and-human-sciences/themes/international-migration/glossary/cultural-diversity

Vatrapu, R. and Suthers, D. (2007). Culture and computers: A review of the concept of culture and implications for intercultural collaborative online learning. In *Intercultural collaboration*, pp. 260–275. Berlin, Heidelberg: Springer.

Young, P. A. (Ed.) (2009). *Instructional design frameworks and intercultural models.* Hershey, PA: IGI Global.

Zhang, X., De Pablos, P. O., & Xu, Q. (2014). Culture effects on the knowledge sharing in multi-national virtual classes: A mixed method. *Computers in Human Behavior, 31*, 491–498.

# Part IV

# Engagement and Motivation

# 23

# Modern Meditation Training

## An Innovative Technique to Increase Employee Learning and Achievement

*Thomas F. Valone*

*Integrity Research Institute*

More and more people are now achieving major improvements in mental outlook, ability, youthfulness, and peacefulness that have been proved to be attributable to meditation. Furthermore, a growing number of corporations—including Ford, Target, Deutsche Bank, Google, Aetna, Goldman Sachs, Apple, AOL, McKinsey & Co., Davos, Adobe, and Hughes Aircraft—are offering meditation classes to their workers.[1] This chapter deals with modern meditation for Westerners, demonstrating dramatic benefits and a generic approach that includes all prospective participants, with an emphasis on the workplace. Looking at the scientific evidence in recent media and journal articles,[2] it is evident that modern meditation practice is now becoming mainstream. In 2017, a billboard along the East Coast US Route 95 used a meditating woman's arm and leg profile, facing the ocean, to promote a Florida scene. In the *Time* magazine article referenced previously, the following points relating to the work environment are made, in the context of a stockbroker who says he has only survived the high-pressure job, where his associates have moved on to positions elsewhere, by daily meditation:

- meditation helps regulate emotions,
- meditation helps people get along,
- meditation improves productivity,
- meditation prevents stress-related illnesses,
- meditation reduces absenteeism.

Upon completing this chapter, the employee, supervisor, director, manager, or president may find the combination of meditation instruction and scientific findings so convincing that he or she will just have to add a new daily routine in their own lifestyle and introduce it to employees with the help of an outside trainer. However, this chapter is designed as a convincing introduction to the online slideshow used by the author, which may be used by anyone interested in presenting three-step Modern Meditation Training to a group of employees, friends, or colleagues.

*The Wiley Handbook of Global Workplace Learning*, First Edition.
Edited by Vanessa Hammler Kenon and Sunay Vasant Palsole.

In 1967, I picked up a tiny book called *Metaphysical Meditations* by Paramahansa Yogananda which inspired me to try meditating, even if only with the guided meditations in the book, which I diligently dictated into my tape recorder for playback. A few years later, I bought, *The Science of Being and the Art of Living* by Maharishi Mahesh Yogi and read it from cover to cover. Shortly afterwards, I wrote to the publisher to find out where Transcendental Meditation (TM) was being taught and in 1972 I took the training when it first became available in Buffalo, NY, at student rates. A few years later, I subscribed to the Self-Realization Fellowship Lessons,[3] which include three separate meditation techniques. After teaching physics and electrical technology courses at Erie Community College for several years, I developed a training seminar for a successful meditation technique that incorporates the best basic components of the various meditation practices. The Modern Meditation technique is being taught by this author regularly, on a quarterly basis at the US Patent and Trademark Office and as an annual seminar at a Natural Living Expo, as well as to other organizations like the American Cancer Society, the Food and Agriculture Organization of the UN, the US Psychotronics Association, the International Conference on Science and Consciousness, and corporations in the DC area.

## Optimal Cognitive Function

The practice of meditation can begin with a simple attempt to try it occasionally and only eventually let it evolve into a daily habit. The beginner will start to discover that meditation is the only time during the day where she or he might have no thoughts at all for a few moments but also receive ideas that help solve their most difficult problems. Of course, while the first few sessions may be rosy and very peaceful, beginners will also most likely go through an unconscious compensation experience that meditators call "dumping," when the unconscious finds an open door for that period and dumps the emotional baggage that we all carry back on the ego. Dr. Paul Brunton, who wrote books like *Search in Secret India* which relate actual experiences and miracles of advanced yogis, cautions "When the beginner sits down to meditate, he is still largely held back by all sorts of strong worldly feelings and thoughts." He therefore advises (as in all books on meditation) that to succeed in meditation one should reduce the number of thoughts. The encouraging "light at the end of the tunnel" for the meditator is that this mental detox will not last for very long, especially if we are diligent in a daily routine of meditation. Thereafter, bridging the gap from pleasant initial experiences to later, more satisfying meditation practice, requires daily practice. This diligence is rewarded in all meditators as they proceed toward the sunshine of the benefits outlined in this chapter.[4] The reason is simple: there is much more long-term good to come of regular practice than merely a release of all the emotional, distracting mental noise. Everyone who practices meditation will attest to this simple discovery. Furthermore, meditation gets "deeper" as the years go by, with profound physical changes that are only recently being discovered. Experienced meditators have been scientifically proven to benefit from a number of health and longevity benefits,[5] including the recently discovered, remarkable ability to generate gamma brain waves,[6] which integrate distributed neural processes into highly ordered cognitive and affective functions, according to the open access National Academy of Sciences study.[7] Other studies in the same theme include comparing brain images from 50 adults who meditate and 50 adults who do not meditate, which found that experienced meditators (people with years of practice) had more folds in the outer layer of their brain (gyrification), which may increase the brain's ability to process information. Further, several studies suggest that meditation practice may slow, stall, or even reverse changes that take place in the brain due to normal aging.[8]

A daily practice for millions of people around the world, akin to prayer, meditation is now welcomed in many health professional areas, such as psychoneuroimmunology, that have accepted, in fact helped to prove, its efficacy. *Time* magazine has published cover stories on meditation several times, such as on August 6, 2003, and recently, the *New York Times* ran an article that was closer to a piece of visual art, an animated video series to train people in mindfulness,[9] a more subtle form of meditation. Medical doctors like D. S. Khalsa, author of *Brain Longevity*, say that meditation produces "optimal cognitive function" and have found that it is positively rejuvenating for the brain and physiologically harmonizing for the body.[10] In his book, Dr. Khalsa states that meditation creates the effects summarized in Table 23.1. Dr. Khalsa's book is also available in an audiobook format.

He tells the story of teaching meditation to his medical students, who then scored the highest grades with 90 percent passing the national medical boards, when the average pass rate is 50 percent. He makes a point of mentioning that he also teaches meditation to his patients. Further on in this chapter, there will be more information about his results. The Modern Meditation Training developed by this author has incorporated the best studies in its delivery for motivating the audience and simplified the essence of meditation into an assembly of three basic exercises (breathing, affirmation, visualization) (Figure 23.1).

The subject of meditation applies to the mind. There is a wealth of research and developments that show the direct bearing of the mind on the body. Dr. Carl Simonton, author of *How to Meditate* and *Getting Well Again*, notes that a breakthrough was made in this area when *Nature* magazine published the finding that white blood cells have "neuroreceptors" on their surfaces. Thus, the physical

**Table 23.1** Benefits of meditation

| A decrease in: | An increase in: |
|---|---|
| Oxygen consumption | Healthspan |
| Blood lactate | Lifespan |
| Heart rate | Hearing |
| Blood pressure | Vision |
| Respiration rate | Youthfulness |
| Cortisol production | Vitality |

*Source:* Adapted from Khalsa (1997), *Brain Longevity.*

**Figure 23.1** The author's book, with a reminder of a possible visualization on the cover, for the training outlined in this chapter

connection between the mind and the immune system has been finally established. From the simplest example of pain control, which I have experienced, to the most extraordinary superhuman feats, it is concentration, visualization, and a meditative calm that achieves the results. Recently, Joyce the dental assistant said to me after a drilling without anesthetic, "I do not know how you do it. I have watched you and you are so calm. Some guys try to be macho and tense up. Do you study something to do that?" I said, "Yes, yoga and meditation practice." When I was a teenager learning about meditation practices through Indra Devi's book *Yoga for Americans* (Prentice-Hall), I saw an oriental martial arts expert drill a one-inch-deep hole into a solid brick with his finger. I was able to talk with him afterwards and examine the normal, heavy red brick as well. This was one of many feats that stuck in my mind as being physically difficult to explain but probably a great example of mind over matter. Other examples which show the extraordinary power of the mind over physical circumstances are included in the anthology, *Energetic Processes*.[11]

## History of Meditation in the West

In the past century, it was not until "for the first time in India's history a Swami was officially received by the President [of the United States]" that meditation became popular with Westerners. The event was when Swami Yogananda, the founder of the Self-Realization Fellowship,[12] met President Calvin Coolidge at the White House, as reviewed on the front page of the *Washington Herald* (January 25, 1927—see Figure 23.2). That popularity was also evident when Yogananda subsequently filled Carnegie Hall to capacity, as well as many other lecture halls across the nation. Other meditation teachers also came before and after him: Swami Vivekananda, Meher Baba, and of course, Maharishi Mahesh Yogi, who gave a new resurgence to meditation with a "transcendental" flair in the 1960s, and attracted the Beatles and actress Mia Farrow. Today, Transcendental Meditation (or "TM") is probably the most familiar type of meditation known to Westerners, though Buddhist meditation is also very popular.

Without meditation, Zen archers would miss their target. Without meditation, Qigong masters could not perform superhuman feats. Without meditation, Christian mystics would never have become saints. Without years of Transcendental Meditation practice, best-selling authors Deepak Chopra, MD and John Gray, PhD would never have become famous and the filmmaker David Lynch would never have formed his foundation. Furthermore, medical doctors

Copies of Microfilm News Archives from the Library of Congress

The Washington Herald

Sage Sees Coolidge

PRESIDENT GREETS SWAMI YOGANANDA

Swami Yogananda, East Indian educator and philosopher, was presented to President Coolidge yesterday at 12:30 by J. Balfour, second secretary of the British Embassy.

He was greeted with evident pleasure by Mr. Coolidge, who told him he had been reading a great deal about him. This is the first time in the history of India that a Swami has been received officially by the President, and "the event will be the occasion of greatest gratification in that country," when the cable news is received, according to the Swami.

Questioned as to his impression of the President after the interview the Swami said: "I found him looking much healthier than his pictures would indicate. He was very calm and quiet, and I felt that he required health and calmness in order to discharge his many duties."

During the interview, which lasted several minutes, the Swami said: "Mr. President, it is only spiritual understanding between all nations that can bring lasting peace. If the navy is scrapped and the machine guns are destroyed, that will not stop war, for the people still would fight, if their weapons were but stones."

Continuing, the Swami declared that he was interested in America because it is a very powerful factor in the world.

To this the President replied: "That is very true. It is only the spiritual understanding between nations that can bring lasting peace."

SWAMI YOGANANDA

AUDITORIUM—
*Swami Yogananda*

Tonight will mark the opening of the third and last week of the series of lectures at the Auditorium by Swami Yogananda, who has achieved such phenomenal success in presenting his theories of the "Art of Living." The subject tonight will be the "Highest Technique of Meditation and Success. Tuning Yourself With the Cosmic Law of Supply." On Tuesday evening the Swami will discuss "Spiritual Marriage. How to Scientifically Attract Your Ideal Soul Companion," and on Wednesday he will reach the heights of his power as an orator and lecturer in the final talk of his series on "Highest Science of Super-Concentration and All-Round Success—Yogoda."

The lectures have been cumulative in their development of philosophical thought combined with highly practical teaching, so that those of this week have a special value, according to the Swami. On Friday evening the first Yogoda class will hold its opening session at 7:30 p. m. in the Rose Room of the Washington Hotel. These classes are to be personally taught by the Swami.

Amazing Demonstration of
RECHARGING THE BODY THROUGH YOGODA
SWAMI YOGANANDA
Last Three Lectures
WASHINGTON AUDITORIUM
1900 E St. N. W.

**Figure 23.2** Articles from the *Washington Herald*, January 1927 obtained by the author from the library of congress.

Andrew Weil, Bernie Siegel, Dharma Singh Khalsa, and Mimi Guarneri are promoting meditation in popular magazines and books these days. Dr. Andrew Weil practices daily meditation and recommends it for his patients. He practices what he preaches at his desert home near the University of Arizona at Tucson. Today, there are plenty of other, not so famous, people who also attribute their success to meditation. The historical integration of yoga and meditation into modern Western society only took about 50 years to accomplish. Now, it is usually included at the end of most yoga classes across the country. It is even taught at the South Pole Station and offered daily in some government agencies: it is one of the most popular of many fitness classes at the Patent and Trademark Office, where the author returns quarterly to conduct Modern Meditation Training.

Today, meditation is so acceptable that a variation called "mindfulness-based stress reduction" (MBSR) is also becoming popular. The practice involves a moment-to-moment awareness and acceptance of one's thoughts, emotions, and physical sensations while seated in a meditation posture with the eyes closed. What is amazing about MBSR is that a six-month study conducted at the University of Maryland with 63 rheumatoid arthritis (RA) patients found a 35 percent reduction in psychological distress and an increased sense of well-being compared with a control group. The study found that mindfulness meditation eases the psychological distress of rheumatoid arthritis by 35 percent after an eight-week training course.[13] As reported in an issue of *Arthritis Health Monitor* magazine, MBSR has been used for many years to help people to cope with stress, anxiety, chronic pain, headaches, stomach problems, sleep difficulties, fatigue, and high blood pressure. A psychotherapist with RA reported in the article that, "If you are just present, there is a sense of peacefulness that makes everything better."[14]

Once again, an ancient science has proven effective in providing modern remedies.

## The Science Behind the Results

Meditation has so many wonderful benefits that some of the more prominent studies are show-stoppers, as summarized here along with the published references which cite these amazing research conclusions. An important immune system study demonstrated that a meditation group had a significantly larger increase in antibodies than the controls, at both 4 and 8 weeks after receiving a vaccine.[15] This has direct implications for the workplace in reducing employee sick time,[16] drop in personal errors on the job, reduction in addiction to tobacco, drugs, alcohol, and binge overeating, besides lowering stress levels, all of which have been substantiated by clinical research on benefits of meditation.[17] Particularly impressive is Dr. Herbert Benson's study. Taking samples of blood samples before and within minutes after meditating for 10–20 min., Benson proved that through epigenetic changes, beneficial genes had become more active in the meditators, cellular mitochondria became more efficient, insulin production was boosted, and the NF-kappaB master gene was less active, thus reducing inflammation, blood pressure, heart disease, bowel disease, and cancer (Figure 23.3).[18]

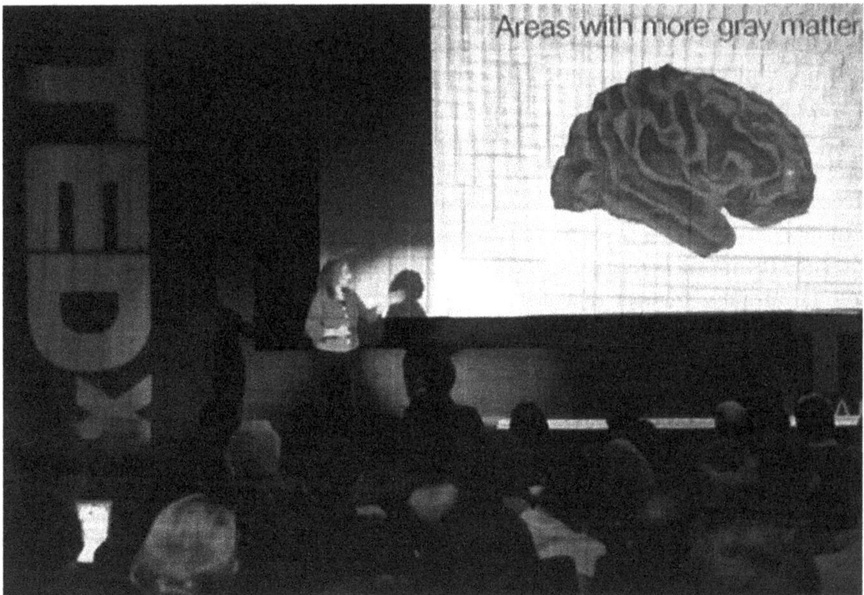


**Figure 23.3** Cambridge University TEDx 2011—Dr. Lazar shows data of older meditators maintaining pre-frontal cortex thickness of 25-year-olds

Dr. Dharma Singh Khalsa also reports the surprising results of improved vision and hearing with regular meditation practice, in addition to an increase in youthfulness and vitality, which is quite unusual. However, perhaps the most significant discovery from meditation practice is the thickening of the prefrontal cortex that normally thins with age. Dr. Sara Lazar found with MRI scanning that 50-year-old meditating subjects had 25-year-old prefrontal cortex thickness. She therefore concluded that:

> meditating actually increases the thickness of the cortex in areas involved in attention and sensory processing, such as the prefrontal cortex and the right anterior insula ... wider blood vessels, more supporting structures such as glia and astrocytes, and increased branching and connections.[19]

This is a seminal study, where all 50-year-old and above non-meditator controls exhibited typical thinning of the prefrontal cortex which is also directly related to memory, learning, and attention. Therefore, it may be suggested that employee learning and achievement can be maintained with regular meditation practice. Related to this is discovery that meditating on non-referential compassion can result in the highest brain EEG frequencies (80–120 Hz) ever recorded—gamma waves—in a study of long-term meditators. The researchers conclude that if the amplitude of the gamma waves is related to the number of neurons synchronizing and the degree of precision with which the cells oscillate, massive distributed neural assemblies are involved in producing this state. The study also concludes that this ability of long-term meditators may reflect a certain degree of attention and possibly higher-order cognitive and affective processes of a flexible skill that can be trained.[20]

Eastern philosophy and yoga offer a viewpoint that the mind is more fundamental than matter. Demonstrating the power of meditation in consciously accomplishing physical abilities has been shown by the Menninger Foundation. Studies of Tibetan monks increasing their body temperature through the practice of "Tumo" or of yogis buried underground for extended periods of time are good examples.[21] The article about the underground burial shows the electrocardiogram (ECG) records as the yogi's heart voluntarily stops and then, 8 days later, starts up an hour before the crypt is opened. They are fascinating accounts, very convincing and motivating to me.

More recently, a modern yogi named Sri Chinmoy, whom I personally met before he passed away, also amazed many researchers. Many people know of his music and involvement with sports figures. Sri Chinmoy also led peace meditations at the United Nations, Congress, and at the British Parliament on a regular basis for years. However, not many may know of his extraordinary accomplishments in weightlifting. In two separate witnessed and photographed events, with specially prepared equipment and media present, Sri Chinmoy lifted 7,063 pounds dead weight with one hand and even more with two hands. He was not a musclebound person either. So how did he do it? Through meditation one can convince the mind–brain, or more scientifically, program our "biocomputer," to believe something is possible, with practice. The motivational speaker Anthony Robbins, author of *Unlimited Power*, tells us that it is only our beliefs that are holding us back and that changing them is a technique that can be learned. Robbins is known for curing addictions in one session and training sharpshooters for the military, both achieved by changing his subjects' belief systems.

Today, more and more Eastern techniques are emerging which have an ancient history, such as "Qigong" (*chi-gong*). It is related to the better-known practice of Tai Chi and teaches one how to move the life energy, *chi* or *prana*, through the body. Recently, a medical doctor from mainland China, Yan Xin, has trained and healed thousands of people throughout the world with qigong methods.[22] In 1991, when President Bush Sr. met Dr. Yan Xin, he called him "a contemporary sage." A "relaxed and quiescent" state is very important to the practice that Dr. Xin speaks of; a nervous or restless mind is not compatible with Qigong. This is also true of meditation and so specific techniques are needed to apply meditation to the Western mind in the workplace successfully.

It should be noted that the bestselling book *The Secret*, by Rhonda Byrne, records that *everyone* ("without exception") she interviewed for the book, movie and CD practices meditation daily.[23] These are people who have applied *The Secret* in their daily lives to dramatically fulfill their grandest wishes by affirming and believing that they are already fulfilled and then acting accordingly. She recommends 3–10 minutes per day for meditation.

## Exercise #1—Breathing to Relax

### Why Do We Mediate?

"We meditate to find, to recover, to come back to something of ourselves we once dimly and unknowingly had and have lost without knowing what it was or where or when we lost it" says Dr. Lawrence LeShan, author of *How to Meditate*, whom I met at his seminar years ago. I remember him stating that a scientist at a conference once told him that his opinion of meditation was "like coming home." This, in a nutshell, summarizes the essence of this mysterious *fourth state* of consciousness (waking, dreaming, and sleeping being the other three). Dr. LeShan also notes, in his book, that meditation seems to produce a physiological state of deep relaxation coupled with a wakeful and highly alert mental state.

However, meditation is not an excuse to sleep while sitting up! When done properly, meditation provides deeper rest than deep sleep, according to research done at Maharishi International University. Meditation produces subtle rewards that increase over time and often-surprising insights in just a few minutes of practice. It creates a balance between your inner and outer world. It also contributes to greater self-acceptance and therefore, greater self-esteem when you begin to carry what the yogis call a "portable paradise" within you. Meditation helps us to live more consciously as well, since our sensitivity and receptivity increases. Lastly, meditation contributes to an inner feeling of positive personal growth being created day after day, as if we are continually evolving each time we meditate. Some believe that meditation actually helps us evolve both mentally and physically (Figure 23.4).

The bubble diagram of TM, from the book *The Science of Being and the Art of Living* by Maharishi Mahesh Yogi shows a possible route for the meditator

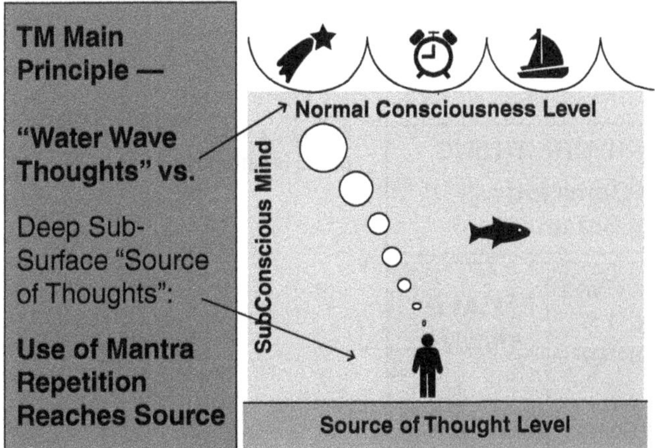


**Figure 23.4** Instructional bubble diagram of deep meditation from Maharishi's 1963 Signet Book

tracing the thought of a mantra (a repeated word or sound) back to its source deep below the normal level of consciousness. This diagram helps us understand that *all of our restless thoughts are on the surface of our "level" of consciousness (A).* As we meditate, we follow a "mantra" thought below the surface to create a new, deeper, more profound experience at level Z. One can also visualize all other distracting thoughts being small bubble boats passing overhead on the "water waves" of consciousness; it is important for the meditator to succeed in detaching from them during the practice of Modern Meditation.

## Breathing Exercise

Everyone takes breathing for granted, as something controlled by the sympathetic nervous system, so much so that it remains mostly unconscious. In yoga, we strive to gain conscious control over the breath as a mean toward gaining control over our states of consciousness. Breathing is thus viewed as a vehicle for *prana* or life energy.

*Exercise #1* is the first stage of meditation practice because it immediately induces a tranquil, relaxation response (guaranteed!), gently dilates the brain's blood vessels, and makes it so much easier to enter a meditative state of consciousness readily. It also increases healthy heart rate variability, as does meditation, which lowers the chance of a heart attack.[24]

It is called a "Ten–Ten–Ten Breathing Exercise" which temporarily makes breathing conscious. Sit with spine straight, preferably away from the back of the chair with the eyes closed:

1) inhale slowly for the count of 10,
2) hold for a count of 10 and look upward toward your inner visual screen with the eyes closed,
3) then, slowly exhale for a count of 10.
4) Repeat a few times (Figure 23.5).

| Exercise #1 10-10-10 BREATHING<br>Oxygenating Conscious Control of Breath | | |
|---|---|---|
| INHALE deeply | Close Eyes HOLD & LOOK UP | EXHALE slowly |
| To a Count of 10 | To a Count of 10 | To a Count of 10 |

**Figure 23.5** Exercise #1—Equally timed breathing in three parts

By practicing this three-part equally timed breathing exercise, before meditation, in order to move and awaken life energy by consciously controlling the breath, we dramatically accomplish the following:

> quickly interrupt the internal dialog,
> improve the depth of meditation, and
> produce better and more satisfying results in a shorter period of time.

Doing just <u>one</u> of these 10–10–10 breaths is also what I call "speed meditation" or "power meditation" and *can be done anywhere* to increase your concentration power immediately, *even in a car.* Yoga teaches that breath is the cord that ties the soul to the body. Practicing even this simple "*pranayama*" will lead one to having more influence over the autonomic nervous system activity, including the natural change in breathing during meditation, called the "quieting of the breath in deep meditation," so it is imperceptible. This in turn also aids dramatically in creating a deeply peaceful state of conscious awareness during meditation. Physiologically, the experience of restfulness for the advanced meditator has been found to be "deeper than deep sleep." One can sometimes substitute a half hour or more of meditation by sitting up in the middle of the night in place of an hour of sleep to take advantage of such benefits, especially if one has insomnia, is restless, anxious, or simply has trouble sleeping that night for any reason.

## Electrophysiology of Meditation

### What can we expect from mediation?

Research psychologist, Dr. Lawrence LeShan, suggests in his book that central to the response to meditation is the lowered rate of metabolism, the lowered rate of using oxygen and producing carbon dioxide. Furthermore, he notes that these decreases are due to a lowered metabolic rate rather than to a slower or shallower breathing since both oxygen use and carbon dioxide production decrease equally and the ratio between them remains the same. This would not be true if the effects were due to alterations in respiration. Typically in meditation, there is also a slowing of the heartbeat and the concentration of lactate in the blood decreases sharply, nearly four times as fast as it does in people resting quietly, while the skin's electrical resistance increases, sometimes by as much as 400 percent.

Thus, meditators show a profound lack of tension and anxiety, accompanied by an increase of slow alpha waves of the brain. Meditation can be scientifically described as a means for the brain to *electrically resonate.* As proven by EEG recordings, the practice bathes the brain in the harmonic frequencies most conducive to homeostasis (alpha and theta) that becomes pleasurable the longer you meditate. Compared to the usual "electrically noisy" waking state of the brain, meditation increases the "signal-to-noise" ratio as well. One study that I reviewed, performed by scientists from Maharishi International University, showed the strong alpha and theta waves of the brain dominating the neuronal EEG patterns in a "waterfall" frequency plot over time. This study of the resonant modes of the brain drew the analogy of a laser cavity tuned to one major coherent frequency. As one stills the random, restless thoughts, meditation convinces the practitioner that he/she can be fully conscious and even blissful, without thinking thoughts. We then start to learn the profound truth taught by yogis that "we are not the mind." A single thought or word, such as a carefully chosen mantra (see next section), is the main vehicle to practicing the Modern Meditation technique successfully.

Meditation also increases the awareness of the self that is apart from the ego. Sometimes referred to as "self-actualization," self-realization has also been taught by many great philosophers like Hegel, Bradley, and Green as the "realization of the true self." It is a gradual process of connectedness that makes one feel more centered, aware of a larger Self and a necessary part of the universe.

Meditation tends to remarkably "expand consciousness" which can be accelerated with visualization exercises. The expansion of consciousness is difficult to describe in Western terms but the experience is breathtaking when it happens to the meditator. Here "teaching by analogy" works best for the uninitiated, "The little fishes of ideas make quite a stir in shallow minds while the whales of inspiration make hardly a ruffle in oceanic minds." This quote from an ancient yogi gives an idea of how less perturbed one becomes when patience improves and calmness is a daily, learned habit. Another benefit is that one's intuition improves, which was amazing to me since as a 20-year old my intuition was practically dead. I thought only women had the gift of intuition. Ideas which are accurate but *seem to come from nowhere*, as well as synchronicities, start occurring with more regularity as one perseveres with daily meditation practice. Meditation had other important benefits in my life too, such as relieving nervousness and even a tendency to stutter under stress, as I turned 21.

Another arena of electrophysiology research that most people have never heard of is from Rollin McCraty and colleagues. I visited the Institute for Heart Math in Boulder Creek, CA when this group first started analyzing the human heart ECG spectrum and then initiated testing during different meditative states with conscious intent. It was fascinating to see the results of a normal, incoherent ECG spectrum, compared with the very coherent and resonant ECG spectrum of a test subject with deep appreciation intent.[25] Which heart rhythm would you rather have? The Institute teaches the concept of the heart as an intelligent organ, thus promoting a "mathematics of the heart." Their research shows a surprising insight into the heart's complex processing ability which is much more expressive than its usual image of being simply a pump. The Heart Math Institute's publications demonstrate conscious effects on the autonomic nervous system and a surprisingly mathematical, complex frequency content of the ECG.

#### Electronic mediation

Some people believe that learning meditation is not necessary since there are many machines, many of which are patented, that put the brain in a state of meditation. Examples are James Gall's "Method and System for Altering Consciousness" Patent #5,123,899, Robert Monroe's Patent #5,356,368 of almost the same title, and Tye Rubins' "Brain Wave Synchronizer" Patent #5,409,445. These were referred to as "electronic drugs" about 10 years ago when they became very popular. I have tried a few of them, especially the ones with blinking lights in front of the eyes and low-frequency tones for the ears. Though your brain may be driven to produce theta waves, your awareness can actually fight the experience since it may seem unexpected and often intrusive. They may work for some people but they do not allow the deep awareness to emerge from within, which takes practice and bodily relaxation as well. Electronic drugs also can produce a dependency and a limit to the depth and scope of the experience. Therefore, I do not recommend them as a shortcut.

## Exercise #2—Positive Affirmation

This section is the second key to successful meditation ability (the first was a breathing exercise). Often a mandala or "yantra" is used to focus the mind to an interiorized state. A *Time* magazine article on Buddhism noted that enlightenment is regarded as the "awakening to the true nature of reality" but also, "a little below Nirvana." In the Hindu tradition, the final state of Samadhi is equivalent to Nirvana, but enlightenment is regarded as the highest goal. To reach this goal, the ancient eightfold path of Patanjali's *Yoga Sutras* is the accepted roadmap for the path of yoga taught in the schools of Raja Yoga, Kundalini Yoga, Kriya Yoga, and so forth.[26]

### The Power of Affirmation

Another area of great help to meditators is the science of affirmation. Affirmations are like guided meditations but using one word or phrase. They are an integral part of the "interiorization" that is necessary for meditation. They also can work in conjunction with your goals. Furthermore, they have been shown to program your subconscious "biocomputer" with new habits and produce healthful results when chosen wisely. Another less well-known result is the appearance of beneficial synchronistic events from affirmation practice, such as the *first insight* in *The Celestine Prophecy.*[27] As mentioned earlier, the effect of the concentrated conscious mind over objective reality usually surpasses normal expectations. Affirmation practice is the key to creating major changes in one's life.

What we strongly believe usually becomes true for us, whether good or bad. Therefore, be careful, as Anthony Robbins warns, of negative affirmations said during periods of anger or fear, such as "How could I be so stupid?" or "What if something bad happens?" for the mind will diligently try to answer every question posed by the ego. Instead, wise men suggest creating new, beneficial beliefs slightly beyond your comfort zone, repeat them mentally and see what positive things begin to happen. With the directions from his wonderful pocketbook, *Scientific Healing Affirmations,*[28] Yogananda suggests:

> Free the mind from restlessness and worries. Choose your affirmation and repeat all of it, first loudly, then softly and more slowly, until your voice becomes a whisper. Then gradually affirm it mentally only ... until you feel that you have attained a deep, unbroken concentration—not unconsciousness, but a profound continuity of uninterrupted thought.

Once background mental repetition in a rhythmic fashion is achieved, the affirmation takes on a life of its own and we notice that it sort of "echos" in the mind as it keeps repeating (similar to a popular song after being heard). However, with its hidden power, days or weeks later, we find a change has taken place in our lives, which is beneficial and sometimes surprising. This is how the yogis change physical reality. Some longer phrase examples are below:

> There is a hidden strength within me to overcome all obstacles
> I am ever protected by omnipresent goodness,

*Read it out loud a few times until it is memorized and then repeat mentally over and over as you release it.* (This still can apply to the one-word affirmations, which are much easier to memorize.) Other affirmations that I use often are: "I send love and goodwill to others." Memorize a few of them, to have a fully equipped arsenal with you at all times, to use as needed on a moment's notice, especially for emergencies! Thoughts are things. Concentrated affirmation practice will prove it to the reader.

Figure 23.6 shows many common affirmations, also called "mantras," to choose from, including single-word affirmations which have been proven in studies to be effective. The one that asks the question, "Who is trying to still the mind?" comes from a 1939 book by Dr. Paul Brunton, *Discover Yourself*,[29] who suggests other affirmations like "Who am I?" that are designed to provoke an answer. Mimi Guarneri, MD, from the Scripps Center for Integrative Medicine, states that she uses the same technique of offering a list of mantras to her patients, when teaching them to meditate, though she developed it independently.[30]

Choose an affirmation, also called a "mantra," from Figure 23.6 to overcome distractions during meditation. It will be mentally repeated in rhythm with the

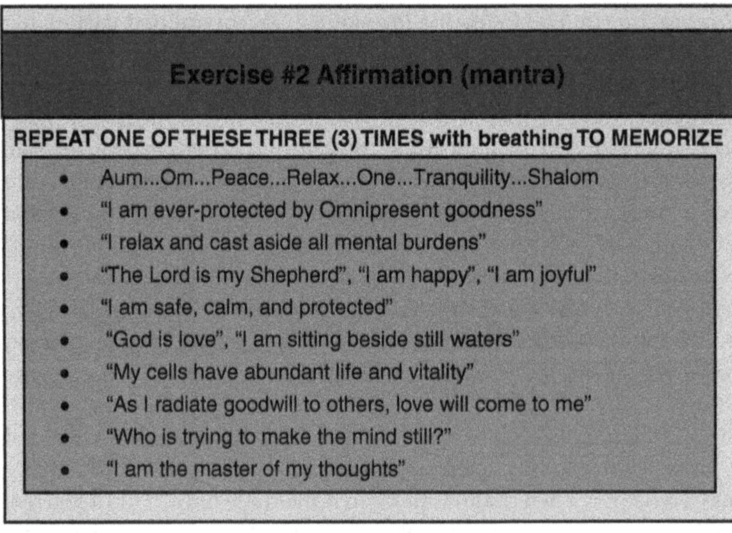


**Figure 23.6** Exercise #2 Pick one affirmation (Mantra)

breathing. Returning to the affirmation after any distraction or spurious thought actively engages the mind and trains it to be "one-pointed" which also improves concentration ability. After a short period, one notices the benefits of peacefulness, a feeling of joy, or even a feeling of love, besides an inspiration that helps solve one's immediate problems. Meditators value their mantra and keep it as a chariot to carry them into the inner realm of consciousness.

Do not discount any of the exercises in this book as trivial. Each one can be practiced independently and builds on the next so that the final modern meditation practice will be powerfully effective in your life!

### Insurance for Mediation

Popular magazines like the *Washingtonian, Self, Time, SPA, Yoga Journal, New Scientist, Scientific American,* and *Let's Live* have all had articles on meditation and yoga, with experts like Dr. Andrew Weil suggesting that inducing a state in which you are relaxed and emotionally comforted can have substantial health benefits. Insurance benefits are also available if you are a veteran or working at IBM or GM. The Veterans Administration, IBM, and GM all pay for part of Transcendental Meditation training under the category of "stress management."

## Exercise #3—Visualization

> Half an hour's meditation each day is essential, except when you are busy. Then a full hour is needed.
>
> —*St. Francis de Sales*

As we enter the third and final exercise before combining them all into one meditation practice, it is good to reflect upon the value of this training as expressed by St. Francis de Sales. While the world demands attention and time from us, we will find that giving a short period to meditation each day increases our efficiency and effortlessness during performance of our work.

#### Visualization

One of the best visual symbols that I feel is very powerful for human evolution is the plant, flower, or tree (Figure 23.7). All three of these symbols drawn from the plant kingdom can teach us a lot. They reach toward the light and pull in sustenance from their outstretched limbs, as well as from their roots. Therefore, this chapter has the tree as its symbol for the meditative process. In Modern Meditation Training, I like to have the participants stand up, inhale deeply, and extend their hands to reach for the sky. Then, as we sit to meditate, the best visualization is to have the brain cells at the top of the cortex all reach out just as the hands and arms did during the practice to become one with everything in the universe. Remember what the Buddhist monk said to the hot dog salesman? "Make me one with everything." This is how the proverbial "thousand petal lotus" at the crown charka works to open up and create a "cosmic consciousness"

**Figure 23.7** Clip art tree symbol as a powerful visualization aid for meditation

experience for us. It just needs an intention, visualization, and emotion to make it happen, along with daily repetition. You may also use any peaceful image, such as a lake or seaside, for this visualization exercise which is done in sequence, after the first two are performed. Simmer for a few years of meditation practice and presto, your consciousness will have changed permanently!

In the book, *The Non-Local Universe*,[31] physicist Robert Nadeau explains quantum entanglement. He notes that experiments with entangled photons separated by a long distance "obliged physicists to conclude that nonlocality or nonseparability is a global or universal dynamic of the life of the cosmos." Thus, we can also conclude that physics teaches our body's atoms are also inseparable from the universe, so it is also appropriate and beneficial to visualize this as another option for this exercise (Figure 23.8).

The practice of looking upward with the eyes closed also tends to draw the consciousness upwards, toward the prefrontal cortex. This can be physically perceived during meditation, with all of our nervous and conscious energy drawn

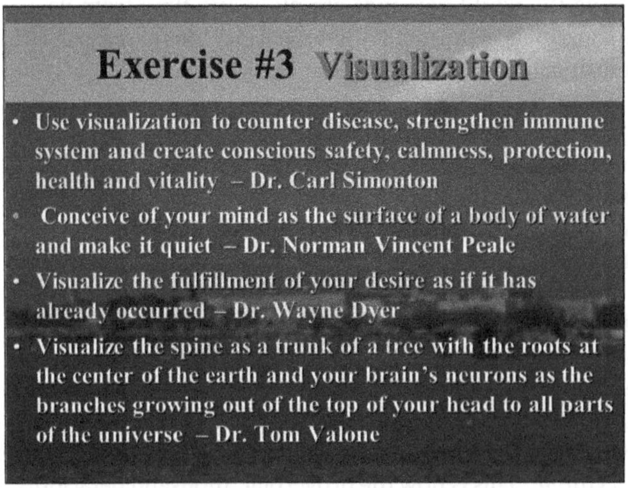

**Exercise #3 Visualization**

- Use visualization to counter disease, strengthen immune system and create conscious safety, calmness, protection, health and vitality – Dr. Carl Simonton
- Conceive of your mind as the surface of a body of water and make it quiet – Dr. Norman Vincent Peale
- Visualize the fulfillment of your desire as if it has already occurred – Dr. Wayne Dyer
- Visualize the spine as a trunk of a tree with the roots at the center of the earth and your brain's neurons as the branches growing out of the top of your head to all parts of the universe – Dr. Tom Valone

**Figure 23.8** Exercise #3—Visualization topics that work best for meditation

upwards to the cerebral region. By letting your gaze drop downwards during meditation, you will invariably go into a sleep state, which is averse to meditation and makes one tend to unconsciousness. Make sure you have enough rest before meditation, or ample concentration ability, so that sleep will not become any part of your meditation. This is very important because habits are strong and I have seen meditators at group meditations who are recognizable because their heads are down against their chest during meditation. We can only hope they will eventually look up while meditating. However, even if we are sleep-deprived, as often happens to new parents, surprisingly, studies have proven that a 20–40-min meditation is much better for psychomotor vigilance than the same amount of sleep. Such meditation in a sleep-deprived state, can actually replace sleep and the subject performs much better on a psychomotor test than the control who takes a nap.[32]

Another additional aid in getting the spinal energy to help your meditation is to visualize a white vertical tube for the spine, shining like a fluorescent light; a powerful but advanced technique.

An additional suggestion is that it is very helpful to mentally "retreat to the spine and brain" and visualize a small white, glowing ball of energy ascending from the perineum "base of the spine" upwards to rest at the point between the eyebrows and even to the top of the head. In deep meditations, this visualization aids in making one detach from the consciousness of the body. It starts to happen slowly as time goes on, starting from the lower part of the body and moving upwards, until it seems that only the spine and brain are present in your field of awareness. That is when the mental space of meditation, or "the darkness behind closed eyes" begins to expand and "lighten."

## Is Meditation Powerful Enough?

### More Suggestions

In the beginning of meditation practice, the most important task you can accomplish, which may take all of your willpower and determination, is to sit still, in silence, for at least 10 min. each day. If you can promise yourself or someone else, that you will keep such a commitment to create this beneficial habit, it will become your resource. *Yoga Journal* once stated, "The more trouble you have allocating twenty minutes a day for meditation, the more desperately you probably need it." Having your own "meditation room" in the house is a great reinforcement for the importance of this practice. I was also happy to see that BWI Airport in Baltimore MD has a meditation room. Going to a weekly meditation group, such as an Employee-Sponsored Meditation Group (like the one that the Pentagon has maintained for over 20 years), can become an oasis of peacefulness and restoration in an otherwise hectic week.

At first, the subconscious mind tends to use the time to "dump" on you, as mentioned previously. All of your worries, troubles, desires, and so forth. will at first plague many or most of your meditations. A lot of people get discouraged at this point if day after day it seems that they are not really meditating. However, that is a trap created by the ego. Instead, this experience of "clearing" the mind of "garbage thoughts," as meditators call them, is *very therapeutic*. It makes way for the clear inspirations to come and the "space between thoughts" which becomes blissful. By the way, "bliss" is the Eastern phrase for the very subtle joy that wells up from deep within everyone who becomes proficient at meditation. It is so peaceful, transforming and expansive that meditators sometimes call it "transcending" because, in reality, it is like a new level of consciousness. Often it lasts for a while after meditation period is over, even up to a week if you meditate for a longer time. More so, it is directly proportional to the length and depth of meditation. In other words, if you meditate for an hour or so but not very deeply, another "deeper" meditation may be more refreshing and have lasting effects, though it is shorter (Figure 23.9).

## Centers of Consciousness

Looking up while your eyes are closed activates the frontal lobe of the brain, which provides our advanced insights and our sense of inspiration if activated properly. By looking downward, one will start to feel sleepy, even while sitting up. Another finding is that the concept of "higher consciousness," like higher vibration levels, is a physical phenomenon as well. What we focus upon with concentration, we often can bring into being. Therefore, by concentrating upwards with our eyes closed during meditation, we can awaken the frontal lobe and what the Eastern mystics call "the spiritual eye" (Ajna center), the tunnel of light, as well as the highest "crown chakra" center of consciousness, (Sahasrara) at the top of the head. Recall that many paintings of saints show a "halo" around the top of the head because the crown chakra has opened in that saint which covers the entire crown or top of the head. Research has also shown that long-term meditators have "significantly greater cortical thickness in the anterior regions of the brain, located in

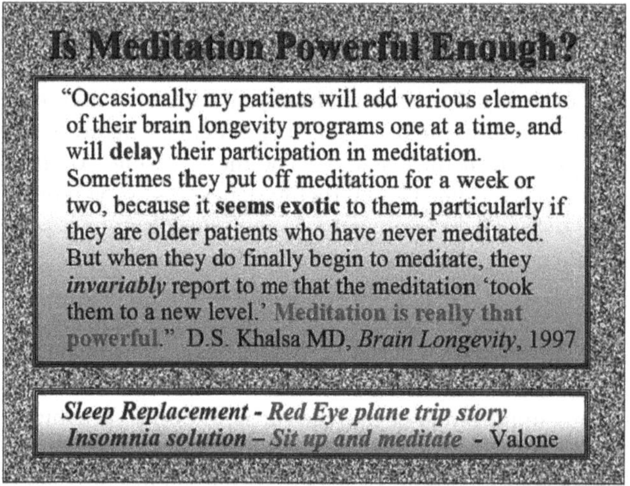


**Figure 23.9** Is meditation powerful enough?

frontal and temporal areas, including the medial prefrontal cortex, superior frontal cortex, temporal pole and the middle and interior temporal cortices."[33]

The practice of looking upward with the eyes closed also tends to draw the consciousness upwards, which can easily be physically perceived during meditation. Regarding the higher centers of consciousness normally activated during meditation, one indication that they are opening is the internal experience of light. Inexperienced meditators may laugh but remember that the pineal gland, esoterically connected to the crown chakra, *responds to light* though deep in the brain. This mystery of it being "optically activated" has been related to the reception of direct sunlight on the eyes. Esoterically, what I have found, especially during longer meditations, lasting a few hours, is that it appears to the meditator that someone has "turned on the ceiling light" in the room. This may be a result of meditation directly stimulating the pineal gland. Other times, various deep colors will be seen on the internal mental screen, such as a white, opal glow or a deep blue glow will be perceived as one relaxes into a deep meditation.

### Power Mediation: A Quick Shortcut

As mentioned before, this shortcut helps in times of drowsiness, especially while driving or working long hours (doing overtime for example). "Power Meditation" (also called "speed" meditation) will give you in a few seconds a close approximation to a regular meditation. It is the same as doing ONE of the breathing Exercise #1 but it helps to spell it out so everyone can try it immediately. (I met a CEO of a waterbed company years ago who said he holds his breath instead of meditating, which gave me this idea.) Holding the breath, even briefly, dilates the blood vessels in the brain immediately. As a reminder:

1) Inhale and draw energy up the spine and look up;
2) Hold the breath as you concentrate at the point between the eyebrows;
3) Exhale *only after a minimum of 10 seconds.* It only takes 10–15 seconds or so to feel the tingling sensation in the middle of the forehead and the expanding blood vessels in the brain, which will invariably awaken even a sleepy driver or a drowsy office worker.

Holding the breath has been proven to cause the brain's blood vessels to expand or dilate in compensation. This immediately improves brain circulation and alertness. Practicing this each day will also directly improve the employee's mental faculties and prevent mental decline from hardening of brain blood vessels with age. It also helps induce more heart rate variability which keeps the heart healthy.

### Ancient Meditation and Prayer

It can be said that the connection between meditation and religion is obvious. In a recent survey, respondents who used *meditative prayer* were twice as likely to feel a "strong relationship with God" than if they stuck to the usual petitionary style of prayer. When we reflect that the word "religion" comes from the Latin "*religio*" meaning "to link back," it reminds us of Dr. LeShan's statements about "coming home," in regards to meditation.[34] Thus, meditation is inherently compatible with any religion, though it is most often taught and practiced without any religious connotation. The practice of meditation is effective, even if regarded simply as a technique. Many people just meditate for what Dr. Herbert Benson called "the relaxation response" in his book with the same title. The main reasons professionals have for prescribing meditation for their patients are for *stress reduction* as well as *improving health* and *mental clarity*.

Meditation was once regarded as a preoccupation of hermits, mystics, and saints. The Chinese practiced a Taoist form of meditation, trying to reduce all striving for a goal; in the Islamic mystical tradition, Sufis sit in solitude repeating the name of Allah without ceasing; Buddhist meditators will often use a mandala, an elaborate symmetrical, circular design representing the cosmos, to focus their attention; Jewish followers of the Kabbalah meditate on the treelike "sefiroth" or the chariot "Merkabah" to carry their consciousness upwards; and meditation has also been a practice of Christian contemplatives and mystics, including St. Francis, St. Ignatius Loyola, and St. Teresa of Avila. Many spiritual leaders of various religions go even further by teaching that anything is possible through prayer. What better state of mind for an effective prayer, clear of mental "noise and static," than just after meditation? Dr. Larry Dossey, also emphasizes the single-blind study proving the efficacy of prayer, which was performed on a coronary care unit.[35]

Meditation is referred to in the Biblical sayings, "Be still and know that I am God," "If thine eye be single, thy whole body shall be filled with light," and "The kingdom of God is within you." These sayings can have great significance when explored during deep meditation by using them as a mantra. With three national opinion polls (CNN, Gallup, NBC) all in agreement with the finding that 90 percent of Americans believe in God, the short injection during Modern Meditation Training of the connection between meditation and an optional prayer addition during meditation practice can awaken some of the more religious employees in the audience to improve their spiritual growth and feeling of closeness to the Divine.[36]

For me, the striving for stillness, even of the breath and heart, along with the concentrated focus of one-pointed devotion within the depths of meditation, after a prayer, have been very important tools, which have created memorable breakthroughs for me in meditation.

In the next section, we will combine the last three exercises into one to start you on your meditation journey of a lifetime. If you are not sure whether you can attain the status of a "highly spiritual" person, take heart. Research has shown that those who describe themselves as highly spiritual tend to exhibit an asymmetry in the thalamus of their brain. However, those who persevere training in meditation skills will develop the same feature.[37] The process can take as little as 8 weeks, so I invite all of my audiences and readers to take the Eight-Week Challenge to see the difference in their lives of doing Exercise #4 in the next chapter each day for 8 weeks. Who knows, you might enjoy the multiple benefits so much that you decide to continue indefinitely.

## Exercise #4—Modern Meditation Technique

### Mantra Meditation

Meditating "about" something is essentially contemplation, which Patanjali's Yoga Sutras define as *Dhyana*, where the concentration (*Dharana*) is narrowed and focused on the object of meditation. This process will happen naturally as we mentally concentrate on the repetition of an affirmation or mantra. To quote Evelyn Underhill from her 500-page treatise called *Mysticism*, written in 1911,

> The modern American schools of mental healing and New Thought recommend concentration upon a carefully selected word as the starting-point of efficacious meditation.[38]

Examples that are popular today include Exercise #2 with the words such as, "one," "aum," "tranquility," "peace," or a direct command like "relax." One can also ask a single identity question as an advanced meditation technique, as Paul Brunton suggests with the question,

> Who is it that is trying to make the mind still? Then you must wait reverently. The answer will be heralded by an intuition, a gentle sense, and something very indeterminate. You cannot force it. You must pay the keenest attention and yield yourself up to it. That is the higher meditation, when you let the interior world reveal itself to you.[39]

This carefully chosen line of questioning, from my experience, can create a *consciousness breakthrough* when used as a point of concentration with earnest sincerity.

To summarize the basics, follow these *three simple steps* for your meditation practice. As a preliminary preparation, stretch forward, back, and side to side briefly if possible and then sit upright with the eyes closed, relaxing the body and calming the mind, while putting aside all outward thoughts, giving this time exclusively to meditation. One may also begin with a prayer if you are religiously inclined to help elevate your consciousness, add a personal investment, and thereby spiritualize the experience. Many airport meditation rooms which this author has visited also label them as a "meditation and prayer room" for example (Figure 23.10).

1) Do the 10–10–10 breathing exercise from the previous section, (Exercise #1), thus gaining conscious control over the breath and autonomic nervous system.
2) Pick a single word or phrase (mantra) which has meaning for you. In a similar fashion as affirmation practice, repeat the mantra in your mind, returning to the mantra when you get distracted (Exercise #2).
3) Simply watch the breath, gently bringing the mind back to your single purpose, as you continue to relax and let go of every thought except one, adding a visualization to your meditation to give it even more dynamic power (Exercise #3) and immediate presence.

Exercise #4 Meditation
• Sit upright with eyes closed.
• Do Breathing Exercise #1
• Relax from top of head to bottom of feet
• Do Affirmation Exercise #2
• Watch the breath as you repeat mantra
• Do Visualization Exercise #3
• If thoughts intrude, just say, "relax" and go back to your mantra of choice

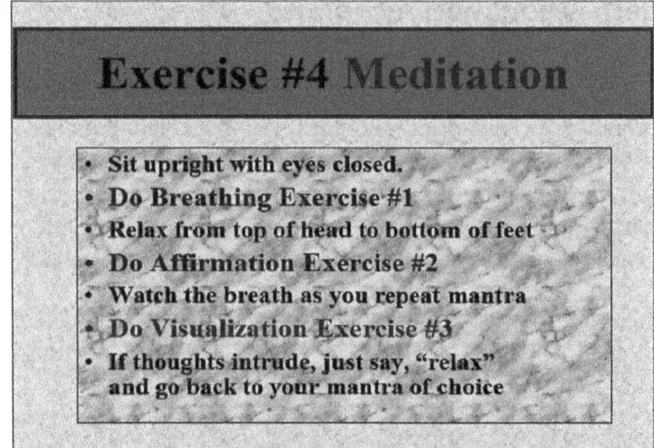

**Figure 23.10** Modern meditation summary combining three simple exercises

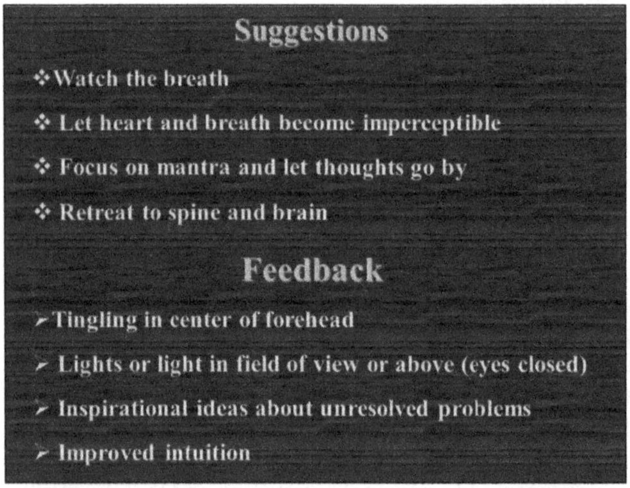

Suggestions
❖ Watch the breath
❖ Let heart and breath become imperceptible
❖ Focus on mantra and let thoughts go by
❖ Retreat to spine and brain
Feedback
➢ Tingling in center of forehead
➢ Lights or light in field of view or above (eyes closed)
➢ Inspirational ideas about unresolved problems
➢ Improved intuition

**Figure 23.11** Suggestions and personal, subjective feedback

Practice on a regular basis, for 10–15 min. (Dr. Carl Simonton[40] suggests that we can also start with once a week, then twice a week, then finally daily.) The vast majority of meditators find daily practice well worth the effort and learn to depend upon it, especially when mental stability is needed.

*Suggestion*: it is important while the meditation habit is being formed, one should strive to practice regularly, with an empty stomach if possible, even if only for 5 minutes at the same time each day, rather than only "once in a while." Another point raised by a participant is the question of what to do if breathing becomes so shallow that it is imperceptible. The answer is to continue the rhythm of the mantra mentally, since that is the vehicle carrying the meditator along. The personal state of mind will confirm to the meditator that he/she is doing everything right at that point and can relax more deeply into the revitalizing experience (Figure 23.11).

Visualizing a white vertical tube for the spine, shining like a fluorescent light, has helped me focus on "retreating to the spine and brain," which is a powerful but advanced technique. Yogis suggests that whenever you see a quiet pond without waves, stop and meditate nearby with eyes partly open, concentrating on quieting the mind to make it as calm as the pond. Merging and expanding one's awareness of light, peace, love, or joy, is the certainly the best course to take, while consciously feeling gratitude in one's heart, such as mindfulness meditation teaches. Then we can understand why the ancient Bhagavad Gita from India, says that meditation induces "radiance of character."

## Signs of Progress in Meditation

### Hatha Yoga and Pranayama

A natural approach to relaxation and flexibility is Hatha Yoga stretching, which helps tune the body for sitting still in meditation. Often a deep state of mind centered on one thought can only be optimized if the body is free from tension, pain and distraction. Yoga *asanas* or Hatha Yoga postures, offered at many fitness centers, can be very beneficial for toning and stretching the ligaments, muscles, and spine so relaxation may happen effortlessly. I go to a one-hour yoga class once a week. Yoga teaches that maintaining a flexible spine ensures the flow of *kundalini* energy upwards during meditation. Furthermore, doing a *pranayama* exercise (moving prana energy with the breath and concentrated visualization) such as the fire breath, *khapalabhakta* breathing, or the gentle Kriya Yoga technique, helps clear the spinal "blockages" as does other pranayama breathing exercises, such as the Modern Meditation Exercise #1, which will quiet the breath and help focus the attention at the highest spinal centers. Hatha yoga and pranayama are companion techniques that help prepare the body and mind for meditation.

### Purification by Fasting

After going through a difficult time, I attended my first 10-day yoga retreat by Yogi Amrit Desai at Ursinus College in 1975, fasted for 3 days on watermelon, and ate mostly live vegetarian food for the rest of the retreat. Near the end, some of us saw several clouds line up in the sky in a formation, which I later found to resemble the Tun hexagram from the I Ching, which is entitled "retreat." This qualified as a major synchronicity, as Dr. Carl Jung would say, that connected my consciousness with the event as a meaningful coincidence. Along with the pranayama breathing exercises, this purifying yoga experience convinced me that consciousness can be favorably and profoundly changed without drugs so the motivation to continue daily practice only increased. Furthermore, the saying that meditation practice improves intuition became abundantly clear to me afterwards, with several meaningful synchronicities starting to happen to me after the retreat experience. Fasting on water and fruit juice, for example, is something that my wife and I now do for one day almost every week and recommend it as a purifying method for the body and brain. Books on fasting describe how the body dumps toxins during a fast.

My thinking and meditations become clearer during and after fasting, even if it is only done for one day, so it is recommended as a complimentary activity to meditation.

## Conclusion

Meditation today is proven to be psychologically and physiologically transformative for employee learning and achievement, while also recommended by doctors. To review, we have learned the practice of Modern Meditation Training, where it is recommended to stick with one mantra (affirmation, Exercise #2) you choose for at least a month or more before trying another one. We also practiced a powerful breathing Exercise #1 that helps awaken brain cells and dilate blood vessels through oxygen therapy and brief holding of the inhaled breath. We also included a "speed meditation" technique (one repetition of Exercise #1) for those extra moments to help you get ahead.

The employee or supervisor may choose to take meditation lessons locally from a yoga center or through one of the many correspondence courses offering meditation instructions. There are services that offer workplace meditation training and tips for launching a meditation program at work.[41] I believe that the David Lynch Foundation program[42] can be implemented for a work environment with the same degree of success. Therefore, I have used the language of a high-performance work environment when teaching Modern Meditation Training in the Workplace, and bypass much of the yoga and higher-consciousness details included in this chapter, when presenting the slideshow. The *Modern Meditation Training Slideshow* is online at http://tinyurl.com/modmed2015 and includes four audio segments which are very motivating and explanatory for the participants. However, the PDF file needs to be downloaded to the laptop or tablet for the audio segments to have active links: the presenter, who may be the Human Resources, Personnel, Social Sciences Department representative, or perhaps a supervisor or manager, then needs to look for the icon which looks like a small loudspeaker and click on that center spot on the slide, in order to activate the audio track (each of them are 1–2 min long). Make sure to have an audio plug hooked to the auditorium speakers so it will be audible to everyone. When one gets to the "Exercise #4" slide, this is the prompt to ask everyone to repeat Exercises #1, #2, and add #3 and then limit the meditation time to *only five (5) minutes* for the first training period. That is all the beginner needs in order to experience the transformative effect of real meditation practice! Asking how people feel immediately when the 5 minutes are up will prove to the presenter that the Modern Meditation Training has been successful, since the majority will express their appreciation spontaneously. The subsequent few slides online after Exercise #4 will give them some takeaway information, which includes the Handout Card at the end of this chapter. It is noted that the David Lynch program, implemented with grants from his foundation, mandates a 15-min daily period called "Quiet Time," with a host of benefits certified on his website. The average workplace may also implement the same protocol, as many companies have already done, and reasonably expect a vast range of similar benefits. It just took one individual with determination (this author) to succeed in seeing it through as a regularly offered training program in a government agency (the US Patent and Trademark Office) for example (Figure 23.12).

As employees consider where to meditate, it is nice to have a meditation room set aside at home but any room will do, such as the bedroom or the living room, or the office when the door is closed. However, I have also used the Metro subway, office cubicle, and even the restroom stall when necessary, so anyone at work can benefit with similar resourcefulness. The benefits outweigh the awkwardness of the surroundings! Carl G. Jung, founder of analytical psychology, said that yoga and meditation promise undreamed-of possibilities. Meditate to improve alertness, mindfulness, general health and well-being, while enhancing one's spiritual practice, whatever that may be ... or as Yogananda says, "Why not unite all your smaller lights, letting them shine forth in one splendid effulgence to illumine the bodily house in which you dwell?"[43] The discussion of kundalini and the chakras, vital to the advanced yogi, gave a basis for the deeper benefits that can be achieved through regular meditation. Also helpful in transforming the conscious mind is the addition of visualization (Exercise #3), implanted in the mind by concentrated repetition. Thus, as one progresses in breath control, affirmation, visualization, combined as the Modern Meditation technique, everyone may rightly expect some or all of the features illustrated in (Figure 23.13.

Thus, increasing employee learning and achievement, as well as job satisfaction, health, and mental acuity, has been demonstrated to be optimally created with the Modern Meditation Training. Its innovative approach to a simple, basic practice has proven to be very popular among all audiences and workplaces where it has been presented. A training narrative script for prospective presenters, to accompany the online slideshow, is also available from the author

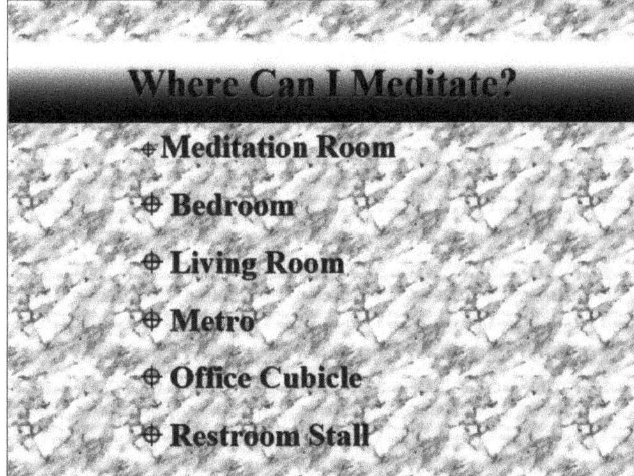


**Figure 23.12** Where can I meditate?

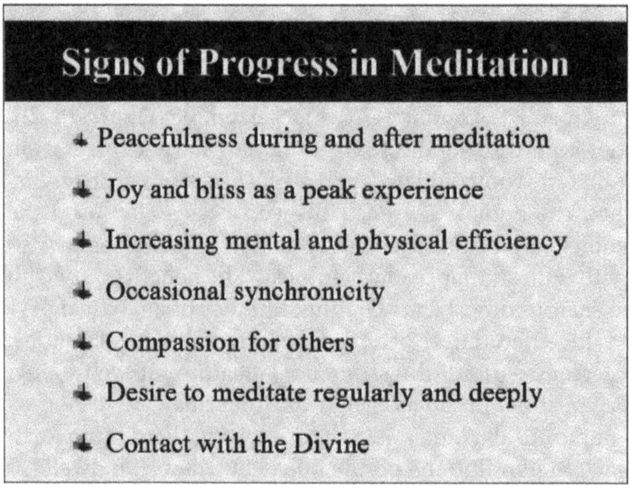

**Signs of Progress in Meditation**

- Peacefulness during and after meditation
- Joy and bliss as a peak experience
- Increasing mental and physical efficiency
- Occasional synchronicity
- Compassion for others
- Desire to meditate regularly and deeply
- Contact with the Divine

**Figure 23.13** Signs of progress in meditation

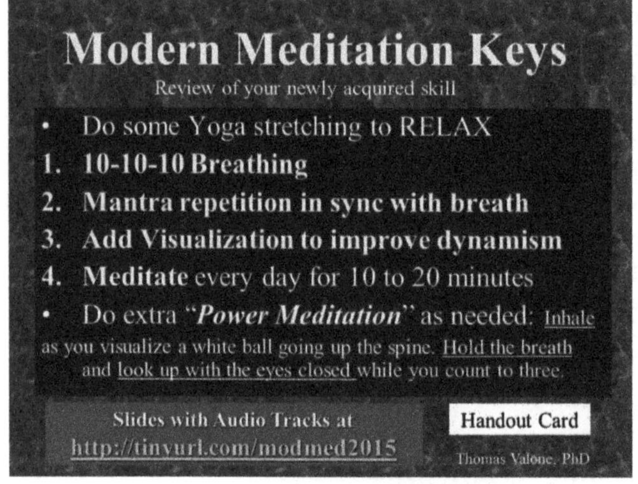


**Figure 23.14** Handout card: Modern Meditation Keys

by emailing iri@starpower.net. The entire presentation takes only about 45 minutes and invariably has enthusiastic responses from all of the participants.

It is suggested that Figure 23.14 may also be reprinted and handed out to each participant as a guide and reminder of the steps to follow, along with the URL for the slideshow, which helps to encourage daily practice. The Human Resources Department at the US Patent and Trademark Office (USPTO) has found this presentation so worthwhile for employees that the author is scheduled to present it on a quarterly basis, as mentioned before, and also has provided a narrated version for the USPTO Learning Center to accommodate teleworkers who can take the course online at their leisure. Companies interested in such a human resources service for their employees are welcome to contact the author for assistance.

## Notes

* Ricard, M., Lutz, A., & Davidson, R. J. (2014). Mind of the Mediator: Contemplative practices that extend back thousands of years show a multitude of benefits for both body and mind. *Scientific American*, 311(5), 39–45.

† Cullen, Lisa. (2006, Jan 10) How to get smarter, one breath at a time. *Time Magazine*. p. 93.

1 Pinsker, Joe. (2015, March 10) Corporations' newest productivity hack: Meditation. *The Atlantic*. Available at: https://www.theatlantic.com/business/archive/2015/03/corporations-newest-productivity-hack-meditation/387286

2 *Broader comprehension and improved ability to focus.*Pelletier, K. R. (1974). Influence of transcendental meditation upon autokinetic perception. *Perceptual and Motor Skills*, 39, 1031–1034.

*Broader comprehension and improved ability to focus*Dillbeck, M. C., Assimakis, P. D., Raimondi, D., Orme-Johnson, D. W., & Rowe, R. (1986). Longitudinal effects of the Transcendental Meditation and TM-Sidhi program on cognitive ability and cognitive style. *Perceptual and Motor Skills*, 62, 731–738.

Decreased cigarette, alcohol, and drug use.Alexander, C. N., Robinson, P. & Rainforth, M. (1994). Treating and preventing alcohol, nicotine, and drug abuse through Transcendental Meditation. *Alcoholism Treatment Quarterly*, 11, 13–87.

Decrease in stress hormone cortisol.Jevning, R., Wilson, A. F., & Davidson, J.M. (1978). Adrenocortical activity during meditation *Hormones and Behavior*, 10, 54–60.

Deeper level of relaxation.Dillbeck, M. C., & Orme-Johnson, D. W. (1987). Physiological differences between transcendental meditation and rest. *American Psychologist*, 49, 879–881.

Development of intelligence, with an increase in IQ.Dillbeck, M. C., Assimakis, P. D., Raimondi, D., Orme-Johnson, D. W., & Rowe, R. (1986). Longitudinal effects of the Transcendental meditation and TM-Sidhi Program on Cognitive Ability and Cognitive Style. *Perceptual and Motor Skills*, 62, 731–738.

Development of intelligence, with an increase in IQ.Cranson, R. W., Orme-Johnson, D. W., Gackenbach, J., et al. (1991). Transcendental meditation and improved performance on intelligence-related measures: A longitudinal study. *Personality and Individual Differences*, 12, 1105–1116.

Eighty percent of hypertensive patients have lowered blood pressure and decreased medications – 16 percent are able to discontinue all of their medications. These results lasted at least three years.Leserman J., Stuart, E. M., Mamish, M. E. et al. (1989). Nonpharmacologic intervention for hypertension: Long-Term follow-up. *Journal of Cardiopulmonary Rehabilitation*, 9, 316–324.

Improved health and more positive health habits.Alexander, C. N., Swanson, G. C., Rainforth, M. V. et al. (1993) Effects of the transcendental meditation program on stress reduction, health, and employee development: A prospective study in two occupational settings, *Anxiety, Stress & Coping*, 6, 245–262.

Improved perception and memory.Dillbeck, M. C. (1982) Meditation and flexibility of visual perception and verbal problem solving. *Memory and Cognition*, 10, 207–215.

Improved relations at work; increased productivity.Frew, D. R. (1974). Transcendental meditation and productivity. *Academy of Management Journal*, 17, 362–368.

Increased creativity with Torrance test of creative thinking.Gowan, J. C. (1978) The facilitation of creativity through meditational procedures. *Journal of Creative Behavior*, 12, 156–160

Increased self-actualization compared to other forms of relaxation.Alexander, C. N., Rainforth, M. V., & Gelderloos, P. (1991). Transcendental meditation, self-actualization, and psychological health: A conceptual overview and statistical meta-analysis. *Journal of Social Behavior and Personality*, 6, 189–248.

Increased strength of self-concept.Van den Berg, W. P., & Mulder, B. (1976). Psychological research on the effects of the Transcendental Meditation technique on a number of personality variables. *Gedrag: Tijdschrift voor Psychologie (Behaviour: Journal of Psychology)*, 4, 206–218.

Lower blood pressure. Goldstein, C. M., Josephson, R., Xie, S., & Hughes, J. W. (2012). Current perspectives on the use of meditation to reduce blood pressure. *International journal of hypertension*, 578397.

Meditation: In depth meditation and the brain. NIH National Center for Complementary and Integrative Health. Web. https://nccih.nih.gov/health/meditation/overview.htm

Natural change in breathing.Wallace, R. K., Benson, H., & Wilson A. F. (1971). A wakeful hypometabolic physiologic state. *American Journal of Physiology*, 22, 795–799.

Physiological reversal of aging process by twelve years as compared to chronological age.Wallace, R.K., Dillbeck, M., Jacobe, E., & Harrington, B. (1982). The effects of the Transcendental Meditation and TM-Sidhi program on the aging process. *International Journal of Neuroscience*, 16, 53–58.

Reduced need for medical care.Orme-Johnson, D. (1987) Medical care utilization and the transcendental meditation program. *Psychosomatic Medicine*, 49, 493–507.

Significant decrease in cholesterol in hypercholesterolemic patients.Cooper, M.J., & Aygen, M. M. (1979). A relaxation technique in the management of hypercholesterolemia. *Journal of Human Stress*, 5, 24–27.

The Benefits of Diet and Nutrition on Nurturing the Older Brain and Mind. (2012, Feb 15). *Age-Proof Your Brain*. Web. https://healthymemory.wordpress.com/tag/alzheimers-disease and http://aarp.org/health/brain-health/info-01-2012/boost-brain-health.html

Women with severe PMS have a 57 percent reduction in physical and psychological symptoms.Goodale, I. L., Domar, A. D., Benson, H.(1990). Alleviation of Premenstrual Syndrome symptoms with the relaxation response. *Obstetrics and Gynecology*, 75, 649–655.

3 Self-Realization Fellowship, www.yogananda-srf.org, offering weekly, mailed correspondence meditation and yoga philosophy, called "SRF Lessons" lasting about two years, with mentoring available for no extra cost.

4 An expanded version with reprints of references is published as *Modern Meditation: Science and Shortcuts*, by Thomas Valone, Integrity Research Institute, 2009, www.integrityresearchinstitute.org

5 Chronic pain patients reduce their physician visits by 36 percent.Caudill M., Schnable, R., & Zuttermeister, P. (1991) Decreased clinic use by chronic pain patients: Response to behavioral medicine intervention. *Clinical Journal of Pain*, 2, 305–310.

There is approximately a 50 percent reduction in visits to a HMO after a relaxation-response based intervention which resulted in estimated significant cost savings.Hellman, C. J., Budd, M., Borysenko, J., McClelland, D. C., & Benson, H. (1990). A study of the effectiveness of two group behavioral medicine interventions for patients with psychosomatic complaints *Behavioral Medicine*, 16, 165–173.

Eighty percent of hypertensive patients have lowered blood pressure and decreased medications – 16 percent are able to discontinue all of their medications. These results lasted at least three years.Leserman J., Stuart, E. M., Mamish, M. E. et al. (1989) Nonpharmacologic intervention for hypertension: Long-term follow-up. *Journal of Cardiopulmonary Rehabilitation* Vol 9. p 316–324.

One hundred percent of insomnia patients reported improved sleep and 91 percent either eliminated or reduced sleeping medication use.Jacobs, G. D., Benson, H., & Friedman, R. (1996). Perceived benefits in a behavioral-medicine insomnia program: A clinical report. *American Journal of Medicine,* 100, 212–216.

Infertile women have a 42 percent conception rate, a 38 percent take-home baby rate, and decreased levels of depression, anxiety, and anger.Domar, A. D., Friedman R., & Zuttermeister, P.C. (1999). Distress and conception in infertile women: A complementary approach. *Journal of the American Medical Women's Association*, 54, 196–198.

Inner city middle school students improved grade score, work habits and cooperation and decreased absences.Benson H., Wilcher M., Greenberg B., et al. (2000). Academic performance among middle-school students after exposure to a relaxation response curriculum. *Journal of Research and Development in Education*, 33, 156–165.

High school students exposed to a relaxation response-based curriculum had significantly increased their self-esteem.Benson, H., Kornhaber, A., LeChanu, C., Mila, N. (1994). Increases in positive psychological characteristics with a new relaxation-response curriculum in high school students. *Journal of Research and Development in Education*, 27, 226–231.

6 Kaufman, Marc. (2005, January 3) Meditation gives brain a charge, study finds. *Washington Post*. P. A05. Web. http://www.washingtonpost.com/wp0dyn/articles/A43006-2005Jan2.html.

7 Lutz, Antoine, et al. (2004, November) Long-term meditators self-induce high-amplitude gamma synchrony during mental practice. *PNAS,* 101(46), 16369–16373.

8 Meditation: In depth meditation and the brain. NIH National Center for Complimentary and Integrative Health. Web. https://nccih.nih.gov/health/meditation/overview.htm#hed4

9 Gelles, D. How to meditate. (2016, September 12). *New York Times*. Web. https://www.nytimes.com/well/guides/how-to-meditate?contentCollection=smarter-living&hp&action=click&pgtype=Homepage&clickSource=story-heading&module=second-column-region®ion=top-news&WT.nav=top-news

10 Khalsa, Dharma Singh. (1997). Brain longevity: The breakthrough medical program that improves your mind and memory. New York: Warner Books.

11 Valone, T. F. (2001). Energetic Processes: The Interconnection Between Matter, Energy, and Consciousness. Bloomington, IN: XLibris.
12 http://www.yogananda-srf.org
13 Mind over arthritis.*A rthritis Health Monitor*. (Reprinted from *Arthritis Care & Research*. Feb/March 2008, Vol 15: 1.)
14 More information is available at http://www.umassmed.edu/cfm/mbsr.
15 Brunette, Lisa. (2006, February 6) Meditation produces positive changes in the brain. News. University of Wisconsin-Madison. http://news.wisc.edu/meditation-produces-positive-changes-in-the-brain
16 "Meditate that cold away." (2012). University of Wisconsin-Madison. After eight weeks of meditation practice, 150 participants missed 76 percent fewer work days from September through May than control.
17 Meditation produced a larger reduction in tobacco, alcohol, and illicit drug use than standard substance abuse treatments or prevention programs. Whereas effects of conventional programs normally decrease significantly by three months, effects of meditation on total abstinence from tobacco, alcohol, and illicit drugs ranged from 50 percent to 89 percent over 18 to 22 months.Alexander, P. et al. (1994) Treating and preventing alcohol, nicotine, and drug abuse through Transcendental Meditation. *Alcoholism Treatment Quarterly*, 11, 13–87.

Middle school students exposed to relaxation and meditation techniques over a three year period scored higher on work habits, cooperation, attendance and had significantly higher GPAs than non-meditating students.Benson et al. (2000). Increases in positive psychological characteristics with a new relaxation–response curriculum in high school students. *Journal of Research and Development in Education*. 27, 226–231

Meditation as beneficial as aerobic exercise in preventing most cardiac events. Fields, J. Z., Walton, K. G., Schneider, R. H. et al. (2002). Effect of a multimodality natural medicine program on carotid atherosclerosis in older subjects: a pilot trial of Maharishi Vedic Medicine. *American Journal of Cardiology*, 89(8), 952–958.

After eight weeks of meditation practice, activity in the left side of the brains increased significantly. Workers reported feeling happier, with a renewed sense of enthusiasm for life and work. The control group showed no change. At the end of the 8 weeks, both groups received flu shots to test immune responses. The mediators developed more antibodies against the flu virus than the non-mediators.Davidson, R. J., Kabat-Zinn, J., Schumaker, J. et al. (2003). Alterations in brain and immune function produced by mindfulness meditation. *Psychosomatic Medicine*, 65(4), 564–70.

Donovan, S., & Murphy, M. (1997) The physical and psychological effects of meditation. Institute of Noetic Sciences. Web. http://library.noetic.org/library/publication-bibliographies/physical-and-psychological-effects-meditation

Those trained in meditation were able to reduce chronic pain by more than 50 percent. This gain was maintained even four years after the initial training.Kabat-Zinn, J., Lipworth, l., Burncy, R., & Sellers, W. (1986 Four-year follow-up of a meditation-based program for the self-regulation of chronic pain: Treatment outcomes and compliance *Clinical Journal of Pain*, 2(3):159–774.

Meditative self-awareness can reduce binge overeating. In a study of overweight women, meditation training and awareness practice while eating (slowly savoring the flavor of a piece of cheese, being aware of how much is enough), reduced eating binges from an average of 4 per week to 1.5 per week.Kristeller, J. L., & Hallett, C. B. (1999) An exploratory study of a meditation-based intervention for binge eating disorder. *Journal of Health Psychology*, 4, 357–363.
Meditation and relaxation therapies are effective in treating chronic pain, and can markedly ease the pain of low back problems, arthritis, and headaches. NIH. (1996). Integration of behavioral and relaxation approaches into the treatment of chronic pain and insomnia. NIH Technology Assessment Panel on Integration of Behavioral and Relaxation Approaches into the Treatment of Chronic Pain and Insomnia. JAMA, 276(4), 313–318.
Mediators showed hospitalization rates 87 percent less than non-mediators for heart disease, 55 percent less for benign and malignant tumors, 30 percent less for infectious diseases, and 50 percent less for outpatient doctor visits.Orme-Johnson, D. (1987) Medical care utilization and the transcendental meditation program. *Psychosomatic Medicine*, 49, 493–507.
Ornish, D., Brown, S. E., Billings, J. H. et al. (1990). Can lifestyle changes reverse coronary heart disease? *The Lancet*, 336(8708), 129–133.
Physiological reversal of aging process by twelve years as compared to chronological age.Wallace, R.K., Dillbeck, M., Jacobe, E., & Harrington, B. (1982). The effects of the Transcendental Meditation and TM-Sidhi program on the aging process. *International Journal of Neuroscience*, 16, 53–58.

**18** Coghlan, A. (2013, May) Meditation boosts genes that promote good health. *New Scientist*, 218 12–15.

**19** Motluk, A. (2005, November) Meditation builds up in the brain. New Scientist. https://www.newscientist.com/article/dn8317-meditation-builds-up-the-brain

**20** Greater orderliness of brain functioning and EEG coherence.Badawi, K., Wallace, R. K., Orme-Johnson, D., & Rouzeré, A.-M. (1984). Electrophysiologic characteristics of respiratory suspension periods occurring during the practice of the Transcendental Meditation program. *Psychosomatic Medicine*, 46, 267–276.

**21** Anand, B. K., Baldev Singh, Chinn, G. S. (1961). Studies on Shri Ramanand Yogi during his stay in an air-tight box. *Indian Journal of Medical Research*, 49(1), 82–89.

**22** Yan Xin. (1997).The Secrets and Benefits of Qigong. Amber Leaf Publishing.

**23** Byrne, Rh. (2006) The secret. Simon and Schuster.

**24** McGonigal, K. (2012) The willpower instinct. Avery-Penguin, pp 24–25, 37.

**25** McCraty, R. et al. (1995) The effects of emotions on short-term power spectrum analysis of heart rate variability. *American Journal of Cardiology*, 76(14), 1089–1093.

**26** Taimni, I. K. (1961) The science of yoga: Yoga-Sutras of Patanjali in Sanskrit with transliteration in Roman, translation in English and commentary. Madras, India: Theosophical Publishing House.

**27** Redfield, J. The Celestine Prophecy. New York: Bantam Books.

**28** Yogananda, Swami. (1925). Scientific healing affirmations. (Reprinted from Los Angeles, CA: Self-Realization Fellowship Publishers).

29 Brunton, P. (1939, reprinted 1990). *Discover Yourself.* Newburyport, MA: Red Wheel/Weiser.
30 Guarneri, M. (2012). *The Science of Natural Healing.* The Great Courses. http://www.thegreatcourses.com/courses/the-science-of-natural-healing.html.
31 Nadeau, R. (1999). *The Non-Local Universe.* Oxford: Oxford University Press.
32 Kaul, P. et al. (2010). Meditation acutely improves psychomotor vigilance, and may decrease sleep need. *Behavioral and Brain Functions*, 6, 47.
33 Kang, D. H., Jo, H. J., Jung, W. H., et al. (2012). The effect of meditation on brain structure: cortical thickness mapping and diffusion tensor imaging. *Social Cognitive and Affective Neuroscience*, 8(1), 27–33.
34 Religio.(1963) *Funk & Wagnalls' Standard College Dictionary.*
35 Byrd, R. (1998) Positive therapeutic effects of intercessory prayer in a coronary care unit population. *Southern Medical Journal*, 81(7), 826.
36 Yogananda, Paramahansa. How you can talk with God. Self-Realization Fellowship
37 Kurth, F., MacKenzie-Graham, A., Toga, A. W., & Luders, E. (2014). Shifting brain asymmetry: the link between meditation and structural lateralization. *Social Cognitive and Affective Neuroscience*, 10(1), 55–61.
38 Underhill, Evelyn (1911, reissued 2011). *Mysticism.* CreateSpace Independent Publishing Platform.
39 Brunton, *Discover Yourself* (see note 26).
40 Simonton, Carl. How to meditate. Hay House Audio Books.
41 Wolfe, Brad. (2015, June 8) Five tips for launching a meditation program at work. Greater Good Science Center, University of California at Berkeley, http://greatergood.berkeley.edu/article/item/five_tips_for_launching_a_meditation_program_at_work
42 David Lynch Foundation program: www.davidlynchfoundation.org
43 Yogananda, Paramahansa. (1992) Self-realization magazine. Spring.

# 24

# Improving Leadership Communication Competencies and Skills through Training

*Andreas Rupp*

*Reutlingen University*

In recent decades, the importance of communication for leaders and managers has been emphasized in many research works (Worley & Doolen, 2006). Communication has been identified as one of the major fields that leaders and managers should master. This is in line with expectations that companies have concerning their leaders and managers to improve their communication competences and skills. Companies provide large budgets to improve those competences and skills, yet, very often, the training programs that are offered do not fulfill the requirements and needs of the companies and their participants. On the one hand, the offered training programs are valued highly by participants. On the other hand, however, the outcome of these training programs is weak and does not bring any significant improvement for the hoped for results to learn the effective skills and competences that can be applied to the daily work.

Nowadays, there are still no evidence-based training programs which integrate theories, training design and effective training methods. The main activities of leaders and managers, however, are well-researched and described (Luthans, 2012) and include, for example, planning and organizing, managing human resources, controlling the workflow and delegating responsibility as well as "the ability of an individual to influence, motivate and enable others to contribute toward the effectiveness and success of the organizations of which they are members" (House, Hanges, Javidan, Dorfman, & Gupa, 2004, p. 15). To implement all these activities, leaders need effective and appropriate communication competences and skills.

The goal of this study is twofold: first, to describe an evidence-based communication training program for training methods, the contextual framework, the content, the skills and competences, and, second, to evaluate a well-designed training program in replicated studies. A survey/ questionnaire was therefore developed to evaluate whether participants can successfully apply general communication leadership competences and specific communication skills they have learned. The appraisal interview was chosen as a frequent situation in the daily life of a manager to train specific communication skills. The participants of the study were managers and leaders in mid-sized firms (*Mittelstandsfirmen*).

*The Wiley Handbook of Global Workplace Learning*, First Edition.
Edited by Vanessa Hammler Kenon and Sunay Vasant Palsole.

The data were collected in the first half of the year 2016 in five two-day sessions as well as in one one-day session in different companies located in the southwest of Germany. In the study, the evidence for success using and adapting the skills and competences was found.

The training program was set up as follows: delivering two leadership concepts and effective and observable communication skills. For the training situation, a formalized fundamental communicative situation was chosen, which each leader and manager is faced with daily, which is a frequent performance review and staff appraisals. The research questions for this study were, thus, formulated as follows:

- Does the training program for a task-oriented leadership competences (e.g., setting goal and management by objectives) help to implement and to adapt the competences immediately after the training and also after eight weeks of use, based on a participant questionnaire?
- Does the training program for a task-oriented leadership competences (e.g., general staff appraisal; task-oriented face-to-face communication and sharing of information) help to implement and adapt the competences immediately after the training and after eight weeks of use, based on a participant questionnaire?
- Does the training program for relationship-oriented leadership competences (friendliness, respect and feedback) help to implement and adapt the competences immediately after the training and after eight weeks of use at the workplace, based on a participant questionnaire?
- Do participants evaluate the training program to be effective in enhancing their communication competences at the workplace, based on a reliable course instructor questionnaire?

## Training Benefits

The training should aim at the development or acquisition of knowledge or special skills and has a benefit for individuals, teams, organizations and the society at large (Aguinis & Kraiger, 2009). Aguinis and Kraiger provide a comprehensive review which covers the training literature from 2000 to 2009. The benefits they found in meta-analyses (e.g., Arthur, Bennett, Edens, & Bell, 2003) are positive, related to job performances, technical skills, strategic knowledge, self-management skills, training for managers and leaders (e.g., Collins & Holton III., 2004), cross-cultural training, team communication and, especially, crew resource management (CRM) training.

## Design of Training and Framework for Interpersonal Communication and Leadership

The training literature for interpersonal communication and leadership training is still strongly influenced by simplistic approaches and advice and dominated by practitioners. One famous slogan is "gained in practice, for use in practice"; but what, if the practice proves wrong?

Advances in organizational psychology can emerge from theories and methods, from other fields and subdisciplines like: educational psychology, social psychology and sociology. Kurtz, Marshall, and Banspach (1985) point out and address the appropriateness, the time and the situation for developing training programs. Tannenbaum and Yukl (1992) describe guidelines for effective training. These include: instructional events, including cognitive and physical elements, actively practicing behavior, memorizing information, using principles in doing tasks, using feedback, precisely and timely enhancing of one's self-efficacy so that the training will be successful and valued. Aguinis and Kraiger (2009) refer to error training as a strategy to avoid mistakes in the future. In a software course, trainees who were encouraged to make errors, learned from these and performed significantly better.

Klinzing and Floden (1991) conceptualized a model with five ability groups for the development and design of training programs, mostly for classroom teaching skills as an interactive process. They include the ability to:

- Use conceptual structures to analyze interactions.
- Generate hypotheses for action for the ongoing situation. The hypotheses are based on the best available knowledge from research and/or reflected experience.
- Carry out the skills appropriately and effectively.
- Reflect on the executed behavior and learn from these experiences.

This model was used for the development and design of the training program.

## Training Methods

The question: What is a good training method for a leadership training? should be supplemented with the questions: Good for which objectives? Good for whom? Good under which circumstances? To search for the most effective training method alone will not lead to success (Joyce, Weil, & Calhoun, 2004). There is no single method that fulfills all requirements (Salas & Cannon-Bowers, 2001). Many powerful methods to help participants to be effective learners have been designed to help trainers to teach and support learners effectively (Hattie, 2013). However, they are often not appropriately adopted. If one, for example, chooses lecturing as a method to deliver knowledge, this will be very effective (Klinzing, 1998), but other objectives, like the development of interactive communication skills and behavior or working effectively, will not be effective or may even obstruct learning of he intended behavior. Each training method carries indirect effects and has an additional impact. Direct impacts refer to the accomplishment of acquiring knowledge or skills. An indirect impact is imparted through experience and the environment. In this paper, the focus is on both direct and indirect effects.

When choosing training methods, it is not only important to be clear what kind of effects are desired directly, but also what is imparted indirectly. Each method was designed for a certain goal (Joyce et al., 2004). Also crucial are external circumstances: these might be audience, facilities, staff, allocated time for the training, preparation time, technology, and content. Reviews (Latham, 1988; Salas & Cannon-Bowers, 2001; Tannenbaum & Yukl, 1992; Wexley, 1984), chose different methods: collaborative training protocols and team training, behavioral role modeling, stress exposure training, web-based training, simulation-based training (widely used by military and aviation industry) and games (groups with game experience performed better), CRM training (a kind of team training). Video training is also widely used in leadership training. One systematic approach using technology and video is micro-teaching to learn specific behavior in leadership training.

## Micro-Teaching

Micro-teaching was developed and effectively used in teacher education. Its use as a training method was developed in the early 1960s in the United States (e.g., Allen & Ryan, 1969) and independently in the 1960s in Germany (Zifreund, 1966). These different approaches for developing classroom teaching skills reduced the complexity of the settings and the skills to master both. For this study, it was used as a training method because of its effectiveness in the training of communication behavior. However, it is not often used in leadership communication training, although Rupp (1998, 2010) and Klinzing (2010) for example, show very positive results in communication leadership training for different situations such as moderating and leading discussions, giving presentations and team training. The next section summarizes recent research done on the effectiveness and the impact of micro-teaching as a training method and how it was used in training programs.

Variations in the procedure have been established. For example, teaching lessons can be brief (5–10 min) or long (20–30 min); the group size can vary from three to twenty (more does not make any sense); groups can be heterogeneous or homogeneous; the topic can change in the second session and the kind of skills can vary from simple to complex. There is a great variation in the use of micro-teaching and related approaches.

## What does the Research Say and how Effective is Micro-Teaching?

Klinzing (2002) gives an overview on a 35-year period of micro-teaching and its effectiveness. Micro-teaching is mainly used in the development of teaching skills in teacher education, and has been well examined from different perspectives. The findings of the research contain encouraging results on benefits. Some authors only acknowledge that skills will be learned "rapidly and to a high degree of proficiency" (Hansford & Copeland, 1979, p. 70). But authors did not find much evidence that micro-teaching has a direct influence on behavior in classrooms. Other studies and reviews, however, strongly support the effectiveness of micro-teaching in practice (see Cruickshank & Metcalfe, 1990; Cruickshank,

Jenkins, and Metcalf (2012); Klinzing & Floden, 1991; Klinzing & Tisher, 1993; Peck & Tucker, 1973; Sadker & Cooper, 1972, cited in Klinzing, 2002; Hattie, 2013).

These contradictions can be explained through the diversity and variations of using different approaches and submethods for micro-teaching (Klinzing, 2002). For his review, Klinzing refers only to programs containing the following elements:

- Providing theoretical background knowledge
- Methods for the cognitive acquisition of specific skills
- Exercises in an experimental setting
- Feedback

Following this approach, Klinzing (2002) focuses in his review on two questions:

- Do training programs increase the probability of acquiring certain behaviors effectively and efficiently?
- Can the skills acquired be transferred into daily situations?

Klinzing explored 225 studies that addressed one or more of the above questions. To answer the first question, he distinguishes two types of micro-teaching: The classical—micro-teaching with small groups of students, (Allen & Ryan, 1969), and peer-teaching—micro-teaching with small groups of pre-service teachers and teachers.

Thirty-four out of 39 studies from the classical micro-teaching approach show significant positive results for the following skills: higher cognitive questions, value questions, prompting questions, human relation skills or a combination of skills, like reinforcement, varying of the stimulus, illustrating and using examples, set induction, closure, clarity of presentation, lecturing- and discipline skills. Five out of the 39 studies showed no significant, but tending to the positive, results.

Studies executed with the peer-teaching micro-teaching approach were developed to save costs (it is cheaper to realize the studies inside a university together with the students rather than organizing training outside of school) and to be more flexible in organizing programs. These micro-teaching peer-teaching programs have not only been used in the context of training teachers and pre-service teachers, they have been widely used to optimize basic forms of communication in adult/peer groups; for instance, moderation of discussions, presentation of content and non-verbal communication (e.g., Klinzing, 1998; Rupp & Klinzing, 1997).

Fifty-nine out of 74 studies showed significant positive results for verbal and non-verbal skills, such as prompting questions, higher cognitive questions, clarity of communication, moderation of communication, presentation techniques, aspects of non-verbal communication; 15 studies showed little or no behavioral improvements. Klinzing (2002) points out that most of these trainings lack of duration and intensity, and especially opportunity to practice. But he still answers "yes" to the question as to whether micro-teaching will help to acquire behavioral skills fast and effectively.

For the second question, whether micro-teaching can transfer acquired skills into our daily work, Klinzing looked at 113 studies. Forty-six out of 56 studies using the classical micro-teaching approach showed significant positive results concerning skills like probing questions, non-verbal behavior, non-directive teaching and classroom discussion. Twenty-six studies were carried out by the Far West Laboratory for Educational Research and Development to evaluate the effectiveness of an in-service micro-teaching program. They evaluated different training programs (called mini-courses) to following subjects, for example, effective questioning, higher cognitive questioning, individualizing instructions in mathematics, divergent thinking and role-playing in the classroom. All these courses showed significant positive results. Klinzing (2002) summarizes that recent research shows very positive results and that we can also expect positive results for the future as long we do not expect miracles from a training method. He recommends micro-teaching particularly for highly interactive professions.

Klinzing reported in 2010 on a group of micro-teaching-peer teaching studies conducted since 2002. Nine experimental studies confirmed that this method was effective and efficient in improving non-verbal sensitivity and non-verbal expressiveness. Also, it was effective in enhancing global personality characteristics (mostly significantly) like charisma, extraversion, self-efficacy expectation and internality (Klinzing & Gerada Aloisio, 2010). Stift (2009)reported on 11 studies. His review appraised mostly studies carried out before or no later than 2004, nearly all of which are included in Klinzing (2002) or Klinzing (2010). Based on these very positive results for developing different kinds of behavior and on the encouraging findings about participants transferring skills into their daily work, the micro-teaching approach was selected as a good method to train participants.

Following the reports and appraisals cited above, micro-teaching was used in the training program as follows:

1) The participants are given basic information on leadership theory and communication skills.
2) They are then given assignments to improve their understanding of different skills.
3) They demonstrate their skills in a staff/ appraisal interview of five to seven minutes in groups of two. After this video session, everybody, including the supervisor, completes a feedback questionnaire.
4) Each participant will receive feedback and then reflect on the feedback questions and the video from the supervisors. The purpose of this phase is to develop and improve the next skill demonstration.
5) Repetition of the demonstration with the possibility of integrating new behavior. At the end of the exercise, each participant receives feedback.

## Selection of the Leadership Content for the Training Program

For leaders, it is important to pay attention to essential requirements, show effective behavior and have competences related to these features. For the content of the training program, research-based literature was selected from leadership literature. In addition to the development of leadership skills in the training program, a key aim was to gain a better understanding of what leadership and leadership behavior is.

## Categories of Leadership Behavior

Leadership involves a wide range of behavior, and has been formally or informally discussed "more than any other single topic" noted Fred Luthans (2002), p. 575). Perhaps we can use his expression "black box" to describe leadership. Of the hundreds of definitions of leadership available, this study defines it as a process that tries to influence employees, groups inside an organization or the organization in total.

Today, the terms behavior, skill and competence are often used as equivalents. The early studies in the 1950s and 1960s used the term "behavior" to describe the activities of leaders; in the 1960s and 1970s, the term "skill" was used more frequently; and from the 1980s onwards, the term "competence" has become popular to describe the actions and activities of leaders. However, the major questions in leadership research are about the importance of behavior categories and the integration of different behavior and competences in a conceptual framework.

Hundreds of studies exist examining the correlation between leadership roles, leadership behavior and variables like effectiveness and competences. Two historically important studies on leadership, the Michigan State Studies (Katz & Kahn, 1952) and the Ohio State Leadership Studies (Stodgill, Goode, & Day, 1962), found two main styles of leadership: task-oriented and relationship-oriented. Task-oriented leadership means, for example, initiating structures, monitoring and clarifying; relationship-oriented leadership means recognizing individual needs, support and consulting. The two categories' dimensions are described as different from each other and show how leaders perform their leadership function. Yukl, Gordon, and Taber (2002), in their meta-analysis, describe a third category: change-oriented leadership. This category is characterized by external monitoring, envisioning change, encouraging innovative thinking and taking personal risks to implement change. A fourth category is proposed by the GLOBE Project, one that underlines the impact of cultural variables on leadership (House, Dorfman, Javidan, Hanges, & Sully de Luque, 2014). Brodbeck (2014) notes that cultural values in leadership, according to the GLOBE study, can probably explain 25 % of the variance of productive leadership.

Based on these understandings of leadership, the four categories were taught in combination with the behavior of leaders described by the Leaders Observation Scale (LOS) (Luthans & Lockwood, 1984). LOS analyzes the activities of successful and effective leaders from all levels and types of organizations in the Midwest and describes 12 managerial activities (i.e., planning, staffing, training/ developing; processing paperwork, exchanging routine information; monitoring; motivating/ reinforcing; disciplining; interacting with outsiders; managing conflict; socializing/ politicking) derived from free observation. Finally, the authors summarize these categories into four types of activities and relate the time they spend with these management activities to lead the enterprise: routine communication (29 %);

traditional management (32 %), networking (19 %) and human resource management (20 %). Two results are notable: first, there are activities that provide evidence across cultures; second, there are activities that effective managers/leaders undertake in their day-to-day interactions, such as giving information and feedback, answering questions, negotiating conflicts, or communicating. In addition to the LOS, there are other taxonomies, like the C–K Scale (the Conger–Kanungo Leadership Scale; Conger & Kanungo, 1998) and the LPI (the Leadership Practices Inventory; (Kouzes & Posner, 1995).

## Managing Performance through Goal Setting

Beside the general information presented to the participants on the four categories of leadership, the concept of goal setting was determined as an additional practical and effective tool for appraising overall performance. For the training program described below, goal-setting theory (Locke & Latham, 1990) was used. Goals describe a result that a person or organization wants to reach at a certain time. According to the goal-setting theory of Locke and Latham (1990), goals have an impact on the performance because they determine the direction, the intensity and the persistence of individual activities. The process is reinforced if the employee will accept and commit to the goals outlined or suggested. In numerous studies, for example, Locke and Latham identified central variables for an effective goal setting (see Luthans, 2002): goal acceptance, participation and commitment.

- Specific goals are necessary to improve the performance. The employees must accept and be committed to the goals.
- Self-efficacy is the perception or belief in one's own ability to complete and manage specific tasks and to reach goals.
- Objective and timely feedback. Providing feedback can help progress toward difficult goals.

Management by Objectives (MbO) is probably the best-known application of goal setting, as applied by Odiorne (1967) and developed by Drucker (2005). MbO does not favor a specific leadership style. A process-related approach is recommended to develop goals. It is used in training programs to develop employees' goals on a behavioral level. The recommendation for this model is based on four main assumptions: first, goal acceptance occurs if managers and employees can develop mutually agreed objectives related to the general objectives of the company; second, it is possible to learn how to use objectives as a communication leadership skill in a two-day training; third, if the company does not have an official MbO system or leadership concept (and a lot of small and medium-sized companies do not), participants in a training course can be part of the model below without introducing the complete system into their company; and fourth, goals and objectives are everywhere in our society and easy to explain. Most participants are familiar with the concept.

The following goal-setting steps were provided in the training program: general objectives, adaptation organizational structures, objectives for managers and employees, mutually agreed objectives, feedback, periodic comparison of the results, and adaptations for the next period (Odiorne, 1967). The objectives were to be developed with SMART criteria. Goals had to be specific, measurable, workable, achievable relevant and meaningful; they also needed to be transferable to other situations. As well as introducing the concept of MbO for leaders, the challenge for the participants was to communicate specific goals in a training situation.

## Leadership Skills, Competences and Culture

In addition to leadership behavior and activities, substantial efforts have also been made in the past 70 years to identify effective leaderships skills and competences. Numerous skills are outlined in practitioner-oriented literature, fewer in scientific-oriented literature. Most of the skills and competences recommended in the literature were a matter of fashion. The skills offered are not wrong, but in many situations they are not helpful.

Nevertheless, there are some effective skills and competence models that seem to be yielding promising results in research. These projects have provided guidelines for the development of training programs for the future.

For example, Whetten and Cameron (1991) developed a model for personal and interpersonal skills. Personal skill levels include three clusters: developing self-awareness, managing stress and solving problems creatively. The interpersonal skill level includes four clusters: communicating supportively, gaining power and influence, motivating others and managing conflicts. Boyatzis (1982, 2008) developed an integrated competence model of management to offer guidance for an organization to solve problems. The model shows the relationship between management functions, tasks and competence clusters. Management functions included were: planning, organizing, controlling, motivating and coordinating. The tasks for planning are: determining the goal of the organization connected to the competences in the goal and action management clusters. The task communicating is connected to competences in the leadership cluster.

Different perspectives and approaches have been developed for communication competences based on the definition offered by White (1959) who argues: "I shall attempt a conceptualization which gathers up some of the important things left out by drive theory. To give the concept a name I chose the word competence which is intended in a broad biological sense rather that in its narrow everyday meaning" (p. 297),.

Johansson, Miller, and Hamrin (2014) conceptualize a framework for analyzing and developing the leaders' communication competence which includes communication awareness, communication acquaintance, communication attitude and communication ability. Other authors instead focus on interpersonal competences (Wiemann & Kelly, 1981) and competent interactions with the task of fulfilling communicative effectiveness and interpersonal appropriateness (Spitzberg & Cupach, 1981). There is a large amount of research on competent communication, yet very little research has been done to study the influences of managers' or supervisors' communication competences. Some findings show that there is a direct relationship between the perceived communication competence of managers and employees' satisfaction (Berman & Hellweg, 1989) as well as their level of organizational identification (Myers & Kassing, 1998).

In the GLOBE Project (House et al., 2004) nine cultural competences were identified: performance orientation, assertiveness orientation, future orientation, human orientation, institutional and in-group collectivism, gender egalitarianism, power distance and uncertainty avoidance. The concept of cultural leadership can be adapted to serve competences directed toward globalization.

Communication is a crucial, arguably the crucial, skill for leaders (Morreale, Osborn, & Pearson, 2000). Communication helps us to exchange knowledge, empathy, experiences and recognitions and to get in contact with others. Leadership needs communication to organize processes and interactions, and so effectiveness of communication between employees and leaders is crucial for the success of the enterprise. Exchange of information, whether formalized (e.g., an appraisal interview) or informal (in a casual meeting) is crucial. These are only some reasons why it is so important that leaders have the ability to communicate appropriately and effectively. Inappropriate and ineffective communication behaviors lead to conflict and strained working environments. However, there are only a few evidence-based training programs available to develop effective communication skills and communication competences for leaders and managers.

## Detailed Content of Communication for the Training Program

After introducing leadership concepts and goal setting, and establishing that effective leading and managing is focused on communication, we progress to choosing a formalized fundamental communication situation for training: performance review/ staff appraisals. To develop the content for the communication part of the training program for this study, not only was research in the fields mentioned above taken into account, but also seminal and research-based literature in the fields of education, humanities and social and educational psychology (Argyle, 1972; Bridges, 1979; Brophy & Good, 1986; Gage & Berliner, 1986; Rosenshine, 1971; Wiemann & Bradac, 1989; Woolfolk, 2008), and communication theory (Watzlawick, Beavin, & Jackson, 1985; Bligh, 2000; Habermas, 2011; Knapp, Hall, and Horgan (2013). Skills were identified and assigned, and dimensions based on the research literature. The general and specific research-based information on communication was partly used for the acquisition of theoretical knowledge.

## Effectiveness and Appropriateness

Skills must fulfill requirements when being used. They must be effective and appropriate. But how can appropriateness be defined? Aristotle may give a direction when stating "(...) anybody can become angry, that is easy; but to be angry with the right person, and to the right degree, and at the right time, for the right purpose, and in the right way, that is not within everybody's power and is not easy" (Aristotle, Nicomachean Ethics Book II, 1109a.27). If we adapt Aristotle's example of anger, which is an emotion, to different kinds of communication situations, we are confronted with the question: How can we learn to show the right skills, to the right degree, at the right time and in the right way, and for the right purpose?

The answer is simple, yet not very popular: one needs the opportunity to fail in communicative interaction, and the people one communicates with should have a tolerant attitude. To experience different kinds of communicative behavior in such situations is crucial, as a child, as a student or as a leader. There should always be the possibility and the tolerance of learning from all these situations, as this will increase the appropriateness for competences and skills. But to be appropriate is not enough, one needs to also be effective.

Effective skills in communicative situations are essential. For example, structured information in a conversation or lecture will increase the memory power, and the ability to decode non-verbal behavior correlates with success in workplaces (Klinzing & Gerada Aloisio, 2010). Spitzberg and Cupach (1981), p. 1) state: "Competent interaction can be viewed as a form of interpersonal influence, in which an individual is faced with the task of fulfilling communicative functions and goals (effectiveness) while maintaining conversational and interpersonal norms (appropriateness)." To combine appropriateness and effectiveness is crucial for developing training programs for effective leadership skills and communication. However, to merely be effective does not lead to success in communication situations. We need both: appropriateness and effectiveness.

## Skills and Dimensions

Training can improve communication competence and interaction behavior (Rubin, 1990). To develop a training program, it is important to first define dimensions and skills for a specific communicative situation. Why is this so important? The reasons are twofold: first, during an interaction, we perceive behavioral dimensions, and we use dimensions as criteria to evaluate and categorize interactions (Argyle, 1972); second, we can operationalize dimensions that will lead us to manageable units of behavior.

The use of dimensions in our daily life can be clarified through the following example. If a friend asks: "How was your conversation last night?" a current answer might be, "Very good, I liked it!" The answer "good" is made on a very high abstract level. We all have our own interpretation of "good." Now we might change the topic of the conversation, or ask another question: "What was good about it?" A training program should focus on skills and on a specific communication situation: in this training program the focus will be on performance review/ staff appraisals, and the requisite skills and dimensions.

The starting point for the development of dimensions and skills is one of Watzlawick et al.'s (1985) axioms: every communication has a content and a relationship aspect. Content and relationship are two general dimensions we will find in every communicative situation. The question: "Are you not able to do things the right way?" includes on a content level the information that the action was not accomplished in the adequate way. On a relation level, the message transports contempt. If you transport this message through non-verbal signals in an ironic tone, the receiver of the message will not hear technical advice, but rather contempt.

The challenge is to be aware of actions and activities on both content and interpersonal levels and to describe and structure them in a way that we can use them to improve our behaviors and skills. This will create opportunities to improve conscious control of our actions. The following effective skills and dimensions for the content and relationship level are supposed to help employees and managers to accomplish effective and appropriate performance reviews and appraisal interviews in daily communication situations.

## Dimensions for the Content and Relationship Levels

Table 24.1 shows the dimensions and Table 24.2 the dimensions and skills of the content level. Table 24.3 shows the dimensions and skills of the relationship level. All participants are systematically trained for both dimensions and skills.

**Table 24.1** Dimensions for the content level and the relationship level

| Content Level | | Relationship Level | | |
|---|---|---|---|---|
| Control | Facilitation | Respect | Friendliness | Feedback |

**Table 24.2** Dimensions and skills of the content level

| Dimensions | Skills |
|---|---|
| Control | Information: Includes structuring: mentioning topic and goal, making the importance of relevant information clear (e.g., using transition).Improving the manner of speaking: being precise, honing and completing sentences, varying pitch and loudness.<br>Questions: closed and open |
| Facilitation | Taking note of one's counterpart<br>Clarifying<br>Summarizing<br>Focusing<br>Probing questions<br>Extending<br>Praise |

**Table 24.3** Dimension and Skills of the Relationship Level

| Dimensions | Skills |
|---|---|
| Respect | Respectful verbal and non-verbal messages, concerned greetings, giving thanks. |
| Friendliness | Friendly verbal and non-verbal messages, paying attention, showing apprehension, encouraging. |
| Feedback | Clarity and empathy, attention to the task, engagement. |

## Dimension Control

Dimension control includes behavior like presenting information at the beginning and from time to time later, explanations, opinions, instructions, questioning and structuring. But what are the functions of presenting information? In a face-to-face situation, we want to express our ideas and the goals of the conversation. We pave the way for how and which information will be perceived. To provide active information, explanations and opinions are crucial elements in each conversation. They are components for effective remembering and initiating higher cognitive processes, which influence our attitude and motivate the counterpart. This is why we must make sure that we provide clear, comprehensible and effective information at the beginning and each time when we explain something or present more information. To present clear and comprehensive information improves the results and quality of a conversation.

Dimension control includes information and facilitation. Such global dimensions are built through subdimensions and concrete and describable skills and skill patterns. For an effective use, frequency, appropriateness and qualified performances are necessary.

For each subdimension, we identified and assigned skills in the research-based literature that show positive results concerning various aspects such as an increase in remembering information or an improvement in the transparency of structures (Gage & Berliner, 1986; Rosenshine, 1971; Woolfolk, 2008).

To increase the transparency of structure in a conversation, the following skills were recommended:

- Mentioning the topic and goal of the conversations at the beginning.
- Making the importance of relevant information clear (you must show this on a verbal and non-verbal level: verbal, using the word "importance"; non-verbal, raising the voice slightly).
- Marking transitions to the next topic on a verbal and on a non-verbal level: verbal, the next point will be ...; non-verbal, pausing).

To improve one's style and quality of speaking, one must be aware of timing, pitch and loudness (Argyle, 1972) be variable; be precise; hone your sentences (Langer, Schultz von Thun, & Tausch, 1974). Frequency is crucial; occasionally one will not have the right timing, not be loud enough or fail to deliver rounded, finished sentences. This is normal. But if it happens too often, listeners will perceive you as incompetent as competence is widely understood to be directly related to effective communication behavior.

Questions also belong to dimension control. Asking questions is a key element in any conversation. We can distinguish between closed and open questions. Closed questions refer to facts, concrete problems and knowledge; ideally, a counterpart can answer such questions quickly and reliably (Klinzing & Klinzing-Eurich, 1988). Closed questions have the positive impact that precise facts and data can provide, which in turn can help objectify emotional situations. Open questions encourage and maintain a dialog. After presenting clear information, responding to open questions encourages the conversation process. Waiting a while between questions and answers is very important. Waiting time refers to the amount of time a manager gives a counterpart to respond to a question and has a positive impact on the quality of the answers (Fagan, Hassler, & Szabao, 1981). For example, three seconds waiting time is recommend after having asked a question which will increase the evidence and enhance logical argument in problem-solving behavior (Rowe, 1974). The clarity of questions influences the quality of the answers as well (Rupp, 1998). If open questions are too complex or abstract, the counterpart will not understand the question, which influences the overall quality of the conversation.

However, control is not the only requirement for effectiveness in a conversation, the dimension of facilitation makes conversations more meaningful and increases the acceptance of what has been said. Facilitating helps to make statements and give information, and makes the process of having conversation more productive. It also improves clarity of participants' thoughts.

## Dimension of Facilitation

The dimension of facilitation includes the following skills: taking note of someone, clarifying, summarizing, focusing, probing, developing and praising. The opposite of taking note of someone is ignoring them, and nobody likes to be ignored. The first step in listening is to take note of statements that have been said. This can be shown through a simple "yes, hmm, OK" on the verbal level, and eye contact or nodding one's head on the non-verbal level. Clarifying statements or answers involves modifying by rephrasing them or conceptualizing them in your own words, or acknowledging ideas by repeating the main points, comparing ideas with those expressed earlier (Flanders, 1970). Another possibility is to abstract, concretize and distinguish statements. Summarizing emphasizes the main topics that have been discussed. This can be done at the end or sometimes even during a performance interview. By focusing on something your counterpart has said, the talk flows smoothly without a sharp break. Thus, the supervisor can move on with the talk without dominating it (Bligh, 2000). Probing questions are questions that follow questions and have the function to deepen, improve and enrich an earlier response. They can be used to solicit additional information related to an earlier statement or to determine a clarifying answer to an earlier answer (Doenau, 1987).

Research by Yukl et al. (2002) on the hierarchical taxonomy of leader behavior puts forward three meta-categories: task, relation, and changing behavior. In addition to supporting, the meta-category relation includes developing, consulting and empowering, and recognizing. Recognizing includes praise and appreciation of others with the objective of an effective performance. Praise by the supervisor can increase employee performance significantly (Wikoff, Anderson, & Crowell, 1983). On the other hand, Yukl et al. (2002) show in their meta-analysis that "results for effects on performance are less consistent in the survey studies." Praise is a difficult construct and there is a lot of misunderstanding and misinformation on it. Praise, for example, does not help you to learn (Hattie, 2013). Brophy (1981) in his famous article describes the functions of praise as an effective reinforcement: praise as a spontaneous expression of surprise, as a balance for criticism, as a positive guidance or an avoidance of criticism or as an ice-breaker. When dealing with other people in a work context, increasing feedback is helpful.

## Relationship Level

Besides skills such as informing, questioning and structuring on the content-management level, there are other skills focusing on the relationship level. The goal is to make contact and to maintain social interaction to establish a productive and respectful communication climate. For a performance interview, the dimensions of respect and appreciation, friendliness and encouragement are important (Rupp & Klinzing, 1997). For each dimension, skills founded on the research-based literature were identified and assigned that show positive results in three dimensions. Table 24.3 stresses the dimensions and skills needed for an effective performance/ appraisal interview.

## Dimension of Respect

The value and importance of the manner of a performance review to direct and motivate behavior is well known. Meaningful, positive feedback can guide and support effective behavior. Negative feedback is indicated in many studies to be destructive. Steelman and Rutkowski (2004), however, underline in their study that unfavorable feedback can have a positive impact on employees under certain conditions.

Respect and appreciation toward other dialog partners is revealed through a certain behavior without showing any previous conditions or admonitions. Your counterpart must be perceived as an independent person with equal rights, or, to express it differently: "human dignity is inviolable." Professional, competent supervisors and managers should acknowledge their counterparts and respect their dignity, even if the behavior of the counterpart during the encounter does not match our own notions/ conceptions or basic attitudes. A lack of respect and appreciation might be expressed by repressing the thoughts, emotions and possibility for action of your counterpart. Hence, a lack of respect and attention are often the source of conflict.

We can show respect by the way we greet someone or say good-bye. These are very easy verbal messages, but only helpful and effective if combined with attentive non-verbal behavior shown by one's facial expressions. The posture must be directed to the counterpart. Effective non-verbal behavior is crucial for effectiveness on the interpersonal level.

## Dimension of Friendliness

There is very little research on friendliness in leadership literature. Often, it is included in other dimensions like encouragement or motivation. Watzlawick et al. (1985) analyze friendliness and point out that it needs confirmation. They indicate that without a confirmatory impact there is no development within communication. According to them, to be confirmatory is one of the main purposes of communication, not only the exchange of information. To achieve constructive working relationships, therefore, friendliness is important (Schmidt & Swaffin-Smith, 1992). Friendliness occurs by using friendly wording accompanied by eye contact, gestures and friendly facial expressions. Paying attention at the beginning and the end of a performance interview and showing understanding of someone else's situation also underlines friendliness.

## Dimension of Feedback

Feedback is crucial in every organization and a powerful way to learn from others, either employees learning from their supervisors or colleagues learning from each other. However, employees tend to seek feedback from supervisors and rather than from colleagues. Feedback is an important source of information about working processes and the status quo of a project. Positive feedback has a high value and importance and can guide and reinforce effective behaviors. Negative feedback neither supports individual development nor the values of organizations (Steelman & Rutkowski, 2004). Kluger and DeNisi (1996) find in a meta-analysis that in one-third of the cases, negative feedback has a negative result. Various motives for employees to seek performance feedback are discussed by Ashford and Cummings (1983). One motive is to reduce uncertainty regarding task performance; a second is to signal that certain values, like quality, are important goals for the organization. A supportive environment encourages feedback-seeking behavior, facilitates the employees' performance and should provide credibility and tactfulness with regards to subordinates (Dahling, Chau, & O'Malley, 2012). According to Steelman and Rutkowski (2004), supportive feedback is given and employees are highly motivated when feedback is delivered clearly and empathetically, positive and negative when necessary, of high quality, in a constructive manner, and, what is also important, with credibility.

## Criticism and Feedback

If dissatisfied with certain behaviors, some people tend to reproach or criticize. The range of what is defined under critique and negative reactions is quite wide. Flanders (1970) describes criticism as statements made with the intention of changing behavior from unacceptable to acceptable patterns. Criticism means showing precisely that we reject certain points in a statement, or that we do not agree with what has been said.

## The Treatment/ Program

At the beginning of the course, all the participants were introduced to the objectives, methods, content and organization of the training course. The training itself started by introducing the participants to one another and explaining expectations for the training, whether the participants knew each other or not.

A presentation about leadership behavior, its efficacy, benefits and practicability (Drucker, 2005) was the next step. This was followed by a discussion on task-, relationship-, change- and value-oriented leadership based on the content described above. This was followed by a group activity to discuss tasks and traits of leaders from participants' perspectives (Luthans, Rosenkrantz, & Hennessey, 1985). This group work was followed by a presentation and discussion on categories of dialogical communication and its function in a daily work situation. This included a brief information on negotiation, conversation, discussion, moderation, problem-solving discussions and conflict management as well as their goals, benefits and functions. Finally, the focus was moved onto staff appraisals/ performance interviews as an important work situation.

These activities were followed by the training of individual skills for staff performance review/ staff appraisals consisting of two parts, distributed over two days (16 hours, including breaks). A third part of the training was devoted to self-evaluation of the participants and the evaluation of the training course.

Part 1 focused on the content aspect of communication, with the dimensions of control and facilitation. The dimension of control includes skills such as instruction, questioning and structuring. The dimension of facilitation includes skills such as summarizing and clarifying. The participants were to acquire the skills described above by listening to the lectures, conducting an exercise to structure a disordered text and a discrimination exercise about questioning. Micro-teaching was used to impart the communication skills for performance review/ staff appraisal of Part 1, as described above.

Part 2 focused on relationships and interpersonal communication with the dimensions of respect, friendliness and feedback (Klinzing, 1998; Rupp, 2010; Wiemann, 1977; Wilen, 2003). The dimension of respect includes skills like not patronizing someone and ensuring that only one party talks at time (Wieman, 1985). The dimension of friendliness includes skills like noticing someone (not ignoring others) (Tausch & Tausch, 1978). The skills were imparted by descriptions of behaviors followed by encouraging participants to develop positive examples in role-playing games. Micro-teaching was used as a method for imparting the communication skills of Part 2 as described above. (See appendix.)

## Data Collection

A questionnaire (BLSCQ) developed for this study, which focused on a set of 13 different competences and skills, was used to collect effective data about communication leadership skills. The competences and skills investigated by the questionnaire are based on the skills described above. Table 24.4 shows the questions used in the questionnaire. The questionnaire has a 6-point Likert scale, where 1 means to strongly agree and 6 to strongly disagree.

At the end of the entire training, the Course Instructor Evaluation Questionnaire (CIEQ) was used. The instrument was developed by Alemoni and colleagues (Alemoni and Stephens (1986), Alemoni (2010)) and translated

**Table 24.4** Basic Leadership Skills and Competence Questionnaire (BLSCQ)

| |
|---|
| 1. Development of objectives/setting goals |
| 2. Management by objectives |
| 3. General staff appraisal |
| 4. Task-oriented face-to-face communication |
| 5. Sharing of information |
| 6. Inquiring of information |
| 7. Instructing directives |
| 8. Structuring information |
| 9. Summarizing information |
| 10. Interpersonal communication |
| 11. Respect toward my dialog partner/colleague |
| 12. Friendliness toward my dialog partner/colleague |
| 13. Formulating criticism and feedback |

into German by Klinzing and Rupp (1989). It consists of 21 questions measuring five dimensions:

- General course attitude (four items);
- Method of instruction (four items);
- Course content (four items);
- Interest and attention (five items);
- Instructor (four items).

Information regarding reliabilities, validity and norms is provided by Alemoni and Stephens (1986).

The following competences and behaviors have been found to be helpful in day-to-day work in appraisal interviews

## Results

The effects of the training program were replicated in six studies using a post-test-only design. Post-test 1 was done immediately after the training. Post-test 2 was conducted two months later. At this stage each participant received the BLSCQ again, with a request to send the questionnaire back. All the participants were informed about this procedure. They were told to focus on one or two skills learned in the seminar each week. The respond rate was 100 %. A better design of pretest–post-test could not be performed because of the context of the training. There was no possibility of gaining access to the companies for example for a pre-test; and interviews or coaching after the training to depend the skills and behavior learned.

Studies 1–4 refer to selected managers from their company. All managers were obliged to attend the training course as part of internal human resource management programs to train managers in leadership. Studies 5 and 6 refer to managers who voluntarily visited a training course offered by a chamber of commerce located in southwestern Germany. The participants in Studies 5 and 6 chose the training course for various reasons, such as the absence of offers in their own company, absence of such training courses in-house, and distance of training location from where they live.

Leadership competences and behaviors concerning appraisal interview were measured by the 13-item BLSCQ developed by Rupp (2016). The items were measured on a 6-point Likert-type scale ranging from 1 = strongly agree to 6 = disagree.

Table 24.5 shows the results for the competences and skills of items 1–9. Items 1–4 (setting goals, management by objectives, general staff appraisal and task-oriented face-to-face-communication) show leadership competences according the leadership theories and categories described above; items 5–9 (sharing of information, inquiring of information, instructing directives, structuring of information and summarizing of information) represent the skills trained in the seminar especially for appraisal interview. All of these competences are assigned to the category of task-oriented leadership and the subdimensions of control and facilitation.

The skills and competences uncovered by the BLSCQ show a moderate positive linear to a strong linear relationship. However, there is no study that shows more than three skills with a moderate to strong positive linear relationship. The differences may result from different questions and expectations of the participants. It might also be that during the training seminar, certain aspects were discussed in more detail, for example during the feedback for a longer period of time and the participants became more aware of the competences and skills for their daily work.

Table 24.6 shows the results for the competences and skills of items 10–13. These four items show the relationship dimension (interpersonal communication, respect toward dialog partner, friendliness toward dialog partner, formulating criticism and feedback). All the dimensions were part of the training program, with specific skills described above.

The relationship-oriented leadership skills and competences varied from a moderate to a strong linear relationship. The differences may also result from different questions and expectations of the participants. It might be also that, during the training, certain aspects were discussed in more detail for a longer period-of-time and the participants became more aware of the competences and skills for their daily work. There is also no difference between obligatory and voluntary participants if one looks at Study 2 and Study 3. However, they show, in the general dimension, interpersonal communication and in the subdimension respect toward the dialog partner, friendliness toward the dialog partner, formulating criticism and feedback having moderately to strong positive relationships. The findings in Study 3 show for respect toward the dialog partners and formulating criticism and feedback a moderate relationship and for interpersonal communication and friendliness toward the dialog partner a strong positive relationship, whereas in the study the findings are weak or there is no positive relationship at all.

**Table 24.5** Results for leadership competences and skills of the Basic Leadership and Competences Questionnaire (BLSCQ) Items 1–9

| Skills and competences | Study 1 CH N = 10 8 hr | | Study 2 KN N = 6 16 hr | | Study 3 FB N = 8 16 hr | | Study 4 SG N = 9 16 hr | | Study 5 GT N = 13 16 hr | | Study 6 SH N = 9 16 hr | |
|---|---|---|---|---|---|---|---|---|---|---|---|---|
| | M | SD | M | SD | M | SD | M | SD | M | SD | M | SD |
| 1. Setting goals | | | | | | | | | | | | 2.5 |
| Post-test 1 | 1.8 | .78 | 1.8 | .40 | 2.6 | .74 | 2.3 | .86 | 2.3 | .75 | 1.01 | |
| Post-test 2 | 1.8 | .63 | 1.8 | .40 | 2.5 | .75 | 2.4 | .52 | 2.4 | .66 | 2.3 | .70 |
| r | **.53** | | −.02 | | **.63** | | **.73** | | −.14 | | **.05** | |
| 2. Management by objectives | | | | | | | | | | | | |
| Post-test 1 | 2.1 | .56 | 2.0 | .89 | 2.2 | 1.03 | 2.1 | .33 | 2.1 | .55 | 2.3 | .70 |
| Post-test 2 | 2.2 | .91 | 1.8 | .40 | 2.6 | 1.06 | 2.3 | .50 | 2.5 | .66 | 2.6 | .88 |
| r | −.04 | | −.54 | | **.77** | | −.25 | | **.66** | | **.13** | |
| 3. General staff Appraisal | | | | | | | | | | | | |
| Post-test 1 | 1.6 | .84 | 1.5 | .54 | 1.3 | .74 | 1.7 | .44 | 1.7 | .72 | 1.5 | .52 |
| Post-test 2 | 1.9 | .56 | 1.1 | .40 | 1.8 | .64 | 1.8 | .33 | 1.6 | .48 | 1.7 | .44 |
| r | −.09 | | **.44** | | −.18 | | **.66** | | **.49** | | **.05** | |
| 4. Task-oriented face-to-face communication | | | | | | | | | | | | |
| Post-test 1 | 1.9 | .87 | 1.3 | .51 | 2.1 | 1.12 | 2.1 | .60 | 2.0 | 1.03 | 1.6 | .50 |
| Post-test 2 | 1.9 | .56 | 1.3 | .51 | 1.5 | .75 | 1.7 | .44 | 2.0 | .57 | 1.7 | .66 |
| r | **.42** | | **.25** | | **.41** | | **.10** | | **.27** | | **.50** | |
| 5. Sharing information | | | | | | | | | | | | |
| Post-test 1 | 2.2 | .63 | 1.8 | .75 | 2.0 | .75 | 1.5 | .72 | 2.5 | .51 | 2.0 | .86 |
| Post-test 2 | 2.1 | .73 | 1.8 | .40 | 1.8 | .99 | 2.0 | .70 | 2.0 | .64 | 2.2 | .83 |
| r | −.28 | | **.54** | | **.57** | | 0 | | **.11** | | **.69** | |
| 6. Inquiring information | | | | | | | | | | | | |
| Post-test 1 | 2.3 | .48 | 1.3 | .51 | 2.7 | .70 | 2.1 | .60 | 2.3 | .63 | 2.3 | 1.00 |
| Post-test 2 | 2.8 | .78 | 1.8 | .40 | 2.0 | .75 | 2.2 | .66 | 2.5 | .77 | 2.3 | 1.00 |
| r | **.46** | | **.31** | | **.26** | | **.55** | | **.65** | | −.25 | |
| 7. Instructing directives | | | | | | | | | | | | |
| Post-test 1 | 2.3 | .94 | 1.8 | .75 | 1.8 | .83 | 1.7 | .44 | 2.0 | .59 | 2.4 | 1.23 |
| Post-test 2 | 2.5 | .52 | 1.5 | .54 | 1.8 | .83 | 2.1 | .78 | 2.0 | .57 | 2.1 | .78 |
| r | **.11** | | −.72 | | **.17** | | .08 | | **.22** | | **.58** | |
| 8. Structuring | | | | | | | | | | | | |
| information | 2.0 | 1.05 | 2.5 | .54 | 1.7 | .70 | 2.1 | .60 | 2.0 | .39 | 2.7 | .97 |
| Post-test 1 | 2.3 | 1.15 | 2.1 | .75 | 1.8 | .64 | 2.1 | .60 | 2.3 | .48 | 3.0 | .86 |
| Post-test 2 | 0 | | **.72** | | −.39 | | **.65** | | **.42** | | **.29** | |
| r | | | | | | | | | | | | |
| 9. Summarizing information | | | | | | | | | | | | |
| Post-test 1 | 2.1 | .99 | 2.0 | .89 | 1.8 | .64 | 1.6 | .86 | 2.3 | .50 | 2.8 | 1.36 |
| Post-test 2 | 2.0 | .47 | 2.3 | .81 | 1.6 | .74 | 2.3 | .50 | 2.3 | .63 | 2.5 | .88 |
| r | −.23 | | **.54** | | −.11 | | 0 | | **.38** | | **.16** | |

Note. Study 1 CH, placement test = Birkenfeld, in-house training, obligated; Study 2 KN = placement test = Konstanz, voluntary; Study 3 FB, placement test = Görwhil, in-house training obligated; Study 4 SG = placement test Lörrach obligated = ; Study 5 GT, placement test = Hohentengen, obligated; Study 6 SH, placement test = Schopfheim, voluntary.

**Table 24.6** Results for the general leadership competences and skills of the Basic Leadership and Competences Questionnaire (BLSCQ) Items 10–13.

| | Study 1 CH N = 10 8 hours | | Study 2 KN N = 6 16 hours | | Study 3 FB N = 8 16 hours | | Study 4 SG N = 9 16 hours | | Study 5 GT N = 13 16 hours | | Study 6 SH N = 9 16 hours | |
|---|---|---|---|---|---|---|---|---|---|---|---|---|
| **Skills and competences** | **M** | **SD** | **M** | **SD** | **M** | **SD** | **M** | **SD** | **M** | **SD** | **M** | **SD** |
| 10. Interpersonal communication | | | | | | | | | | | | |
| Post-test 1 | 1.8 | .63 | 1.8 | .75 | 1.7 | 1.16 | 1.6 | .70 | 2.0 | .57 | 2.4 | 1.23 |
| Post-test 2 | 2.1 | .73 | 1.8 | .40 | 1.7 | .88 | 2.2 | .40 | 2.0 | .81 | 2.2 | .83 |
| r | **.28** | | **.54** | | **.76** | | −.13 | | 0 | | **.62** | |
| 11. Respect towards my dialogue partner | | | | | | | | | | | | |
| Post-test 1 | 1.7 | .48 | 2.3 | 1.50 | 2.1 | 1.12 | 1.7 | .44 | 2.0 | .70 | 2.6 | 1.0 |
| Post-test 2 | 2.1 | .73 | 2.0 | .63 | 2.12 | .64 | 1.8 | .78 | 1.9 | .75 | 2.4 | .72 |
| r | **.09** | | **.84** | | **.56** | | **.64** | | **.15** | | **.22** | |
| 12. Friendliness towards my dialogue partner | | | | | | | | | | | | |
| Post-test 1 | 1.8 | .63 | 2.6 | 1.36 | 2.5 | 1.06 | 1.5 | .72 | 2.0 | .91 | 2.6 | 1.00 |
| Post-test 2 | 2.4 | .51 | 1.6 | .51 | 2.1 | .64 | 2.1 | .78 | 2.0 | .64 | 2.4 | 1.04 |
| r | −.06 | | **.66** | | **.72** | | −.12 | | 0 | | **.04** | |
| 13. Formulating criticism and feedback | | | | | | | | | | | | |
| Post-test 1 | 2.2 | 1.22 | 1.8 | .40 | 1.7 | .70 | 1.8 | .60 | 2.0 | .57 | 2.5 | 1.13 |
| Post-test 2 | 2.0 | .47 | 1.8 | .75 | 1.8 | .64 | 2.0 | .50 | 2.1 | .68 | 2.1 | 1.05 |
| r | **.38** | | −.10 | | **.55** | | **.41** | | **.41** | | **.25** | |

Note. Study 1 CH, placement test = Birkenfeld, in-house training, obligated; Study 2 KN = placement test = Konstanz, voluntary; Study 3 FB, placement test = Görwhil, in-house training, obligated; Study 4 SG = placement test, Lörrach obligated = ; Study 5 GT, placement test = Hohentengen, obligated; Study 6 SH, placement test = Schopfheim, voluntary.

As the results in Table 24.7 indicate, the training program was rated favorably by the participants. The best results in total are seen in Study 1 and 4. Both courses were obligatory for the participants. Very often, obligatory training courses are not very popular. Results from the oral evaluation by the participants in a final discussion confirmed those from CIEQ.

## Conclusion

Communication is the most important skill for leaders, and communication leadership training is widely recommended and offered. But there is still a lack of research-based and evaluated training programs. The reasons are varied. One is that it is difficult to find companies willing to support field research. The post-test-only design in this study is due to this fact. The program was tested and evaluated for its applicability in six studies with leaders and managers of midsize enterprises in Germany.

**Table 24.7** Results of the Course Instructor Evaluation Questionnaire (CIEQ). Means for the Five Subscales of the Instrument for Studies 1–6

| Dimension | Study 1 (CH) N = 14 8 hr Mean | Study 2 (KN) N = 6 16 hr Mean | Study 3 (FB) N = 8 16 hr Mean | Study 4 (SG) N = 9 16 hr Mean | Study 5 (GT) N = 13 16 hr Mean | Study 6 (SH) N = 10 16 hr Mean |
|---|---|---|---|---|---|---|
| General Course Attitude | 1.24 | 1.20 | 1.37 | 1.16 | 1.41 | 1.35 |
| Method of Instruction | 1.28 | 1.62 | 1.46 | 1.30 | 1.68 | 1.65 |
| Interest and Attention | 1.21 | 1.29 | 1.21 | 1.27 | 1.59 | 1.52 |
| Course Content | 1.28 | 1.58 | 1.37 | 1.38 | 1.55 | 1.52 |
| Instructor | 1.25 | 1.23 | 1.29 | 1.17 | 1.47 | 1.37 |
| Total | 1.25 | 1.38 | 1.34 | 1.25 | 1.54 | 1.48 |

Note. Study 1 CH, placement test = Birkenfeld, in-house training, obligatory; Study 2 KN = placement test = Konstanz, voluntary; Study 3 FB, placement test = Görwhil, in-house training obligatory; Study 4 SG = placement test Lörrach, obligatory =; Study 5 GT, placement test = Hohentengen, obligatory; Study 6 SH, placement test = Schopfheim, voluntary. Four-point scales: 1 = strongly agree; 4 = strongly disagree.

A high level of skills seems necessary. For this reason, a program was designed using the micro-teaching approach (Klinzing & Floden, 1991; Klinzing & Gerada Aloisio, 2010; Rupp, 1998) which combines participants' acquisition of knowledge and abilities: the acquisition of theoretical knowledge on leadership, the ability to use concepts as organizing tools like management by objectives, to generate hypotheses, to make and test decisions, to skillfully carry out actions and to reflect on the execution of behaviors and their consequences (Klinzing & Floden, 1991).

This program was tested for its applicability and value in six studies with managers and leaders of different levels in the first half of 2016.

The results of the studies testing the direct applicability on behavioral changes were encouraging:

Studies 1 and 6 (for three skills), Studies 3 and 4 (for four skills) and Studies 2 and 5 (for five skills) show a weak to moderate relationship. We can find a weak to moderate positive relationship for each skill and competence. Study 5 shows a positive relationship from weak to moderate for five skills for the dimension of content level, but for the dimension of relationship there is only a weak relationship for one skill. Obviously, in this company, the relationship-oriented leadership needs a more frequent and intensive training. Studies 1, 3 and 4 show a moderate to strong relationship for setting goals. In all three companies, the concept of management by objectives was known, but the participants did not know how to use the concept effectively in their daily work at their workplaces.

The training program encouraged and enabled them to use the skill effectively and appropriately. In studies 2, 5 and 6, there was no relationship for setting goals. In these companies, the concept was not used and not known.

Studies 2 and 3 show a moderate and strong relationship for the competence of friendliness, which is a notable result. In both companies, the participants complained at the beginning of the training program about a lack of friendliness in their company between managers/ leaders and employees. The participants obviously could implement and adapt these competences at their workplace.

For all target behaviors, changes could be achieved. All skills were used, but obviously, applicability was not always possible, or there was no need for these skills. The different culture and values of the company may also play a role in the use of certain skills.

Furthermore, the training program was evaluated exceptionally well by the participants at the end of the training for all categories (general course attitude, method of instruction, interest and attention, course content, instructor).

Overall, this training program concerning task-oriented and relationship-oriented leadership competences and skills can be recommended and shows positive results. Also, the training methods and the course content, besides the other dimensions, were evaluated positively. Additional research and development should be carried out to see how the understanding of these components of leadership training, especially communication, can be extended to offer a wide range of research-based training programs for leadership development.

## References

Aguinis, H., & Kraiger, K. (2009). Benefits of training and development for individuals and teams, organizations, and society. *Annual Review of Psychology, 60*, 451–474.

Alemoni, L. M. (2010). Why is faculty evaluation so one sided? In A. Rupp (Ed.), *Moderne Konzepte der betrieblichen und universitären Aus- und Weiterbildung. Festschrift für Hans Gerhard Klinzing. 3. erweiterte Auflage. (Modern concepts in business and university pre- and in-service education.) (3rd expanded ed)* (pp. 145–161). Tübingen, Germany: dgtv-Verlag.

Alemoni, L. M., & Stephens, J. J. (1986). *Arizona Course/Instructor Evaluation. Questionnaire (CIEQ): Results interpretation manual.* Tucson, Arizona: University of Arizona: Office of Instructional Research and Development.

Allen, D. W., & Ryan, K. A. (1969). *Micro-teaching.* Reading, MA: Addison-Wesley.

Argyle, M. (1972). *Soziale Interaktion. (Social interaction).* Köln, Germany: Kiepenheuer and Witsch.

Aristotle, Nicomachean Ethics, Book II, 1109a.27. The quotations come from these or other translations: *The Works of Aristotle.* Ed. W. David Ross. 12 vols. Oxford: Clarendon, 1908; *The Complete Works of Aristotle: The Revised Oxford Translation.* Ed. Jonathan Barnes. 2 vols. Princeton, NJ: Princeton Univ. Press, 1984.

Arthur, W. J., Bennett, W. J., Edens, P., & Bell, S. T. (2003). Effectiveness of training in organizations: a meta-analysis of design and evaluation features. *Journal of Applied Psychology, 88*, 234–245.

Ashford, S. J., & Cummings, L. L. (1983). Feedback as an individual resource: Personal strategies of creating information. *Organizational Behavior and Human Performance, 32*, 370–398.

Berman, S. J., & Hellweg, S. A. (1989). Perceived supervisor communication competence and supervisor satisfaction as a function of quality circle participation. *Journal of Business Communication, 26*, 103–122.

Bligh, D. (2000). *What's the point in discussion?*. Exeter, UK: Intellect Books.

Bridges, D. (1979). *Education, democracy and discussion*. Windsor, Berks, UK: NFER Publishing Company.

Brodbeck, F. C. (2014). *Internationale Führung. (International leadership)*. Berlin, Germany: Springer.

Brophy, J. E. (1981). Teacher praise: A functional analysis. *Review of Educational Research, 51*, 5–32.

Boyatzis, R. E. (1982). *The competent manager*. New York, NY: Wiley.

Boyatzis, R. E. (2008). Competences in the 21st century. *Journal of Management Development, 27*(1), 5–12.

Brophy, J., & Good, T. (1986). Teacher behavior and student achievement. In M. C. Wittrock (Ed.), *Handbook of research on teaching* (3rd ed.) (pp. 328–375). New York, NY: Macmillan Publishing.

Collins, D. B., & Holton, E. F. III. (2004). The effectiveness of managerial leadership development programs: a meta-analysis of studies from 1982 to 2001. *Human Resource Development Quarterly, 15*, 217–248.

Conger, J. A., & Kanungo, R. (1998). *Charismatic leadership in organizations*. Thousand Oaks, CA: Sage Publications.

Cruickshank, D. R., Jenkins, D. B., & Metcalf, K. K. (2012). *The act of teaching* (6th ed.). Boston, MA: McGraw-Hill.

Cruickshank, D. R., & Metcalfe, K. K. (1990). Training with teacher preparation. In W. R. Houston (Ed.), *Handbook of research on teacher education* (pp. 469–497). New York, NY: Macmillan.

Dahling, J. J., Chau, S. L., & O'Malley, A. (2012). Correlates and consequences of feedback orientation in organizations. *Journal of Management, 38*(2), 531–546.

Doenau, S. J. (1987). Structuring. In M. Dunkin (Ed.), *The international encyclopedia of teaching and teacher education* (pp. 39–407). Oxford, UK: Pergamon Press.

Drucker, P. F. (2005). *Management*. Revised Edition. Harper Collins e-book URL: http://youth-portal.com/wp-content/uploads/2014/10/Peter-F-Drucker-Management-Rev-Ed.pdf, Accessed February 9, 2016.

Fagan, E. R., Hassler, D. M., & Szabao, M. (1981). Evaluation of questioning strategies in language arts instruction. *Research in the Teaching of English, 15*, 267–273.

Flanders, N. A. (1970). *Analyzing teaching behavior*. Reading, MA: Addison-Wesley.

Gage, N. L., & Berliner, D. C. (1986). *Pädgogische Psychologie. (Educational psychology)* (4th ed.). Weinheim, Germany: Beltz.

Habermas, J. (2011). *Theorie des kommunikativen Handelns. (The theory of communicative action)* (8th ed.). Frankfurt, Germany: Suhrkamp Verlag.

Hansford, B. C., & Copeland, W. D. (1979). Microteaching as a tool for teachers: Some current considerations. *South Pacific Journal of Teacher Education, 7*, 68–75.

Hattie, J. (2013). *Lernen sichtbar machen. (Visible learning)*. Baltmannsweiler, Germany: Schneider Verlag Hohengeren.

House, R. J., Hanges, P. J., Javidan, M., Dorfman, P. W., & Gupa, V. (2004). *Culture, leadership, and organizations: The GLOBE Study of 62 societies*. Thousand Oaks, CA: Sage Publications.

House, R. J., Dorfman, P. W., Javidan, M., Hanges, P. J., & Sully de Luque, M. F. (2014). *Strategic leadership across cultures. The GLOBE Study of CEO leadership behavior and effectiveness in 24 countries*. Los Angeles, CA: Sage.

Johansson, C., Miller, V. D., & Hamrin, S. (2014). Conceptualizing communicative leadership. *Corporate Communications: An International Journal, 199*(2), 147–165.

Joyce, B. R., Weil, M., & Calhoun, E. (2004). *Models of teaching*. Needham Heights, MA: Allyn and Bacon.

Katz, D., & Kahn, R. L. (1952). Some recent findings in human relations research. In E. Swanson, T. Newcomb, & E. Hartley (Eds.), *Readings in social psychology*, (pp. 650–665). New York, NY: Holt, Rinehart and Winston.

Klinzing, H. G., & Klinzing-Eurich, G. (1988). Questions, responses and reactions. In J. T. Dillon (Ed.), *Questioning and discussion: A multidisciplinary study*, (pp. 212–239). Norwood, NJ: Ablex Publishing.

Klinzing, H. G. and Floden, R. E. (1991). The development of the micro-teaching movement in Europe. Paper presented at the annual meeting of the American Educational Research Association, Chicago, IL.

Klinzing, H. G., & Tisher, R. P. (1993). The development of classroom teaching skills. In H. Vonk, L. Kremer-Hayon, & R. Fessler (Eds.), *Teacher professional development* (pp. 167–195). Lisse, The Netherlands: Sweets/Zeitlinger.

Klinzing, H. G. and Rupp, A. (1989). *Course Instructor Evaluation Questionnaire (CIEQ)*: German Version. Tübingen.

Klinzing, H. G. (1998). Interagieren als Experimentieren. In H. G. Klinzing (Ed.), *Neue Lernverfahren. Zweite Festschrift für Walter Zifreund. (New teaching methods)* (pp. 231–341). Tübingen, Germany: dgvt-Verlag.

Klinzing, H. G. (2002). Wie effektiv ist Micro-teaching? Ein Überblick über fünfunddreißig Jahre Forschung. (How effective is micro-teaching?). *Zeitschrift für Pädagogik, 48*(2), 194–214.

Klinzing, H. G., & Gerada Aloisio, B. (2010). "Charisma", nonverbale Kompetenzen und Persönlichkeitsdimensionen. (Charisma, nonverbal competences and personality dimensions). In A. Rupp (Ed.), *Moderne Konzepte der betrieblichen und universitären Aus- und Weiterbildung. Festschrift für Hans Gerhard Klinzing. 3. Erweiterte Auflage. (Modern concepts in business and university pre- and inservice education) (3rd expanded ed)* (pp. 313–358). Tübingen, Germany: dgvt-Verlag.

Klinzing, H. G. (2010). Training nonverbaler Wahrnehmungsfähigkeit. In A. Rupp (Ed.), *Moderne Konzepte der betrieblichen und universitären Aus- und Weiterbildung. Festschrift für Hans Gerhard Klinzing. 3. Erweiterte Auflage. (Modern concepts in business and university pre- and inservice education.) (3rd expanded ed)* (pp. 289–312). Tübingen, Germany: dgvt-Verlag.

Kluger, A. N., & DeNisi, A. (1996). The effects of feedback interventions on performance: a historical review, a meta-analysis, and a preliminary feedback intervention theory. *Psychological Bulletin, 119*, 254–284.

Knapp, M. L., Hall, J. A., & Horgan, T. G. (2013). *Nonverbal communication in human interaction*. Boston, MA: Wadsworth.

Kouzes, J. M., & Posner, B. Z. (1995). *The leadership challenge: How to get extraordinary things done in organizations*. San Francisco, CA: Jossey-Bass.

Kurtz, P. D., Marshall, E. K., & Banspach, S. W. (1985). Interpersonal skill-training research: A 12-year review and analysis. *Counselor Education and Supervision, 24*, 249–263.

Langer, I., Schultz von Thun, F., & Tausch, R. (1974). *Verständlichkeit in Schule, Verwaltung, Politik, Wissenschaft. (Comprehensibility in schools, administration, politics and science)*. München, Germany: Ernst Reinhardt Verlag.

Latham, G. P. (1988). Human resource training and development. *Annual Review of Psychology, 64*, 239–246.

Locke, E. A., & Latham, G. P. (1990). *A theory of goal setting and task performance*. New York, NY: Prentice Hall.

Luthans, F., & Lockwood, D. L. (1984). Toward an observation system for measuring behavior in natural settings. In J. G. Hunt, D. Hosking, C. Schriesheim, & R. Stewart (Eds.), *Leaders and managers* (pp. 122). New York, NY: Pergamon.

Luthans, F., Rosenkrantz, S. A., & Hennessey, H. W. (1985). What do successful managers really do? An observation study of managerial activities. *The Journal of Applied Behavioral Science, 21*(3), 255–270.

Luthans, F. (2002). *Organizational behavior* ((9th ed) ed.). Boston, MA: McGraw-Hill.

Luthans, F. (2012). *Organizational Behavior: An evidence-based approach* (12th ed) ed.). New York, NY: McGraw-Hill.

Morreale, S. P., Osborn, M. M., & Pearson, J. C. (2000). Why communication is important: A rationale for the centrality of the study of communication. *Journal of the Association for Communication Administration, 29*, 1–25.

Myers, S. A., & Kassing, J. W. (1998). The relationship between perceived supervisory communication behaviors and subordinate organizational identification. *Communication Research Reports, 15*, 71–81.

Odiorne, G. S. (1967). *Management by objectives. (Führung durch Vorgabe von Zielen)*. Landsberg, Germany: Verlag Moderne Industrie.

Peck, R. F., & Tucker, J. A. (1973). Research on teacher education. In R. M. W. Travers (Ed.), *Second handbook of research on teaching* (pp. 340–378). Chicago, IL: Rand McNally.

Rosenshine, B. (1971). *Teaching behaviors and student achievement*. London, UK: National Foundation for Educational Research.

Rowe, M. B. (1974). Pausing phenomena: Influence on the quality of instruction. *Journal of Psycholinguistic Research, 3*, 203–224.

Rubin, R. (1990). Communication competence. In G. M. Phillips, & J. T. Wood (Eds.), *Speech communication: Essays to commemorate the 75th anniversary of the Speech Communication Association* (pp. 94–129). Carbondale, IL: Southern Illinois University Press.

Rupp, A. (1998). Training von Diskussionsleiter – und teilnehmerverhalten oder Die Entwicklung kommunikativer Kompetenz in Diskussionen - (Training of discussion leader and discussion participant behavior or the development of communicative competence in discussions). In H. G. Klinzing (Ed.),

*Neue Lernverfahren. Zweite Festschrift für Walter Zifreund. (New teaching methods.)* (pp. 231–341). Tübingen, Germany: dgvt-Verlag.

Rupp, A. (2010). Trainingsprogramm: Effektive Konfliktlösungen in Organizationen. (Training program: Effective conflict resolution in organizations). In A. Rupp (Ed.), *Moderne Konzepte der betrieblichen und universitären Aus- und Weiterbildung. Festschrift für Hans Gerhard Klinzing. 3. Erweiterte Auflage. (Modern concepts in business and university pre- and inservice education.) (3rd expanded ed)* (pp. 65–85). Tübingen, Germany: dgvt-Verlag.

Rupp, A. (2016). *Basic Leadership Skills and Competences Questionnaire (BLSCQ)*. Reutlingen, Germany: Institute of Medical Device, Knowledge Foundation@ Reutlingen University.

Rupp, A., & Klinzing, H. G. (1997). *Training von Diskussionsleiter- und Teilnehmverhalten*. (Training of discussion leader behaviors). *Didaktisches Design, 2*, 81–90.

Sadker, M., & Cooper, J. M. (1972). What do we know about micro-teaching? *Educational Leadership, 29*(6), 547–550.

Salas, E., & Cannon-Bowers, J. A. (2001). The science of training: a decade of progress. *Annual Review of Psychology, 52*, 471–499.

Schmidt, S. M., & Swaffin-Smith, C. (1992). *Organization life: Initiating change and being appreciated. Interfaces, 22*(4), 109–111.

Spitzberg, B. H. and Cupach, W.R. (1981). *Self-monitoring and relational competence*. Paper presented at the Speech Communication Association Convention, Anaheim, CA.

Steelman, L. A., & Rutkowski, K. A. (2004). Moderators of employee reactions to negative feedback. *Journal of Managerial Psychology, 19*(1), 6–18.

Stift, D. (2009). *Micro-teaching und Peerteaching in der Lehreraus- und fortbildung. Aktuelle Forschungsbefunde im deutsch und englischsprachigen Raum. (Micro-teaching and peer-teaching in teacher education)*. Saarbrücken, Germany: VDM Verlag Dr. Müller.

Stodgill, R. M., Goode, O. S., & Day, D. R. (1962). New leader behavior description subscales. *Journal of Psychology, 54*, 259–269.

Tannenbaum, S. I., & Yukl, G. (1992). Training and development in work organizations. *Annual Review of Psychology, 42*, 399–441.

Tausch, R., & Tausch, A. M. (1978). *Erziehungspsychologie. (Educational Psychology)* (8th ed.). Göttingen, Germany: Hofgrefe.

Watzlawick, P., Beavin, J. H., & Jackson, D. D. (1985). *Menschliche Kommunikation. (Pragmatics of human communication. A study of interactional patterns, pathologies, and paradoxes)* (8th ed.). Bern, Switzerland: Verlag Hans Huber.

Wexley, K. N. (1984). Personnel training. *Annual Review of Psychology, 35*, 519–551.

Whetten, D. A., & Cameron, K. S. (1991). *Developing management skills* (2nd ed.). New York, NY: HarperCollins.

White, R. W. (1959). Motivation reconsidered: The concept of competence. *Psychological Review, 66*(5), 297–333.

Wiemann, J. M. (1977). Explication and test of a model of communicative competence. *Human Communication Research, 3*, 195–213.

Wieman, J. M. (1985). Interpersonal control and regulation in conversation. In R. L. Street, & J. N. Capella (Eds.), *Sequence and pattern in communicative behavior* (pp. 85–102). London, UK: Edward Arnold.

Wiemann, J. M., & Bradac, J. J. (1989). Metatheoretical issues in the study of communication competence: Structural and functional approaches. In B. Dervin, & M. J. Vight (Eds.), *Progress in communication sciences* (Vol. 9) (pp. 261–284). Norwood, NJ: Ablex.

Wiemann, J. M., & Kelly, C. W. (1981). Pragmatics of interpersonal competence. In C. Wilder-Mott, & J. H. Weakland (Eds.), *Rigor and imagination: Essays from the legacy of Gregory Bateson* (pp. 283–297). New York, NY: Praeger.

Wikoff, M., Anderson, D. C., & Crowell, C. R. (1983). Behavior management in factory setting: Increasing work efficiency. *Journal of Organizational Behavior Management, 4*, 97–128.

Wilen, W. W. (2003). Conducting effective issue-based discussions in social studies classrooms. *International Journal of Social Education, 18*(1), 99–109.

Woolfolk, A. (2008). *Pädagogische Psychologie. (Educational Psychology.)* (10th ed.). München, Germany: Pearson.

Worley, J. M., & Doolen, T. L. (2006). The role of communication and management support in lean manufacturing implementation. *Management Decision, 44*(2), 228–245.

Yukl, G., Gordon, A., & Taber, T. (2002). A hierarchical taxonomy of leadership behavior: Integrating a half century of behavior research. *Journal of Leadership and Organizational Studies, 9*, 15–32.

Zifreund, W. (1966). *Konzept für ein Training des Lehrverhaltens mit Fernseh-Aufzeichungen in Kleingruppen-Seminaren. (Conceptualization of training teaching behavior with video-recordings in small groups).* Berlin, Germany: Cornelsen.

# Appendix A

## Guidelines Day 1 (8 hours)

- Welcome
- Introductions among participants
- Leadership theories part I
- Competences and skills for content level
- Lunch break
- Micro-teaching video session 1
- Break
- Feedback and small group discussion

## Guidelines Day 2 (8 hours)

- Review
- Leadership theories part II
- Break
- Competences and skills for relationship level
- Lunch break
- Micro-teaching video session 2
- Break
- Feedback and small group discussion
- Evaluation (questionnaire and oral feedback)

# 25

# An Examination of Key Factors That Influence Employee Learning in the Workplace

*G. J. Schwartz*

*South African Police Service*

This chapter is based on findings of a recent study conducted by the author on workplace learning in a law enforcement context. The study was conducted to better understand the ways in which senior managers and personnel involved in the teaching of research learn in the workplace. While the organization has emphasized the development of research skills as a necessary and important problem-solving skill for its senior management cadre, most senior managers do not share the same sentiment. Senior managers are required to attend specific skills development learning programs such as the Executive Development Learning Program (EDLP), which, along with leadership and management modules, contains a research module. The research module requires learners to conduct research on a specific problem in the workplace and to propose solutions to the organization's management to address the problem and similar problems elsewhere in the organization. This study further explored how the organization learned to teach research methodology and how the learning program evolved over time. The findings of this study confirmed several arguments in the workplace learning debate and point to aspects that need further investigation. I share the main findings by approach and the broader debate on workplace learning.

Illeris (2011, p. 37) argues that recent studies, such as the one referred to above, tended to focus on either the individual's knowledge acquisition process in which employees are expected to meet the qualification requirements of the workplace, or on organizational learning in which individuals' learning stimulate the development of the enterprise (Illeris, 2011, p. 38). The focus on the individual's effort is also found in adult education in which the experience and interest of the individual in learning is acknowledged. Other perspectives, which focus on the workplace (the learning organization), show interest in what the organization learns over and above, or independent from the sum of the learning of the individuals. Theories of situated learning of Lave and Wenger (1991) and Community of Practice of Wenger (1998a) for instance focused on the workplace as point of learning. These theories are based on the belief that the individual will automatically move from legitimate peripheral participation, toward a central competent

*The Wiley Handbook of Global Workplace Learning*, First Edition.
Edited by Vanessa Hammler Kenon and Sunay Vasant Palsole.

position by means of a learning process in the workplace (Illeris, 2011, p. 38). In yet another stance to workplace learning, the focus is on the interaction between the social and the individual (Illeris, 2011, p. 38). Billett and Choy (2013, p. 270) later argued that the relationship between personal and social contributions to learning through and for work warrants further elaboration. To this end, this chapter explores aspects of work, place and personal and social contributions to learning. However, while this chapter elaborates on the factors that influence learning in a law enforcement environment in which strong militaristic organizational culture impacts on learning, the study extends the work of Campbell who studied learning of police recruits in a police culture. He concludes that

> ... development in adults needs to account for the pre-existing dispositions, histories and ontogenetic selves which the adult learner brings to the new practice experience. These constructs guide and shape the effortful task of learning and therefore determine the pathway and outcomes of processes of development... *(Campbell, 2012, p. 81)*

Billett and Choy (2013, p. 264) studied learning through work to uncover emerging perspectives and challenges related to work, place and learning as ingredients of workplace learning. The authors argue that due to changes in the workplace and in the education system where there is a growing need for practical experience in the workplace to be offered as part of the curriculum, learning is greatly focused on what is needed for a particular job or requirement in the workplace. The workplace requires employees not only to learn how to master particular skills to do a job, but also places an additional expectation on its employees to learn from and engage with others, such as supervisors, to learn from them certain insights, procedures and dispositions (Billett & Choy, 2013, p. 265). Yet, workplace learning is influenced by the individual's own purpose and interests in the vocation and workplace (Billett, 2009, p. 831). It follows that there has to be some consideration for the individual and social contributions to learning. To this end, Billett and Choy (2013, p. 266) argue that there are three emerging concepts that explain learning in circumstances of work. These are changes in the requirements for work, conceptual understandings about the processes of learning, and elaborated views of relations between the social and personal contributions to learning and development (Billett & Choy, 2013, p. 266). For Malloch and Cairns (2010, p. 3), the concepts of work, place and learning should be considered more broadly due to the considerable changes of the last number of years and due to the new thinking inspired by the combination of these concepts. In this chapter, I highlight the key factors that influenced workplace learning in an organization during the teaching of research methodology.

## The Changing Nature of Work, Workplace and Learning

My study strongly confirmed Malloch and Cairns' (2010, p. 4) statement that work is much more than the mere completion of tasks. For them, work is done either individually or with another, to contribute to productive endeavors or achieving goals in exchange for payment, or without payment. While the output of such activities may result in positive recognition or remuneration from others, work also has a negative connotation because of its history of forced labor and slavery. The concept of work has therefore different meanings for different people. Workplaces where work traditionally was done and homes where work was traditionally not done, were, until recently, seen as two inherently different places. In the workplace, work is the act of carrying out labor. At home, our normal day-to-day tasks were regarded as something different to the act of carrying out labor. This idea, as argued by Malloch and Cairns (2010, p. 4), is outdated, as several homes have become workplaces for home-based enterprises in recent years. The workplace has therefore become a personal and negotiated location where one often does work without being paid, or where employed time may not be spent working. Executives in my recent study, consistently explained how they had done their work at home if they had spent time on their research projects during office hours, or vice versa. Working on their research project (learning) was regarded as part of the job which they were being paid for, even if it was done in their private time. Executives' practice of doing "work" in their own time in order to complete their learning points me to Malloch and Cairns' (2010, p. 6) conclusion that work is intentional; as it requires effort and purpose. The critical element in this argument is found in the purpose or motivation for doing the work. It makes sense that concerting efforts for tasks related to one's employment at work or in private time, whether or not for remuneration, would be considered work. Conversely, effort to learn a new hobby or social activity that do not relate to one's employment will not be regarded as work in the general conception of work as the purpose for the activity is other than for work. Remuneration is for all practical reasons not a necessary element of the concept of work.

In support of Malloch and Cairns (2010, p. 4), Billett and Choy (2013, p. 266) argue that the nature of work is changing and that learning acquired for entry into the workplace is not enough to last a lifetime of employment. There is a growing reliance on conceptual and symbolic knowledge, often brought about by electronic technologies that are introduced to perform job activities. Ways of learning these new skills in the workplace therefore introduce new challenges and these challenges or changes affect both employers and employees (Billett & Choy, 2013, p. 266). However, the type of work that one does in or for the workplace matters as Chappell, Farrell, Scheeres and Solomon (2000, p. 3) argue that some knowledge cannot be transferred in a workplace, but has to be generated at the site of work, which often is located at a separate location than the boundaries of the actual workplace of the organization. For example, learning to function within a multinational team at a construction site in a different country with its own unique regulatory requirements may create an opportunity to construct knowledge of different working conditions and cultures at a working site away from the normal workplace. Knowledge is also becoming increasingly short term due to constant change in the workplace. The authors explain that learning in the workplace is an ongoing process that signals the transitory nature of knowledge and emphasizes the importance of situated formal and formal learning. Formal learning opportunities are generally structured interventions with classroom and a degree of experiential learning in the form of assignments to be completed in the workplace. Situated formal learning points to the value of experience in the construction of learning in real life working activities where workers are confronted by various activities and resources (Lee & Ross, 2003, p. 16). The importance of the situated learning is demonstrated in one of the four cases studied by Chappell et al. (2000). Evidence suggested that the actors (new teachers) relied on previous experience to perform better in their new environments. The teachers emphasized the practical over the theoretical, applied knowledge over academic knowledge, experiential knowledge over disciplinary knowledge and contextualized knowledge over generalizable knowledge (Chappell et al., 2000, p. 6). Similarly, executives that had been confronted by real problems in the workplace generally completed their research projects and produced better products. These points fit in with Jacobs and Park's (2009) proposed conceptual framework for workplace learning in the sense that it emphasizes the importance of the location of learning, in particular the on-the-job learning dimension.

Sambrook (2005) looked at work by differentiating between learning at work and learning in work. In Sambrook's (2005) argument, the idea of attending some sort of planned training intervention represents the act of learning *at work*. Learning *in work* refers to learning while working, or learning as a result of working. Activities such as observing others when they work, asking questions, solving problems, participating in discussions and mentoring others form part of the informal learning taking place. Sambrook (2005) expands this idea by arguing that opportunities for workplace learning exist outside the boundaries of the work setting (outside work), such as when two or more separate organizational teams work together on an initiative or skills that you develop on your own. The term "work" therefore does not necessarily mean actively contributing to the product or service of the organization, but can include the act of learning how to contribute to the product or service of the workplace. Moreover, such learning does not have to occur at the employee's normal place of work. Finlay (2008, p. 73) provided more insights in this regard. Finlay (2008, p. 73) explored the learning and development of further education lecturers in both university and workplaces. He conducted his study in the framework of Engeström's (2001) contemporary activity theory, which holds that learning takes place across boundaries. In this view, learning takes place across different activity systems that interact with one another, such as the workplace and a university. Employees who work together on a joint project of the workplace and the university, for instance, will learn from each other during project meetings (or boundary clinics as Finlay refers to it) where they "pick up" the language, culture and technical knowledge of the other workplace for use in their own workplace or activity system (Finlay, 2008, p. 86). According to Finlay (2008, p. 86), his participants utilized various resources such as a reflective journal, ideas, teaching strategies, fellow students and a community of teachers to shape their identity and to make sense of their practice and workplace. Participants in my study sought guidance from their peers in other settings within the organization, regardless of obvious differences between the settings, research methods or topics.

Jacobs and Park (2009, p. 143) describe three variables in the workplace that affect learning. First, the location of the learning experience plays a role. Learning takes place in the actual work setting when "on-the-job," while learning occurs away from work when the employee is "off-the-job." Jacobs and Park (2009, p. 145) argue that when learning takes place on-the-job, the learning takes place near or at the actual work setting, but off-the-job learning takes place off-site in another facility away from the actual work site. Second, the degree of planning involved in work activities makes learning structured or unstructured. When learning is unstructured, there is little evidence that a systems approach was followed as the outcome was not planned for. When there is evidence that a systems approach was followed in the learning process, such learning is regarded as structured, as the outcomes of the learning are defined. Third, the role of the trainer in learning at work determines the level of learner engagement and initiative. The trainer is passive when he or she plays a limited role in the facilitation of learning. In this case the trainee engages the trainer as and when needed during the learning process. The trainer is regarded as active when playing a direct role throughout the learning process. Jacobs and Park's (2009) proposed framework positions learning either in or outside the actual site of work. In this regard, executives indicated that they often found themselves thinking about their research projects and their attempts to uncover the causal factors of their problems at work when they are driving, preparing for work or when they discuss their projects at social events. The tendency of thinking about work when not at work breaks down the boundaries between work and home. In fact, for executives, such boundaries only exist in the mind of the individual, because they made no distinction between their actual task and learning when they worked after office hours on their research projects.

For Torraco (1999, p. 256) the integration of learning and work, such as whether or not there are still clear boundaries between work and learning, needed more clarity. Järvensivu and Koski (2012) explicated in this regard that employees and employers are contractually tied together and that the employer has the right to determine how the contracted working hours are spent, whether on work or learning. The authors found that in modern organizations the employer still defines the content and times of learning. The employer determines what should be learned, a notion that presents a challenge to the concepts of adult education and learning. Antila (2005 in Järvensivu & Koski, 2012) argues that the borders of work are blurring and that working life is being extended to voluntary overtime at home. Working hours are therefore no longer clearly separated from free time. Learning that is commissioned by the employer will thus extend into free time as employees take their work home. Workplace learning is consequently not necessarily done during office or working hours (Järvensivu & Koski, 2012).

The term "place" has several interpretations as it can relate to the place where the job is done as site of work or to a virtual location. Malloch and Cairns (2010, p. 6) explain that the most common connotation of a workplace is in line with a modern view of it being a physical location, but it might also be spiritual when viewed from an anthropological point of view. Brookfield (1991) regards the workplace as a resource for thinking, acting and reflecting. Billett (2002a, p. 56) supports this view. He explains that when it comes to learning, educational settings and workplaces are seen as places of learning because they represent different instances of social practices in which learning occurs through participation. Billett (2002a, p. 56) asserts that the needs of workplaces and educational institutions have evolved over time due to their particular cultural requirements. The term "place" therefore does not necessarily refer to an unchanging or stagnant space or location, but in fact to a space that is evolving, and where learning takes place. Billett (2002a, p. 57) draws the attention to the workplace as a site for learning as it represents the only and most viable location for many workers to learn and develop their vocational practice. Understanding workplaces therefore remains an urgent matter as they form the center of lifelong learning practices. The workplace offers opportunities to engage in work, provides the type of tasks that individuals are permitted to participate in, and provides a place where they can get guidance in their work. These aspects are needed in order to evaluate what and how employees learn at work (Billett, 2002a, p. 57). From a psychological perspective, the term place can refer to where we find ourselves in our minds at any given time. The mind is the place where we think, solve problems and consider ourselves. Malloch and Cairns (2010, p. 7) summarize their thoughts about the term "place" as follows:

> Place ... in relation to learning and cognition ... cover a wide range of ideas and situations ... refer to physical or spiritual locations and also relate to spaces in which we see ourselves as people and learners ... [and] can refer to where it is we think we operate cognitively as we think and learn (Intra-Personal Place)

The workplace may thus be trapped in our minds when we are not at work, yet still pondering over work-related matters and our roles at work. This raises the issue of belongingness. Warhurst (2006, p. 112) studied participatory learning among peers in a university setting by using the insights of situated theory. In his deliberation, Warhurst (2006, p. 114) explicates that membership of a community is an intrinsic condition for learning and that belonging to a community results in participation in practices at work. He also mentions how some participants in his study expressed feelings of "being isolated." In other words, there was distance between the individual (learner), the social group (colleagues) and work (practice) that resulted in limited learning and development. Perhaps this is indicative of distance between the employee or learner and the workplace or space due to the emotional disconnect between the employee and the place of learning. Other participants in Warhurst's (2006, p. 115) study stated that they really felt part of something, expressing their belongingness to the group and place. Again, in this positive stance, the employee or learner made a psychological connection with the workplace as explained by Malloch and Cairns (2010, p. 7). Pondering over work when not at work could constitute acts of learning as a consequence of reflecting on whether or not we belong in a social setting. In my study, participants explained how they thought of ways to provide better support to senior managers when the develop research skills. Participants felt part of a research team and regularly reflected on their learners' progress when they were not at work.

It follows then that as the role of work is changing employees find themselves alternating between the space in which they work and learn. As employees work, they learn. Much of this learning experience, wherever acquired, is carried into other social settings where workers reflect on the day's work. In such instances, the employee might find themselves neither at work, nor working, but still by learning when meaning is attached to the activities of the job. The workplace has changed from being a physical structure or virtual place to also include a psychological location, the mind of the worker.

## Factors Influencing Workplace Learning

Regardless of one's stance toward the workplace or what is considered to constitute work and learning, one cannot ignore the factors that influence learning in the workplace. These factors may vary in nature as it may be inherent to the institution or to the individual or it may be attributed to factors that are independent of the institution or individual.

### Organizational Factors

Workplaces differ, which means that there is no single way to do things as far as workplace learning pedagogy is concerned. Before embarking on a specific workplace learning pedagogy, several workplace learning-influencing factors need to be considered. Consider, for instance, adequate support structures and systems for workplace learning. Many learners' inability to complete their programs or apprenticeships can be contributed to a workplace that either fails to provide support to learners or is challenging or confronting in its nature (Billett & Choy, 2013, p. 271). Providing learning experience is not enough. Learners should be able to gain adequate experience and support in the workplace and access opportunities to integrate them with educational programs. Moreover, on order to ensure that the quality of their learning is enhanced, support throughout the entire process—pre-, during and post-learning experience—must be provided to learners (Billett, 2011, p. 15).

The workplace environment and organization further impacts workplace learning. While workplaces that offer limited career growth and development opportunities may not be perceived as an enabling learning environment, Tynjälä (2008, p. 141) argues that the most important contextual factor related to workplace learning is the way in which work is organized. This follows the logic that, where work is organized in a narrow scope, there is little opportunity to learn and for making autonomous decisions because such work is normally repetitive in nature. Meanwhile, in work situations where employees are confronted with new challenges, experience job rotation and are exposed to opportunities for autonomous decision-making, they will be in a position to learn more.

The changing nature of work places further influence workplace learning. Workplaces tend to attract entry-level employees with high-level technical skills and once such learners are in the workplace, they are offered very little learning opportunities or experiences (Council on Higher Education [CHE], 2011, p. 20). The differences between workplace and university knowledge and structures make it difficult for learners to understand and derive meaning from what they encounter. Universities' theoretical knowledge and workplaces' contextualized knowledge pose a challenge for meaningful articulation between them (CHE, 2011, p. 21).

Mentors, in the form of qualified co-workers, also carry with them the ability to influence an individual's workplace learning. When experts are disinclined to provide support, advice or mentoring opportunities, the learning outcomes may be constrained (Billett, 1995, p. 25). Qualified co-workers may play a valuable role in disseminating expert knowledge in the workplace and novices in the workplace need to embrace the opportunity and find, access and learn from such knowledge (Torraco, 1999). In doing so, it allows novices a chance to become old-timers that form part of the community of practice (Torraco, 1999). Situations where there is a lack of expertise or no access to such expertise may cause employees to seek expertise outside the workplace.

Another aspect that may influence workplace learning pertains to incentives. When there are no actual or perceived rewards or incentives for individuals, it may curb their motivation to enter workplace training programs. Individuals form perceptions of the value of learning or incentives, based on their own interpretations of the real world that they are living and working in (Mullins, 1999, p. 824).

It has been posited that forming part of a community of practice is an intrinsic condition for learning (Warhurst, 2006, p. 114). Such participation in the distinctive practices of a specific community will see learning become inevitable and incidental (Warhurst, 2006, p. 114). Learners learn in relation to other members of a community (Lave & Wenger, 1991, p. 93). Moreover, membership in a community of practice allows learners to construct the meaning underpinning practice (Warhurst, 2006, p. 115).

Billett (1995, p. 25) explicates that not all knowledge that workers construct in the workplace is desirable. Employees may develop inappropriate skills if such skills are present in the culture and practice of the workplace. The effectiveness of learning that is embedded in communities of practice, is dependent on guided access to the authentic activities of the community of practice. Without access to authentic activities, there might not be appropriate or desired learning. Additionally, when one argues that learning results from participation in work practices, such participation must be based on the invitational qualities of a workplace. These invitational qualities are influenced by factors that are associated with the norms and practices of the workplace (Billett, 2004, p. 318). Learning is a product of the affordances resulting from the continuity of activities within the practice. The continued development of skills through mentoring activities in a workplace, for example, could be a method of ensuring continuity of work processes. An organization's culture and practices regarding workplace learning may thus influence workplace learning.

That being said, it is important to bear in mind that though workplaces may regulate participation, learning still dependent on the individual's agency and intent to engage with the practice of learning in the workplace. Learners are thus active parties in workplace learning (Billett, 2004, p. 319).

## Individual Factors

It is evident that workplace learning is also influenced by individual factors such as learner agency. Much of what employees learn is controlled by the employee self: employees' personal agency determines what they learn and when they learn, especially since they also exercise their discretion in harnessing opportunities for development in the workplace. As such, learners exercise what Bandura (2001 in Malloch & Cairns, 2010, p. 10) terms "agentic intent" in their interaction with others and the social environment.

In the same way, individuals' attitudes and identities influence their workplace learning in that affects their access to and retention of workplace learning. For instance, Blåka and Filstad (2007) argue that learning in a CoP is more complex than Wenger (1998a) described. Novices do not automatically form part of the CoP, but it is rather the case that the novices' own expectations, abilities and desires to become a member of the CoP determines whether they are accepted into the CoP. Access to a CoP is therefore reliant on the novices' initiative and engagement with invitational qualities in the workplace. Consequently, one must consider novices' learning processes in conjunction with their expectations and abilities as this will determine the extent of their relationships with established members of the CoP.

Furthermore, individuals' ability to critically analyze and reflect influences their workplace learning experience. Boud, Keogh and Walker (1985, p. 19) refers to reflective learning, a process which sees individuals generating meaning from experience. However, learning from reflection depends on the degree to which individuals share their learning with others. Contextual factors such as the organizational climate, interpersonal relationships and the characteristics of the work itself may influence the individual's willingness and opportunity to share their learning (Billett, 2001). In addition, before learning can take place, individuals must have the ability to draw conclusions from their abstractions when they reflect on their experience. There has to be a certain willingness and readiness to reflect on their practice to learn from and to share the learning. Blanchard and Thacker (2007) point to personal factors such as having limited intellectual ability and memory limitations as barriers for learning in the workplace.

From this, it is evident that the individual's own personal factors (motivation, reflection, attitudes etc.) may influence their workplace ability. However, while there are factors that can be attributed to the individual or the organization, there are outside factors that may also influence workplace learning.

## External Factors

Torraco (1999, p. 256) posits that the nature of present instructional models of learning in tertiary institutions do not address the features of the task environment. The result is that entry level employees often do not have the required skills sets to function effectively from the start. Such employees may thus feel overwhelmed by the new conditions in the work environment, leaving them underprepared for learning challenging workplace tasks from the onset.

For Ezeokoli (2014, p. 71), who studied psychological factors on adult learning in Nigeria, learning can be severely affected by illiteracy and inability to communicate in English in the workplace. Although this is viewed as an individual aspect that influences learning, it really points to the external environment that does not prepare adults for the workplace.

While external development opportunities and the availability for scholarships and grants may encourage employees to work harder and learn faster, it seldom reaches the level of the lower end workers at those in managerial positions, who control learning in the organization, take up most of these better learning opportunities.

## Learning

### Workplace Learning Is Mostly Informal

One of the key findings in my study centered on the nature of learning, particularly that workplace learning is mostly informal, often unnoticed and not acknowledged. Participants generally indicated that they had learned more from their practical research projects than learning theory in class. Executives thus learnt to do research through working on real life problems in their work environments. Jacobs and Park (2009, p. 141) argue that informal learning recognizes that the acquisition of knowledge and skills in the work setting does not occur from organized programs only. They assert that informal learning occurs in situations that are usually not intended for learning, especially in the workplace. Individuals learn in the workplace because of their intellectual curiosity, self-directedness and self-efficacy (Beckett & Hager, 2002). Billett (2002b) explains that workplace learning involves both structured and unstructured learning that takes place through on-the-job activities. While formal learning is mostly presented in a structured way, such as in a classroom setting, informal learning can be structured or unstructured, planned or unplanned (Lohman, 2005, p. 44) and is usually experiential in nature, involving dialectical processes of action and reflection (Marsick, Volpe and Watkins, 1999 in Lohman, 2005, p. 44).

Lohman (2005, p. 44) draws from Doornbos, Bolhuis, and Simons (2004) when she asserts that workplace learning is activated by activities that require the handling of novel, ambiguous problems. These activities may also form part of some structured or sanctioned effort to enable learning, such as mentoring, coaching, job rotation, job shadowing and projects (Billett, 2003; Marsick & Watkins, 1997) or may form part of some self-initiated study (Jacobs & Park, 2009, p. 141). Activities such as reflection on oneself in relation to the job, learning from mistakes, vision sharing, challenging group think, asking for feedback, experimentation, sharing knowledge and awareness of employability promote informal workplace learning (Van Woerkom, Nijhof, & Nieuwenhuis, 2002, p. 376 in Lohman, 2005, p. 44). Workplace learning should therefore not be underestimated as approximately 87% of learning that impacts on one's job is informal in nature and takes place over time and in the social context of the workplace (Cross, 2007). Watkins and Marsick (1992, p. 292) had a similar view of Cross' findings. They explicated that individuals learn through collaboration, mutual problem-solving and the sharing of experience in the workplace. For Tynjälä (2008, p. 133) informal learning in the workplace is unintentional learning which is supported by intentional learning, characterized by the absence of formal curricula and prescribed outcomes, is contextual and relying on contextual reasoning. Informal learning is also focused on tool use and mental activities, produces implicit and tacit knowledge and situation specific competencies or learning outcomes that are not always predictable. The emphasis is on work and experiences that are based on the learner as worker. Informal learning is collaborative, built on practical wisdom and resulting new competences are treated holistically with no distinction between knowledge and skills.

Executives showed a tendency to rely on two very practical approaches in their attempt to complete their research projects. They treated their research projects as actual work problems that had to be resolved and regularly reflected on their progress.

## Reflection in Workplace Learning

Dewey's reflective thinking conceptualization (1978, Original work published 1910) pictured reflection on an individual level as complex and multifaceted. For Dewey (1978), reflection included the triggering stimulus that challenges existing habits to create an environment of uncertainty. In return, these uncertainties block the usual responses and lead to reflective thought. Dewey therefore explicated that reflective thinking is an "active, persistent, and careful consideration of any belief or supposed form of knowledge ... and the further conclusions ... to establish belief upon a firm basis of evidence and rationality" (Dewey, 1978, p. 118). Dewey (1978) regarded reflection as a process that includes framing, anticipatory thinking, testing and elaboration, but the core of reflection is the conscious ability to apply former experience to new problem-solving situations. Boud et al., (1985, p. 19) expanded Dewey's (1978) notion of critical thinking with their concept of learning. They argue that reflection as far as learning is concerned, is a generic term for "intellectual and affective activities in which individuals engage to explore their experiences in order to lead to new understandings and appreciations." They subsequently describe reflection as "the intermediate that allows people to generate meaning from an experience" and explain that reflective learning are based on one's own experience, including one's thoughts, feelings and actions before and after the experience. These reflective processes involve the return to experience, re-attending to feelings and the re-evaluation of experience.

Participants in my study, without exception, referred to situations where they had taken a break from their research projects to discuss their progress with their study leaders, or to discuss their findings with peers. In their discussion with colleagues, participants reflected on practical exercises and class activities to overcome challenges in the workplace such as to read reports more critically, to prepare better before attending management meetings and to engage in critical discussion before making judgment. Elkjaer (2004) asserts that individual acquisition of skills and knowledge result from these reflective thinking processes and experience. Further, that the integration of learning through reflection in workplace practice rests on the collaboration of co-workers and interaction with peers. This notion, that reflection is socially practiced when individuals learn through self-regulation and participation in workplace activities, is supported by Warhurst (2006, p. 117) and Knipfer, Kump, Wessel and Cress (2013, p. 30). Knipfer et al. (2013, p. 30) argue that a learner's reflection might also be based on relevant peer or colleagues' experience when the learner makes sense of the experience in terms of his or her own practice at work. There has to be a conscious evaluation of an experience to learn from it and to utilize such enlightenment in future situations (Knipfer et al., 2013, p. 38). Taking a broader view of reflection, Knipfer et al. (2013, p. 36), posit that reflection could also result from experience of rules and routines in a workplace. The shared practice in the workplace is then used to reflect on for the construction of new knowledge, often in collaborative practices found in communities of practice, where practice of specific knowledge is generated.

## Learning Through Problem-Solving

Hodkinson et al., (2004, p. 21) propose enhancing learning opportunities to improve workplace learning by creating more expansive learning environments that are in line with what learners' want, their needs and what they respond to. Theoretically, this implies that learning opportunities that learners want should then be prioritized over those that management think they need, but in practice such notion will be impractical as employers determine what skills are needed in the workplace. Learning opportunities therefore have to take into account pervasive power differentials and workplace inequalities. In my study, very few participants showed interest in developing research skills, but as it formed part of their executive development, they had to comply with the organizational rules. Participants indicated that organizational needs took priority over their personal development in the workplace. They also received little support for their research projects in the workplace. Their learning experience therefore largely involved solving their research problems while dealing with their daily work challenges. Solving problems at work is part of workplace learning. To this end, Vaughan (2008, p. 4) proposes several different approaches to workplace learning that may assist employers in the development of their workers. These include:

- Off-the-job training that entails learning assignments that are related to problem-solving and task-centered activities linked to the organization's business intent;
- Structured learning in the workplace that is managed and validated by external providers of training in partnership with the employer or co-workers. In this case, there should be strong links between the classroom learning and the workplace activities to serve as motivation to learn;
- Informal, pervasive learning that forms the basis of the context that informs the practices, routines and behaviors of the workplace, and enables the formation of communities or the joining of communities and the reconstruction of professional identities. Learning involves the employee becoming an insider of such communities, learning to speak their language and his/her aligning

individual behavior to that of the community by acquiring the community's subjective views; and

- Intentional on the job learning that is structured and organized according to specific pedagogy. On the job learning is intended to develop specific employee competencies. This is done through the support, structure and monitoring of progress by structuring workplace learning through processes such as job rotation and exposure to more challenging tasks. This can also be done through participative action-reflection sessions where employees work together to brainstorm to solve problems and also hold debriefing sessions during which feedback is given on experiences (Vaughan, 2008, p. 5).

Gosling and Moon (2001 in CHE, 2011, p. 19) provide a model to implement Vaughan's strategies effectively in the workplace. It holds that workplace learning opportunities must provide for concrete experience in which learners actively take part in the activities. This aspect requires more engagement than just observing the activity at work. Learners must be exposed to reflective observation, which requires learners to experience and observe particular elements of the activity, and to reflect on that activity later to consider what has happened there. Learners must go through a process of abstract conceptualization in which they use inductive reasoning to analyze observations, explain these and formulate theories about their conclusions. In the final step, learners should be allowed to actively experiment with what they have learned by testing their theories or conceptions of new learning in the workplace.

As was experienced by executives in my study, the challenges facing workplace learning are mostly found in workplaces where there are inadequate structures and systems to support workplace learning (CHE, 2011, p. 20). Participants referred to the inability of co-workers to comprehend what they were doing during their research projects. They could not seek assistance within the workplace other than communicating with their study leaders. Participants ascribed their challenges to senior managers being experts in particular fields of work only. It was therefore difficult for them to develop research skills in the workplace where little research expertise are present. In Torraco's (1999) view, the qualified co-worker holds the expert knowledge that is distributed in the workplace, and newcomers need to find, access and learn from this knowledge, but certainly, this knowledge refers to the practice or core business of the organization. Billett (2011, p. 12) adds that affordances in social settings, such as the support offered by more experienced workers, may be welcomed by some learners, while others may find such support unhelpful (Billett & Choy, 2013, p. 273). Learning through everyday practice might not be enough to maintain currency of knowledge or to sustain employability (Billett & Choy, 2013, p. 272).

## Organizational Support Needed for Integration of Learning into Practice

While participants struggled to understand why they had to develop research skills as part of their executive development, they still complied with the instruction of their superiors. They completed the research methodology part of the research module successfully in the classroom, but several learners failed to complete their research projects in the field. Those who completed their studies ascribe their success to supportive commanders or working conditions, but those who could not complete their projects blamed the organization for not supporting them in the workplace. As senior managers, they had to take care of their core business first and then after work try to work on their research. This measure proved inadequate as they could not access data sources after hours. Billett (2002a, p. 56) explains that such tendency of structuring learning experiences in workplaces are often directed to sustain practice. This has the effect that workplaces are developing their employees in narrow scopes of competences or skills for which the workplace (organization) is given funding specifically to develop employees in terms of the skills needs of the country. Despite this developmental effort, workplaces are often confronting and challenging or unsupportive of workplace learners, resulting in many learners not completing their programs (Billett & Choy, 2013, p. 271). There is also no guarantee that workers will learn what they have to, because learners construct knowledge based on what they know (cognitive experience) and what they have experienced (pre-mediate experience). Their learning is thus unpredictable (Billett, 2011, p. 13) and to overcome this, workplaces have to provide authentic learning experiences.

## Authentic Work Experience

Whereas participants in my study frequently mentioned the lack of understanding and support in the workplace during their research projects, they also found it hard to access research experts in the workplace. Participants indicated that they expected to find mentors in the field, but this was unlikely as organizational research was situated at the Head Office only. To this end, Billett and Choy (2013, p. 268) argue that affordances to learn from experienced workers are but one aspect of learning in the workplace. The other is the level of interest, motivation and ability to learn intentionally through such engagements. Another aspect that needs clarity is why engagement in authentic work activities is so effective in building the required knowledge needed for work performance. What is certain is that learning through work is a process (Billett & Choy, 2013, p. 269). In this regard, my study showed that authentic learning experiences are closer related to the practice (policing, legal expertise, accounting, etc.) than the development of research skills, which the organization viewed as important problem-solving skills for senior managers.

Billett and Choy (2013, p. 270) explicate that the mediating factors of situation, society and culture are central to understanding, learning and advancing the knowledge and skills needed for work, even though learning is a process in which the individual must be engaged. However, two surfacing concepts that explain the relation between personal and social contributions to learning are the "practice of communities" and "bounded agency." The concept of "practice in communities" (CoP) refers to practices of working communities where people's participation and the enactment of these practices are salient. "Bounded agency" refers to the means by which individuals use discretion to negotiate between what they are able and willing to do (Billett & Choy, 2013, p. 270). Crossing such set boundaries, both personal and organizational, promotes the inevitability of learning. The concept of boundaries and boundary crossing in learning, therefore, not only refers to institutional facts but also contains personal facts. Institutional rules and culture may serve as boundaries in the workplace that have to be crossed in order to "enter" into a position from which learning can take place. Crossing personal boundaries in relation to workplace learning can refer to taking the leap from a current skills level to engaging in activities that require a much higher level of skill, or even learning to trust co-workers when working together in teams. To this end, my findings indicate that even though the organization has a very clear policy on workplace learning, it is not known or implemented by managers. Participants were thus largely left to devise their own ways and means to complete their projects. The majority of the senior managers and executives found it too troublesome to execute their projects. This fact emphasized the need for commitment and will of employees to engage in learning opportunities in the workplace.

## Deliberate Actions Needed for Workplace Learning

With regard to affordances to learn from other in a CoP, my study confirmed that even though invitational qualities are present to join a CoP, participants exercised discretion whether or not they wanted to take part in the activities of the community. Invitational qualities refer to those aspects (such as working in a pleasant working environment, level of collaboration and collegiality, type of work and the perception of being successful) present in a CoP that would attract co-workers that are not part of the CoP to seek association with such CoP. Li, Grimshaw, Nielsen, Judd, et al. (2009) explain the elements that impact on the individual's discretion to take part in a CoP activities. Firstly, the domain should create common ground and outline the boundaries for employees to decide what is worth sharing and how to do that. Secondly, the community should create the social structure that will facilitate learning through interaction and relationships with others. Lastly, the practice should stipulate the shared repertoires of resources, which include documents, ideas, experiences, information and ways of addressing recurring problems. In addition, the group needs to have a facilitator or supervisor to manage the day-to-day activities. In this case, the term group refers to a CoP, which Wenger, McDermott, and Snyder (2002) portray as different to a group of interest. Organizations can optimize the dissemination of knowledge by focusing on the domain, community and practice elements of a CoP (Wenger et al., 2002), but the decision to learning in a CoP still lies with the individual. Wenger (1998b, p. 100) asserts that the approximation of participation must engage individuals, especially newcomers, and provide a sense of how the CoP operates.

Warhurst (2006, pp. 111–122) takes a more general approach to workplace learning by emphasizing a number of important considerations. He argues that formal teaching should be supported by contextual learning in the workplace.

The individual should be exposed to practice in a setting that is true to that particular practice. Learning takes place as a facet of belonging to communities of practice in the workplace. Learning will be an inevitable and incidental occurrence arising from the act of participation in the distinctive practice of a specific community. Learning in the workplace results from the construction of meaning and meaning-making of experience. Meaning is dependent on the constant juxtaposition between the possibilities that language offers and the constraints it imposes on learners. Learning is a consequence of doing and experiencing legitimate peripheral participation. This entail that learners must be engaged in authentic, legitimate practice, be accepted as legitimate participants by established colleagues and need to start their learning from the periphery of practice and experience a centripetal trajectory over time to the core of the community's practice. Learning takes place in the process of becoming someone or something in the workplace and the construction of identity. Learning takes place over time as the individual transforms and gains a new professional identity during which the outcome of learning is a way of being. Learning is both social and individual. Learning is social in nature when constructed through participation and individual when constructed through self-regulation and reflective practices. (Warhurst, 2006, pp. 111–122).

Finally, for Jawitz (2009), who focused on the individual habitus in the workplace, the context of new learning sites needs to be understood before being introduced to learners, especially when creating opportunities for learning within CoPs. The downside of not being sensitive to the learning context is that individual learners may have to learn in isolation. Jawitz (2009, p. 613) subsequently argues for the need to support relationships within CoPs to enable understandings and negotiations around the distributed knowledge of practice.

## Unintended Learning

When the employer affected more pressure on the senior managers to complete their studies, several of them reverted to unethical research methods or submitted heavily plagiarized reports. They tried to cheat the system. This raised a concern as the managers had learned to deal with pressure in inappropriate ways, which does not fit well with the ethos of senior managers. To this end, Billett (1995, p. 25) posits that there are several challenges in the workplace that impede on learning. He explicates that not all knowledge that workers construct in the workplace is desirable. Employees may develop inappropriate skills if such skills are present in the culture and practice of the workplace. The effectiveness of learning that is embedded in communities of practice, is dependent on guided access to the authentic activities of the community of practice. Without access to authentic activities, there might not be appropriate or desired learning. In addition, the reluctance of experts to provide advice, mentoring or support may inhibit the outcomes of learning. Situations where there is a lack of expertise or no access to such expertise may cause employees to seek expertise outside the workplace. Lastly, learners may not be capable of developing conceptual knowledge through workplace learning (Billett, 1995, p. 25).

### Organizational Readiness for Workplace Learning

A number of participants in my study expressed feelings of being overwhelmed by their research projects when they returned to their workplaces. They became used to the support provided to them while at the training academy. Part of their challenge was to hold their superiors to their promises of support given before the start of the learning time. Participants generally received little support when they left the academy as they had to account for their contractual performance obligations. The organization could not afford learners the time to learn because the learners' core responsibilities were not shared by co-workers. Yet, Billett (2011, p. 15) proposes that learners should be supported before, during and after their learning experiences to enhance their quality of learning. This is possible by implementing specific pedagogical practices, which if applied carefully, can support workplace learning (Billett & Choy, 2013, p. 271). First, before entering the workplace, learners need to be orientated to the requirement to effectively engage in the workplace, to be aware of expectations, to know what they have to learn and to understand the means of undertaking that learning. Second, learners need to possess certain capacities to undertake the activities that they could reasonably be expected to master. Third, the expectations about the purpose of support during the learning process and the roles and responsibilities of other parties should be clarified. Fourth, learners, being dependent and interdependent in the workplace, should understand their own roles and responsibilities as their learning is self-directed. Their observations, engagement and interaction should contribute to their learning. Fifth, learners need to be prepared for circumstances where their encounters are unpleasant or confronting in order for them to manage these situations for their own well-being and sense of self (Billett & Choy, 2013, p. 272). However, in my study, I found that it is important to reinforce key concepts after training to support and reinforce the theoretical knowledge. Support can be everything from performance support systems or job aids to managerial support, but unless management reinforces training on the job, workers may resort to short-cuts instead of following the procedure learned in class. To this end, I found that even if the organization had committed to allowing time during office hours (1 day per week for 20 weeks) for senior managers to complete their research projects, it was not enough to see learners through. Employees therefore need to have the desire to learn and to accept responsibility for their development, and the employer has to assess the ability and motivation of employees to master skills, particularly if those skills are not directly linked to the core business of the organization. The study also pointed out that divergence in the workplace can obstruct workplace learning, especially when top management openly disagree about the need for research skills for senior managers. The bulk of senior managers subsequently could not link research skills to their core business and showed little commitment to complete their assignments. When the organization put pressure on them to complete their research projects, they simply submitted work of low quality or colluded not to submit anything at all. Individuals mostly learned to survive and to cope with pressure of the workplace instead of developing research skills.

## Learning Is Greatly Due to Personal Agency

Employees have control over what they learn and when they learn due to personal agency and the discretionary utilization of development affordances in the workplace. In order to learn, learners exercise agentic intent in their interactions with the social environment and with others (Bandura, 2001, pp. 1, 13). Employees learn of their own accord when they observe, imitate and initiate work activities and interactions, but these efforts are not enough to make informed judgments (Billett & Choy, 2013, p. 267). Such individual learning methods do not enable learning of that which is hidden from view or sensation. Learning for work requires tacit knowledge, which is gained through repetitive engagement until it becomes implicit, as well as explicit, as procedural and conceptual knowledge. The concern is that the exact implications of human progress in learning through practice or in the workplace is not known. While older generations have learnt through work and managed to develop conceptual capacities, it is unclear if younger generations can access emerging forms of knowledge through individual effort alone, or whether or not they need access to experts or instructional resources to access learning (Billett & Choy, 2013, p. 267). Different generations of workers may thus require exposure to alternative learning opportunities and methods to encourage their engagement with the learning opportunity. Employees further extend their knowledge from alternative interactions in the social or cultural contexts rather than from their independent effort at work (Tynjälä, 2008, p. 132).

To this end, when one argues that learning results from participation in work practices, such participation must be based on the invitational qualities of a workplace. These invitational qualities are influenced by factors that are associated with the norms and practices of the workplace (Billett, 2004, p. 318). Firstly, learning is a product of the affordances resulting from the continuity of activities within the practice. The continued development of skills through mentoring activities in a workplace, for example, could be a method of ensuring continuity of work processes. Secondly, even though participation in work can be regulated by workplaces, learning still resides in the individual's agency and intention to engage with the practice in the workplace. Learning is not just dictated by the situation, but is rather a product of learner agency and intent to negotiate participation in learning activities. Learners are thus not passive parties in learning in the workplace (Billett, 2004, p. 319). This is an important aspect of workplace learning. Whatever the situation at work, workers will either learn something useful from it or develop undesirable attitudes or skills when they respond to invitations to engage.

## Learning Is in Communities of Practice

In essence, there were three small groups of actors in my study. The first group was the research trainers and administrators who were involved with the learners from day one until the certification of the successful learners. The second group was the Research Committee who dealt with the approval of research topics and proposals, and the third group constituted the research panels who consisted of three permanent members and one or two ad hoc members. Each of these three groups had its own way of working and learning. Billett (2004, p. 119) asserts that the thinking and acting of individuals who form part of these three groups are influenced by the practices in their workplaces. The research team, responsible for teaching and administration, and the research panels operated as CoPs. Regular meetings and open communication drew the actors in the setting together, to such extent that they developed their own way of doing things and their own processes and rules that were different to that of the main campus or the organization at large.

A subculture, which was closer to an academic setting, developed so strongly that it challenged the culture practiced at the main campus or larger organization. This is a strong indication that the development of a CoP is indeed an informal collective, which is defined by its members by the shared ways of working, their rules and ways of responding to research challenges resulting from their interpretation of events (Gherardi & Nikolini, 2002). This finding also fits Wenger's (1998a) explanation of the makeup of a CoP. For Wenger, a CoP is a joint enterprise as understood and continually renegotiated by its members, consisting of relationships of mutual engagement which bind the members together in a social entity, and the capability such as routines and vocabulary that it has produced over time.

Vygotsky's Zone of Proximal Development, explains that employees extend their knowledge much further than independently possible when they learn from more experienced colleagues in the social setting where the work is done (Billett & Choy, 2013, p. 268). The data revealed several examples of how the participants extended their own knowledge by learning from another team member. Yet, Vygotskian views suggest that learning is largely dependent on the learner's agency and not on a reliance on expert partners (Billett & Choy, 2013, p. 268). The trainers' willingness to learn from each other enabled their construction of knowledge. Other participants explained how they participated willingly, even in their private time, and how they were guided in the way in which the research module was presented and how to align the administrative process with new developments. This behavior is consistent with Billett's (2001) view that it is through the individual's participation in activities, their intentional engagement in available learning opportunities, the guidance afforded in the workplace and the invitational qualities that influence how individuals learn and what they learn.

To this end, Warhurst (2006, p. 114) explicates that membership of a community is an intrinsic condition for learning and that learning will be both incidental and inevitable due to participation in the distinctive practice of a specific community. This proposition is in line with Lave and Wenger's (1991, p. 93) argument that individuals learn in relation to other individuals of a community. He further denotes that belonging to a practice community enables learners to construct the meaning that underpins practice, and that meaning-making through shared language is the second analytical component of the situated learning model (Warhurst, 2006, p. 115). Another analytic component of situated learning theory is argued to be that learning is a process of engaging in practice, a process of doing during which the individual experiences a process of "legitimate peripheral participation" as theorized by Lave and Wenger (1991, p. 29). Warhurst (2006, pp. 116–117) explains that this means that individuals will, first of all, be engaged in authentic and legitimate practice, and secondly, such individuals must be accepted as legitimate participants by established colleagues of that community. Lastly, individuals need to begin learning from practice on the periphery of practice and experience a centripetal trajectory over time to the core of their community's practice. In the end, Warhurst (2006, p. 118) argues, since practice is construed socially from the situated learning perspective, a key outcome of learning is "a way of being," a type of person in a specific practice context.

When individuals participate in shared practices, they learn new ways of being in the worlds they live and participate in, and, as a result, contribute to constituting these worlds. Blåka and Filstad (2007) argue that newcomers do not automatically become part of a CoP. Newcomers' expectations and abilities to get access, or their desire to get access, to several communities of practice determine their acceptance into such CoP. Access into a CoP rests on the newcomer's initiative and engagement with invitational qualities in the workplace. Newcomers' learning processes need to be considered in relation to their expectations and abilities as these elements determine to what extent they belong and build relationships with established members of the CoP. In addition, newcomers' pre-existing identities influence their construction of new professional identities to such an extent that these newcomers shaped their respective identities in their own unique ways (Blåka & Filstad, 2007, p. 72). Newcomers do not automatically become part of a community of practice. They evaluate their expectations and abilities to determine to what extent they can belong to and build relationships with established members of the community of practice (Blåka & Filstad, 2007, p. 72). I found two scenarios in my study that indicated that newcomers' abilities, expectations and belongingness do affect their response to invitational gestures of established communities of practice, in this case the research team. In one scenario, the receptionists could not join the research team because of their job description and non-commitment to the workplace. The receptionists did not feel that they belonged there. In the other scenario, the other trainers had no intention of engaging with research even though they were afforded opportunities to attend outsourced research courses. The other trainers' stance reiterated Billett and Choy's (2013, p. 268) argument that even though the trainers were afforded opportunities to learn from experienced research trainers, their workplace learning depended on their level of interest, motivation and ability to learn.

## Learning and Organizational Culture and Identity

In this section, I highlight an extreme example in which organizational culture and identity can hamper workplace learning. My study indicated that there was very little understanding by commanders for the peculiar position that EDLP learners found themselves in. EDLP learners are senior managers who were selected and trained in a culture that emphasize compliance to instruction rather than allowing them discretion in their work. Further, work is strictly supervised, which leaves little room for debate or exploration of alternative methods of problem-solving. The strong organizational culture is based on standing orders, procedures and rules. In a law enforcement environment, people are not expected to argue about facts, because it is a disciplined environment in which work gets done upon instruction. Doing research is different to following instructions. While research requires learners to read and compare, to think and reason about things, to understand and solve a problem, the learners' supervisors expect learners to follow their instructions in order to solve a problem in the way that their supervisors deem appropriate and adequate. Support for learning in the workplace was as a result minimal. Once in the workplace, learners were usually left to complete their projects without support or supervision. In addition, having a strong organizational identity dictated to the learners that the demand to meet targets of fighting crime were superseding the learning initiative by far. However, regardless of these circumstances, the organization demanded a good return on its investment.

It is clear that learning does not occur in isolation from others or the organizational culture. While Tynjälä (2008, p. 132) posits that it is now widely acknowledged that learning is situated in specific cultural contexts, I argue that not all organizational cultures are supportive of or enabling for workplace learning. In such environments where the organizational culture is so strong and so heavily guarded, individuals will informally construct knowledge, but if this new knowledge does not fit in with the organization's practice and culture, it will largely go unnoticed and unrecognized, or may even become a treat to the existing organizational culture. CoPs that develop subcultures which grow more prominent than the bigger organizational culture, may face pressure to dissolve. This is an aspect which needs further exploration.

## Summary and Implications

Much progress has been made in the workplace learning discourse. I have deliberated on some of the key factors that influence employee learning in the workplace by drawing from my own study in a policing environment. My study has provided substantial support for several debates about workplace learning. I have confirmed that workplace learning is mostly informal and not only done at work, but also in the minds of employees when they think about their work while they are not at work. Work also includes learning through reflection and problem solving during workers' private time. The study has confirmed that employees' learning result from their conscious decision to engage with learning opportunities as individuals or as part of a group, team or community in a social setting such as the workplace. Workplaces can support workplace learning by providing legitimate and authentic learning experiences. Establishing CoPs is an method of helping workers to develop new skills, but there are specific actions to be taken. If not carefully managed, employees and CoPs may develop undesirable skills that could harm the organization in some way. In this regard, the effect of strong subcultures in CoPs on organizational culture may warrant further research.

Organizations need to take organizational culture, language and other cultural factors into consideration when embarking on practical research projects in the workplace. It prompts one to consider the impact of one's work in a broader context in terms of the difference research could make in society, the impact on economic stability and growth in the long run. This aspect illuminates the need for better marketing strategies and management of structured workplace learning. More important though, is the implication for leadership in acknowledging the role of research as a problem-solving mechanism to find lasting solutions in developing countries. Recognition of the value of workplace learning will need stronger policy as workplace learning is a relatively cheap investment in preparing the workforce for the future. The cost aspect is an important one for developing countries that are struggling to grow their economies. Workplace learning could become an important mechanism to prepare employees for solving problems in a more scientific or informed manner, especially for those employees who have been marginalized through inadequate education systems.

## References

Bandura, A. (2001). Social cognitive theory: An agentic perspective. *Annual Review of Psychology, 52*, 1–26.

Beckett, D., & Hager, P. (2002). *Life, work and learning: Practice in postmodernity*. London, UK: Routledge.

Billett, S. (1995). Workplace learning: Its potential and limitations. *Education and Training, 37*(5), 20–27.

Billett, S. (2001). Learning through work: Workplace affordances and individual engagement. *Journal of Workplace Learning, 13*(5), 209–214.

Billett, S. (2002a). Toward a workplace pedagogy: Guidance, participation, and engagement. *Adult Education Quarterly, 53*(1), 27–43.

Billett, S. (2002b). Critiquing workplace learning discourses: Participation and continuity at work. *Studies in the Education of Adults, 34*(1), 56–67.

Billett, S. (2003). Workplace mentors: Demands and benefits. *Journal of Workplace Learning, 15*(3), 105–113.

Billett, S. (2004). Workplace participatory practices: Conceptualising workplaces as learning environments. *Journal of Workplace Learning, 16*(6), 312–324.

Billett, S. (2009). Realising the educational worth of integrating work experiences in higher education. *Studies in Higher Education, 34*(7), 827–843.

Billett, S. (2011). *Curriculum and pedagogic bases for effectively integrating practice-based experiences*. Sydney, Australia: Australian Learning and Teaching Council.

Billett, S., & Choy, S. (2013). Learning through work: Emerging perspectives and new challenges. *Journal of Workplace Learning, 25*(4), 264–276.

Blåka, G., & Filstad, C. (2007). How does a newcomer construct identity? A socio-cultural approach to workplace learning. *International Journal of Lifelong Education, 26*(1), 59–73.

Blanchard, P. N., & Thacker, J. W. (2007). *Effective training: Systems, strategies, and practices* (3rd ed.). Upper Saddle River, NJ: Pearson Prentice Hall.

Boud, D., Keogh, R., & Walker, D. (1985). *Reflection: Turning experience into learning*. London, UK/New York, NY: Routledge.

Brookfield, S. D. (1991). *Developing critical thinkers. Challenging adult to explore alternative ways of thinking and acting*. San Francisco, CA: Jossey-Bass.

Campbell, M. (2012). Constructs of self within the emerging professional identity of beginning police officers. Культурно Историческая Психология, *1/2012*, 82–82.

Chappell, C., Farrell, L., Scheeres, H., & Solomon, N. (2000). *Organization of identity: 4 cases. Working knowledge: The new vocationalism and higher education*. Stony Stratford, UK: Open University Press.

Council on Higher Education. (2011, August). *Work Integrated Learning: Good Practice Guide* HE Monitor 12. Pretoria: Council on Higher Education.

Cross, J. (2007). *Informal learning: Rediscovering the natural pathways that inspire innovation and performance*. San Francisco, CA: Pfeiffer.

Dewey, J. (1978). How we think. In J. A. Boydston (Ed.), *John Dewey: The Middle Works, 1899-1924: Vol. 6. 1910 1911* (pp. 177–356). Carbondale: Southern Illinois University Press Original work published 1910.

Doornbos, A. J., Bolhuis, S., & Simons, P. R. (2004). Modeling work-related learning on the basis of intentionality and development relatedness: A noneducational perspective. *Human Resource Development Review*, *3*(3), 250–274.

Elkjaer, B. (2004). Organizational learning the third way. *Management Learning*, *35*(4), 419–434.

Engeström, Y. (2001). Expansive learning at work: Towards and activity theoretical reconceptualization. *Journal of Education and Work*, *14*(1), 1–24.

Ezeokoli, R. N. (2014). Psychological factors as predictors of adult learning in selected study centres in Ibadan Metropolis, Oyo state. *IFE PsychologIA*, *22*(10), 71–79.

Finlay, I. (2008). Learning through boundary-crossing: Further education lecturers learning in both the university and workplace. *European Journal of Teacher Education*, *31*(1), 73–87.

Gherardi, S., & Nikolini, D. (2002). Learning the trade. A culture of safety in practice. *Organizations London*, *9*, 191–233.

Gosling, D., & Moon, J. A. (2001). How to use learning outcomes and assessment criteria. In Council for Higher Education (Ed.), *Work-integrated learning: Good practice guide* HE Monitor 12: August 2011. Pretoria: Council on Higher Education.

Hodkinson, P., Hodkinson, H., Evans, K., Kersh, N. et al. (2004). The significance of individual biography in workplace learning. *Studies in the Education of Adults*, *36*(1): 6–24.

Illeris, K. (2011). Workplaces and learning. In M. Malloch, L. Cairns, K. Evans, & B. N. O'Connor (Eds.), *The Sage handbook of workplace learning* (pp. 32–45). Los Angeles, CA: Sage.

Jacobs, R. L., & Park, Y. (2009). A proposed conceptual framework for workplace learning: Implications for theory development and research in human resource development. *Human Resource Development Review*, *8*(2), 133–150.

Järvensivu, A., & Koski, P. (2012). Combatting learning. *Journal of Workplace Learning*, *24*(1), 5–18.

Jawitz, J. (2009, June). Academic identities and communities of practice in a professional discipline. *Teaching in Higher Education, 14*(3), 241–251.

Knipfer, K., Kump, B., Wessel, D., & Cress, U. (2013). Reflection as a catalyst for organizational learning. *Studies in Continuing Education, 35*(1), 30–48.

Lave, J., & Wenger, E. (1991). *Situated learning, legitimate peripheral participation.* Cambridge, UK: Cambridge University Press.

Lee, S., & Ross, W. (2003, June). Re-mapping the landscape: Science educators within a community action network. *Perspectives in Education, 23*(2), 15–30.

Li, L. C., Grimshaw, J. M., Nielsen, C., Judd, M., et al. (2009). Evolution of Wenger's concept of community of practice. *Implementation Science, 4*, 11.

Lohman, M. C. (2005). A survey of factors influencing the engagement of information technology professionals in informal learning activities. *Information Technology, Learning, and Performance Journal, 25*(1), 43–53.

Malloch, M., & Cairns, L. (2010). Theories and theoretical frameworks. In M. Malloch, L. Cairns, K. Evans, & B. N. O'Connor (Eds.), *The Sage handbook of workplace learning* (pp. 1–14). Los Angeles, CA: Sage.

Marsick, V. J., & Watkins, K. E. (1997). *Informal and incidental learning in the workplace.* London, UK: Routledge.

Mullins, L. J. (1999). *Management and organizational behavior* (5th ed.). London, UK: Prentice Hall.

Sambrook, S. (2005). Factors influencing the context and process of work-related learning: Synthesizing findings from two research projects. *Human Resource Development International, 8*, 101–119.

Torraco, R. J. (1999). Integrating learning with working: A reconception of the role of workplace learning. *Human Resource Development Quarterly, 10*(3), 249–270.

Tynjälä, P. (2008). Perspectives into learning in the workplace. *Educational Research Review, 3*, 130–154.

Van Woerkom, M., Nijhof, W. J., & Nieuwenhuis, L. F. M. (2002). Critical reflective working behaviour: A survey research. *Journal of European Industrial Training, 26*(8), 375–383.

Vaughan, K. (2008). *Workplace learning: A literature review.* Competenz, New Zealand: New Zealand Council for Educational Research.

Watkins, K., & Marsick, V. (1992). Toward a theory of informal and incidental learning in organizations. *International Journal for Lifelong Education, 11*, 287–300.

Warhurst, R. P. (2006). "We really felt part of something": Participatory learning among peers within a university teaching-development community of practice. *International Journal for Academic Development, 11*(2), 111–122.

Wenger, E. (1998a). *Communities of practice.* Cambridge, UK: Cambridge University Press.

Wenger, E. (1998b). *Communities of practice: Learning, meaning and identity.* Cambridge, UK: Cambridge University Press.

Wenger, E., McDermott, R. A., & Snyder, W. (2002). *Cultivating communities of practice.* Boston, MA: Harvard Business School Press.

# 26

# The Effectiveness of Learning Communities in Increasing Employee Learning

*George Sellu[1] and Cynthia Carter Ching[2]*

[1] *Butte College*
[2] *University of California*

With the expansion in global markets and the advancement in technology and innovation, the requisite skills for entry-level jobs in multinational corporations are rapidly changing. Educational institutions and management teams for multinational corporations are developing strategies to address the skills gap. Global corporations are diverting more resources toward activities that enhance workplace learning. Firms have developed different forms of employee learning groups to enhance learning without jeopardizing quality and standards. The effectiveness of these learning groups within global firms has had mixed results. In this chapter, we examine workplace learning with a particular focus on the efficacy of learning communities in multinational corporations. Additionally, this chapter examines useful frameworks for understanding workplace learning and the implications for practice and success of global organizations.

## Defining Workplace Learning

The ways in which employees learn is fundamentally different from the ways in which organizations perceive learning. This creates a disconnect between organizational planning regarding employee learning and giving employees the option to select their preferred method of learning. Although working, learning and innovating are closely related activities in the daily operations of everyday human activity, organizations tend to view them as distinctly different and conflicting activities. Learning is viewed as the accumulation of abstract knowledge, while practice is associated with work (Lave & Wenger, 1991). This misalignment between work and learning has influenced how organizations plan learning opportunities for employees. Specifically, organizations have invested heavily in developing training manuals and training events based on the inaccurate belief that employees will learn and internalize abstract knowledge. Organizations plan training events and develop training manuals in locations away from work,

*The Wiley Handbook of Global Workplace Learning*, First Edition.
Edited by Vanessa Hammler Kenon and Sunay Vasant Palsole.

where employees acquire abstract knowledge with no contextual connection to their workplace. Employees are then expected to apply this abstract knowledge to work problems that arise later. This type of structured learning opportunity which we would rather refer to as a top-down approach to training has down-skilled the workforce of organizations and has stifled authentic workplace learning and innovation (Brown and Duguid, 1991).

Researchers (Lave, 1988; Lave & Wenger, 1991) have challenged the idea of separating learning from integrated practice. To this end, researchers (Billet, 2016; Fuller, Hodkinson, Hodkinson, & Unwin, 2005), argued that the definition of workplace learning has been limited because it has focused primarily on using schools as the context for formal learning. Fuller et al. (2005) suggested that the workplace provides suitable and dynamic context for learning that may not be available in schools. This allows for learning and practice to occur simultaneously in the workplace. Workplace learning opportunities appear to be better suited for the diverse workforce and work environment within global organizations.

In order to address some of the limitations in prior definitions of workplace learning, researchers (Eraut, 2004; Malcolm, Hodkinson, & Colley, 2003) have used formal and informal learning for the purpose of clarification. A handful of researchers in the field of adult learning (Dale & Bell, 1999; Stacey, Smith, & Barty, 2004) have suggested that informal learning could be a successful mechanism for acquiring workplace knowledge if used in conjunction with formal learning opportunities. Conlon (2004) suggested that informal learning could be an integral component for improving global workplace learning.

> Workplace learning includes training as formal learning, informal and incidental learning can achieve both individual and organizational performance by individual learning. It will be more logical to employ the term workplace learning more than "training" as it would demonstrate various learning activities. *(Jacobs & Park, 2009)*

This does not imply that global organizations should not have any formal training for their employees. Rather, it suggests that while formal training is important in the workplace, it should be integrated with informal learning, thereby enabling employees to create new knowledge at the workplace that is relevant to their local community or environment (Brown, Collins, & Duguid, 1989).

Based on the description above, Jacobs and Park (2009) suggested that corporate trainings are too formal and geared toward knowledge acquisition and not learning. Employees could enhance workplace learning when they are allowed to participate in the learning process (practice), thereby addressing problems that may be unique to a particular job site for multinational firms. Some individuals may not have the skills to directly solve problems encountered at their local work site. However, they could use auxiliary tools acquired through work to develop solutions (Igira & Gregory, 2009).

To this end, researchers (Brown et al., 1989; Reardon, 2010) suggested that the learning process may be viewed as comprising three interdependent factors: learning activities, concepts, and culture. In global organizations it would seem that these three factors are usually separated, sequenced, and treated distinctly. Effective learning however, should employ an integrated approach that blends all three. Researchers, (Brown et al., 1989) posited that many multinational organizations address no more than two of the three factors. For example, if the concept and activity are sound, omission of the cultural factor would make workplace learning irrelevant in certain regions of the world. In these situations, employees are expected to use learning tools without incorporating culture. The omission of cultural concepts could have varying effects on organizational goals. Cole and Engestrom (1993) argued that culture is distributed differently within communities and subjects or individuals experience culture differently.

While the definition of workplace learning continues to be refined, researchers Gil and Mataveli (2017) suggested that workplace learning is multilayered and thus warrants a layered analysis. Gil and Mataveli (2017) posited that workplace learning takes place at three levels; individual, group and institutional. Learning at each level has different requirements and generate varied affordances for employees. As such, it is important for organizations to understand the type of learning that takes place at each level and provide appropriate support to enhance learning. A clear understanding of the learning levels, learning culture, and deploying the appropriate learning facilitators could help shape learning within global organizations. However, a lot of global organizations have used canned corporate trainings, simulations, online trainings, blogs, and chatrooms to enhance employee learning. The aforementioned learning activities do not always address the different levels of learning, cultural differences across regions and, as such, these activities may not be relevant to certain job sites and groups of employees across the globe (Billett, 2001; Lucas & Kline, 2008). This is one reason why corporate trainings fail to effectively address the learning needs of global organizations.

## Forms of Workplace Learning Communities

Wenger and Snyder (2000) suggested that the challenge of international development extends beyond finances, and includes the development of culturally relevant knowledge that is aligned with the overall strategy of global organizations. Forward-thinking organizations are convening Communities of Practice (CoPs) to allow practitioners to build relevant knowledge that will be applicable across different regions of the world (Wenger, 2006). CoPs have taken different forms within organizations. In the next section, we examine CoPs and other forms of work groups that have been used to enhance workplace learning.

## Communities of Practice versus Project Teams/ Task Groups

Although CoPs have been around for a long time, only a few organizations have fully embraced and formally nurtured them. Some researchers (Wenger, 2006; Wenger & Snyder, 2000) posited three reasons for the slow adoption of the concept of CoPs; (a) unfamiliarity with the concept; (b) limited resources for the installing CoPs; and (c) difficulty integrating CoPs within organizations. In recent years, many organizations have developed organizational groupings around tasks/

functions and have referred to them as CoPs. Organizational groupings are organized around job tasks and they are established and controlled by managers (Hutchins, 1995). As such, management rather than self-selection by employees determines membership and participation within such groups. Therefore, there is little or no flexibility for members to engage in informal learning activities that create new knowledge. This may be due to the fact that informal learning is not generally considered a viable source of workplace learning (Eraut, 2004). Hence, organizations have invested fewer resources to support informal learning.

In multinational organizations, there is a tension between proponents of informal networks and formal learning groups, which are primarily formed and led by employees and management respectively (Conlon, 2004; Thompson, 2005). This is because while global organizations create project/ task groups to accomplish specific tasks across regions, informal networks are developed between employees as they participate in formal task groups. Orr (1990a) found that employees learned more from informal networks compared to formal workgroups. In order to create a workplace that embraces formal and informal learning without jeopardizing quality, the current learning communities should be thoroughly examined. Wenger and Snyder (2000) presented a framework for comparing CoPs with other work/task groups that may exist within global organizations as shown in Table 26.1. We adapted Table 26.1 by adding the last column (*who starts and controls it?*).

## Task Groups/Work Groups

From Table 26.1, it is plausible to suggest that formal task groups and project teams are the most pervasive groups within organizations. Formal work groups are easy to manage because they are organized around tasks/ functions. The use of task groups has allowed global firms to assign different production tasks to groups across the world. For example, a fabric company may have a cotton-growing operation in Nebraska in the United States, a cotton-processing plant in Bangladesh and a T-shirt-making facility in Colombia. Employees at each site are trained to meet specific production standards. The structure of global organizations such as the fabric company, provide little or no flexibility for employees to participate in authentic workplace learning. Employees within task groups become specialized in only the task(s) assigned to their groups (downskilling). Cole and Engestrom (1993) suggested that compartmentalization of expertise within organizations could result in open or latent disturbances between task groups and subsequently undermines organizational success.

For instance, in the fabric company, employees stationed in Bangladesh, are not trained or expected to be familiar with processes associated with producing and harvesting cotton, which takes place in Nebraska. They are only trained to process cotton, which limits their ability to work outside their task group. More importantly, the structure, boundary, and functions of task groups are developed by management that are usually far removed from different work sites across the globe. This could engender a lot of problems related to varied learning at different levels within the organization and adaptability of task groups in solving localized problems (Weldy & Gillis, 2010).

**Table 26.1** Comparison between workplace learning communities

| | What's the purpose? | Who belongs? | Who holds it together? | How does it last? | Who starts and controls it? |
|---|---|---|---|---|---|
| Community of Practice | To develop members' capabilities; to build and exchange knowledge | Members who self-select | Passion, commitment, and identification with group's expertise | As long as there is interest in maintaining the group | Initiated by members with the support of management but controlled by members |
| Formal work group | To deliver a product or service | Everyone who reports to the group's manager | Job requirements and common goals | Until the next reorganization | Initiated and controlled by management |
| Project Team | To accomplish a specific task | Employees assigned by senior management | The project's milestone and goals | Until the project has been completed | Initiated and controlled by management |
| Informal Network | To collect and pass on business information | Friends and business acquaintances | Mutual needs | As long as people have a reason to connect | Initiated and controlled by members |

*Source:* Adapted from Wenger and Snyder (2000).

The culture of employees varies across the world and hence would lead to differences in group dynamics and success. Task groups are used within global organizations to support formal learning that takes place primarily through trainings. Management leads these task groups and they provide little or no opportunities to support informal learning or incorporate the workplace culture of employees. The absence of informal learning and social interaction, distinguishes work groups and project teams from other learning communities shown in Table 26.1. Lave and Wenger (1991) would argue that there is little or no workplace learning taking place in such formal work groups or project teams. They argued that employees need to interact around the work content to create new knowledge. Global firms for their part would contend that work/ task groups are communities of practice that engage around given tasks/ functions. The only problem here is that while management assumes that employees are learning as a consequence of participating in work groups, employees could be benefitting more from informal networks (unintended learning). For instance, some of the employees at the cotton-processing site in Bangladesh may have prior experience growing and harvesting cotton, which may be useful at the processing site. However, employees may not be asked to contribute to the learning process related to growing or processing cotton. Therefore, if employees encounter anomalies in the cotton product during processing that could be related to production, their personal experiences may not be solicited, to solve such problems because they have not been formally trained to produce cotton. This anomaly in the cotton product may be familiar to some of the workers or members of their local communities. The anomaly may be a reoccurring problem and hence, a learning community could be a useful resource for addressing the problem. However, lack of flexibility to allow employees to use community resources to solve workplace problems could have adverse effects on the success of the fabric firm. Wenger and Snyder (2000) suggested that the absence of CoPs within global firms could be associated with the overall corporate failure of some organizations.

## Informal Networks

As mentioned earlier in this chapter, informal networks could emerge from formal interactions. In fact, researchers (Conlon, 2004; Gannon-Leary & Fontainha, 2007; Orr, 1990b) found that employees benefitted from informal networks that were created during formal interactions. From Table 26.1, we see that informal networks are created and managed by members, which in this case will be employees. However, there are several challenges associated with establishing informal networks within global firms: (a) They receive little to no support in terms of resources from management; (b) they are not embedded within the structure of the workplace; (c) they are limited in their ability to recruit members from different task groups in the workplace. Based on these challenges, it is difficult for informal networks begin and persist within global firms. In order to address the lack of informal communities within multinational corporations, some firms have established online or virtual communities. Researchers (Madge, Meek, Wellens, & Hooley, 2009; Skeels & Grudin, 2009) suggested that virtual communities have been used effectively to support learning in global firms such as Facebook and LinkedIn across the world. The success of virtual learning communities in global firms could be attributed to the differences in the nature of work, infrastructure as well as social and cultural values across regions. In particular, virtual and online communities have been used with more success in multinational technology firms (Allan & Lewis, 2006; Matsuo, 2015; Stacey et al., 2004; Tian, Yu, Vogel, & Ron Chi-Wai Kwok, 2011). For the most part, these virtual communities are seeded and controlled by management. Hence, they function more or less as project teams or task groups rather than communities of practice.

Informal groups on the other hand, are not always incorporated into the structure of multinational corporations (Conlon, 2004; Weldy & Gillis, 2010). This is because organizations may be unaware of the valuable contribution of informal networks to the organizational objectives. As a result, there has been tension between employees and managers regarding the contribution to project teams/task groups and informal networks toward workplace learning. Unlike some managers, employees value the contribution of informal networks to workplace learning (Gannon-Leary & Fontainha, 2007). In order to defuse this tension, authentic workplace learning communities should incorporate the unique features of formal and informal learning networks. From Table 26.1, we see that CoPs combine the structure and functions of both informal networks and project teams/work groups.

### Communities of Practice (CoP)

CoPs have been proposed as vehicles for addressing the gaps in workplace learning that exist in global firms (Rehm, 2009; Wenger, 1998; Wenger & Snyder, 2000). Specifically, Wenger and Snyder (2000) posit that in order for firms to benefit from CoPs, managers should understand CoPs, embrace their potential for developing knowledge and be able to integrate them within organizations. Lave and Wenger (1991) in defining CoPs, examined the structure and epistemology of organizations. Epistemology deals with the ways in which people think, participate, and learn (practice). Thompson (2005) opined that accepting the existence of a CoP suggests that one has taken an epistemic position about how a particular group interacts, thinks and learn. Therefore, multinational firms that accept the importance of CoPs should invest resources in seeding them. Organizations tend to struggle in maintaining a balance between seeding and controlling CoPs. In fact, Wenger, McDermott, and Snyder (2002) suggested that the success of CoPs is dependent on how they are structured and developed. Wenger (1998) suggested that establishing boundaries based on function and locus of control, allow members to self-select the CoP they are interested in and the level of participation they intend to invest. Once a CoP is established, members should be allowed to take control and lead groups. This delicate balance between structural seeding of a CoP and controlling the CoP after it is established ensures the persistence of effective CoPs. When organizations seed CoPs, they need to be able to assess whether or not members are prepared to take over control so that management may relinquish control. If that determination is not made in time, management may continue to exert control for a prolonged period of time, which in most cases would stifle flexible social interactions, innovation, and the generation of knowledge.

While some multinational firms struggle to establish CoPs on the one hand, supportive organizations on the other end of the spectrum have been overzealous about seeding CoPs. This has led to the rapid growth of CoPs, which has led in turn to several challenges. First, management may attempt to recruit members instead of allowing employees to self-select. Second, there may be a lot of novices taking on leadership roles within a CoP as a result of rapid growth. The combination of inexperienced leadership and inappropriate membership recruitment could undermine the stability and effectiveness of CoPs. We suggest that while CoPs are useful in enhancing workplace learning, they should be carefully structured and controlled to ensure effectiveness.

Researchers (Wenger, 2006; Wenger et al., 2002; Wenger & Snyder, 2000) posited that multinational organizations are using CoPs to enhance the knowledge and skills of their employees. While CoPs have had some success, there have been questions about the success of CoPs in formal learning situations. Rehm (2009) suggested that Communities of Learning (CoLs) could address some of the weaknesses of CoPs. This is because CoLs are structured collaborative learning groups that also provide opportunities for employees to reflect on their practice and use these reflections to solve future problems. In short, CoLs provide opportunities for dynamic learning within organizations via ongoing reflection and adaptation.

The on-going adaptation that takes place after reflection increases the complexity of workplace learning even in the absence of cultural differences. Since multinational corporations operate across different regions, culture is an integral component of workplace learning. In order to fully understand workplace learning in global firms, it will be helpful to examine the culture, histories and learning activities of employees.

## Cultural Historical Activity Theory (CHAT)

Cultural Historical Activity Theory (CHAT) provides a framework for organizing and analyzing the complex learning opportunities that exist in the workplace. Specifically, cultural historical perspective provides another lens for examining workplace learning that takes place in multinational firms. For organizations that are pursuing flatter organizational structures, the activity system framework provides agency for individuals, or groups of individuals in decision making within organizations. In short, CHAT provides bottom-up remediation and participants/employees may have more input in the change process (Gil & Mataveli, 2017).

Cole and Engestrom (1993) argued that cultural historical perspective is a product of the work of several theorists (Leontiev, 1932; Luria, 1928; Vygotsky, 1929; 1987). Vygotsky (1978) argued that culture mediates cognition. Since culture is not static, as culture changes so the type of mediation that takes place changes. This is particularly important because multinational firms are situated in different cultural settings across the world. In order to understand how changes in culture and histories affect cognition over time, Cole and Engestrom (1993) extended Vygotsky's model into CHAT. The work of Cole and Engestrom

(1993) will guide the initial discussion of workplace learning, because their model (the modified mediational triangle) addresses some of the complexities of learning that are mediated through activity systems in multinational organizations such as the fabric company example. Moreover, the work of Cole and Engestrom (1993) provided a theoretical foundation for current models such as Developmental Work Research (DWR) that are currently used to examine global workplace learning. The mediational triangle as proposed by Cole and Engestrom (1993) is made up of three components; activity, subject, and object. Engestrom writes: "[The] activity system integrates the subject, the object, and the instrument (materials tools as well as signs and symbols) into a unified whole" (2001, p. 67). Engestrom uses "subject" to refer to learners/ employees and "object" to describe the motivation of individuals or groups of individuals within an activity system. In multinational organizations there are individuals or groups of individuals that directly or indirectly affect organizational success. Hence it is critical to understand how the motivation of target and non-target groups affect the success of global organizations. Activity systems are units of analysis that provide insights into the learning processes that take place within and between target and non-target communities. Hence, identifying activity systems within organizations and using them as units of analysis provides a robust and long-lived tool for analyzing institutionalized activities (Cole & Engestrom, 1993).

Foot (2014) posited that activity systems are multivoiced and multilayered that could be used to analyze the actions of participants with different roles, positions, perspectives and values. The object developed in an activity system is based on the needs and values of one or more participants. These needs are sometimes not clearly defined. However, the orientation of subject(s), their personal experiences engender motives for what should be acted upon. A motive emerges when needs are linked unto objects (Ripamonti & Galuppo, 2016).

In a multinational organization, there could more than one activity system, which, could result complex learning activities. The participants in each activity system are not homogenous hence activity systems are prone to contradictions and tension (Engestrom, 1993). CHAT provides a framework for analyzing workplace practice (previous, present and future) through multilevel sociocultural, political and institutional lenses (Foot, 2014). CHAT enables practitioners and researchers identify the different activity systems within organizations. Objects of activity systems could be rooted in several activity systems. Using activity systems as units of analysis makes it easier to identify contradictions or tensions that could otherwise be latent when examined at an organizational level (Blacker, 2009).

In the activity system shown in Figure 26.1, job guidelines and standards (mediator) are used as instruments to analyze the alignment between organizational objectives and practice. Employees interact with the rules, their community and mediator. Figure 26.1 shows the type of learning that takes place within a workplace activity system that integrates culture and allows for employee participation in the learning process.

The guidelines and standards for the cotton-production plant in Nebraska are different from the cotton-processing site in Bangladesh. However, if the fabric company had a second processing facility at a different location,

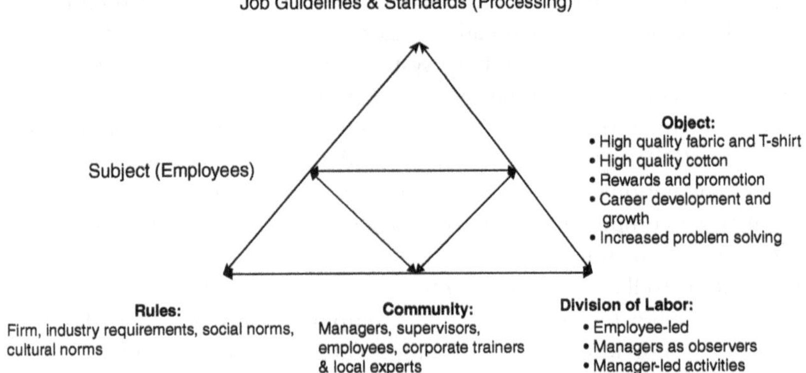


**Figure 26.1** Fabric company activity system

employees would follow the same guidelines and standards as the plant in Bangladesh. While the guidelines and standards remain unchanged for the processing plants, the object at each site could be different as a result of the differences in employee backgrounds and the workplace culture at each location (Harvey, Novicevic, & Garrison, 2004; O'Keefe, 2003). These differences in object could lead to contradictions between processing divisions across locations. In fact, these differences and contradictions suggest that the processing division within the fabric company could have different activity systems. Furthermore, activity systems could transcend locations, or departments within global organizations. Hence, these divisions should be analyzed individually to identify the sources of tension using different activity systems.

From Figure 26.1, we see that the job activity system extends beyond these strict guidelines and standards for processing cotton. The rules for training, interaction, and socialization at the processing site are based on industry standards for fabric firms. The learning community in the fabric company example is comprised of company employees, supervisors, trainers, and community members. From the earlier discussions, supervisors and employees could be members of different and overlapping activity systems. The overlapping of activity systems could lead to tension and contradictions. Ripamonti and Galuppo (2016) posited that disturbances and contradictions within each activity system help shape the object in each activity system and hence the object within global organizations with overlapping activity systems. The managers and the employees interact differently with the standards and guidelines of the organization, thereby creating different motivations or objects for each group (Harvey et al., 2004; O'Keefe, 2003). We argue that these differences in motivation between managers and employees could be latent within an organizational activity system.

For example, the Nebraska site could foster more interaction between employees compared to the T-shirt site in Colombia, where employees are expected to pay closer attention to details related to standards. The level of interaction within the fabric company will be influenced by the task, role of individuals, workplace culture, community values and the flexibility of supervisors and managers in embracing learning through interaction. From the discussion above,

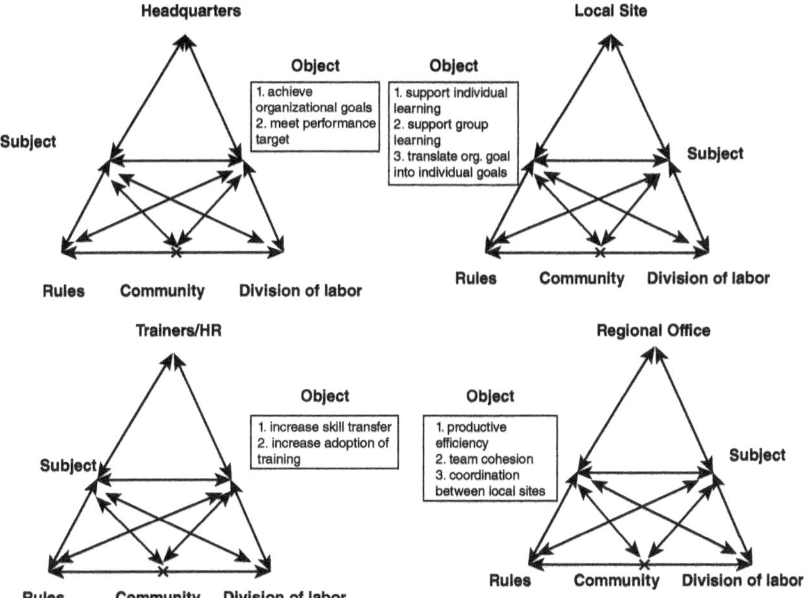


**Figure 26.2** Overlapping activity systems in global organizations. *Source:* Adapted from Ripamonti and Galuppo (2016)

it is clear that different interactions could engender activity systems that overlap with one another. Overlapping activity systems could lead to different workplace learning opportunities. as shown in Figure 26.2.

Figure 26.2 provides a framework for examining global workplace learning using overlapping activity systems. Engestrom (2001) identified and described the three generations of CHAT: mediated action, individual and collective activity, and multiple interacting activity systems. Igira and Gregory (2009) argued that the third generation of CHAT (multiple activity systems) exploits some of the latent challenges in the two previous generations. Specifically, the third generation of CHAT uses multiple activity systems as units of analyses compared to one activity system. The interaction between multiple activity systems produces different perspectives, networks, and epistemologies. Furthermore, as the activity systems interact and overlap, subjects and objects are constantly negotiated and adapted. The interaction between activity systems create unique contexts that integrate subject, object tools, norms and rules, community, and division of labor into whole activity systems. From this discussion, we see that CHAT expands our understanding of how objects or motivations are adapted within global organizations as a result of overlapping activity systems. Although CHAT provides a useful tool for analyzing the contradictions and tension between overlapping activity systems, it does not provide tools for solving future problems.

Igira and Gregory (2009), suggested that the third generation of CHAT provided the basis for theoretical empirical methodologies such as DWR. DWR integrates the active and reflective participation of employees/learners/subjects in analyzing individual/group needs and structuring/restructuring object(s) and developing models for addressing problems and monitoring intervention. DWR is based on the idea that changes in history advances expansive cycles[1] of learning. DWR provides a robust methodology for examining current practice, reflect on past practices and develop skills for solving problems. In a global organization where the location, culture, history, political situation, and the background of employees is constantly changing, DWR could be a useful tool for understand workplace learning and the associated implications for organizational success.

## Legitimate Peripheral Participation

In the previous section, we discussed CHAT as a framework for analyzing workplace learning. In this section, we use Legitimate Peripheral Participation (LPP) as a tool for understanding workplace learning. Lave and Wenger (1991) coined the term LPP, which does not refer to an instructional method nor does not involve the transfer of knowledge or learning about practice. Rather, it refers to learning through participation (learning through practice). Using the fabric company example, employees participate in practice about cotton production, processing, or T-shirt making at the different sites. At each site, employees learn more about practice (cotton production, processing, and T-shirt making) through participation in each process. Employees develop a deeper understanding (learning) about the processes at each site through participation in practice. Increased and sustained participation increases learning and creates opportunities upward mobility within their learning community or the organization.

However, in countries where local communities are organized in hierarchies, knowledge, skills and histories are also distributed based on these hierarchies. As such, older community members may have primacy over local knowledge, skills, and histories and they may not be willing to share experiences with younger members of society for fear of losing control or leadership roles. Similarly, long-term employees within organizations could hold tremendous institutional knowledge that they may otherwise not be willing to pass down to new employees. Both scenarios described here could create skills gaps within organizations. While these hierarchies exist, in workplace and local communities, multinational corporations have embarked on training-the-trainers model as a means of addressing the skills gap or improving workplace learning. This is because some multinational firms assume that a handful of trained employees would facilitate the distribution of cognition among workers (Orr, 1990b). However, in communities where hierarchies extend into the workplace, local trainers will be less likely to share knowledge and skills with all employees. As such, employees may have limited access to core knowledge and skills within the organization (limited peripheral participation). There are several challenges associated with what we refer to as *limited peripheral participation*. First, workplace learning will be stagnated and could affect personal growth and job satisfaction of employees. Second, cost would increase because only a handful of employees would have a deeper understanding of the processes within the firm. As a result, the firm would need to constantly pay to train small groups of employees to address the ongoing skill gap. Finally, the leadership pipeline within the firm would diminish because the number of employees with deeper understanding of the firm's operations will always remain small. Hence, the pipeline for training technicians and technical managers will remain shallow.

## The Role of Learning Communities in Workplace Effectiveness

### Personal growth and development

As discussed earlier in this chapter, workplace learning communities are important in helping employees develop skills for solving problems that are relevant to the workplace. More importantly, learning communities allow for interaction between employees, former employees and local communities to develop new knowledge that would be useful in solving problems. Authentic workplace learning communities attract members from different task groups and levels within the organization. The diversity in the background of workplace learning communities extend employee learning beyond the scope of the company's formal training. There are several implications for the employee and the firm. First, it increases employees' repertoire of skills to solve problems that may be unique to specific locations across the globe (Orr, 1990b). This would improve personal satisfaction for employees and most likely higher productivity and contribution to the overall success of the firm. Second, participation in workplace learning communities prepares employees to take on leadership roles at different levels within the firm. In short, increase in employee participation in workplace learning communities could increase the chances of upward mobility within the organization. Nevertheless, employees that only participate in task groups would have limited opportunities for upward mobility outside their task group.

### Maintaining quality and standards

From earlier discussions in this chapter, we have seen several researchers (Boud and Garrick, 1999; Illeris, 2011; Lave, 1988; Orr, 1996; Wenger, 1998) draw attention to the tension between formal and informal learning in the workplace. One of the main concerns for management is related to standardization of practice. That is, firms want to maintain the same quality and standard of production across different locations. It is for this reason that multinational firms develop training materials at their corporate headquarters and implement them across the globe. These trainings are rigid with little or no flexibility for employees to contribute toward workplace learning. A CoP for example, could support informal learning while maintaining quality and standards. Although, a handful of researchers have (Brown & Duguid, 1998; Orr, 1990b; Thompson, 2005) found that employees reported higher job satisfaction and motivation as a result of participating in informal workplace learning communities, though many multinational firms are still reluctant to embrace flexible informal learning communities. It is possible to incorporate informal learning in the workplace without compromising standards. Creating learning activities that embrace informal learning does not exclude maintaining quality and standards. In fact, it should enhance quality and standards because employees who engage in informal learning activities could be more motivated and so more likely to deliver higher-quality work.

### Cost savings

The ultimate goal of multinational firms is to cut costs and increase profits. Therefore, it is important for management to explore practices that reduce cost without compromising quality and standards. In the fabric firm example, a CoP could be helpful in reducing production cost. A typical CoP at the cotton-processing site for the fabric company would address competencies related to receiving, cleaning, processing, and packing cotton. This CoP could develop employee competencies in basic repair of the cotton processing machines, which, in most cases would be outside the tasks of employees at this site. As such, when there is a minor technical failure with machinery, management would have to ship technicians from a different location to address this problem. This will be a tremendous cost for the fabric firm each time such a problem arises. Such minor technical problems reoccur quite often in multinational firms (Orr, 1990a). Longtime employees may become familiar with recurring technical problems within a firm.

However, employees may not be consulted to help address such problems because it may be outside their job description. Each time such technical problems occur, the site may be out of operation, while they wait for technicians to arrive and perform repairs. In addition to the cost of flying the technician to the job site, there will be a loss in revenue due to a temporary halt in operation. Some firms have avoided this pitfall by training a handful of employees at different locations to address tasks such as machine repairs that are outside the scope of daily operations. This approach may be a temporary fix because when employees retire or take vacation, the job site is still left without adequate technicians. An effective CoP could enhance employee skills to perform the tasks of technicians. The type of knowledge that is embodied within the CoP would be available to new employees that join the CoP over time. As a result, the CoP would always have employees with the skills to perform the tasks of technicians at no cost to the employer.

## Creating and Managing Effective Workplace Learning Communities

Some multinational corporations with sound business objectives and goals may have different outcomes across regions depending on endogenous and exogenous factors. Even learning communities would have varying impacts on organizational objectives as a result of endogenous and exogenous factors.

### Endogenous factors

Multinational corporations such as the fabric company have control over their objectives, values, resources, employees, and leadership. Global organizations have established objectives and values that guide business operations. These values should be adaptable to different cultures around the world. For example, employees working for the fabric company at the Colombia site may need Sundays off to attend church, while employees in Bangladesh might need Fridays off for Muslim prayers. This is particularly important, because these are the majority religions in both countries and citizens of these countries usually take an entire day off for religious rites and family time. Supportive multinational firms or corporations could provide flexible schedules for employee to meet their religious rites. Such flexibility could build stronger community among employees, which may translate into effective workplace learning communities and increased productivity. From earlier discussions in this chapter, we suggested that institutional resources are usually required to establish successful workplace learning communities. As such, the leadership of organizations that understand the purpose of workplace learning communities should be willing to direct resources toward these communities. Finally, management is responsible for hiring employees therefore they need to hire individuals that meet organizational objectives and fits within the current dynamics of the organization. In short multinational firms have control over endogenous factors that could influence the effectiveness of workplace learning communities. Although global firms have the ability to adapt endogenous factors, they have little to no control over exogenous factors. However, leadership within multinational firms could adopt practices that mitigate the negative impact of exogenous factors on organizational success.

### Exogenous factors

One of the major causes of failure for international development agencies and other multinational firms is the lack of understanding of exogenous factors in different countries. For example, the Green Revolution program, which was developed to address food shortage and hunger in developing countries such as Philippines, India, and several countries in sub-Saharan Africa. The success of the Green Revolution program[2] varied across countries. From the perspective of scientists and project planners, the project concept and implementation was sound and was expected to succeed. The program was successfully implemented in the Philippines and India but failed in West Africa. According to Khush (Personal communication, April 8, 2009), one of the leading architects of the Green Revolution project, the major reason for the failure in West Africa was a lack of effective governance institutions. Good governance is an exogenous factor that could have significant impact on the operation of global firms. In some countries there could be political instability that could interfere with the stability of employees and hence the quality of workplace learning communities. In addition, cultural or social values in some regions of the world support hierarchy and class system. Hierarchies and class systems could impact the formation of effective workplace learning communities. We posit that the failure of multinational programs such as the Green Revolution could be attributed to one or several of the aforementioned factors. In order to mitigate the negative impact of exogenous factors, organizations should be aware of these factors and develop strategies for minimizing their impact on organization success.

## Conclusion

The objective of this chapter was to examine effective communities of practice and their influence on workplace learning. In this chapter, we acknowledge that while it is difficult to address the gaps in employee learning in multinational firms, organizations could mitigate these differences through effective learning communities. Forward-thinking global firms have used varied forms of learning communities to address the gaps in employee learning. However, some of the learning communities have not been effective in addressing these gaps in employee learning. Based on the different learning communities examined in this chapter, we recommend CoPs as the most effective vehicle for mitigating the gap in employee learning within global firms. While we believe that CoPs could mitigate the gaps in employee learning, we anticipate that the structure and membership of CoPs should be dynamic because workplace learning needs change as frequently as exogenous and endogenous factors within and around organizations evolve. Global firms should address this threat to CoPs by creating learning environments that foster on-going adaptation in CoPs that reflect changes in both exogenous and endogenous factors.

The success of global firms therefore, could be enhanced by the initiation, management and support of effective communities of practice, that can adapt to changes in job tasks, employee backgrounds and exogenous factors such as governance, cultural values, religious beliefs that are outside the control of multinational firms.

## Notes

1 Expansive cycle is made up of six stages: examine current practices and activities; identify tensions, controversies, and conflicts within and between activity systems; consider new models and metaphors and develop new solutions; test and evaluate the new model in actual setting; reconceptualize, revise and implement the new model; consolidate and reflect on the new practices.

2 A research, development and technology transfer that was designed to address food shortage by developing high-yielding crop varietals for developing nations.

## References

Allan, B., & Lewis, D. (2006). Virtual learning communities as a vehicle for workforce development: a case study. *Journal of Workplace Learning*, 18(6), 367–383.

Billet, S. (2016). Critiquing workplace learning discourses: Participation and continuity at work. *Studies in the Education of Adults*, 34(1), 56–67.

Billett, S. (2001). Learning through work: Workplace affordances and individual engagement. *Journal of Workplace Learning*, 13(5), 209–214.

Billett, S. (2001). Learning in the workplace: Strategies for effective practice. Sydney, Australia:: Allen and Unwin.

Blacker, F. (2009). Cultural-historical activity theory and organizational studies. In A. Sannino, H. Daniels, & K. D. Gutierrez (Eds.), Learning and expanding with activity theory (pp. 19–39). Cambridge, UK: Cambridge University Press.

Brown, J. S., Collins, A., & Duguid, P. (1989). Situated cognition and the culture of learning. *Educational Researcher*, 18(1), 32–42.

Brown, J. S., & Duguid, P. (1991). Toward a Unified View of Working, Learning, and Innovation. *Organization Science*, 2(1).

Brown, J. S., & Duguid, P. (1998). Organizing knowledge. *California management Review*, 40(3), 90–111.
Cole, M., & Engestrom, Y. (1993). A cultural-historical approach to distributed cognition. In G. Salomon (Ed.), Distributed cognitions: Psychological and educational considerations (pp. 1–46). Cambridge, UK: Cambridge University Press.
Conlon, T. J. (2004). A review of informal learning literature, theory and implications for practice in developing global professional competence. *Journal of European Industrial Training*, 28(2), 283–295.
Dale, M., & Bell, J. (1999). Informal learning in the workplace. London: Department for Education and Employment.
Engestrom, Y. (2001). Expansive learning at work. Toward an activity–Theoretical reconceptualisation. *Journal of Education and Work*, 14(1), 133–156.
Engestrom, Y. (1993). Developmental studies of work as a testbench of activity theory: The case of primary care medical practice. In S. Chaiklin, & J. Lave (Eds.), Understanding practice: Perspectives on activity and context (pp. 64–103). Cambridge, UK: Cambridge University Press.
Eraut, M. (2004). Informal learning in the workplace. *Studies in Continuing Education*, 26(2), 247–273.
Foot, K. A. (2014). Cultural-historical activity theory: Exploring a theory to inform practice and research. *Journal of Human Behavior in the Social Environment*, 24(3), 329–346.
Fuller, A., Hodkinson, H., Hodkinson, P., & Unwin, L. (2005). Learning as peripheral participation in communities of practice: A reassessment of key concepts in workplace learning. *British Educational Research Journal*, 31(1), 49–68.
Gannon-Leary, P. and Fontainha, E. (2007). Communities of practice and virtual learning communities: Benefits, barriers and success factors. eLearning Papers, 5 September.
Gil, A. J., & Mataveli, M. (2017). Learning opportunities for group learning: An empirical assessment from the learning organization perspective. *Journal of Workplace Learning*, 29(1), 65–78.
Harvey, M., Novicevic, M. M., & Garrison, G. (2004). Challenges to staffing global virtual teams. *Human Resource Management Review*, 14, 275–294.
Hutchins, E. (1995). Cognition in the wild. Cambridge, MA: MIT Press.
Igira, F. T., & Gregory, J. (2009). Cultural historical activity theory. In Y. Dwivedi, B. Lal, M. Williams, S. Schneberger, & M. Wade (Eds.), Handbook of research on contemporary theoretical models in information systems (pp. 434–454). Hershey, PA: IGI Global.
Illeris, K. (2011). The fundamentals of workplace learning: Understanding how people learn inworking life. London, UK: Routledge.
Jacobs, R. L., & Park, Y. (2009). A proposed conceptual framework of workplace learning: Implications for theory development and research in human resource development. *Human Resource Development Review*, 8(2), 133–150.
Lave, J. (1988). Cognition in practice: Mind, mathematics and culture in everyday life. Cambridge, UK: Cambridge University Press.
Lave, J., & Wenger, E. (1991). Situated learning: Legitimate peripheral participation. Cambridge, UK: Cambridge University Press.

Leontiev, A. N. (1932). Studies of cultural development of the child, 3: The development of voluntary attention in the child. *Journal of Genetic Psychology*, 37, 53–81.

Lucas, C., & Kline, T. (2008). Understanding the influence of organizational culture and group dynamics on organizational change and learning. *The Learning Organization*, 15(3), 277–287.

Luria, A. R. (1928). The problem of the cultural development of the child. *Journal of Genetic Psychology*, 35, 493–506.

Madge, C., Meek, J., Wellens, J., & Hooley, T. (2009). Facebook, social integration and informal learning at university: It is more for socializing and talking to friends about work than for actually doing work. *Learning, Media and Technology*, 34(2), 141–155.

Malcolm, J., Hodkinson, P., & Colley, H. (2003). The interrelationships between formal and informal learning. *Journal of Workplace Learning*, 15(7), 313–318.

Matsuo, M. (2015). Human resource development to facilitate experiential learning: The case of yahoo Japan. *International Journal of Training and Development*, 15(2), 127–132.

O'Keefe, T. (2003). Preparing expatriate managers of multinational organizations for the cultural and learning imperatives of their job in dynamic knowledge-based environments. *Journal of European Industrial Training*, 27(5), 233–243.

Orr, J.E. (1990a). Sound, feel, and practice: Some examples from diagnosis of machines. Palo Alto, CA: Systems Science Laboratory, Xerox Palo Alto Research Center SSL Report SSL-90-42v.

Orr, J. E. (1990b). Sharing knowledge, celebrating identity: Community memory in a service culture. In D. Middleton, & D. Edwards (Eds.), Collective remembering (pp. 169–189). London, UK: Sage.

Orr, J. E. (1996). *Talking about machines*: An ethnography of a modern job. Ithaca, NY: Cornell University Press.

Reardon, R. F. (2010). The impact of learning culture on worker response to new technology. *Journal of Workplace Learning*, 22(4), 201–211.

Rehm, M. (2009). Unified in learning–separated by space. *Industry and Higher Education*, 23(4), 331–341.

Ripamonti, S. C., & Galuppo, L. (2016). Working transformation following the implementation of an ERP system: An activity-theoretical perspective. *Journal of workplace learning*, 28(4), 206–223.

Skeels, M.M., and Grudin, J. (2009). When social networks cross boundaries: A case study of workplace use of Facebook and LinedIn. Proceedings of *GROUP, May 10–13, 2009* (pp. 95–103). Tampa, FL.

Stacey, E., Smith, P. J., & Barty, K. (2004). Adult learners in the workplace: Online learning and communities of practice. *Distance Education*, 25(1), 107–123.

Thompson, M. (2005). Structural and epistemic parameters in communities of practice. *Organization Science*, 16(2), 151–164.

Tian, S. W., Yu, A. Y., Vogel, D., & Ron Chi-Wai Kwok, R. C. (2011). The impact of online social networking on learning: A social integration perspective. *International Journal of Networking and Virtual Organizations*, 8(3/4), 264–280.

Vygotsky, L. S. (1929). The problem of the cultural development of the child, vol II. *Journal of Genetic Psychology*, 36, 414–434.

Vygotsky, L. S. (1987). Thinking and Speech. New York: Plenum.
Vygotsky, L. S. (1978). Mind in society. Cambridge, MA: Harvard University Press.
Weldy, T. G., & Gillis, W. E. (2010). The learning organization: Variations at different organizational levels. *The Learning Organization*, 17(5), 455–470.
Wenger, E. (1998). Communities of practice: Learning, meaning, and identity. Cambridge, UK:: Cambridge University Press.
Wenger, E. (2006). Communities of practice: A brief introduction Retrieved from http://www.ewenger.com/theory
Wenger, E., & Snyder, W. M. (2000). Communities of practice: The organizational frontier. *Harvard Business Review*, R00II0, 139–145 Boston, MA: Harvard Business School Publishing.
Wenger, E., McDermott, R., & Snyder, W. M. (2002). Cultivating communities of practice. Boston, MA: Harvard Business School Press.

[illegible] (198[illegible]). [illegible] New York: Pergamon.
[illegible] Harvard University Press.
[illegible]
[illegible]
[illegible]
[illegible]
[illegible]
[illegible]
[illegible]
[illegible]
[illegible]
[illegible]

# Part V

# Workplace Technology Learning Trends

# 27

# A Study of Attitude and Utilization of Interactive Whiteboards among Teacher Educators

*Sunday Ayodele Taiwo*[1] *and Emmanuel Olufemi Adeniyi*[2]

[1] *Federal College of Education (Special), Oyo, Nigeria*
[2] *Federal College of Education, Abeokuta*

The Federal Government of Nigeria recognizes the key role of education toward the attainment of sustainable development, and has made qualitative education a key component of a seven-point Agenda. However, attainment of qualitative education requires improving on teaching and learning. This in turn requires introducing Information and Communication Technology (ICT) into the educational system because it plays a vital role in promoting such an improvement (Federal Republic of Nigeria (FRN), 2010). The government, realizing this fact, is leaving no stone unturned to take advantage of the opportunities offered by the technology in furthering ICT-driven education goals at the institutional level. One of the initiatives and strategies put in place to realize ICT-driven education is the massive provision of ICT infrastructure at the institutional level.

One emerging aspect of ICT is the interactive whiteboard (IWB). This medium is rapidly becoming the new chalkboard in the classroom. An IWBs is a large touch-sensitive display panel that can function as an ordinary whiteboard, a projector screen, an electronic copy board or as a computer projector screen on which the computer image can be controlled by touching the surface of the panel instead of using a mouse or keyboard (Kennewell & Morgan, 2003). The technology allows the user to write or draw on the surface, print the image, save it to a computer or distribute it over a network. The user can also project a computer screen image onto the surface and then control the application either by touching the board directly or by using a special pen. In addition, the computer image can be annotated or drawn over, and the annotations saved (Kennewell & Morgan, 2003).

Recent studies indicate that effective use of IWBs brings about benefits. British Educational Communications and Technology (BECTA, 2004) suggests that among other benefits, IWBs enables enhanced presentation of content, allows students to absorb information more easily and to participate in classroom discussions by freeing them from copious note taking and saves teachers valuable preparation time.

*The Wiley Handbook of Global Workplace Learning*, First Edition.
Edited by Vanessa Hammler Kenon and Sunay Vasant Palsole.

It is hoped that the introduction of IWBs into the formal education setting would improve the academic performance of teacher educators by encouraging them to improve their ability to use and apply technology and software in their jobs. IWB capacity-building programs have been organized for teacher educators to become proficient in their use of the technology. This is coupled with in-service training opportunities in different subject areas across age groups and settings. It is expected that teachers' use of IWBs in education will improve educational outcomes, increase technological skills and reduce anxiety when preparing lectures.

The use of an interactive whiteboard beyond just use as chalkboards requires prior experience in using a computer and some prior skills in manipulating software applications. Consequently, for this study it is necessary to be aware of the factors that may affect teacher educators' competence and attitudes in using IWBs as these factors may in turn affect how they adopt the use of IWBs for teaching.

The success of implementing ICT in education depends greatly upon the attitudes of the teachers and their willingness to embrace such technology. Therefore, teachers should possess not only ICT knowledge and skills, but also the right attitudes toward ICT (Kennewell & Morgan, 2003). This is because their toward ICT will have a marked influence on their readiness to utilize technology in their teaching strategies.

Since a substantial amount of time, money, and effort is invested in the technology, it must exhibit learning value not only for students but also for teacher educators. There is little published research on IWBs in Nigeria, hence there is insufficient established data on the technology. Assessments of the IWB is needed so as to determine its effectiveness. Furthermore, since IWBs are relatively new and their use in classroom is still rising, knowing the attitude of the user (i.e., teacher) is essential.

Therefore, the aims of this study are to determine (a) the attitude that teacher educators have toward the use of IWBs; (b) teacher educators' level of use of IWBs; (c) whether significant correlation exists between the teacher educators' gender and their attitude toward IWBs; (d) if there is any significant relationship between teacher educators' use of IWBs and their attitudes toward IWBs; and (e) whether significant difference exists in the characteristics of teacher educators on IWBs based on their area of specialization.

The aim of the study will be investigated under the following research questions and hypotheses.

**Research Questions**

1) Will the attitude of the respondents to IWB usage be the same?
2) Will the respondents have the same attitude to IWB usage based on their academic qualification?
3) Will the respondents have the same attitude to IWBs usage based on their gender?
4) Will the respondents' IWBs skill demonstration be the same in the area of specializations of study?

**Research Hypotheses**

$H_{01}$: Attitude of teacher educators toward the use of IWBs is independent of skills acquired

$H_{02}$: There is no significant difference in the attitude of teacher educators toward the use of IWBs based on their level of educational qualification.

$H_{03}$: There is no significant difference in the attitude of teacher educators toward the use of IWBs based on gender

$H_{04}$: There is no significant relationship between teacher educators' attitude to the use of IWBs and their utilization of IWBs

$H_{05}$: There is no significant difference in the characteristics of teacher educators on IWBs skill acquired based on their area of specialization.

## Literature Review

Attitudes can be considered both the determinants and consequences of learning experiences. Every educational reform should take into consideration teachers' knowledge, skills, beliefs, and attitudes. One important concept of area of specialization reform is the human element, which encompasses emotions, feelings, needs, beliefs, and pedagogical assumptions. According to Ralf Linton, cited in (Yapici & Hevedanli, 2012), attitude is an implicit response. It could be negative–positive or neutral and cannot be directly observed. In order to be able to decide on what attitude an individual holds toward a specific object or event, the individual's response to that object should be observed in various environments (Turel & Johnson, 2012). Turel and Johnson (2012) state... that beliefs and attitudes play a fundamental role in the way that teachers deal with IWBs in the classroom. In other words, dealing effectively with IWBs relates not only to knowledge of the capability, limitations, applications, and implication of IWBs, but also to individuals' attitudes and perceptions regarding IWBs. Mathews-Aydinli and Elaziz (2010) state that the effective implementation of IWBs depends upon users' having positive attitudes toward them. They posited that area of specializations can go only so far to encourage IWBs use, and that actual take-up depends largely on teachers' personal feelings, skills, and attitudes toward IWBs. This implies that teachers who have positive attitudes toward IWBs and perceive them to be useful in promoting learning will integrate IWBs in their classroom more easily than others (Kennewell & Morgan, 2003; Turel & Johnson, 2012). IWB attitude can be defined as a person's general evaluation or feeling of favor or antipathy toward IWBs and specific computer-related activities (Kubiatko & Halakova, 2009).

A review of research on the introduction of IWBs in UK classrooms (Smith, Higgins, Wall, & Miller, 2005) revealed a clear preference for their use by both teachers and pupils. This had been noted previously by Kester (2002), who stated that all the teachers in her study were enthusiastic about the tools this new technology offered to help structure their lessons, to save time scribing, to attract and retain children's attention and to provide large attractive text and images (Jones & Vincent, 2010).

According to Jang and Tsai (2012), the IWBs can serve as a facilitative technological tool in the classroom to promote teaching effectiveness and to help teachers develop various pedagogical approaches with this technological integration (Winzenried, Dalgarno, & Tinkler, 2010). The integration of its functions into pedagogical strategies to improve teaching effectiveness has been studied with pre-service teachers (Murcia, 2008) and with in-service teachers for science (Jang, 2010) and mathematics (Miller, Glover, & Averis, 2005). Generally, the use of IWBs has been shown to positively influence teachers' integrative skills with developing their pedagogical approaches and students' learning as associated outcomes (Jang & Tsai, 2012).

Moseley and Higgins (1999) studied the attitudes of a small sample of teachers. They found that teachers who successfully made use of ICT had the following characteristics:

- A positive rather than negative attitude toward ICT. Teachers who have positive attitudes toward ICT itself will be positively disposed toward using it in the classroom.
- Pupil choice rather than teacher direction. Teachers who preferred directive styles of teaching tended to rate their own competence as low and made use of helpers with ICT.
- Pupil empowerment as learners rather than pupils receiving instruction.
- A preference for individual study rather than pupils receiving instruction.

Willis, Thompson, and Sadera (1999) draw together the main threads of what the research tells us today; for example, that teachers have very positive attitudes toward the use of technology in education, but are far less confident about their ability to actually use the technology and do not think that their teacher training programs prepared them to use technology in innovative ways. Also, that teacher training faculties, although positive about IT, do not have a strong background in integrating that into teacher education courses they teach.

Of the factors that have been listed to affect the successful use of technology in the classroom are teachers' attitudes toward technology, and these attitudes, whether positive or negative, affect how teachers respond to technologies. This in turn affects the way students view the importance of technology in schools (Teo, 2006) and affects current and future computer usage.

No matter how sophisticated and powerful the state of technology is, the extent to which it is implemented depends on teachers having a positive attitude toward it (Huang & Liaw, 2005).

## Method

### Instrument

The questionnaire developed for this study was guided by reviewing past literature (Beauchamp, 2004; Gomleksiz, 2004; Turel & Johnson, 2012).

The questionnaire comprised three sections: the first section highlighted participants' demographic background, the second section listed the type of IWBs skills used, while the third section sought to discover attitude toward IWBs.

The second section comprised a list of 20 different types of IWBs skills; participants were required to indicate their frequency of use for each skill. The items were measured by a five-point Likert type scale, ranging from never, rarely (average of 1 hour per week), sometimes (average of between 1 and 3 hours per week) often (average of between 3 and 6 hours per week) and always (average of more than 6 hours per week).

A panel of three expert judges validated all the items in the questionnaire. In terms of reliability, the Cronbach's alpha reliability coefficient for frequency of use subscale was 0.84.

In the third section of the instrument, 23 items measured attitudes toward IWBs. (Gomleksiz, 2004). The attitude scale was modified to meet the attitude objective of this investigation. Each item was measured against a four-point Likert-type scale ranging from strongly agree to strongly disagree.

## Sample

A multistage stratified sampling technique was used for this study. Three zones were selected - South West, South East, and North Central—out of the six geopolitical zones in Nigeria through random sampling. Two colleges of education were purposively selected from each zone. From these, 600 academic staff members (343 males and 257 females) were randomly sampled.

## Data Analysis

Frequency counts and percentages were used to describe the demographic variables in the study, Cross tabulations and percentages were used to answer the research questions while Spearman Rank correlation coefficient and Chi square test of independence were used to analyze the research hypothesis at 0.05 level of significance (Figure 27.1).

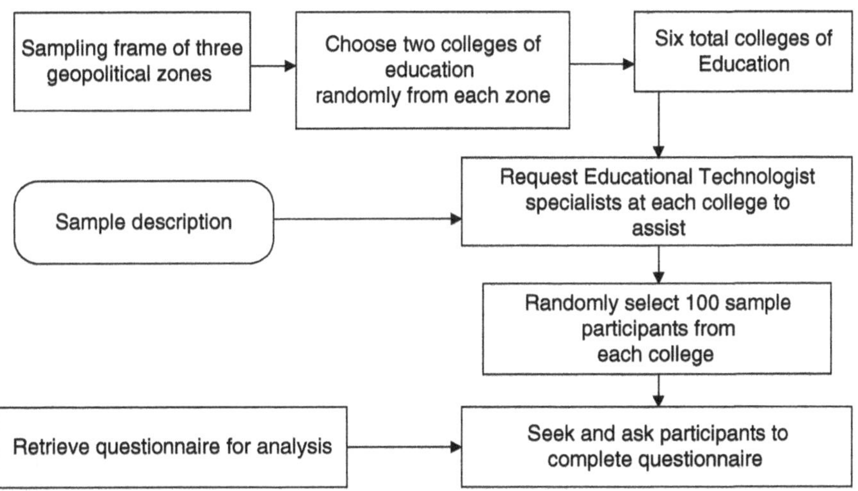


**Figure 27.1** Sampling and data collection method

## Results

### Descriptive Statistics

From Table 27.1, it is evident that out of 600 respondents, 343 (57.2 %) were male while 257 (42.8 %) were female. Seventy six (12.6 %) of the respondents were below 26 years, 145 (24.2 %) between 26 and 35 years, 109 (18.2 %) between 36 and 45 years, 152 (25.3 %) between 46 and 55 years while the remaining 118 (19.7 %) were above 55 years. One hundred and thirty-one (21.8 %) of the respondents stated their area of specialization to be education, 116 (19.3 %) nominated sciences, 124 (20.7 %) nominated vocational and technical education, 109 (18.2 %) nominated languages while the remainder, 120 (20 %) had theirs to be arts and social sciences. Two hundred and fifty-one (41.8 %) of the respondents had a bachelor's degree, 280 (46.7 %) have a master's degree while the remaining 69 (11.5 %) have a doctorate.

## Research Question

RESEARCH QUESTION 1: Will the attitude of the respondents to IWBs usage be the same?

From Table 27.2, out of the total of 600 respondents, 106(18 %) rarely demonstrated IWB skills in the class, 177 (30 %) sometimes demonstrated IWB skills in the class, 258 (43 %) often demonstrated IWB skills in the classroom. Twenty-three

**Table 27.1** Number and percentage of respondents by demographics, N = 600

| | Status | Frequency | Percent |
|---|---|---|---|
| Gender of Respondents | Male | 343 | 57.2 |
| | Female | 257 | 42.8 |
| Age Range of Respondents | Below 26 Years | 76 | 12.6 |
| | 26–35 Years | 145 | 24.2 |
| | 36–45 Years | 109 | 18.2 |
| | 46–55 Years | 152 | 25.3 |
| | Above 55 Years | 118 | 19.7 |
| Area of Specialization | Education | 131 | 21.8 |
| | Sciences | 116 | 19.3 |
| | Voc. And Tech. Edu | 124 | 20.7 |
| | Languages | 109 | 18.2 |
| | Arts And Social Sciences | 120 | 20 |
| Academic Qualification | Bachelor | 251 | 41.8 |
| | Masters | 280 | 46.7 |
| | Ph.D. | 69 | 11.5 |

(4 %) of the respondents always demonstrated IWB skills in the classroom while the remaining 37 (6 %) disagreed with the demonstration of IWB skills in the classroom.

RESEARCH QUESTION 2: Will the respondents have the same attitude to IWBs usage based on their academic qualification?

In Table 27.3, from the total of 600 respondents, 235 (39.2 % of the total respondents) with bachelor's degrees had a positive attitude to IWB skill demonstration, as did 262 (43.7 %) with master's degrees, 67 (11 %) with PhD degrees; the remaining 36 (9 %) had a negative attitude to the demonstration of IWB skills in the classroom.

RESEARCH QUESTION 3: Will the respondents have the same attitude to IWBs usage based on their gender?

From Table 27.4, it can be observed that out of the total of 600 respondents, 322 male respondents (53.7 % of the total respondents) had a positive attitude toward IWBs skill demonstration, 242 female respondents (40.3 %) had a positive

**Table 27.2** Distribution of attitude of respondents to IWB usage

| **Attitude to IWBS Usage** | | | | |
|---|---|---|---|---|
| **IWBS Skills Demonstrated** | **Agree** | **%** | **Disagree** | **%** |
| Rarely | 106 | 18 | 6 | 1 |
| Sometimes | 177 | 30 | 7 | 1 |
| Often | 258 | 43 | 6 | 1 |
| Always | 23 | 4 | 17 | 3 |

**Table 27.3** Frequency distribution of attitude of respondents to IWB usage based on academic qualification

| **Attitude to IWBs** | | | | |
|---|---|---|---|---|
| **Academic Qualification** | **Good** | **%** | **Bad** | **%** |
| Bachelor | 235 | 39.2 | 16 | 2.7 |
| Masters | 262 | 43.7 | 18 | 3 |
| Ph.D. | 67 | 11.2 | 2 | 0.3 |

**Table 27.4** Frequency distribution of attitude of respondents to IWB usage based on gender

| **Attitude to IWBs** | | | | |
|---|---|---|---|---|
| **Gender of Respondents** | **Good** | **%** | **Bad** | **%** |
| Male | 322 | 53.7 | 21 | 3.5 |
| Female | 242 | 40.3 | 15 | 2.5 |

attitude toward IWB skill demonstration, 21 male respondents (3.5 %) had a negative attitude toward the demonstration of IWBs while the remaining 15 female respondents (2.5 %) had a negative attitude toward IWB skill demonstration.

RESARCH QUESTION 4: Will the respondents' IWB skill demonstration be the same in the area of specializations of study?

In Table 27.5, from the total of 600 respondents, in the area of specialization of education 24 (4 % of the total respondents), 43 (7.2 %), 52 (8.7 %) and 12 (2 %) rarely, sometimes, often and always demonstrate IWBs skills in the classroom respectively. In the area of specialization of sciences 15 (2.5 % of the total respondents), 44 (7.3 % of the total respondents), 50 (8.3 %) and 7 (1.2 %) rarely, sometimes, often and always demonstrate IWB skills in the classroom respectively. In the area of specialization of vocational and technical education 25 (4.2 % of the total respondents), 26 (4.3 %), 66 (11 %) and 7 (1.2) rarely, sometimes, often and always demonstrate IWB skills in the classroom respectively. In the area of specialization of languages 24 (4.0 % of the total respondents), 32 (5.3 %), 43 (7.2 %) and 10 (1.7) rarely, sometimes, often and always demonstrate IWB skills in the classroom respectively. In the area of specialization of Arts and social science 24 (4.0 % of the total respondents), 39 (6.5 %), 53 (8.8 %) and 4 (0.7 %) rarely, sometimes, often and always demonstrate IWBs skills in the classroom respectively.

## Research Hypothesis

### Hypothesis 1

$H_0$: Attitude of teacher educators toward the use of IWBs is independent of IWBs skills acquired.

$H_1$: Attitude of teacher educators toward the use of IWBs is dependent on IWBs skills acquired.

#### Decision

From Table 27.6, since the Pearson Chi-Square asymptotic significant (2-sided) value of 0.000 is less than alpha value of 0.05, the null hypothesis is rejected, and

**Table 27.5** Frequency distribution of IWB skill demonstrated based on area of specialization

| **IWB Skills Demonstrated** | | | | | | | | |
|---|---|---|---|---|---|---|---|---|
| **Area of Specialization** | **Rarely** | **%** | **Sometimes** | **%** | **Often** | **%** | **Always** | **%** |
| Education | 24 | 4.0 | 43 | 7.2 | 52 | 8.7 | 12 | 2.0 |
| Sciences | 15 | 2.5 | 44 | 7.3 | 50 | 8.3 | 7 | 1.2 |
| Vocational and Technical Education | 25 | 4.2 | 26 | 4.3 | 66 | 11.0 | 7 | 1.2 |
| Languages | 24 | 4.0 | 32 | 5.3 | 43 | 7.2 | 10 | 1.7 |
| Arts and Social Sciences | 24 | 4.0 | 39 | 6.5 | 53 | 8.8 | 4 | 0.7 |

**Table 27.6** Chi square tests showing the dependency of the use of IWBs on attitude of teacher educators

| | Value | df | Asymp. Sig. (2-sided) |
|---|---|---|---|
| Pearson Chi-Square | 102.644[a] | 3 | .000 |
| Likelihood Ratio | 54.250 | 3 | .000 |
| Linear-by-Linear Association | 15.992 | 1 | .000 |
| N of Valid Cases | 600 | | |

[a] 1 cell (12.5 %) has expected count less than 5. The minimum expected count is 2.40.

it was concluded that the attitude of teacher educators toward the use of IWBs is dependent on IWB skills acquired.

## Hypothesis 2

$H_0$: There is no significant difference in the attitude of teacher educators toward the use of IWBs based on their level of educational qualification.

$H_1$: There is a significant difference in the attitude of teacher educators toward the use of IWBs based on their level of educational qualification.

### Decision

From Table 27.7, Since the Pearson Chi-Square asymptotic significant (2-sided) value of 0.514 is greater than alpha value of 0.05, the null hypothesis is not rejected, and it was concluded that there is no significant difference in the attitude of teacher educators toward the use of IWBs based on their level of educational qualification.

## Hypothesis 3

$H_0$: There is no significant difference in the attitude of teacher educators toward the use of IWBs based on gender.

**Table 27.7** Chi square tests showing the differences that exist in the use of IWBs based on their level of educational qualification of respondents

**Chi-Square Tests**

| | Value | df | Asymp. Sig. (2-sided) |
|---|---|---|---|
| Pearson Chi-Square | 1.330[a] | 2 | .514 |
| Likelihood Ratio | 1.590 | 2 | .452 |
| Linear-by-Linear Association | .634 | 1 | .426 |
| N of Valid Cases | 600 | | |

[a] 1 cell (16.7 %) has expected count less than 5. The minimum expected count is 4.14.

$H_1$: There is a significant difference in the attitude of teacher educators toward the use of IWBs based on gender.

**Decision**

From Table 27.8, Since the Pearson Chi-Square asymptotic significant (2-sided) value of 0.884 is greater than alpha value of 0.05, the null hypothesis is not rejected, and it was concluded that there is no significant difference in the attitude of teacher educators toward the use of IWBs based on gender.

## Hypothesis 4

$H_0$: There is no significant relationship between teacher educators' attitude to the use of IWBs and their utilization of IWBs.

$H_1$: There is a significant relationship between teacher educators' attitude to the use of IWBs and their utilization of IWBs.

**Decision**

From Table 27.9. the Spearman rank correlation coefficient of 0.147 indicate a positively weak correlation between teacher educators' attitude to the use of IWBs and their utilization of IWBs while the approximate significant value of 0.000 which is less than 0.05 indicates a significant correlation. Hence the null hypothesis is rejected, and it was concluded that there is a significant relationship between teacher educators' attitude and their utilization of IWBs.

## Hypothesis 5

$H_0$: There is no significant difference in the characteristics of teacher educators on IWBs skill acquired based on their area of specialization.

**Table 27.8** Chi square tests showing the differences that exist in attitude of the teacher educators toward the use of IWBs based on their gender

**Chi-Square Tests**

| | Value | df | Asymp. Sig. (2-sided) | Exact Sig. (2-sided) | Exact Sig. (1-sided) |
|---|---|---|---|---|---|
| Pearson Chi-Square | .021[a] | 1 | .884 | | |
| Continuity Correction[b] | .000 | 1 | 1.000 | | |
| Likelihood Ratio | .021 | 1 | .884 | | |
| Fisher's Exact Test | | | | 1.000 | .514 |
| Linear-by-Linear Association | .021 | 1 | .884 | | |
| N of Valid Cases | 600 | | | | |

[a] 0 cells (0.0 %) have expected count less than 5. The minimum expected count is 15.42.

[b] Computed only for a 2 × 2 table.

**Table 27.9** Correlation tests showing the relationship that exist teacher educators' attitude and their utilization of IWBs

**Symmetric Measures**

| | | Value | Asymp. Std. Error[a] | Approx. T[b] | Approx. Sig. |
|---|---|---|---|---|---|
| Interval-by-Interval | Pearson's R | .163 | .054 | 4.050 | .000[c] |
| Ordinal-by-Ordinal | Spearman Correlation | .147 | .052 | 3.624 | .000[c] |
| N of Valid Cases | | 600 | | | |

[a] Not assuming the null hypothesis.
[b] Using the asymptotic standard error assuming the null hypothesis.
[c] Based on normal approximation.

**Table 27.10** Chi square tests showing the differences that exist in attitude of the teacher educators toward the use of IWBs based on their area of specialization

**hi-Square Tests**

| | Value | df | Asymp. Sig. (2-sided) |
|---|---|---|---|
| Pearson Chi-Square | 17.162[a] | 12 | .144 |
| Likelihood Ratio | 17.816 | 12 | .121 |
| Linear-by-Linear Association | .906 | 1 | .341 |
| N of Valid Cases | 600 | | |

[a] 0 cells (0.0 %) have expected count less than 5. The minimum expected count is 7.27.

$H_1$: There is a significant difference in the characteristics of teacher educators on IWBs skill acquired based on their area of specialization.

**Decision**

From Table 27.10, since the Pearson Chi-Square asymptotic significant (2-sided) value of 0.144 is greater than alpha value of 0.05, the null hypothesis is not rejected, and it was concluded that there is no significant difference in the characteristics of teacher educators on IWBs skill acquired based on their area of specialization.

## Discussion

The results imply that the use of IWBs in Nigerian colleges of education has reached a moderate level for different types of IWBs use, namely, matching items, coloring important content, lesson recording, snapshot, flipping back and forth between content, annotating important content, and importing existing graphics. Their attitude has been discovered to have played significant role in their IWBs skill demonstration in classrooms, which is in line with the opinion of Turel and Johnson (2012) who believe that attitudes play a fundamental role in the way that teacher deal with IWBs in the classroom. Their attitudes toward the use of IWBs are independent of educational qualification, gender and area of specialization as they are all enthusiastic about the tool, which corroborates the view of Kester (2002), who stated that all the teachers in her study were enthusiastic about the tools since this new technology offered to help structure their lessons, and this was regardless of their educational qualification, gender, or area of specialization. This implies that the money the federal government is expending on ICT is beginning to yield desirable results. The majority of the participants showed a positive attitude toward the use of IWBs. It is reasonable to expect this, since all participants passed through pre-service teacher education programs where they were required to take one or two technology courses taught by an educational technology expert. This type of course is normally designed to assist teacher candidates to develop a variety of technical skills. The lack of IWB attitude differences between genders in this study is consistent with research that revealed changing attitudes among female technology users (Teo, 2008).

The teacher educators have embraced the use of IWBs in their colleges. However, the usage of advanced IWB skills was still at low level among teacher educators and perhaps this may be due to their limited competency in using IWBs. This is consistent with the findings of Moursand and Bielefeldt (1999) who claimed that the technology course teacher educators took in their pre-service teacher education program was not sufficient to prepare them to teach with technology in the classroom. This impact may be due in part to the way the technology course was taught.

The majority of teacher educators considered IWBs to be a veritable instructional tool which helped them to achieve the aims and objective of teaching learning process. The finding of this research confirmed previous work (Armstrong et al., 2005; Beauchamp, 2004; Levy, 2002; Slay, Sieborger, & Hodgkinson-Williams, 2008; Smith et al., 2005; Turel & Johnson, 2012).

The finding of the study also indicated a weak positive correlation between teacher educators' use and their attitude toward IWBs. This result was consistent with the literature that emphasized a positive attitude toward a new technology is important for its successful implementation (Armstrong et al., 2005; Teo, 2008). The positive attitudes toward IWBs shared by teacher educators constitute a critical factor in the effective use of IWBs.

The use of IWBs appears to be independent of demographic characteristics of the respondents. No significant difference could be established in the utilization of IWBs by teacher educators' gender, area of specialization, or academic qualifications.

In general, this study contributes significantly to the literature in that it shows that successful implementation of IWBs in Nigerian classroom can be guaranteed only by developing in the user a positive attitude toward the use of such technology.

The results of this study have implications for policy-makers who are aiming to encourage the use of IWBs among academic staff. Heads of institutions should consider the attitudes of would-be users before deciding whether the technology is going to be used or not. It is recommended that periodic seminars and workshops be conducted for all staff members so as to provide them with basic information about IWBs and their benefits. Similarly, when widely implementing IWB-based classrooms, an inmportant prerequisite may be the condition that the users (teacher educators) should have positive attitudes toward the system.

## Conclusion

Successful implementation of technology integration in the classroom depends to a large extent on teachers who are the users. It is pertinent for them to have positive technology attitudes since attitudes have been found to be linked to usage and intention to use technology in the classroom (Teo, 2008).

The limitation of this study is that it did not investigate the effect of computer knowledge on IWBs utilization or attitude. Future studies should consider these factors and further research with larger samples be conducted.

## References

Armstrong, V., Barnes, S., Sutherland, R., Curran, S., Mills, S., & Thompson, I. (2005). Collaborative research methodology for investigating teaching and learning: The use of interactive whiteboard technology. *Educational Review, 57*(4), 457–569.

Beauchamp, G. (2004). Teacher use of the interactive whiteboard in primary schools. Towards an effective transition framework. *Technology Pedagogy and Education, 13*(3), 327–348.

British Educational Communications and Technology. (2004). *Getting the most from your interactive whiteboard. A guide for secondary schools.* Coventry, UK: BECTA.

Federal Republic of Nigeria. (2010). Science and Technology Standard for Teacher Educators in Nigerian Colleges of Education. Abuja, Nigeria: NCCE.

Gomleksiz, M. N. (2004). Use of education technology in English classes. *Turkish Online Journal of Technology, 3*(2), 8–16.

Huang, H. M., & Liaw, S. S. (2005). Exploring users' attitudes and intentions toward the web as a survey tool. *Computers in Human Behavior, 21*, 729–743.

Jang, S. J. (2010). Integrating the interactive whiteboard and peer coaching to develop the TPACK of secondary science teachers. *Computers and Education, 52*(4), 1744–1751.

Jang, S. J., & Tsai, M. F. (2012). Reasons for using or not using interactive whiteboards: Perspectives of Taiwanese elementary mathematics and science teachers. *Australian Journal of Educational Technology, 28*(8), 1451–1465.

Jones, A., & Vincent, J. (2010). Collegial mentoring for effective whole school professional development in the use of IWBs technologies. *Australian Journal of Educational Technology, 26*(4), 477–493.

Kennewell, S. and Morgan, A. (2003) Student teachers' experiences and attitudes towards using interactive whiteboards in the teaching and learning of young children. In Proceedings of Young Children and Learning Technologies Conference. Sydney; International Federation for Information Processing.

Kester, S. (2002). The use of IWBs in the classroom. *Innovation in Technology, 52*(4), 121–134.

Kubiatko, M., & Halakova, Z. (2009). Slovak high school students' attitudes to ICT using in biology lesson. *Computers in Human Behaviour, 25*, 743–748.

Levy, P. (2002). Interactive whiteboards in learning and teaching in two Sheffield schools. A developmental study. Department of Information Studies, University of Sheffield (retrieved 6 March 2013). http://dis/shef.ac.uk/eirg/projectswboards.htm

Mathews-Aydinli, J., & Elaziz, F. (2010). Turkish students' and teachers' attitudes toward the use of interactive whiteboards in EFL classrooms. *Computer Assisted Language Learning, 23*(3), 235–252.

Miller, D., Glover, D. and Averis, D. (2005). Developing pedagogic skills for the use of the interactive whiteboard in mathematics. Glamorgan, UK: British Educational Research Association,. (Retrieved 6 August 2014). www.keele.ac.uk/media/keeleuniversity/fachumsocsci/sclpppp/education/interactivewhiteboard/BERA%2Paper%20Sep%202005.pdf

Moseley, D., & Higgins, S. (1999). *Ways forward with ICT: Effective pedagogy using information and communications technology for literacy and numeracy in primary schools.* London, UK: Teacher Training Agency.

Moursand, D., & Bielefeldt, T. (1999). *Will new teachers be prepared to teach in a digital age? National survey on information technology in teacher education.* Santa Monica, CA: Milken Exchange on Educational Technology. Retrieved from https://eric.ed.gov/?id=ED428072

Murcia, K. (2008). Teaching for scientific literacy with an interactive whiteboard. *Teaching Science, 54*(4), 17–21. Retrieved from http://smartboardita.pbworks.com/f/Teaching%2Bfor%2Bscientific%2B%2Bliteracy%2Bwith%2Bank%2B%interactive%2Bwhiteboard.pdf

Slay, H., Sieborger, I., & Hodgkinson-Williams, C. (2008). Interactive whiteboards: Real beauty or just "lipstick"? *Computers and Education, 5*(3), 1321–1341.

Smith, H. J., Higgins, S., Wall, K., & Miller, J. (2005). Interactive whiteboards. Boon or bandwagon? A critical review of the literature. *Journal of Computer Assisted Learning, 21*, 91–101.

Teo, T. (2006). Attitudes toward computers: A study of postsecondary students in Singapore. *Interactive Learning Environments, 14*, 17–24.

Teo, T. (2008). Pre-service teachers' attitudes towards computer use: A Singapore survey. *Australian Journal of Educational Technology, 24*(4), 414–424.

Turel, Y. K., & Johnson, T. E. (2012). Teachers' belief and use of Interactive Whiteboards for Teaching and Learning. *Journal of Educational Technology and Society, 15*(1), 381–394.

Willis, J., Thompson, A., & Sadera, W. (1999). Research on technology and teacher education: current status and future directions. *Journal of Curriculum and Instruction, 47*(4), 29–45.

Winzenried, A., Dalgarno, B., & Tinkler, J. (2010). The interactive whiteboard: A transitional technology supporting diverse teaching practices. *Australasian Journal of Educational Technology, 26*(4), 534–552.

Yapici, I. U., & Hevedanli, M. (2012). Pre-service biology teachers' attitudes towards ICT using in biology teaching. *Procedia—Social and Behavioural Sciences, 64,* 633–638.

# 28

# Gamification for Learning and Workforce Motivation

*Kenneth R. Pierce*

*Texas State University*

Online courses are great for providing anytime anyplace education; but they still face issues of design in terms of keeping students on task, developing self-efficacy, and motivating students to succeed. Although online education is widespread and generally accepted, it still faces the stigma of being inferior to education delivered in person by subject-matter experts. But, since online education is generally a cheaper and many times a less time-consuming alternative to traditional education, it is important that it continue to evolve to a point where it is perceived to deliver equal or greater results than in-person education. Therefore, any strategy that appears to enhance the learning outcomes of online education needs attention paid to it. Gamification is one of those strategies.

Gamification strategies can be adopted to generate the same excitement and motivation for an online course as is seen in modern electronic games. Whether we realize it or not, we already encounter the principles of gamification in just about every aspect of our lives, for example, loyalty cards for petrol or groceries, bonus payments, energy saving schemes, squash/bridge/tennis rankings (Dale, 2014). The use of gamification dynamics within a course has three overall goals: Improve students' motivation and learning; provide students with adaptive course content; and implement effective management strategies for the subject matter experts' online workload and ongoing course maintenance. To make the course scalable and automated in some components (which is required in a gamified scenario), students must take formative assessments, which are graded automatically and provide student immediate feedback (Markopoulos, Kasidiaris, and Davim, 2015).

Well-designed online courses have been shown to have equivalent outcomes to traditional face-to-face courses. The process of "gamifying" the course can provide invaluable insights for the course designer and result in a more effective course. Preliminary data suggests that students in gamified courses outperform students in the traditionally designed online course. In addition to the learning outcomes, gamified educational experiences will achieve higher

*The Wiley Handbook of Global Workplace Learning*, First Edition.
Edited by Vanessa Hammler Kenon and Sunay Vasant Palsole.

student engagement without requiring the instructor to spend more time on the course when enrolled students increase in number.

Gamification strategies that involve rethinking the philosophy of student engagement may provide a greater benefit rather than a high value investment of game creation. A stratified approach to gamification provides gains in student engagement and learning throughout the learning period, leading to better learning outcomes. Organizations whose employees, and customers are deeply engaged will outperform those that cannot engender authentic motivation (Werbach and Hunter, 2012). These strategies could be very meaningful as courses scale, because they leverage principles of self-actuation and prompt feedback to keep the learners motivated toward achieving their learning goals. While the time spent in rethinking and redesign might sound daunting, the resulting payoff in a high degree of learner engagement without a corresponding increase of instructor workload makes it a worthy investment.

In her article "Gamification: Recipe for Successful Learning-or Just One Ingredient?," Carol Leaman promotes a recipe for learning success as being "1 part personalization, 1 part brain science, and 1 part gamification" (Leaman, 2015). While we are only focusing on gamification here, it is important to note there can be tight linkages to other strategies that will also provide the opportunity to greatly enhance learning success.

## What is a Game?

For us to understand gamification techniques and strategies, we must first be able to articulate exactly what a game is, and what makes something become a "game." According to the Merriam-Webster dictionary, a game is "any activity undertaken or regarded as a contest involving rivalry, strategy, or struggle." We have all played games during our lifetime, and probably for different reasons. For some, playing a game is for personal reasons such as simply enjoying the competition it offers. Many play games to better themselves at some mental or physical activity. For others, games offer an opportunity to demonstrate their supremacy at something, or an opportunity for financial success via professional activity (sports, etc.). To sum it all up, games are popular simply because they are fun to play!

While much has been written regarding games and game theory, most research shows there are a set of characteristics which make a game a game. In general, these characteristics are: (a) participation must be voluntary; (b) a game has rules; (c) games have a beginning and an end; (d) there is freedom of choice; and (e) there are rewards.

If you engaged in an activity that you could control the outcome every time because you could change the rules at will, you would probably be bored as the competitive nature you are wanting to engage in would be lost. In that case, it wouldn't really be considered a game. Additionally, if you were not free to make decisions or choices, then you would have no control or influence over the outcome. This too would make for a very unchallenging and boring activity. Unfortunately, this is also the manner in which education courses have traditionally been designed.

## What is Gamification?

Now that we understand what a game is, we can extend the concept to gamification. Again, according to the Merriam-Webster dictionary, gamification is "the process of adding games or game like elements to something (as a task) so as to encourage participation." One of the more popular definitions is "the use of game elements and game thinking in non-game environments to increase target behavior and engagement." In other words, gamification is a process of converting something potentially tedious or "not fun" into something that is more challenging or fun. Notice that we did not state that we are turning something that is not a game into a game. In the gamification process, we are simply applying the characteristics, attributes, or mechanics of a game to non-game activities to make them more enjoyable and engaging. More recently, gamification has become a powerful instructional method in K-12 education, as well as top colleges and universities. Health care is still in the early stages of embracing gamification in education; however, some of this may be due to a knowledge deficit related to what gamification is and how it could be applied in the health care setting (Brull and Finlayson, 2016).

Successful gamification involves two kinds of skills. It requires an understanding of game design, and it requires an understanding of business techniques (Werbach and Hunter, 2012). The core of the gamification strategy is based on a leaderboard, points, and badges, combined with a customizable course "roadmap" and dynamic course modules.

Gamification achieves effectiveness by accessing our natural craving for competition and measured achievement. Implementation of gamification has greatly expanded with the proliferation of software and electronic devices. It is often a core feature of websites or mobile applications. According to Gartner, more than 50% of organizations that manage innovation processes will gamify them. Extensive applications of gamification can be found in almost all functional areas of HR including talent acquisition, training and development, talent management and performance management, as organizations try to find newer ways of keeping employees engrossed (Sarangi and Shah, 2015). For example, most health-related wearable technologies (such as Fitbit) use gamification to motivate users to achieve personal goals such as weight-loss or measured activity. Simply put, the advancement of technology has made gamification strategies easier to implement; and therefore, more available. As we will see later in this chapter, applying gamification strategies to educational activity can lead to improved engagement and outcomes for learners.

Additionally, there continues to be a growing scholarly interest in gamification. According to recent findings, "gamification" is a potentially fruitful topic for scholars to continue to explore. In addition, ongoing research is merited in light of scholars' continued interest in the topic (Harman and Koohang, 2014).

The results of a gamification strategy should end up with a more human-focused design. Most systems are inherently "function-focused," that is, designed to get the job done quickly. This is like a factory that assumes its workers will do their jobs because they are required to, not because they necessarily want to perform the associated tasks (Chou, 2015). Gamification is founded in the fundamentals of human psychology and behavioral science, and rests on three primary factors: motivation, ability level and triggers (Dale, 2014).

## Motivation

One of the main reasons we apply gamification to a situation is to motivate the participants to complete a task with a certain result (although motivation is not always the only reason). Alongside the motivation must be a rewards system which defines for the participant what they receive for successful completion. It is important when gamifying an experience that the designer understand some basic motivational principles, typically referred to as the Self-Determination Theory, or SDT.

Self-Determination Theory distinguishes between two different types of motivation: intrinsic motivation and extrinsic motivation. The basic distinction between them is the reward. With Intrinsic motivation, the reward is generally the positive experience or the feeling one gets by doing something. Extrinsic motivation involves doing something because it leads to a separable outcome such as a prize or token. Research shows the quality of both experience and performance can significantly vary when participants are behaving intrinsically versus extrinsically.

To put this theory into perspective, consider your motivation for exercising. If you are motivated intrinsically to exercise, you do it because it makes you feel good and you are investing in your health. These are personal feelings that motivate you to continue to exercise. If you were acting extrinsically, you would be exercising because there is something you receive (physical or virtual) in return for the activity, such as a discount on insurance.

Intrinsic motivation has emerged as an important phenomenon for educators—a natural wellspring of learning and achievement that can be systematically catalyzed or undermined by parent and teacher practices. Because intrinsic motivation results in high-quality learning and creativity, it is especially important to detail the factors and forces that engender versus undermine it (Ryan and Deci, 2000).

Therefore, when implementing gamification, it is important to employ the most suitable and effective rewards strategy, remembering that in general developing an intrinsic motivation will usually outperform a design solely based on extrinsic motivation. Gabe Zichermann developed the SAPS model, which classifies rewards in four categories: Status, Access, Power, and Stuff. Two "rules" apply to this classification:

1) Costs generally increase from 1 to 4. In other words, "Stuff" is more expensive to give away than "Status."
2) The "stickiness" decreases from 1 to 4. Over the long term, "Status" is more effective than "Stuff."

Giving away a new tablet computer doesn't require a lot of creativity. In other words, "Stuff" is usually the *easiest* to give away. However, there's usually a *better* reward available.

Another key consideration in motivation is managing the relationship between challenge and skill. At the heart of the success of games is an idea called "flow." Mihaly Csikszentmihalyi, a Hungarian psychologist and Distinguished Professor of Psychology and Management at Claremont Graduate University established what he called the "flow channel," which is the optimum channel for an activity to prevent anxiety when skill levels are low and the challenge is too great, and boredom when the skill level is high and the activity is too easy (Zicherman and Cunningham, 2011).

## Gamification in Education

Motivating students or employees to stay engaged until the end of a training event is not easy. Involvement (engagement) is one of the significant challenges in education and training, especially when the subject matter is not of personal interest to the learner. The idea of sitting in a classroom to learn essential information not only is cost prohibitive but doesn't provide a delivery format needed to keep the younger generation engaged (Brull and Finlayson, 2016). Educational providers could greatly benefit by gamification to foster engagement in the learning activity. The parallels between gaming and learning make for a good match. Education is about obtaining knowledge or a skill, advancement in grades, or scoring well on exams. In gaming, overcoming obstacles relates to the attainment of knowledge and skills, completing levels relates to grade advancement, and completing tasks relates to the passing of exams. A key element to modern games (especially online multiplayer games) is social interaction. Social interaction enhances the gaming experience, and has been shown to also improve educational outcomes when incorporated into the learning design. These correlations make gamification of education seem almost natural. Social gamification aims to bring together gamification and social networking to combine the potential of both approaches to create compelling, socially-driven user experiences. From an educational perspective, it can harness the motivational aspects of gamification to stimulate participation and engagement with learning contents and with other participants. The combination of both can create a kind of multiplication effect in which gamification can be used to promote social desirable learning behaviors, and actions in the social network can be used to design gamification props that produce motivational boosts in educational settings (de-Marcos, Garcia-Lopez, and Garcia-Cabot, 2016).

E-learning courses are usually linear courses. This kind of content structure can allow us to easily gamify the content. The basic idea is to uncover content progressively, put more focus on exercises while offering the theoretical means for them to be solved and offer points for correctly solving them (Muntean, 2011). Gamification capitalizes on the assumption that the adult learner will be intrinsically motivated to learn when provided with the flexibility and convenience to do so at his or her own pace (Brull and Finlayson, 2016). In the future, we can expect even greater use of gamification in education. Progress in technology and software, and the knowledge of gamification will bring an even a higher degree of personalization in e-learning (Urh, Vukovic, Jereb, and Pintar, 2015).

## Attributes and Expectations of a Gamified Experience

There are a few other considerations that need to be addressed with incorporating gamification into a situation, and they deal with the expectations of participants which, if not met, can be disastrous when it comes to reaching the goal of the effort.

### Immediacy

In terms of gamification, it refers to the participant always knowing how they are doing and where they stand. Immediacy needs to be addressed in any gamification scenario. Consider playing a slot machine in Las Vegas. You put in your money, and you pull the lever (OK, today not many machines still have usable levers as they have been replaced by buttons) and the wheels start spinning. Instead of watching the images stop in front of you one by one, you get a message that says, "come back in an hour and we'll tell you if you won." I'm guessing if that happened you wouldn't be playing slot machines for much longer! Why? Because the immediacy that is expected for that activity is not an hour, but seconds. Not meeting that requirement would drive off patrons.

When it comes to immediacy in gamification within education and training, it is important to establish reasonable expectations of learners and incorporate the appropriate mechanisms to satisfy the immediacy requirements. This could include redesigning tests to be electronic, or for existing electronic tests redesigning the questions so they can be electronically graded thereby providing instant feedback upon completion of the test. The results can then be piped directly to other gamification elements such as point totals, badge awards, or leaderboards.

### Accuracy

Throughout the experience, if the participant perceives that the data being provided is not accurate (which could also be because of an immediacy problem), there could be disengagement by the participant. Accuracy is akin to integrity in the mind of the participant, and therefore gamification designs should ensure that accuracy is always maintained. Within an educational or training environment, striving for more objective grading mechanisms over subjective ones is preferred.

### Progression

Participants have an expectation that as they master knowledge or skills their "score" reflects that status. Typically, this can be handled with points and badges if using those elements, but sometimes there is a need for additional metrics. One should also consider the motivational side of these metrics and whether they are positively motivating or negatively motivating. Within an educational or training environment, the design of the course or curriculum should be done with progression milestones in mind. Very distinguishable completion points such as percentage complete or overall score are important.

### Decision Making

As we noted earlier, the ability of a participant to make decisions in a game scenario is key to the experience and the outcome. Designing in ways for students to make decisions on their own pathway through education material is a very good way to incorporate this concept.

### Competition

Competition is another key element that should be considered in the design of a gamified experience. While it may not always be present, if should be incorporated if possible to strengthen the opportunity to increase the intrinsic motivational factor discussed earlier. For some, the thought of winning is a strong intrinsic motivator.

## The Bread and Butter of Gamification

As with most design strategies, gamification has a generally accepted foundation or starting point that can be applied to the situation. In this case, however, it is essentially a recognized set of tools where one or more of them are present in most instances. In this section, we explore these tools and their role in the design of a gamified educational experience.

## Points, Badges, and Leaderboards

Points, badges and leaderboards (often called "PBL's") are the most utilized game elements when it comes to gamification. In nearly every gamified experience people encounter in their daily lives, one of these three elements (if not all three) is present, mainly because they tend to be the easiest to implement. However, simply affixing PBL's to an existing activity without looking at the design of the whole activity does not ensure a successful gamification implementation as it is doubtful that the once boring activity will automatically become fun or exciting. This is something to be aware of, as many gamification platforms you might look at utilizing are simply adding PBLs in a scalable or automated manner, often giving you a false sense of security that you have gamified your product. Remember, the reason for gamifying your product is to make an impactful change that improves results.

But don't get the impression that points, badges, and leaderboards are not valuable. They do have their place in game design, which is why they have been used so pervasively. They have the inherent ability to motivate and influence people to perform certain actions.

### Points

The key functions of points are to keep score, provide up to date feedback, and provide progress toward the win state. Points also can have a connection to the rewards component of the activity. Earning points can have a dramatic effect on participants' behavior even when the points have no monetary value. They also offer flexibility to employees by targeting their specific needs (Sarangi and Shah, 2015).

## Badges

The key function of badges is to provide a representation or acknowledgement of achievement. Badges can be synonymous with credentials, or a collection of badges can be used to create a credential. While badges are generally personal achievement representations, they are typically shared on social display to generate positive feedback or acknowledgement from others. They are the tangible accomplishments that instill the sense of pride and purpose that are critical to employee engagement (Sarangi and Shah, 2015).

## Leaderboards

The key function of a leaderboard is to provide feedback on competition via a visible ranking system accessible by participants. See Figure 28.1. Leaderboards are especially effective when participants can compare themselves to people they know, such as friends or relatives. They encourage healthy competition. They are used as trackers for enhancing employee performance and development (Sarangi and Shah, 2015).

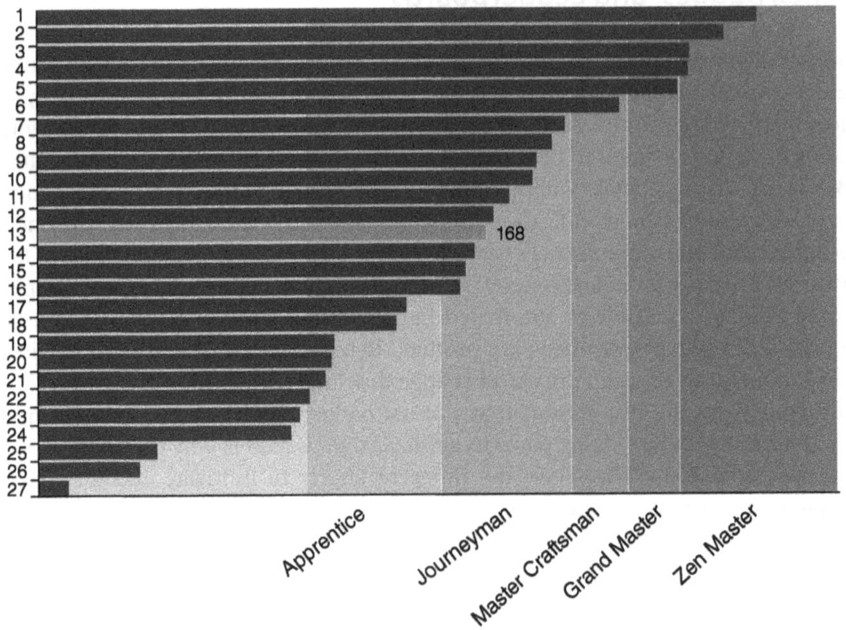


**Figure 28.1** Sample Course Leaderboard

**Table 28.1** Traditional versus gamified education

| | Traditional College Course | Gamified Requirement |
|---|---|---|
| Immediacy | Students sometimes wait days or weeks to receive feedback on the work they submit | Players receive timely feedback on their attempts or activities (instant or no more than 24 hours) |
| Accuracy | Much scoring is done manually and subjectively depending on the subject | Most scoring is handled electronically and is therefore inherently accurate and objective |
| Progression | Students start at 100 and through mistakes (such as missed questions) watch their score decrease | Player starts at 0 and through successful completion of items improves their score toward 100% |
| Decision Making | Students usually don't have the ability to make decisions within a course, other than extra credit possibilities | Players make decisions throughout the activity |
| Competition | Students only know of their own scores progress and do not have near real time comparative data with other students | Players always know where they rank in relation to other players |

Remember, gamification is more than just PBLs. Experts only familiar with how to implement PBL mechanics often miss the point of user engagement, and can insult participants by presenting them with seemingly shallow shell mechanics.

However, if you look at our traditional educational models in secondary and post-secondary education, you see there are some parts of the design that just don't align. For example, looking at a traditional college course, its overall design does not align with gamification principles. Table 28.1 depicts the differences between the two.

## The Gamification Design Framework

To make gamification effective, a plan that addresses business goals, behaviors, and the target audience needs to be created. To help with this, Professor Kevin Werbach of Pennsylvania State University created the Gamification Design Framework. This framework is designed to assist professionals in designing a gamified solution that encourages particular behaviors and stimulates engagement. The six steps in the Gamification Design Framework are:

1) DEFINE the business objectives (What's the ultimate business goal?)
2) DELINEATE target behavior (what are the concrete specific steps that you would want people to take?)
3) DESCRIBE the players—(they are people who are voluntarily playing the game)
4) DEVISE the activity loops (the structure of how the gamified system works and what keeps the players playing)

5) DON'T forget the fun (would people actually find this fun and engaging?)
6) DEPLOY the appropriate tools (Find the appropriate tools, whether it is software platforms or other kinds of mechanisms)

## Example Course Utilizing Gamification Strategies

Gamification has come a long way since it was first propounded. It is working successfully in organizations like L'Oreal, Deloitte and Starbucks. It has found application in engaging employees by infusing vigor, making them dedicated and enabling them to be absorbed in their work (Sarangi and Shah, 2015). In this section I will provide an example of using gamification strategies to redesign an educational course in information systems.

Let's assume you are taking an instructor led course in information technology. If this were a standard course design, as most are, you would have a pre-defined experience that was not alterable by you, the student. For a course in information technology, you would expect a course outline something like:

1) Introduction to Information Systems
2) History of Computers and Information Technology
3) Information Systems in the Global Enterprise
4) The Internet, Networks, and Telecommunications
5) Computer Hardware
6) Categories of Computer Software
7) Computer Software Development
8) Information Security
9) Information Technology Organizations and Infrastructure
10) Cloud Computing
11) The Future of Computing and Information Technology

This generally designed course would have you completing a series of modules or chapters, in concert with your fellow classmates, with all assignments and tests and/or quizzes taken at the same time. In other words, the course's instructor has complete control over the content, pace, and rules of the course. As the student, you simply follow directions in the order given and hope that in the end you will receive a grade you are happy with. Your experience will mimic the same experience you have had in virtually all other courses you have taken. Other than the scores for assessments or assignments provided to you occasionally, you will not have any other feedback as to your progress or mastery of the subjects.

Obviously, this sort of course design has been in place for centuries; probably because it is undoubtedly the easiest to produce and deliver. It is the foundational design of most secondary and post-secondary education, and for the most part has been the design for corporate training programs.

However, as the internet has become a highly useful medium for delivering training, those responsible for that training have merely moved what they previously showed in presentation software in a room to a webinar type platform; without changing anything else about the training.

Now that we have a baseline for how this course would be laid out traditionally, let's look at the design of the course with some basic gamification elements and strategies included.

## The Course Structure

First, we look at one premise behind the way the course is designed. For the traditional version of the course, it is designed around the premise that everyone in the course should get the same results from of it. In other words, everyone is in the course for the same reason and wanting the same outcome. However, that is potentially not true.

The first step of redesigning the course is to account for the varied outcomes for different students—although all will have a common foundational mastery of certain topics. This will happen through the modular design of the course, breaking it down into smaller elements. Here is an example of how it may be broken down differently.

By design, each module in the course is identified as either "core" or "upgrade" depicting content that is core to the course and must be completed by all students or content that is in addition to the core. A roadmap such as Figure 28.2 performs many critical functions for a gamified course, including:

1) Shows the student the entire "playing field" showing all the course elements
2) Outlines the dependencies between content modules
3) Distinguishes content that is required and that which is optional
4) Depicts the contribution of each module to the total score

In general, this roadmap provides clarity to the student regarding the overall rules of the course and, most importantly, allows them to see the options they can choose throughout the course. In this scenario, there are two types of decisions the student will make:

1) Which order to I want to take the modules in?
2) Which "Upgrade" modules do I want to choose to complete?

Already, we are seeing a marked difference in the operation of the course, and the need for student engagement. This step begins to take care of one of the important aspects of a game which is that players need to be able to make decisions and establish strategy.

## Points (The Grading Schematic)

Let us now turn to the topic of grading. Traditionally, courses work off a percentage basis, with the generally accepted standard being A = 90–100, B = 80–89, C = 70–79, D = 60–69, and an F is anything below 60%. While this method could be utilized in a gamified design, it is typically not well suited for it without the added component of repetition and mastery, which is

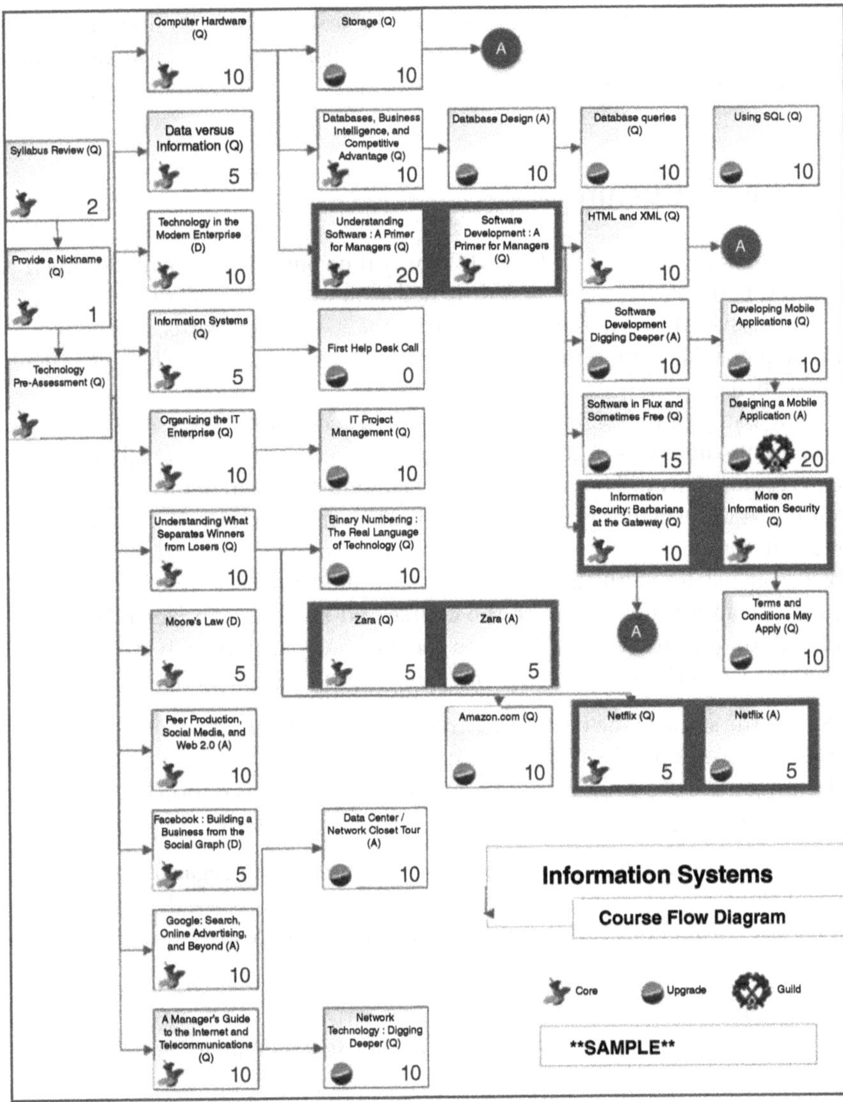


**Figure 28.2** Course flow diagram for the sample information systems course

discussed later. More typically one would find a point system that begins with zero and has a maximum that could be attained should all work be completed perfectly.

Suppose a student could earn the grade of their choosing by completing a set of modules including the core modules, plus a variable set of upgrade modules, that totals a score for that particular grade. Therefore, students who perform better in the core modules may be required to complete fewer upgrade modules to achieve the same grade. In this course example, Table 28.2 is a potential grading chart:

**Table 28.2** Sample course grading chart

| To get this grade: | A | B | C | D |
|---|---|---|---|---|
| Takes this many points: | 305 | 270 | 235 | 225 |

If all core modules are completed with a perfect score, the student might theoretically need to acquire an extra 120 points in upgrade modules to get into the "A" range. However, a student who performed slightly lower and only received 80% of the total points available in the core modules would need to acquire 150 points in the upgrade modules to get into the "A" range. This affords both students the opportunity to get an "A" throughout the duration of the course, thereby providing motivation for both students and not undermining the lesser performing student's (on the core modules) motivation to receive a top score.

Therefore, when you combine the decision-making component of the design with the grading structure, you have the possibility of two separate student outcomes:

1) You have a student whose knowledge is very strong on the core topics, and very strong on a smaller set of custom topics. This student's learning profile is one we would call "deep but narrow."
2) You have a student whose knowledge is good on the core topics, and good to very strong on a larger set of custom topics. This student's learning profile is one we would call "shallow but wide."

The variance between these two as far as learning or skills attainment goes is a function of the course design and individual module completion requirements.

The easiest way to miss the potential of gamification is to focus too heavily on the rewards and not enough on the appeal of the experience. This problem can be seen in the unthinking assumption that any business process can be gamified and improved simply by adding points to it, and motivating users to engage with the system just for the love of collecting points (Werbach and Hunter, 2012).

## Badges

Many of us have interacted with activities or communities where badges have long been employed as a strategy to motivate and provide distinction between levels of mastery or achievement. A couple that come to mind are The Boy Scouts of America with their Merit Badge Program and Junior Olympics mastery badges. In elementary school, your badges may have been in the form of gold stars. It is doubtful that any of us have gone our entire lives without being exposed to some program with a badge program.

Websites, social communities, and mobile-based business are increasingly employing badges as a key motivational feature of their product. In fact, many heavily depend on them for successful client engagement with their product. For example, Starbucks uses badges to entice its customers to perform tasks it wants them try, like recharging their account with their debit card or buying a gift card. Online games like World of Warcraft use Achievements as their badging mechanism, incenting users to change their game play priorities to acquire a reward for the achievement, or in many cases providing the play only with the sense of accomplishment for completing the challenge.

The key role badges play in gaming activity is to give a sense of accomplishment to the participants, generating an elevated status to distinguish themselves within the community for which the badge is relevant.

In an educational sense, badges play the same role as they do in games: generating motivation and distinguishing participants within their community (i.e., the class). Using badges to entice students to extend their mastery of certain areas or to explore additional areas to supplement their foundation can be very effective.

In our example course, a badging program could provide some additional motivation to steer students toward certain modules or to take on extra activities above and beyond what is required. Table 28.3 is a sample of some of the badges applied to this course:

Another important aspect of badging is social recognition. Advertising to the community that a member of the community has earned a badge is in itself a motivational strategy. Many are incented not just by the acquisition of a badge, but also the recognition by others in the relevant community that the badge was earned. Therefore, it is probably not beneficial to advertise on Facebook that someone in a particular class received a badge as the Facebook community is too broad to provide the necessary social connection.

One term we used earlier regarding badges is the term "relevant." It is important to note the importance of aligning a badge and its reward (if there is one) to something relevant within the community where the badge is made available. For example, a Starbucks badge for recharging your card could come with additional stars toward a free drink, which is relevant for the user and the value proposition is within the context of the overall rewards program. Such a Starbucks badge probably will not get you elevated recognition on Yelp or Foursquare (social media sites). Therefore, it is important that when designing a badge program for your educational program that its relevance has a meaning and value (intrinsic or extrinsic) within that same educational program.

Badging can greatly enhance a gamified educational experience providing a well-rounded program for achievement and recognition. It should be relevant to the material and to the audience, and provide intrinsic and/or extrinsic value to the holder.

## The Leaderboard

While we have discussed gaming elements related to decision making, mastery and repetition, and grading/scoring, we have not yet hit on a key motivational factor: competition. All humans have an innate desire to compete (and win), although it is obviously greater in some individuals than others. In gamification

**Table 28.3** Sample of course badge inventory

| Badge name | Badge criteria |
|---|---|
| I Drank Every Drop | Complete every module in the course |
| Programmer at Heart | Complete the following modules related to software development and programming with a score of 60 % or better:<br>1) Quiz: Understanding Software: A Primer for Managers<br>2) Quiz: HTML and XML<br>3) Quiz: Software in Flux: Partly Cloudy and Sometimes Free<br>4) Assignment: Software Development: Digging Deeper<br>5) Quiz: Developing Mobile Applications |
| It's all about the Data | Complete the followings modules related to databases and data with a score of 60 % or better:<br>1) Quiz: Databases, Business Intelligence, and Competitive Advantage<br>2) Assignment: Designing a Database—A more Detailed Look<br>3) Quiz: Using SQL to Interact with Databases |
| Math Geek! | Score 80 % or greater on the Binary Numbers quiz |
| On Your Way | Reach Level 2 in the Leaderboard with 110 points |
| Failure is Not an Option | Reach Level 3 in the Leaderboard with 150 points |
| No Standing in the way of Progress | Reach Level 4 in the Leaderboard with 205 points |
| A Master Within | Reach Level 5 in the Leaderboard with 230 points |
| Tour la Techie | Complete both the Data Center Tour and the Networking Tour. |
| I Learned Something! | Score 30 or more on the Technology Post Assessment Quiz which is greater than your initial score in the Pre-Assessment. |

strategy, we are looking to harness a person's competitive nature and convert it into motivational energy. This motivational energy will provide additional motivation for the student to excel through mastery of the material, and can usually be provided by a leaderboard.

The purpose of the leaderboard is to provide the student with their standing relative to their classmates. Do you remember playing an electronic game (for older folks it would be something like pinball games or arcade games) where they show you the leaderboard? As you played the game, your desire was to make it on the leaderboard so you deposited quarter after quarter for that chance? That is the power of the leaderboard. It is understood that privacy concerns such as FERPA (the Family Education Rights and Privacy Act) come into play, but these can be easily handled.

In the sample course, a leaderboard that is combined with the grading strategy was generated graphically with the lowest number of points on the bottom and the most amount of points on the top. The individual student's bar is a different color than the others, and the names of class participants are merely numbers, thereby providing complete anonymity. The diagram below shows how this can be implemented.

This is something most people would not expect in a training class, as the initial impression is that it might violate some sort of privacy or single a participant out. However, my own experience demonstrated that this is a highly effective tool at providing motivation, and also offers the student a comparative analysis of their progress in the class. The labels in the diagram were created specifically for the sample course, and could be replaced with any set of categories relevant to the course.

The leaderboard is only effective if can be generated in near-real time and in an automated fashion. This requirement refers to the concept of immediacy in game mechanics.

## Repetition and Mastery

As we further the conversation on skills and knowledge attainment, we must discuss the final goal of a course, which is hopefully to generate a level of mastery. Assume you were playing a video game that had 10 levels you could complete, with each level being a bit harder than the previous one. If the game designer gave you only one chance to play a level, and if you did not complete it, you could never play that level or any other levels above it, I would presume the game manufacturer would be out of business quite quickly as no one would want to invest in the game. In these types of games, repeating content is the core capability of the design to produce mastery, and a true gamified design will allow for this repetition. Companies that want to boost their internal training programs are also looking at gamification as a way to increase engagement and friendly competition. The willingness to play, to fail, and to try again, could be said to be the essence of what makes learning a compelling activity (Dale, 2014).

To embrace this idea, you need to embrace the idea that someone who can assemble a widget perfectly in 10 s 100% of the time after 1 lesson and a person who can assemble the same widget perfectly in 10 s 100% of the time after 5 lessons both have the same mastery at assembling the widget. This is similar to a game player replaying a game at a particular level until he completes it and is ready to move on to the next level.

Designing this in a course provides students the opportunity to learn from their mistakes, and reattempt to achieve mastery without being penalized. Most courses do not allow students to go back after an exam and work on what they missed and get a second chance at improving their score. To a student motivated (or borderline motivated) to achieve mastery on a topic, this is a de-motivator.

Repetition can be easily handled in many cases (if you are talking about knowledge acquisition) by creating a pool of questions for exams or quizzes that can be randomly chosen at test time, allowing for each test for the student to be different than the previous one. This does require additional work on the part of the course content designer, but can certainly yield higher knowledge and capabilities of the student. Most online testing engines and learning management systems support the question pool notion.

In the example information system courses, many of the tests were designed to support the multi-attempt concept.

## Summary

Gamification has come a long way since it was first propounded. It is working successfully in organizations like L'Oreal, Deloitte and Starbucks. It has found application in engaging employees by infusing vigor, making them dedicated and enabling them to be absorbed in their work (Sarangi and Shah, 2015). Gamification can provide a significant contribution to all types of educational offerings, whether it is in secondary, post-secondary, or corporate education programs. It is not about creating a game, but using game design and elements to create a more human-centric design for educational delivery. Whether we like it or not, employees love their smartphones, apps, and games. Providing education using gaming techniques provides an innovative platform for educators to use when developing curricula. (Brull and Finlayson, 2016) Companies use gamification to improve productivity within the organization in order to foster innovation, enhance camaraderie, or otherwise derive positive business results through their own employees (Werbach and Hunter, 2012). When done correctly, gamification provides an experience that is inherently engaging and, most importantly, pro-motes learning. The elements of games that make for effective gamification are those of storytelling, which provides a context, challenge, immediate feedback, sense of curiosity, problem-solving, a sense of accomplishment, autonomy and mastery (Dale, 2014).

While gamification has the potential to become an integral part of the workplace, it must be done right. Considering how difficult it is to build a hit game, it should come as no surprise that building successful gamification within a work environment is no different; there are many more ways to do it wrong than right. From small mistakes that waste your time to disasters that can turn users against you (Dale, 2014).

The people who continue to write off games will be at a major disadvantage in the coming years. Those who deem them unworthy of their time and attention won't know how to leverage the power of games in their communities, in their businesses, in their own lives. They will be less prepared to shape the future (McGonigal, 2011).

## References

Brull, S., & Finlayson, S. (2016). Importance of gamification in increasing learning. *The Journal of Continuing Education in Nursing*, 47(9), 372–375. https://doi.org/10.3928/00220124-20160715-09

Chou, Y.-K. (2015). Actionable gamification—beyond points, badges, and leaderboards. Octalysis Media.

Dale, S. (2014). Gamification: Making work fun, or making fun of work? Business information. *Business Information Review*, 31(2), 82–90. https://doi.org/10.1177/0266382114538350

de-Marcos, L., Garcia-Lopez, E., & Garcia-Cabot, A. (2016). On the effectiveness of game-like and social approaches in learning: Comparing educational gaming, gamification and social networking. *Computers and Education*, 95, 99–113. https://doi.org/10.1016/j.compedu.2015.12.008

Harman, K., & Koohang, A. (2014). Scholarly interest in gamification: A citation network analysis. *Industrial Management and Data Systems*, 14(9), 1438–1452. https://doi.org/10.1108/IMDS-07-2014-0208

Leaman, C. (2015, September 15). Gamification: Recipe for successful learning—or just one ingredient? *Learning Solutions Magazine*, September 15, 2015.

Markopoulos, A. P., Kasidiaris, P. D., & Davim, J. (2015). Gamification in engineering, education, and profiessional training. *International Journal of Mechanical Engineering Education*, 43(2), 118–131. https://doi.org/10.1177/0306419015591324

McGonigal, J. (2011). Reality is broken: Why games make us better and how they can change the world. New York, NY: Penguin Books.

Muntean, C. I. (2011). Raising engagement in e-learning through gamification. International Conference on Virtual Learning. Cluj-Napoca, Romania.

Ryan, R. M., & Deci, E. L. (2000). Intrinsic and extrinsic motivations: Classic definitions and new directions. *Contemporary Educational Psychology*, 25, 54–67. https://doi.org/10.1006/ceps.1999.1020

Sarangi, S., & Shah, S. (2015). Individuals, teams and organizationsscore with gamification. *Human Resource Management International Digest*, 23(4), 24–27. https://doi.org/10.1108/HRMID-05-2015-0074

Urh, M., Vukovic, G., Jereb, E., and Pintar, R. (2015). The model for introduction of gamification into e-learning in higher. 7th World Conference on Educational Sciences, (WCES-2015). 197, pp. 388–397. Athens, Greece: Procedia Social and Behavioral Sciences.

Werbach, K., & Hunter, D. (2012). For the win: How game thinking can revolutionize your business. Philadelphia, PA: Wharton Digital Press.

Zicherman, G., & Cunningham, C. (2011). Gamification by design: Implementing game mechanics in web and mobile apps (1st ed.). Sebastopol, CA: O'Reilly Media, Inc.

# 29

# The Use of Gamification in Workplace Learning to Encourage Employee Motivation and Engagement

*Hazel Grünewald, Petra Kneip, and Arjan Kozica*

Reutlingen University

When we think about playing a game, be it a card game, board game, sport, or video game, we generally associate the act of playing with a positive experience like having fun, enjoying the interaction with others or feeling a greater motivation to reach a certain goal. By contrast, workplace learning is often perceived as being dull. Employees are likely at some point in their career to find themselves stuck in a rigidly defined seminar for a long period of time or in front of their computer navigating through a mandatory e-learning course on a dry topic such as standards of business conduct or safety policies.

In recent years, organizations have tried to leverage the motivating quality of games for more serious learning contexts. Gamification entails transferring those elements and principles from games to a non-gaming context that improve user experience and engagement. In this chapter, we will specifically focus on the context of workplace learning. A game-like environment has the power to transform the activity of learning a new skill or onboarding new employees into an exciting challenge. Gamification has increasingly won acceptance by learners in the workforce who recognize the benefits of receiving immediate feedback on their learning progress or of being able to adapt the learning speed to their individual needs.

This chapter will begin by addressing what gamification is and how it has impacted workplace learning. We will outline the benefits that gamified learning can bring to an organization's bottom line. Drawing on the findings of motivational psychology, we will demonstrate how gamification can turn learners into active information-consumers who take initiative and drive their personal development forward without the constant push of Learning and Development departments. Several practical cases of gamified learning and development initiatives will be presented. Some demonstrate good practices where solutions are used to drive business objectives. Others serve as a warning of the traps that organizations fall into when introducing gamification without adequate thought and planning.

*The Wiley Handbook of Global Workplace Learning*, First Edition.
Edited by Vanessa Hammler Kenon and Sunay Vasant Palsole.

## What is Gamification?

Despite the growing interest by academics, practitioners and educators from a variety of domains, the term "gamification" is still novel (Seaborn & Fels, 2015). British computer programmer and consultant, Nick Pelling, coined the expression in 2002. He applied the term to hardware where he talked of applying a "game-like" accelerated user interface design to make electronic transactions fun and fast. The term "gamification" did not really take on until 2010 when it appeared on Google trends and was used more specifically to describe the integration of social/reward aspects of games into software.

A universally accepted definition for gamification does not exist, frequently cited definitions stem from blogs, news or practitioner oriented books (e.g., Burke, 2014). There is a broad consensus among scholars with respect to gamification being defined as the use of game elements and game design techniques or mechanisms in non-game contexts (Burke, 2014; Deterding, Dixon, Khaled, & Nacke, 2011; Seaborn & Fels, 2015; Werbach & Hunter, 2012). Some authors attribute a specific intention to gamification, and so forth, to change behavior, develop skills, engage people in innovation (Burke, 2012) or to motivate and engage end-users (Seaborn & Fels, 2015). Others consider gamification as "the process of making activities more gamelike" (Werbach, 2014, p. 267). Although the majority of gamified applications are digital, gamification should not be limited to digital technologies.

Companies have been applying principles of games to business contexts for some time, often without realizing the full potential of those solutions. The use of game mechanisms in business environments is not a scientifically developed pedagogical tool, but rather based on practitioners experimenting with new ways of motivating and engaging employees and triggering behavioral changes. Many companies introduce mechanisms such as collecting points and redeeming them for products to increase customer loyalty. Rewards memberships, frequent flyer programs, interactive health and fitness accessories and profile completion bars are all examples of gamification (see Table 29.1).

A point of contention raised by scholars concerns the extent to which gamification can be distinguished from terms like (serious) games and (digital) game-based learning remains. Let us look firstly, at the term "serious games." For Deterding et al. (2011) serious games are fully-fledged games to address non-game users and designed for purposes other than entertainment, for example,

**Table 29.1** Application of gamification in the real world

| Real-life application | Game elements |
|---|---|
| Sales competition, logistics pick and pack performance | Challenge, leaderboards |
| Frequent flyer programs and loyalty cards | Points, levels |
| Profile completion bars in business networks, e.g., LinkedIn | Progression |
| Fitness tracker, e.g., Fitbit | Badges |

with the aim of increasing educational, political, social, or workforce interaction. Players may enjoy the challenge of collecting points on their way to a project management certification or the challenge of the monthly sales competition, but they will not leave reality, the business context, they are in. Often game designers create realistic, immersive learning environments to enhance connectivity with players. Well-crafted games place learners in a graphically-rich simulated world and engage them through compelling and realistic storylines ensuring a fast transfer of the experience to the desired target in real life. Popular examples of such games are flight simulators.

Moving on to the concept of (digital) game-based learning (DGBL), we see that difference from gamification is similarly not clear-cut. Both may pursue similar goals—they are trying to solve a problem, motivate, and promote learning using game-based thinking and techniques. Gamification, however, turns the entire learning process into a game, applying game elements and principles to it (e.g., earning points, managing a challenge, or receiving badges for accomplished tasks). (D)GBL, on the other hand, takes a game and uses it for teaching knowledge, and skills (Kapp, 2014). Gamification is also distinguished from playfulness or playful design. Whereas playing refers to a free-form expressive, improvisational recombination of behaviors and meanings, gaming is characterized rule-bound, goal-oriented play (Deterding et al., 2011; McGonigal, 2011).

Scholarly interest in gamification is on the increase and will play an important role in defining the phenomenon further. Current research is largely dedicated to analyzing its effects on learning and engagement (Robson, Plangger, Kietzmann, McCarthy, & Pitt, 2015; Seaborn & Fels, 2015), defining gaming mechanisms and elements, and considering how the term relates to other concepts such as serious games, games with a purpose, gamified learning or even game theory (Deterding et al., 2011; Werbach & Hunter, 2012).

## Workplace Learning and the Trend toward Gamification

Workplace learning is integral to the success of today's organizations operating in a dynamic global environment. In the contemporary digital age, employees are required to adapt quickly to new situations and expand or update their skills to match rapidly changing organizational or customer needs. Despite the huge need for workplace learning, organizations find themselves faced with numerous difficulties when trying to deliver appropriate training solutions. Scheduling and bringing learning to employees in different locations or connecting corporate training to their individual goals and ensuring necessary behavioral changes can prove to be both challenging and costly. For this reason, increasingly more companies are turning to digital training solutions as a means of offering training in timely fashion to large learner bases.

According to Roland Berger Strategy Consultants, corporate e-learning can be seen as one of the most impressive growth segments in the education industry (Vernau & Hauptmann, 2014). Since 2000 the global e-learning market has grown by 900 % (Wildi-Yune & Cordero, 2015). Today, already 77 % of US companies offer e-learning programs in their professional development programs (Vernau & Hauptmann, 2014). When deployed meaningfully, e-learning solutions can positively grow an organization's bottom line. However, to reap the expected rewards, sufficient thought must be applied to instructional design, context or goals. Gamified learning in which content is attached to real-life on-the-job scenarios can provide a step toward engaged learners and increased return on investment, make learning memorable, stimulating and worthwhile.

Badgeville, an award-winning business gamification company, readily shares customer success stories. One of its clients, Sodexo, purchased a virtual learning environment (VLE) with gamification elements. The solution resulted not only in increased participation in annual training events, but also brought a significant reduction to the company's training costs. "Moving our training online has saved our company time and money," stated Michele Supronowicz, Sodexo's senior director of training and development. "The VLE is an innovative talent-management system that drives engagement and positive learning outcomes consistently and cost-effectively" (Buckner, 2014).

Despite the anecdotal evidence that such stories provide for the benefits of digital learning solutions in the workplace, research struggles with bringing clear empirical evidence for the their usefulness. When it comes to intentional workplace learning, a central challenge for Learning & Development departments remains the engagement and motivation of learners. In this chapter, we will concentrate specifically on intentional learning rather than incidental or random learning which is characterized as unorganized, unstructured, and unintentional. Many employees consider designed elements of workplace learning as discouraging them from doing their "real" jobs, increasing workload and fostering additional work (Noe, Tews, & McConnell Dachner, 2010).

The process of knowledge or skill acquisition in the workplace can be dull and arduous unless employees feel an immediate sense of gratification through accomplishment. As we will try to show in the rest of this chapter, gamification offers a wide range of engagement tools and techniques as potential solutions to problems in workforce learning.

## Beyond the Hype: Gamification Goes Mainstream

Until a few years ago gamification was considered to be a fad earmarked for Web 2.0 startups and the e-learning industry. Like numerous other new trends and emerging technologies, gamification found itself approaching the peak of Gartner Hype Cycles in 2014. Gartner predicted that by 2015, 40 % of Global 1 000 organizations would be using gamification as the primary mechanism to transform their business operations (Gartner, 2014). The expected slide into the "trough of disillusionment" has not yet come about and in 2015 gamification was removed altogether from the Gartner model, signaling for many the idea that "gamification is here to stay." Not that the entire business world is as enthralled by gamification as perhaps earlier predicted. Gartner revised its estimation of market penetration to a mere 5–10 % in 2015. In a further study of over 100 line-of-business managers conducted by Sunrise Software, only about one in three respondents (30 %) considered that gamification was here to stay, while a fifth (21 %) still believed it to be a passing fad and half (49 %) remain uncertain (Sunrise Software, 2014).

Engagement surveys, such as those conducted by Gallup and Mercer, highlight the growing need for organizations to provide incentives to achieve the level of engagement necessary for the transformation of business operations. The hype and popularity of deploying gamification tools for engagement purposes has been well documented in business literature over the past years (Robson et al., 2015; Werbach & Hunter, 2012).

Yet, the popularity of the concept of gamification poses a potential danger for corporations that intend to introduce gamified elements. As research on managerial fashion shows (Abrahamson, 1996), modern and timely concepts are often introduced because they are *en vogue*, not because they work as intended. Even though introducing up-to-date practices might have positive implications (such as increased legitimization through being seen to be progressive and conforming with societal expectations), it remains crucial that solutions are rationally selected and appropriate.

Training executives on the lookout for best practices are advised to ensure that tools are deployed in a meaningful way that is closely aligned with business objectives (Callan, Bauer, & Landers, 2015). It is not enough to have in mind creating an enjoyable experience for learners. At the end of the day, investors will expect measurable results. Experts also warn against the tendency to "overhype" and the inherent desire to jump on the bandwagon. Brian Burke of Gartner draws attention to the pitfalls of gamification and need for due consideration before deploying innovative solutions. He uses a particularly vivid example of a company seeking to leverage gamification to urge administrative staff to go beyond the call of duty and fill in expense reports for sales staff. The direct response is: "No, gamification is not going to help you get administrative staff to do someone else's dirty work" (Burke, 2014, p. 8).

In their chapter, *How to avoid the dark side of gamification: Ten business scenarios and their unintended consequences*, Callan et al. (2015) present ten scenarios in which gamified interventions in organizations failed to achieve the intended goals and were even counterproductive. Organizations may unintentionally encourage superficial engagement by introducing extrinsic motivators to improve performance. One issue is that the authors highlight is that when the motivators are removed, employees are likely return to old habits.

Other issues mentioned by the authors include offering rewards for metrics that have not been well thought out. Awarding sales staff points, for example, for the volume of sales they net may not take into account differing complexity in tasks. Therefore, one salesperson may struggle to achieve the same performance results as a peer, because they have been assigned to a more difficult territory. The scholars also show that rewarding managers for getting their performance appraisals completed on time is similarly problematic. The intervention may encourage speed rather than accuracy.

Finally, the authors stress the serious implications of gamified interventions in terms of promoting negative behaviors such as dishonesty. They present the fictitious scenario of an organization introducing gamification in a selection process where applicants compete against one another. Candidates move up a leaderboard on account of their results in personality or knowledge tests. The risk is that applicants fake the tests and misrepresent themselves to appear more socially desirable. We can conclude that practitioners need to be aware of and avoid such pitfalls of gamification, which may prevent them achieving their intended goals.

## To What Extent is Gamification a Potential Game Changer in Corporate Learning?

The incorporation of games in the work domain has been documented in research since the 1930s, but there is evidence that workplace games were used to motivate workers as far back as ancient Egypt (Edery & Mollick, 2009). A growing body of research stresses the positive effects games and play can have. Well-designed games can foster learning (Crookall, 2010; Perryer, Scott-Ladd, & Leighton, 2012; Popescu, Romero, & Usart, 2012) and can lead to improved self-efficacy (Perryer et al., 2012; Popescu, Romero, & Usart, 2013) and healthy behavioral change (Lenihan, 2012). A comprehensive review of computer games and serious games underlines the potential positive impact of gaming on knowledge acquisition, skill (motor, cognitive, social, and emotional) development, motivational outcomes and behavioral changes (Connolly, Boyle, MacArthur, Hainey, & Boyle, 2012; Hamari, Koivisto, & Sarsa, 2014).

Games are rapidly becoming one of the world's favorite pastime. An estimated 183 million individuals, in the United States alone, play computer or video games on a regular basis (McGonigal, 2011, p. 3). The results, based on self-reports, indicate that individuals play on average 13 hr per week. The global game industry (including console, tablet, browser PC, (smart)phone, and boxed/ downloaded PC games) has been growing rapidly, becoming a $108.9 billion industry in game revenues 2017 (McDonald, 2017). For many people, gaming may still be a waste of time, merely helping the gamers to escape from reality, but it is hard to ignore the numbers. People of all ages, men and women, around the globe, are choosing to spend a considerable amount of their time playing video and computer games. According to game designer and researcher Jane McGonigal individuals are increasingly engaged in gaming, because in contrast to reality, games are able to fulfill basic human needs such as the need to be socially connected or the striving to feel in command of one's life, and games provide rewards which people very often miss in their real world (McGonigal, 2011).

A growing interest in gamification as a motivator in the workplace is signaled by the fact that 55 % of Americans say they are interested in working for a company that uses gamification to increase productivity (Saatchi & Saatchi, 2011). Gamification combines technology with psychology in a non-gaming context to increase productivity. Findings in the field of neuroscience support the argument that techniques similar to those deployed by game designers to keep players hooked present a possible means of developing the engagement desired by organizations.

According to a report by Accenture (Ryan, Sleigh, Wee Soh, and Li (2013, p. 2), "The potential power of such game-based applications and ventures has been magnified by the convergence of two major trends: the coming of age of Generation Y, and the overcrowding of the digital space, which makes it harder for companies to stand out." Generation Y, or the Millennials, the demographic cohort born between 1980 and 2000, has been born into a digital world. Many are keen online gamers and help drive the development of the global gaming industry. Attention should be paid to their wants and needs, both as consumers and employees. In 2012, Gartner estimated that the deployment of gamified services for consumer goods marketing and customer retention would become as significant as Facebook (Davey, 2015). In terms of predominant values and characteristics, scholarship has documented time and again that Gen Y are early adopters and hence open for new technologies and learning styles. They seek challenges, feedback and recognition, freedom, the chance to grow and the desire to strike a good work-life balance. Gamification can indeed respond to these needs. What will, however, remain a challenge is that the generation is perceived as incredibly fickle, making it difficult for industry leaders to predict trends and acceptance with any certainty.

## Why Gamification Makes Good Business Sense

Organizations widely offer online learning solutions as a means of reaching large employee communities. However, drop-out rates are alarmingly high. Gamification offers a potential antidote since it provides high leverage and works best with large communities. Single solutions can be deployed for an almost unlimited number of players. In many cases, the more players, the more diversity—the better the results (Burke, 2014). Gamification promotes healthy competition among learners, keeping them on the edge to perform better and score higher points than their counterparts. Further, some games allow them to share their scores and strategies with friends and peers on the social media platforms. Built-in analytics enable analysis of employee behavior.

Information garnered on attitudes toward skill upgrades, speeds, and so forth. can be leveraged to develop and customize systems making them even better suited to learners.

Gamification potentially improves engagement and the completion of online learning. Moreover, it can boost the retention and application of knowledge. Based on an experimental study, Brull, Finlayson, Kostelec, Macdonald, and Krenzischeck (2017) argue that learners use and retain more knowledge when they are trained in a gamified learning experience rather than in a training experience that only focuses on appropriate didactics or on online learning groups without gamified elements. Gamification in e-learning aims to create experiences that fully engage learners. Learners do not do not simply receive information. They have to process and apply it. If made to feel positive about their learning process, learners become actively engaged and are better able to absorb the information and commit it to their long-term memory.

The sense of achievement that games generate, for example, as learners move up a level or receive a reward helps to stimulate endorphin release (Lazarro, 2004). This not only increases the sense of well-being in the learner, it also fosters knowledge retention. A growing body of knowledge about gamification indicates the benefits of gamified training in terms of improved knowledge acquisition. The enterprise software giant SAP, for example, implemented a MindTickle platform to enhance its college recruitment process, incorporating leaderboards, points, and badges. When the company compared new hires who received gamified training to their predecessors who had not, they noted a 75 % rise in awareness of the company values and its products (MindTickle, 2013). Not only that, gamification eliminated the need for four classroom training sessions. It also led to 70 % savings in senior management coaching time and reduced administrative costs by 60 %.

Serious gaming provides a further business argument for the use of gamification in the workplace. Learners must be able to access and apply the knowledge they have acquired when needed in the real world. Serious gaming seeks to merge digital and real world social environments. Often designers create realistic, immersive learning environments to enhance connectivity with players. Well-crafted games place learners in a graphically rich simulated world and engage them through compelling and realistic storylines ensuring a fast transfer of the experience to the desired target in real life. Popular examples of such games are flight simulators. Other examples are *Innov8: CityOne,* a online single player marketing game, custom-designed by IBM, in which players experience what is like to run a city and make it smarter (IBM, 2012).

McDonalds provides an example of how gamified learning solutions can positively affect business and contribute significantly to bottom line results. The fast-food giant approached City & Guilds Kineo seeking a solution to train their employees on a new cash register and ordering system. The company wanted to keep mistakes to a minimum and avoid frustrating customers through increased waiting times. Kineo designed a game which approximated the real work situation. The staff members could learn and practice in a safe environment with the comforting knowledge that making errors was of no consequence. Implementation of the training led to a reduction of 7.9 s for each till service. In the UK the average check increased by 15 p, which led to an overall revenue impact to the tune of GBP 23 million (Kineo, n.d.).

## The Psychology of Gamification—How and why Gamification Motivates User Behavior

In this section, we will draw on game and motivation theories to offer an understanding on how gamification taps into key motivators as a way of encouraging engaged behavior and boosting productivity in the workplace. Gamification uses reward systems that go beyond simple competitions ("the employee of the year receives an award") toward the purposeful inclusion of elements from designed games (such as video games, board games, and sports) to increase the enjoyment factor or effectiveness of a game in a work environment

(Deterding et al., 2011). We will demonstrate how gamification design, on the one hand, aims for self-purposeful and hedonistic use, yet organizations ultimately seek to make use of it to utilitarian ends to support extrinsic and valuable business or learning outcomes outside the gamification system (Hamari et al., 2014). Moreover, we will look specifically at the way in which given game components trigger motivation.

Findings in areas such as neuroscience, cognitive science, behavioral economics, and motivation theory have had an impact on the design and application of many of today's gamified offerings. Engaging games respond to the fundamental intrinsic needs of human beings outlined in traditional needs-based theories of motivation (Richter, Raban, & Rafaeli, 2014). These desires or needs include such things as recognition, status, achievement, self-expression, competition, and altruism. At the other end of the spectrum, theories such as Expectancy Value Theory and Skinner's Reinforcement inform the way in which games make use of extrinsic rewards to induce learners to perform actions or behaviors (Richter et al., 2014).

Game-based solutions seek to deploy game mechanics in a meaningful way to create addictive experiences. The goal is to motivate users to take specific actions, and to return more frequently. Whereas earlier research into gamification focused on fun, pleasure and flow as central aspects of game play, current debate is more concerned with how to harness the motivational power of games to foster participation, persistence and achievement (Richter et al., 2014).

Gamification combines both intrinsic and extrinsic motivators to change people's behavior. Game designers identify desired behavior such as knowledge-sharing or task accomplishment and offer instant rewards when the individual behaves accordingly. Such extrinsic rewards trigger motivation and can influence behavior. Gamified activities aim to stimulate the amygdala and condition the brain's limbic system. Well-designed systems can thereby culminate in individuals engaging more intensively with designated activities and even being enticed to pursue higher levels of accomplishment than usually expected.

Designed games incorporate reinforcing contexts, structure, look and feel, interactions, and mechanisms that establish an immersive sense of play while advancing instrumental organizational goals (Zimmerman & Salen, 2005). Many workplace learning solutions incorporate real-life job aspects to transform activities into highly motivational experiences which respond to and satisfy basic human desires.

Although the "fun" aspect of games is often associated with intrinsic motivation, self-determination theory (SDT) demonstrates how this is only partially true. SDT is one of the most established theoretical frameworks within gamification and game motivation research (Landers, Bauer, & Callan, 2015; Richter et al., 2014; Seaborn & Fels, 2015). Its usefulness comes from the fact that it presents a spectrum of intrinsic and extrinsic motivations. The theory purports that intrinsic motivation refers to behavior driven by internal rewards. In other words, individuals pursue an activity for enjoyment's sake (Gagne & Deci, 2005; Ryan & Deci, 2000). In gamification, employees do not complete tasks out of pure volitional interest. Rather, there is an instrumental value to be gained. Gamification works on the assumption that tasks are generally not inherently rewarding or engaging, but disguises the non-motivating nature of activities behind a layer of fun. Gaming literature refers to this phenomenon as "chocolate covered broccoli" (Bruckman, 1999). Game elements, such as points, badges, levels and leaderboards can act as extrinsic rewards, but insofar as they raise users' desire to achieve mastery, autonomy and a sense of belonging (Sailer, Hense, Mandl, & Klever, 2013), they also foster intrinsic motivation.

Mollick and Rothbard claim that, "gamification, while not intended to make the work more interesting in and of itself, is focused on improving the employee's affective experience at work, making the environment more exciting and thus increasing the positive affect employees feel at work" (2014, p. 10). They refer to research on neurological activity in the brain which demonstrates that gameplay activates reward-related neural circuits. Well-designed games set carefully regulated challenges and give continuous, measured rewards in order for players to have the feeling that they are progressing and achieving success in the world of the game. It is suggested that positive affective events can be related to improved performance on account of greater cognitive availability and flexibility.

Returning to the issue of intrinsic motivation, Mollick and Rothbard highlight the contentious issue of gamification as essentially being a form of "mandatory fun" prescribed by companies to improve performance. To resolve this paradox and derive a long-term positive outcome from gamification, employees need to consent to this "mandatory" form of fun. The scholars purport consent to be a cognitive response which can be operationalized and to some degree measured by the means of three indicators: *understanding the rules, perceived fairness and justice*, and *active engagement* (Mollick & Rothbard, 2014, p. 35). Employees are shown to give their consent when they perceive the game as legitimate, in other words a "desirable and proper activity" (p. 17) and when they have a sense of individual agency and "some choice and thus control over the gamification process" (p. 18). An important finding of the research is that when employees consent to a gamification initiative in the workplace, it is likely to increase their positive affect. If consent is not given, the positive affect and, hence, the motivation decreases (p. 39).

## Game Mechanics—The Key to Successful Gamification Tools

Game elements, which are at the core of the definition of gamification, are not easy to specify. Several authors have tried to categorize game elements into lists (Kapp, 2012; Werbach & Hunter, 2012; Zichermann & Linder, 2013), either of more universal value or specific to certain games. Such lists are far from exhaustive. In this section, our concern is less with comprehensively detailing all possible game components. Instead, we will focus on some of the most common elements and consider them in relation to motivational perspectives. This should help us better understand what it is that makes gamification successful in engaging users.

**Table 29.2** Comparison of different classification frameworks

| Robson et al. (2015) | Werbach and Hunter (2012) |
|---|---|
| **Mechanics:** basic elements of the gamified context (setup, rule and progression mechanics | **Mechanics:** basic processes that drive the action forward and create player engagement |
| **Dynamics:** activities which unfold player progresses | **Dynamics:** highest level of abstraction, big picture aspects of the gamified solution |
| **Emotions:** players' state of mind | **Components:** specific instantiations of mechanics and dynamics |

The MDE-framework from Robson et al. (2015) presents a useful way of organizing elements that contribute to a gamified experience. The model classifies these components into mechanics, dynamics, and emotions. Table 29.2 compares this model to the classification presented by Werbach and Hunter (2012).

In the MDE framework, mechanics are the basic elements of the gamified context, such as the principle learning environment, the rules, the context and the specific setting. Considering a sport like soccer, mechanics would regulate that this is a team sport, where two teams compete in one game, and that there might be one winner or that the game ends in a tie, based on the goals. Mechanics can be divided into setup, rule mechanics, and progression mechanics. The general environment is part of the setup mechanics. In digitally supported workplace learning, the gamified experience takes place at the intersection of the real and digital world. Hence, game designers need to regulate which part is in which world and how they shape the intersection and boundaries. Rule mechanics include the rules about how the game plays out, including the decision about what is allowed and what not. Progression mechanics are the instruments that designers integrate into the game in order to motivate people as they progress. These may be levels to be reached or rewards to be gained (such as victory points). Such progress indicators signal to players that they are on the right track toward success—and (if appropriately linked with the underlying objective of the gamified experience) on their way toward achieving the learning goals.

Organizations adopt game thinking and game mechanics in a variety of innovative ways to solve problems and engage users. The use of point systems in conjunction with leaderboards can trigger driven behavior in achievement- and status-oriented users. Some games use point systems as instrumental motivators, by offering players the chance to redeem points, for example, to gain access to exclusive content.

Dynamics refer to the activities which unfold as the player progresses. Typically, players structure their activities by pursuing specific goals (achieving the next level), and/or by deploying certain strategies (e.g., interacting with others to join forces if the mechanics allow such behavior). Due to the time-based nature of dynamics, it is difficult to predict how exactly they are shaped by the game mechanics. Player creativity can, for example, strongly influence dynamics. Moreover, besides intended player behavior, unintended behavior can emerge. The latter poses a strong challenge to game designers who have to review the unfolding gamified situations critically and consider how to adapt the mechanics to achieve the desired behavior or learning results that are expected.

While several authors (Hunicke, LeBlanc, & Zubek, 2004; Zichermann & Cunningham, 2011) use the expression "esthetics" in their frameworks, Robson et al. (2015) introduce the term "emotions" believing this to be a better fit to the engagement outcomes that businesses can expect from target groups. Emotions arise when individuals are personally and directly affected by the gamified experience and react with feelings of happiness, surprise, wonder, euphoria and the like. Players might also react with more negative emotions such as stress, anger, or disappointment. While negative emotions (e.g., the disappointment of not succeeding in the game, and the anger that the colleague in the same department has won) can also motivate positive learning behavior, positive emotions need to outweigh them in order to create an overall sustainably enticing, motivating, and engaging learning experience.

Werbach and Hunter (2012) take a different approach toward classifying game elements. Similar to the MDE-framework they identify three categories of game elements, which they organize hierarchically. Dynamics, the highest level of abstraction, encompass constraints, emotions, progression and relationships in the sense of social interactions. To achieve one or more of the dynamics, *mechanics* are used. These constitute the fundamental processes that act as an impetus for the action and generate player engagement. Examples include challenges like puzzles, competitions, rewards and feedback.

Although they have no monetary value, mechanics such as points and leaderboards, for example, satisfy certain basic needs of some users. They can be tremendous motivators for achievement-oriented learners who thrive on gaining credit for their efforts. Visible recognition of their accomplishments can serve to raise employees' self-esteem, reinforce their value to the organization, improve self-image and encourage them to accomplish even greater results in the future.

Finally, the scholars talk of *components* which tie to one or more higher-level elements and can be seen as more-specific forms that mechanics and dynamics can take. The most well-known examples are those falling within the PBL triad—***P***oints, ***B***adges, And ***L***eaderboards. There are, of course, many more. Each component can be visually represented and are the most obvious surface-level gamification features for users. Table 29.3 displays a non-exhaustive list of game elements.

By incorporating aspects of reality, gamification transforms activities into highly motivational experiences that respond to and satisfy basic human desires. Well-designed systems can thereby culminate in individuals engaging more intensively with designated activities and maybe even being enticed to pursue higher levels of accomplishment than usually expected. Within games, learners experience autonomy, competence and relatedness (Ryan & Deci, 2000). As such, we see a departure from the somewhat outdated belief that the main drivers of engagement worth focusing on are extrinsic financial motivators such as money or gifts or purely instrumental motivations (e.g., information seeking).

This idea of using game mechanics and dynamics to encourage participation and engagement by using predominantly extrinsic motivation needs closer examination. Research suggests that using extrinsic rewards may result in a phenomenon

**Table 29.3** Examples of game elements (Hunicke et al., 2004; Seaborn & Fels, 2015; Werbach & Hunter, 2012)

| Term | Definition |
|---|---|
| Points, scores | Numerical units indicating progress |
| Badges, trophies | Visual icons signifying achievements |
| Leaderboards, scoreboard, rankings | Display of ranks for comparison |
| Progression bars, levels | Milestones indicating progress |
| Status, title, ranks | Textual monikers indicating progress |
| Rewards | Tangible, desirable items |
| Roles | Role-playing elements of character |

known as the *undermining* or *overjustification effect* (Lepper, Greene, & Nisbett, 1973; Rheinberg, 2010). Players no longer play to learn, but are extrinsically motivated, for example, to stay at the top of a leaderboard. Extrinsic reward overtakes intrinsic motivation (Deci & Ryan, 1980, 1985). More often than not such effects are attributable to poor design. There is still much groundwork to be done to better understand what effect these mostly extrinsic game mechanics have on intrinsic motivation and how exactly they affect motivation, both positively and negatively.

## From the Simple to the Sophisticated: Transforming the Way in Which Employees are Engaged Through Gamified Learning

Following on from our previous discussion, in which we elaborated on the psychological fundament of gamification, we will now see what insights can be derived from practical cases of gamification being introduced into workplace learning. Examples range from basic e-learning courses to quite sophisticated models, which demonstrate the appeal of gamification and the recognized business results it brings in terms of improving learning and motivation in the workforce. Israel-based data security company, NICE, released a short publication in which they presented ten mechanics that they claim motivate employees and transform organizations (Aftergut, 2016). They validate their claim with practical examples of organizations that have successfully leveraged such mechanics to encourage engagement and inspire employees to change workplace behaviors or to collaborate, share and interact in some activity or community.

Cisco is an example of a company that takes a level- /title-based approach in its deployment of gaming. The company helps its employees and contractors build up a social media skillset by offering courses at three levels of certification. In addition, it provides four sub-certification levels for HR, external communications, sales and internal partner teams. Team challenges with respect to earning social media certifications have contributed a further competitive element to the model, increasing learning engagement as enterprise employees try to outdo each other.

The Indian mobile advertising firm, InMobi, introduced a simple reward-based gaming construct that led to considerable improvement in short-term engagement. The company underwent rapid international expansion with an increased monthly headcount of 10 %. The HR team was neither primed nor adequately staffed to handle this phenomenal growth. So, the company partnered with MindTickle, a training startup, to gamify their onboarding process. New hires got to experience company orientation via an online social game in a team setting with badges, points, and prizes for high scorers. Not only did this help the company overcome issues of onboarding delays, but they were able to establish an engaged and productive workforce faster than previously experienced (Buggie, Appukuttan, and Digital Transformation Research Institute, 2013).

The case of Deloitte provides a compelling argument for introducing gamified elements like badges, leader boards and status symbols to improve participation and completion times of training courses. Deloitte's virtual Leadership Academy encourages and promotes the skills the company considers to be most important to their future leaders (Meister, 2013). The company uses a learning platform which embeds missions, badges, and leaderboards and combines them into a user-friendly structure consisting of three categories of content: videos, in-depth courses, and self-assessments in the form of tests and quizzes. Learners are also encouraged to build a community by interacting with each other's status updates in a format similar to social media sites like Facebook. Deloitte applies the principles of gamification and behavioral science to motivate learners to achieve their learning goals. For Deloitte, gamification is not just fun. The company seeks to measure success by tracking metrics such as the increase in the number of users returning to the site each week and the number of badges users receive for completed online learning modules indicating the learning progress (Meister, 2013). Built-in analytics enable analysis of employee behavior. Information garnered on attitude toward skill upgrades, speeds, and so forth. can be leveraged to develop and customize the system.

## Learning from Mistakes and Successes

What we have learned in this chapter is that gamification has become a widespread trend within workforce learning. Despite the growing fascination with the phenomenon and evidence of its usefulness, many organizations still struggle to deploy it in a way that responds appropriately to workforce learning needs and adequately addresses organizational objectives. The chapter has argued that learning professionals should be wary of deploying gamified solutions without adequate reflection as this may simply result in a fleeting interest, which can rapidly dissipate leaving learners even more disengaged before the introduction.

Gamification becomes a powerful tool in workplace learning if well integrated into the overall learning strategy. Training professionals need to define the key competencies required to achieve business goals, have a clear understanding of the target group and what may engage and motivate them. The technology should never be the main focus. Rather, it should be selected to fit in with the content and teaching concept. As Werbach and Hunter (2012) stress, selecting appropriate game mechanisms and components is the last step of a carefully designed roadmap.

Long-term learner engagement can only be secured if both intrinsic as well as extrinsic motivators are considered in the overall game design. Tangible external rewards such as praise, money, or status succeed in driving players who are extrinsically motivated to learn. Sustainable learning solutions, however, urge players to complete learning activities by also trying to create a genuine desire to do so. They try to create an environment in which players see learning as something more than a means to an end. Learners rather experience internal rewards like enjoyment, positive feelings, and happiness. Key success factors in unleashing the potential for intrinsic motivation include creating a sense of fairness for players, providing meaningful rewards and establishing a clear understanding of the rules so that players consent in a quasi-voluntary fashion to pursue activities. Nonetheless, workplace-learning solutions need to achieve something beyond playfulness. Serious games provide the potential to allow learners to solve real-world problems in an enjoyable way.

It is difficult to predict whether gamification will be a sustainable avenue in workplace learning. Success within gamified learning concepts is still limited to singular company cases. What is needed is systematic research into metrics that will help clearly measure gamification's contribution to business success. As with other digital learning solutions, decision makers have to consider the full implications of introducing gamified solutions to workplace learning. Not only does it affect the individual learning experience, but it also shapes the overall learning culture within a company. Companies that choose to adopt this style of learning support a paradigm shift with respect to life-long learning, one that backs independently organized, customizable learning, which allows employees to take responsibility for their own development and to have fun.

## References

Abrahamson, E. (1996). Management fashion. *Academy of Management Review*, 21(1), 254–285.

Aftergut, A. (2016, November 29). 10 mechanics that drive gamification. Driving employee engagement by applying game mechanics in the workplace [Web log post]. Retrieved October 10, 2017, from http://www.nice.com/engage/blog/10-Mechanics-That-Drive-Gamification-2228

Bruckman, A. (1999, March). Can educational be fun? Retrieved December 21, 2018, from https://www.cc.gatech.edu/~asb/papers/conference/bruckman-gdc99.pdf

Brull, S., Finlayson, S., Kostelec, T., Macdonald, R., & Krenzischeck, D. (2017). Using gamification to improve productivity and increase knowledge retention during orientation. *Journal of Nursing Administration*, 47(9), 448–453.

Buckner, C. (2014, November 5). Five benefits of employee training software [Web log post]. Retrieved October 10, 2017, from https://badgeville.com/five-benefits-of-employee-training-software

Buggie, M., Appukuttan, P., and Digital Transformation Research Institute (2013, April 9). Let the games begin—using game mechanics to drive digital transformation. Retrieved October 10, 2017, from Capgemini Consulting website: https://www.capgemini.com/consulting/resources/let-the-games-begin-using-game-mechanics-to-drive-digital-transformation

Burke, B. (2012, November 5). Gamification 2020: What is the future of gamification? Retrieved October 10, 2017, from Gartner website https://www.gartner.com/doc/2226015/gamification--future-gamification

Burke, B. (2014). Gamify: How gamification motivates people to do extraordinary things. Brookline, MA: Gartner Inc.

Callan, R. C., Bauer, K. N., & Landers, R. N. (2015). How to avoid the dark side of gamification: Ten business scenarios and their unintended consequences. In T. Reiners, & L. Wood (Eds.), Gamification in education and business (pp. 553–568). Cham, Switzerland: Springer.

Connolly, T. M., Boyle, E. A., MacArthur, E., Hainey, T., & Boyle, J. (2012). A systematic literature review of empirical evidence on computer games and serious games. *Computers and Education*, 59(2), 661–686. https://doi.org/10.1016/j.compedu.2012.03.004

Crookall, D. (2010). Serious games, debriefing, and simulation/gaming as a discipline. *Simulation and Gaming*, 41(6), 898–920. https://doi.org/10.1177/1046878110390784

Davey, N. (2015, March 9). Why it's not game over for gamification. Retrieved October 10, 2017, from http://www.mycustomer.com/experience/engagement/why-its-not-game-over-for-gamification

Deci, E. L., & Ryan, R. M. (1980). The empirical exploration of intrinsic motivational processes. In L. Berkowitz (Ed.), Advances in experimental social psychology (pp. 39–80). New York, NY: Academic Press.

Deci, E. L., & Ryan, R. M. (1985). Intrinsic motivation and self-determination in human behaviour. New York, NY: Plenum.

Deterding, S., Dixon, D., Khaled, R., and Nacke, L. (2011, September). From game design elements to gamefulness: defining gamification. In *Proceedings of the 15th international academic MindTrek conference: Envisioning future media environments* (pp. 9–15). New York, NY: Association for Computing Machinery.

Edery, D., & Mollick, E. (2009). Changing the game: How video games are transforming the future of business. New York, NY: Financial Times Press.

Gagne, M., & Deci, E. L. (2005). Self-determination theory and work motivation. *Journal of Organizational Behavior*, 26(4), 331–362. https://doi.org/10.1002/job.322

Gartner (2014, August 11). Gartner Hype Cycle [Press release]. Retrieved October 10, 2017, from http://www.gartner.com/newsroom/id/2819918

Hamari, J., Koivisto, J., and Sarsa, H. (2014). Does gamification work?—A literature review of empirical studies on gamification. In *Proceedings of the 47th Annual Hawaii International Conference on System Sciences* (pp. 3025–3034). doi: https://doi.org/10.1109/HICSS.2014.377 Retrieved December 21, 2018 from https://ieeexplore.ieee.org/document/6758978

Hunicke, R., LeBlanc, M., and Zubek, R. (2004). MDA: A formal approach to game design and game research. In *Proceedings of the Challenges in Game AI*

*Workshop,* Nineteenth National Conference on Artificial Intelligence (pp. 1–5). Retrieved October 10, 2017, from http://www.cs.northwestern.edu/~hunicke/MDA.pdf

IBM. (2012). Serious games: An innovative way to accelerate deep skills. Retrieved October 10, 2017, from http://www-935.ibm.com/services/multimedia/IBM_Serious_Games_Capabilities.pdf

Kapp, K. M. (2012). The gamification of learning and instruction: Game-based methods and strategies for training and education. San Francisco, CA: Pfeiffer.

Kapp, K. M. (2014, March 19). Gamification: Separating fact from fiction. *Chief Learning Officer*. Retrieved October 10, 2017, from http://www.clomedia.com/2014/03/19/gamification-separating-fact-from-fiction

Kineo. (n.d.) McDonald's Till Training Game Case Study. Retrieved October 10, 2017, from http://www.kineo.com/case-studies/mcdonalds-till-training-game

Landers, R., Bauer, K., & Callan, R. (2015). Gamification of task performance with leaderboards: A goal setting experiment. *Computers in Human Behavior*, 71 June 2017, 508–515. https://doi.org/10.1016/j.chb.2015.08.008

Lazarro, N. (2004). The 4 Keys 2 Fun [White paper]. Retrieved October 10, 2017, from http://www.xeodesign.com/category/the-4-keys

Lenihan, D. (2012). Health games: a key component for the evolution of wellness programs. *Games for Health Journal: Research, Development, and Clinical Application*, 1, 233–235. https://doi.org/10.1089/g4h.2012.0022

Lepper, M. R., Greene, D., & Nisbett, R. E. (1973). Undermining children's intrinsic interest with extrinsic reward: A test of the "overjustification" hypothesis. *Journal of Personality and Social Psychology*, 28(1), 129–137. https://doi.org/10.1037/h0035519

McDonald, E. (2017, April 20). The Global Games Market Will Reach $108.9 Billion in 2017 With Mobile Taking 42 %. Retrieved December 21, 2018 from: https://newzoo.com/insights/articles/the-global-games-market-will-reach-108-9-billion-in-2017-with-mobile-taking-42

McGonigal, J. (2011). Reality is broken: Why games make us better and how they can change the world. New York, NY: Penguin Press.

Meister, J. C. (2013, January 2). How Deloitte made learning a game, *Harvard Business Review*, Retrieved December 21, 2018 from https://hbr.org/2013/01/how-deloitte-made-learning-a-g

MindTickle. (2013). How SAP Saved Senior Management Time by 70% and Reduced Costs by 60 % [Case Study]. Retrieved October 10, 2017, from http://mstest.mindtickle.com/customers/new-hire-sap

Mollick, E. R., and Rothbard, N. (2014). Mandatory fun: Consent, gamification and the impact of games at work. The Wharton School Research Paper Series. Retrieved December 21, 2018 from https://papers.ssrn.com/sol3/papers.cfm?abstract_id=2277103 doi: https://doi.org/10.2139/ssrn.2277103

Noe, R. A., Tews, M. J., & McConnell Dachner, A. (2010). Learner engagement: A new perspective for enhancing our understanding of learner motivation and workplace learning. *The Academy of Management Annals*, 4(1), 279–315. https://doi.org/10.1080/19416520.2010.493286

Perryer, C., Scott-Ladd, B., & Leighton, C. (2012). Gamification: implications for workplace intrinsic motivation in the 21st century. *Asian Forum on Business Education Journal,*, 5, 371–381.

Popescu, M., Romero, M., and Usart, M. (2012). Using serious games in adult education serious business for serious people-the MetaVals game case study. In *ICVL 2012–7th International Conference on Virtual Learning* (pp. 125–134). Bucharest, Romania: Bucharest University Press.

Popescu, M., Romero, M., & Usart, M. (2013). Serious games for serious learning using SG for business, management and defence education. *International Journal of Computer Science Research and Application*, 3(1), 5–15.

Rheinberg, F. (2010). Intrinsic motivation and flow. In J. Heckhausen, & H. Heckhausen (Eds.), Motivation and action (4th ed.) (pp. 365–388). Cambridge, UK: Cambridge University Press.

Richter, G., Raban, D. K., & Rafaeli, S. (2014). Studying gamification: The effect of rewards and incentives on motivation. In T. Reiners, & L. Woods (Eds.), Gamification in education and business (pp. 21–46). Cham, Switzerland: Springer International Publishing. https://doi.org/10.1007/978-3-319-10208-5

Robson, K., Plangger, K., Kietzmann, J. H., McCarthy, I., & Pitt, L. (2015). Is it all a game?: Understanding the principles of gamification. *Business Horizons*, 58(4), 411–420. https://doi.org/10.1016/j.bushor.2015.03.006

Ryan, M., Sleigh, A., Soh, K. W., & Li, Z. (2013). Why gamification is serious business. *Outlook–The Journal of High-Performance Business (Accenture)*, 1, 1–6 Retrieved October 10, 2017, from https://www.accenture.com/us-en/insight-outlook-why-gamification-is-serious-business

Ryan, R. M., & Deci, E. L. (2000). Self-determination theory and the facilitation of intrinsic motivation, social development and well-being. *American Psychologist*, 55(1), 68–78.

Saatchi and Saatchi. (2011). Engagement unleashed: Gamification for business, brands and loyalty. Retrieved October 10, 2017, from http://saatchi.com/en-us/news/engagement_unleashed_gamification_for_business_brands_and_loyalty

Sailer, M., Hense, J., Mandl, H., & Klever, M. (2013). Psychological perspectives on motivation through gamification. *Interaction Design and Architecture(s) Journal*, 19, 28–37.

Seaborn, K., & Fels, D. I. (2015). Gamification in theory and action: A survey. *International Journal of Human-Computer Studies*, 74, 14–31. https://doi.org/10.1016/j.ijhcs.2014.09.006

Sunrise Software (2014). Sunrise Software gamification survey results. [White paper]. Retrieved October 10, 2017, from https://www.sunrisesoftware.com/whitepapers/white-paper-gamification-survey-results-2014.

Vernau, K., & Hauptmann, M. (2014). Corporate learning goes digital: How companies can benefit from online education. Munich, Germany: Roland Berger Strategy Consultants.

Werbach, K. (2014). (Re)defining gamification: A process approach. In A. Spagnolli, L. Chittaro, and L. Gamberini (Eds.), Persuasive technology: 9th International Conference, PERSUASIVE 2014 (pp. 266–272). Cham, Switzerland: Springer.

Werbach, K., & Hunter, D. (2012). For the win: How game thinking can revolutionize your business. Philadelphia, PA:: Wharton Digital Press.

Wildi-Yune, J., and Cordero, C. (2015). Corporate Digital Learning: How to Get It "Right". (KPMG/IMD position paper). Retrieved October 10, 2017, from the

KPMG website https://assets.kpmg.com/content/dam/kpmg/pdf/2015/09/corporate-digital-learning-2015-KPMG.pdf

Zichermann, G., & Cunningham, C. (2011). Gamification by design: Implementing game mechanics in web and mobile apps. Sebastopol, CA: O'Reilly Media.

Zichermann, G., & Linder, J. (2013). The gamification revolution: How leaders leverage game mechanics to crush the competition. New York, NY: McGraw-Hill Education.

Zimmerman, E., & Salen, K. (2005). The game design reader: A rules of play anthology. Cambridge, MA: The MIT Press.

# 30

# Impact of Gamification on Learning and Motivation of Workforce

## A Student-Based Study

*Ahmed Deif*

*California Polytechnic State University*

## Gamification Overview

### What is Gamification?

Gamification is the use of game design elements and game mechanics in non-game contexts. In order to have a better understanding of gamification as a concept, we need to start by defining the concept of a "game". Salen and Zimmerman (2003) compared eight academic definitions, and then defined a game as "a system in which players engage in an artificial conflict, defined by rules, that results in a quantifiable outcome" (p. 76). Others like Kim (2009) have defined a game as: "a structured experience with rules and goals that's fun." Thus, gamification is attributed to using the game approach to engage a group of people in designed activity within a specific context.

That context can be, for example, marketing, entertainment or education. Educational gamification proposes the use of game-like rule systems, player experiences, and cultural roles to shape learners' behavior. Gåsland (2011) reported on the wide application of gamification at both the industrial and educational fronts by referring to the number of commercial companies rising up to provide gamification services, technology, and platforms. Some visionaries, like game designer Jesse Schell, envision a kind of "gamepocalypse," a hypothetical future in which everything in daily life becomes gamified, from brushing one's teeth to exercise (Schell, 2010).

### Gamification Classification

In the literature, gamification belongs to the wider field of studying simulation in education and learning. Research work has identified three categories of simulation-based learning: role play, gaming, and computer simulation (Feinstein, Mann, & Corsun, 2002; Hsu, 1989). These categories are different in their design, objective and scope of application. In a role playing exercise, participants demonstrate

*The Wiley Handbook of Global Workplace Learning*, First Edition.
Edited by Vanessa Hammler Kenon and Sunay Vasant Palsole.

the role of a specific job or worker in a particular situation following a set of rules and interacting with other role players. As for gaming the key elements entail interaction within a predetermined context, often involving forms of competition, cooperation, conflict, or collusion.

These interactions are constrained by a set rules and procedures. Finally, computer simulations aim to replicate system characteristics using mathematics or simple object representations (Feinstein et al., 2002). Ellington (2001) differentiates between game-based simulations depending on their format. Specifically, his differentiation depends on the distinction made between manual exercises and electronic exercises. Examples of manual exercises identified by Ellington include card, board, and field games. Lean, Moizer, Towler, and Abbey (2006) summarize these classifications in Figure 30.1.

## Gamification Dimensions

In the following sections, I outline the three fundamental dimensions in which gamification can serve as an intervention in learning and motivation.

### Cognitive dimension

Games provide complex systems of rules for learners to explore through active experimentation and discovery. They engage learners through the mastery pro-

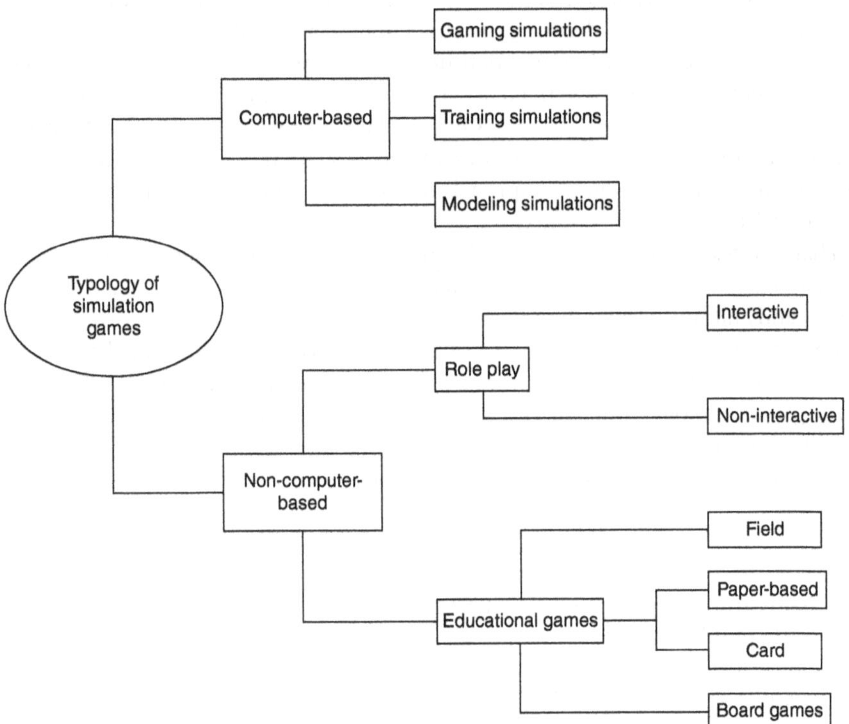


**Figure 30.1** Typology of Simulation (*Source:* Adopted From Lean et al., 2006)

cess and the pre-designed difficult tasks (Koster, 2004). One critical game design technique is to deliver concrete challenges that are tailored to each learner's skill level, increasing the difficulty as the player's skill expands. Specific, moderately difficult, immediate goals are motivating for learners (Locke & Latham 1990; Bandura, 1997), and these are precisely the sort that well-designed games provide (Gee, 2008). Games also provide multiple routes to success, allowing players to choose their own subgoals within the larger task. This, too, supports motivation and engagement (Locke & Latham, 1990).

#### Emotional dimension

Games invoke a range of powerful emotions, from curiosity to frustration to joy (Lazzaro, 2004). Furthermore, they help learners overcome negative emotional experiences and sometimes transform them into positive ones. A clear example of such transformation in a game is demonstrated in the concept of failure. Since games involve repeated experimentation, they also involve repeated failure. In fact, for many games, the only way to learn how to play the game is to fail at it repeatedly, learning something each time (Gee, 2008). Games maintain this positive relationship with failure by making feedback cycles rapid and keeping the stakes low. The former means players can keep trying until they succeed; the latter means they risk very little by doing so.

#### Social dimension

Games permit learners to experience different roles, asking them to make in-game decisions from their new vantage points (Squire, 2006). Learners can also discover new sides of themselves in the safe space of play. Gamification can provide social credibility and recognition for various learning achievements, which might otherwise remain invisible or even be denigrated by other learners. Recognition can be provided by the teacher, but gamification can also allow learners to reward each other (Lee & Hammer, 2011). Finally, games enhance various teamwork ethics among learners whether in their teams or across different teams. This is achieved through promoting positive cooperative and competitive social spirits.

## Gamification and Workforce Learning Process

Gamification is used in the workforce learning process for multiple reasons. These reasons are usually referred to as advantages of gamification over alternative pedagogies and are typically classified into three categories (Anderson & Lawton, 2009):

### Learning

1) Teach the workforce the terminology and principles of their work in a general or specific discipline.
2) Help the workforce grasp the interrelationships among the various functions of their work environment (marketing, maintenance, production, and so forth).

3) Demonstrate the difficulty of executing different work policies that appear relatively simple.
4) Enhance the retention of knowledge. (Participation in an activity yields greater retention of concepts and relationships than does a more passive educational pedagogy.)
5) Enable the workforce to transfer learning to their relative real work world.

### Attitudinal

1) Improve the workforce's attitudes toward their discipline and work.
2) Provide a common experience for collective discussion among the workforce.
3) Engage the workforce in the learning process.

### Behavioral

1) Teach the workforce to apply the concepts and principles of their different disciplines to make effective decisions.
2) Improve the workforce's ability to interact with their peers. (Because most trainers using gamification have their attendees work in groups, the belief exists that the workforce will learn interpersonal skills during the course of play.)
3) Give the workforce practice at making work-related decisions.
4) Improve the workforce's work-related decision skills.

These lists shows the various factors that motivate trainers and educators to implement gamification within the workforce environment. These factors are not mutually exclusive and in many cases can be fulfilled simultaneously. Furthermore, the ability of gamification to motivate, engage and influence behaviors of the workforce, serious games are being used for three key processes in organizations, namely; Training, Recruitment and Marketing and Sales. A Gartner research report indicated that by 2020, 70 % of large organizations will have 'gamified' at least one business process (Gartner 2012). According to an M2 Research report on gamification in 2012, 56 % of organizations purchasing "gamified" solutions are seeking to improve workforce engagement and motivation. Successful implementation examples of gamification approach in different work environments can be found in ClickSoftware (2014).

Research studies support the previously reported market trends highlighting the impact of gamification on workforce learning. Examples include the work of London and Hall (2011) discussing how the use of games in an e-learning setup can improve the support and efficiency of organizations' workforce. Farrington (2011) also surveyed the increase of gamification use in corporations and its wide application at different areas within organizations. O'Rourke (2016) discussed the positive outcome of gamification in vocational training for a young workforce.

Finally, it is important to note that the implementation of gamification within the workforce environment comes with associated challenges. For example, games are time-consuming to create, sometimes costly, and take time to play. Not all learning warrants this investment in time and money. Also, gamification in learning is usually focused on encouraging certain social behaviors, but this may have unintended consequences depending on the workforce's background and expectation. More of these challenges will be addressed in this article.

## Assessment of Gamification Impact on Learning and Motivation

In this article, we report on a research experiment conducted at California Polytechnic State University (Cal Poly) to assess the impact of gamification on the learning performance of students while studying Lean Thinking principles and tools. The internalizing motivation theory or sometimes referred to as intrinsic motivation theory (Stipek, 1988) is the general guiding framework for our assessment of gamification impact. This theory suggests that an education curriculum is successful in promoting intrinsic (internal) motivation of students to seek and retain knowledge if it can get students to evolve through four stages. The first stage starts by external motivation then approval seeking followed by understanding and ending with the target internalization. The external motivation and the approval seeking stages of the internalizing motivation theory are captured through different elements of what is referred to in this study as motivational processing.

The understanding stage of the theory framework is captured through what we refer to as the cognitive processing part of the assessment. Finally, the last stage of internalization by the students is captured through both motivational and social processing assessment. The details of these motivational, cognitive, and social processes are explained in the following paragraph.

The motivation processing is measured using the attention, relevance, confidence, and satisfaction (ARCS) model of motivational design (Keller, 1987a; 1987b). This model is widely applied in instructional design processes that connect learning motivation with performance (Ames, 1992; Anderman & Maehr, 1994; Bandura, 1997; Keller, 2008). The model suggests that learning motivation is dependent on four perceptual components: attention, relevance, confidence, and satisfaction (Keller, 2008). Attention refers to the learner's response to perceived instructional stimuli provided by the instruction. Relevance helps learners associate their prior learning experience with the given instruction. Confidence stresses the importance of building learners' positive expectation toward their performance on the learning task. Satisfaction comes near the end of the learning process when learners are allowed to practice newly acquired knowledge or skills. The ARCS model focuses on the interactions between learners and the instructional programs.

Its main thesis is rooted in the expectancy-value theory that views human behaviors as evaluative outcomes among expectations (beliefs), perceived probability for success (expectancy), and perceived impact of the success (value) (Palmgreen, 1984).

Cognitive processing was assessed through requesting the students to self-report the mental effort investment level and the difficulty level associated with the learning task on a nine-point symmetrical Likert scale. The reason for selecting these two cognitive processing dimensions is to try to capture the intrinsic cognitive load via the mental effort experienced and also the germane cognitive load via rating the difficulty the students encountered through the game (Huang, 2011).

Social processing was captured through a group of questions that integrated both cooperative as well as competitive interactions. Cooperation will create many important group dynamics that relate to multiple aspects of lean systems. On the other hand, competitive interaction will increase students' engagement enhancing the overall educational experience.

## A Case Study on Gamification as a Motivational and Learning Tool

The research setup in this experiment involved a total of 60 students across two classes where every student was asked to fill a designed questionnaire that captures the three discussed assessment components after each game. The students were engaged in seven different games over the duration of their Lean Thinking course for 3 months. The course curriculum was redesigned to include games that demonstrated different Lean principles and tools in a competitive way among students' teams. The selected games included physical sets of systems that mimicked production lines and service environments. Students used these sets to compete using predefined performance metrics (such as cost, quality, and time) to see which team would implement the best lean tool (such as pull system, line balancing, or value stream mapping).

An example of one of these games was a manufacturing simulation based around a small line assembling torches. The game was to examine how the different students' teams would use the concepts of line balancing and quality at the source (as typical Lean Thinking tools) to improve this assembly line. The initial state of the line was unbalanced and included a number of components that have been modified to cause defects during assembly. Another game was dedicated to get the students to understand the importance of visual management in a Lean environment. This was done through competing teams to see which one will assemble a product composed of ten components in an unorganized workplace with no instructions or standards versus the case with an environment applying visual control tools and standards. After each of the games teams debriefed on what they learned and how it was related to what they studied.

Figure 30.2 shows a sample of students playing one of the selected games.

Table 30.1 lists the summary of the average scores for all reported questions by the students after each of the seven played games.

Before looking into the different insights revealed by the reported data, analysis of variance was conducted. The main objective of the analysis was to ensure that student's bias as a parameter was masked and that the different assessment scores reported were varying mainly due to the different games setups. A summary of the ANOVA results is shown in the Appendix.

The overall average of each of the four aspects constituting the motivational processing assessment criterion is shown in Figure 30.3. One can observe that the relevance scale has the highest mean of 7.8 while the confidence scale has the

**Figure 30.2** Picture of students engaged in one of the lean games

lowest mean at 2.53. Satisfaction and attention scales were close at 7.48 and 7.3 respectively. It is important to note that the questions for the confidence-assessment criterion were articulated so that lower scores would reflect a better confidence performance. Thus, the reported scores reflect a good motivational performance since the four ARCS model components scored around the top third of the used 1–9 Likert scale. This finding suggests that gamification positively impacts students' motivation to engage in the learning process and aligns with similar results such as those found in Huang (2011).

Among the reasons why the ARCS components reflect students' willingness to engage is that they theoretically measure the amount of effort invested by learners to achieve the learning goal (Small, 2000) as well as reflecting both intrinsic and extrinsic motives.

The high satisfaction score can also be explained through the scores of the other three aspects of the (ARCS). The students found the games attracting their attention through perceptual arousal, inquiry arousal, and variability. Also, the played games were relevant to them in terms of their goal orientation to learn about how Lean principles and tools improve systems and thus their motive to play the games matched their expectations. In addition, their confidence increased due to the clear learning requirements and the success opportunities available in the games in addition to being able to have personal responsibility through the different roles required by the gamified systems.

Figure 30.4 captures the overall averages of the three learning assessment criteria; motivational processing, cognitive processing, and social processing. Social processing had the highest score among the three, highlighting the importance of the social interaction in the gamification learning approach. The internal dynamics among the team as well as the competitive spirit between teams contributed to the positive learning experience of students.

Table 30.1 Reported average scores for learning performance questionnaire

| Items for Motivation<br>Absolutely disagree (1)–Absolutely agree (9) | Reported Level |
|---|---|
| **Attention** | |
| There was something interesting at the beginning of the game that attracted my attention | 7.39 |
| The design of the game is eye-catching | 7.39 |
| The quality of the game kit helped to hold my attention | 7.23 |
| I enjoyed the game so much that I would like to know more about this topic | 7.13 |
| The way the tasks were arranged in the game helped keep my attention | 7.35 |
| The game has things that stimulated my curiosity | 7.35 |
| I really enjoyed learning with the game | 7.46 |
| The wording of feedback or comments after the exercises helped me feel rewarded for my effort | 7.42 |
| The variety of reading passages, exercises, illustrations, etc., helped keep my attention on the game | 6.82 |
| I could relate the content of the game to things I have seen, done or thought about in my own life | 7.55 |
| It was a pleasure to work on such a well-designed game | 7.17 |
| **Relevance** | |
| It is clear to me how the content of the game is related to things I already know | 7.93 |
| There were examples that showed me how the game could be important to some people in the learning setting | 7.88 |
| The content of the game is relevant to my interests | 7.68 |
| **Confidence** | |
| The game was more difficult to understand than I would like for it to be | 2.97 |
| The game had so much information that it was hard to pick out and remember the important points | 2.76 |
| The game is so abstract that it was hard to keep my attention on it | 2.4 |
| The exercises in the game were too difficult | 2.26 |
| I could not really understand quite a bit of the material in the game | 2.25 |
| **Satisfaction** | |
| It felt good to successfully complete the game | 7.48 |

| Items for cognitive processing<br>Very low mental effort (1)–Very high mental effort (9) | Reported level |
|---|---|
| How much mental effort did you invest to learn the content from the game? | 5.45 |
| How difficult was it for you to learn the content from the game? | 3.87 |

| Items for Social Processing<br>Absolutely disagree (1)–Absolutely agree (9) | Reported level |
|---|---|
| A spirit of teamwork and cooperation existed in my team | 7.8 |
| The competition enhanced my engagement in the game | 7.45 |
| My team communicated effectively with other teams | 7.41 |

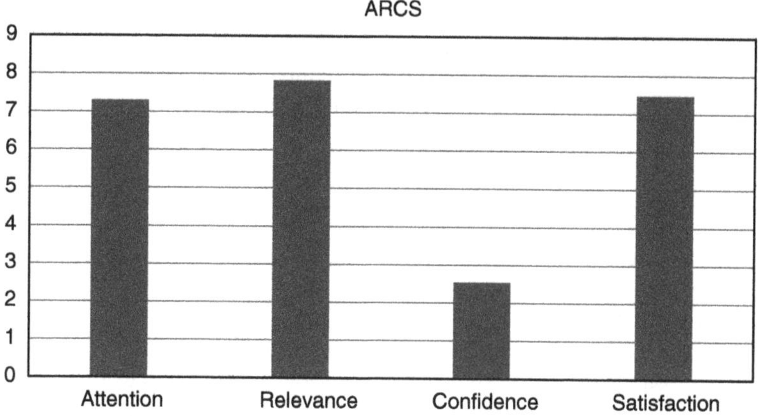


**Figure 30.3** Average of the motivational processing aspects

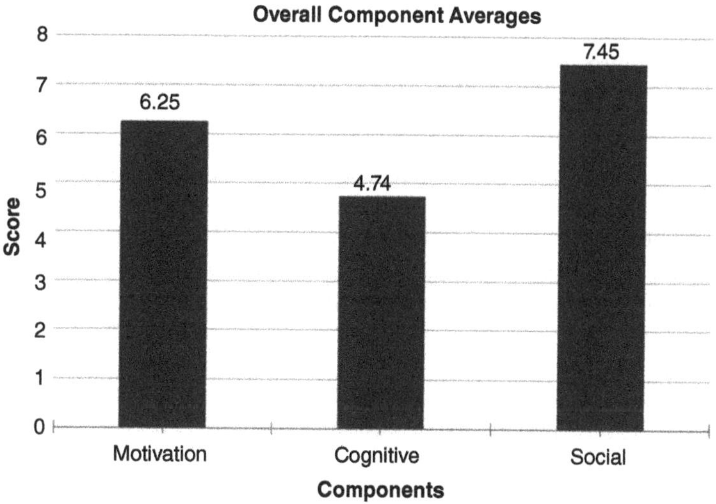


**Figure 30.4** Overall averages for the performance learning assessment components

Cognitive processing scored the lowest as students reported above average in their mental effort investment to learn the content game while they reported below average in the difficulty to learn the game content. The cognitive challenge in gamification learning is very important. Researchers argue that cognitive load can demotivate learners (Sweller, van Merriënboer, & Paas, 1999). In the conducted study, the general above-average performance of cognitive processing can be attributed to the lecturing components that usually preceded each game where the target Lean principle or tool was generally explained; thus, relating the game content to that principle or tool was easier for the student.

The three assessment components constitute the requirements for a typical learning cycle (exploration which is captured through motivation elements followed by concept development which was approached through cognitive processing, and finally concept application as illustrated in social processing). However, their different scores reflect the ways in which learners would interact differently with each of these components. In a higher education setup, students usually prefer social processing followed by motivation processing, and interact least with cognitive processing, as illustrated by the reported results.

## Summary and Discussion

This study was designed to explore the impact of gamification on the motivation and learning of a workforce through a sample of undergraduate students, using internalizing motivation as a general framework for assessment. It used the ARCS model to capture the motivation processing of the leaners.

Motivation processing together with cognitive and social processing were used to assess the impact of gamification on the learning of the workforce (students in this case). Data were gathered after having the students learning different Lean thinking principles and tools using physical games that mimic real manufacturing and service environment over the course of 3 months. In general, reported results showed that gamification seems to enhance students' motivation, cognitive and social processing leading to an improved learning process. Some of the further recommendations that can be derived from the conducted study are mentioned as follows:

1) The gamification design dimensions in the study were intended to align with the learning cycle that usually starts with motivation and then cognitive exercise within a social setup. The effort to align with the learning cycle helps gamification to be one of the efficient mechanisms that can enhance learning among workforce in any given workplace.
2) The reported results also pointed to the effectiveness of non-computer based games as they appeal more to students. This can be attributed to the level of personal interaction (as reflected in the social processing scores) as well as the more realistic sense that such game topology offers to students. This observation would likely be the same in other workforce contexts.
3) The cognitive processing component in the gamification learning approach was shown to be critical as it could impact learners' perceived satisfaction levels. Learners with a high level of intention to pursue the performance goal of the game could be either encouraged or frustrated at the end of the game due to the experienced high cognitive load. In the academic context, this can be managed with different educational techniques; however, in a workplace context, attention needs to be paid to the workforce skills level and expectation in order to avoid unsatisfactory learning experiences.
4) From a sustainability standpoint, the above-average scores suggest that students will most likely engage in more games as they perceived gamification to be motivational and satisfactory. This is a very important aspect in the general workforce learning management process since it is crucial to maintain the interest of the workforce to continuously learn how to improve their workplace.
5) Furthermore, it is recommended that people responsible for workforce learning can apply this assessment approach and its scores as a cycle for continuous improvement of motivational support when developing workforce learning and training materials and tracking its impact on the workforce.

6) Future work would include exploring the interaction between the different learning assessment components and extending the analysis to include the impact of more social and cognitive aspects.
7) Finally, the application of the proposed assessment approach to specific workforce environments will enhance the understanding of the impact of gamification on learning process beyond the academic investigated setup in this study into various workforce applications.

## References

Ames, C. (1992). Classroom: Goals, structures, and student motivation. *Journal of Educational Psychology, 84*, 261–271.

Anderman, E. M., & Maehr, M. L. (1994). Motivation and schooling in the middle grades, review of educational research. *Journal of Educational Psychology, 64*, 287–309.

Anderson, P. H., & Lawton, L. (2009). Business simulations and cognitive learning developments, desires, and future directions. *Simulations and Games, 40*(2), 193–216.

Bandura, A. (1997). *Self-efficacy: The exercise of control.* New York, NY: Freeman.

ClickSoftware. (2014). Retrieved from: https://www.clicksoftware.com/blog/top-25-best-examples-of-gamification-in-business

Ellington, H. (2001) 'Using games simulations and case studies to develop key skills', in M. Boyle and Y. Smith (eds) *simulation and gaming research yearbook*, SAGSET

Farrington, J. (2011). From the research: Myths worth dispelling: Seriously, the game is up. *Performance Improvement Quarterly, 24*(2), 105–110.

Feinstein, A. H., Mann, S., & Corsun, D. L. (2002). Charting the experiential territory: Clarifying definitions and uses of computer simulation games and role play. *Journal of Management Development, 21*(10), 732–744.

Gartner Research Report. (2012), *Gamification 2020: What is the Future of Gamification?*

Gåsland, M. (2011). Game mechanic based e-learning. Norwegian University of Science and Technology, *Master Thesis.*

Gee, J. P. (2008). Learning and games. In Katie Salen (Ed.) *The ecology of games: Connecting youth, games, and learning* (John D. and Catherine T. MacArthur Foundation series on digital media and learning). Cambridge, MA: The MIT Press.

Hsu, E. (1989). Role event gaming simulation in management education: A conceptual framework and review. *Simulations and Games, 20*(4), 409–438.

Huang, W. H. (2011). Evaluating learners' motivational and cognitive processing in an online game-based learning environment. *Computers in Human Behavior, 27*, 694–704.

Keller, J. M. (1987a). Strategies for stimulating the motivation to learn. *Performance and Instruction, 26*, 1–7.

Keller, J. M. (1987b). The systematic process of motivational design. *Performance and Instruction, 26*(9/10), 1–8.

Keller, J. M. (2008). An integrative theory of motivation, volition, and performance. *Technology, Instruction, Cognition and Learning, 6*, 79–104.

Kim, A. J. (2009). Putting the Fun in Functional: Applying Game Mechanics to Functional Software. *Google Tech. Talks.* https://www.youtube.com/watch?v=ihUt-163gZI

Koster, R. (2004). *A theory of fun.* New York, NY: Paraglyph Press.

Lazzaro, N. (2004). Why we play games: Four keys to more emotion without story. Retrieved from: http://www.xeodesign.com/xeodesign_whyweplaygames.pdf

Lean, J., Moizer, J., Towler, M., & Abbey, C. (2006). Simulations and games: use and barriers in higher education. *Active Learning in Higher Education, 7*(3), 227–242.

Lee, J. J., & Hammer, J. (2011). Gamification in education: What, how, why bother? *Academic Exchange Quarterly, 15*(2), 1–5.

Locke, G., & Latham, E. (1990). Self-regulation through goal setting. *Organizational Behavior and Human Decision Processes, 50,* 212–247.

London, M., & Hall, M. J. (2011). Web 2.0 support for individual, group and organizational learning. *Human Resource Development International, 14*(1), 103–113.

M2 Research, Gamification in 2012, Market Update, Consumer and Enterprise Market Trends.

O'Rourke, M. (2016). Using student voice in the design of game-based learning. In S. Barker, S. Dawson, A. Pardo, and C. Colvin (Eds.), Show Me The Learning. Proceedings ASCILITE 2016 Adelaide (pp. 481–486).

Palmgreen, P. (1984). Uses and gratifications: A theoretical perspective. In R. N. Bostrom (Ed.), *Communication yearbook, 8* (pp. 61–72). Beverly Hills, CA: Sage..

Salen, K., & Zimmerman, E. (2003). *Rules of play: Game design fundamentals.* Cambridge, MA: MIT Press.

Schell, J. (2010). DICE 2010. *Design Outside the Box Presentation.* Available at: http://www.g4tv.com/videos/44277/dice-2010-design-outside-the-box-presentation

Small, R. V. (2000). Motivation in instructional design. *Teacher Librarian:, 27,* 29–31.

Squire, K. (2006). From content to context: Videogames as designed experience. *Educational Researcher, 35*(8), 19–29.

Stipek, D. (1988). *Motivation to learn: From theory to practice.* Englewood Cliffs, NJ: Prentice Hall.

Sweller, J., van Merriënboer, J. G., & Paas, F. G. W. C. (1999). Cognitive architecture and instructional design. *Educational Psychology Review, 10*(3), 251–296.

# A. Appendix

## A.1 Analysis of variance for attention

| Source | DF | Adj SS | Adj MS | F-Value | P-Value |
|---|---|---|---|---|---|
| Game Name | 7 | 17.21 | 2.4589 | 2.59 | 0.014 |
| Name | 55 | 234.05 | 4.2554 | 4.48 | 0.000 |
| Error | 222 | 210.93 | 0.9501 | | |
| Total | 284 | 477.14 | | | |

## A.2 Analysis of variance for relevance

| Source | DF | Adj SS | Adj MS | F-Value | P-Value |
|---|---|---|---|---|---|
| Game Name | 7 | 10.57 | 1.5101 | 2.33 | 0.026 |
| Name | 55 | 118.23 | 2.1496 | 3.32 | 0.000 |
| Error | 222 | 143.65 | 0.6471 | | |
| Total | 284 | 276.50 | | | |

## A.3 Analysis of variance for confidence

| Source | DF | Adj SS | Adj MS | F-Value | P-Value |
|---|---|---|---|---|---|
| Game Name | 7 | 83.04 | 11.863 | 6.28 | 0.000 |
| Name | 55 | 227.73 | 4.140 | 2.19 | 0.000 |
| Error | 222 | 419.61 | 1.890 | | |
| Total | 284 | 741.02 | | | |

## A.4 Analysis of variance for satisfaction

| Source | DF | Adj SS | Adj MS | F-Value | P-Value |
|---|---|---|---|---|---|
| Game Name | 7 | 140.3 | 20.040 | 3.00 | 0.005 |
| Name | 55 | 894.9 | 16.271 | 2.44 | 0.000 |
| Error | 267 | 1784.1 | 6.682 | | |
| Total | 329 | 2826.0 | | | |

## A.5 Analysis of variance for cognitive

| Source | DF | Adj SS | Adj MS | F-Value | P-Value |
|---|---|---|---|---|---|
| Game Name | 7 | 67.34 | 9.620 | 4.87 | 0.000 |
| Name | 55 | 400.67 | 7.285 | 3.69 | 0.000 |
| Error | 223 | 440.50 | 1.975 | | |
| Total | 285 | 910.42 | | | |

## A.6 Analysis of variance for social

| Source | DF | Adj SS | Adj MS | F-Value | P-Value |
|---|---|---|---|---|---|
| Game Name | 7 | 43.34 | 6.192 | 5.45 | 0.000 |
| Name | 55 | 355.24 | 6.459 | 5.69 | 0.000 |
| Error | 223 | 253.23 | 1.136 | | |
| Total | 285 | 681.45 | | | |

# 31

# Using Technology-Oriented, Problem-Based Learning to Support Global Workplace Learning

*Emma O'Brien*[1], *Ileana Hamburg*[2], *and Mark Southern*[1]

[1] *The University of Limerick*
[2] *Institut Arbeit und Technik, Westfalische Hochschule*

## Changing World of Work

Over the past decade, the world in which we work has been subject to an increasing pace of change (Organization for Economic Cooperation and Development [OECD], 2017; Paccagnella and Organization for Economic Cooperation and Development [OECD] (France), 2016; Puncreobutr, 2016). There are three main drivers to these changes: technology, globalization, and demography (Eurofound, 2016; Frey et al., 2016; OECD, 2016a; Paccagnella and OECD, 2016; Wilson et al., 2016).

Technology has brought about changes in the way we work and socialize. The digitization of professional and personal lives has led to an exponential increase in the amount of data available to individuals. (Walker, 2015). This has resulted in more informed customers who have a greater understanding of their needs, thereby, placing significant demands on product and service providers to satisfy their individual requirements. Consequently, business is now more competitive, with companies offering customized products and instant product and service delivery (Brancher, 2016).

Technology has also enabled a global economy in which companies can now access markets and suppliers beyond geographical boundaries. Many companies are dispersed, with operations in multiple locations to allow them to avail of cost savings and economies of scale. Globalization has also impacted consumers who have access to a wider variety of products and services, significantly increasing competition. On a personal level, individuals now socialize and work with people they have never physically met, resulting in a growth in cross-cultural dimensions to work.

Globalization has caused a constant shift in demographics due to migration, resulting in a mobile, more diverse workforce (EUROSTAT, 2015). Furthermore, decreasing family sizes and improvements in healthcare will result in an aging population and a longer working life (Wilson, 2013).

*The Wiley Handbook of Global Workplace Learning*, First Edition.
Edited by Vanessa Hammler Kenon and Sunay Vasant Palsole.

The impact of these changes will be significant over the coming years. Technology will lead to an automation of routine work; the third industrial revolution will result in many "left brain" activities being automated and a demand for "right brain thinking" (Wilson, 2013). It is estimated that up to 57 % of job tasks will become automated (Frey et al., 2016). Most at risk will be economies that have failed to invest in education and skills (Frey et al., 2016). Developing countries will be most affected as automation will increase productivity and will result in "premature deindustrialization" with many companies relocating manufacturing "back home." For example, manufacturing will take place at point of sale using technology such as additive printing. As routine tasks will be undertaken by machinery, job roles will become more complex resulting in increased unemployment levels for mid- to low-skilled workers, which will widen social inequalities (Wilson, 2013).

The digitization of work practices will allow routine collection of data, and analytics will embody everyday work practices. The expectation will be that workers have to interpret these data and investigate why these underlying trends occur. This will drive the need for employees who are problem solvers rather than data processors (Walker, 2015).

The increase in speed of change will require people to be more adaptable, undertaking several job roles through the course of their longer working life. Furthermore, the emergence of an informal economy will result in unconventional and flexible work arrangements in working conditions, with self-employment becoming increasingly common (Wilson, 2013). To allow individuals to meet these emerging changes new skills will be required (Liddle & Lerais, 2007; OECD, 2017).

## Skills Needs in an Emerging Workplace

Due to accelerating change, discipline specific knowledge will continuously need to be updated. Learning to learn and becoming self-determined, autonomous learners will become increasingly important in the emerging workplace (OECD, 2015b). To build this capacity, it is necessary to develop skills that allow individuals to rapidly adapt to change (Paccagnella and OECD, 2016). Rather than teaching learners content that will become quickly obsolete, it is important to assist learners in the workplace to:

1) Think creatively to identify solutions to problems and new ways of doing business.
2) Develop knowledge and skills they require, on demand, to solve such problems.
3) Apply the relevant knowledge to a given situation or problem.

Problem solving, communication, entrepreneurship, and digital skills are necessary to allow workers to embrace digitization and a faster paced, complex, global, working environment (Frey et al., 2016; Walker, 2015; Wilson, 2013). Problem solving and entrepreneurship or initiative taking are transferable to multiple contexts and in European Union (EU) policy classified as transversal skills. Communication is seen as a traditional skill and digital skills as a basic necessity. All are identified as key competencies for future workplaces (European Commission, 2016).

There is currently a dearth of skills in problem solving, it is estimated that only 30 % of adults have the skills to enable them "to evaluate problems and find solutions" (Frey et al., 2016; OECD, 2013). Skills to enable problem solving in technology rich environments are at a large deficit (2016b; OECD, 2015a).

As Information Technology (IT) takes over routine tasks, "soft skills" such as communication and creative thinking will become more important as they are difficult to digitize (OECD, 2017; Puncreobutr, 2016).

The increasing technological orientation of tasks gives rise to the requirement of digital skills for virtually every job. This is cause for concern as currently 45 % of European citizens have insufficient digital skills (Richer, 2017).

To ensure success in an emerging workplace, learners need to initiate change, adapt quickly, become excellent problem solvers, and work in global teams. Therefore, skills such as entrepreneurial thinking, problem solving, digital skills, and communication are key. Currently, the discipline-oriented approach in academia places emphasis on teaching specific content and a prescribed curriculum rather than these skills (Costley & Dikerdem, 2011).

A flexible approach to learning is required, not only in terms of time, place, and learning style but also flexibility in content which is relevant to the student's professional needs. The next section will explore pedagogical theories, which can facilitate the development of skills for an emerging workplace.

## Workbased Learning: Developing Emerging Skills

In the future, boundaries between formal and informal education will become ill-defined. Learning will take place in various locations, and contexts outside formal educational institutes. Traditionally the workplace is seen as an informal learning environment, but policy has driven the need to formalize workplace learning through accreditation (European Commission, 2010). This has been reinforced by research that highlights the challenges associated with the unstructured nature of informal learning (Eraut, 2004).

However, the increasing need for individuals to maintain employability while learning sees the workplace as gaining credibility as a vital learning environment (Fouad & Bynner, 2008; Savickas & Porfeli, 2012). Through the application of learning, the workplace facilitates skills development (OECD, 2016a). In addition, EU policy on workplace learning highlights the role of the workplace as a learning environment that empowers people by "acquiring skills that are not only occupational" (European Commission, 2010).

In support of this, many advocates of work-based learning have argued that pedagogies should focus on teaching learners the process by which to construct knowledge in the workplace, rather than discipline specific knowledge. This approach requires the individuals learning situation to dictate the curriculum (Costley & Dikerdem, 2011; Kettle and HEA, 2013).

Pedagogies used in formal education can be restrictive by prescribing content and learning approaches that are not always relevant to the individuals learning needs. In contrast, informal learning is configurable to the learner. Billett (2002), proposed workplace pedagogies should provide opportunities, guidance and consider individual engagement. Fuller and Unwin (2002) did an extensive study into existing workplace pedagogies and identified five theoretical strands these are (a) Transmissional theories which are concerned with formal teaching of skills; (b) Informal and incidental learning which consists of unintended learning (c) Social and collective learning which addresses the work conducted by Lave, 1991 on communities of practice. (d) Competence-based theories in which skills developed align to particular job roles, these are developed in a formal manner using vocational education. (e) Those based on activity theory, which emphasizes the role of social and formal activities on learning. It can also comprise of work done by Argyris and Schön (1996), Garvin, 1993, and Senge (1990), on organizational learning and learning organizations.

Theories in category (a) to (d) focus exclusively on formal, informal, or social learning. Those based on activity theory recognize the importance of social and collective learning and sees informal or formal methods of tools that can be used to learn. However, the theories based on activity theory do not address the complex chaotic nature of work and the constant changing environment. They see reflection as a tool to learn and not an integral part of allowing learners to apply what they have learned to new contexts in addressing change.

Heutagogy is an emerging form of pedagogy based on complexity theory, which realizes that education is preparing learners for a constantly changing work environment. To allow them to succeed and progress, it is important that they can transfer what they have learned to different contexts (Hase & Kenyon, 2007). Current formal pedagogical approaches, such as the competency based and transitional models, limits this as it requires tutors to project the skills they think learners will need in the future and teaches these skills in a particular context. When the learner is faced with unfamiliar situations, they find it difficult to transfer what they have learned.

Heutagogy is based on the principle of self-determined learning, where the learner decides what is to be learned. It is a living curriculum, where the workplace is the subject of what you learn (Hase & Kenyon, 2007). It also focuses on collaboration and highlights the importance of double-loop learning which integrates theories associated with social and collective learning. Table 31.1 illustrates the characteristics of heutagogy.

As a result, heutagogy develops a student's capability to reapply knowledge to a wide variety of contexts, it does this by focusing on the process of learning and reflection (through double-loop learning). The learning content is driven by a change or predicted change in their environment.

The concept of a flexible, individualized curriculum, which does not prescribe a list of learning outcomes and how they can be assessed can be difficult to translate into an academic program (Hase, 2009).

However, the theory of heutagogy is very applicable to the development of skills in an emerging workplace, given the increasing multifaceted nature of organizations (Hase, 2009). Furthermore, its collaborative nature encourages the

**Table 31.1** Characteristics of heutagogy (Blaschke, 2012; Hase & Kenyon, 2007)

| Characteristic | Explanation |
|---|---|
| **Learning is initiated based on a need** | The learner identifies a need to learn something based on a change or predicted change in their environment |
| **Double-loop learning** | What the individual learns impacts on their underlying assumptions and beliefs |
| **Flexible curriculum** | The curriculum is a "living curriculum" and changes based on the learners needs which evolve over time |
| **Learner centered** | Focus on self-determined learning |
| **Non-linear** | Learning is iterative and non-sequential involving periods of reflection and adapting |
| **Emphasis on learning process rather than content** | The learner is aware of how they learn and if it is successful or not and how to acquire new knowledge and skills |
| **Collaborative** | Learners work together to solve a problem and learn |
| **Focus on developing learner capability** | Giving learners the confidence to apply their learning to unfamiliar situations |

development of communication skills, while its orientation toward a change in the learner environment fosters a flexible employee with skills in problem solving and creative thinking.

As heutagogy is an emerging concept it has not been widely applied. There have been some studies of its application in practice. Hase, Tay, and Goh (2006) identified how action research can facilitate the development of heutagogical characteristics in learners by studying their progression to self-directed learners while engaging action research projects. They found, over a period of time, students transitioned from dependent to self-determined learners. In addition, distance and e-learning approaches have been argued as favorable environments to employ a heutagogical framework (Hase, 2009). Abraham and Komattil (2017), highlighted the potential ability of PBL to develop autonomous and capable learners, two key characteristics of heutagogy. However, to date this has not been explored. The next section will examine how heutagogical principles align to the characteristics of problem-based learning and work-based learning and argue the suitability of PBL as a method for delivering a heutagogical curriculum in the workplace.

## Heutagogy in Practice: Problem-Based Learning in an Emerging Workplace

Problem-Based Learning (PBL) is a constructivist approach to learning that has been widely used and advocated in higher education. It is a method of inquiry-based learning and focuses on experiential learning advocated by Dewey (1938). Experiential learning is widely used in work environments (Armstrong, 1990).

PBL is a learner centered, collaborative approach to learning in which a teacher facilitates the activity by guiding the learner in a process of inquiry. Thus, the teacher plays the role of a mentor. It is known to positively affect learning outcomes and develop the skills that are critical in today's workplace, namely problem solving, logical thinking, creative thinking and communication (Şendağ & Ferhan Odabaşı, 2009).

The characteristics of PBL significantly overlap with those of work-based learning and heutagogy. See Table 31.2 for a comparison between PBL, work-based learning and heutagogy.

However, PBL can be challenging for some learners. The absence of prescribed learning material can cause anxiety and difficulties in the initial stages of the process (Fiddler & Knoll, 1995). In addition, PBL might be difficult for learners who cannot grasp the concept of meta-cognition and reflection. Scaffolding is key in assisting students to overcome this issue (Hmelo-Silver, 2004). These issues may also relate to heutagogy, particularly due to the characteristics of flexible learning and reflection. This is an area, which needs to be explored further.

To ensure PBL is based on the employees learning needs, it is important that it is delivered in the workplace and in a manner that allows the employee to immediately apply what they are learning to their environment. With the help of modern technologies, the delivery of PBL in the workplace, or workplace PBL (w-PBL)

**Table 31.2** Comparison between PBL, WBL and heutagogy (Foster, 1996; Hung, Harpole Bailey, & Jonassen, 2003; McKee & Burton, 2005; Wood, 2003)

| Characteristic | PBL | WBL | Heutagogy |
|---|---|---|---|
| Problem solving | Problem-based—concerned with solving a problem | Problem-based—concerned with work-based problems | Reflection on problem solving process |
| Teamwork | It is collaborative.<br>It is conducted in small groups | Collaborative—involves several people working in a team | Emphasis on learners working with others |
| Self-directedness | Self-directed, the learner is responsible for their own learning and reflecting on the adequacy of what they have learned<br>Learner-centered- the learner takes the lead role and the tutor acts as a mentor | Requires the learner to be self-motivated and responsible<br>Employee is responsible for their own learning | Emphasis on self-determined learning |
| Outcome | Concerned with achieving pre-specified learning outcomes<br>There is no one solution or right and wrong answer. | Performance-related—requires learners to satisfy organizational objectives<br>Innovative—requires the learner to look for new ways of working | Emphasis on the learning process rather than the outcome |

can be supported by providing additional learning materials and collaborative space to solve problems. Hung, Jonassen, and Liu (2008) categorized two uses of technology to deliver PBL. One is the combination of PBL with distance or online learning; the second is the use of multimedia for communication and the transfer of information in PBL, such as text, sound, and video.

Online PBL can offer a space for collaborative work and to exchange materials. There have been several reported advantages associated with delivering PBL online such as:

Increased flexibility
Learning of skills in cross cultural and virtual communication
If managed correctly, increased communication

(Brodie, 2009; De Jong, Könings, & Czabanowska, 2014; Ng, Bridges, Law, & Whitehill, 2014; Said & Syarif, 2016).

However, many are skeptical about the delivery of problem-based learning through technology. They feel that technology will affect the PBL ethos of working in teams and communication and may result in PBL becoming more teacher-focused (Cheaney & Ingebritsen, 2006; de Jong et al., 2014; Savin-Baden & Wilkie, 2006). However, in an emerging workplace working in virtual teams to solve problems is a key skill. Furthermore, PBL requires a transitioning period and many are concerned that technology-orientated PBL may isolate learners (McLinden, McCall, Hinton, & Weston, 2006). These issues must be considered when developing a workplace problem-based learning environment.

However, the real challenge lies in delivering a flexible curriculum based around the workplace needs of the learner and allowing them to develop skills that can be reapplied. This could be addressed by guiding the learner to choose a problem for PBL.

To meet the needs of workplace learners and address the challenges associated with technology oriented PBL, the traditional PBL model needs to be adapted. As a result, the next section will explore the design and implementation of a w-PBL program. To assist the development of skills for the future workplace, there is a need for a w-PBL model to place emphasis on many of the traits of heutagogy, particularly, encouraging collaborative learning, identifying and framing a workplace problem (traditionally this is done by a tutor), aiding double-loop learning and helping them to reflect on how they can reapply what they have learned to different contexts. The proceeding case study will outline a w-PBL methodology and the empirical research undertaken to determine how it can develop the heutagogical characteristics in workplace learners.

## Case Study: Technology-Oriented Problem-Based Learning in The Global Workplace

### Background

Archimedes is a European project that explored the application of Problem-Based Learning within the workplace. The project developed an ICT platform and PBL program to support and accredit the deployment of PBL in a workplace environment (w-PBL). The project also examined the ability of the w-PBL program to address the learning needs of adults in Small to Medium Enterprises (SMEs).

To date, there is no dedicated IT platform to support PBL, although the use of various technologies has been explored (Hung et al., 2008). Therefore, Archimedes developed an IT platform to support the delivery of problem-based learning in the workplace. The platform provided:

Video and digital text-based learning material, on how to complete each stage of the PBL process.

A collaborative space, to allow the problem-based learning group to work on the problem in a structured manner. This was necessary as group members were dispersed across several EU countries.

Communication functionality, synchronous meeting software was used by each PBL group to meet weekly (synchronously). Between meetings they used discussion forums.

To enable the program to be delivered in SMEs, a 13-step workplace w-PBL process was designed to align with the heutagogical principles. This allowed learners to develop the relevant skills for an emerging workplace. Note that steps 1 to 3 were designed to alleviate any learner issues outlined in the literature review and enable them to choose a problem relevant to their individual needs. Steps 4 to 12 were part of the traditional PBL methodology as identified by Wood, 2003; Helelä & Fagerholm, 2008. Step 13 was focused on the reapplication of learning to different contexts. For each step, the learner was provided with digital learning material guiding them how to complete each step:

1) **Step 1: Preparation**—This step aided the transition from a dependent to independent learner, enhancing learner capability. To do this, learners were informed of the PBL process and what was expected of them. They were also asked to review solved PBL problems on the IT platform and reflect on how successfully they were solved and why.
2) **Step 2: Problem identification**—To make the curriculum flexible and adaptable to their needs, the work-based learners reflected on their current work environment. They were guided to identify a problem that they would like to address through PBL. This allowed the learner to ensure the learning is based on their individual needs. The learner posted the problem on the IT platform and other learners could choose to collaborate. The collaboration formed a PBL group which met weekly using the IT platform.
3) **Step 3: Team formulation**—This step was used to prepare learners how to collaborate in a virtual team. Learners were encouraged to reflect on instances where they had previously worked in a team and what they learned from those experiences, they posted these experiences to a discussion forum on the IT platform.
4) **Step 4: Clarify terms**—On the platform learners were asked to list any of the terms in the problem that were ambiguous. Other learners clarified the meaning of terms. Following this step, the first online PBL group meeting was held using the synchronous meeting tool.

5) **Step 5: Define problem**—The learners reflected on the problem in a group. This was done through structured questioning to allow them to fully understand the problem. A guide on appropriate questioning strategies was provided in the learning material. Following the meeting, the agreed problem definition was posted on the IT platform.
6) **Step 6: Brainstorm solutions**—Prior to the second PBL meeting, students studied learning material on best practice approaches to brainstorming. On the IT platform, they each uploaded their proposed solutions to the problem. At the second PBL meeting, these solutions were discussed, classified and learning objectives are agreed upon.
7) **Step 7: Classify**—The PBL group classified the solutions and agreed on a solution to investigate further.
8) **Step 8: Develop learning objectives**—The group agreed upon learning objectives to allow them to investigate the proposed solution(s) fully and allocated these to individual learners for self-study.
9) **Step 9: Reflection**—Learners reflected on the initial stages of PBL, if they were completed successfully and if they had enough information to progress to the latter stages. If not, they are asked to host another PBL meeting to allow them to obtain enough information to allow them to progress to Step 10.
10) **Step 10: Self-study**—This step focused on the principles of work-based information literacy. It taught learners how to search for and gather quality information associated with their learning objectives.
11) **Step 11: Synthesis**—The PBL group met for a third time. Each learner presented their findings and the group synthesized this into an implementable solution.
12) **Step 12: Reflection**—The learner reflected on the PBL process, its effectiveness, and how they would have improved the process.
13) **Step 13: Reapplication**—Learners were asked to develop an action plan of how they would apply what they have learned to other areas of the business. This was introduced to encourage the learners to reuse their skills and continue work-based learning, integrating it fully into the organization. It facilitates the transfer of learner to other contexts.

Below is a summary of how the 13-step w-PBL methodology addresses some of the key characteristics of heutagogy (see Table 31.3).

## Methodology

Between April 25 and July 31, 2016, a module entitled problem-based learning for business professionals was delivered to 42 learners in Europe.

A random sample of 250 learners in SMEs in Ireland, Romania, Lithuania, Germany, and Portugal was targeted. Of those targeted, 180 expressed interest in taking the program. Of those individuals, 161 registered on the online PBL platform developed as part of the project. Of the 161 students, 59 did not log into the IT platform to participate in the program. Of the remaining 102 students, exactly half withdrew from the program within the first three weeks, without notifying the tutor. Initially, the program was scheduled to take 10 weeks;

Table 31.3 Alignment of the Archimedes 13-step w-PBL to heutagogical principles

| Heutagogical principle | How it is incorporated into PBL | PBL stage |
|---|---|---|
| **Learning is initiated based on a need** | Learner identifies the problem they wish to work on. The program is driven by a learner need | Step 2: Problem Identification |
| **Double-loop learning** | Guided reflection | Steps 9 and 12: Reflection |
| **Flexible curriculum** | Learning material depends on the problem to be solved the learner is taught how to gather this material | Step 2: Problem identification<br>Step 8: Individual learning objectives |
| **Learner centered-self-directed/self-determined** | Tutor is a guide and the learner is responsible for driving their own learning | Problem-based learning meetings are run by the learners; tutorials are used to answer any learner questions |
| **Non-linear** | Learner is required to iteratively reflect on the work completed and if it was successful and if not are asked to revisit | Learner reflects on<br>1) The initial PBL stages and their effectiveness in step 9.<br>2) The overall PBL process in Step 12. |
| **Emphasis on learning process rather than content** | Learning content teaches the learner how to reflect and acquire new knowledge | Learning content non-discipline specific. Focuses on the process of doing PBL and reflecting on its effectiveness |
| **Collaborative** | Formation of PBL groups | Step 3: Learner is asked to reflect on previous team work and its effectiveness<br>Learners work virtually in groups to solve problems |
| **Focus on developing learner capability** | Reapplication stage | Step 13 |

however, collaboration in the first weeks of the program proved difficult to foster, and an additional 2 weeks were added to the schedule to allow time for the students to familiarize with each other, this had a significant impact on the dropout rate.

In the remaining weeks nine students left the program, these students contacted the tutor and cited time management and personal issues. It should be noted that online programs are notorious for their low student retention rate with completion rates being approximately 10–20 % lower than face-to-face courses (Frydenberg, 2007).

Students attended a weekly tutor-led online question and answer session, and formed pan-European PBL groups to solve problems using the w-PBL approach. This PBL group was learner-led and met weekly.

The following data were gathered to evaluate the ability of the program to address the needs of workplace learners.

- Pre-questionnaires were completed by students prior to starting the PBL program. In total, 104 of the 161 students that registered completed the questionnaire. The questionnaire asked students using a five-point Likert scale to rate their confidence level at particular tasks, such as learning, gathering information, and solving problems.
- A post-questionnaire was disseminated to students following completion of the 12-week program. In total 52 students who started the program completed the questionnaire. The survey asked students to rate their confidence level at the same tasks in the pre-program questionnaires. It evaluated their confidence as a learner, in gathering information and solving problems. The questionnaire also gathered information on the learner's experience, benefits of the program, challenges learners experienced, skills acquired, and reuse of learning material.
- Interviews were conducted with 19 learners. These interviews were conducted face-to-face or over the phone and students were asked questions regarding their learning experience, satisfaction with the program and challenges.
- A content analysis was conducted on the reflective learning entries of 19 students. Thematic coding was used for the analysis, the main themes were learner experience, skills acquired, challenges, and benefits of the program.

## Analysis

The pre-program questionnaire and post-program questionnaire data were analyzed using a comparison of the pre- and post- mean confidence level of the individual in learning, gathering information to solve problems, and solving problems. A two-sample t-test assuming unequal variances was also conducted to determine the reliability of the results. The alpha value of the test was 0.05.

The post survey questionnaire was analyzed using a percentage response rate to questions regarding learner satisfaction, challenges, skills developed, and benefits of the program.

Interviews were transcribed, and the transcription was analyzed using the same thematic codes as the reflective learning diaries; learner experience, skills acquired, challenges and benefits of the program.

## Results

### Learning experience

The post-course questionnaire illustrated that there was a 100 % satisfaction rate with the program, with all remaining students stating that they enjoyed the program.

This was reinforced from interviews and learning diaries, with all learners who completing the program stating they found it interesting. One respondent stated that they were "*Yes, very satisfied. Expectations at the beginning were poorly defined but, after to overcome the initial constraints (organizational and personal issues) I can say that was very positive.*"

In the post course survey, 92 % of students found the program of value to them, noting the collaboration and PBL process elements as most beneficial. *"Yes.You learn a lot by how others approach an issue. Using the steps to work through the process was beneficial"*

> *"The PBL process is useful, we already use this in everyday work, but not so methodologically. Now we have new skills and will be able operate in another level"*

Despite the satisfaction with the cohort who complete the program there were several challenges faced by participants.

**Challenges faced with PBL methodology**

Participants experienced several challenges, particularly in the initial stages of the program. This can be illustrated by a 50 % retention rate in the first three weeks. As PBL is largely self-directed, this and lack of structure were things that the learners found difficult. These emerged as themes in the learning diaries. It was obvious that for most groups there was a clear contrast between the initial and final steps. As the learner progressed through the process their confidence increased due to familiarity with the process, problem, and group. These findings coincide with those experienced by Hase (2009) regarding the progression from pedagogy to heutagogy in action research. This was particularly evident in the interviews and learning diaries which can be illustrated from the below extracts. These illustrated that the learners had difficulty grasping the PBL concept.

> *"Steps 1 to 5 were a challenge ... Reversing the way, we would normally solve problems was quite challenging at first..."*
>
> *"During the later stage of the process when group members had a clear learning objective the group performed much better than the early stages. The first 2 weeks were uncertain times..."*
>
> *"The main challenges faced during the PBL process were firstly understanding the PBL process and adapting this as a method of problem solving...The second challenge was finding the time to learn the process, collaborate and communicate. This would be less of a factor the next time PBL is used..."*

These challenges were also combined with professional and personal issues. In the post-course survey when asked what issues they faced the main concerns identified were.

- Time (25 %)—This was reinforced by extracts from the interviews and learning diaries *"My biggest issue was the current workload in my job and it severely impacted my ability to dedicate enough time to successfully finish the program to a high standard"*
- Team work (25 %)—Supported by extracts from the interviews and learning diaries *"Trying to get the team together to meet to work on the project"* and *"hard to conciliate with some professional or delicate moments"*
- Assignments (14 %)—*"carrying out assignments"* and *"uploading the assignments"*

To overcome such issues, efforts should be made to foster collaboration in the early stages of the program and further integrate the course into the workplace environment of the learners to reduce time constraints.

**Relevance of the PBL methodology to the workplace and heutagogy**

The program provided learners with several professional and personal benefits in terms of skills acquisition and new methods of conducting activities

From the post program survey, 43 % of participants found an immediate benefit such as "solved long standing company problem (38 %)," "improved the productivity of a process" (28 %), "increased the number of customers" (16 %)

Those that did not note an immediate benefit to their workplace, predicted benefits such as cost savings, productivity and customer satisfaction.

Only 8 % did not realize any benefit from the program at the time of completing the survey. In the post-course survey, those that found the program beneficial identified the greatest benefits in

- Collaborating with others (24 %) *"I liked the working together with my colleagues and finding proper solution"* and *"interacting with people from a different culture"*
- PBL process (36 %) *"The core content that breaks down a problem and identifies the steps in researching solutions"* and *"To be able to approach work issues differently, more constructively with an open mind"*
- Problem solving (16 %) *"The different way of looking at a problem"* and *"The assignments that put me face to face with concrete problems"*

Several, different heutagogical learner traits were developed throughout the program. At the center of heutagogy is the concept of the self-determined learner. During the 12-week program learner capability at solving problems increased significantly. Earlier, in Table 31.1 the main characteristics of heutagogy were outlined. From the pre- and post-program questionnaires, reflective learning diaries and interviews there was evidence that of four of these heutagogical characteristics were developed in learners during the program. These are double-loop learning, emphasis on the learning process, focus on learner capability and self-determined learners and collaboration (including cross-cultural).

***Double-loop learning***

It was evident from interviewing learners and their reflective learning diaries that the w-PBL program impacted their beliefs about themselves and others:

> *"... by simply challenging your mind to do things in another way, the results are much better"*
>
> *"I learned ... mainly about other people's "way" of learning. By understanding that an, it gives one a greater insight into how a team can work together to solve a problem"*

**Emphasis on learning process rather than content**

Learners expressed the fact that the w-PBL program gave them an insight into how people learn and apply their learning in a more methodological way. This was highlighted in 12 of the learning diaries and interviews, some extracts of which are below

> *"To learn more methodically, to organize problem solving in more structured way"*
>
> *"... gave me an insight into PBL and a new way of looking at how I can learn"*
>
> *"The most valuable piece was around understanding HOW people learn. This makes it easier for me to understand others and how to best resolve problems"*

**Focus on developing learner capability and self-directedness/self-determined learning**

Questionnaires were distributed to learners to measure their learner confidence before and after undertaking the w-PBL program. The null hypothesis indicated that there was no change in learner confidence levels. On analysis of the results learner confidence increased from 3.9 to 4.0, _however the t-value of 0.6 does not make this statistically significant and the null hypothesis cannot be rejected.

Learner confidence in the capability to acquire the relevant knowledge themselves increased from 3.8 to 4.0. Again, the t-value of 0.1 does not indicate any significant findings. However, an increase in learner confidence to solve problems increased from 3.6 to 4. The t-result of 0.004 indicates a significant outcome and allows us to reject the null hypothesis. Illustrating that the w-PBL program resulted in an increase in learner confidence at solving problems.

In addition, the post-course satisfaction survey illustrated that an overwhelming 97% would use PBL in their organization again, and in interviews respondents gave several examples to illustrate how they would do so. An example of one of these extracts is below:

> *"I would like to analyze the ways to increase employee's productivity; motivation...within different organizations and plant sites for common issues e.g. energy reduction"*

**Collaboration (including cross-cultural)**

From the post course survey 33% of learners identified one of the main benefits of the program was collaboration, this was reinforced by several interviews and learning diary extracts, some of which are illustrated below

> *"How to collaborate or work as part of a team"*
>
> *"....to communicate with colleagues and approach problems with openness and ingenuity"*
>
> *"I liked the working together with my colleagues and finding proper solutions ... interacting with people from a different culture"*

## Deploying PBL in the Workplace (W-PBL)

It is evident that heutagogy provides a pedagogical framework to facilitate skills development in an emerging workplace. The application of a technology oriented w-PBL methodology illustrates how heutagogy can be applied in practice. The workplace problem-based learning program developed learners, which were reflective, and aware of their learning processes, collaborative and self-directed. They also transitioned into more confident learners and were capable of reapplying their learning. Furthermore, learners acquired skills in communication and problem-solving. Learners did not report that they acquired digital skills; however, communication, problem-solving, and acquisition of learning material were conducted using technology. Therefore, it is expected that some level of digital skills would have been developed.

Despite the high dropout rate, those that remained in the PBL program found the overall experience very beneficial. The most enjoyed aspects of the program were collaboration, a new way of learning and new ways of problem solving. Several learners reported an immediate benefit to their company.

However, there were several different obstacles. Time was a major issue faced by many learners and is cited by work-based learners as an ongoing barrier to participation in learning. The unstructured, chaotic and uncertain nature of the PBL process was also a difficulty for many learners, in the initial stages and could be one of the reasons attributed to the high dropout rate. It is projected that these challenges could be an issue when workers are transitioning in the emerging workplace due to its increasing complex nature.

As a result, further research needs to be conducted into how to support learners to become capable and self-directed. The familiarity and dependence of learners on didactic approaches to learning make it more difficult to transition students to an unstructured chaotic learning process. Learners are accustomed from a young age to become dependent on educators to teach and guide learners to apply content, a less structured approach to teaching needs to be gradually introduced from a young age to minimize the impact of this transition. Problem-based learning could provide a safe environment that allow employees to prepare for these complex changes. Such an approach can facilitate the transition from competence based to capable learners empowering people to keep pace with accelerating change. However, additional studies need to be completed to determine how to address the challenges faced by learners and scaffold them in the transition to self-determined learning.

## Acknowledgments

This research is part of a project called Archimedes, which has been funded by the Erasmus plus program of the European Union grant agreement number 2014-1-IE01-KA200-000342_E.

## References


Abraham, R., & Komattil, R. (2017). Heutagogic approach to developing capable\ learners. *Medical Teacher, 39*(3), 295–299. https://doi.org/10.1080/0142159X.2017.1270433

Argyris, C., & Schön, D. A. (1996). *Organizational learning II: Theory. Method, and practice, reading*. Reading, MA: Addison Wesley.

Armstrong, R. K. (1990). How do managers learn? unpublished research paper, Lancaster University CSML.

Barnes, S.-A., & Brown, A. (2016). Stories of learning and their significance to future pathways and aspirations. *British Journal of Guidance and Counselling, 44*(2), 233–242. https://doi.org/10.1080/03069885.2016.1145194

Bessen, J. (2015). *Learning by doing: The real connection between innovation, wages, and wealth*. New Haven, CT: Yale University Press.

Billett, S. (2002). Toward a workplace pedagogy: Guidance, participation, and engagement. *Adult Education Quarterly, 53*(1), 27–43. https://doi.org/10.1177/074171302237202

Blaschke, L. (2012). Heutagogy and lifelong learning: A review of heutagogical practice and self-determined learning. *International Review of Research in Open and Distance Learning, 13*(1), 56–71. https://doi.org/10.19173/irrodl.v13i1.1076

Brancher, C. (2016). Additive and the ideal of "batch of one" manufacture. *Metal Powder Report, 71*(5), 339–343.

Brodie, L. M. (2009). eProblem-based learning: Problem-based learning using virtual teams. *European Journal of Engineering Education, 34*(6), 497––509. https://doi.org/10.1080/03043790902943868

Cheaney, J. D., & Ingebritsen, T. (2006). Problem-based learning in an online course: A case study. *The International Review of Research in Open and Distributed Learning,* 6(3), Retrieved December 22, 2018 from doi: https://doi.org/10.19173/irrodl.v6i3.267

Costley, C., and Dikerdem, M. A. (2011). Work based learning pedagogies and academic development. Retrieved December 22, 2018 from~; http://eprints.mdx.ac.uk/8819/

De Jong, N., Könings, K. D., & Czabanowska, K. (2014). The development of innovative online problem-based learning: A leadership course for leaders in European public health. *Journal of University Teaching and Learning Practice, 11*(3), Retrieved March 7, 2018 from https://www.learntechlib.org/p/159453

Dewey, J. (1938). *Experience and education (the kappa delta pi lecture series)*. New York, NY: Touchstone.

Ecorys UK: Digital skills for the UK economy. (2016). Retrieved March 07, 2018, from https://www.gov.uk/government/publications/digital-skills-for-the-uk-economy

Eraut, M. (2004). Informal learning in the workplace. *Studies in Continuing Education, 26*(2), 247–273.

Eurofound. (2016). New forms of employment. Retrieved December 22, 2018, from the European Foundation for the Improvement of Living and Working Conditions: https://www.eurofound.europa.eu/new-forms-of-employment

European Commission. (2010). The Bruges Communiqué on enhanced European Cooperation in Vocational Education and Training for the period 2011–2020, Bruges, Belgium (2010), European commission. Retrieved March 7, 2018 from https://ec.europa.eu/education

European Commission. (2016). A New Skills Agenda for Europe, Brussels, Belgium, European Commission. Retreived March 7, 2018 from http://ec.europa.eu/social/main.jsp?catId=1223&langId=en

EUROSTAT. (2015). People in the EU -Statistics on demographic changes Retrieved December 4, 2017 from http://ec.europa.eu/eurostat/statistics-explained/index.php/People_in_the_EU_%E2%80%93_statistics_on_demographic_changes

Fiddler, M. B., & Knoll, J. W. (1995). Problem-based learning in an adult Liberal learning context: Learner adaptations and feedback. *Continuing Higher Education Review, 59*, 13–24.

Foster, E. (1996). Work-based Learning Project: final report 1994–1996. University of Leeds. Retrieved from https://doi.org/10.1080/01421590601046088

Fouad, N. A., & Bynner, J. (2008). Work transitions. *American Psychologist, 63*(4), 241–251. https://doi.org/10.1037/0003-066X.63.4.241

Frey, C. B., Osborne, M. A., Holmes, C., Rahbari, E., Garlick, R., Friedlander, G. and Wilkie, M. (2016). Technology at Work v2. 0: The future is not what it used to be. Citi GPS: Global Perspectives and Solutions. University of Oxford. Retrieved March 7, 2018 from https://www.oxfordmartin.ox.ac.uk/downloads/reports/Citi_GPS_Technology_Work.pdf

Frydenberg, J. (2007). Persistence in university continuing education online classes. *The international review of research in open and distributed Learning, 8*(3). https://doi.org/10.19173/irrodl.v8i3.375

Fuller, A., and Unwin, L. (2002). Developing pedagogies for the contemporary workplace. Working to learn: transforming learning in the workplace, 95–111.

Garvin, D. A. (1993). Building a learning organization (Vol. *71*, No. 4, pp. 78–91). *Harvard Business Review*. Retrieved March 7, 2018, from https://hbr.org/1993/07/building-a-learning-organization

Hase, S., & Kenyon, C. (2007). Heutagogy: A child of complexity theory. *Complicity: An International Journal of Complexity and Education, 4*(1), Retrieved March 7, 2018, from https://journals.library.ualberta.ca/complicity/index.php/complicity/issue/view/562

Hase, S., Tay, B. H., and Goh, E. (2006). Developing learner capability through action research: from pedagogy to heutagogy in the workplace. Graduate College of Management Papers, 154. Retrieved from https://www.researchgate.net/publication/37357852_Developing_learner_capability_through_action_research_from_pedagogy_to_heutagogy_in_the_workplace

Hase, Stewart. (2009). Heutagogy and e-learning in the workplace: Some challenges and opportunities. *Impact: Journal of Applied Research in Workplace E-Learning* Retrieved December 22 from doi:https://doi.org/10.5043/impact.13.

Helelä, M., and Fagerholm, H. (2008). *Tracing the roles of the PBL tutor: A journey of learning*. Helsinki. Finland: HAAGA-HELIA University of Applied Sciences. Retrieved March 7, 2017 from http://myy.haaga-helia.fi/~liibba/PBLguide.pdf

Hmelo-Silver, C. E. (2004). Problem-based learning: What and how do students learn? *Educational Psychology Review, 16*(3), 235–266. https://doi.org/10.1023/B:EDPR.0000034022.16470.f3

Hung, W., Harpole Bailey, J., & Jonassen, D. H. (2003). Exploring the tensions of problem based learning: Insights from research. *New Directions for Teaching and Learning, 2003*(95), 13–23.

Hung, W., Jonassen, D. H., & Liu, R. (2008). Problem-based learning. In J. M. Spector, J. G. van Merrienboer, M. D. Merrill, & M. Driscoll (Eds.), *Handbook of research on educational communications and technology* (3rd ed.) (pp. 485–506). New York, NY: Lawrence Erlbaum Associates.

Kettle, J., and HEA (Higher Education Academy (United Kingdom)). (2013). *Flexible pedagogies: Employer engagement and work-based learning.* Flexible pedagogies: Preparing for the future series. York, UK: Higher Education Academy.

Lave, J. (1991). Situating learning in communities of practice. In L. Resnick, J. Levine, & S. Teasley (Eds.), *Perspectives on socially shared cognition* (pp. 63–82). Washington, DC: APA.

Liddle, R., and Lerais, F. (2007). A consultation paper from the bureau of European policy advisers, Europe's social reality. Luxembourg: European Commission. Retrieved from http://europa.eu/rapid/press-release_MEMO-07-83_en.htm

McKee, A., and Burton, J. (2005). Recognizing and valuing work based learning in primary care. Work-Based Learning in Health Care: Applications and Innovations. Retrieved from https://doi.org/10.5367/000000007782311821

McLinden, M., McCall, S., Hinton, D., & Weston, A. (2006). Participation in online problem-based learning: Insights from postgraduate teachers studying through open and distance education. *Distance Education, 27*(3), 331–353. https://doi.org/10.1080/01587910600940422

Ng, M. L., Bridges, S., Law, S. P., & Whitehill, T. (2014). Designing, implementing and evaluating an online problem-based learning (PBL) environment–a pilot study. *Clinical Linguistics & Phonetics, 28*(1–2), 117–130.

OECD (Organization for Economic Cooperation and Development) (2015a). *Adults, computers and problem solving: "what's the problem?".* OECD skills studies. OECD Publishing.

OECD (Organization for Economic Cooperation and Development.). (2016a). *Trends shaping education 2016.* FR: Centre For Educational Research and Innovation.10.1787/trends_edu-2016-en

OECD (Organization for Economic Cooperation and Development). (2016b). Skills for a digital world: 2016 ministerial meeting on the digital economy. background report. Paris: OECD Publishing.10.1787/5jlwz83z3wnw-en

OECD (Organization for Economic Cooperation and Development). (2017). Future of work and skills: Paper presented at the 2nd Meeting of the G20 Employment Working Group 15–17 February 2017 Hamburg, Germany. OECD Publishing, Paris.

OECD (Organization for Economic Co-Operation, and Development). (2015b). *OECD science, technology and industry scoreboard 2015 [ePub] - innovation for growth and society.* FR: OECD Publishing.

OECD (Organization for Economic Cooperation and Development (France)). (2013). *OECD skills outlook 2013: First results from the survey of adult skills.* Paris: OECD Publ.10.1787/9789264204256-en

Paccagnella, M., and OECD (Organization for Economic Cooperation and Development, France). (2016). *Age, ageing and skills: Results from the survey of adult skills.* OECD education working papers, no. 132. OECD Publishing

Puncreobutr, V. (2016). Education 4.0: New challenge of learning. *St. Theresa Journal of Humanities and Social Sciences, 2*(2), 94–95 Retrieved from www.stic.ac.th/ojs/index.php/sjhs/article/view/Position%20Paper3

Richer, A (2017). Industry 4.0 and Higher Education, EURASHE Conference 2017, La Havre, France, 30-31 March

Said, A., & Syarif, E. (2016). The development of online tutorial program design using problem-based learning in open distance learning system. *Journal of Education and Practice, 7*(18), 222–229.

Savickas, M., & Porfeli, E. (2012). Career adapt-abilities scale: Construction, reliability, and measurement equivalence across 13 countries. *Journal of Vocational Behavior, 80*(3), 661–673. https://doi.org/10.1016/j.jvb.2012.01.011

Savin-Baden, M., and Wilkie, K. (2006). *Problem-based learning online*. McGraw-Hill Education (UK).

Şendağ, S., & Ferhan Odabaşı, H. (2009). Effects of an online problem based learning course on content knowledge acquisition and critical thinking skills. *Computers & Education, 53*(1), 132–141. https://doi.org/10.1016/j.compedu.2009.01.008

Senge, P. M. (1990). *The fifth discipline: The art and practice of the learning organization* (1st ed.). New York, NY: Doubleday/Currency.

Walker, S. J. (2015). Big data: A revolution that will transform how we live, work, and think. *International Journal of Advertising, 33*(1), 181–183. https://doi.org/10.2501/IJA-33-1-181–183

Wilson, R. (2013). Skills anticipation-the future of work and education. *International Journal of Educational Research, 61*, 101–110. https://doi.org/10.1016/j.ijer.2013.03.013

Wilson, R., Sofroniou, N., Beaven, R., May-Gillings, M., Perkins, S., Lee, M., Glover, O., Limmer, H. and Leach, A. (2016). Working Futures 2014–2024. Commission for Employment and Skill (2017). Wath upon Dearne: UK Retreived March 7, 2018 from https://www.gov.uk/government/organizations/uk-commission-for-employment-and-skills

Wood, D. F. (2003). ABC of learning and teaching in medicine: Problem-based learning. *BMJ: British Medical Journal, 326*(7384), 328.

# Index

10–10–10 Breathing exercise 424–425

*a*

academic rationale, education internationalization 335–337
accreditation
  gamification 546, 551–552
  internationalization 337
  value of 78
accuracy, in gamification 544
ACE *see* American Council on Education
acknowledgement, of need to develop 41–42
action research 264–268
activity systems 509–512
adaptation, intercultural competence 296
advantages of gamification 562–563, 579–581
aesthetics 247
affective variables 101
affirmations 427–429
age, and agility 52
agency, and learning 485, 494
"agentic intent" 485
agility 45–65
  and age 52
  Bosch Group 57–59
  challenges 49–57
  and communication 46–47, 48, 54–55, 58
  concepts 46–49, 61–62
  and culture 48–49, 55–56
  elements of 46
  environmental factors 46
  and groupthink 47, 56
  holistic practice 55–56
  Hugo Boss AG 59–61
  individuals 46, 52–53, 56
  manager opinions 53–57
  organizational impacts 57–61
  and strategy 49, 55–57, 59–60
  study data collection 50–51
  study results 51–57
  success factors 49–57
  talent management 48, 56
  working learners 68–69
Ajibade, E.S. 8
Ajna center 432–433
Allport, G. 217–218
Allwood, J. 303
Al Nahyan, Z., Sheikh 327–328
American Council on Education (ACE) 69–70
AMOEBA design framework 405–407
analysis, talent management 161–162
analyzers (communication style) 375, 382–385, 388–389
apprentice chefs 249–251
appropriateness
  of communication 456–457
  and culture 281–282
  intercultural 287–289
  of labels 87
Arab generations 193–194

*The Wiley Handbook of Global Workplace Learning*, First Edition.
Edited by Vanessa Hammler Kenon and Sunay Vasant Palsole.

Archimedes project 597–605
artifacts, role in learning 361–363
ASCOT initiative 127–131
assessment frameworks
English language proficiency 350
experiential learning models 95–117
gamification 545–546, 549–551
inclusive education 89–90
rationale for 95–96
attention, relevance, confidence, and satisfaction (ARCS) model 581, 583–585
attitudinal advantages to gamification 580
attributes of gamification 544–545
authentic work experience 490
authoritarian leaders 4–5, 8, 17
authority-compliant managers 9
autobiographical lens 266
AVE *see* average variance extracted
average variance extracted (AVE) 106

## b

Baby Boomers 183
*see also* generational differences
badges in gamification 546, 551–552, 568
barriers
to executive development 39–42
to working learners 73–74
Bartlett's test 106–107
Bayelsa State, Nigeria
secondary school leadership 3–25
implications 18
methodology 14–15
questionnaires 22–25
results 16–18
sources 15, 22–25
Beechler, S. 155–156
behavior
communication styles 374–376, 382–385, 388–389
and culture 282
gamification advantages 580
of leaders 4–5, 453–454
learning disability symptoms 227
behavioral variables 102
beliefs, and culture 281, 396–397
belonging
and learning 482
virtual teams 371
Benson, H. 420, 434
Bernstein, B. 98
Billett, S. 70, 478, 479, 482, 484, 485
biopsychosocial model (BPSM) 224
Bloemroad, I. 202
Bosch Group, agility 57–59
boundaries, communities of practice 306
bounded agency 490–491
BPSM *see* biopsychosocial model
*Brain Longevity* 417
branch courses, Switzerland 248
Brazil, university partnerships 203–209
breathing to relax 423–427
bridging the cultural gap 355–367
Broderick, M. 142
Brookfield, S. 266
Brunton, P. 416–417
budgets, and talent management 166
business case for gamification 563–564
business development, and agility 57
buy-in, and effectiveness 35–36
Byrne, R. 422

## c

Cairns, L. 478–479, 481–482
Campbell, M. 478
Canada, generational differences 191–192
CAP *see* cultural adaptation process model
career expectations, generational differences 185–186
career and technical education (CTE)
apprentice chefs 249–251
digital methods for creativity 241–261
ICT competence initiatives 243–244
surgery-room technicians 251–253
*see also* vocational education and training

Cartesian Plane of Intercultural Competence (CPIC) 288–289
Castells, M. 285
CAT *see* communication accommodation theory
CBM *see* culture-based model
centers of consciousness 432–433
Centre for Educational Research and Innovation (CERI) 13–14
CERI *see* Centre for Educational Research and Innovation
certification
 internationalization 337
 value of 78
CFA *see* confirmatory factor analysis
challenges
 to agility 49–57
 problem-based learning 602–603
 of qualitative research 204
 in talent management 162–167
Chappell, C. 479–480
CHAT *see* cultural history activity theory
chefs, mobile learning 249–251
*chi-gong* 422
China
 culture of 282
 generational differences 191
Chinese language and cultural training 171–179
 *see also* Confucius Institute
Chinmoy, S. 422
Chomsky, N. 312–313
Choy, S. 478, 479
CI *see* Confucius Institute
Cisco 569–570
CofP *see* communities of practice
cognitive dimension of gamification 578–579
cognitive function, optimal 416–419
cognitive variables 102
Cole, M. 508–512
collaboration
 and agility 58–59
 and problem-based learning 604
 "we-creativity" 246
colleagues' experiences, as a lens 266
collectivism, generational differences 191–194
college students, numbers working 72
common workplace needs 124–125, 478–483, 591–593
communication
 accommodation theory 304–305
 and agility 46–47, 48, 54–55, 58
 appropriateness 456–457
 communities of practice 305–307
 compensation for lack of non-verbal cues 371
 contrastive analysis 310–312
 conversation analysis 309–310
 cooperative principle 307–309
 and culture 302
 English language proficiency 343–354
 ethnography of 312–314
 face threatening acts 308–309
 high- vs. low-context cultures 374
 leadership competence training 447–475
  behavior categories 453–454
  content selection 452–453
  data collection 463–464
  frameworks 448–449, 455–462
  goal setting 454–455
  methods 449–450, 462–463, 475
  micro-teaching 450–452
  results 464–467
 styles 374–376, 382–386
 virtual teams 369–394
 *see also* digitally mediated communication; intercultural communication; non-verbal cues
communication accommodation theory (CAT) 304–305
communication power 285
communication theory of identity (CTI) 373
communities of practice (CofP) 305–307, 490–492, 494–496, 503–504, 507–508
compensation methods, digitally mediated communication 381–382, 384–386

competences
current expectations 124–125, 478–483, 591–593
emerging 592–597
English language proficiency 343–354
intercultural 285–296
in society 285–293
in workplaces 293–296, 314–317
*see also* intercultural communication; intercultural competence
intrapreneurship 127–131
*see also* workplace competences
competing interests, as a barrier 40–41
competition, in gamification 545, 546–547, 552–554
competitive advantage 143
conceptual flexibility 56
confidence 271, 272
confirmatory factor analysis (CFA) 107
conflicts
of working learners 73–74
*see also* barriers
Confucius Institute (CI) 171–179
education platform building 176
role in organizing training 175
selection criteria 172–174
STARTALK program 177–178
technologies in training 176–177
training methods 174–175
construction
of identity 315
of social space 359
context indicators, experiential learning 100–101
contextual success factors, intrapreneurship 129–131
Contingency Theory 7
Contrastive Analysis 310–312
controllers (communication style) 375, 382–386, 388–389
conversational implicature 307
Conversation Analysis 309–310
cooperation, generational attitudes 189–190
cooperative principle (CP) 307–309
Corker, M. 87
Costley, C. 89
cost savings of learning communities 514
country club manager 9
CP *see* cooperative principle
CPIC *see* Cartesian Plane of Intercultural Competence
creative professional development
concepts 245–247
digital learning 241–261
and experience 246–247
hypervideo 251–253
mobile learning 249–251
skills 244–245
supportive processes 245–247
visual display benefits 247–248, 251–253
creativity
and experience 246–247
as a skill 244–245
supportive practices 245–247
critical approaches, multicultural curricula 202–208
critical reflective practice 264–268
criticism 462
cross-cultural communication 303, 395–412
*see also* intercultural communication
cross-cultural workplace learning 201–213
decolonialization 202–208
framework 202–203
leadership 209–210
university partnerships, Brazil 203–209
crown chakra 432–433
CTE *see* career and technical education
CTI *see* communication theory of identity
cultural adaptation process model (CAP) 404–405
cultural history activity theory (CHAT) 508–512
cultural identity 283–284

culture
  and agility 48–49, 55–56
  Chinese 282
  and communication 302, 370–371
  concepts 280–283, 302, 396–397
  and design 399–400
  of diversity 217–223
  generational differences 181–194
  and global workplace learning 395, 400–409
  and humor 316–317
  and identity 283–284
  of learning 29–30
  and learning 397–399
  organizational 357–358
  sociocultural perspectives 355–367
culture-based model (CBM) 401–402
culture reflective knowledge 290
culture specific knowledge 289–290
curiosity, intercultural 291–292
customer-focus, and agility 59–60

### d

Davis, J. 87
DCU *see* Dublin City University
Deardoff, D.K. 286–287
decision-making
  in gamification 545
  strategic planning 147–151
decolonialization 203, 204, 207
deferment of responsibility 86
deindividuation 371
Deloitte 570
democratization, leadership 3–25
den Heijden, V. 145
descriptors 89
design
  AMOEBA framework 405–407
  and culture 399–400
  experiential learning assessment framework 95–117
    affective variables 101
    behavioral variables 102
    cognitive variables 102
    concepts 98–102
    context indicators 100–101
    discussion 112–113
    generic feedback loop 99–100
    hypothesis testing 104, 110–113
    impact indicators 102
    implications of study 113–114
    input domains 99, 101
    interviews 110–112
    methodology 103–104
    output indicators 102
    process indicators 101–102
    results 104–110
    structure of 98–100
    transformations 99–100, 101–102
  gamification frameworks 547–548, 566–569
  multiple cultures model 407–408
developmental work research (DWR) 509, 511–512
Devi, I. 418
Dewey, J. 265–266, 487
De Wit, H. 331
*Dhyana* 435–437
dialog
  face-to-face English 347
  and intercultural communication 294
digital education 241–261
  gamification 539–590
  hypervideo 251–253
  interactive whiteboards 523–537
  mobile learning 249–251
  visual display benefits 247–248
digitally mediated communication (DMC) 369–394
  belonging 371
  communication styles 374–376, 382–386
  compensation methods 381–382, 384–386
  high- vs. low-context cultures 374
  human resources development 387–388
  implications 372–374, 386–389
  research methods 376–379
  results 380–386
  trust 371–372
  web-based conferencing 388–389

Digital Natives 184–185
see also generational differences
dimension control 459
dimensions
of gamification 578–579
of leadership communication 459–462
national cultural model 401–404
disability
biopsychosocial model 224
criticism of terminology 88
and diversity 217–223
General Systems Theory 223–224
holistic model 224–226
labeling 86–87
organizational learning 232–234
theories of 223–228
workplace development 228–234
see also inclusive learning; learning disabilities; special educational needs
discipline, secondary schools 11
diversity
concepts 217–223
of culture 283
frameworks 219–222
inclusive education 83–94
multicultural curricula 201–213
organizational learning 232–234
United Arab Emirates 337
workplace development 228–234
Diversity Wheel 220
dominance, and languages 315–316
double-loop learning 603–604
Drucker, P. 144–145
Dublin City University (DCU) 263–276
DWR see developmental work research

## e

economic rationale, for education internationalization 333–335
EDLP see Executive Development Learning Programme
educational development, United Arab Emirates 326–327
Education Entrepreneurial Approach (EEA) 264–268
education reform, United Arab Emirates 327–330
Education and Training Management (eLearning) MSc, Dublin City University 263–276
findings 268–274
methods 267–268
theoretical underpinning 264–267
EEA see Education Entrepreneurial Approach
EEG see electroencephalograms
Eelen, G. 309
effectiveness, intercultural 287–289
Elbaz-Luwisch, F. 202
e-learning, gamification 543
electroencephalograms (EEG) of meditators 421–422, 425–427
electronic mediation 426–427
elements
of agility 46
of gamification 545–547, 549–554, 568
ELP see English Language Proficiency
emerging trends 96–97
emerging workplace skills 592–597
Emiratization 333
emotional dimension of gamification 579
empathy, and intercultural competence 295–296
employability, of working learners 74
employee learning disabilities 215–240
disability theories 223–228
diversity 217–223
organizational learning 232–234
workplace development 228–232
employee learning factors 477–500
authentic work experience 490
communities of practice 490–492, 494–496
external 485–486
individuals 485
informality 486–487
organizational 483–484, 489–490, 493, 496–497

personal agency 494
problem-solving 488–489
reflection 487–488
unintended learning 492
employee satisfaction 185–186
empowerment, inclusive education 84–86
endogenous factors, learning communities 514–515
Engestrom, Y. 508–512
English language
face-to-face dialog 347
focal skills 349, 350
generalizable skills 349
instruction programs 349–350
internal communications 347–348
as a lingua franca 315–316
proficiency 343–354
UAE internationalization 332–333
English Language Proficiency (ELP) 343–354
assessment 350
face-to-face 347
focal skills 349, 350
generalizable skills 349
for global workplace 346–347
impacts of 345–346
internal communications 347–348
environmental factors
agility 46
employee learning 483–484
establishment of learning communities 514–515
ethnography
of communication 312–314
of insurance companies 362–363
Europe, common workplace needs 124–125
European Convention for Human Rights 87
evaluation, strategic planning 152
*Every School is a Good School: The Way Forward for Special Educational Needs (SEN) and Inclusion* 88
evolutionary methods, strategic planning 145
evo-revolution 75
executive coaching
Raelin's model 30–31
readiness levels 31–32
task-orientation 38
usefulness of tools 36–39
Executive Development Learning Programme (EDLP) 27–44
barriers to implementation 39–42
facilitators 32–35
leaderful strategy 30–31
organizational support 35–36
task-orientation 38
usefulness of tools 36–39
exogenous factors, learning communities 515
expectations, of gamification 544–545
experiential learning
affective variables 101
assessment development 95–117
discussion 112–113
hypothesis testing 104, 110–113
implications of study 113–114
interviews 110–112
methodology 103–104
results 104–110
behavioral variables 102
cognitive variables 102
concepts 98–102
context indicators 100–101
creativity 246–247
generic feedback loop 99–100
heutagogy 594–597
impact indicators 102
input domains 99, 101
output indicators 102
process indicators 101–102
sociocultural theory 359–360
structure of 98–100
transformations 99–100, 101–102
*see also* problem-based learning
experimentation, and creativity 245–246

external factors
  employee learning 483–484
  talent management 156
extrinsic motivation 186, 565, 568–569

**f**

face threatening acts (FTAs) 308–309
face-to-face communication, English language proficiency 347
facilitation by leaders 460
facilitators, strengths and preferences 32–35
factors influencing employee learning 477–500
  authentic work experience 490
  communities of practice 490–492, 494–496
  external 485–486
  individuals 485
  informality 486–487
  organizational 483–484, 489–490, 493, 496–497
  personal agency 494
  problem-solving 488–489
  reflection 487–488
  unintended learning 492
Farrell, L. 479–480
fasting 437–438
feedback by leaders 462
feedback loops, experiential learning 99–100
fire breath 437
flexible working 187–188
focal skills, English language proficiency 347–348, 350
Foot, K.A. 509
formal education
  functions of principals 9–11
  goal-orientation 11–12
  inclusive education 83–94
  instructional programs 10
  interactive whiteboard utilization 523–537
  intrapreneurship competence 127–131
  multicultural curricula 201–213
  student welfare 10–11
  transition to work 121–122
  vocational 121–139
  Work Colleges 70
  workplace competence measurement 125–127
  *see also* higher education institutions; schools; secondary schools
Four Layers of Diversity Model 220–221
*fourth state of consciousness* 423
Fox, W. 337
frameworks
  diversity 219–222
  gamification design 547–548, 566–569
  integrated talent management 159
  intercultural competence 286–290
  leadership communication competencies training 448–449, 455–462
  work and learn options 74–78
Franklin, P. 303
freelancing, and working learners 68–69
friendliness of leaders 461–462
FTAs *see* face threatening acts
functions, of principals 9–10

**g**

games
  concepts 540–542
  history of 562
gamification 539–590
  advantages 562–563, 579–581
  attributes 544–545
  badges 546, 551–552, 568
  business rationale 563–564
  case studies 569–570, 581–586
  concepts 540–542, 558–559, 577–579
  course flow diagram 551
  design framework 547–548
  dimensions 578–579
  in education 543
  elements 545–547, 549–554, 568
  example course 548–554
  expectations 544–545

game mechanics 566–569
leaderboards 546–547, 552–554, 568
learning impacts 581–586
mastery 554
and motivation 542–543, 564–566, 569, 581–586
overview 577–590
points 545–546, 549–551, 568
psychology 564–566
repetition 554
trend toward 559–560
GCC *see* Gulf Cooperation Council
generalizable English skills 349
General Systems Theory (GST) 223–224
Generation 2020 184–185
Generation…, *see also* generational differences
generational differences 181–199
career expectations 185–186
categories 183–185
global 190–194
soft knowledge 188–189
"sweet spot" 194–195
teamwork attitudes 189–190
working hours 187–188
workplace learning attitudes 185
Generation X 184
Generation Y 184, 195–196, 563
Generation Z 184–185, 196
Generic Assessment Feedback Loop 99–100
Gen Tech 184–185
Georgetown University Center on Education and the Workforce report 72
Germany, ICT competence initiatives 243
*gestalten* 245
GFI *see* Goodness-of-Fit Index
global awareness, as a learning outcome 336
"global culture" 285
*see also* intercultural communication
global generational differences 190–194
globalization
and English language proficiency 343–354
and intercultural communication 279–299, 355–367
and strategic planning 143
and talent management 155–157
global strategic planning 141–154
in context 144–146
evaluation 152
evolutionary methods 145
implementation 151–152
monitoring 152
phases of 150–151
process of 146–147
processual methods 145
rationalist methods 145
risk management integration 153
strategy development 147–151
global talent management 155–170
budgets 166
challenges 162–167
framework 159
infrastructure 162
measurement efficacy 166
mindsets 164
primary activities 162–163
retention 165
scenario planning 166–167
talent analysis 161–162
talent life cycle 158–162
talent value chain 160–161
technological solutions 165
turnover 155–156, 164–165
global workplace learning
AMOEBA framework 405–407
challenges 356–357
cross-cultural theories 395–412
cultural adaptation process model 404–405
culture-based model 401–402
definitions of 501–503
multiple cultures model 407–408
national cultural dimensions 401–404
organizational culture 357–358
sociocultural theory 355–367
training deficits 359–360

goal-attainment, and leadership style 17–18
goal-orientation
  leadership communication competencies training 454–455
  schools 11–12
Goffman, E. 308–310
Goodness-of-Fit Index (GFI), experiential learning assessment 107–110
Google 47
grasping experience, modes of 99
Gregory, J. 511–512
Grice, H.P. 307, 309–310
grounding, of individuals 28
groupthink 47, 56
growth, retention of 165
GST *see* General Systems Theory
Gudykunst, W.B. 303
Gulf Cooperation Council (GCC) 325–326

## h

Hackman, J.R. 357
Hanban, Confucius Institute 171–179
Hatha Yoga 437
Heijden, V., den 145
HEIs *see* higher education institutions
HEQCO *see* Higher Education Quality Council of Ontario
heutagogy 594–597
high-context cultures 374
higher education institutions (HEIs)
  action research 264–268
  Confucius Institute 171–179
  internationalization 324–325
  master's programs 263–276
  multicultural curricula 201–213
  United Arab Emirates 323–342
Higher Education Quality Council of Ontario (HEQCO) 68, 76–78
high school students, numbers working 72
high-touch learning options 75–76
high turnover, of management 40
history of meditation 419–420
Hoadley, C. 363–364
Hofstede, G. 401–404
holism, and agility 55–56
holistic model of disability 225–226
*How to Meditate and Getting Well Again* 417–418
Hoy, W.K. 7
HRD *see* Human Resource Development
Hugo Boss AG, agility 59–61
human capital 157
Human Resource Development (HRD)
  agility 48, 56
digitally-mediated training 387–388
  inclusive 228–232
  South African Police Services 27, 35–36
humility, intercultural competence 295
humor, workplace culture 316–317
Hymes, D.H. 313
hypervideo, surgery-room technician training 251–253
hypothesis testing
  experiential learning assessment framework 104, 110–113
  interactive whiteboard utilization 530–533
  a skill 84–85

## i

identity
  communication theory of 373
  construction 315
  and culture 283–284
  and labeling 86–87
  linguistic 314
iGeneration 184–185
  *see also* generational differences
Igira, F.T. 511–512
immediacy, and gamification 544
immune system 417–418
impact indicators, experiential learning models 102
implementation
  interactive whiteboards 523–537
  strategic plans 151–152

impoverished managers 9
imprinting 280–281
*Improving School Leadership* 14
inclusive education 83–94
 assessment criteria 89–90
 deferment of responsibility 86
 descriptors 89
 empowerment 84–86
 labeling 86–87
 learning disabilities 215–240
 learning outcomes 89–90
 organizational learning 232–234
 ownership 90
 quality assurance 89–90
 workplace development 228–234
income, and English language proficiency 346
individual intercultural competence 293
individualism, generational differences 191–194
individuals
 agility 46, 52–53, 56
 challenges in modern labor market 121–122
 conceptual grounding 28
 human capital 157
 intrapreneurship competence factors 131
 learning factors 485
 readiness levels 31–32
 talent 156–157
 uniqueness 157
industry 4.0, ICT competence 243–244
informal education 486–487
informal networks 506–507
information and communications technology (ICT)
 in creative development 241–261
 gamification 539–590
 interactive whiteboards 523–537
 intercultural communication 363–364
 vocational education and training 243–244
 *see also* digital education; technology
infrastructure, talent management 162
Ingiabuna, E.T. 8
InMobi 570
input domains, experiential learning 99, 101
Institute for Heart Math 426
institutional context factors, intrapreneurship 130–131
instructional programs
 AMOEBA design framework 405–407
 cultural adaptation process model 404–405
 English language 349–350
 multicultural curricula 201–213
 multiple cultures model 407–408
 national cultural dimensions model 401–404
 school principals 10
 web-based conferencing 388–389
integrated talent management (ITM) 155–170
 budgets 166
 challenges 162–167
 framework 159
 infrastructure 162
 measurement efficacy 166
 mindsets 164
 primary activities 162–163
 retention 165
 scenario planning 166–167
 talent analysis 161–162
 talent life cycle 158–162
 talent value chain 160–161
 technological solutions 165
 turnover 155–156, 164–165
integrative model of diversity 221–222
"interaction order" 309
interactive whiteboards (IWB) 523–537
 data analysis 527
 hypothesis 530–533
 questionnaires 526–530
 results 528–530

intercultural communication 279–322
  adaptation 296
  AMOEBA framework 405–407
  as an organizational strategy 386–389
  and communication 302
  communication accommodation theory 304–305
  communities of practice 305–307
  competences 279–299
    frameworks 286–290
    in society 285–293
    in workplaces 293–296, 301–304, 314–317
  concepts 284–285
  contrastive analysis 310–312
  conversation analysis 309–310
  cooperative principle 307–309
  cultural adaptation process model 404–405
  and culture 280–283, 302
  culture-based model 401–402
  definitions 303
  dialog 294
  empathy 295–296
  ethnography 312–314
  face threatening acts 308–309
  and global workplace learning 395–412
  high- vs. low-context cultures 374
  human resources development 387–388
  humility 295
  and identity 283–284
  multilingual workplaces 301–322
  multiple cultures model 407–408
  national cultural dimensions 401–404
  organizational culture 357–358
  politeness 307–309
  sensibility 294–295
  sociocultural perspectives 355–367
  technological solutions 363–364
  theories of 304–314
  virtual team non-verbal cue compensation 369–394
    implications 372–374, 386–389
    research methods 376–379
    results 380–386
intercultural competence 285–296
  adaptation 296
  appropriateness and effectiveness 287–289
  Cartesian Plane of 288–289
  and communication 302
  components of 289–293
  curiosity 291–292
  dialog 294
  empathy 295–296
  ethnography of communication 312–314
  Face Threatening Acts 308–309
  frameworks 286–290
  humility 295
  open-mindedness 291
  respect 291
  sensibility 294–295
  in society 285–293
  systemic 293
  tolerance 292
  turn-taking 309–310
  in workplaces 293–296, 301–304, 314–317
interculturalism 201–213
  *see also* multicultural curricula
intergenerational sweet spot 194–195
intergroup contact hypothesis 217–218
internal communications, English language proficiency 347–348
internationalization
  concepts 324–325
  higher education in UAE 323–342
    academic rationale 335–337
    economic rationale 333–335
    political rationale 330–333
    sociocultural rationale 337–338
  and national identity 331–332
interpersonal communication
  leadership training 447–475
    behavior categories 453–454
    content selection 452–453

data collection 463–464
frameworks 448–449, 455–462
goal setting 454–455
methods 449–450, 462–463, 475
micro-teaching 450–452
results 464–467
intrapreneurship (IP) 127–131
contextual success factors 129–131
measurement and visualization 127–129
intrinsic motivation 186, 565–566
intuition 426
IP *see* intrapreneurship
Ismail, M. 332
ITM *see* integrated talent management
IWB *see* interactive whiteboards

*j*

Jacobs, R.L. 480–481
Järvensivu, A. 481
*jiao yu* (education) 282

*k*

Kaiser–Mayer–Olkin (KMO) test 106–107
key performance areas (KPAs) 42
Khalsa, D.S. 417, 421
*khapalabhakta* 437
KMO test *see* Kaiser–Mayer–Olkin test
Knight, J. 335
"knowing-in-action" 266
knowledge
culture reflective 290
culture specific 289–290
knowledge acquisition, separation from practice 359–360
knowledge capital, generational differences 188
knowledge creation 479–490
knowledge economy 69–71
*see also* learning economy
knowledge and skills enablers (KSE) 97–98, 110
knowledge work 98
Koski, P. 481
KPAs *see* key performance areas
Kriya Yoga 437
KSE *see* knowledge and skills enablers

*l*

labeling 86–87
labor market
current needs 121–123, 124–125, 478–483
current trends 121
Labovian paradigm 304
lack of understanding, as a barrier 39–40
Lakoff, R. 307
language
and culture 302
and identity 314
and power 315–316
*see also* intercultural communication
language identity 314
Language in the Workplace Project (LWP) 316
Latin America, generational differences 192
Lawler, E.E. 357
Lazar, S. 421–422
LD *see* learning disabilities
leaderboards 546–547, 552–554, 568
leaderful strategy 30–31
leadership
behavior categories 453–454
communication competencies training 447–475
behavior categories 453–454
content selection 452–453
data collection 463–464
frameworks 448–449, 455–462
goal setting 454–455
methods 449–450, 462–463, 475
micro-teaching 450–452
results 464–467
concepts of 4–8, 30–31
definitions 3
dimension control 459

leadership (*cont'd*)
  dimensions
    facilitation 460
    feedback 462
    friendliness 461–462
    respect 461
  executive coaching 30–31
  global strategic planning 144–146
  multicultural curricula 209–210
  relational skills 461–462
  as shared practice 3–25
  South African Police Service 27–44
  styles 4–6, 8–9
    and attainment 17–18
    secondary school principals 13–14, 17–18
Leaders Observation Scale (LOS) 453–454
learners
  creativity supportive processes 245–247
  effects of working 72–74
  inclusive education 83–94
  labeling 86–87
  mobile learning 249–251
  readiness levels 31–32, 69–70
  visual display benefits 247–248
  *see also* working learners
learning
  artifacts, role of 361–363
  communities of practice 305–307, 490–492, 494–496
  external factors 485–486
  gamification advantages 579–580, 581–586
  individual factors 485
  influencing factors 477–500
    authentic work experience 490
    communities of practice 490–492, 494–496
    external 485–486
    individuals 485
    informality 486–487
    organizational 483–484, 489–490, 493, 496–497
    personal agency 494
    problem-solving 488–489
    reflection 487–488
    unintended learning 492
  performance-driven 69–71, 74–78
  personal agency 494
  and problem-solving 488–489
  and reflection 266–267, 272–273, 487–488
  repetition 554
  sociocultural theory 358–359, 361–363
  unintended 492
  web-based conferencing 388–389
learning communities 501–519
  communities of practice 305–307, 490–492, 494–496, 503–504, 507–508
  cost savings 514
  creation and management 514–515
  cultural history activity theory 508–512
  establishment and management 514–515
  forms of 503
  informal networks 506–507
  legitimate peripheral participation 496, 512–513
  personal growth and development 513
  quality assurance and standards 513
  task groups/work groups 504–506
learning disabilities (LD)
  criticism of terminology 88
  and engagement 226–227
  labeling 86–87
  organizational learning 232–234
  symptoms 227
  and workforce learning 215–240
  workplace development 228–232
  *see also* inclusive education; special educational needs
learning economy 67–81
  certification 78
  conflicts 73–74
  evolution of 69–71

fluidities 68
future framework 74–78
techno-economic paradigm 69
and working learners 71–73
work-to-study model 71
learning outcomes
global awareness 336
inclusive education 89–90
Leech, G. 307–308
legitimate peripheral participation (LPP) 496, 512–513
*Lernortkooperation* 248–249
LeShan, L. 425
life cycles
integrated talent management 158–162
talent analysis 161–162
limited peripheral participation 512–513
lingua francas 315–316
linguistic identity 314
local context factors, intrapreneurship 130
Loden, M. 219
looking upwards 432–433
LOS *see* Leaders Observation Scale
low-context cultures 374
low-touch learning options 75–76
Loxley, A. 83–89
LPP *see* legitimate peripheral participation
Lundvall, B. 69
LWP *see* Language in the Workplace Project

*m*

McCraty, R. 426
McDonalds 564
Malloch, M. 478–479, 481–482
management
agility perceptions 53–57
generational differences 181–199
high turnover 40
involvement of 41
learning communities 514–515
management by objectives (MbO) 454–455
mantras 428, 435–437
Master of Science (MSc), Education and Training Management, Dublin City University 263–276
mastery, through gamification 554
Maxwell, J.C. 6
MbO *see* management by objectives
MDE-framework 567–568
measurement
intrapreneurship competence 127–131
talent management 166
vocational education and training outcomes 121–139
workplace competence 125–127
*see also* assessment frameworks
meditation 415–446
breathing to relax 423–427
centers of consciousness 432–433
history of 419–420
mantras 428, 435–437
optimal cognitive function 416–419
positive affirmation 427–429
power meditation 425, 433
and prayer 433–434
science of 420–423
signs of progress 437–438
visualization 429–433, 437
metabolism and meditation 425
Microsoft 190
micro-teaching 450–452
Middle East, generational differences 193–194
middle-of-the-road managers 9
midwives 305
Millenials 184, 195–196, 563
*see also* generational differences
mindfulness 420
*see also* meditation
mindfulness-based stress reduction (MBSR) 420
mind over matter 417–418
mindsets
agile 46–49, 56
in talent management 164
*see also* meditation

Ministry of Education and Youth (MOEY), United Arab Emirates 326–327
Miskel, C.G. 7
m-learning *see* mobile learning
MNCs *see* multinational corporations
mobile learning (m-learning), apprentice chefs 249–251
model fit, experiential learning 107–110
modern leadership frameworks 6–8
Modern Meditation Training *see* meditation
MOEY *see* Ministry of Education and Youth
Mohrman, S.A. 98
monitoring, strategic planning 152
motivation
  ARCS model 581, 583–585
  and gamification 542–543, 564–566, 569, 581–586
  generational differences 183–186, 195–196
  leadership factors 4
MRI scans of meditators 421
multicultural curricula 201–213
  decolonialization 202–208
  framework 202–203
  leadership 209–210
  university partnerships, Brazil 203–209
multilingual workplaces 301–322
  *see also* intercultural communication; intercultural competence
multimedia learning theory 244
multinational corporations (MNCs)
  challenges 356–357
  English language proficiency 343–354
  organizational culture 357–358
  sociocultural theory 355–367
  strategic planning 146
  talent management 155–170
  training deficits 359–360
multiple cultures model of instructional design 407–408

*n*

Nadeau, R. 430
national cultural dimensions (NCD) model 401–404
national identity, and internationalization 331–332
National Policy on Education, Nigeria 4
nature of work 478–483
NCD model *see* national cultural dimensions model
negotiation, of identity 314–315
Nepal, computers in schools 364
network societies 285
  intercultural competence 285–293
  *see also* intercultural communication
neural synchrony 421–422
new learning economy 67–81
  certification 78
  conflicts 73–74
  future framework 74–78
  techno-economic paradigm 69
  and working learners 71–73
  work-to-study model 71
Ng, E.S. 202
NICE 569
Nigeria
  interactive whiteboard utilization 523–537
    data analysis 527
    hypothesis 530–533
    questionnaires 526–530
    results 528–530
  secondary school leaders 3–25
    implications 18
    methodology 14–15
    questionnaires 22–25
    results 16–18
    sources 15, 22–25
Niteroi, Brazil, multicultural curricula development 203–209

non-verbal cues
compensation in virtual teams 369–394
high- vs. low-context cultures 374
human resources development 387–388
implications 386–389
preferred methods 381–382, 384–386
research methods 376–379
results 380–386
web-based conferencing 388–389
importance of 370–371
"normalcy" 226
norms 281

**o**

OECD *see* Organization for Economic Cooperation and Development
Ojo 8
"One Child Generation" 191
open-mindedness, intercultural 291
operationalization, intrapreneurship 127–131
optimal cognitive function 416–419
organizational culture 357–358, 496–497
organizational factors in employee learning 483–484, 489–490
organizational goals, democratizing 3–25
organizational impacts, agility 57–61
organizational learning 232–234
organizational readiness 493
organizational support 35–36, 489–490
Organization for Economic Cooperation and Development (OECD)
ICT competence needs 243–244
school leadership 13–14
Osuji, E.E. 8
"othering" 315
outcome measurement, vocational education and training 123–131
output indicators, experiential learning models 102
overjustification effect 569
ownership
generational differences 188
inclusive education 90
Oyebamiji, M.A. 8

**p**

Park, Y. 480–481
participation 362
AMOEBA design framework 405–407
communities of practice 305–307, 490–492, 494–496
participative leaders 8
partnership, inclusive education 84–86
Path–Goal Theory 7
PBL *see* problem-based learning
PBL (points, badges, leaderboard) triad 545–547, 549–554, 568
performance-driven learning 69–71, 74–78
perioperative nurses 252–253
personal agency, and learning 494
personal development
action research 264–268
leadership communication competencies 447–475
behavior categories 453–454
content selection 452–453
data collection 463–464
frameworks 448–449, 455–462
goal setting 454–455
methods 449–450, 462–463, 475
micro-teaching 450–452
results 464–467
learning communities 513
master's program effects 263–276
and reflection 266–267, 272–273
*see also* meditation
personal identity 284
persuasive leaders 8
pitfalls of qualitative research 204, 208
"place" 481–482
"players" 157
points in gamification 545–546, 549–551, 568

police organizations, South Africa 27–44
politeness, intercultural communication 307–309
political rationale, for education internationalization 330–333
Porter, L.W. 357
Porter Value Chain Framework 160–161
positive affirmations 427–429
post-colonialism 202–208
post-structuralism 83–94
power
  and language 315–316
  and politeness 309
power of affirmation 427–429
power meditation 425, 433
practice and knowledge acquisition 359–360
Pranayama 437
preferences of facilitators 32–35
prejudice, definition of 217
primary talent management 162–163
principals
  expectations in Nigeria 9
  functions of 9–11
  leadership styles 13–14, 17–18
  multicultural curricula 209–210
  secondary schools 3–25
problem-based learning (PBL) 591–609
  Archimedes project 597–605
  and creativity 245
  and employee learning 488–489
  heutagogy 594–597
process indicators, experiential learning models 101–102
processual methods, strategic planning 145
productivity, retention of 165
proficiency
  English language 343–354
  knowledge acquisition 359–360
progression, in gamification 544
promoters (communication style) 375, 382–385, 388–389
purification by fasting 437–438
Pym, A. 303

*q*
Qigong 422
qualitative research, pitfalls 204, 208
quality assurance
  inclusive education 89
  learning communities 513
questionnaires
  interactive whiteboard utilization 526–530
  secondary school leadership research 22–25

*r*
Raelin, J. 27–31
rationalist methods, strategic planning 145
readiness levels
  of learners 31–32, 69–70
  organizational 493
recruitment 155–170
  and agility 48, 56
  challenges 162–167
  Confucius Institute criteria 172–174
  external factors 156
  infrastructure 162
  primary activities 162–163
  supply vs. demand 155–156
  talent analysis 161–162
  talent life cycle 158–162
  talent value chain 160–161
  working learners 74
  *see also* integrated talent management; talent management
reflection
  and awareness 272–273
  concepts of 266
  and employee learning 487–488
regional variations, school leadership styles 13–14
reification 362–363
relationship skills, of leaders 461–462
relaxation, breathing 423–427
"the relaxation response" 434

respect
  intercultural 291
  by leaders 461
retention, integrated talent management 165
risk management, strategic planning integration 153
Robbins, A. 422
Robert Bosch GmbH, agility 59–61
Roth, W.F. 143, 151
Royce, W. 45

***S***
Sahasrara 432–433
Sambrook, S. 480
SAPS *see* South African Police Service
Sashkin, M. & M.G. 7
Saudi Arabia, school leadership 13
scenario planning, talent management 166–167
Scheeres, H. 479–480
Schein, E. 357
Schön, D. 266
schools
  democratizing leadership 3–25
  discipline 11
  functions of principals 9–11
  goal-orientation 11–12
  inclusive education 83–94
  instructional programs 10
  leadership styles 13–14, 17–18
  National Policy on Education, Nigeria 4
  student welfare 10–11
  transition to work 121–122
  Work Colleges 70
  *see also* secondary schools
science of meditation 420–423
*Scientific Healing Affirmations* 427–428
SDT *see* self-determination theory
secondary schools
  discipline 11
  functions of principals 9–11
  goal-orientation 11–12
  instructional program 10
  leadership 3–25
  Nigeria 3–25
    implications 18
    methodology 14–15
    National Policy on Education 4
    questionnaires 22–25
    results 16–18
    sources 15, 22–25
  student welfare 10–11
  transition to work 121–122
selection criteria, Confucius Institute teachers 172–174
self-actualization 426
self-determination theory (SDT) 542, 565–566, 594–597
SEN *see* special educational needs
sensibility, intercultural competence 294–295
Sergiovanni, T.J. 6–7
shared practice
  leadership as 3–25
  learning 305–307, 490–492, 494–496
Shore, L.M. 221–222
signs of progress in meditation 437–438
silence 310
Simonton, C. 417–418
SIPP *see* Survey of Income and Program Participation
SIP theory *see* social information processing theory
Situational Theory 7
skills
  communities of practice 305–307, 490–492, 494–496, 503–504, 507–508
  creativity 244–245
  cultural history activity theory 508–512
  emerging workplaces 592–597
  English language proficiency 343–354
  gamification advantages 554
  informal networks 506–507
  for leadership 457–462
  legitimate peripheral participation 496, 512–513
  organizational attrition 164–165
  task groups/work groups 504–506

skills development
  current labor market 121–123
  repetition 554
skills enablers 97–98, 110
Sleeter, C. 204, 206
social context factors, intrapreneurship 130
social dimension of gamification 579
social identity 284
social information processing (SIP) theory 372
social space 359
sociocultural rationale for education internationalization 337–338
sociocultural theory 355–367
  artifacts, role in learning 361–363
  cases 360–364
  challenges to learning 356–357
  learning 358–359, 361–363
  organizational culture 357–358
  social space 359
  as a tool 358–359
  training deficits 359–360
soft knowledge, generational differences 188–189
Solomon, N. 479–480
sources
  agility study 50–51
  experiential learning assessment framework 103–104
  Nigerian secondary school leaders study 15, 22–25
South African Police Service (SAPS) 27–44
  barriers to implementation 39–42
  executive coaching 30–31
  facilitators 32–35
  leaderful strategy 30–31
  model 28–31
  organizational support 35–36
  readiness levels 31–32
  task-orientation 38
  usefulness of tools 36–39
special educational needs (SEN)
  concepts 84
  deferment of responsibility 86
  empowerment 84–86
  inclusive education 83–94
  labeling 86–87
speed meditation 425, 433
Spencer-Oatey, H. 303
Spitzberg, B.H. 288–289
"spread" 225
Sri Chinmoy 422
standards and learning communities 513
STARTALK program 177–178
stereotypes 225–226, 315
strategic planning 141–154
  definitions 142
  evaluation 152
  evolutionary methods 145
  in global context 144–146
  globalization effects 143
  implementation 151–152
  monitoring 152
  multinational corporations 146
  phases of 150–151
  process of 142–143, 146–147
  processual methods 145
  rationalist methods 145
  risk management integration 153
  strategy development 147–151
strategy 27–44
  and agility 49, 55–57, 59–60
  barriers to implementation 39–42
  development 147–151
  facilitator strength and weaknesses 32–35
  implementation 151–152
  leaderful 30–31
  organizational support 35–36
  Raelin's framework 27–31
  and readiness levels 31–32
  task-orientation 38
  usefulness of tools 36–39
  *see also* strategic planning
strategy–planning process 146–147
strengths, of facilitators 32–35
students, discipline 11
students'/learners' eyes, as a lens 266
student welfare, secondary schools 10–11

styles of communication 374–376, 382–389
styles of leadership 4–6, 8–9
 and attainment 17–18
 secondary school principals 13–14, 17–18
success factors
 for agility 49–57
 intrapreneurship competence 129–131
 talent acquisition 156
supply, versus demand of talent 155–156
supporters (communication style) 375, 382–385, 388–389
support processes
 creative development 245–247
 talent management 162
surgery-room technicians 251–253
Survey of Income and Program Participation (SIPP) 72
Sweden, school leadership 13
sweet spot, intergenerational 194–195
swift trust, theory of 371–372
Switzerland
 ICT competence initiatives 243
 vocational education and training 248–249
SWOT analysis 144–145
symptoms, learning disability 227
system intercultural competence 293

## t

tacit knowledge, generational differences 188
"tact maxim" 307–308
talent, concepts 156–157
talent analysis 161–162
talent life cycle (TLC) 158–162
talent management (TM) 155–170
 agility 48, 56
 analysis 161–162
 budgets 166
 challenges 162–167
 external factors 156
 framework 159
 generational differences 185–190
 infrastructure 162
 life cycle 158–162
 measurement efficacy 166
 primary activities 162–163
 retention 165
 scenario planning 166–167
 supply vs. demand 155–156
 turnover 155–156, 164–165
 value chain 160–161
 working learners 74
 *see also* integrated talent management
talent value chain (TVC) 160–161
task groups 504–506
task-orientation 38
teachers
 Confucius Institute training 171–179
 creativity mentoring 246
 interactive whiteboard utilization 523–537
team managers 9, 18
teamwork, generational attitudes 189–190
technical knowledge
 and intrapreneurship competence 127–131
 need for acquisition 97, 122–123
 as vertical discourse 98
techno-economic paradigm 69
technology
 Chinese teacher training 176–177
 intercultural communication 363–364
 talent management solutions 165
technology skills
 need for acquisition 97
 vocational education and training 121–123
Ten–Ten–Ten Breathing exercise 424–425
Thailand, generational differences 192
*The Non-Local Universe* 430
theory of swift trust 371–372
"the spiritual eye" 432
"The Wrong Tool for the Right Job" 364
Thomas, G. 83–89

TLC *see* talent life cycle
TM *see* talent management; Transcendental Meditation
Todd, J. 83–94
tolerance, intercultural 292
tools, usefulness of 36–39
Torrance, E.P. 245
totalising identities 87
traditionalist generation 182–183
  *see also* generational differences
traditional leadership frameworks 6
training methods
  Confucius Institute 174–175
  leadership communication competencies 449–452, 475
  *see also* gamification
Trait Theory 7
Transcendental Meditation (TM) 419, 423–424, 429
transformational leadership 38–39
transforming experience, modes of 99–100
trust, virtual teams 371–372
turnover
  of management 40
  of staff 155–156, 164–165
turn-taking, intercultural differences 309–310
TVC *see* talent value chain

**u**

UAE *see* United Arab Emirates
undermining effect 569
understanding, lack of, as a barrier 39–40
undervaluing of working learners 74
unemployment 121–122
UNESCO *see* United Nations Educational, Scientific, and Cultural Organization
unintended learning 492
uniqueness of employees 157
United Arab Emirates (UAE)
  diversity 337
  educational development 326–327
  education reform 327–330
  general information 325–326
  generational differences 193–194
  higher education internationalization 323–342
    academic rationale 335–337
    economic rationale 333–335
    political rationale 330–333
    sociocultural rationale 337–338
United Nations Educational, Scientific, and Cultural Organization (UNESCO), intercultural competence 287
United Parcel Service (UPS) 73
United States (US)
  generational differences 191–192
  Work Colleges 70
university partnerships
  Brazil 203–209
  Confucius Institute 171–179
University of Texas at San Antonio (UTSA) 171–179
UPS *see* United Parcel Service
"upward convergence" 304–305
urban multilingual workplaces 301–322
  cases 316–317
  communication in 314–316
  *see also* intercultural communication; intercultural competence
US *see* United States
usefulness of tools, executive coaching 36–39
UTSA *see* University of Texas at San Antonio

**v**

validity assessment, experiential learning 104
value, of educational options 78
value chains, talent management 160–161
values
  critical evaluation 273
  and culture 281
  generational differences 182–185, 191–194
vertical discourse 98
virtual classrooms 176–177

virtual teams
  attribution 371
  belonging 371
  high- vs. low-context cultures 374
  intercultural communication 372–374
  non-verbal cue compensation 369–394
    implications 386–389
    preferred methods 381–382, 384–386
    research methods 376–379
    results 380–386
  trust 371–372
visual displays
  educational benefits 247–248, 251–253
  hypervideo 251–253
  interactive whiteboards 523–537
visualization
  and creativity 247
  intrapreneurship competence 127–131
  meditation 429–433, 437
  workplace competences 125–127
vocational education and training (VET) 121–139
  age of ICT 243–244
  assessment frameworks 123–131
  chefs 249–251
  creative development 241–261
    case studies 248–253
    concepts 245–247
    skills 244–245
    supportive practices 245–247
    visual displays 247–248, 251–253
  digital education 241–261
  hypervideo 251–253
  ICT competence initiatives 243–244
  intrapreneurship competence 127–131
  mobile learning 249–251
  needs of 121–125
  surgery-room technicians 251–253
  Switzerland 248–249
  visual display benefits 247–248, 251–253
  workplace competence 125–127
Von Bertalanffy, L. 223
Vygotsky, L.S. 361, 495

***W***

"war for talent" 156
WBL *see* work-based learning
web-based conferencing, training implications 388–389
"we-creativity" 246
Wenger, E. 362–363
*Wen hua* (culture) 282
western history of meditation 419–420
white blood cells 417–418
Wilbers, K. 244
willingness, readiness levels 31–32
Woodward, I.C. 155–156
work, changing nature of 478–483
work-based learning (WBL)
  artifacts, role of 361–363
  authentic work experience 490
  Confucius Institute 171–179
  emerging skills development 593–595
  generational differences 185
  global 355–367
    artifacts, role of 361–363
    cases 360–364
    challenges 356–357
    organizational culture 357–358
    training deficits 359–360
  and inclusive education 83–94
  influencing factors 477–500
    authentic work experience 490
    communities of practice 490–492, 494–496
    deliberate actions 491–496
    external 483–484, 485–486
    individuals 485
    informality 486–487
    organizational 483–484, 489–490, 493, 496–497
    personal agency 494
    problem-solving 488–489
    reflection 487–488
    unintended learning 492
  knowledge acquisition 359–360, 479–480

work-based learning (WBL) (*cont'd*)
problem-based 488–489, 591–609
Raelin's model 28–31
sociocultural theory 355–367
structure of 98–100
technology for intercultural communication 363–364
web-based conferencing 388–389
Work Colleges 70
work experience, authenticity 490
workforce planning *see* integrated talent management; talent management
work groups 504–506
working hours, generational differences 187–188
working learners 67–81
agility 68–69
conflicts 73–74
definition 71
future framework 74–78
performance-drive 69–71
work-integrated learning 75–78
definition 70
gamification trends 559–562
*see also* work-based learning
work and learn options *see* new learning economy; working learners
work–life balance, generational differences 187–188
workplace competences 121–139
current needs 121–125, 478–483, 591–593
emerging 592–597
intercultural communication 293–296
intrapreneurship 127–131
measurement and visualization 125–127
workplace learning, definitions of 501–503
workplace problem-based learning (w-PBL) *see* problem-based learning
work-to-study model 71
w-PBL (workplace problem-based learning) *see* problem-based learning

**x**
Xerox 360–361
Xin, Y. 422

**y**
Yoga 437
*Yoga for Americans* 418
Yogananda 427–428
Young, P.A. 399, 401
Yucatec Mayan midwives 305

**z**
Zayed Universtity (ZU) 336
zone of proximal development 495
ZU *see* Zayed Universtity